Advanced Data Analysis Techniques, Theory, and Applications

Sofia D. Anastasiadou
https://orcid.org/0000-0001-6404-5003
University of Western Macedonia, Greece

Theodore G. Chadjipadelis
Aristotle University of Thessaloniki, Greece

Nikos Koutsoupias
https://orcid.org/0000-0003-1664-5404
University of Macedonia, Greece

Angelos Markos
https://orcid.org/0000-0002-4204-3573
Democritus University of Thrace, Greece

George C. Menexes
https://orcid.org/0000-0002-1034-7345
Aristotle University of Thessaloniki, Greece

IGI Global
Scientific Publishing
Publishing Tomorrow's Research Today

Vice President of Editorial	Melissa Wagner
Director of Acquisitions	Mikaela Felty
Director of Book Development	Jocelynn Hessler
Production Manager	Mike Brehm
Cover Design	Jose Rosado

Published in the United States of America by
IGI Global Scientific Publishing
701 East Chocolate Avenue
Hershey, PA, 17033, USA
Tel: 717-533-8845 | Fax: 717-533-7115
Website: https://www.igi-global.com E-mail: cust@igi-global.com

Library of Congress Cataloging-in-Publication Data

LCCN: 2026003297 (CIP Data Pending)
ISBN13: 9798337369266
Isbn13Softcover: 9798337369273
EISBN13: 9798337369280
British Cataloguing in Publication Data
A Cataloguing in Publication record for this book is available from the British Library.

Table of Contents

Detailed Table of Contents

In 2015, the United Nations introduced 2030 agenda for Sustainable Development focusing on Sustainable Development Goals (SDGs) and 167 specific targets which are adopted by 193 member countries. The goals serve as a global blueprint for achieving inclusive, equitable and sustainable growth. The present study evaluates the sustainability performance of leading companies listed on the NIFTY50 index to assess how effectively for top performing firms have integrated SDG principles into their strategic planning, disclosure practices and operational frameworks. The resulting scores provide a quantifiable measure of company's alignment with global SDG agenda. Also, the study analyzes the financial performance indicators specifically for stock returns and volatility using NIFTY50 as benchmark. It reveals a positive relationship between higher SDG scores and improved stock performance as well as a negative correlation for volatility suggesting that companies with stronger sustainability engagement tend to offer better risk-adjusted returns.

The tools discussed in this chapter offer guidelines for assessing qualitative data from social media platforms, without requiring prior coding knowledge, thus supporting social science research. This chapter provides an overview of user-friendly social media analytical tools that can be easily replicated for research purposes. These tools are relevant across any industry that utilises social media platforms such as Facebook, Instagram, or X to connect with users and followers. Influencers and digital marketers can employ these tools to measure their social media presence and engagement, enabling them to make well-informed strategic decisions to enhance reach and performance. Academics can also use these methods for research and to teach social media analytics courses to students with little or no coding experience skills.

Data engineering forms the backbone of modern analytics and machine learning by designing, building, and maintaining data pipelines. Yet, research often emphasizes downstream analytics over upstream infrastructure. This review presents a systematic bibliometric analysis of Scopus indexed peer-reviewed publications to map methodological trajectories and conceptual frameworks. Four core domains emerge: ETL processes with cloud-native storage, schema and metadata design, real-time stream processing, and workflow orchestration. Key shifts include movement from sequential to ELT models, schema-on-read in data lakes, and real-time engines like Flink and Spark Streaming, alongside orchestration tools such as Airflow. Despite progress in scalable ingestion and pipeline automation, challenges persist in metadata governance, dynamic scheduling, and integrating feature engineering into ML workflows. Future research should advance self-tuning orchestration, metadata-first models, and unified frameworks to enhance reliability and integration with predictive systems.

This chapter explores the evolution and conceptual structure of artificial intelligence and machine learning research in business and economics. Drawing on bibliometric and science-mapping analysis of Scopus-indexed publications (1984–2025), it maps the field's intellectual landscape through descriptive indicators, keyword co-occurrence, thematic mapping, trend visualization, country-level citation analysis, and Multiple Correspondence Analysis. Findings show a shift from classical methods toward broader frameworks involving predictive modelling, deep learning, and NLP, with rising focus on analytics-driven decision-making, business intelligence, and strategy. Emerging themes like sustainability, fintech, and generative AI show expanding applications. The chapter offers a structured, replicable overview of key themes, methods, and global influence, deepening understanding of the field’s growth and diversification.

Chapter 5

Zacharenia Kyrana, School of Agriculture, Aristotle University of Thessaloniki, Greece
Nikolaos Papafilippou, School of Agriculture, Aristotle University of Thessaloniki, Greece
Emmanouil D. Pratsinakis, School of Agriculture, Aristotle University of Thessaloniki, Greece
Christos Dordas, School of Agriculture, Aristotle University of Thessaloniki, Greece
Angelos Markos, School of Education, Democritus University of Thrace, Greece
Georgios C. Menexes, School of Agriculture, Aristotle University of Thessaloniki, Greece

Data cubes are p-dimensional data structures ($p \geq 3$). This study proposes alternative clustering strategies for four-dimensional data cubes ($p = 4$) with independent slices. In biological sciences, the key point of Statistical-Data Analysis is the study of variability focusing on its structure and components, while interactions between slices and hyper-slices are often of scientific interest. The dimensionality reduction strategy decomposes the cube's total variability into variability between and within slices and hyper-slices. The first clustering strategy projects the extracted principal components as points in Euclidean space, the second projects them onto a differentiable manifold, and the third is based on Procrustes distances among matrices. The real dataset "Basil" is used, consisting of three irrigation levels (hyper-slices), five basil varieties (slices), seven quantitative traits, and 60 basil plants. These strategies highlight the need for a holistic approach to the cube, so that its underlying sources of variability can be studied in depth and from different perspectives.

and forty-two (142) respondents, living in the Punjab State of India Country is the research framework. The emerging data is analyzed using statistical tool of Regression Analysis.

Artificial intelligence (AI) has unprecedented applications across education. AI algorithms learn from data, make in-formed decisions, interact with their environment, and integrate seamlessly into educational settings. AI can support personalized learning, facilitate language acquisition, address individual student needs, offer real-time feedback, and enhance teacher-student interactions. This research investigates students' attitudes by exploring their emotional responses, perceptions of cognitive impact, and resulting behavioral intentions regarding AI. The SATAI scale (Students' Attitudes Towards Artificial Intelligence) was employed to measure these attitudes. The scale comprises 26 statements rated on a five-point Likert scale, divided into three dimensions: affective, cognitive, and behavioral factors. A total of 216 students participated in the study. Data analysis was conducted using factor analysis. Results indicated that emotional and cognitive factors significantly shape students' behavioral intentions toward AI integration in educational contexts.

This chapter examines Grade 12 students' mental strategies when solving functional tasks in a graphical environment. Forty-two students in Greece participated in clinical interviews requiring mental computation without external tools. They

Preface

INTRODUCTION

The rapid expansion of data across scientific, economic, technological, and social domains has fundamentally reshaped how knowledge is generated, interpreted, and applied. Advanced data analysis is no longer confined to specialized disciplines; rather, it has become a foundational pillar supporting decision-making, innovation, and discovery across nearly every field of inquiry. From complex computational infrastructures to human-centered applications in education and policy, the capacity to analyze and interpret multidimensional data has become essential to addressing contemporary global challenges. This edited volume emerges from this transformative context, bringing together diverse perspectives that reflect both methodological rigor and applied relevance.

As editors, we envisioned this book as a platform for integrating theoretical advancement with real-world application. While statistical and computational methods continue to evolve at an unprecedented pace, their true significance lies in how they are operationalized to understand systems, behaviors, and phenomena that are increasingly complex and interconnected. The contributions in this volume reflect this dual commitment: they not only advance methodological sophistication but also demonstrate how analytical techniques can illuminate sustainability, education, healthcare, social behavior, economic systems, and governance. The result is a collection that bridges foundational theory with domain-specific insight.

Equally important is the interdisciplinary character of the work presented here. The chapters represent collaborations among scholars from diverse academic traditions, reflecting the growing recognition that contemporary data challenges cannot be addressed within disciplinary silos. By presenting methodological innovations alongside empirical investigations, the volume provides readers with both conceptual frameworks and practical models of application. It is our hope that this book will serve researchers, practitioners, and students alike as a comprehensive resource for understanding the evolving landscape of advanced data analysis.

CHAPTER OVERVIEW

This volume is organized to reflect the breadth of modern data analysis, moving from sustainability and digital analytics to methodological innovation and domain-specific applications across business, education, healthcare, and policy.

Chapter 1 examines the strategic integration of Sustainable Development Goals within leading corporations, offering a multidimensional assessment of sustainability performance and its relationship with financial outcomes. The chapter demonstrates how data-driven evaluation can connect environmental responsibility with market performance and risk dynamics.

Chapter 2 provides a practical and accessible framework for utilizing social media analytical tools in research and professional practice. Emphasizing usability and replicability, it presents methods that enable researchers and practitioners to analyze qualitative digital data without extensive coding expertise.

Chapter 3 presents a systematic review of data engineering research, mapping the conceptual and methodological evolution of data infrastructure. By identifying major domains such as cloud-based architectures, real-time processing, and workflow orchestration, the chapter highlights both progress and persistent challenges in modern data ecosystems.

Chapter 4 explores the intellectual development of artificial intelligence and machine learning within business and economics through bibliometric and science-mapping techniques. It offers a structured perspective on emerging themes, global research influence, and the expanding integration of predictive analytics in decision-making.

Chapter 5 introduces innovative clustering strategies for multidimensional data cubes, presenting advanced techniques for analyzing variability within complex structured datasets. Through methodological experimentation and empirical application, it demonstrates how high-dimensional data structures can be interpreted more holistically.

Chapter 6 investigates dimensionality reduction in mixed-type healthcare data, comparing alternative encoding strategies and analytical approaches. The chapter highlights methodological trade-offs and emphasizes the importance of flexible analytical frameworks when working with heterogeneous datasets.

Chapter 7 analyzes the influence of social media advertising on brand equity, employing statistical modeling to examine consumer awareness, perception, and retention. It provides insight into how digital engagement metrics can inform strategic marketing decisions.

Chapter 8 explores student attitudes toward artificial intelligence in educational contexts. Using psychometric measurement and factor analysis, the chapter examines how emotional, cognitive, and behavioral responses shape acceptance of AI technologies in learning environments.

Chapter 9 investigates students' mental strategies in algebraic problem solving through multivariate and multidimensional analysis. The study reveals how cognitive processes emerge through interaction between representation, context, and reasoning.

Chapter 10 examines the convergence of generative AI and learning analytics, addressing both methodological opportunities and regulatory challenges. Particular attention is given to governance, transparency, and compliance frameworks for responsible implementation.

Chapter 11 introduces the Energy Quadrilemma Index, expanding traditional energy assessment frameworks by incorporating technological and institutional capacity. The chapter demonstrates how composite indicators can support comparative policy analysis across national contexts.

Chapter 12 applies multi-criteria decision-making methods to analyze preferences for medium of instruction in secondary education, incorporating uncertainty through neutrosophic modeling. It highlights how advanced analytical tools can inform educational policy in linguistically diverse settings.

Chapter 13 investigates university students' perceptions of school bullying using factorial correspondence analysis, revealing patterns of experience and behavioral response. The chapter illustrates the role of data analysis in understanding social and psychological phenomena.

Chapter 14 examines the intersection of language, religion, and geographic settlement patterns in early twentieth-century Greece. Through historical data analysis, the chapter demonstrates how quantitative methods can illuminate demographic and cultural complexity.

Together, these chapters collectively demonstrate the range of analytical possibilities enabled by contemporary data methodologies, spanning theoretical development, methodological innovation, and applied investigation.

CONCLUSION

The contributions gathered in this volume collectively demonstrate that advanced data analysis is not simply a technical endeavor but a critical framework for understanding complex systems and informing meaningful action. Across diverse domains, the chapters reveal how methodological sophistication enables deeper insight into sustainability, education, economics, governance, and human behavior. By integrating statistical rigor with real-world application, the book reflects the evolving role of data analysis as both a scientific discipline and a practical instrument of knowledge creation.

Another central theme that emerges throughout the volume is the importance of methodological adaptability. As data environments grow more heterogeneous and dynamic, analytical approaches must remain flexible, integrative, and context-sensitive. The studies presented here illustrate how researchers are responding to this challenge—developing new frameworks, refining existing techniques, and expanding analytical boundaries to address increasingly complex questions. This adaptive orientation represents not merely a technical evolution but a conceptual shift toward more holistic and interdisciplinary forms of inquiry.

As editors, we hope this volume contributes meaningfully to ongoing conversations about the future of data analysis and its role in shaping research and practice. We offer this collection as both a reference and an invitation—encouraging readers to engage critically with emerging methods, explore new applications, and continue advancing the analytical tools that support discovery across disciplines. In an era defined by data abundance and complexity, the capacity to analyze, interpret, and apply information responsibly remains one of the most essential scholarly and professional competencies.

This volume honors the Greek professor Ioannis Papadimitriou, a leading figure in mathematics, statistics, and data analysis. Drawing on methods from the French school of Data Analysis, Professor Papadimitriou has developed innovative approaches to complex problems across a wide range of fields, including finance, literature, economics, applied informatics, politics, and education. His distinguished academic career is defined by major contributions to scientific research and remarkable mentorship. Inspired by his commitment and passion, his students continue to make progress in Data Analysis and Multivariate Statistical Analysis. We offer our deepest gratitude and admiration to this outstanding scholar and scientist.

Chapter 1

A Multi-Dimensional Analysis of NIFTY50's Strategic Integration and Performance on the United Nations' Sustainable Development Goals

Shanu Singh
http://orcid.org/0000-0002-1863-0364
Christ University, India

Surbhi Srivastava
http://orcid.org/0000-0001-9572-1983
Christ University, India

Yashmita Awasthi
http://orcid.org/0000-0002-9497-8514
Christ University, India

ABSTRACT

In 2015, the United Nations introduced 2030 agenda for Sustainable Development focusing on Sustainable Development Goals (SDGs) and 167 specific targets which are adopted by 193 member countries. The goals serve as a global blueprint for achieving inclusive, equitable and sustainable growth. The present study evaluates

DOI: 10.4018/979-8-3373-6926-6.ch001

the sustainability performance of leading companies listed on the NIFTY50 index to assess how effectively for top performing firms have integrated SDG principles into their strategic planning, disclosure practices and operational frameworks. The resulting scores provide a quantifiable measure of company's alignment with global SDG agenda. Also, the study analyzes the financial performance indicators specifically for stock returns and volatility using NIFTY50 as benchmark. It reveals a positive relationship between higher SDG scores and improved stock performance as well as a negative correlation for volatility suggesting that companies with stronger sustainability engagement tend to offer better risk-adjusted returns.

1. INTRODUCTION

The NIFTY50 index, established in 1996, is one of the most prominent and widely tracked equity indices in the Indian financial market. It represents the performance of 50 of the largest and most actively traded companies listed on the National Stock Exchange (NSE) across key sectors of the economy. Because of a diverse sectoral representation, the NIFTY50 is often seen as a barometer of the Indian economy's overall health and direction. The 2030 Agenda for Sustainable Development is a global agreement spearheaded by the United Nations Sustainable Development Goals. The Goals aim to inspire coordinated action of front-line nations in an effort to achieve solutions to environmental, social, economic, political, and global issues. They are a set of ambitious objectives that can be attained only through synergy by governments, corporations, non-profit entities, and citizens. Each objective has significant targets, and their attainment is quantified through various indicators.

As countries around the world work to align their policies with the United Nations' Sustainable Development Goals (SDGs), the corporate sector is becoming a key player in this process. Mishra et al. (2024) investigated the progress, challenges, opportunities, trends and prospects of SDGs through bibliometric analysis providing insight into the evolution and understanding for the various scientific research into the field. Saha et al. (2024) explored that in India, where the economy is growing quickly and the corporate sector is diverse, many companies have started to include the SDGs in their financial planning. In India, leading companies listed on NIFTY50 index in financial markets, play a vital role in shaping sustainable development trajectory. As of March 28, 2025, the Nifty 50 index represented approximately 55.48% of the NSE's free-float market capitalization (NSE Indices, 2025). These companies represent a significant portion of industrial influence and market capitalization, their alignment with SDGs is very essential for the broader national effort in order to achieve 2030 agenda. Chhabra (2020) discussed that beyond regulatory compliance, stakeholders expect companies to integrate sustainability into core business functions and disclose measurable impacts across environmental, economic and social dimensions. While the companies have realized the significance of contributing to the success of SDGs, there is no direct Sustainable Development Research Institute (SDRI) yet which can explain about an individual company's performance towards SDGs. The current study examines the incorporation of United Nations Sustainable Development Goals (SDGs) into companies' strategic frameworks ad approaches that they adopt to measure the corporate sustainability. While earlier studies provide valuable insights into SDG adoption and reporting practices, they rarely have explored the direct link between stock market performance and SDG initiatives. Moreover, there is no established scale available which can track SDG progress and connect it to important financial dimensions such as risk and return. Addressing the gap, the present study offers a major contribution by developing a framework in order to evaluate how effectively companies integrate SDGs into their core operations and by analyzing the potential positive impact on stock prices. This perspective strengthens the foundation for assessing commitment of the corporates to sustainability as well as it enables important comparisons with previous research, offering new insights into the financial value of sustainable practices. Hence, the conceptual alignment ensures methodological consistency with policy frameworks providing a credible base for evaluating corporate contributions to SDGs. It further defined principal objectives, issues being targeted and the significance of developing SDG-focused index for the evaluation of companies' performance.

2. LITERATURE REVIEW

The integration of United Nations Sustainable Development Goals (SDGs) into corporate and investment strategies has become very important in aligning business growth with global sustainability imperatives. Since the adoption of SDGs in 2015, it has provided a framework to various organizations to address societal challenges while creating a long-term shareholder and stakeholder value (UN, 2015). However, there is lack of standardized frameworks for reporting and inconsistencies in corporate engagement which continue to challenge the credibility and comparability of such sustainable efforts (Calabrese et al., 2021). Recent studies underscore the growing need for robust mechanisms that link SDG adoption with measurable financial and market performance, particularly in emerging economies like India (Felix & Saha, 2024; Meqbel et al., 2025). In this regard, Sharma et al. (2025) found that SDG adoption by NSE 500 firms significantly reduced firm risk through enhanced investor confidence and reduced agency costs, while Chen et al. (2025) reported that higher SDG performance in Chinese firms was associated with lower excess stock returns, suggesting market underpricing of sustainability-linked value. Vega et al. (2025) further observed that in developed markets, SDG-focused firms benefit from a lower cost of capital, reinforcing the economic relevance of SDG integration.

2.1 SDG Engagement and Value Creation for Corporates

Recent literature emphasizes the strategic relevance of SDGs as a vehicle for corporate resilience and value creation. Schramade (2017) argued that firms aligning with SDGs can achieve societal impact while enhancing shareholder returns. Ghauri (2022) stressed that multinational enterprises (MNEs) must evolve beyond shareholder primacy to include marginalized stakeholders. Extending this view, Patel et al. (2024) observed that among NIFTY50 firms, proactive SDG integration correlates positively with enhanced brand equity and investor trust, especially in IT and financial sectors. In a global context, Vega et al. (2025) demonstrated that SDG-focused firms in developed markets achieve statistically significant reductions in cost of capital, with sustainability disclosures acting as proxies for lower firm-specific risk. Beretta et al. (2024) further established that SDG disclosure acts as a partial mediator between sustainability performance and return on equity (ROE), underscoring its strategic importance in value creation.

2.2 Sustainability in Stock Markets

The relationship between sustainability performance and stock market behavior remains nuanced. Caporale et al. (2022) found no significant persistence differences between ESG and non-ESG indices globally. However, Singh & Rahman (2021) has examined the basket of major global challenges i.e the UN SDGs are well connected with the three pillars of corporate sustainability where firstly, the author has used a stakeholder approach to establish the organic linkages between the triple bottom line (TBL) approach and SDGs, secondly, the author has used quantitative content analysis to examine the alignment of the top 100 Indian companies with the SDGs. Similarly, Dutta et al. (2024) proposed an ESG-based pairs-trading model in Indian equities, outperforming conventional trading algorithms and indicating the financial relevance of sustainability strategies. Spulbar et al. (2019) investigated the profitability of momentum portfolios within the framework of India's emerging market, specifically the Bombay Stock Exchange (BSE), and also articulated that sustainable investing entails the act of investing with deliberate attention to environmental, social, and governance (ESG) factors showcasing short term momentum effect for the Indian stock market is a local anomaly that may have been influenced by behavioral and risk-based portfolio construction factors. In the specific context of SDGs, Chen et al. (2025) highlighted that higher SDG performance in Chinese firms lowered idiosyncratic risk and eased financing constraints, but paradoxically led to lower excess returns, indicating potential market mispricing.

2.3 Corporate SDG Reporting Practices

SDG reporting remains fragmented across industries and geographies. Lan Song et al. (2022) reported that only 32.6% of Fortune 500 firms aligned existing business practices with SDGs, with few developing robust tracking tools. In emerging markets, Erin & Bamigboye (2021) highlighted weak SDG disclosures in Nigerian firms due to regulatory challenges. Van Zanten et al. (2021) categorized economic activities into levels of SDG alignment to support tailored strategies. Bebbington & Unerman (2020) revealed slow engagement of accounting literature with SDG research. Fahad & Rahman (2020) studied governance and CSR disclosure in Indian firms using Bloomberg ESG scores. Bhagawan & Mukhopadhyay (2024) found CSR spending positively affects firm value. In the Indian context, Sharma et al. (2025) found a positive association between structured SDG disclosures and foreign institutional investor (FII) inflows. Additionally, Khayed et al. (2025) noted that institutional ownership often limits SDG disclosure levels, whereas foreign ownership tends to enhance them in Indian firms proposing an SDG adoption index for NSE 500 firms and demonstrated its effectiveness in reducing firm risk and improving investor confidence.

2.4 Sector-Specific Engagement and Financial Outcomes

The interplay between sectoral SDG engagement and financial performance has gained attention in recent years. Lassala et al. (2021) identified mixed financial outcomes from SDG adoption in European markets. In contrast, Singh & Rahman (2021) showed that Indian energy and FMCG firms prioritizing SDG 7 (affordable energy) and SDG 12 (responsible consumption) achieved superior ROE compared to sector peers. Moreover, Iqbal et al. (2024) examined Middle Eastern markets and reported that proactive SDG initiatives significantly contributed to market capitalization growth over a five-year horizon. Ferrero-Ferrero et al. (2023) analyzed qualitative and quantitative techniques that are used in finding consistency in reporting of SDGs based on alignment in material characteristics, corporate aims, and performance indicators to SDGs that are mostly relevant to the hotel industry. Khanchel et al. (2023) concluded ESG and green innovation influence financial performance positively. Erin et al. (2022) emphasized the role of accounting in SDG integration, noting a lack of tools and standardization in Africa, however, Saha et al. (2024) corroborated these findings by highlighting that environmental SDGs drive positive impacts on return on assets (ROA), while strong governance moderates the financial implications of social SDGs. Later, Erin et al. (2024) revealed public sector interest in Nigeria but noted lack of standard tools for SDG monitoring. In a European multi-industry panel, Beretta et al. (2025) found a significant positive link between SDG disclosure levels and Tobin's Q, reinforcing the valuation benefits of transparent SDG engagement whereas Silva (2021) analyzed how companies address their contribution to the United Nations Sustainable Development Goals (SDGs) to manage their legitimacy.

2.5 Knowledge Gaps and Contribution of the Present Study

The preceding literature highlights growing corporate engagement with SDG frameworks and their potential links to financial performance. However, studies examining the influence of SDG adoption on firm-level financial outcomes remain limited, especially in the Indian context. Vicente-Pascual et al. (2024) studied agri-business firms with B Corp certification, linking impact to SDGs. Recent evidence suggests sector-specific variations in SDG reporting and its potential to impact market-based indicators like stock returns and volatility (Sharma et al., 2025). Yet, there is a lack of comprehensive indices quantifying the extent of SDG engagement among leading Indian corporates and connecting these efforts to firm performance in capital markets. While few studies such as Sharma et.al (2025) and Chen et al. (2025) explore the effects of SDG adoption on firm risk and stock returns, they do not integrate both accounting-based and market-based performance measures within an Indian capital market context. This study fills that gap by developing a composite SDG engagement index for leading Indian firms and linking it to both financial metrics (ROA, ROE) and stock market outcomes (Tobin's Q, volatility), thereby providing a dual-lens assessment of SDG adoption's economic implications. In doing so, it extends the literature beyond risk-focused or single-market measures and adds empirical depth to emerging market evidence. Although comprehensive, the literature review mainly summarizes prior studies without critically evaluating conceptual gaps or methodological limitations (Bebbington & Unerman, 2020; Van Zanten et al., 2021). It also insufficiently addresses debates on SDG materiality, greenwashing, and measurement challenges (Calabrese et al., 2021; Lan Song et al., 2022), limiting the manuscript's demonstration of originality.

3. RESEARCH OBJECTIVES

The current study aims to quantify the progress in integrating the SDGs of the international community into their internal operating and strategic framework of the companies. It implies an understanding of the extent that these companies contribute to the world's sustainability agenda and the business operations that would fall in alignment with the SDGs. Following are the objectives of the current research article:

- To construct a Sustainable Development Goal Index (SDG Index) using secondary data to quantify and compare the extent of corporate engagement.
- To assess the financial performance of NIFTY50 companies through key market indicators - stock returns and return volatility.
- To examine the relationship between sustainability performance and financial outcomes to interpret sectoral patterns to identify sustainability leaders and laggards across industries.

4. RESEARCH METHODOLOGY

Based on a quantitative methodological framework, secondary data has been gathered from annual reports and published sustainability reports submitted by NIFTY50 corporations over the past five years form the bases of this analysis. A detailed scrutiny has been conducted in order to identify and measure important performance indicators (KPIs) relevant to SDGs. corporate-reported SDG initiatives were cross-verified with SEBI's mandatory BRSR disclosures to reduce the risk of selective reporting bias. Out of the 50 companies listed in NIFTY50 index, 20 companies have been selected for creating the SDG-focused index based on their demonstrable and consistent commitment to the United Nations Sustainable Development Goals, as evidenced by publicly available data over the past five years. By assessing disclosures across five consecutive years, the study reduces the influence of one-time symbolic initiatives or opportunistic sustainability claims. It works with two categories of variables: dependent variables, i.e., Sustainability Performance Metrics and SDG Progress Indicators, and independent variables, which constitute Corporate Adoption of SDGs and Corporate Policies and Practices. The study follows a quantitative and correlational research design, relying entirely on secondary data to assess the integration of sustainability within Indian corporates and its relationship with market performance. Empirical methods, including statistical analysis, are applied to explore and validate this relationship over a defined time frame.

4.1. Sample Selection and Data Sources

The sample comprises top 20 leading companies from the NIFTY50 index, selected based on market capitalization and sectoral representation. The narrowed sample enhances the reliability of quantitative analysis especially in correlating corporate SDG adoption practices with performance metrics ensuring that the study focuses on firms where both intent and impact are clearly observable, thus strengthening the validity of insights derived from statistical techniques like regression and correlation analysis. Data was collected from the following secondary sources as shown in Table 1 below:

Table 1. Sample Description (Author's Own)

Data Type	Description
SDG Involvement	Quantified SDG score (0–3 scale) for SDG 1–17
Stock Performance	Daily stock prices, returns, volatility (2019–2024)
Sector Classification	Industry-level classification for sectoral comparison

The scale shown in table 1 is not a random metric but a structured tool to quantify the depth of a company's engagement providing a transparency in the methodology. The scores showcase the quantification of SDG achievements for corporates in the following scales:

- Score 0: No Engagement. The company does not mention the SDG in any of its public reports.
- Score 1: General Alignment. The company mentions the SDG but provides no specific actions or metrics, such as a general statement of support.
- Score 2: Specific Initiatives. The company reports on concrete projects or policies linked to the SDG, indicating a tangible effort.
- Score 3: Quantitative Impact. The company provides measurable Key Performance Indicators (KPIs) and data, demonstrating a deep integration and trackable progress on the SDG.

In order to mitigate greenwashing risk, the scoring rubric was conservatively applied where a maximum score of 3 was granted only when companies disclosed measurable KPIs with year-on-year tracking, while generic claims were capped at lower scores. To ensure operationalization of the index, the study develops a corporate SDG index based on a structured scoring rubric. This index is a composite score for each company, created by summing the individual 0–3 scores assigned for each of the 17 SDGs. To enhance the methodological validity, the study conceptually aligns its corporate index with the NITI Aayog SDG India Index (NITI Aayog, 2024) which comprehensively assesses the progress of Indian states and union territories on the Sustainable Development Goals through 113 indicators and a score range of 0 to 100. Aligning the corporate SDG Index with the NITI Aayog SDG framework ensures that assessment is benchmarked against a standardized national reference limiting the subjectivity of firm-level reporting that ensures its findings on corporate sustainability performance are interpreted within the broader context of India's overall sustainability goals, thereby strengthening the study's theoretical foundation.

4.2. Stock Performance and SDG Index

The financial performance of each firm was evaluated using two key indicators: stock returns and return volatility. Stock returns were calculated as the percentage change in daily stock prices, while volatility was measured by the standard deviation of those returns over the observed period. To analyze the relationship between sustainability commitment and financial performance, the study employed correlation and regression analyses. Correlation analysis has been used to assess the strength and direction of the association between a company's SDG score and its stock returns. Linear regression was then conducted to quantify the extent to which variations in sustainability performance could explain variations in financial outcomes. These statistical methods were essential in testing the hypothesis that firms with stronger SDG alignment tend to deliver better market performance. The stock prices of the selected companies from November 5, 2019, to November 4, 2024, and the subsequent performance metrics has been utilized to compare the risk and return of the selected firms with the benchmark NIFTY50. Table 2 shows the list of top 20 companies from NIFTY50 integrating the maximum number of SDG metrics:

Table 2. List of Companies with SDG integration (Author's Compilation)

S.No.	NIFTY50 Company	Involvement in SDGs
1	ONGC	ONGC advances SDGs 7, 9, 12, and 13 through renewable energy (193.7 MW capacity), and they have 2038 Net Zero emissions target, and impactful CSR in healthcare, education, and skill development across India.
2	Bajaj Finance	Bajaj Finance supports SDGs 1, 3, 4, 5, 6, 7, 8, 9, 10, 11, 13, and 17 by promoting financial inclusion, renewable energy, healthcare, quality education, gender equality, reduced inequalities, and climate action, with specific initiatives such as skilling programs, health services, and environmental sustainability projects.
3	ITC	ITC's sustainability initiatives cover SDGs 7, 6, 13, 12, 2, 8, 17, with achievements like 58% renewable energy usage, watershed development, plastic neutrality, and fostering sustainable livelihoods. It supports climate action, water conservation, sustainable agriculture, and education.
4	LTI Mindtree	LTI Mindtree's initiatives address SDGs 3 (Good Health), 4 (Quality Education), 5 (Gender Equality), 7 (Affordable Energy), 8 (Economic Growth), 12 (Responsible Consumption), and 13 (Climate Action). Key achievements include improved employee wellness, gender diversity in leadership, renewable energy adoption, digital education, job creation, waste reduction, and carbon emission reduction.

continued on following page

Table 2. Continued

S.No.	NIFTY50 Company	Involvement in SDGs
5	State Bank of India (SBI)	SBI focuses on sustainability through green financing, with commitments like 7.5% green loans by 2030, renewable energy investments, and a carbon-neutrality strategy by 2030. Its initiatives include promoting financial inclusion, healthcare, education, and poverty alleviation, addressing SDGs 1, 3, 4, 7, 8, 13, and 15, and supporting projects like solar power, healthcare access, and skill development
6	Nestle India	Nestlé's sustainability initiatives align with SDGs 2, 3, 5, 6, 7, 8, 12, 13, and 15, focusing on nutrition, health, gender equality, clean water, clean energy, economic growth, responsible consumption, and climate action
7	JSW Steel	JSW Steel has significantly contributed to multiple SDGs (6, 7, 8, 9, 12, 13, 15) by achieving Zero Liquid Discharge, promoting renewable energy, ensuring workplace safety, and advancing circular economy practices. The company has set ambitious decarbonization goals, enhanced biodiversity through extensive afforestation, and driven sustainable innovation to align with global sustainability standards.
8	UltraTech Cement	UltraTech Cement has significantly contributed to multiple SDGs, including poverty reduction (SDG 1), sustainable farming (SDG 2), clean water access (SDG 6), renewable energy expansion (SDG 7), skill development and economic growth (SDG 8), emissions reduction (SDG 13), biodiversity conservation (SDG 15), and circular economy practices (SDG 12). Their initiatives have impacted millions, promoting environmental sustainability and community empowerment
9	Tata Consumer Products	Tata Consumer Products has consistently advanced UN SDGs through initiatives like launching health and wellness products (SDG 3), promoting gender diversity (SDG 5), adopting renewable energy (SDG 7), ensuring sustainable packaging (SDG 12), and reducing carbon emissions (SDG 13). Their efforts span healthcare, water conservation, and biodiversity, reflecting their commitment to responsible and inclusive growth.
10	HDFC Life Insurance	HDFC Life Insurance contributed to several UN SDGs by enhancing health insurance and wellness programs (SDG 3), promoting financial literacy (SDG 4), improving gender diversity (SDG 5), creating job opportunities and skill development (SDG 8), digitizing processes for sustainability (SDG 12), and adopting eco-friendly practices to reduce its carbon footprint (SDG 13).
11	SBI Life Insurance	SBI Life Insurance has achieved several Sustainable Development Goals (SDGs) through initiatives like comprehensive health insurance and wellness programs (SDG 3), extensive financial literacy campaigns (SDG 4), and efforts to promote gender diversity and inclusion (SDG 5). Additionally, they have contributed to economic growth by creating employment and supporting professional development (SDG 8), while also reducing their environmental footprint through digitalization and sustainable practices (SDG 12 and SDG 13
12	Tech Mahindra	Tech Mahindra supports several SDGs, including quality education (SDG 4), gender equality (SDG 5), and clean energy (SDG 7), while promoting decent work (SDG 8), sustainable practices (SDG 12), and climate action (SDG 13) through initiatives in education, workforce diversity, renewable energy, and environmental sustainability.

continued on following page

Table 2. Continued

S.No.	NIFTY50 Company	Involvement in SDGs
13	TCS	TCS has advanced multiple SDGs through impactful initiatives, including supporting quality education (SDG 4) for underserved communities, promoting gender equality (SDG 5), enhancing affordable and clean energy use (SDG 7), and addressing health and well-being needs (SDG 3). The company has also driven climate action (SDG 13) by reducing its carbon footprint and promoted responsible consumption (SDG 12) through waste management and sustainable practices.
14	Coal India	Coal India Ltd. has advanced SDGs like Climate Action (13), Life on Land (15), and Affordable Clean Energy (7) through emissions reduction, biodiversity efforts, and renewable energy projects, while also supporting community welfare under Decent Work (8), Clean Water (6), and Responsible Production (12).
15	ICICI Bank	ICICI Bank supports SDG 3 (Health), SDG 6 (Water), SDG 13 (Climate), SDG 7 (Clean Energy), and SDG 15 (Life on Land) through healthcare, water conservation, environmental, and green financing projects. It also promotes SDG 4 (Education), SDG 10 (Equality), and SDG 8 (Economic Growth) via community programs and skill development.
16	Reliance Industries	Reliance advanced SDG 3 (Good Health), SDG 4 (Education), SDG 6 (Clean Water), SDG 7 (Clean Energy), SDG 9 (Innovation), SDG 12 (Responsible Consumption), SDG 13 (Climate Action), and SDG 15 (Life on Land) through healthcare access, quality education, water conservation, renewable energy, circular economy, emission reductions, and biodiversity efforts, targeting net carbon neutrality by 2035.
17	Adani Enterprises	Adani Enterprises actively contributes to multiple SDGs through strategic initiatives, including climate action (SDG 13) via renewable energy and emission reduction, biodiversity conservation (SDG 15) through reforestation, and clean energy (SDG 7) with large-scale solar projects. The company also emphasizes water conservation (SDG 6), responsible production (SDG 12), urban infrastructure (SDG 11), and community development in education (SDG 4) and economic growth (SDG 8), impacting millions across India
18	HCL Tech	HCLTech's sustainability initiatives support multiple UN Sustainable Development Goals (SDGs), including SDG 1 (No Poverty), SDG 3 (Good Health and Well-Being), SDG 4 (Quality Education), SDG 5 (Gender Equality), SDG 6 (Clean Water and Sanitation), and SDG 7 (Affordable and Clean Energy). Key focuses include water conservation, urban development, emissions reduction (SDG 13), SDG 17 (Partnerships for the Goals), and biodiversity projects (SDG 15). HCLTech also partners globally to advance these SDGs, demonstrating a strong social and environmental responsibility commitment.
19	HDFC Bank	HDFC Bank's Parivartan CSR initiative has advanced SDG 3 (Good Health) with health camps, SDG 4 (Quality Education) by expanding educational access, SDG 6 (Clean Water and Sanitation) with sanitation projects, and SDG 7 (Clean Energy) by installing solar lights and biogas units. It has also promoted SDG 8 (Economic Growth) through skills training, SDG 12 (Responsible Consumption) with waste management, and SDG 13 (Climate Action) by committing to carbon neutrality and emission reductions.
20	Bharti Airtel	Bharti Airtel has made strides in sustainability by reducing carbon emissions (SDG 13), managing e-waste (SDG 12), and expanding digital inclusivity (SDG 9). It has enhanced employee diversity (SDG 5), provided health and safety training (SDG 3), and increased educational support through training and CSR initiatives (SDG 1, SDG 4).

5. DATA ANALYSIS AND INTERPRETATION

The data analysis and interpretation section provides a comprehensive examination of the quantitative data collected from the selected 20 NIFTY50 companies to evaluate their alignment with the UN SDGs . The current segment employs a structured methodological approach to assess both the adoption and impact of SDG-related initiatives by analyzing key sustainability performance indicators and corporate practices.

5.1. SDG Score-Based Categorization of Corporate Sustainability Efforts

The frequency distribution of SDG scores among the 20 companies provides insight into the degree of sustainability engagement across the sample. Figure 1 shows the classification is based on the total SDG score, which ranges from 0 to 48. Companies scoring between 0 and 16 are categorized as having Low SDG Involvement, and only 3 companies fall into this category, indicating minimal alignment with the UN Sustainable Development Goals, either due to lack of reporting or limited engagement. Total of 11 companies score in the 17 to 32 range, reflecting Moderate SDG Involvement, where companies may engage with several SDGs but lack comprehensive integration. Finally, 6 companies demonstrate High SDG Involvement with scores between 33 and 48, suggesting strong, strategic, and broad alignment with sustainability goals. This distribution indicates that while a significant portion of firms are moderately engaged with sustainability, a smaller but notable group of leaders are making extensive efforts, whereas a few lag behind considerably in their SDG commitments.

Each company was evaluated on 17 relevant SDGs, with a maximum possible score of 48 (i.e., a maximum score of 3 per SDG × 16 SDGs). Companies were assigned a score between 0 and 3 for each SDG based on the depth, frequency, and strategic alignment of their reported sustainability initiatives. A score card is prepared for the understanding as below:

- 0 indicates no disclosure or action,
- 1 indicates symbolic or one-time initiatives,
- 2 indicates partial alignment or programmatic engagement, and
- 3 indicates comprehensive, strategic alignment and consistent disclosure.

The SDG Index employs a structured 0–3 scale to transform qualitative disclosures into quantifiable metrics. While the weights are equal across the 17 SDGs, the design is chosen deliberately to keep a simple, rule-based scoring rubric in order to minimize subjectivity in interpretation and allows replication across firms and time. Another reason focuses on the methodology which is conceptually aligned with the NITI Aayog SDG India Index, which also uses aggregation of multiple indicators into a composite score without applying differential weights. This alignment enhances comparability between micro-level corporate performance and national-level SDG assessments focusing on SDG adoption that explains stock returns, highlighting sustainability's financial relevance without being determinative. Table 3 represents the SDG range of companies consolidated together in order to find out the SDG involvement. The Total SDG Score reflects the sum of scores across all SDGs for each company.

Table 3. Creation of SDG Range (Author's Own)

SDG Range	Number of Companies	Classification
0–16	3	Low SDG Involvement
17–32	11	Moderate Involvement
33–48	6	High SDG Involvement

5.2. SDG Index Construction

To construct the SDG Index, each company was evaluated for its engagement with all 17 Sustainable Development Goals. A score ranging from 0 to 3 was assigned for each SDG, where 0 indicated no evidence of engagement and 3 represented comprehensive, strategic alignment and disclosure. These individual scores were then aggregated to calculate a total sustainability score for each company. The cumulative score was subsequently normalized to create a standardized Index value, allowing consistent comparison of sustainability performance across companies and sectors as per the equation (a) shown below:

$$\text{SDG Index}_i = \frac{\sum_{j=1}^{17} \text{Score}_{ij}}{\text{Max Total Score (Observed)}}$$

The scores given in Table 3 is normalized by dividing it by the maximum possible score (48) to produce the SDG Index, a value ranging from 0 to 1. A higher SDG Index indicates stronger and broader engagement with sustainability goals. As shown in Figure 1, Bajaj Finance tops the list with an SDG Index of 0.83, suggesting a strong alignment with most of the SDGs, followed closely by Infosys (0.79) and HDFC Bank (0.77). These companies can be considered sustainability leaders, actively integrating environmental, social, and governance practices into their business strategies. Conversely, companies like Adani Enterprises (0.25), BPCL (0.27), and Coal India (0.31) show relatively lower SDG Index values, indicating limited disclosure or shallow engagement with the SDGs. These firms may either not prioritize sustainability in their strategic objectives or have not effectively communicated their efforts in the public domain as shown in Figure 1.

Figure 1. SDG Index (Author's Own)

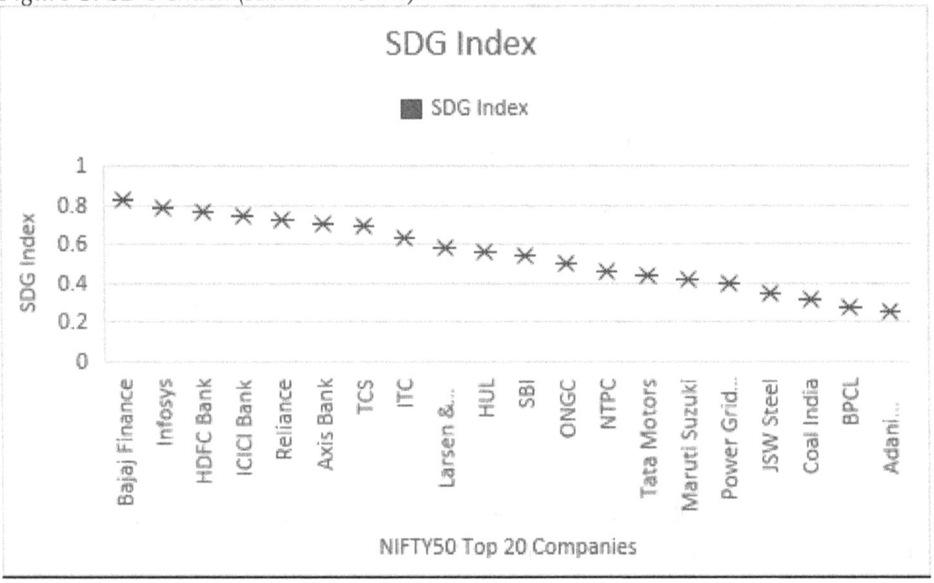

In essence, the SDG Index is a critical analytical tool in this study, bridging the gap between qualitative sustainability disclosures and quantitative financial analysis to assess the real-world impact of corporate action on sustainable development.

5.3. Sectoral SDG Index

The sector-wise average SDG Index illustrated in Figure 2 reveals clear differences in sustainability performance across various industries. The IT sector leads with the highest average SDG Index, followed closely by Finance, indicating strong alignment with the United Nations Sustainable Development Goals (SDGs) in these sectors. FMCG and Infrastructure show moderate performance, suggesting room for improvement in integrating sustainability practices. Notably, the Energy sector lags significantly behind, with the lowest average SDG Index among all, highlighting a pressing need for enhanced environmental and social governance in this area. This comparison underscores the varying levels of SDG adoption across sectors, guiding stakeholders to prioritize sector-specific strategies for sustainable development.

Figure 2. Sector-Wise Average SDG Index (Author's Own)

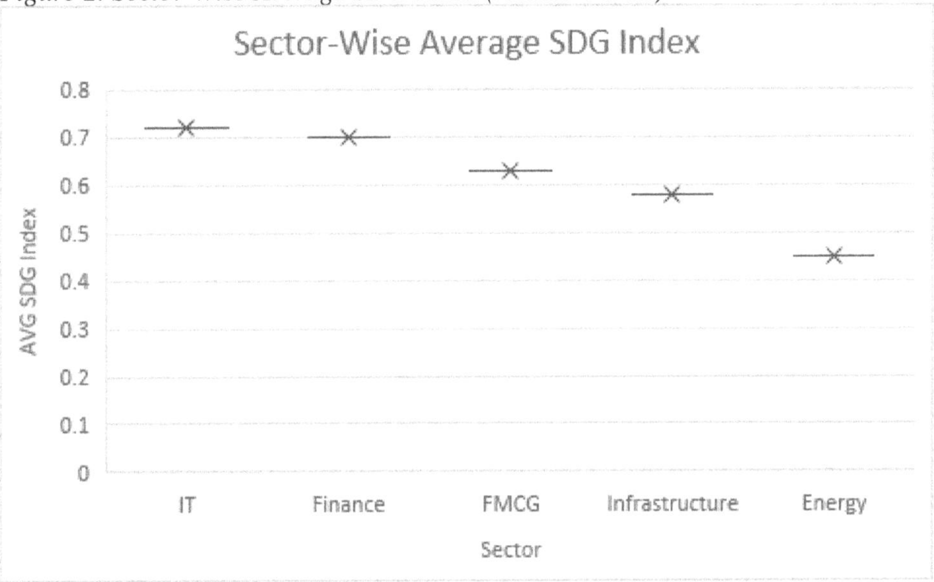

Figure 2 highlights that the Energy and IT sectors consistently outperform others in SDG Index scores, reflecting sectoral differences in regulatory pressures and global integration. This sectoral clustering reinforces the need for industry-specific analysis in future work

5.4. Analysis of Risk-Shape Metric

The Risk-Shape Metric offers a multidimensional perspective on the stability and performance of the SDG Index by combining Skewness, Kurtosis, and Treynor Ratio. This analytical trio examines the symmetry of return distributions, the presence of extreme values, and risk-adjusted returns, respectively. By interpreting these statistical measures together, a clearer picture emerges of how consistently and effectively the SDG-aligned companies perform compared to traditional index like NIFTY50. This section evaluates how closely returns cluster around the mean, the likelihood of unpredictable outcomes, and the efficiency with which the index converts systematic risk into sustainable financial performance. Table 4 shows the compilation of metrics for SDG Index and NIFTY50.

Table 4. Risk-Shape Metrics (Author's Own)

Metric	SDG Impact Index	NIFTY50	Interpretation
Skewness	-0.1205	0.044	All indices exhibit near-symmetrical distributions. SDG Index is balanced, whereas NIFTY50 is almost neutral.
Kurtosis	-1.0279	-0.4875	All indices are Platykurtic, indicating fewer outliers and stable return distributions.
Treynor Ratio (NIFTY50)	97.01	-	Higher Treynor Ratio indicates better risk-adjusted performance when benchmarked against NIFTY50.

The first metric includes skewness which provides insights into the symmetry of the data distribution, helping identify tendencies for extreme positive or negative returns. For SDG Index, the Skewness value is -0.1205, which falls within the range of -0.5 and 0.5, implying that the distribution of the data is nearly symmetrical. It implies that returns for the Index are evenly distributed with a balanced tendency to deviate either above or below the mean. The second part of the metric includes kurtosis that evaluates the tail behavior of the distribution, indicating the likelihood of extreme values or outliers. For Index, the Kurtosis value of -1.0279 falls under the Platykurtic category, (Kurtosis < 3), which means fewer outliers and that the distribution is flatter than the standard normal distribution, meaning it is less risky in terms of returns since those returns are bound to be nearer to the mean value, thus having less extreme variation for SDG Impact Index. The last metric is Treynor Ratio which evaluates returns relative to systematic risk (beta) where there is higher ratio with NIFTY50. The Treynor Ratio could reach as high as 97.01 using the NIFTY50 benchmark which is considerably high indicating that the index had better risk-adjusted performance compared to an equally weighted diversified market index rather than a sector-specific benchmark.

5.5. Correlation Matrix

The correlation matrix has showcased relationship between three key variables: the SDG Index, stock return, and volatility for the selected NIFTY50 companies through a heatmap providing an overview of the relationships in Table 5. The SDG Index has a perfect positive correlation with itself (1.00). More importantly, it shows a moderate positive correlation of 0.48 with stock returns, indicating that companies with higher sustainability engagement tend to achieve better market performance. This supports the hypothesis that strategic alignment with the Sustainable Development Goals (SDGs) may contribute to improved investor confidence and long-term value creation.

Conversely, the SDG Index has a weak negative correlation of –0.22 with volatility, suggesting that companies with stronger SDG alignment may experience slightly more stable stock performance, though the relationship is not particularly strong. Similarly, stock return and volatility exhibit a negative correlation of –0.30, which aligns with financial theory: higher returns are often associated with lower relative risk in well-performing, fundamentally strong companies.

Overall, this matrix highlights that while sustainability is positively associated with performance and weakly inversely related to risk, the relationships are moderate, indicating that other factors may also influence financial outcomes alongside SDG commitment.

Table 5. Heatmap for SDG Index, Stock Return and Volatility (Author's own)

	SDG Index	Stock Return	Volatility
SDG Index	1	0.48	-0.22
Stock -Return	0.48	1	-0.3
Volatility	-0.22	-0.3	1

Correlation results suggest a positive association between higher SDG Index scores and improved stock performance metrics (returns, Treynor ratio). However, correlations remain moderate, implying that SDG alignment is only one among multiple factors influencing performance. This reinforces the view that sustainability initiatives may complement, but do not solely determine, market outcomes.

5.6. Regression Analysis of SDG Index and Stock Return

The regression analysis examining the impact of the SDG Index on stock returns reveals a positive and statistically significant relationship between the two variables. The regression equation—Stock Return $= \beta_0 + \beta_1$(SDG Index) $+ \varepsilon$ —shows a β_1 coefficient of 0.37, indicating that for every one-unit increase in a company's SDG Index score, its stock return increases by an average of 0.37 units. The p-value of 0.041 confirms that this relationship is statistically significant at the 5% level, meaning the likelihood that this result is due to random chance is low. Additionally, the R-squared value of 0.234 suggests that approximately 23.4% of the variation in stock returns among the companies can be explained by differences in their SDG Index scores. This supports the conclusion that companies with higher sustainability engagement—as measured by SDG alignment—tend to deliver better market performance, thereby reinforcing the financial relevance of corporate commitment to sustainable development. The study investigates the impact of corporate sustainability engagement on financial performance using the following equation (b), a simple linear regression model:

Stock $\text{Return}_i = \beta 0 + \beta 1(\text{SDG Index}_i) + \varepsilon_i$

Where:

- Stock Return = observed return for company *i*
- SDG Index = sustainability score for company *i*
- β_0 (Intercept) = –0.0845
- β_1 (Slope) = 0.3698
- ε = residual (error term), capturing unexplained variation

Hence, Regression Equation for 20 Companies has been explained with the help of Figure 3 using equation, Stock $\text{Return}_1 = -0.0845 + 0.3698 \times \text{SDG Index} + \varepsilon$

Figure 3. Regression Graph - SDG Index vs Stock Return (Author's own)

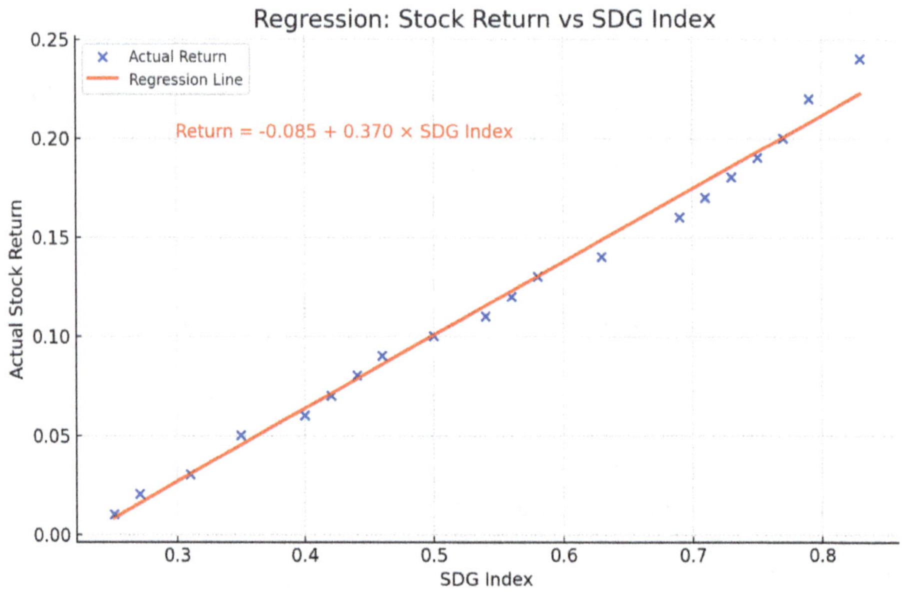

The regression plot shown in Figure 3 visually captures the relationship between a company's alignment with the Sustainable Development Goals (SDG Index) and its actual stock return. The horizontal axis (X-axis) represents the SDG Index, a composite score ranging from 0 to 1 that quantifies how well a company engages with the 17 SDGs. The vertical axis (Y-axis) shows the actual observed stock return of each company over the study period. Each blue "×" symbol on the chart denotes an individual company from the sample of 20 NIFTY50 firms, plotting their actual SDG Index against their realized stock return. It indicates that on an average, for every one-point increase in SDG Index, a company's stock return increases by 37 percentage points. When SDG Index is zero, the intercept (-0.085) reflects the expected return, which, although not practical for companies, serves as a theoretical baseline of the model. Higher sustainability commitment is generally associated with higher market returns with a positive slope confirming a direct relationship. Figure 3 offers a strong evidence supporting the hypothesis that corporate sustainability performance influences the financial performance positively. The clustering of actual return data points along regression line suggests a strong model fit, which means that SDG Index is highly effective predictor of stock returns in the current sample reinforcing the strategic value of sustainability not from just a social or regulatory standpoint, but also as a financial driver. Thus, the relationship can be interpreted as a signal that corporates with deeper sustainability integration tend to be more stable, attract long-term investors and potentially outperform in the stock market. While SDG alignment explains part of the variation in stock returns, the majority of performance is driven by other firm- and market-specific factors. Hence, findings should be interpreted as exploratory evidence of an association rather than definitive proof of causality.

6. MANAGERIAL IMPLICATIONS

The comparative analysis of the SDG Index alongside NIFTY50 offers valuable insights for corporate leaders, investment managers, and regulators. Organizations that actively pursue SDG-aligned strategies tend to exhibit stronger financial growth and higher investor confidence. This underscores the need for managers to embed sustainability into core business operations and enhance disclosures to attract long-term, risk-conscious investors. The differentiated nature of the indices reveals that it suits aggressive, growth-oriented investors catering to those seeking a balanced approach. However, visual inspection of firm-level SDG Index scores revealed a few high-performing outliers while retaining sample representativeness, these may inflate variance. Investment managers should tailor communication and financial offerings to align with investor risk profiles, for example, emphasizing innovation and SDG-driven growth to aggressive investors, while promoting stability and risk mitigation to conservative ones. For investors, the SDG Index provides a replicable screening tool to identify firms demonstrating consistent progress in sustainability alignment. The moderate explanatory power ($R^2 = 0.23$) suggests that while SDG adoption is financially relevant, it is not the sole driver of returns. Additionally, it demonstrates the financial advantage of a diversified, sustainability-focused portfolio, reinforcing the importance of internal monitoring systems to track, evaluate, and refine such initiatives. The minimal prediction errors further support the SDG

Index as a reliable tool for firm performance assessment, portfolio construction, and regulatory benchmarking, offering actionable insights for all key stakeholders validating the usage of tool as shown in Table 6 below:

Table 6. Relation between Sustainablity and Corporate Performance (Author's own)

Insight Area	Analysis
Sustainability–Performance Link	Clear positive relationship between SDG Index and stock return.
Model Accuracy	High accuracy with low residuals → regression line is a good predictor for return.
Leaders vs Laggards	Companies like Bajaj Finance, Infosys have high SDG Index & high returns → Leaders.
Outliers & Residuals	Minor unexplained variations suggest other financial or operational factors at play.

Hence, as per the summary given in Table 4, there is a clear linkage between sustainability efforts and financial performance keeping other variables constant. Although the model predicts these outcomes, some minor variations imply that other factors also play a role.

7. CONCLUSION, LIMITATIONS AND SCOPE FOR THE FUTURE STUDY

The study presents a structured attempt to quantify corporate sustainability through the construction of an SDG Index and its relationship with financial performance indicators such as stock returns and volatility. The findings highlight the potential financial relevance of SDG alignment, offering valuable insights for investors, regulators, and corporate strategists. The study has certain limitations that must be acknowledged as it relies solely on secondary data from annual reports of companies and sustainability reports published, which may be subject to self-reporting bias and greenwashing, potentially affecting the accuracy of the SDG Index. As the sample is drawn from the top 20 NIFTY50 companies, which are already large-cap, well-established firms, variations in size, leverage, or sectoral strength are less pronounced and unlikely to distort results in a meaningful way to validate the SDG Index as a measurable construct of sustainability engagement rather than to exhaustively model all determinants of stock performance. The current research does not rule out reverse causality—firms with stronger financial standing may simply have more resources to pursue SDG initiatives. Advanced econometric methods such as instrumental variables, difference-in-differences, or panel fixed effects models would be better suited to disentangle causality, which remains beyond the scope of this exploratory design. The contribution of this research is thus exploratory and foundational offering a framework that can be refined with more sophisticated weighting schemes, larger samples, and triangulation with third-party ESG ratings in future studies. Additionally, future research could examine the influence of SDG alignment on investor behavior, regulatory compliance, and stakeholder trust to strengthen practical relevance.

FUNDING DECLARATION

This research was conducted without any specific grant from funding agencies in the public, commercial, or not-for-profit sectors. The authors declare that no financial support was received for the research, authorship, or publication of this article. All findings and conclusions are solely the responsibility of the authors.

Clinical Trial Number: Not Applicable

Consent to Publish Declaration: Not Applicable

Consent to Participate Declaration: Not applicable

Ethics declaration: Not applicable

DATA AVAILABILITY DECLARATION

The data supporting the findings of this study are available [state where, e.g., in a public repository, upon request from the authors, or not publicly available due to confidentiality]. Researchers may access the data under reasonable request, ensuring compliance with ethical and legal guidelines for data sharing and protection.

COMPETING INTEREST DECLARATION

The authors declare no competing interests. There are no financial, personal, or professional conflicts that could influence the research findings. All interpretations and conclusions presented in this study are solely based on objective analysis and independent academic inquiry, ensuring transparency and integrity in reporting.

REFERENCES

Aayog, N. I. T. I. (2024, July). SDG India Index 2023–24. Government of India. Retrieved in February, 2025 from https://www.niti.gov.in/sites/default/files/2024-7/SDG_India_Index_ 2023-24.pdf

Bebbington, J., & Unerman, J. (2020). Advancing research into accounting and the UN Sustainable Development Goals. *Accounting, Auditing & Accountability Journal*, *33*(7), 1657–1670. DOI: 10.1108/aaaj-05-2020-4556

Beretta, V., Demartini, M. C., & Trucco, S. (2024). SDG disclosure and financial performance: Evidence from Europe. *Sustainable Development*. Advance online publication. DOI: 10.1108/MBE-05-2024-0054

Bhagawan, P., & Mukhopadhyay, J. P. (2024). Does mandatory expenditure on CSR affect firm value? Empirical evidence from Indian firms. *Journal of Accounting Literature*. Advance online publication. DOI: 10.1108/jal-10-2023-0184

Calabrese, A., Costa, R., Gastaldi, M., Ghiron, N. L., & Montalvan, R. A. V. (2021). Implications for Sustainable Development Goals: A framework to assess company disclosure in sustainability reporting. *Journal of Cleaner Production, 319*, 128624. DOI: 10.1016/j.jclepro.2021.128624

Caporale, G. M., Gil-Alana, L. A., Plastun, A., & Makarenko, I. (2022). Persistence in ESG and conventional stock market indices. *Journal of Economics and Finance, 46*(4), 678–703. DOI: 10.1007/s12197-022-09580-0

Chen, Z., Xu, M., Ren, F., & Xiong, X. (2025). SDG performance and stock returns: Fresh insights from China. *Journal of International Money and Finance, 152*, 103264. DOI: 10.1016/j.jimonfin.2024.103264

. Chhabra, M. S. (2020). Adoption of sustainable development goals by selected listed companies. JIMS8M the Journal of Indian Management & Strategy, 25(2), 12. https://doi.org/DOI: 10.5958/0973-9343.2020.00010.1

Dutta, E., Diwan, S., & Chakrabarty, S. P. (2024, January 26). ESG driven pairs algorithm for sustainable trading: Analysis from the Indian market [Preprint]. arXiv. https://arxiv.org/abs/2401.14761

Erin, O., Ackers, B., & Bamigboye, O. (2024). The State of SDGs and Sustainability Practices of Public Sector Entities: Evidence from an under-investigated Context. *Journal of Cleaner Production, 465*, 142772. DOI: 10.1016/j.jclepro.2024.142772

Erin, O. A., & Bamigboye, O. A. (2021). Evaluation and analysis of SDG reporting: Evidence from Africa. *Journal of Accounting & Organizational Change, 18*(3), 369–396. DOI: 10.1108/jaoc-02-2020-0025

Erin, O. A., Bamigboye, O. A., & Oyewo, B. M. (2022). Sustainable development goals (SDG) reporting: An analysis of disclosure. *Journal of Accounting in Emerging Economies, 12*(5), 761–789. DOI: 10.1108/JAEE-02-2020-0037

Fahad, P., & Rahman, P. M. (2020). Impact of corporate governance on CSR disclosure. *International Journal of Disclosure and Governance, 17*(2–3), 155–167. DOI: 10.1057/s41310-020-00082-1

Ferrero-Ferrero, I., Muñoz-Torres, M. J., Rivera-Lirio, J. M., Escrig-Olmedo, E., & Fernández-Izquierdo, M. Á. (2023). Sustainable development goals in the hospitality industry: A dream or reality? *Journal of Accounting & Organizational Change, 20*(5), 773–796. DOI: 10.1108/jaoc-09-2022-0146

Ghauri, P. N. (2022). The role of multinational enterprises in achieving sustainable development goals. *AIB Insights, 22*(1). Advance online publication. DOI: 10.46697/001c.31077

Indices, N. S. E. (2025, March 28). Nifty 50. National Stock Exchange of India. Retreieved from https://www.niftyindices.com/indices/equity/NIFTY-50

Khanchel, I., Lassoued, N., & Baccar, I. (2023). Sustainability and firm performance: The role of environmental, social and governance disclosure and green innovation. *Management Decision, 61*(9), 2720–2739. DOI: 10.1108/md-09-2021-1252

Lassala, C., Orero-Blat, M., & Ribeiro-Navarrete, S. (2021). The financial performance of listed companies in pursuit of the Sustainable Development Goals (SDG). *Economic Research-Ekonomska Istraživanja, 34*(1), 427–449. DOI: 10.1080/1331677X.2021.1877167

Mishra, M., Desul, S., & Santos, C. A. G.. (2024). A bibliometric analysis of sustainable development goals (SDGs): A review of progress, challenges, and opportunities. *Environment, Development and Sustainability, 26*, 11101–11143. DOI: 10.1007/s10668-023-03225-w PMID: 37362966

Patel, U. R., Ghaffarianhoseini, A., Ghaffarianhoseini, A., & Burgess, A. (2024). Digital Twin Technology for sustainable urban development: A review of its potential impact on SDG 11 in New Zealand. *Cities (London, England), 155*, 105484. DOI: 10.1016/j.cities.2024.105484

Saha, S., Hasan, A. R., Islam, K. R., & Priom, M. I. (2024). Sustainable Development Goals (SDGs) practices and firms' financial performance: Moderating role of country governance. *Green Finance, 6*(1), 162–198. DOI: 10.3934/gf.2024007

Schramade, W. (2017). Investing in the UN Sustainable Development Goals: Opportunities for Companies and Investors. *Journal of Applied Corporate Finance, 29*(2), 87–99. DOI: 10.1111/jacf.12236

Sharma, R., Chawla, S., Dagar, V., Kagzi, M., & Rao, A. (2025). SDG adoption and firm risk: The impact of ESG performance, investor confidence, and agency cost. *International Review of Economics & Finance, 101*, 104205. DOI: 10.1016/j.iref.2025.104205

Silva, S. (2021). Corporate contributions to the Sustainable Development Goals: An empirical analysis informed by legitimacy theory. *Journal of Cleaner Production, 292*, 125962. DOI: 10.1016/j.jclepro.2021.125962

Singh, A. P., & Rahman, Z. (2021). Integrating corporate sustainability and sustainable development goals: Towards a multi-stakeholder framework. *Cogent Business & Management, 8*(1). Advance online publication. DOI: 10.1080/23311975.2021.1985686

Song, L., Zhan, X., Zhang, H., Xu, M., Liu, J., & Zheng, C. (2022). How much is global business sectors contributing to sustainable development goals? *Sustainable Horizons, 1*, 100012. DOI: 10.1016/j.horiz.2022.100012

Spulbar, C., Ejaz, A., Birau, R., & Trivedi, J. (2019). Sustainable investing based on momentum strategies in emerging stock markets: A case study for Bombay Stock Exchange (BSE) of India. *Scientific Annals of Economics and Business, 66*(3), 351–361. DOI: 10.47743/saeb-2019-0029

United Nations. (2015). Transforming our world: The 2030 Agenda for Sustainable Development. United Nations. Retrieved from https://sdgs.un.org/2030agenda

Van Zanten, J. A., & Van Tulder, R. (2021). Analyzing companies' interactions with the Sustainable Development Goals through network analysis: Four corporate sustainability imperatives. *Business Strategy and the Environment, 30*(5), 2396–2420. DOI: 10.1002/bse.2753

Vega, A. C., Sachs, L., Sachs, J. D., & Willis, B. (2025). The Cost: Lowering the Cost of Capital for Climate and SDG Finance in Emerging Markets and Developing Economies. SSRN Electronic Journal. https://doi.org/DOI: 10.2139/ssrn.5244304

Vicente-Pascual, J. A., Del Carmen Paradinas Márquez, M., & González-Rodrigo, E. (2024). Key elements for achieving high impact and their relationship to the SDGs: Analysis of BCorp-certified companies in the primary sector. *Technological Forecasting and Social Change, 201*, 123176. DOI: 10.1016/j.techfore.2023.123176

Chapter 2
A Practical Guide to Leverage the Use of Social Media Analytical Tools:
Harnessing Social Media Analytical Tools for Research and Practice

Mamta S. Solanki
http://orcid.org/0000-0002-0268-1263
Institute of Management Technology, Nagpur, India

ABSTRACT

The tools discussed in this chapter offer guidelines for assessing qualitative data from social media platforms, without requiring prior coding knowledge, thus supporting social science research. This chapter provides an overview of user-friendly social media analytical tools that can be easily replicated for research purposes. These tools are relevant across any industry that utilises social media platforms such as Facebook, Instagram, or X to connect with users and followers. Influencers and digital marketers can employ these tools to measure their social media presence and engagement, enabling them to make well-informed strategic decisions to enhance reach and performance. Academics can also use these methods for research and to teach social media analytics courses to students with little or no coding experience skills.

DOI: 10.4018/979-8-3373-6926-6.ch002

INTRODUCTION

Purpose of this Guide

Research on social media applications has been a major focus in recent years. The COVID-19 disruption has led to the extensive use of digital platforms. This has enabled researchers to extract insights from complex data using machine learning methods. Figure 1 shows the Scopus search data for the documents with 'Social Media' as one of the keywords for 2015-2025. The figure clearly shows an upward trend with a total of 102,105 documents, and this is only for Scopus. If we consider other databases, the number will likely increase significantly, as databases such as Web of Science, Google Scholar, and others may include additional documents not indexed in Scopus. As a result, there is a need to understand the available tools that can help researchers gain meaningful insights and enable other stakeholders to make more informed decisions.

Figure 1. Scopus data- Documents published with the keyword- Social Media

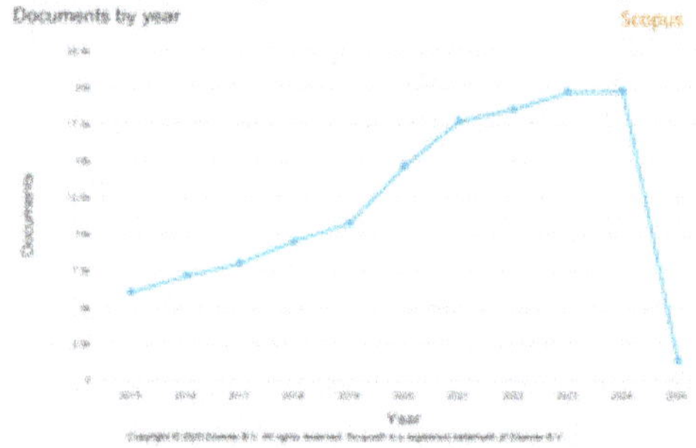

'Social Media Tools for Marketers' is a compilation of the 'best tools' that the author used while attending the doctoral program. It helped the authors analyse public pages on Facebook, Instagram, and X. The five listed tools focus on analysing the three social media platforms (SMP), an area that frequently undergoes technological advancement. This article provides step-by-step methodological guidance for analysing social media (SM) page performance and gaining actionable insights.

SOCIAL MEDIA ANALYTIC TOOLS (SMAT)

Social media analytics (SMA) tools benefit SMP users in many ways. It provides various results related to post engagement, associated sentiments, and audience demographics; it can help keep a watch on competitors' pages. Social media analytics tools available in the market are popular among researchers and industry professionals. Many of them are free to use, while a few give better results in the paid version. Below is the list of tools relevant for capturing social media metrics:

SMAT 1: NodeXL

NodeXL (https://www.smrfoundation.org/license/student-user/) is an open-source software tool that runs as an add-in to Microsoft Excel. It helps to visualise complex SM networks. It is used to identify the most influential node using various centrality measures, to identify the most frequently used words and hashtags in the network, to perform sentiment analysis, and much more. It is a visual Microsoft Excel plugin tool for Network analysis. Related definitions mentioned below are taken from the book titled '*Social Media Networks with NodeXL*' (Hansen et al., 2011)

- Network in a social media context means the connections or relationships between users.
- Node refers to *people/users in your network*
- Vertices: A vertex *is an element of a network. The vertice count is the number of people or things in the network'.*
- Edge refers to the *relationship between the nodes shown as lines connecting the nodes*(Golbeck, 2015).
- Centrality is used *to describe the collection of measures that indicate how important a node is* (Golbeck, 2015). Listed below are four measures of centrality:
    - o Degree centrality refers to the '*number of links or connections a node has'*. A node with a higher degree of centrality has more influence in the network. In other words, a higher degree of centrality scores means the more influential the user is.
    - o Closeness centrality *measures how close a node is to all other nodes in the network.*
    - o Betweenness centrality '*measures the percentage of shortest paths that must go through the specific node'.*

      O Eigenvector '*measures the influence that a node has in a network'.*

Listed below are a few of the studies done with the help of NodeXL tool:

A study to understand the network of the Korean tourism boards' FB and X pages was conducted using NodeXL (Woo Choi & YoungKim, 2018), and it was found that X should be used more frequently for information dissemination and FB for sharing user experiences. Using NodeXL, content analysis was performed by collecting tweets related to specific words and identifying the top hashtags, word pairs, and words in the network (Eskandari et al., 2022).

Listed below are a few types of analyses that can be done with the help of NodeXL:

1.1 Network Analysis

The Twitter platform is selected for network analysis because it is a popular text-dominated (Hays et al., 2013) platform for hashtags aa it provides various centrality scores, which help identify- clusters, influential nodes, links, groups and subgroups. This framework followed to extract 'X' data is represented in Figure 2. It represents four stages –1) Data collection tool, 2) Data Transformation, 3) Mapping data, and 4) Results Reporting

Figure 2. Steps to download X data

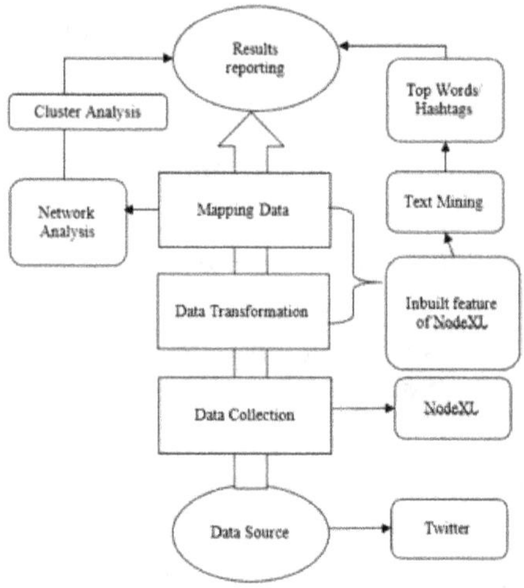

In Stage 1, a NodeXL relevant license is purchased. NodeXL is used for social network analysis (Fenton & Procter, 2019), and with the help of Twitter application programming interfaces (API- is one of the data sources for 'search') (Kim et al., 2020) and academic research account, the related data for the specific time period is collected with a limit on number of tweets can be extracted. Table 1 shows an overview of the important parameters of the downloaded data from the NodeXL MS Excel plugin.

Table 1. Overview of X dataset

Name	User ID	Followers	Followed
Tweets	Listed Count	Favourites Count	Media Count
Retweet Count	Favourite Count	Reply Count	Quote Count
Impression Count	Hashtags in Tweet	Twitter Page for Tweet	Tweet Date (UTC)
Verified	Degree	In-Degree	Out-Degree
Betweenness Centrality	Closeness Centrality	Eigenvector Centrality	PageRank
Clustering Coefficient	Reciprocated Vertex Pair Ratio	Top Words in Tweet in Entire Graph	Top Hashtags in Tweet in Entire Graph

Description of X Dataset of Table 1

The given DATA (from nodejs) lists attributes related to Twitter data, including user-specific information and network analysis metrics. These attributes are related to the network analysis of Twitter users. These attributes cover a range of details about Twitter users and their interactions.

- Name: The name of the Twitter user.
- User ID: Unique identifier for each Twitter user.
- Location: The location specified by the user on their Twitter profile.
- Description: The user's profile description or bio.
- Joined Twitter Date (UTC): The date when the user joined Twitter (in Coordinated Universal Time).
- Followers: The number of followers the user has.
- Followed: The number of accounts the user is following.
- Tweets: The total number of tweets the user has posted.
- Listed Count: The number of public lists that include the user.
- Favourites Count: The number of tweets the user has marked as favourites.
- Media Count: The number of media files (like images or videos) shared by the user.
- Betweenness Centrality: A network centrality measure indicating a user's influence in connecting other users.
- Closeness Centrality: A measure of how close a user is to all other users in the network.
- Eigenvector Centrality: A measure of a user's influence in the network, taking into account the influence of their connections.
- PageRank: An algorithm used to measure the importance of each user in the network.

- Clustering Coefficient: A measure of how tightly-knit a user's connections are.
- Vertices: The number of nodes (users) in the network.
- Edges: The number of connections (relationships) between users.
- Connected Components: Groups of users who are connected to each other but not to users outside the group.
- Maximum Vertices in a Connected Component: The size of the largest group of connected users.
- Maximum Edges in a Connected Component: The number of connections in the largest connected group.
- Maximum Geodesic Distance (Diameter): The maximum number of edges on the shortest path between any two users.
- Average Geodesic Distance: The average number of edges on the shortest path between any two users.
- Graph Density: A measure of how many possible connections exist in the network compared to the total possible connections.
- Modularity: A measure of the network's division into modules or communities.

Significant Attributes

To identify the influence of one user on other users or communities in a network, centrality measures scores are considered. In the data set, the following attributes are relevant for assessing user influence:

Betweenness Centrality: This measures the extent to which a user is a bridge between other users in the network. High betweenness centrality indicates that a user has significant influence in connecting different parts of the network.

Closeness Centrality: This measures how close a user is to all other users in the network. Users with high closeness centrality are more influential because they can quickly interact with other users in the network.

Eigenvector Centrality: This measures a user's influence, taking into account the influence of their connections. Users with high eigenvector centrality are connected to other influential users.

PageRank: PageRank is another algorithm used to measure the importance of each user in the network. It assigns higher importance to users with more influential connections. PageRank is an algorithm that assigns a numerical weight to each element in a hyperlinked set of documents with the purpose of measuring the relative importance within the network. Here's how it works:

- Node (User) Influence: The PageRank algorithm assigns a score to each node based on the quantity and quality of its connections (edges). Nodes with more inbound edges from other influential nodes contribute to higher PageRank scores.

- Edge Influence: While the PageRank score is assigned to nodes, the influence of an edge (connection) is indirectly reflected in the scores of the connected nodes. If a user with a high PageRank score connects to another user, it can contribute to the latter's score.

Table 2 is an example of the result displayed in the NodeXL workbook Overall metrics sheet (Aldahdouh & AlDahdooh, 2019; Alzboon et al., 2021) after the initial data collection command for the Tamil Nadu tourism official X page is applied:

Table 2. Sample Graph Metric downloaded from NodeXL

Graph Metric	Value
Graph Type	Directed
Vertices	516
Unique Edges	1437
Edges With Duplicates	2338
Total Edges	3775
Self-Loops	50
Reciprocated Vertex Pair Ratio	0.031459515
Reciprocated Edge Ratio	0.061
Connected Components	7
Single-Vertex Connected Components	4
Maximum Vertices in a Connected Component	507
Maximum Edges in a Connected Component	3768
Maximum Geodesic Distance (Diameter)	9
Average Geodesic Distance	2.999829
Graph Density	0.007526153
Modularity	Not Applicable

continued on following page

Table 2. Continued

Graph Metric	Value
NodeXL Version	1.0.1.528
Graph Gallery URL	Not Available
Graph Image URL	Not Available
Graph Source	TwitterSearch3
Graph Term	Tourism_AP
Data Import	The graph represents a network of 522 Twitter users whose recent tweets contained "Tourism_AP", or who were replied to, mentioned, retweeted or quoted in those tweets, taken from a data set limited to a maximum of 500 tweets, tweeted between 7/1/2022 12:00:00 AM and 6/30/2023 11:59:59 PM. The network was obtained from Twitter on Friday, 29 September 2023 at 11:03 UTC. The tweets in the network were tweeted over the 1303-day, 3-hour, 5-minute period from Thursday, 05 March 2020 at 13:28 UTC to Friday, 29 September 2023 at 16:33 UTC. There is an edge for each "replies-to" relationship in a tweet, an edge for each "mentions" relationship in a tweet, an edge for each "retweet" relationship in a tweet, an edge for each "quote" relationship in a tweet, an edge for each "mention in retweet" relationship in a tweet, an edge for each "mention in reply-to" relationship in a tweet, an edge for each "mention in quote" relationship in a tweet, an edge for each "mention in quote reply-to" relationship in a tweet, and a self-loop edge for each tweet that is not from above.

The next - Stage 2, was to to find the most frequently used words and hashtags and to perform cluster analysis.

1.2 Network Top Items

The built-in NodeXL application is used to identify frequently used words and hashtags in the network. The extracted data included the top ten frequently used words and hashtags in the network, along with their frequency of occurrence. This helps to identify if the brand's name or hashtags are often used in the network or any other words the marketers intend to reflect in the network.

1.3 Text Analytics

With the help of text in the network, text analysis, trend analysis, topic extraction, and sentiment analysis can be performed.

The users can go for the licensed version of Node XL Pro Student, which helps to analyse the text. The steps followed are:

Node XL workbook → Import (from open workbook) → import the Excel sheet for text analysis→ Graph Metrics → Words and word pairs → Options Select the desired options (including stopwords) → Calculate Metrics.

The above steps can be repeated for separate pages. Then, the raw data should be cleaned and processed according to the study requirements.

1.3.1 Sentiment Analysis

Sentiment analysis is categorised into - Sentiment context (opinion mining), Sentiment level (text analytics), Sentiment subjectivity (determine whether the communicated text is opinion or factual), Sentiment orientation/polarity (opinion in the text is positive, neutral or negative), and Sentiment strength (intensity of emotions in the text: weak, mild or strong).

In NodeXL sentiment analysis can be done with the help of its in-built feature. Alternatively, the data can also be analysed with another tool, for instance, Azure Machine Learning tool and Meaning Cloud Analytics tool. Both are add-in for MS-Excel that can be used to perform various types of text analysis.

SMAT 2: Orange Data Mining Software

Orange data mining toolkit (https://orangedatamining.com/) is an open-source data visualization tool ideal for analysing qualitative data. It is a freely available, easy-to-use software that does not require any prior coding knowledge. With the help of various widgets image analysis, text mining, and network analysis can be done. It is also an excellent tool for visual representation. Figure 3 shows the performed steps for the hierarchical clustering of Image of Instagram pictures and Figure 4 is the result of the analysis done.

Figure 3. Steps for Image analysis

Figure 4. Hierarchical analysis

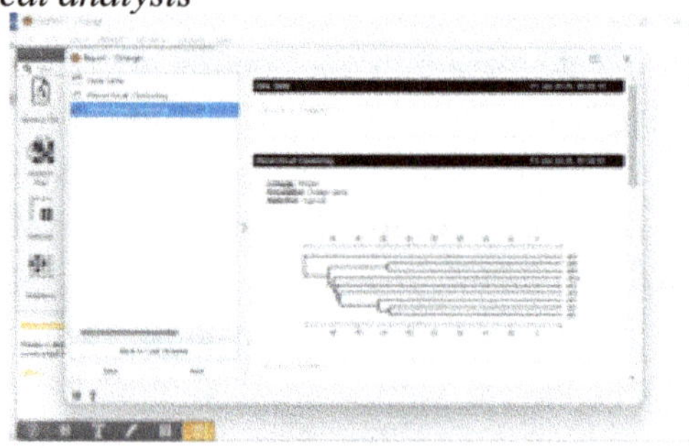

The orange data mining software also generates the word cloud. Flores-Ruiz et al. (2021) studied public sentiments of Andalusia, a southern region in Spain, and found that for a simple exploratory data analysis, word cloud, along with other techniques, is a key element in analysing and visualising the data related to behaviour and emotion detection.

Gulati (2022) studied public sentiments in X platform related to three Indian heritage sites with the help of Word Cloud visualisation and there be a mechanism to act proactively on negative sentiments in the Word cloud by the Destination Management Organizations.

For wordcloud generation the Corpus is created, and then the text is pre-processed. The uploaded text needed to be pre-processed, so the first step is to strip out the HTML code, followed by tokenisation, stopwords, stemming, and n-grams. The steps followed for the word cloud generation is shown in Figure 5 and Figure 6 shows the frequently used words in the content of Delhi (Capital of India) Tourism's Facebook page (https://www.facebook.com/delhitourism):

Figure 5. Word cloud steps in Orange.

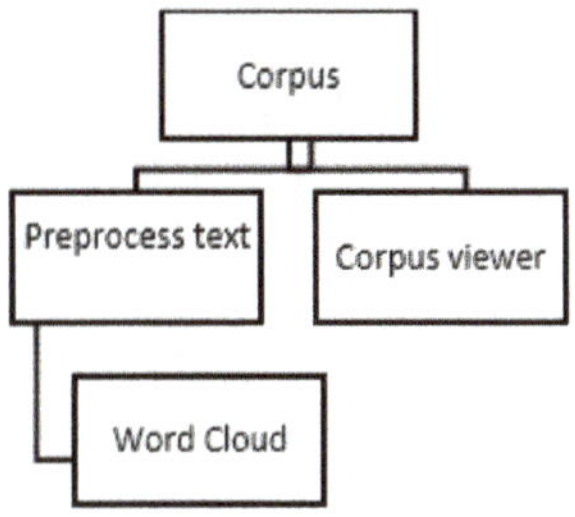

Figure 6. Word cloud representation of FB content

Figure 6 clearly shows Delhi is frequently using its name as one of the attributes in its content. It also uses this platform to invite users to join for event.

For the Instagram platform, images are collected through MassDownloader, a Google extension.

SMAT 3: RapidMiner

RapidMiner (https://altair.com/altair-rapidminer), owned by Altair Engineering, is an open-source software data science platform for text and data mining for which coding skills are not required. Its self-learning tools have operators like drag and drop and extensions that help to analyse social media data easily, build models, and make predictions. Below are few studies who have used this software for data analysis:

- Pitchayadejanant & Nakpathom (2018) used Rapid Miner 7.3. to analyse the association of tourist activities in orchards to stimulate their intention to travel to these agro-tourism farms.

- Yu & Egger, (2021) with the help of Rapid Miner's Auto Model Tool, evaluated the tourist's IG pictures and found 24 image categories.
- N A Deraman et al., (2021) studied the COVID-19 effect on Malaysian tourism; they used Rapid Miner software for thematic analysis of Twitter and found three themes: tourism destination, user sentiments, and future planning.

SMAT 4: Instagram Image Analysis

Based on the extensive literature review, a methodological framework for analysing Instagram images is developed (Zhan et al., 2024). This framework is represented in Figure 7. It describes four stages – 1) Image scrapping tool, 2) Data Cleaning, 3) Image coding, and 4) Results reporting.

In Stage 1, Mass Downloader (Google extension scrapping tool), through which all the images for specific period can be downloaded (Figure 7). The Mass Downloader has the feature of downloading all the posts for that given period; hence, the videos were also downloaded, so the following Stage 2 was to remove all the videos from the downloaded post.

Figure 7. Steps for IG image analysis

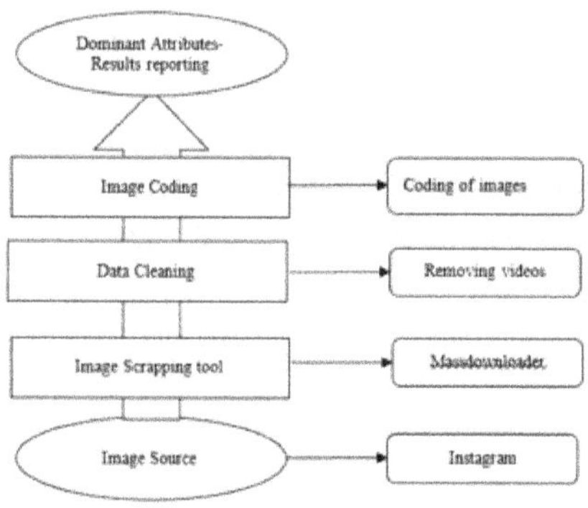

SMAT 5: Export Comments

"EXPORT COMMENTS API enables you to programmatically manage and run your exports and retrieve extracted data" (*API Documentation - EXPORTCOMMENTS.COM*, n.d.). This website has a download daily limit of 100 posts

performance, and as per the pricing, the features vary. The social media page URL is pasted in the export comments website, and the results are downloaded in an MS Excel sheet. It is ideal for Facebook page analysis as the dataset collected from FB consists of 18 parameters (Table 3). This exercise can be done multiple times if the paid version is there. It also has a free version but it comes with limitations. Figure 8 shows the research design adopted for downloading FB data. The rationale behind choosing Facebook for the engagement metrics is that this is the only platform that provides different types of reaction-related matrices for analysis, such as like, love, support, wow, haha, and sorry. In contrast, Twitter and Instagram have only like and share buttons. The free version sometimes does not capture all the quantitative data accurately. Usually the total reactions, comments and shares results are accurate but not the number for other emoji's It is recommended to verify the data manually for each url in the downloaded file before data anlayzing.

Figure 8. Steps to download FB data

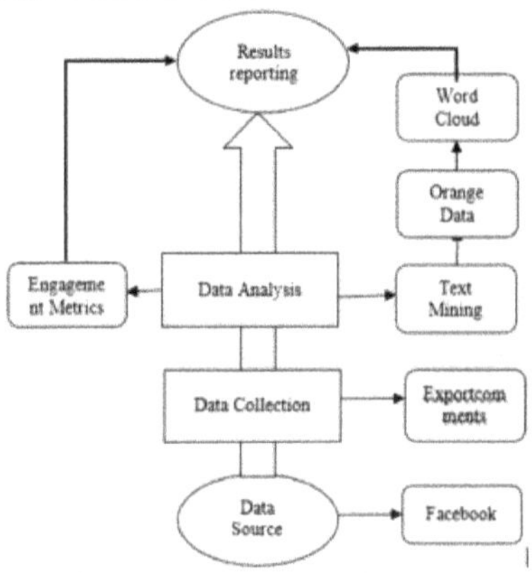

The downloaded MS-Excel had the parameters mentioned in Table 3

Table 3. FB parameters

FB Parameters		
Post ID	**(view source)**	**Love**
Name	Comments Count	Support
Publication Date	Reactions Count	Haha
Publication Date	Shares Count	Wow

continued on following page

Table 3. Continued

FB Parameters		
Post ID	**(view source)**	**Love**
Message	Views Count	Sorry
Post Url	Like	Anger

Below is the description of FB Parameters for content analysis mentioned in Table 3 are:

- Post ID: It is the unique id of the page post usually in numeric
- Name: Name of the page
- view source: Direct clickable link which opens to directly view the post
- Post Url: It is the Url (Uniform Resource Locator) of the post
- Message: The message posted on the corresponding Post ID.
- Publication Date: The date and time on which the post is uploaded.
- Comments Count: The total number of comments posted by users to the corresponding post
- Reactions Count: It is the total number of reactions the post has received to date. It is the sum of all the emoji's (Like, Love, Support, Haha, Wow, Sorry, and Anger) the post received.
- Shares Count: The number of shares the post has to date
- Like: Total number of 'Thumbs up' emoji given by the user to the corresponding post
- Love: Total number of 'Heart' emoji given by the user to the corresponding post
- Support: Total number of 'Care' emoji given by the user to the corresponding post. It is a "Yellow smiley face with a hugging heart"
- Haha: Total number of 'haha' emoji, known as "Grinning Squinting Face", given by the user to the corresponding post
- Wow: Total number of 'Wow' emoji given by the user to the corresponding post, usually to express admiration, impression or surprise
- Sorry: Total number of 'sad' emoji given by the user to the corresponding post
- Anger: Total number of 'anger' emoji given by the user to the corresponding post, usually to express displeasure or anger.

CONCLUSION

Social media applications are powerful tools for connecting with a larger audience. It is a low-cost platform, and marketers are leveraging its potential to stay connected to their potential customers. The growing popularity has enabled the researchers to provide meaningful insights into consumer behaviour, sentiments, industry trends, user interests, and demographics. The tools and websites mentioned in the article- NodeXL, Orange data mining software, Azure machine learning tool, Mass Downloader, and ExportComments are easily available and can be used by all types of professionals. These tools differ from traditional analytical tools, such as Python or R. With these tools, marketers can strategically plan their digital strategies, and researchers can conduct qualitative research with ease.

Conflict of Interest/ Competing Interests: The authors declare no competing interests.

REFERENCES

Aldahdouh, M. M., & AlDahdooh, R. M. (2019). Social media network analysis with NodeXL. *International Journal of Innovative Research in Computer and Communication Engineering*, *7*(9).

Alzboon, M. S., Aljarrah, E., Alqaraleh, M., & Alomari, S. A. (2021). NodeXL tool for social network analysis. *Turkish Journal of Computer and Mathematics Education*, *12*(14), 202–216.

API documentation - EXPORTCOMMENTS.COM. (n.d.). ExportComments. Retrieved May 17, 2024, from https://exportcomments.com/api

Deraman, N. A., Samah, K. A. F. A., Jono, M. N. H. H., & Isa, S. M. A. M., & Saad, [Initial(s)]. (2021). A social media mining using topic modeling and sentiment analysis on tourism in Malaysia during COVID-19. *IOP Conference Series. Earth and Environmental Science*, *704*, 012020. Advance online publication. DOI: 10.1088/1755-1315/704/1/012020

Eskandari, F., Lake, A. A., & Butler, M. (2022). COVID-19 pandemic and food poverty conversations: Social network analysis of Twitter data. *Nutrition Bulletin*, *47*(1), 93–105. DOI: 10.1111/nbu.12547 PMID: 36045084

Fenton, A., & Procter, C. (2019). Studying social media communities: Blending methods with netnography. In *Sage research methods cases*. SAGE Publications., DOI: 10.4135/9781526468901

Flores-Ruiz, D., Elizondo-Salto, A., & Barroso-González, M. D. L. O. (2021). Using social media in tourist sentiment analysis: A case study of Andalusia during the COVID-19 pandemic. *Sustainability*, *13*(7), 3836. Advance online publication. DOI: 10.3390/su13073836

Golbeck, J. (2015). Analyzing networks. In *Introduction to social media investigation* (pp. 221–235). Elsevier., DOI: 10.1016/B978-0-12-801656-5.00021-4

Gulati, S. (2022). Tapping public sentiments on Twitter for tourism insights: A study of famous Indian heritage sites. *International Hospitality Review*, *36*(2), 244–257. DOI: 10.1108/IHR-03-2021-0021

Hansen, D. L., Shneiderman, B., & Smith, M. A. (2011). *Analyzing social media networks with NodeXL: Insights from a connected world*. Elsevier.

Hays, S., Page, S. J., & Buhalis, D. (2013). Social media as a destination marketing tool: Its use by national tourism organisations. *Current Issues in Tourism*, *16*(3), 211–239. DOI: 10.1080/13683500.2012.662215

Kim, Y., Nordgren, R., & Emery, S. (2020). The story of goldilocks and three twitter's APIs: A pilot study on twitter data sources and disclosure. *International Journal of Environmental Research and Public Health*, *17*(3), 864. Advance online publication. DOI: 10.3390/ijerph17030864 PMID: 32019070

Pitchayadejanant, K., & Nakpathom, P. (2018). Data mining approach for arranging and clustering the agro-tourism activities in orchard. *Kasetsart Journal of Social Sciences*, *39*(3), 407–413. DOI: 10.1016/j.kjss.2017.07.004

Woo Choi, J., & Young Kim, H. (2018). Tourism trend and network analysis utilizing big data on social media. International Journal of Engineering & Technology, 7(2.12), 312. https://doi.org/DOI: 10.14419/ijet.v7i2.12.11313

Yu, J., & Egger, R. (2021). Color and engagement in touristic Instagram pictures: A machine learning approach. *Annals of Tourism Research*, *89*, 103204. Advance online publication. DOI: 10.1016/j.annals.2021.103204

Zhan, L., Cheng, M., & Zhu, J. (2024). Progress on image analytics: Implications for tourism and hospitality research. *Tourism Management*, *100*, 104798. Advance online publication. DOI: 10.1016/j.tourman.2023.104798

Chapter 3
A Systematic Review and Thematic Analysis of Data Engineering Research:
Methods and Frameworks

Nikos Koutsoupias
http://orcid.org/0000-0003-1664-5404
University of Macedonia, Greece

Marios Nosios
http://orcid.org/0009-0007-6161-3854
University of Macedonia, Greece

ABSTRACT

Data engineering forms the backbone of modern analytics and machine learning by designing, building, and maintaining data pipelines. Yet, research often emphasizes downstream analytics over upstream infrastructure. This review presents a systematic bibliometric analysis of Scopus indexed peer-reviewed publications to map methodological trajectories and conceptual frameworks. Four core domains emerge: ETL processes with cloud-native storage, schema and metadata design, real-time stream processing, and workflow orchestration. Key shifts include movement from sequential to ELT models, schema-on-read in data lakes, and real-time engines like Flink and Spark Streaming, alongside orchestration tools such as Airflow. Despite progress in scalable ingestion and pipeline automation, challenges persist in metadata gover-

DOI: 10.4018/979-8-3373-6926-6.ch003

nance, dynamic scheduling, and integrating feature engineering into ML workflows. Future research should advance self-tuning orchestration, metadata-first models, and unified frameworks to enhance reliability and integration with predictive systems.

INTRODUCTION

Data engineering, as a technical and conceptual domain, concerns the systematic construction, optimization, and maintenance of data pipelines that operationalize the computational infrastructure underpinning both statistical analytics and Machine Learning (ML) in contemporary organizations. This domain encompasses the extraction of unstructured or semi-structured data from heterogeneous and often distributed sources; the transformation, normalization, and semantic refinement of such data; and its subsequent integration into storage architectures designed for high-efficiency querying and scalable retrieval. Crucially, this end-to-end architecture constitutes the infrastructural precondition for meaningful data-driven inquiry and decision-making (Inoubli et al., 2018). The canonical big data life cycle comprises a sequence of interdependent phases, commencing with data acquisition, followed by syntactic and semantic preprocessing, commonly referred to as information extraction, then advancing to persistent storage, proceeding through inferential modeling and analytical interpretation, and culminating in the dissemination of results to end-users or downstream computational systems. A predominant emphasis on downstream analytics, absent commensurate investment in upstream engineering, tends to occlude the epistemic potential of large-scale data ecosystems. Literature consistently identifies the integration of heterogeneous data modalities and the real-time ingestion of high-volume streams as principal technical and architectural challenges. In response, a substantial body of scholarship has developed around methodological and infrastructural solutions spanning Extract-Transform-Load (ETL) paradigms, conceptual data modeling, event stream processing, orchestration frameworks, and cloud-native, horizontally scalable infrastructures (Jagadish et al., 2014). The present study undertakes a systematic review and thematically structured analysis of this evolving landscape, synthesizing peer-reviewed contributions to elucidate the current state of the art in data engineering practice and theory.

A foundational architectural element in traditional data warehousing, ETL processes continue to serve as a core operational mechanism within contemporary data engineering. The paradigm encompasses the systematic extraction of data from source systems, its transformation through operations such as cleansing, aggregation, and reformatting to conform to established schemas or quality thresholds, and the subsequent loading of the curated data into target repositories, including data warehouses and data lakes. Early research in the field contributed to the formalization of

ETL workflow semantics and proposed optimization strategies designed to improve both computational efficiency and systemic reliability. For instance, Simitsis et al. (2005) modeled ETL activities as directed graphs and proposed state-space optimization methods to improve the performance of data warehousing pipelines. In a typical ETL scenario, data from multiple operational sources is consolidated into a unified schema. Differences in data formats and semantics across sources often complicate this integration step. Academic literature emphasizes that integrating heterogeneous data is a crucial challenge for leveraging big data, as combining information from many sources is key to extracting knowledge. Big data's well-known "3 Vs" (Volume, Variety, Velocity) highlight that it is not only the volume but also the variety of data that make integration difficult (Jagadish et al., 2014). Modern ETL frameworks have evolved in response to these challenges. In the era of Hadoop and cloud warehouses, many organizations shifted from traditional ETL to an ELT approach, loading raw data first into a scalable storage cluster, then performing transformations in situ using distributed processing frameworks. This shift is enabled by frameworks like Apache Hadoop and Spark, which can apply transformation logic to large datasets in parallel across commodity hardware clusters. Research surveys note that recently proposed big data platforms help to store, analyze, and process the data, indicating that integration and transformation tasks can now be handled at scale within these platforms (Inoubli et al., 2018). Additionally, incremental and continuous data ingestion techniques have been developed to handle streaming data sources, reflecting the need for efficient online ETL for real-time analytics (Jagadish et al., 2014). Ultimately, ETL remains a central concern, as contemporary data engineering extends classical principles to accommodate datasets that are increasingly massive in scale, high-velocity, and heterogeneous in structure. Both academic and industry initiatives have increasingly focused on automating data cleaning procedures, designing transformation pipelines that accommodate flexible or evolving schemas, and optimizing data-flow mechanisms to ensure the consistent availability of high-quality data for analysis, all while minimizing manual intervention.

Deliberate data modeling underpins practical data engineering by shaping how data is structured for both storage and analysis. In traditional relational data warehouses, data modeling typically follows a schema-on-write approach: data is first organized into structured schemas, such as star or snowflake configurations in dimensional modeling, prior to loading, thereby enforcing consistency and enabling efficient SQL-based querying. However, the emergence of NoSQL and big data platforms has introduced new challenges and opportunities for data modeling. NoSQL databases, including document stores, key-value stores, column-family stores, and graph databases, adopt a range of data models and generally relax the requirement for a predefined global schema, prioritizing flexibility and scalability (Cattell, 2011). This heterogeneity implies that schema or data model design is frequently implemented at the application level and may vary significantly across systems. Asaad and Baïna (2018) note that NoSQL databases are typically designed at the physical level, adhering to the specific constraints and conventions of each system, and often lack a unified modeling methodology. As NoSQL technologies have matured, researchers have increasingly sought unified, or at least systematic, approaches to schema design within these diverse platforms. The literature documents numerous efforts to reconcile the rigorous modeling traditions of relational databases with the schemaless flexibility characteristic of NoSQL systems (Asaad & Baïna, 2018). In practice, data engineers must carefully balance flexibility and performance: while schema flexibility and denormalization can enhance read performance and better accommodate semi-structured data, poor modeling decisions can lead to data quality issues or inefficient queries. There is growing recognition that even ostensibly "schema-free" systems benefit from a degree of logical coherence and semantic structure. For instance, unplanned storage of JSON documents in a document database can lead to data duplication and update anomalies, prompting the emergence of design guidelines that aim to reduce redundancy while leveraging the database model's inherent strengths. A parallel development is the schema-on-read paradigm, increasingly employed in data lakes and specific NoSQL contexts, wherein raw data is stored without a predefined schema and structural interpretation is deferred until query execution. This model maximizes flexibility for heterogeneous data ingestion but transfers the modeling burden to the point of consumption, thereby intensifying demands on analytical tools and metadata infrastructure. Scholars have emphasized the importance of robust metadata management in such environments, warning that, without it, data lakes risk degenerating into unstructured and unmanageable "data swamps" (Sawadogo et al., 2019). Data modeling remains a critical topic, as methods have expanded beyond entity-relationship modeling for structured databases to encompass new techniques for semi-structured and polymorphic data. Thematically, current research focuses on imposing sufficient structure to ensure data usability and quality, for example, by employing metadata catalogs, canonical data models, or hybrid approaches, while maintaining the flexibility and scalability required by modern data formats and NoSQL systems.

Furthermore, the velocity dimension of big data has driven extensive research into real-time stream processing methods and frameworks. Many applications today generate continuous data streams, such as sensor readings, website click logs, financial transactions, and social media feeds, which need to be processed with minimal latency to derive timely insights. Traditional batch processing frameworks, most notably the Hadoop MapReduce paradigm, are poorly adapted to scenarios requiring low-latency responsiveness, as they are designed to operate on static datasets and inherently introduce substantial processing delays. To fill this gap, distributed stream processing engines have emerged as a cornerstone of data engineering for real-time analytics. Systems such as Apache Storm, Apache Spark Streaming, and Apache Flink implement scalable stream processing by distributing incoming data streams across clusters of machines and processing events in memory as they arrive. For instance, Apache Storm was one of the early popular platforms for real-time computation, providing a programming model composed of spouts and bolts that together create directed acyclic graphs of operators that process tuples in a record-at-a-time fashion. On Twitter, Storm reliably processed high-volume tweet streams with sub-second latency (Toshniwal et al., 2014). Spark Streaming adopted a micro-batch approach by slicing the stream into small batches and leveraging Spark's engine to process each batch rapidly (Zaharia et al., 2016). Apache Flink builds upon earlier systems to support precise event-by-event processing, offering capabilities such as event-time windows and exactly-once state consistency, while also unifying batch and streaming APIs within a single framework. These frameworks ensure fault tolerance through techniques such as upstream backups and replay logs (e.g., Kafka) to recover lost messages, and they also support scalability by allowing users to add more nodes to handle increased throughput. According to a comparative survey by Inoubli et al. (2018), modern stream processing engines can achieve high throughput on large clusters but differ in terms of latency guarantees and programming abstractions. For instance, Storm offers very low latency and a straightforward tuple processing model, whereas Spark Streaming and Flink provide more comprehensive analytics APIs at the cost of increased latency (Inoubli et al., 2018). A crucial architectural concept in this domain is Lambda architecture, which integrates a batch layer designed for accurate and comprehensive results computed over long time windows with a speed layer that delivers approximate real-time results on newly ingested data, thereby balancing the dual demands of accuracy and low latency (Kiran et al., 2015). Modern stream processing has matured into a critical and dynamic field within data engineering, shaped by developments in cloud-native architecture, the integration of streaming SQL functionality, and advances in complex event processing and windowing models. Recent systems increasingly embed stream processing as a foundational component of their infrastructure, reflecting its rising importance in enabling real-time, data-driven applications (Fragkoulis et al., 2024).

While real-time stream processing frameworks address the velocity challenge in modern data pipelines, coordinating the numerous ingestion, transformation, and loading tasks into a seamless workflow demands robust orchestration. Building a data pipeline typically involves coordinating multiple tasks and jobs. For instance, an ingestion job might fetch and stage raw data; a series of transformation jobs might clean and aggregate it; and a loading job might store the processed data in an analytics database. In complex analytics applications, additional steps such as feature extraction, model training, or report generation may also be present. Managing dependencies and scheduling these interrelated tasks is the role of orchestration, or workflow management, in data engineering. This necessity has given rise to dedicated workflow orchestration frameworks such as Apache Airflow, Luigi, Azkaban, and Prefect in industry practice. These frameworks enable data engineers to define workflows as Directed Acyclic Graphs (DAGs) of tasks, where each task can be a script or job, and the edges represent execution dependencies. The orchestration system's scheduler ensures that tasks are executed in the correct order, retries tasks on failure, and provides frequent monitoring, logging, and alerting capabilities. From a research perspective, workflow management is not a novel concept, as it has roots in business process management and scientific computing, exemplified by systems such as Pegasus for scientific workflows. However, the big data context introduces new challenges related to scalability and reliability. Production data pipelines often execute daily or hourly jobs with strict timing constraints and must recover gracefully from faults or data anomalies. Munappy et al. (2020) conducted an industry case study on data pipeline management and reported that practitioners highly value automation, traceability, and fault tolerance in pipeline orchestration. Automating pipeline steps, thereby reducing manual intervention, was found to enhance data quality and consistency by minimizing human error (Munappy et al., 2020). Additionally, traceability, the ability to track data lineage throughout the pipeline, is essential for both debugging and compliance. Modern orchestration frameworks address these requirements by maintaining metadata on task executions and data lineage. They also frequently integrate with cluster resource managers (such as Kubernetes or YARN) to scale out tasks and manage computing resources efficiently.

In conclusion, a salient academic challenge in this domain lies in optimizing the scheduling of pipeline tasks under constrained computational resources and stringent temporal requirements. Simplistic or static scheduling approaches often prove inadequate when confronted with the volatility of real-world workloads. Existing research has frequently framed workflow scheduling as an NP-hard optimization problem and has introduced heuristic and reinforcement learning techniques to enhance throughput and minimize end-to-end latency in data workflows. Despite these advances, operational systems continue to employ rudimentary scheduling methods, including cron-like periodic triggers or manual interventions, typically reinforced by robust fault-tolerance mechanisms. The broader emergence of the term DataOps signals a paradigmatic shift in which orchestration is increasingly understood through the lens of DevOps-inspired methodologies, intending to enable continuous data integration and delivery. This evolution encompasses key practices such as data and code versioning, automated validation of pipeline components, and collaborative pipeline development. As such, orchestration frameworks have become indispensable for achieving reliable, scalable, and production-grade data engineering. Contemporary literature and industry practice converge on three focal developments: pipelines are becoming more declarative, such that the what is specified, and the system determines the how; more observable, through the integration of rich metadata, lineage tracing, and real-time monitoring; and more self-managing, by means of dynamic scheduling and autonomous recovery capabilities. These interrelated trends collectively address the increasing complexity of modern data pipelines as organizations continue to scale their analytic infrastructures.

METHODOLOGY

This study adopted a systematic bibliometric methodology (Bitzenis & Koutsoupias, 2023b; Bitzenis & Koutsoupias, 2024a) to investigate research trends within the data engineering literature, drawing on a curated dataset constructed through a targeted search query executed in the Scopus database (Baas et al., 2020; Bitzenis & Koutsoupias, 2023A; Koutsoupias & Nosios, 2025; Bitzenis & Koutsoupias, 2024B). The search query used for dataset retrieval is as follows:

```
TITLE-ABS-KEY ( "data engineering" AND ( methods OR frameworks OR architectures OR models OR pipelines ) ) AND ( LIMIT-TO ( SUBJAREA , "COMP" ) OR LIMIT-TO ( SUBJAREA , "ENGI" ) OR LIMIT-TO ( SUBJAREA , "DECI" ) OR LIMIT-TO ( SUBJAREA , "MATH" ) ) AND ( LIMIT-TO ( DOCTYPE , "cp" ) OR LIMIT-TO ( DOCTYPE , "cr" ) OR LIMIT-TO ( DOCTYPE , "ar" ) OR LIMIT-TO ( DOCTYPE , "ch" ) OR LIMIT-TO ( DOCTYPE , "bk" ) ) AND ( LIMIT-TO ( LANGUAGE , "English" ) )
```

To uphold methodological rigor and procedural transparency, the review process was structured in accordance with the Preferred Reporting Items for Systematic Reviews and Meta-Analyses (PRISMA 2020) guidelines. These standards organized the sequential phases of study identification, screening, eligibility assessment, and final inclusion, thereby supporting a reproducible and systematic construction of the dataset, as shown in Figure 1 (Page et al., 2021).

Figure 1. PRISMA 2020 flow diagram of the selection process

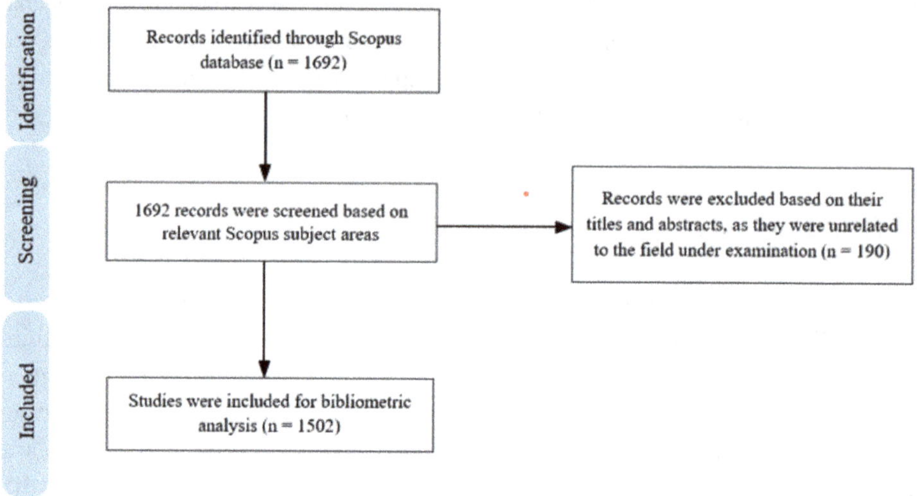

Following the compilation of the dataset, bibliometric analyses were conducted in the R statistical environment utilizing the bibliometrix package and its associated visualization tools (Bitzenis et al., 2025B; Bitzenis et al., 2025C). Initial descriptive indicators were extracted to provide a comprehensive overview of publication dynamics, authorship structures, citation distributions, and document typologies. Concurrently, a suite of bibliometric visualizations was produced, including keyword co-occurrence networks, frequency plots of Keywords Plus, national scientific production maps, and temporal topic trend graphs, which collectively offered a structured synthesis of the field's thematic evolution (Bitzenis et al., 2023; Bitzenis et al., 2025A).

To explore the conceptual structure of the data engineering literature with greater analytical precision, Multiple Correspondence Analysis (MCA) was applied to the author-supplied keyword matrix (Koutsoupias & Nosios, 2025A). MCA, a multivariate technique particularly well-suited for analyzing large-scale categorical data, enables the identification of latent dimensions underpinning term associations. In this study, MCA projected the high-dimensional keyword space onto a lower-dimensional plane, thereby facilitating the detection of thematic clusters and the visualization of conceptual proximity among research topics (Koutsoupias & Nosios, 2025B). The resulting factorial map positioned keywords according to their co-occurrence patterns, with the first two dimensions accounting for the most significant proportion of inertia. These dimensions were further examined using contribution tables, which quantified the relative influence of individual terms in shaping the underlying conceptual structure.

The integration of descriptive bibliometric indicators, network-based visualization, and multivariate conceptual analysis yielded a robust, multilayered methodological framework for reconstructing the intellectual trajectories of data engineering research. This combined approach not only enhanced the study's transparency and replicability but also deepened its analytical granularity by enabling both longitudinal trend analysis and nuanced mapping of thematic configurations. Taken together, these methodological procedures facilitated a systematic, empirically grounded depiction of the evolution of methods, frameworks, and conceptual priorities in the data engineering literature (Zourna et al., 2021).

RESULTS

The results section outlines the principal findings of the bibliometric study, including core publication indicators, analyses of collaboration networks and keyword co-occurrence structures, and the delineation of both established research domains and emerging thematic developments.

Table 1. Descriptive statistics

Description	Results
MAIN INFORMATION ABOUT DATA	
Timespan	1965:2025
Sources (Journals, Books, etc)	728
Documents	1502
Annual Growth Rate %	6.47
Document Average Age	11.8
Average citations per doc	17.49
References	32052
DOCUMENT CONTENTS	
Keywords Plus (ID)	8447
Author's Keywords (DE)	3024
AUTHORS	
Authors	3739
Authors of single-authored docs	119
AUTHORS COLLABORATION	
Single-authored docs	132
Co-Authors per Doc	3.01

continued on following page

Table 1. Continued

Description	Results
International co-authorships %	16.11
DOCUMENT TYPES	
article	333
book	35
book chapter	38
conference paper	882
conference review	214

Table 1 presents core bibliometric indicators. Spanning six decades (1965–2025), the data-engineering corpus comprises 1,502 documents drawn from 728 distinct sources, with an annual growth rate of 6.47 percent and an average document age of 11.8 years. A total of 32,052 references, averaging 17.49 per paper, attests to the field's dense scholarly foundations, drawing integratively on database theory, distributed systems, and analytics. Automated indexing has yielded 8,447 "Keywords Plus" descriptors, more than double the 3,024 author-provided keywords, reflecting a breadth of latent concepts that extend beyond authors' explicit labels.

Authorship patterns further underscore a collaborative ethos. A total of 3,739 unique authors have contributed to the corpus, with an average of 3.01 co-authors per document and only 132 single-authored works. Although international partnerships account for 16.11 percent of collaborations, research clusters remain relatively localized, suggesting opportunities for deeper cross-border exchange. In terms of dissemination channels, the discipline remains strongly conference-driven, with 882 conference papers compared to 333 journal articles, followed by 214 conference reviews, 38 book chapters, and 35 monographs. This distribution reflects the community's prioritization of rapid, iterative sharing of emerging methods and frameworks.

Overall, these metrics depict data engineering as a dynamic and rapidly expanding field, one that is methodologically integrative and community-oriented. The rich citation networks, expansive content descriptors, and prevailing conference culture provide a strong empirical foundation for the thematic and methodological analyses that follow (see Table 1).

Figure 2. Annual scientific production

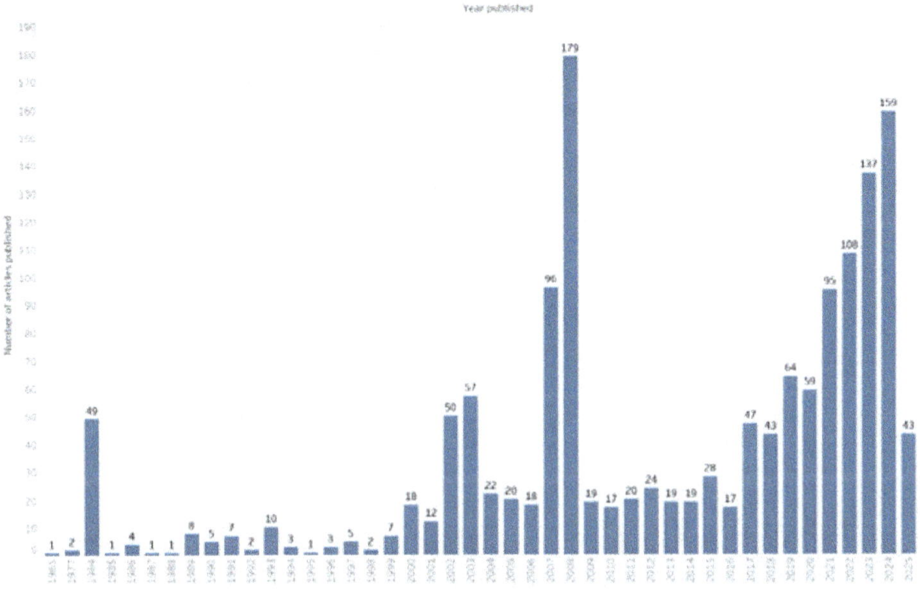

As shown in Figure 2, which presents the annual scientific production, publication activity in data engineering between 1965 and the late 1990s remained sparse and irregular. Annual output seldom exceeded single digits, with only occasional upticks, most notably 49 articles in 1984, before receding once again to minimal levels. These intermittent bursts of scholarship reflected isolated foundational inquiries rather than the development of a cohesive research community.

A more sustained trajectory emerged in the early 2000s, as annual publication counts rose from 18 papers in 2000 to over fifty by 2002–2003. A pronounced surge followed, with 96 articles recorded in 2007 and a peak of 179 in 2008, after which a brief contraction occurred. Subsequently, output stabilized at approximately 17–28 publications per year through 2016. During this period, incremental refinements to distributed processing frameworks and orchestration methods attracted steady, albeit measured, scholarly attention

In sum, from 2017 onward, a renewed and sustained acceleration became evident. Output climbed from 47 contributions in 2017 to 108 in 2022, reaching 159 in 2024. Mid-year figures for 2025 already mirror earlier peak levels, suggesting that this upward momentum is likely to persist. This sustained growth not only underscores the field's maturation but also signals its readiness for deeper methodological refinements and expanded thematic exploration in the years ahead, marking a decisive shift toward a more robust and dynamic research trajectory (see Figure 2).

Figure 3. Most relevant Keywords Plus

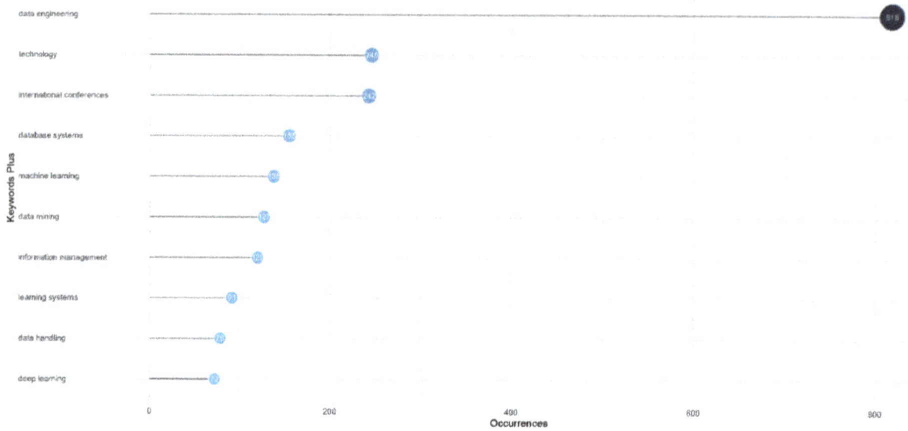

Figure 3 illustrates the most frequently occurring Keywords Plus terms in the dataset. Notably, the term *data engineering* stands out overwhelmingly, being cited 818 times. This striking prevalence suggests that authors are increasingly choosing to explicitly frame their work within the domain of data engineering, rather than categorizing it under related disciplines. Following at a considerable distance are *technology*, with 245 mentions, and *international conferences*, cited 242 times. These two terms form a closely aligned tier, indicating that broader technological advancements propel developments in pipeline methodologies and are predominantly disseminated through major academic conferences. The similarity in their frequencies suggests that conference venues remain a primary medium for the introduction of innovative data-engineering frameworks.

Terms occupying the middle ranks, such as *database systems*, cited 155 times, *machine learning*, cited 138 times, *data mining*, cited 127 times, and *information management*, cited 120 times, reflect the field's bifocal orientation. On one side, database architectures and management strategies continue to provide the structural backbone for efficient data storage and retrieval. On the other hand, analytic techniques, including pattern extraction and predictive model training, are deployed downstream in the data-processing pipeline. This distribution underscores the intermediary role of data engineers, who operate at the intersection of scalable storage solutions and analytic computation.

Ultimately, at the lower end of the top ten, the terms *learning systems*, referenced in 91 instances; *data handling*, appearing 78 times; and *deep learning*, with 72 citations, point to a nascent yet noteworthy interest in end-to-end workflows focused on model training and deployment. While these concepts are clearly recognized in the scholarly discourse, their frequency remains markedly lower than that of foundational topics such as storage and management. This asymmetry in attention foregrounds the current frontier of research: the ongoing expansion of classical pipeline architectures to accommodate the requirements of advanced learning applications (see Figure 3).

Figure 4. Most cited countries

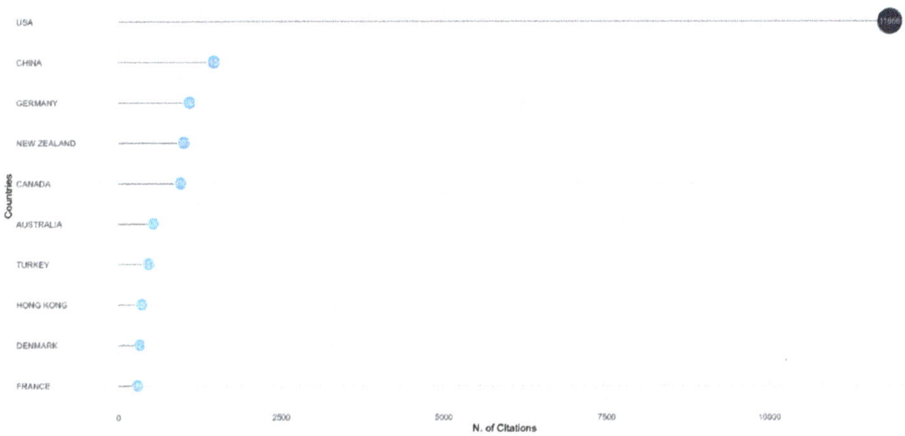

As evidenced in Figure 4, the United States leads all other countries by a significant margin in citation count, with a total of 11,866. This figure represents more than twice the number of citations of the following most-referenced country and reflects the longstanding concentration of research funding, the breadth of institutional participation, and the prominence of major academic venues within the United States. In contrast, China, with 4,584 citations, and Germany, with 3,898, form a distinct second tier, indicating substantial but comparatively moderate contributions to the field.

A middle-ranking group includes New Zealand, with 2,997 citations, Canada with 2,950, and Australia with 2,530. Despite their smaller populations, these countries demonstrate sustained research activity with international visibility, likely supported by active participation in global collaborations and the presence of institutions with expertise in data engineering. At a lower citation level, Turkey has accumulated 1,457 citations, Hong Kong 1,350, Denmark 1,212, and France 1,112. While their overall contributions are more limited in scale, they nonetheless reflect ongoing and meaningful engagement in the field.

Taken together, the citation distribution reflects a research landscape in which North America and Western Europe remain central, while countries in the Asia-Pacific region are increasingly visible. The data suggest that data-engineering frameworks and methodologies continue to be shaped predominantly within established academic centers, even as a broader range of national contexts contributes to the expanding global discourse (see Figure 4).

Figure 5. Trend topics

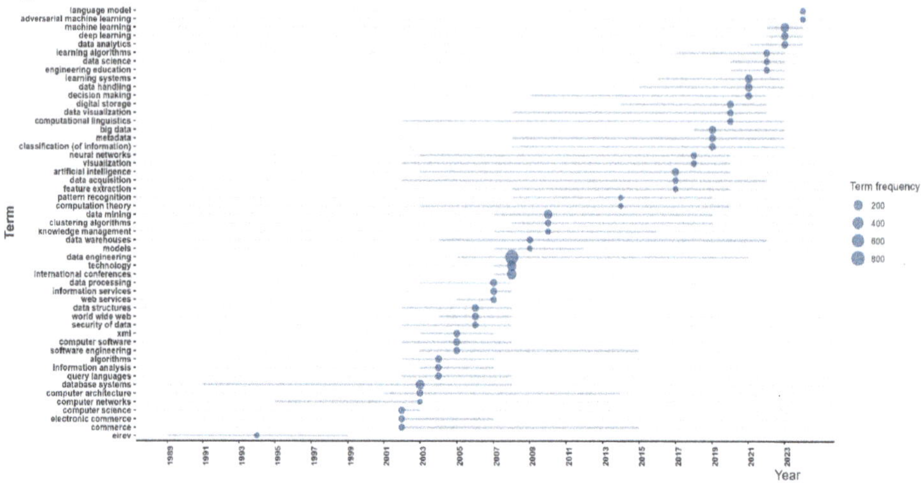

The trend topics graph presented in Figure 5 depicts the temporal span of each term through a horizontal bar, extending from its initial recorded occurrence to its most recent appearance. Each year along this span, the size of the corresponding bubble indicates the term's relative frequency, offering a layered view of both duration and intensity. The persistent visibility of *big data, data warehouses,* and *database systems* points to the field's long-standing preoccupation with infrastructural foundations. Big Data, emerging in the early 2000s and continuing into the present, reflects enduring challenges in accommodating volume, velocity, and structural diversity across large-scale data environments. The recurrence of the term *data warehouse* underscores sustained efforts to refine ETL and ELT processes, which remain central to analytic workflows. Likewise, *database systems* retain their conceptual and technical centrality, with both relational and NoSQL models shaping contemporary approaches to schema enforcement, whether predefined (schema-on-write) or deferred (schema-on-read).

Analytical imperatives are reflected in the sustained rise of *data analytics* and *data science*, alongside the closely related domains of *machine learning* and *deep learning*. Data Analytics has exhibited consistent growth since the early 2010s, marking a broad shift toward low-latency, real-time query capabilities. Data Science, which encompasses elements of engineering, statistical modeling, and data visualization, emerged shortly thereafter and now rivals analytics in both frequency and prominence. The appearance of *machine learning* around 2005, followed by the ascent of *deep learning* from 2008 onward, underscores the growing influence of model training, feature extraction, and computationally intensive neural architectures in shaping contemporary pipeline design.

Fundamental pipeline operations are captured by the recurrent presence of *data acquisition, data processing,* and *query languages*, each maintaining significant visibility over the observed period. Data Acquisition, which encompasses both batch and stream-based ingestion, reflects the enduring infrastructural imperative to secure reliable input mechanisms. Data Processing, a term broadly encompassing data cleansing, transformation, and aggregation, has appeared consistently since the mid-2000s, attesting to its centrality in operational workflows. Query Languages, including most notably SQL and SPARQL, are similarly persistent, emphasizing their instrumental role in validating, profiling, and extracting actionable insights from structured datasets. While *metadata* appears less frequently, its peaks alongside these core terms highlight its essential role in enabling lineage tracking and data governance.

The rise of *web services, information services,* and *data visualization* reflects the expansion of service-oriented architectures within data engineering. Their emergence around 2005 coincides with the transition toward cloud-native, distributed pipeline infrastructures, increasingly accessed and orchestrated through APIs and microservices. Data Visualization, in particular, has evolved into both a terminal analytic product and a diagnostic interface, with its usage stabilizing in the 2010s as pipelines became more complex and interactive.

Collectively, these trends mark a clear evolution from storage-centric architectures to an integrated, layered ecosystem that interweaves scalable infrastructure with analytical sophistication and machine-learning integration. The most persistent and frequently occurring topics thereby stand out as conceptual and technical pillars for a systematic review of the field, offering a foundation from which to articulate the methods, challenges, and frameworks that have shaped and continue to define the trajectory of data engineering (see Figure 5).

Figure 6. Co-occurrence network graph

Figure 6 illustrates the keyword co-occurrence network, with node size indicating term frequency, edge thickness representing co-occurrence strength, and node color denoting clusters identified through community detection analysis. A red cluster is centered on the term *data engineering*, encompassing associated terms such as *data warehousing, decision support systems, information management,* and *metadata.* This grouping reflects a thematic focus on data storage architectures, governance, and metadata frameworks that support the reliability of data pipelines. The observed interconnections within this cluster indicate a close association between research on warehousing and decision support, with metadata practices functioning as a linking element between storage systems and analytical processes.

The green cluster, anchored by "*technology*" and *international conferences*, comprises terms such as *query processing, information retrieval, web services,* and *semantics*. Its composition indicates that data-engineering methodologies are frequently disseminated through established technical venues and are closely associated with research in information retrieval and query optimization. The density of interconnections within this cluster suggests that developments in technologies such as XML, search engines, and query languages are understood as essential components of scalable pipeline architectures.

A distinct blue cluster, positioned to the left of the network, centers on *machine learning* and *predictive analytics*, incorporating terms including *machine learning, deep learning, classification, forecasting,* and *learning algorithms*. The concentration of links in this area indicates that downstream analytical applications often frame and extend data-engineering research. In particular, the proximity of learning systems and forecasting techniques to data-handling processes points to the role of preprocessing and pipeline design in shaping model effectiveness.

Lastly, situated at the center of the network, the *data engineering* node functions as an intermediary among these clusters. Its high betweenness centrality suggests a bridging role across discourses on data-management infrastructures, technological platforms, and analytical methods. This structural position underscores the interdisciplinary orientation of the field, wherein pipeline design, enabling technologies, and ML are integrated into a methodologically cohesive research framework (see Figure 6).

Figure 7. Country scientific production graph

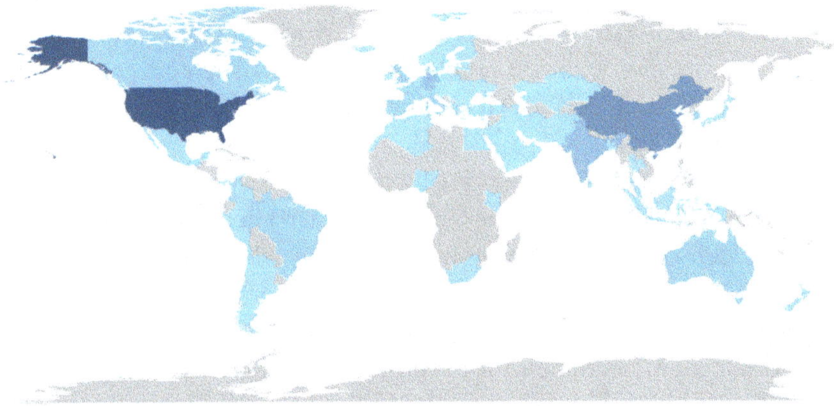

Figure 7 and Table 2 present the national scientific production in data engineering, with shading intensity and tabulated frequencies indicating each country's total number of publications. This graph and table jointly illustrate the geographic distribution and relative magnitude of scholarly output across the most prolific countries.

Table 2. Country scientific production table

Country	**Frequency**
USA	1075
CHINA	533
INDIA	251
GERMANY	245
UK	194
ITALY	139
SPAIN	137

continued on following page

Table 2. Continued

Country	Frequency
FRANCE	121
CANADA	120
SOUTH KOREA	107

As seen in Table 2, the United States demonstrates pronounced preeminence, contributing 1,075 publications. This leadership is underpinned by substantial federal and private funding, the concentration of leading research institutions, and the historical centrality of North American conferences in shaping methodological agendas. China follows with 533 articles, reflecting its strategic prioritization of big-data initiatives and the rapid expansion of domestic research infrastructure over the past decade.

A secondary tier includes India (251 publications), Germany (245), and the United Kingdom (194). In these countries, robust scholarly activity has been catalyzed by academic consortia, government–industry partnerships, and targeted funding programs. India's output signals an accelerated integration of data-engineering methodologies into both academic and commercial contexts, while Germany and the United Kingdom continue to leverage established centers of excellence and interdisciplinary collaborations.

A tertiary cohort comprises Italy (139 publications), Spain (137), France (121), Canada (120), and South Korea (107). Although smaller in volume, their contributions are distinguished by specialized advances in metadata governance, cloud-native orchestration, and scalable storage paradigms. Overall, these patterns reveal a predominantly Western and North American dominance in data-engineering research. Nevertheless, the growing presence of emerging contributors points toward a gradual globalization of the field, enriching it with more diverse methodological perspectives and research priorities (see Figure 7 and Table 2).

Figure 8. Conceptual structure map

Figure 8 presents the conceptual structure map generated through MCA, which arranges the most frequent author keywords into thematic clusters within the broader domain of data engineering. Together, the two MCA dimensions account for a meaningful share of the dataset's total inertia, with Dim 1 explaining 51.12% and Dim 2 contributing 16.27%, thereby indicating the extent to which the spatial configuration reflects underlying co-occurrence relationships. The distribution of terms across the plot reveals distinct conceptual domains that recur throughout the literature, and the relative positions of clusters along the two axes highlight patterns of thematic proximity and the degree to which different research trajectories align with central data-engineering concerns.

The largest and most densely populated cluster, represented in green, comprises terms such as *database systems, data processing, information management, algorithms, query processing, optimization, data structures,* and *data warehouses*. This grouping reflects a long-established body of research focused on the management, organization, and processing of large-scale structured data. The presence of related terms, including information systems, computer software, data reduction, and software engineering, reinforces the cluster's focus on the infrastructural foundations that support data-engineering work. The central placement of *data mining* and *database systems* within this region indicates their frequent co-occurrence with surrounding terms, consistent with their intermediary position that links the storage, transformation, and analytical stages of data pipelines. The configuration of terms within this cluster underscores the prominence of efficient data management, schema design, and computational optimization as continuing priorities in the field.

Adjacent to this region, the light-blue cluster includes *web services, query languages, information retrieval, world wide web,* and *XML.* This grouping captures research themes concerned with accessing, querying, and disseminating data across distributed architectures. The prominence of query languages and information retrieval emphasizes ongoing efforts to develop mechanisms that support effective human-system and system-system interaction with stored data. From a data-engineering perspective, these themes correspond to the interface layers of data pipelines, where data is exposed through APIs, retrieval engines, or search services. The inclusion of web services signals the expansion of service-oriented and cloud-based architectures, reflecting a movement toward modular, interoperable data-delivery frameworks. Overall, this cluster illustrates the operational dimension of data engineering, foregrounding scalable access, interoperability, and the integration of distributed systems.

On the left side of the map, the purple cluster brings together terms such as *machine learning, deep learning, learning algorithms, classification, decision making, metadata, data analytics,* and *big data.* This grouping represents the intersection of upstream data engineering tasks and downstream analytical applications. The co-occurrence of analytical concepts with *metadata* and *data-handling* terminology indicates that research in this domain often highlights not only modeling techniques but also the preparatory engineering activities that make such techniques viable. The presence of *life cycle* and *digital storage* ties these activities to the broader pipeline infrastructure, where decisions about storage, curation, and transformation directly influence the effectiveness of learning algorithms. Although *machine learning* constitutes a distinct research frontier, its proximity to core data-engineering terms reflects the increasing integration of feature preparation, data validation, and metadata structuring into analytical workflows.

A smaller, more isolated red cluster includes terms such as *technology, international conferences, information theory,* and *chlorine compounds*. The general nature of entries, such as technology and international conferences, suggests indexing artifacts rather than genuine thematic coherence. Their separation from the major conceptual regions reflects their limited co-occurrence with the technical lexicon of data engineering.

The boundaries between clusters illuminate areas of conceptual overlap. The green and purple clusters converge around terms such as *data engineering, data mining,* and *metadata*, indicating that studies frequently link pipeline-oriented processes with analytical methodologies. This convergence reflects the increasing incorporation of data transformation, preparation, and validation into machine-learning workflows, a pattern consistent with broader findings in the bibliometric analysis. A similar point of intersection occurs between the green and blue clusters around query processing and search engines, highlighting the dependence of retrieval-focused research on well-structured data management infrastructures, particularly indexing strategies and storage architectures.

The overall dispersion of terms along the MCA dimensions suggests that the field is organized around three principal thematic directions: data-management infrastructures, learning-driven analytical processes, and retrieval-oriented service architectures. Although each cluster highlights a distinct priority, their adjacency demonstrates that data engineering functions as a central connective domain. The map thus portrays a coherent conceptual ecosystem in which storage, processing, retrieval, and analytical preparation constitute interdependent components of a broader data pipeline. The clustering patterns observed in this visualization reinforce the empirical conclusion that data engineering serves as a structural foundation linking database systems, scalable architectures, and increasingly model-driven applications (see Figure 8).

Table 3. Coordinates of keywords on Dimension 1

word	Dim1
information services	2.35
information theory	2.21
world wide web	1.89
web services	1.88
chlorine compounds	1.80
search engines	1.50
information retrieval	1.44
technology	1.42
international conferences	1.42
xml	1.20
query languages	1.19
decision support systems	1.06
query processing	0.97
internet	0.96
semantics	0.92
computer software	0.90
optimization	0.90
data structures	0.88
data processing	0.78

continued on following page

Table 3. Continued

word	Dim1
electronic commerce	0.67
information analysis	0.60
database systems	0.55
information management	0.41
algorithms	0.21
data engineering	0.19
commerce	0.14
data warehouses	0.08
data mining	0.06
computer science	0.06
information systems	0.04

Table 3 presents the contributions of individual keywords to Dimension 1 of the MCA, thereby identifying the terms that exert the most significant influence on the horizontal axis of the conceptual structure map. Higher values in the first dimension indicate more potent effects on the variance accounted for by this axis, whereas lower scores indicate a relatively minor influence on its underlying configuration. Interpreting these contributions offers a data-driven perspective on the distribution of thematic areas along the principal conceptual gradient, elucidating how distinct domains position themselves within the broader conceptual architecture revealed by the MCA solution. The values reported in the table thus clarify which topics most substantially drive the left–right separation of clusters and how these topics correspond to established domains of inquiry in data engineering research.

The keyword contributing most strongly to Dimension 1 is *information services* (2.35), followed closely by *information theory* (2.21), *world wide web* (1.89), *web services* (1.88), and *chlorine compounds* (1.80). Except for the domain-irrelevant term' chlorine compounds', these high-loading keywords correspond to concepts located on the far right of the MCA map, forming a cluster associated with information retrieval, service-oriented architectures, and distributed-access mechanisms. Their elevated Dimension 1 values indicate that research emphasizing service provision, web-based infrastructures, and information-access technologies plays a dominant role in differentiating this conceptual region from the remainder of the thematic space. Within data-engineering discourse, these contributions underscore the centrality of systems that expose, distribute, and operationalize data for downstream use, particularly at pipeline endpoints where data is accessed via APIs, retrieval engines, or web interfaces.

The next tier of high-contributing keywords includes *search engines* (1.50), *information retrieval* (1.44), *technology* (1.42), *international conferences* (1.42), *XML* (1.20), and *query languages* (1.19). These terms generally correspond to mechanisms for locating, structuring, and querying data across distributed systems. Their moderate-to-high contributions suggest that Dimension 1 captures a shift toward topics emphasizing data accessibility, interoperability, and standardized representational forms. The presence of XML and query languages highlights the importance of syntax-governed data exchange and retrieval tools in shaping this axis. These keywords align with core data-engineering concerns, including schema representation, serialization formats, and the interfaces for acquiring, navigating, and consuming data.

Several mid-range contributors occupy positions near the conceptual boundary between retrieval-oriented topics and broader data-management themes. These include *decision support systems* (1.06), *query processing* (0.97), *internet* (0.96), *semantics* (0.92), *computer software* (0.90), *optimization* (0.90), *data structures* (0.88), and *data processing* (0.78). Their locations within the conceptual map correspond to an area that bridges large-scale data management, analytical querying, and system integration. From a data engineering standpoint, these keywords signal infrastructural and procedural elements integral to the operational workflow of data pipelines: structuring data, optimizing storage and retrieval operations, managing semantic layers, and supporting systems that incorporate analytical or decision-support capabilities. Their values indicate that they contribute meaningfully to the gradient separating retrieval-centric research from the more processing-focused literature, which is concentrated toward the left side of the dimension.

Lower-to-mid contributions are associated with terms such as *electronic commerce* (0.67), *information analysis* (0.60), *database systems* (0.55), *information management* (0.41), *algorithms* (0.21), and *data engineering* (0.19). These areas represent well-established, broadly distributed topics that often serve as connective or foundational concepts within the data engineering field. Their relatively modest scores indicate that these terms are more evenly dispersed across the thematic space and thus contribute less to the horizontal differentiation of conceptual clusters. For instance, *database systems* and *information managem*ent appear near the central green cluster in the MCA map, an area characterized by terms related to data organization, schema design, and pipeline architecture. Their lower contributions reflect their omnipresence across multiple thematic contexts, reducing their capacity to polarize Dimension 1.

The lowest loadings of the first dimension are observed for *commerce* (0.14), *data warehouses* (0.08), *data mining* (0.06), *computer science* (0.06), and *information systems* (0.04). These low values correspond to concepts situated on the left side of the MCA map, where topics related to data storage, structural modeling, and algorithmic foundations cluster densely. Their minimal contributions to the first dimension demonstrate that these keywords do not drive the primary conceptual separation; instead, they align with the central core of data-engineering research, a region characterized by overlapping and mutually reinforcing conceptual ground. The presence of data warehouses and data mining at the lowest end underscores their role as central, widely shared elements in the literature rather than as differentiating features along this particular analytical axis.

Collectively, the contributions to Dimension 1 delineate a coherent thematic gradient that extends from web-based, service-oriented, retrieval-focused topics on the right to foundational data-management and processing-oriented topics on the left. This distribution illustrates how Dimension 1 captures the contrast between downstream data-access mechanisms and the upstream infrastructure components that store, structure, and prepare data for subsequent use. In data engineering, this gradient mirrors the conceptual distinction between interfaces that expose data to end users and the architectural systems that underpin data pipelines. Consequently, the values reported in Table 4 provide a measurable, empirically grounded summary of how these concepts collectively shape the field's organization along the MCA solution's horizontal dimension (see Table 3).

Table 4. Coordinates of keywords on Dimension 2

word	Dim2
chlorine compounds	1.70
international conferences	0.91
technology	0.90
information theory	0.35
classification (of information)	0.28
learning algorithms	0.26
decision support systems	0.24
deep learning	0.18
data engineering	0.14
machine learning	0.14
forecasting	0.10
decision making	0.08
learning systems	0.07

Table 4 delineates the contributions of individual keywords to Dimension 2 of the MCA, indicating the extent to which each term shapes the vertical axis of the conceptual map. Higher values in the second dimension signify that a keyword plays a more substantial role in the thematic differentiation captured by this axis, whereas lower values reflect comparatively limited influence. In this sense, the table both complements and deepens the MCA visualization by quantifying the vertical conceptual gradient that structures the field's terminology. Examining these values affords insight into the alignment of topics across the dataset. It clarifies how specific research areas within data engineering diverge when viewed through the lens of the second analytical dimension.

The term with the highest contribution, *chlorine compounds* (1.70), is a domain-irrelevant artifact of the dataset, as its isolation in both the MCA plot and the underlying records inflates its score. Its prominence reflects the structural behavior of an outlier that co-occurs minimally with technical terminology rather than any meaningful conceptual relevance. By contrast, *international conferences* (0.91) and *technology* (0.90) occupy the upper region of the conceptual map and significantly shape the vertical separation. These terms operate primarily as contextual or bibliographic descriptors rather than as methodological concepts. Their contributions thus demonstrate that Dimension 2 captures variance partly associated with metadata-related features of the dataset. Their position along the axis underscores how such descriptors differentiate non-technical terminology from the discipline's substantive clusters, even though they exert little influence on the conceptual core of data-engineering research.

Descending the ranking, keywords such as *information theory* (0.35), *classification (of information)* (0.28), and *learning algorithms* (0.26) contribute moderately to the vertical gradient. These terms are associated with analytical and model-driven research and appear above the central data-management cluster in the MCA plot. Their values indicate that the second axis separates analytically oriented work, particularly research centered on classification, algorithmic modeling, and theoretical constructs, from system-oriented literature. This distinction is consequential for understanding the field's structure: algorithmic and modeling tasks rely heavily on upstream activities such as data structuring, preparation, and transformation, yet they form a conceptually distinct area when examined through keyword co-occurrence patterns. Their contributions thus highlight the differentiated position of analytical research within the broader data-engineering ecosystem.

A similar configuration appears among keywords with mid-range values, including *decision support systems* (0.24), *deep learning* (0.18), *data engineering* (0.14), and *machine learning* (0.14). Their placement suggests that Dimension 2 captures a transitional area where analytical outputs intersect with systems-oriented applications. For example, decision support systems commonly arise in work that links data-processing workflows with organizational or computational decision-making tools. Likewise, *deep learning* and *machine learning* refer to research that relies on data readiness and pipeline orchestration, but extends into modeling and predictive analysis. That data engineering itself contributes moderately to the second dimension and reflects its bridging nature: it appears in proximity to both transformation-oriented and analysis-oriented terminology, consistent with its role at the interface of multiple stages within the data lifecycle.

Lower-end Dim2 contributors, including *forecasting* (0.10), *decision-making* (0.08), and *learning systems* (0.07), also align with downstream analytical tasks but exert less influence on the vertical axis structure. Their modest contributions indicate that, although they participate in shaping the upper thematic region of the map, they do not define it in isolation. Instead, they collectively reinforce the association between Dimension 2 and modeling-oriented research themes. From a data-engineering perspective, these terms refer to outputs or operational uses of engineered data flows rather than to the infrastructural processes that enable them.

Taken as a whole, the contributions of Dimension 2 delineate a vertical gradient that distinguishes analytical and metadata-related terminology from the foundational data-management vocabulary situated lower in the conceptual space. This axis thus illuminates the organization of the field along two broad thematic directions: analytical modeling and contextual descriptors at the upper end, and infrastructural processes and system-level functions at the lower end. Whereas Dimension 1 differentiated access-oriented from storage-oriented topics, Dimension 2 emphasizes the contrast between analytical tasks and the architectural foundations that support them. For data engineering, this reinforces the field's dual mandate: supplying the structured, high-quality data required for modeling while simultaneously defining and maintaining the architectures that support ingestion, transformation, and storage. Overall, the table furnishes a precise, data-driven account of how secondary conceptual patterns shape the dataset. The arrangement of terms along Dim2 reflects the relationship between modeling-focused research and the foundational systems that sustain it, illustrating how data engineering functions as connective tissue across both areas. These contributions therefore provide a rigorous quantitative summary of the vertical thematic structure revealed in the MCA results (see Table 4).

Table 5. Most cited papers

Paper	Total Citations
He H, 2009, Ieee Trans Knowl Data Eng	7394
Hall Ma, 2003, Ieee Trans Knowl Data Eng	986
Zhou B & Pei J, 2008, Proc Int Conf Data Eng	606
Lee J-G, 2008, Proc Int Conf Data Eng	435
Abul O, 2008, Proc Int Conf Data Eng	434

continued on following page

Table 5. Continued

Paper	Total Citations
Zhang L, 2021, Appl Energy	426
Li J, 2009, Ieee Trans Knowl Data Eng	354
Man Ly, 2008, Proc Int Conf Data Eng	310
Nunes De Casto L, 2000, Proc - Brazilian Symp Neural Netw Sbrn	296
Denecke K, 2008, Proc Int Conf Data Eng	281
Jeung H, 2008, Proc Int Conf Data Eng	253
Wang D, 2019, Proc Acm Hum Comput Interact	250
Tian Y, 2008, Proc Int Conf Data Eng	244
AGGARWAL CC, 2008, PROC INT CONF DATA ENG-A	180
Kasneci G, 2008, Proc Int Conf Data Eng	168

Table 5 synthesizes the most frequently cited works in the dataset, indicating their publication venues, total citation counts, and documented methodological contributions. Collectively, these studies engage with a spectrum of themes that intersect directly with core concerns in data engineering, including data preprocessing, privacy protection, trajectory modeling, semantic alignment, clustering, high-dimensional analytics, and large-scale graph processing. Examined together, these contributions provide a structured vantage point for understanding how influential research addresses upstream and mid-pipeline challenges, particularly those involving data quality, scalability, metadata organization, and the management of heterogeneous or sensitive datasets. The breadth of topics represented among the most cited works underscores the expansive methodological foundations on which contemporary data-engineering practices continue to build.

The most highly cited study is He and Garcia's (2009) survey of class-imbalance learning, which has accumulated more than 7,000 citations. Their framework systematically categorizes techniques for handling skewed data distributions, encompassing data-level strategies, algorithmic modifications, hybrid approaches, and evaluation protocols designed for imbalance scenarios. This taxonomy formalizes a long-recognized set of challenges in data preprocessing, where imbalanced class distributions can significantly affect model performance. In data-engineering contexts, the study foregrounds the importance of upstream transformations, such as sampling, weighting, and feature recalibration, preparing datasets for reliable analytical modeling. The authors' attention to data readiness, quantifiable performance trade-offs, and structured processing aligns closely with pipeline design principles that prioritize quality assurance, reproducibility, and systematic handling of data irregularities.

Another foundational contribution is made by Hall and Holmes (2003), who offer a comparative assessment of attribute-selection techniques across multiple datasets using naïve Bayes and C4.5 classifiers. Their analysis of filter-based and wrapper-based methods elucidates clear trade-offs between computational efficiency and predictive accuracy: filters achieve faster processing, whereas wrappers deliver improved performance at higher computational cost. In data engineering practice, these findings highlight feature selection as both a computational and an architectural choice. Dimensionality reduction can reduce storage requirements, accelerate pipeline execution, and improve downstream model performance. Because data engineering routinely involves specifying transformation steps that determine the representational structure of datasets, empirical evidence on feature selection performance remains highly relevant to pipeline-optimization strategies.

Several of the most cited papers focus on privacy preservation in large-scale, structured, or spatiotemporal datasets, an emergent concern in data engineering environments tasked with managing sensitive information. Zhou and Pei (2008) introduce the k-neighborhood anonymity model for social network graphs, demonstrating that anonymization must protect not only node identifiers but also structural properties, such as neighborhood topology. Their method ensures that each one-hop subgraph appears sufficiently often to prevent reidentification based on structural uniqueness. This work situates privacy as inseparable from graph structure, illustrating that metadata and relational patterns must be incorporated directly into anonymization procedures. For data-engineering workflows that store relationship data, such as knowledge graphs or user-interaction networks, these findings indicate that privacy requirements must be embedded in transformation and governance processes rather than applied exclusively at the access-control level.

Furthermore, Abul et al. (2008) extend privacy considerations to trajectory data using the k,δ-anonymity model, which represents movement paths as cylindrical uncertainty regions and applies clustering and translation operations to enforce indistinguishability among sets of similar trajectories. Their demonstration that minimizing distortion is NP-hard underscores the computational difficulty of reinforcing privacy in spatio-temporal systems. These results carry evident implications for data-engineering pipelines that ingest or process streaming mobility data, where privacy must be ensured without undermining the analytical value of location-sequence information. Their framework illustrates how privacy-preserving transformations can be incorporated at data ingestion and preprocessing stages, enabling anonymized trajectories to remain analytically useful for pattern detection and aggregate modeling.

Another cluster of highly cited works focuses on outlier detection, trajectory modeling, and forecasting, areas that depend heavily on systematic data preparation and scalable computation. Lee, Han, and Li (2008) propose TRAOD, a two-level partition-and-detect framework for identifying trajectory outliers. By segmenting trajectories into sub-components and applying hybrid distance- and density-based scoring, their method demonstrates that effective anomaly detection depends on appropriate segmentation and representation of raw movement data. The study thus reinforces the importance of data-modeling decisions within pipeline execution. Because trajectory data often arrive as continuous streams with irregular sampling, TRAOD exemplifies how preprocessing imposes necessary structure on semi-structured temporal data, directly shaping analytical accuracy. The framework mirrors common data-engineering challenges associated with handling heterogeneous temporal data and converting it into formats suitable for large-scale analysis. On the other hand, Zhang et al. (2021) provide a comprehensive review of ML methods for building energy-load forecasting, categorizing prior research by scenario type, feature engineering strategies, algorithm selection, and data management requirements. A central conclusion is that preprocessing steps, including sensor calibration, missing-value imputation, temporal feature generation, and metadata structuring, heavily influence forecasting accuracy. These observations highlight a recurring pattern across the most cited works: upstream transformations consistently shape analytical outcomes. By highlighting pervasive challenges, including data sparsity, irregular sensor streams, and inconsistent temporal granularity, the review aligns with data-engineering research that emphasizes robust ingestion, harmonization, and quality-assurance procedures in time-series pipelines.

Semantic alignment and location-aware computation are among the highly cited contributions, constituting another prominent theme. Li et al. (2008) present RiMOM, a multi-strategy ontology-alignment framework that combines textual and structural similarity measures. By adjusting similarity weights according to ontology characteristics, the framework supports alignment across heterogeneous metadata schemas. In data engineering, this work underscores the enduring need for systematic schema integration as organizations merge structured, semi-structured, and knowledge graph datasets. Ontology alignment remains a central component of metadata management practice, particularly in data lake architectures characterized by varied formats and levels of structure. RiMOM's emphasis on adaptive weighting and multi-source similarity computation parallels ongoing efforts to automate schema harmonization in large-scale heterogeneous environments. Yiu et al. (2008) contribute SpaceTwist, a location-privacy-preserving protocol for k-nearest-neighbor (KNN) queries. By shifting the anchor point through which the query is issued and expanding the search region incrementally, the protocol preserves the correctness of KNN results while masking the user's precise location. This study demonstrates that privacy mechanisms can be embedded directly into query-processing layers without compromising result quality. Given the growing interest in federated architectures, API-driven analytics, and mobile-data pipelines, SpaceTwist offers a practical illustration of how privacy protections can be integrated into the domain of real-time request processing, increasingly relevant to data-engineering systems that expose public-facing interfaces.

Two further influential works represent clustering and high-dimensional analysis. De Castro and Von Zuben (2002) introduce aiNet, an immune-network-inspired clustering algorithm that evolves through proliferation, mutation, and suppression. Although rooted in neural computation, the model addresses a persistent challenge in data engineering: identifying structure within high-dimensional or irregular datasets. aiNet anticipates contemporary efforts to automate elements of data preparation, such as prototype selection and noise reduction, operations now incorporated into automated feature-engineering pipelines. Aggarwal (2008) likewise investigates outlier detection in high-dimensional data, showing how subspace-based approaches mitigate sparsity and noise artifacts common in large-scale analytical datasets. These contributions align with data-engineering concerns about dimensionality, sparsity, and the need for transformation strategies that reduce computational overhead.

The remaining highly cited studies further reinforce the centrality of data structuring and scalable processing in influential research. Jeung et al. (2008) examine trajectory-pattern mining techniques using incremental updates and partition-based representations, showing that practical trajectory mining depends on stable, structured representations that can absorb new data without full recomputation. Their incremental architecture parallels that of contemporary streaming systems, in which data models must support continuous ingestion. Wang et al. (2019), writing in the domain of human–computer interaction, rely on structured extraction, cleaning, and processing of interaction logs, illustrating that reproducible behavioral analysis is fundamentally grounded in robust upstream preparation. Tian and Patel (2008) propose TALE, an approximate subgraph-matching tool based on the Neighborhood Index that enables scalable graph querying by directly encoding structural properties into the index. TALE exemplifies the importance of indexing strategies within data-engineering systems where query performance and scalability are central concerns. Finally, Kasneci et al. (2008) developed methods for extracting semantic relationships from structured datasets, drawing on consistent metadata and preprocessing routines that closely parallel data engineering tasks such as schema normalization, feature integration, and data quality enforcement.

Collectively, the 15 most-cited papers in the dataset emphasize foundational data-engineering priorities. Across diverse domains, including privacy protection, trajectory modeling, ontology alignment, clustering, high-dimensional analytics, and forecasting, these influential studies repeatedly foreground issues such as data preprocessing, metadata structuring, transformation design, scalability constraints, and the management of complex or sensitive datasets. The recurrence of these themes across independently developed research programs underscores the centrality of upstream data-management activities to methodological innovation. Collectively, these works demonstrate that the reliability and scalability of analytical outcomes hinge on deliberate architectural and procedural decisions made early in the data lifecycle. For this reason, the most cited literature provides a coherent illustration of how data engineering continues to function as the structural foundation supporting research across computational, analytical, and applied domains (see Table 5).

CONCLUSIONS

This systematic review and bibliometric analysis offer a comprehensive, empirically grounded account of how research in data engineering has evolved over six decades and how its thematic, conceptual, and methodological foundations have taken shape. Across publication trajectories, keyword structures, co-occurrence networks, country-level contributions, and conceptual mappings, the findings show that the field has progressed well beyond its early concentration on storage architectures and batch-oriented Extract-Transform-Load (ETL) workflows. Instead, the results depict a domain in which data ingestion, transformation, metadata governance, and orchestration increasingly function as interdependent components of a continuously evolving pipeline ecosystem, one that supports analytics, real-time decision-making, and machine-learning applications. The cumulative evidence from bibliometric indicators demonstrates that data engineering has broadened its methodological repertoire while maintaining a coherent identity anchored in scalable data processing and structured computational design.

The longitudinal analysis of publication activity renders this developmental trajectory particularly clear. Early contributions were sporadic, reflecting isolated inquiries into database systems and foundational aspects of data management. Publication growth became more consistent in the early 2000s, coinciding with the emergence of distributed architectures and large-scale ETL optimization strategies. A pronounced expansion from 2017 onward, culminating in peak publication output in 2024 and sustained levels in 2025, signals the consolidation of data engineering as a mature and steadily expanding research area. These temporal dynamics correspond to broader technological transformations, including the rise of cloud-native infrastructure, the increasing availability of high-velocity data streams, and the widespread adoption of orchestration and workflow automation tools. The dataset, therefore, captures a field that has grown in scale, methodological diversity, and applied relevance while remaining firmly grounded in its foundational concern with efficient, reliable data integration and management.

The keyword analyses further substantiate this evolution. High-frequency Keywords Plus terms, such as data engineering, technology, and database systems, demonstrate the continued prominence of infrastructural responsibilities within the field. The sustained presence of machine learning, data mining, deep learning, and learning systems reflects a broader trend in which engineering and analytical activities are increasingly interdependent. Rather than functioning as distinct domains, upstream engineering processes and downstream analytical tasks appear as tightly coupled segments of a unified data pipeline, in which the quality and structure of preprocessed data decisively influence modeling, inference, and evaluation. Temporal topic analysis reinforces this interpretation. Longstanding themes such as big data, data warehouses, and database systems indicate persistent engagement with storage platforms, processing routines, and transformation infrastructures. Recent increases in terms such as data analytics and data science, alongside the growing frequency of machine learning and deep learning, signal the emergence of architectures designed to support model-driven computation and real-time analytical workloads. Taken together, these observations reveal how shifting data environments have expanded the methodological demands placed on data engineering.

The conceptual structure map generated by MCA similarly illuminates the field's thematic architecture. The largest cluster, encompassing database systems, information management, data processing, algorithms, and data structures, represents the established infrastructural core of data engineering. Adjacent to this domain, a second cluster focused on web services, query languages, information retrieval, and XML corresponds to research concerned with accessing, distributing, and disseminating data across distributed and service-oriented systems. A third cluster, defined by machine learning, deep learning, classification, and related analytical concepts, reflects the increasingly integrated relationship between engineering practices and predictive modeling. Their spatial arrangement, as well as the relative proximity of these clusters, illustrates that the field's thematic boundaries coalesce around three major orientations: foundational data-management tasks, service- and query-oriented interfaces, and advanced analytical requirements. The total inertia explained by the first two MCA dimensions (51.12% and 16.27%, respectively) indicates that these clusters capture the principal conceptual structure of the literature and represent stable co-occurrence patterns across diverse research contexts.

The dimensional contributions reinforce these insights. Dimension 1 distinguishes service-oriented and web-based topics from foundational data-processing concepts, revealing a thematic gradient between downstream access mechanisms and upstream pipeline architecture. Dimension 2 differentiates analytical and modeling-related terminology from core engineering topics, highlighting a second conceptual axis centered on the relationship between data management and predictive analytics. These gradients collectively clarify how the field is organized around two central distinctions: (1) storage and transformation versus access and dissemination, and (2) infrastructural engineering versus analytical computation. These structural patterns support the conclusion that data engineering functions as a bridging domain that both grounds system-level design and undergirds model-driven analysis.

Co-authorship and country-level production indicators further contextualize the field's development. The prominence of the United States, alongside substantial contributions from China, India, Germany, and the United Kingdom, reflects the concentration of research capacity in technologically advanced regions. At the same time, the gradual expansion of contributions across Europe and Asia demonstrates the growing diffusion of expertise and institutional participation. Lower levels of international co-authorship (16.11%) indicate that collaborative networks remain comparatively localized, providing opportunities for greater cross-border integration. Nevertheless, the geographic distribution of scholarship aligns with the global spread of large-scale data infrastructures and the widespread deployment of cloud-based processing technologies. These contexts increasingly shape the operational realities of data engineering.

An examination of the most cited papers in the dataset further clarifies recurring methodological priorities. Influential works consistently focus on upstream challenges, data preprocessing, feature selection, trajectory structuring, clustering, privacy protection, and ontology alignment. These contributions aim to enhance data quality, preserve utility, enforce privacy constraints, and establish representational coherence across heterogeneous datasets. Their sustained citation impact suggests that the field's most influential innovations often stem from confronting the practical complexities inherent in preparing, structuring, and governing data for downstream analysis. This alignment between highly cited research and broader bibliometric patterns reinforces the observation that data engineering's intellectual center remains rooted in the design of reliable, scalable, and semantically robust data pipelines.

Despite these advancements, the results also reveal several persistent challenges. Metadata governance, although conceptually central within multiple clusters, remains less visible in publication trends than its importance for lineage tracking, schema consistency, and quality assurance would suggest. Orchestration frameworks continue to attract interest, yet many published approaches rely on static scheduling heuristics that do not fully accommodate real-world variability. Moreover, the conceptual and practical separation between engineering tasks and machine-learning workflows, though narrowing, remains evident in many contexts, complicating reproducibility and obscuring feature-derivation processes. These observations collectively point to areas where methodological integration may be particularly beneficial. Future research may therefore prioritize the development of declarative pipeline specifications that enable more automated and predictable orchestration; the embedding of lightweight metadata services directly into processing frameworks; and the design of adaptive, performance-aware scheduling mechanisms that can respond dynamically to fluctuating workloads. Expanding international collaboration would support comparative investigations into pipeline performance across diverse infrastructural settings, while deeper integration between data engineering and Machine-Learning Operations (MLOps) could facilitate more unified, end-to-end workflow architectures. These prospective directions emerge directly from the bibliometric patterns observed in the present review and reflect areas where methodological innovation appears especially consequential.

Ultimately, this systematic review provides a coherent, data-driven account of data engineering as a field that has progressively broadened its methodological and thematic scope while maintaining a robust conceptual focus on pipeline reliability, scalable computation, and structured data management. Its ongoing evolution reflects growing integration with analytical processes, increased attention to orchestration and metadata governance, and sustained interest in real-time processing and distributed architectures. As data volumes accelerate and analytical demands intensify, data engineering's role as the structural foundation of contemporary computational practice becomes increasingly pronounced. The insights derived from this bibliometric analysis thus furnish a comprehensive portrait of the discipline's development and illuminate the methodological priorities likely to shape its future trajectory.

REFERENCES

Abul, O., Bonchi, F., & Nanni, M. (2008). Never Walk Alone: Uncertainty for Anonymity in Moving Objects Databases. *2008 IEEE 24th International Conference on Data Engineering*, 376–385. https://doi.org/DOI: 10.1109/icde.2008.4497446

Asaad, C., & Baïna, K. (2018). NoSQL Databases – seek for a design methodology. In *Lecture notes in computer science* (pp. 25–40). https://doi.org/DOI: 10.1007/978-3-030-00856-7_2

Baas, J., Schotten, M., Plume, A., Côté, G., & Karimi, R. (2020). Scopus as a curated, high-quality bibliometric data source for academic research in quantitative science studies. *Quantitative Science Studies*, *1*(1), 377–386. DOI: 10.1162/qss_a_00019

Bitzenis, A., & Koutsoupias, N. (2023A). FOREIGN DIRECT INVESTMENT AND SUSTAINABILITY: A VISUALIZED BIBLIOMETRIC REVIEW. *South-Eastern Europe Journal of Economics, 1*, 41–52. https://doi.org/DOI: 10.17605/OSF.IO/PCAXG

Bitzenis, A., & Koutsoupias, N. (2023B, December). Visualizing Economics and Business in the field of Education: A Quantitative Analysis of Scholarly Literature. *Global Business & Economics Anthology. Volumes I, II*. Advance online publication. DOI: 10.47341/gbea.23126

Bitzenis, A., & Koutsoupias, N. (2024A). Big data in economics research. In *Springer proceedings in business and economics* (pp. 1063–1072). https://doi.org/DOI: 10.1007/978-3-031-49105-4_61

Bitzenis, A., & Koutsoupias, N. (2024B). A Scientometric Review regarding FDI in SouthEast Europe (2005–2024). *Global Business & Economics Anthology, I&II*(2024), 117–128. https://doi.org/DOI: 10.47341/gbea.241210

Bitzenis, A., Koutsoupias, N., & Boutsiouki, S. (2023). Business Research and Data Mining: a Bibliometric Analysis. *2023 3rd International Conference on Electrical, Computer, Communications and Mechatronics Engineering (ICECCME)*, 1–6. https://doi.org/DOI: 10.1109/iceccme57830.2023.10252699

Bitzenis, A., Koutsoupias, N., & Nosios, M. (2025A). Artificial intelligence and machine learning in production efficiency enhancement and sustainable development: A comprehensive bibliometric review. *Frontiers in Sustainability*, *5*. Advance online publication. DOI: 10.3389/frsus.2024.1508647

Bitzenis, A., Koutsoupias, N., & Nosios, M. (2025B). Public Perceptions of Tax Evasion and Informal Economy in Greece. *Proceedings of XXIII. International Balkan and Near Eastern Social Sciences Congress Series on Economics, Business and Management*, 80–90. https://doi.org/DOI: 10.17605/OSF.IO/V3YCS

Bitzenis, A., Koutsoupias, N., & Nosios, M. (2025C). Theoretical Advancements in Logistics: Digitalization, Big Data, and Machine Learning in Decision Making. *Proceedings of XXIII. International Balkan and Near Eastern Social Sciences Congress Series on Economics, Business and Management*, 91–101. https://doi.org/DOI: 10.17605/OSF.IO/G7H43

Cattell, R. (2011). Scalable SQL and NoSQL data stores. *SIGMOD Record*, *39*(4), 12–27. DOI: 10.1145/1978915.1978919

Denecke, K. (2008). Using SentiWordNet for multilingual sentiment analysis. *2008 IEEE 24th International Conference on Data Engineering Workshop*, 507–512. https://doi.org/DOI: 10.1109/icdew.2008.4498370

Fragkoulis, M., Carbone, P., Kalavri, V., & Katsifodimos, A. (2023). A survey on the evolution of stream processing systems. *The VLDB Journal*, *33*(2), 507–541. DOI: 10.1007/s00778-023-00819-8

Hall, M., & Holmes, G. (2003). Benchmarking attribute selection techniques for discrete class data mining. *IEEE Transactions on Knowledge and Data Engineering*, *15*(6), 1437–1447. DOI: 10.1109/tkde.2003.1245283

He, N. H., & Garcia, E. (2009). Learning from Imbalanced Data. *IEEE Transactions on Knowledge and Data Engineering*, *21*(9), 1263–1284. DOI: 10.1109/tkde.2008.239

Inoubli, W., Aridhi, S., Mezni, H., Maddouri, M., & Nguifo, E. M. (2018). An experimental survey on big data frameworks. *Future Generation Computer Systems*, *86*, 546–564. DOI: 10.1016/j.future.2018.04.032

Jagadish, H. V., Gehrke, J., Labrinidis, A., Papakonstantinou, Y., Patel, J. M., Ramakrishnan, R., & Shahabi, C. (2014). Big data and its technical challenges. *Communications of the ACM*, *57*(7), 86–94. DOI: 10.1145/2611567

Kiran, M., Murphy, P., Monga, I., Dugan, J., & Baveja, S. S. (2015). Lambda architecture for cost-effective batch and speed big data processing. *2021 IEEE International Conference on Big Data (Big Data)*. https://doi.org/DOI: 10.1109/bigdata.2015.7364082

Koutsoupias, N., & Nosios, M. (2025). Data Engineering Research: A Systematic Review and Thematic Analysis of Methods and Frameworks [dataset]. https://doi.org/DOI: 10.17605/OSF.IO/87XEH

Koutsoupias, N., & Nosios, M. (2025A). Hierarchical Clustering in Social Sciences and Humanities: A Review. In S. D. Anastasiadou, T. G. Chadjipadelis, Nikolaos Koutsoupias, Angelos Markos, & George Menexes (Eds.), *Modern International Developments in Data Analysis and Multivariate Statistical Analysis.* IGI Global Scientific Publishing. https://doi.org/DOI: 10.4018/979-8-3693-9400-7

Koutsoupias, N., & Nosios, M. (2025B). Sentiment and Geopolitical Analysis in Sino-American Relations. In S. D. Anastasiadou, T. G. Chadjipadelis, Nikolaos Koutsoupias, Angelos Markos, & George Menexes (Eds.), *Modern International Developments in Data Analysis and Multivariate Statistical Analysis.* IGI Global Scientific Publishing. https://doi.org/DOI: 10.4018/979-8-3693-9400-7

Lee, J., Han, J., & Li, X. (2008). Trajectory Outlier Detection: A Partition-and-Detect Framework. *2008 IEEE 24th International Conference on Data Engineering*, 140–149. https://doi.org/DOI: 10.1109/icde.2008.4497422

Li, N. J., Tang, N. J., Li, N. Y., & Luo, N. Q. (2008). RIMOM: A dynamic multistrategy Ontology alignment framework. *IEEE Transactions on Knowledge and Data Engineering*, *21*(8), 1218–1232. DOI: 10.1109/tkde.2008.202

Munappy, A. R., Bosch, J., & Olsson, H. H. (2020). Data Pipeline Management in Practice: Challenges and opportunities. In *Lecture notes in computer science* (pp. 168–184). https://doi.org/DOI: 10.1007/978-3-030-64148-1_11

Page, M. J., McKenzie, J. E., Bossuyt, P. M., Boutron, I., Hoffmann, T. C., Mulrow, C. D., Shamseer, L., Tetzlaff, J. M., Akl, E. A., Brennan, S. E., Chou, R., Glanville, J., Grimshaw, J. M., Hróbjartsson, A., Lalu, M. M., Li, T., Loder, E. W., Mayo-Wilson, E., McDonald, S., & Moher, D. (2021). The PRISMA 2020 statement: An updated guideline for reporting systematic reviews. *BMJ (Clinical Research Ed.)*, (71). Advance online publication. DOI: 10.1136/bmj.n71

Sawadogo, P. N., Scholly, E., Favre, C., Ferey, E., Loudcher, S., & Darmont, J. (2019). New trends in databases and information systems. In *Communications in computer and information science*. https://doi.org/DOI: 10.1007/978-3-030-30278-8

Simitsis, A., Vassiliadis, P., & Sellis, T. (2005). State-space optimization of ETL workflows. *IEEE Transactions on Knowledge and Data Engineering*, *17*(10), 1404–1419. DOI: 10.1109/tkde.2005.169

Toshniwal, A., Taneja, S., Shukla, A., Ramasamy, K., Patel, J. M., Kulkarni, S., Jackson, J., Gade, K., Fu, M., Donham, J., Bhagat, N., Mittal, S., & Ryaboy, D. (2014). Storm@twitter. *SIGMOD '14: Proceedings of the 2014 ACM SIGMOD International Conference on Management of Data*, 147–156. https://doi.org/DOI: 10.1145/2588555.2595641

Yiu, M. L., Jensen, C. S., Huang, X., & Lu, H. (2008). SpaceTwist: Managing the Trade-Offs Among Location Privacy, Query Performance, and Query Accuracy in Mobile Services. *2008 IEEE 24th International Conference on Data Engineering*, 366–375. https://doi.org/DOI: 10.1109/icde.2008.4497445

Zaharia, M., Xin, R. S., Wendell, P., Das, T., Armbrust, M., Dave, A., Meng, X., Rosen, J., Venkataraman, S., Franklin, M. J., Ghodsi, A., Gonzalez, J., Shenker, S., & Stoica, I. (2016). Apache Spark. *Communications of the ACM*, *59*(11), 56–65. DOI: 10.1145/2934664

Zhang, L., Wen, J., Li, Y., Chen, J., Ye, Y., Fu, Y., & Livingood, W. (2021). A review of machine learning in building load prediction. *Applied Energy*, *285*, 116452. DOI: 10.1016/j.apenergy.2021.116452

Zhou, B., & Pei, J. (2008). Preserving Privacy in Social Networks Against Neighborhood Attacks. *2008 IEEE 24th International Conference on Data Engineering*, 506–515. https://doi.org/DOI: 10.1109/icde.2008.4497459

Zourna, C., Papavassiliou-Alexiou, I., Koutsoupias, N., & Papakota, A. (2021). *A mixed methods research approach to investigate undergraduate students' perceptions of changes enforced due to COVID-19*. Advance., DOI: 10.31124/advance.13606409.v1

Chapter 4

Artificial Intelligence and Machine Learning for Business and Economic Applications: A Systematic Review and MCA Approach

Nikos Koutsoupias
http://orcid.org/0000-0003-1664-5404
University of Macedonia, Greece

Aristidis Bitzenis
http://orcid.org/0000-0001-7047-9406
University of Macedonia, Greece

Marios Nosios
http://orcid.org/0009-0007-6161-3854
University of Macedonia, Greece

ABSTRACT

This chapter explores the evolution and conceptual structure of artificial intelligence and machine learning research in business and economics. Drawing on bibliometric and science-mapping analysis of Scopus-indexed publications (1984–2025), it maps the field's intellectual landscape through descriptive indicators, keyword co-occurrence, thematic mapping, trend visualization, country-level citation analysis, and Multiple Correspondence Analysis. Findings show a shift from classical methods toward broader frameworks involving predictive modelling, deep learning, and

DOI: 10.4018/979-8-3373-6926-6.ch004

NLP, with rising focus on analytics-driven decision-making, business intelligence, and strategy. Emerging themes like sustainability, fintech, and generative AI show expanding applications. The chapter offers a structured, replicable overview of key themes, methods, and global influence, deepening understanding of the field's growth and diversification.

INTRODUCTION

Over the past two decades, Artificial Intelligence (AI) and Machine Learning (ML) have evolved from specialized technical subjects into central research pillars within business and economics. Driven by the exponential growth of digital data and significant advances in computational power, AI and ML applications have proliferated across various business domains (Baesens et al., 2003; Mullainathan & Spiess, 2017). Unlike traditional analytical models, ML techniques can process vast quantities of structured and unstructured data, generating rapid predictions and decisions without reliance on rigid parametric assumptions (Agrawal et al., 2018). In tandem with the increasing prominence of these technologies, a substantial corpus of bibliometric and systematic reviews has emerged, charting research trajectories, thematic evolutions, and methodological innovations across business and economics (Gao et al., 2024; Kumar et al., 2023).

Research on AI and ML in business and economics can be grouped into several major thematic clusters, each reflecting distinct application domains. In finance and economics, AI and ML have been applied extensively for stock market prediction, algorithmic trading, credit risk evaluation, and fraud detection (Gu et al., 2020). Early studies, such as Baesens et al. (2003), demonstrated that neural networks could significantly enhance credit scoring performance, introducing rule-extraction methods to address interpretability challenges. Over time, Deep Learning (DL) models, particularly convolutional and recurrent architectures, became dominant due to their ability to model complex patterns in financial data (Ozbayoglu et al., 2020). Economists have also begun integrating ML methods into macroeconomic forecasting and policy analysis, although ML's emphasis on prediction rather than causal interpretation created methodological tensions. Mullainathan and Spiess (2017) highlighted this divide, noting that while economists traditionally seek causal explanations, ML methods excel at predictive tasks. Despite differences, ML's predictive superiority has led to greater integration into asset pricing, forecasting, and risk management models (Gu et al., 2020).

In marketing and customer analytics, AI and ML techniques have transformed data-driven decision-making by enhancing customer segmentation, personalization, and targeting. ML models have enabled firms to predict customer churn, optimize marketing strategies, and implement recommender systems that personalize product offerings based on individual behavior. Sentiment analysis powered by DL algorithms has also allowed businesses to extract actionable insights from vast streams of consumer-generated content (Huang & Rust, 2020). Despite the success in improving marketing outcomes, researchers highlight challenges in integrating AI into branding and creative strategy, where data-driven methods may not fully capture consumer emotions and values. Studies also show that using AI in marketing is often associated with improved firm performance, though results vary when it supports dynamic customer engagement (Mariani et al., 2022).

In operations and supply chain management, AI and ML models have improved forecasting, logistics, inventory management, and production planning. Toorajipour et al. (2020) found that the most prevalent AI methods in supply chain management include artificial neural networks, fuzzy logic systems, and genetic algorithms, applied to demand forecasting and optimization. The application of DL in pharmaceutical demand forecasting, as reviewed by Mousa and Al-Khateeb (2023), has improved inventory management and enhanced supply chain efficiency in the pharmaceutical sector. AI applications have also extended into sustainable operations, where algorithms optimize routes, reduce emissions, and support green logistics initiatives (Toorajipour et al., 2020). Researchers have also noted challenges in adoption, particularly related to technological and resource constraints.

Methodologically, the deployment of AI and ML techniques in business and economics has undergone a striking evolution. In the early 2000s, relatively rudimentary models, such as decision trees, neural networks, and support vector machines, were experimentally applied to business problems, often achieving superior predictive performance compared to traditional statistical approaches (Baesens et al., 2003). With the advent of the significant data era during the 2010s, the field witnessed a decisive shift toward more intricate DL architectures, enabled by the unprecedented availability of vast datasets and enhanced computational resources (Ozbayoglu et al., 2020). Surveys from this period document a pronounced movement toward DL approaches across business disciplines. Nevertheless, the growing reliance on so-called "black-box" models has provoked sustained concerns regarding explainability, fairness, and accountability, issues that continue to animate critical debates about the responsible use of AI in organizational contexts.

Recent research has emphasized explainability, causal inference, and hybrid methodologies. Techniques such as SHAP values, LIME, and interpretable neural architectures have been developed to clarify the inner workings of complex models (Arrieta et al., 2019). Athey and Imbens (2019) introduced methods integrating ML with causal inference, enabling researchers to estimate treatment effects while leveraging predictive power. This convergence addresses a key limitation of earlier AI and ML applications: their inability to answer causal questions that are critical for business strategy and policymaking. Most recently, the rise of foundation models and generative AI represents a significant evolution in scale and capability. Large-scale pre-trained models such as GPT-3 have demonstrated the ability to perform a range of business-relevant tasks, from customer service automation to strategic decision support (Bommasani et al., 2021). However, their deployment raises new issues around model governance, fairness, and robustness, which are only beginning to be addressed in empirical research.

Several influential works have shaped the field's evolution. Einav and Levin (2014) provided a roadmap for economists to engage with big data and ML, while Mullainathan and Spiess (2017) clarified how predictive modeling complements traditional econometric approaches. In business domains, Brynjolfsson and Mitchell (2017) framed AI as a "prediction technology" that fundamentally alters the cost structures of decision-making processes. As Ghoddusi et al. (2019) mentioned in energy finance and Nazareth and Reddy (2023) in financial ML, survey articles have provided comprehensive overviews that guide subsequent empirical studies.

Despite substantial progress, several gaps persist. Many AI models remain difficult to interpret, which impedes adoption in regulated industries (Arrieta et al., 2019). Data quality and bias issues continue to affect the reliability of business predictions, particularly in unstructured or customer-generated data (Mariani et al., 2022). The integration of causal reasoning into ML frameworks remains nascent, with opportunities to develop models that predict, explain, and optimize decisions (Athey & Imbens, 2019). Emerging technologies such as generative AI present novel research challenges, including understanding how AI-generated content influences economic behavior and firm strategy (Bommasani et al., 2021). Finally, the literature would benefit from more interdisciplinary research that combines insights from economics, psychology, management, and computer science to address the complex impacts of AI on organizations and markets.

Ultimately, research in AI and ML in business and economics has advanced incrementally, yielding tools for prediction, optimization, and decision-making. The field has developed from isolated applications toward broader strategic integration, although essential challenges related to explainability, bias, causality, and governance remain. Effectively addressing these concerns will be essential to fully harness the transformative impact of these technologies on business practices and economic systems in the coming years.

METHODOLOGY

This study employs a bibliometric and science-mapping methodology to examine research trends in AI and ML within the context of business and economic scholarship

(Donthu et al., 2021). Scopus was used as the primary data source, selected for its extensive disciplinary coverage and its recognized reliability in empirical analyses of scholarly output (Baas et al., 2020). A structured search strategy was developed to identify publications addressing AI- and ML-related methods, applications, and theoretical contributions (Schotten et al., 2017; Burnham, 2006). The query used for data retrieval is as follows:

```
TITLE ( "artificial intelligence" OR "machine learning" OR "deep learning" OR "AI" OR "ML") AND TITLE ( business OR economic OR finance OR "business applications" OR "economic applications" ) AND PUBYEAR > 1974 AND PUBYEAR < 2026 AND ( LIMIT-TO ( SUBJAREA,"COMP" ) OR LIMIT-TO ( SUBJAREA,"BUSI" ) OR LIMIT-TO ( SUBJAREA,"ENGI" ) OR LIMIT-TO ( SUBJAREA,"ECON" ) OR LIMIT-TO ( SUBJAREA,"DECI" ) OR LIMIT-TO ( SUBJAREA,"SOCI" ) OR LIMIT-TO ( SUBJAREA,"MATH" ) OR LIMIT-TO ( SUBJAREA,"MULT" ) ) AND ( LIMIT-TO ( DOCTYPE,"ar" ) OR LIMIT-TO ( DOCTYPE,"cp" ) OR LIMIT-TO ( DOCTYPE,"ch" ) OR LIMIT-TO ( DOCTYPE,"bk" ) )
```

To ensure methodological rigor and replicability, the study selection process adhered to the PRISMA 2020 framework, which provides a standardized protocol for identifying, screening, and assessing eligibility of records (Page et al., 2021). The progression of studies through each phase of the review is depicted in Figure 1.

Figure 1. PRISMA 2020 flow diagram of the selection process

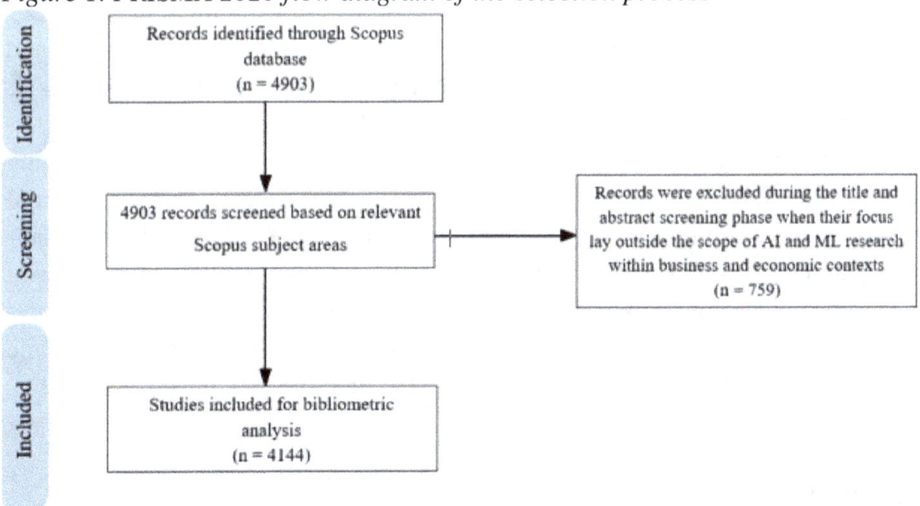

The bibliometric analysis was conducted using the bibliometrix package within the R environment, which facilitated systematic data preprocessing, descriptive evaluation, and the generation of science-mapping visualizations (Bitzenis et al., 2023; Aria & Cuccurullo, 2017). Descriptive indicators, including annual scientific production, authorship patterns, collaboration metrics, and document-type distributions, were calculated to characterize the dataset's structural composition and temporal evolution. These measures offered a quantitative overview of publication volume, citation behavior, and authorship dynamics within the field (Ellegaard & Wallin, 2015).

Beyond descriptive statistics, several science-mapping techniques were employed to investigate the literature's conceptual and intellectual organization (Thomos et al., 2023). Keyword co-occurrence analysis was utilized to identify the most frequently used author-assigned terms and to map the dominant thematic anchors within the corpus (Zourna et al., 2021). A thematic map was subsequently generated to classify keyword clusters by centrality and density, thereby identifying niche, motor, basic, and emerging research themes (Bitzenis et al., 2025; Bitzenis & Koutsoupias, 2023A). In parallel, a country-level citation analysis was conducted to assess the geographic distribution of scholarly influence, measured through aggregated citation counts.

To uncover deeper conceptual structures, Multiple Correspondence Analysis (MCA) was applied to the keyword dataset. This dimensionality reduction technique produced a factorial map positioning terms according to their co-occurrence patterns, thereby revealing distinct thematic groupings (Koutsoupias & Nosios, 2025A). The analysis enabled a nuanced examination of how methodological, managerial, and socio-technical concepts align along the principal axes of variation (Passas, 2024). Complementary visualizations, including trend evolution plots, were also produced to trace shifting research emphases and thematic salience over time (Bitzenis & Koutsoupias, 2024; Bitzenis & Koutsoupias, 2023B).

Collectively, these analytical procedures, ranging from descriptive profiling and co-word analysis to thematic classification, geographic citation mapping, and MCA, construct a multidimensional representation of the field's intellectual landscape (Koutsoupias & Nosios, 2025B). The integration of systematic data retrieval and bibliometric techniques provides a robust and replicable foundation for understanding the evolution of AI and ML scholarship in business and economics, while also illuminating emerging trajectories within the literature (Zupic & Čater, 2014).

RESULTS

In the results section, the analysis is presented through a series of quantitative and visual outputs, including core bibliometric indicators, keyword co-occurrence mapping, thematic cluster visualizations, country-level citation distributions, annual trends in scientific production, and the conceptual structure identified through MCA.

Table 1. Descriptive statistics

Description	Results
MAIN INFORMATION ABOUT DATA	
Timespan	1984:2025
Sources (Journals, Books, etc)	1027
Documents	4144
Annual Growth Rate %	17.14
Document Average Age	2.04
Average citations per doc	10.58
References	31501
DOCUMENT CONTENTS	
Keywords Plus (ID)	12272
Author's Keywords (DE)	8259
AUTHORS	
Authors	10759
Authors of single-authored docs	690
AUTHORS COLLABORATION	
Single-authored docs	771
Co-Authors per Doc	3.25
International co-authorships %	25.6
DOCUMENT TYPES	
article	1791
book	150
book chapter	894
conference paper	1309

The descriptive statistics in Table 1 summarize the dataset's core characteristics and provide an overview of its structure, scope, and composition. These indicators outline basic features of the publication corpus, the authors involved, and the types of documents included. Together, they form a numerical profile of research activity on AI and ML in business and economic contexts.

The dataset spans 1984 to 2025, covering more than four decades of publication activity. This period includes 1,027 sources, comprising articles, books, book chapters, and conference papers. The total number of documents is 4,144, representing a considerable body of indexed literature. The annual growth rate of 17.14% reflects the average rate of increase in publication volume over the recorded timespan. The average document age is 2.04 years, indicating that the dataset contains a substantial proportion of recent publications. On average, each document has received 10.58 citations, and the collection as a whole references 31,501 cited works. Furthermore, the document content indicators report two types of keyword measures: Keywords Plus (12,272 occurrences) and Authors' Keywords (8,259 occurrences). These totals reflect the volume of thematic descriptors assigned throughout the dataset. Keywords Plus typically derive from terms in cited references, whereas Authors' Keywords consist of author-selected descriptors intended to signal the focus of each publication. The difference between the two values suggests that the dataset incorporates a broad range of indexing terms, spanning both author-defined and reference-derived vocabularies.

The authorship statistics show that 10,759 authors contributed to the dataset. Of these, 690 produced single-authored documents, while the remainder participated in collaborative works. The dataset contains 771 single-authored documents. The co-authors-per-document ratio is 3.25, indicating that publications typically involve multiple contributors. Additionally, the share of internationally co-authored documents is 25.6%, indicating cross-country collaboration within the corpus. On the other hand, the document type distribution identifies the kinds of outputs represented. The corpus includes 1,791 journal articles, which form the largest category. Conference papers (1,309 documents) also constitute a substantial share. Books appear less frequently, with 150 entries, whereas book chapters account for 894 documents. These figures indicate that the dataset comprises a mix of peer-reviewed journal articles, conference papers, and book chapters.

Collectively, the descriptive statistics depict a dataset with broad temporal coverage, varied publication sources, diverse authorship patterns, and multiple document types. The span from 1984 to 2025 captures both earlier work and recent studies, while the relatively low average document age suggests that more recent publications account for a large portion of the corpus. The high number of sources and references points to an extensive citation network, and the volume of keywords indicates a wide thematic range. The authorship and collaboration indicators reflect a combination of individual and team-based contributions, including a notable proportion of international co-authorship (see Table 1).

Figure 2. Annual scientific production

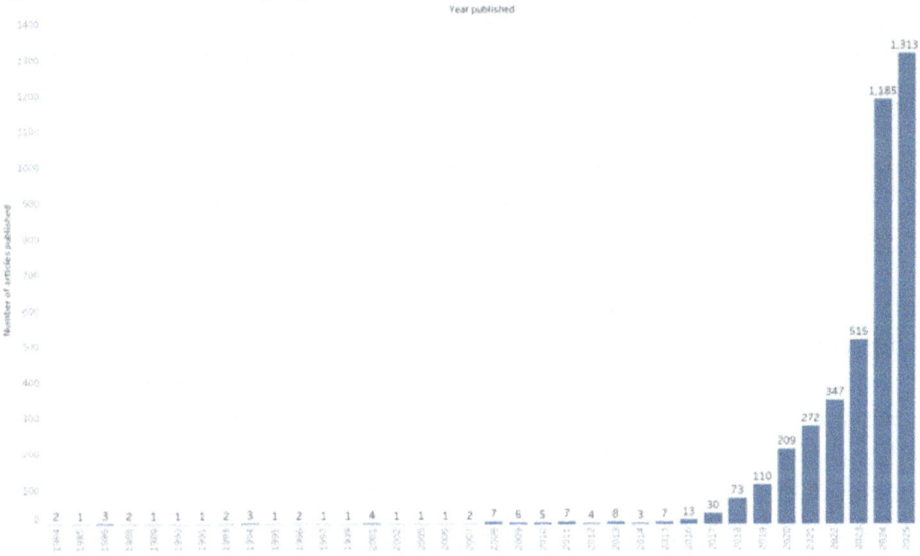

The annual scientific production graph in Figure 2 presents a chronological overview of publication activity from 1984 to 2025, illustrating how the dataset is distributed across time. The earliest years of the timeline are marked by limited output, with only a few publications appearing each year. From the mid-1980s through the late 1990s, the dataset records between 1 and 3 documents per year, indicating a sparse pattern of scholarly activity. For instance, 1984 includes two articles, 1985 one, and 1986 three. This minor fluctuation within a narrow range persists throughout the decade, as evidenced by similarly modest totals in 1988, 1989, and 1990. The early 1990s follow this same pattern, with annual publication counts remaining restricted to one, two, or three articles. Even by the decade's end, this trend continues, as exemplified by the low totals in 1996 and 1997. Collectively, this initial 15-year segment of the timeline reveals a relatively limited body of work and suggests that research output during this early period was minimal and irregular.

As the timeline enters the 2000s, publication activity remains modest, though subtle changes begin to emerge. The year 2001 is notable for producing four documents, marking an early deviation from the prevailing pattern of one or two publications per year. However, this increase does not immediately herald a sustained shift, as subsequent years revert to lower totals. A more discernible transformation becomes apparent in the mid-2000s. The dataset reports two articles in 2007, followed by seven in 2008 and six in 2009. While still modest compared to later figures, these numbers mark a departure from the earlier decades, which were characterized predominantly by single-digit outputs. This period inaugurates a phase of more regular and slightly intensified activity, with multiple consecutive years registering mid-single-digit counts. The early 2010s continue this trajectory: five publications are listed in 2010, seven in 2011, eight in 2013, and seven again in 2015. Although the scale remains relatively limited, publication frequency becomes more consistent, in contrast to the irregularity of the preceding decades.

A more pronounced inflection point occurs in 2016 and becomes especially apparent in 2017. The total number of publications rose to 13 in 2016, the highest annual figure recorded up to that time, signaling a significant departure from the previous trend of single-digit counts. This shift is dramatically amplified in 2017, with 30 publications, indicating an apparent acceleration in scholarly output. The subsequent years demonstrate a pattern of steady expansion: 73 publications are recorded in 2018, 110 in 2019, and 209 in 2020. These figures mark a period of rapid numerical growth, as annual outputs surpass earlier thresholds and begin to reflect sustained increases in research activity. This upward trajectory persists into 2021 and 2022, with annual counts of 272 and 347, respectively. These consecutive increases delineate a segment of the timeline in which publication activity becomes markedly more concentrated and quantitatively robust.

The final three years of the dataset, 2023, 2024, and 2025, constitute the most densely populated period in terms of publication volume. In 2023, annual output reached 515 documents, surpassing the 500-publication threshold for the first time. This is followed by a substantial leap in 2024, with 1,185 articles recorded, more than double the previous year's figure. The trend continues in 2025, which documents 1,313 publications, marking the highest annual total in the dataset. Taken together, these years represent the peak of publication activity within the recorded timeline. Their placement at the end of the period underscores the increasing density and intensity of research production in recent years. However, this observation is offered descriptively and does not speculate on underlying causes or broader implications beyond the scope of the available data.

Across the full four-decade span, the annual scientific production graph shows a marked progression from minimal activity in the earlier decades to substantially higher levels in the most recent years. The shift from one or two articles per year in the 1980s and 1990s to over 1,000 in 2025 illustrates cumulative growth in publication volume. It identifies periods of low, moderate, and high activity without inferring causality or attributing interpretive significance to the observed changes. As presented, the table offers a clear and coherent temporal profile of the corpus, mapping the distribution of publications over time with precision and neutrality (see Figure 2).

Figure 3. Most relevant abstract keywords

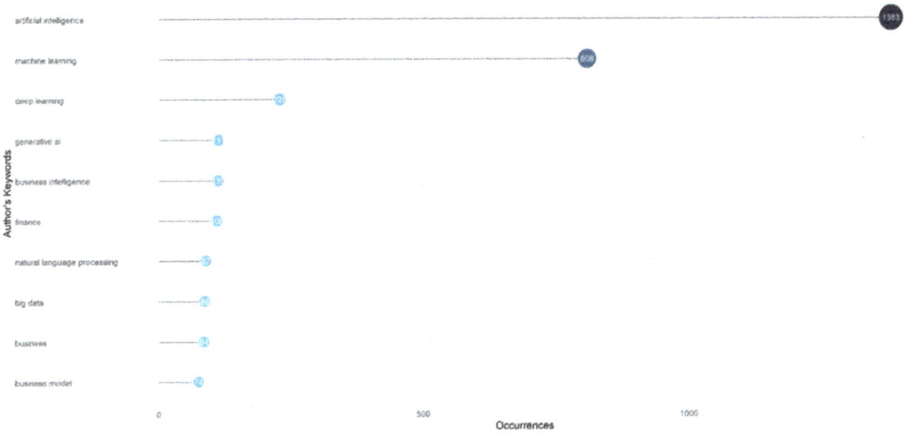

The most relevant author keywords graph in Figure 3 illustrates the frequency distribution of author-assigned keywords in the dataset, providing a direct depiction of the dominant terminology shaping research on AI and ML in business and economic contexts. Each point along the horizontal axis denotes the number of keyword occurrences across the corpus, while the relative size of the markers visually encodes their prevalence. In this respect, the graph functions as an accessible yet analytically meaningful representation of the conceptual lexicon most commonly employed by scholars as they articulate and situate their contributions within this interdisciplinary field.

The most immediate observable feature of the distribution is the prominence of the term *artificial intelligence*, which appears 1,383 times. This concentration indicates that a considerable portion of the literature identifies broadly with the domain of AI rather than adopting more specialized methodological or application-oriented labels. Such usage reflects the way AI commonly functions as a general conceptual category encompassing various analytical approaches and business applications. On the other hand, the keyword *machine learning* was recorded 808 times and forms a second central pole within the dataset. Its high frequency reflects its status as the principal methodological framework through which contemporary business and economic research operationalizes AI-related inquiry. Whereas *artificial intelligence* provides the broader conceptual scaffold, the greater prevalence of *machine learning* underscores the extent to which predictive modeling, data-driven techniques, and algorithmic decision-making constitute the operational core of current scholarship. The disparity in magnitude between the two terms suggests both the breadth of research that invokes AI in general terms and the centrality of ML as the predominant analytic tool within that overarching domain.

The third-most-frequent keyword, *deep learning*, appears 227 times. Its presence signals the increasing incorporation of advanced neural architectures into business- and economics-related research. Although its frequency is considerably lower than that of machine learning, its position among the leading terms nonetheless attests to the steady uptake of computationally intensive techniques. The observed gap likely reflects differences in conceptual scope: while *deep learning* represents a specific methodological subset, *machine learning* and *artificial intelligence* encompass far broader categories of inquiry. Keywords situated in the mid-frequency range, most notably *generative ai* (111 occurrences) and *business intelligence* (110), capture both emerging and established research domains. The visibility of *generative ai* is particularly noteworthy given its relatively recent rise, indicating that the dataset reflects ongoing transformations in the technological and conceptual landscape. By contrast, the stable presence of business intelligence highlights a longstanding intersection between AI-driven techniques and organizational decision-support systems. Together, these terms illustrate how the literature integrates methodological innovation with long-established areas of corporate practice.

Further down the distribution, several business-oriented terms appear with moderate frequency. The term *finance*, with 103 occurrences, emerges as a central application domain, reflecting the extensive body of work on forecasting, risk modeling, algorithmic trading, and financial decision-making. Its prominence is consistent with the well-established relevance of AI and ML to financial analytics, where predictive performance and data intensity are key. The term *natural language processing* (87) also features prominently, pointing to the growing importance of text-based analytical approaches for examining corporate disclosures, consumer sentiment, and other forms of unstructured language data relevant to organizational decision-making. Other keywords, such as *big data* (86), *business* (84), and *business model* (74), reveal the field's sustained engagement with broader organizational and strategic perspectives. Their moderate frequency suggests that, while the methodological vocabulary tends to be dominated by computational terms, there is still significant attention to the managerial, structural, and strategic dimensions of AI adoption. These keywords underscore the interplay between technological innovation and organizational transformation, a recurrent theme in business and economics research.

Collectively, the distribution of author keywords portrays a research landscape anchored in expansive conceptual categories, operationalized through specific computational methodologies, and applied across core business domains. The weight given to *artificial intelligence* and *machine learning* underscores their centrality as both descriptive and organizational constructs. Concurrently, the presence of terms such as *deep learning, generative ai,* and *natural language processing* reflects the field's ongoing methodological diversification. At the same time, keywords related to *finance, business intelligence,* and *business models* underscore the ongoing integration of AI into the core of economic and managerial practice. Overall, the graph provides a succinct yet substantive overview of the thematic anchors shaping current scholarship, thereby offering a descriptive foundation for understanding how AI- and ML-related studies articulate their core concepts within the broader academic conversation (see Figure 3).

Figure 4. Most cited countries

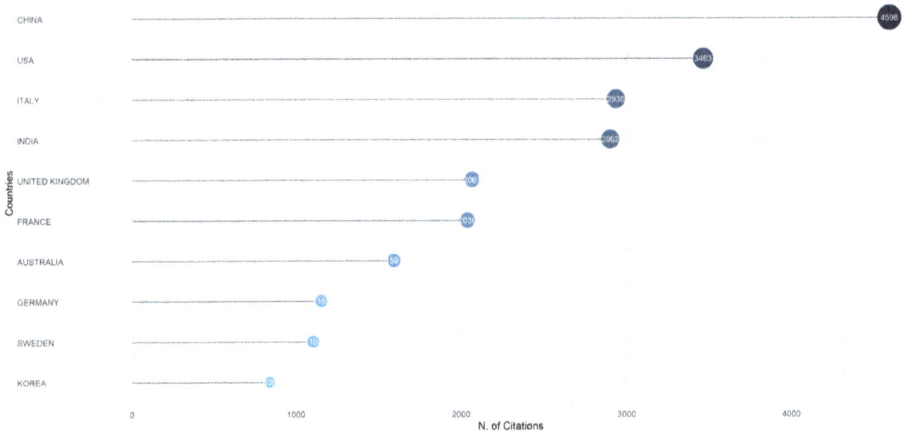

The most-cited countries graph in Figure 4 provides a comparative view of citation counts for publications across different national affiliations. Each point indicates the total number of citations accumulated by works linked to authors from a given country, while the horizontal axis displays citation volume. The size of the markers conveys relative magnitude, enabling clear differentiation between countries with higher and lower citation totals. Accordingly, the figure offers a descriptive overview of how citation activity is distributed geographically within the dataset.

China appears at the top of the distribution, indicated by the most significant marker on the graph, with 4,598 citations. This value identifies China as the country with the highest citation count in the corpus. Its extended placement along the horizontal axis reflects the scale of its citation activity, indicating that publications affiliated with Chinese institutions have accumulated a substantial number of references within the dataset. The United States follows with 3,463 citations, ranking second. The difference between China and the United States reflects a measurable gap in citation volume, but both countries occupy the upper tier of the distribution. Their positions indicate they are the two most-cited national contributors in the dataset, based on the citation counts presented.

Italy and India appear next, with citation counts of 2,939 and 2,902, respectively. Their values are closely aligned, forming a pair of mid-upper-range contributors. The similarity of their totals suggests that publications from these two countries have accumulated comparable citation activity. The United Kingdom and France follow, with 2,067 and 2,038 citations, respectively. Their positions indicate that both lie in a middle segment of the distribution, with nearly equivalent citation volumes. Their marker sizes reflect moderate citation activity compared with the highest contributors.

Australia appears with 1,559 citations, forming a smaller but clearly identifiable marker along the horizontal scale. Its position indicates a discernible decrease in citation volume relative to the preceding countries, placing Australia in a secondary tier of contributors. Germany follows with 1,015 citations, placing it further down the scale but still within the group of countries with citation totals exceeding one thousand. At the lower end of the distribution, Sweden and Korea record 910 and 838 citations, respectively. These values correspond to the smallest markers among the listed countries. Although their citation counts are substantially lower than those of the leading contributors, their presence in the graph indicates ongoing participation within the broader geographical distribution of citation activity.

Ultimately, the graph presents a numerical distribution of citation activity across the countries represented in the dataset. The pattern forms distinct tiers, with higher-, mid-, and lower-level citation groups distinguishable by their horizontal positions and marker sizes. As arranged in the figure, the data provide a clear overview of how citation counts are allocated among national contributors, offering a concise visual summary of the geographic distribution of citations within the corpus (see Figure 4).

Figure 5. Trend topics graph

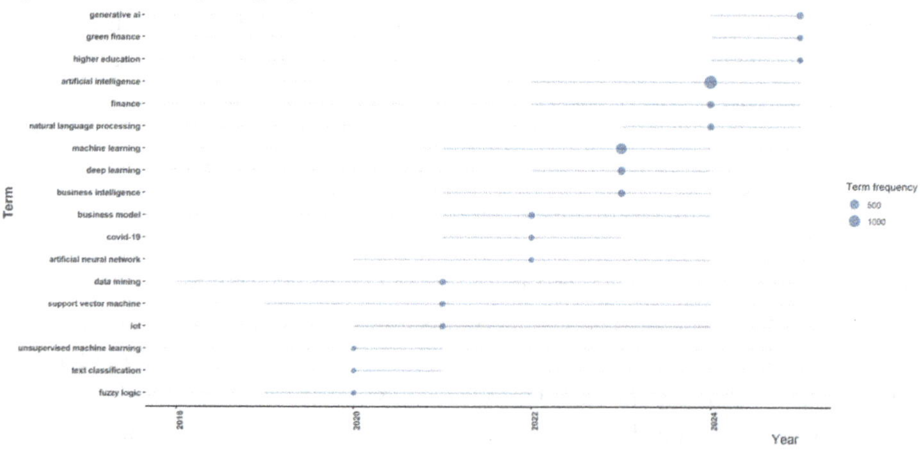

The trend topics visualization in Figure 5 provides a temporal representation of how key terms associated with AI and ML evolve across the dataset from 2018 to 2025. Lines indicate periods of activity for each topic, while bubble size reflects term frequency. Together, these elements outline shifts in methodological emphasis and application areas without assigning directional causality. In the earliest segment of the timeline, the figure shows a concentration of activity among classical ML techniques. This includes the appearance of terms such as *data mining, support vector machine, artificial neural network,* and *fuzzy logic* primarily between 2018 and 2020. Their shorter spans and relatively modest bubble sizes suggest that these approaches, while foundational in earlier research, occupy a more limited position in recent years. Additional early-period topics, *unsupervised machine learning,* and *text classification* exhibit similar temporal characteristics, reflecting methodological orientations that were more prominent at the beginning of the observed interval.

A noticeable change emerges around 2020-2021, with broader methodological categories dominating the timeline. This shift is evident in extended activity for terms such as *machine learning*, which displays one of the longest durations and one of the largest bubble sizes in the figure. Its sustained prominence indicates its role as a central descriptor used across diverse studies rather than a reference to any specific technique. A similar pattern appears for *deep learning*, which gains visibility from 2021 onward, marking increased reliance on neural architectures for tasks such as classification, forecasting, and text processing. Around the same period, *business intelligence* became more visible, pointing to heightened interest in analytics-driven decision support and organizational information systems.

Application-oriented themes gain traction in the middle years of the timeline. This is particularly evident in the emergence of *finance* and *natural language processing*, both of which have become more prevalent since 2022. Their placement reflects increased engagement with financial modelling, risk analysis, sentiment extraction, and text-based applications in business contexts. A cluster of shorter-lived topics, *business model,* and *COVID-19*, appears during 2021-2022, indicating focused periods of research addressing strategic transformation and pandemic-related disruptions. Although these topics do not persist over many years, their presence illustrates the field's responsiveness to specific organizational and contextual challenges.

In the latter portion of the timeline, broader conceptual and institutional themes become more prominent. Terms such as *artificial intelligence, higher education,* and *green finance* appear beginning in 2023 and continue through 2025, with varying frequencies. The large bubble associated with *artificial intelligence* suggests its continued use as an overarching category encompassing both methodological and application-level studies. Meanwhile, *higher education* reflects growing attention to the role of AI in academic settings, including teaching, administration, and skill development. The presence of *green finance* underscores the integration of sustainability-oriented topics into discussions of AI's relevance to economic and managerial decision-making.

The most recent addition to the trend structure, *generative ai*, emerged in 2024 with a short yet clearly defined timeline. Its appearance at the far right of the visualization indicates early but increasing activity in this area. Compared with longer-standing methodological terms, *generative ai* remains in an initial phase of integration, consistent with its still-developing position in thematic and conceptual analyses across the dataset. This suggests that, while the topic is gaining traction, it has not yet formed enduring or central patterns of co-occurrence with other research themes.

Across these developments, the visualization depicts a precise movement from early reliance on algorithm-specific terminology toward broader methodological categories and more diverse domain applications. The sustained prominence of *machine learning, deep learning,* and *artificial intelligence* in later years corresponds with an expanding research base characterized by larger datasets and more complex analytical techniques. Concurrently, the emergence of themes such as *generative ai, green finance,* and *higher education* signals the field's extension into areas shaped by technological development, environmental considerations, and institutional change. Viewed collectively, the distribution of topics across the timeline reflects a research environment in which longstanding analytical foundations coexist with newer areas of inquiry that broaden the scope of AI- and ML-related work in business and economics (see Figure 5).

Figure 6. Thematic map

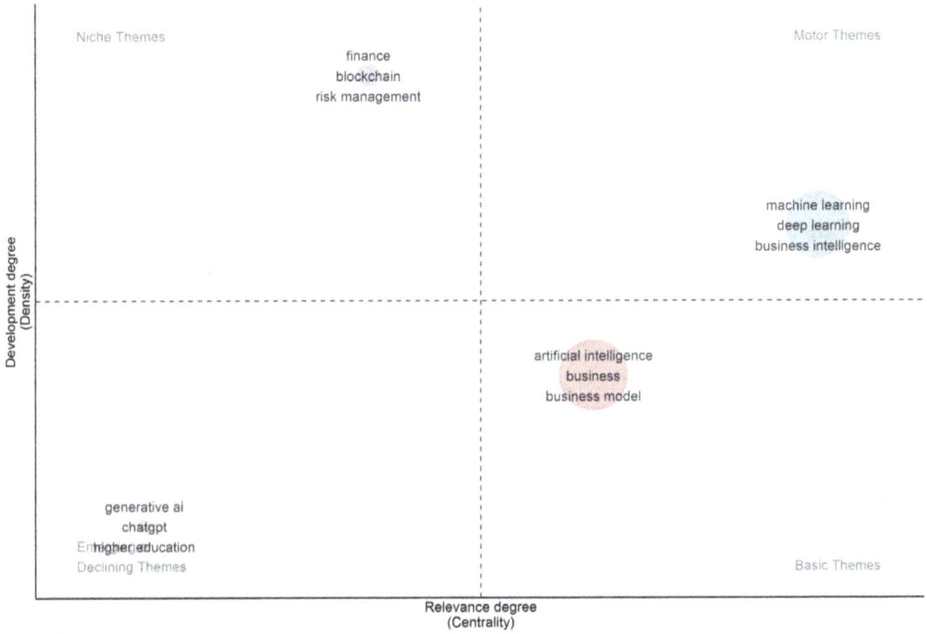

The thematic map in Figure 6 provides a structured visualization of the field's conceptual organization by positioning groups of keywords according to their degree of development (*density*) and their importance within the broader research network (*centrality*). The horizontal axis reflects relevance, indicating the extent to which a theme is connected to others, while the vertical axis captures the internal cohesion of each thematic cluster. Together, these dimensions outline how research topics relate to the central structure of AI and ML scholarship in business and economics.

In the upper-left quadrant, labelled niche themes, the keywords *finance, blockchain,* and *risk management* appear as a compact grouping. Their higher position on the density scale indicates that these topics form internally cohesive clusters within their respective subfields. Their comparatively low centrality, however, places them at some distance from the dataset's primary conceptual focus. This pattern suggests that although finance-related applications of AI and ML are substantively developed and coherent, they operate as specialized areas rather than as central components within the broader research landscape. The presence of *blockchain* alongside *finance* and *risk management* points to an application-oriented domain in which computational techniques support sector-specific analytical aims.

In contrast, the upper-right quadrant contains the motor themes, including *machine learning, deep learning,* and *business intelligence*. These keywords combine relatively strong centrality with higher density, situating them as both well-developed and closely integrated into the broader research network. Their position indicates that they make substantial contributions to the methodological and conceptual foundations of current scholarship. The terms *machine learning* and *deep learning*, in particular, feature prominently in empirical work across business and economics, reflecting their frequent use in predictive modelling, classification tasks, and the analysis of large datasets. The inclusion of *business intelligence* highlights ongoing interest in analytical systems that support managerial decision-making, underscoring the continued relevance of computational tools for organizational contexts.

The lower-right quadrant, associated with basic themes, includes *artificial intelligence, business,* and *business models*. These terms show relatively strong relevance but lower density, indicating that while they occupy essential positions in the field, they encompass broad and diverse bodies of research. The term *artificial intelligence* serves as a central conceptual category that links methodological and application-focused studies. Still, its lower thematic cohesion reflects the wide range of perspectives and uses associated with the term. Similarly, *business* and *business model* represent general frameworks through which scholars address organizational processes, strategic adaptations, and the implications of AI technologies. Their placement suggests that these concepts help connect methodological developments with practical domains, even though they are less thematically concentrated than more specialized clusters.

The lower-left quadrant contains emerging or declining themes, represented by *generative ai, chatgpt,* and *higher education*. Their limited centrality and density indicate that these topics are either at early stages of thematic formation or remain peripheral within the dataset. The themes *generative ai* and *chatgpt* are recent additions to the research landscape, and their placement suggests that although they have begun to attract attention, they have not yet developed extensive thematic cohesion or strong connections to established research clusters in business and economics. Their presence nonetheless signals growing interest in how generative models may affect organizational practices, content production, and decision-support processes. The presence of *higher education* in this quadrant suggests a smaller group of studies addressing educational or institutional aspects of AI adoption, which, according to the map, currently sit apart from the field's main trajectory.

Overall, the thematic map provides a structured view of how the dataset's main topics are distributed by degree of development and relevance. The placement of methodological, applied, and emerging themes illustrates how these areas align within the broader configuration of the literature. Motor themes appear as developed and central components, while basic themes represent widely connected but less cohesively structured areas. Niche and emerging themes occupy more specialized or developing regions of the map. Within the scope of this study, the figure offers a concise visual overview of how the dataset's thematic areas are arranged and how they relate to one another based on their positions in the map (see Figure 6).

Table 2. Coordinates of keywords on Dimension 1

word	Dim1
classification	2.51
sentiment analysis	1.99
random forest	1.69
prediction	1.64
data mining	1.63
lstm	1.53
business analytics	1.32
business intelligence	1.26
neural network	1.24
forecasting	1.17
neural networks	1.12
natural language processing	1.05
deep learning	1.03
machine learning	0.87
predictive analytics	0.71
data analysis	0.50
data analytics	0.47
decision making	0.42
covid-19	0.19
big data	0.14

The distribution of loadings along the first dimension, as seen in the first dimension in Table 2, reveals a discernible progression from narrowly defined ML techniques to more encompassing analytical and contextual terminology. The terms with the highest positive loadings, *classification* (2.51), *sentiment analysis* (1.99), *random forest* (1.69), *prediction* (1.64), and *data mining* (1.63), coalesce around the domain of supervised learning and predictive modeling. Collectively, they constitute a methodological cluster anchored in algorithmic implementation, performance evaluation, and task-specific computational procedures. Their prominent positioning suggests that Dimension 1 primarily captures variance associated with studies that emphasize technical execution and empirical precision over theoretical abstraction or organizational framing.

A second grouping of terms, marked by moderately high loadings, reinforces this methodological orientation while extending its scope to include neural architectures and advanced computational strategies. Terms such as *lstm* (1.53), *neural network* (1.24), *neural networks* (1.12), and *deep learning* (1.03) underscore a continuity with the predictive and classification-focused terminology, situating these architectures within the same analytical axis. The inclusion of *forecasting* (1.17) and *natural language processing* (1.05) in this region further signals the prevalence of time-series and textual data applications, both of which frequently draw on deep learning paradigms or hybrid analytic frameworks.

The presence of *business analytics* (1.32) and *business intelligence* (1.26) among the higher-loading items introduces a managerial dimension to this computational cluster. Their relatively elevated positions imply a strong association between analytics-driven decision environments and technically intensive ML workflows. Rather than constituting a separate conceptual domain, these terms appear to integrate seamlessly into the dimension's technical and predictive emphasis, highlighting the embeddedness of algorithmic approaches within applied organizational contexts.

Lower-tier positive loadings mark a transitional zone, shifting from specialized computational methods toward more generalized methodological descriptors. Terms such as *machine learning* (0.87), *predictive analytics* (0.71), *data analysis* (0.50), and *data analytics* (0.47) represent broad methodological categories with cross-domain applicability. Their placement reflects widespread relevance across the corpus, albeit with less discriminative power in relation to the specific algorithmic intensity captured at the upper end of the dimension. Similarly, *decision making* (0.42) indicates a link to analytics-focused research while remaining somewhat removed from technical implementation.

At the lower extreme of Dimension 1, terms such as *covid-19* (0.19) and *big data* (0.14) exhibit marginal contributions to the dimension's variance. Their low loadings suggest weaker alignment with the computational and predictive focus that characterizes the higher end of the axis. These items function more as contextual or thematic markers, recurring across various methodological approaches without anchoring any particular analytic orientation. In sum, the ordered distribution of terms along Dimension 1 articulates a gradient of methodological intensity. High-loading items cluster around specific, implementation-oriented terminologies related to algorithmic design and predictive modeling. Intermediate and lower loadings reflect increasingly general methodological lexicons and domain-transversal topical tags. As such, Dimension 1 may be interpreted as indexing a continuum from technical specificity to conceptual generality within the discourses of computational and analytical research (see Table 2).

Table 3. Coordinates of keywords on Dimension 2

word	Dim2
business analytics	3.37
decision making	2.98
big data	2.55
data analytics	2.09
business management	2.07
marketing	1.87
decision-making	1.84
predictive analytics	1.29
business intelligence	1.24
risk management	0.97
automation	0.78
finance	0.74
data analysis	0.68
neural network	0.62
data mining	0.58
fintech	0.52
bibliometric analysis	0.36
artificial intelligence	0.29
forecasting	0.28
e-commerce	0.22
machine learning	0.20
blockchain	0.17
business	0.15
internet of things	0.05

The second dimension, as seen in the second dimension in Table 3, is defined by high loadings on terms associated with managerial, organizational, and decision-oriented domains. The most heavily weighted keywords, *business analytics* (3.37), *decision making* (2.98), *big data* (2.55), *data analytics* (2.09), and *business management* (2.07), form a coherent cluster that foregrounds strategic and operational applications of AI and ML. These elevated values indicate that the dimension captures variance associated with the organizational appropriation of analytical tools for planning, performance evaluation, and structuring business operations. The concurrent prominence of *marketing* (1.87) and *decision-making* (1.84) further reinforces this interpretation, underscoring the role of customer insights and evaluative judgment in managerial discourse.

Terms with mid-range loadings extend this organizational emphasis while introducing more specific applications and evaluative frameworks. The terms *predictive analytics* (1.29) and *business intelligence* (1.24) occupy intermediary positions that link managerial strategy to analytical execution, emphasizing the deployment of data-driven methods for operational and tactical purposes rather than their algorithmic underpinnings. The inclusion of *risk management* (0.97), *automation* (0.78), *finance* (0.74), and *data analysis* (0.68) suggests that the dimension also reflects domain-specific functions in which AI and ML are employed to optimize processes, mitigate uncertainty, and support financial decision-making. These placements indicate a continued, albeit more specialized, alignment with organizational efficiency and evaluative control.

Lower positive loadings reflect terms that contribute to the dimensional structure but are not central to its thematic core. Items such as *neural network* (0.62), *data mining* (0.58), and *fintech* (0.52) suggest a degree of overlap with business analytics, yet their associations are markedly weaker than those of explicitly managerial terms. Their presence likely reflects contexts in which technical methods intersect with organizational aims without being primarily shaped by them. Similarly, the appearance of *bibliometric analysis* (0.36), *artificial intelligence* (0.29), and *forecasting* (0.28) points to broader methodological and thematic connections that are not principal structuring forces of the dimension. These terms function more as general-purpose or cross-cutting categories, appearing across diverse areas of research rather than anchoring the dimension itself.

At the bottom end of the scale, *e-commerce* (0.22), *machine learning* (0.20), and *blockchain* (0.17) exhibit minimal loading, suggesting only marginal alignment with the managerial orientation that defines the dimension. These terms likely reflect either generic computational frameworks or domain-specific technologies that operate outside the core managerial narrative. The lowest-loading term, *internet of things* (0.05), further underscores this pattern. Despite its relevance in technologically enabled business environments, its conceptual distance from the strategic, decision-centric themes at the top of the dimension suggests it is not a principal contributor to the axis's structure.

Taken together, the distribution of loadings across Dimension 2 indicates that it functions as a managerial-intentionality axis, distinguishing research that foregrounds the use of AI and ML for business decision-making, strategic analytics, and organizational optimization. High-scoring terms articulate a managerial discourse concerned with control, planning, and applied data use. In contrast, terms with lower loadings either reflect technical methodologies or domain-general themes that are only weakly integrated into this organizational focus (see Table 3).

Figure 7. Conceptual structure map

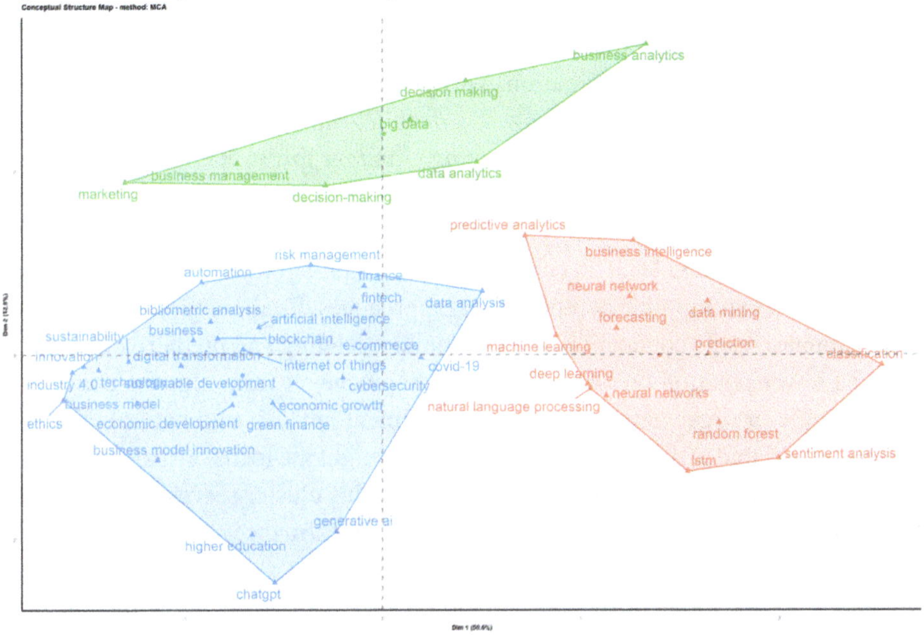

The factorial map in Figure 7 was generated via MCA and offers a spatial representation of the dataset's underlying conceptual structure, derived from patterns of co-occurrence among author keywords. Each plotted point corresponds to a keyword, and the proximity between terms reflects their tendency to appear within the same documents. The map is organized along two principal dimensions: Dimension 1, accounting for 50.65% of the total inertia, captures the dominant axis of variation, while Dimension 2 accounts for an additional 24.85%. Together, the two dimensions represent approximately 75.5% of the total variance, yielding a highly informative two-dimensional projection. Within this space, three distinct clusters, green, red, and blue, can be discerned, each corresponding to a coherent thematic grouping.

Located in the upper-right quadrant, the green cluster comprises a tightly grouped set of keywords focused on decision-making and business analytics. Core terms include *decision-making, business analytics, data analytics, marketing, big data,* and *business management.* Their spatial proximity suggests a thematic convergence on managerial decision-making and data-informed business operations. The presence of *marketing* on the periphery indicates its conceptual alignment with the cluster, albeit with a somewhat more tangential focus. The location of this group, strongly positive along both dimensions, suggests that it is aligned with the strategic application of analytics (Dimension 1) and more abstract, organizational concerns (Dimension 2). The overall configuration reflects a stream of scholarship focused on how AI and

ML tools are deployed to support firm-level decisions, generate customer insights, and execute data-driven strategies.

To the right of the graph, the red cluster occupies the mid- and lower-right quadrants and shows a more diffuse distribution. This grouping includes methodological and technical terms such as *machine learning, deep learning, data mining, prediction, classification, natural language processing, random forest, neural network,* and *sentiment analysis*. The placement of *classification* and *prediction* on the far right indicates their frequent co-occurrence with algorithm-specific keywords, notably *random forests* and *LSTMs*. Conceptually, this cluster is rooted in implementation-level techniques and applied computational approaches. Its alignment along Dimension 1 emphasizes its connection to algorithmic modeling and predictive analytics, while its lower position on Dimension 2 distinguishes it from clusters concerned with strategic or organizational framing. Sentiment analysis and natural language processing, located at the lower-right margin, highlight the focus on textual data and DL techniques in this body of work. As a whole, this cluster serves as the computational heart of AI research, emphasizing model performance, analytical methods, and forecasting capabilities.

In contrast, the blue cluster spans the lower and left-hand areas of the map and exhibits greater internal heterogeneity. Terms such as *artificial intelligence, blockchain, digital transformation, industry 4.0 technologies, sustainability, economic growth, fintech, cybersecurity, bibliometric analysis, e-commerce,* and *green finance* populate this space. Located predominantly on the negative side of Dimension 1, these keywords are associated with broader socio-technical and macroeconomic concerns. The proximity of *artificial intelligence* to *economic development, innovation,* and *blockchain* suggests framing AI as a driver of systemic change and industrial evolution. The inclusion of terms such as *covid-19, higher education,* and *ethics* signals the cluster's engagement with institutional, policy-oriented, and societal dimensions. In addition to the above, *sustainability* and *green finance* further extend this thematic range, reflecting research on AI's potential to address global challenges and support developmental agendas. Notably, the appearance of *chatgpt* at the cluster's lower edge marks the growing, though still emergent, interest in *generative ai*. Overall, this group encompasses a wide-ranging discourse on innovation, disruption, and economic transformation, framed through the lens of emerging technologies.

The spatial configuration of these clusters along the factorial plane reveals meaningful patterns. Dimension 1 serves to separate computational and algorithmic emphases, concentrated on the right, from broader conceptual and transformative discussions situated on the left. This axis effectively distinguishes applied technical work from research concerned with strategic implications and macro-level shifts. Dimension 2 introduces a vertical differentiation, contrasting organizational and decision-making themes (upper half) with operational, tool-based inquiries (lower half). The placement of *neural networks, lstms,* and *classification* near the bottom reflects their centrality to performance-focused, data-intensive applications. By contrast, the elevated position of *decision-making* and *business analytics* underscores their link to managerial reasoning and strategic action. Together, the dimensions articulate a conceptual topology that isolates three relatively distinct yet interrelated spheres: strategic management, ML implementation, and socio-technical innovation.

In summary, the factorial map delineates three principal thematic zones within the AI and ML literature in business and economics. The green cluster reflects a managerial orientation, emphasizing decision-making, analytics, and strategic application. The red cluster foregrounds computational techniques and methodological rigor, capturing the technical core of ML scholarship. The blue cluster, by contrast, addresses systemic and cross-sectoral change, encompassing innovation studies, economic development, and the societal implications of AI. Their distribution across the factorial space illustrates both the field's thematic breadth and structural coherence, offering a concise yet comprehensive visual schema of its prevailing conceptual domains (see Figure 7).

Table 4. Most cited papers

Paper	Total Citations
Di Vaio A, 2020, J Bus Res	859
Wamba-Taguimdje S-L, 2020, Bus Process Manage J	761
Enholm Im, 2022, Inf Syst Front	595
Bahrammirzaee A, 2010, Neural Comput Appl	450
Loureiro Smc et al., 2021, J Bus Res	390
Mhlanga D, 2020, Intern J Financial Stud	378
Akter S, 2022, Ann Oper Res	370
Sjödin D, 2021, J Bus Res	368
Bose & Mahapatra, 2001, Inf Manage	364
Ghoddusi H, 2019, Energy Econ	356
Zhu Y, 2019, Int J Prod Econ	312
Lee J, 2019, J Open Innov: Technol Mark Complex	295
Cao L, 2022, Acm Comput Surv	293
Cubric M, 2020, Technol Soc	292
Chowdhury S et al., 2022, J Bus Res	290

The 15 most-cited papers in the dataset, as shown in Table 4, establish the conceptual and methodological underpinnings of contemporary research on AI and

ML in business and economic contexts. Rather than coalescing around a single theoretical paradigm, these studies articulate a diverse array of perspectives that map how AI is mobilized across strategic management, organizational transformation, computational modeling, and sector-specific applications. Their visibility in the citation hierarchy attests to the extent to which each has served as a critical point of reference for subsequent scholarship, shaping how researchers conceptualize the capabilities, functions, and implications of AI in managerial and economic domains.

At the top of the citation distribution, Di Vaio et al. (2020) and Wamba-Taguimdje et al. (2020) offer two of the most influential frameworks for analyzing organizational engagement with AI. Di Vaio et al. position AI within broader debates on digital transformation and sustainability, detailing how algorithmic technologies restructure processes related to value creation and governance. Their framework highlights the mechanisms through which AI becomes embedded in corporate strategy and operational practice, treating the technology not simply as a computational resource but as a driver of sustainable organizational change. Wamba-Taguimdje et al., working from an IT-capabilities perspective, develop a model that links AI capabilities and AI-enabled transformation projects to organizational and process-level performance outcomes. Rather than treating AI primarily as an adoption decision, they conceptualize it as a bundle of complementary capabilities, digital infrastructure, managerial expertise, and data-driven routines that support value creation and performance improvements. Together, these two studies delineate a conceptual landscape in which AI emerges as both a transformative capability and a catalyst for reconfiguring organizational priorities and processes.

A second group of highly cited works extends this focus on strategic and organizational transformation, with particular attention to the mechanisms through which firms generate business value from AI. Enholm et al. (2022), through a systematic review, synthesize the literature on AI adoption and value realization, identifying the organizational contingencies, such as strategic alignment, data readiness, and implementation enablers, that shape AI's ability to produce meaningful performance outcomes. Loureiro et al. (2021) shift the lens toward customer engagement, examining how AI reshapes firm–client interaction through automation, personalization, and data-driven brand communication. Cubric (2020) contributes a tertiary review of AI adoption across business domains, identifying key drivers, barriers, and social considerations surrounding AI implementation, including job redesign, skills transformation, and the reorganization of work practices. These contributions underscore the interdependence between technological capability, organizational adaptation, and managerial agency in shaping the contours of AI deployment.

Parallel to these organizational investigations is a foundational stream of methodological work that has codified the analytical tools and computational paradigms underpinning AI research in economic and managerial contexts. Bahrammirzaee

(2010) provides one of the most comprehensive typologies of intelligent systems used in financial forecasting, surveying neural networks, evolutionary computation, and hybrid models. His synthesis remains a touchstone for scholars exploring AI applications in economic decision-making. Bose (2001), writing at an earlier juncture, outlines the role and architecture of data-mining techniques in business intelligence, anticipating the centrality of pattern recognition and predictive analytics in corporate data ecosystems. Cao (2022) offers a panoramic review of AI methods for financial problem-solving, mapping the evolution of algorithmic techniques, such as DL and reinforcement learning, across applications including trading, risk management, and fraud detection. These studies serve as methodological keystones, providing researchers with a shared vocabulary and conceptual framework for navigating the evolving terrain of AI techniques.

A distinct thematic axis within the top-cited literature centers on sectoral applications, where algorithmic methods are tailored to the specific exigencies of different economic domains. Mhlanga (2020) offers a detailed account of AI's role in digital financial inclusion, exploring how ML supports tasks such as credit scoring, fraud detection, and service personalization, particularly in emerging-market contexts. Ghoddusi et al. (2019) focus on the energy sector, cataloguing the use of ML in forecasting, consumption modeling, and regulatory analysis. Zhu et al. (2019) extend these insights through the lens of supply chain finance, developing an ensemble ML approach (RS-MultiBoosting) to forecast SMEs' credit risk and demonstrating how algorithmic tools can strengthen financing decisions and risk assessment. Each of these studies highlights how sector-specific constraints and opportunities shape the configuration, implementation, and perceived utility of AI systems.

Equally prominent are investigations into AI's role in driving innovation and enabling capability development. Lee et al. (2019) examine how firms leverage AI to reimagine their business models, arguing that algorithmic tools not only enhance efficiency but also enable novel value propositions. Sjödin et al. (2021) expand on this by tracing the formation of AI-enabled service ecosystems within digital servitization strategies and identifying the organizational conditions necessary for their emergence, including data pipelines, algorithm development routines, and scalable infrastructure. Akter et al. (2022) emphasize the relationship between AI capabilities and operational excellence, demonstrating how digital infrastructure and complementary organizational capabilities interact with firm-level performance metrics. These analyses underscore the extent to which technological adoption is bound up with broader efforts to innovate, differentiate, and restructure organizational competencies.

The final set of contributions widens the intellectual scope by focusing on AI's intersection with creativity, collaboration, and strategic ideation. Chowdhury et al. (2022) investigate how human-AI collaboration, operationalized through employees' AI skills, knowledge-sharing practices, trust, and role clarity, enhances firm performance in creative industries. Although the study's primary outcome variable is business performance, its examination of collaborative problem-solving and knowledge generation adds conceptual depth to understanding AI's role in supporting the creative and exploratory dimensions of organizational work. Revisited here, Loureiro et al. (2021) and Cubric (2020) similarly contribute to this broadened understanding, reinforcing the view that AI's organizational imprint extends beyond operational efficiency to encompass dynamic, adaptive, and generative capacities.

Across these fifteen contributions, several key thematic trajectories emerge. One centers on organizational strategy and transformation, foregrounding how firms evaluate, implement, and adapt AI systems. A second thread consolidates the field's methodological foundations, offering taxonomies and syntheses of analytical tools. A third focuses on industry-specific deployments, mapping the differentiated pathways through which AI technologies take shape in finance, energy, production, and related sectors. A final axis connects AI to innovation and capability development, highlighting its role in reshaping value creation and organizational renewal. While each paper emphasizes distinct concerns, their cumulative prominence illustrates the field's multidimensional character and the variety of analytical vocabularies it sustains.

Ultimately, these studies chart the central contours of AI and ML research in business and economics. Their influence derives not only from the specific insights they offer but from the broader conceptual and methodological scaffolding they provide. Together, they have helped to define the intellectual coordinates of a rapidly evolving domain, offering researchers a durable foundation for examining the organizational, analytical, and strategic implications of intelligent technologies (see Table 4).

CONCLUSION

This study undertook a systematic review to map the evolving landscape of AI and ML research in business and economics. By examining co-occurrence networks of keywords and tracing topic trends across a dataset of 4,144 documents published between 1984 and 2025, the analysis identified two principal thematic orientations. One concentrates on organizational and strategic applications, including digital transformation, decision-support systems, and Industry 4.0 frameworks, while the other foregrounds methodological advancement, particularly developments in deep learning architectures, natural language processing, and sentiment analysis. Alongside these orientations, the MCA and thematic mapping uncovered a third, more macro-level cluster encompassing innovation, sustainability, fintech, economic development, and emerging generative AI tools, underscoring the field's expanding conceptual scope.

Temporal analyses of topic emergence reveal that foundational concepts such as *machine learning, big data,* and *data analytics* have maintained sustained visibility throughout the period examined. In contrast, terms like *economic* and *social effects* and *Industry 4.0* appear more recently, signaling an ongoing shift from technically focused inquiry toward research agendas that embed computational innovation within broader socio-economic contexts. Annual scientific production patterns reinforce this trajectory: after decades of limited activity, publication volume increases sharply beginning in 2017, surpassing 500 documents in 2023 and exceeding 1,300 in 2025, marking a phase of rapid expansion. In parallel, rising citation counts for synthesis-oriented and review-focused publications since 2020 indicate growing efforts to bring conceptual order to an increasingly extensive and heterogeneous research domain.

The geographic distribution of publications and citations reveals concentrated contributions from a small number of countries. China and the United States emerge as the most highly cited producers, followed by Italy, India, the United Kingdom, and France, contexts where strong funding systems and dense collaboration networks appear to support scholarly visibility. Additional contributors such as Australia, Germany, Sweden, and Korea also demonstrate sustained engagement, though at comparatively modest scales. These patterns highlight the ongoing need to strengthen international collaboration and resource-sharing to promote a more balanced global distribution of research activity.

Building on these findings, three priority directions for future research become evident. First, integrating causal inference approaches into bibliometric and review methodologies would allow scholars to move beyond descriptive analyses toward explanations of how research trajectories respond to policy shifts, funding dynamics, or technological advances. Second, as large pre-trained and generative models become increasingly embedded in business environments, evaluating the effectiveness of governance interventions, such as human-in-the-loop validation and algorithmic bias detection, will be essential to ensure that synthesized findings and conceptual frameworks accurately reflect underlying data integrity and fairness considerations. Third, environmental dimensions of AI research, particularly the carbon footprint associated with large-scale computational experimentation, remain insufficiently addressed; incorporating sustainability metrics into trend analyses and thematic studies would support more responsible research practices. The emergent presence of *generative ai* and tools such as *chatgpt* in the thematic and MCA maps also signals the need for continued longitudinal monitoring of how these technologies reshape methodological conventions and business-focused research priorities.

Ultimately, this review demonstrates that AI and ML research in business and economics has matured significantly, both methodologically and thematically, while still confronting unresolved challenges related to methodological integration, governance accountability, and sustainable implementation. The rapid escalation of publication activity, the concentration of influential scholarship within specific geographic regions, and the fragmented positioning of emerging topics all underscore the importance of sustained interdisciplinary synthesis. Addressing these challenges through causal modeling, governance evaluation, and sustainability assessment will be crucial to advancing a more balanced, actionable, and socially responsible research agenda that informs organizational practice and policy development.

REFERENCES

Agrawal, A., Gans, J., & Goldfarb, A. (2018). *Prediction machines: The Simple Economics of Artificial Intelligence*. Harvard Business Press.

Akter, S., Michael, K., Uddin, M. R., McCarthy, G., & Rahman, M. (2022). Transforming business using digital innovations: The application of AI, blockchain, cloud and data analytics. *Annals of Operations Research, 308*(1–2), 7–39. DOI: 10.1007/s10479-020-03620-w

Aria, M., & Cuccurullo, C. (2017). bibliometrix : An R-tool for comprehensive science mapping analysis. *Journal of Informetrics, 11*(4), 959–975. DOI: 10.1016/j.joi.2017.08.007

Arrieta, A. B., Díaz-Rodríguez, N., Del Ser, J., Bennetot, A., Tabik, S., Barbado, A., Garcia, S., Gil-Lopez, S., Molina, D., Benjamins, R., Chatila, R., & Herrera, F. (2019). Explainable Artificial Intelligence (XAI): Concepts, taxonomies, opportunities and challenges toward responsible AI. *Information Fusion, 58*, 82–115. DOI: 10.1016/j.inffus.2019.12.012

Athey, S., & Imbens, G. W. (2019). Machine learning methods that economists should know about. *Annual Review of Economics, 11*(1), 685–725. DOI: 10.1146/annurev-economics-080217-053433

Baas, J., Schotten, M., Plume, A., Côté, G., & Karimi, R. (2020). Scopus as a curated, high-quality bibliometric data source for academic research in quantitative science studies. *Quantitative Science Studies, 1*(1), 377–386. DOI: 10.1162/qss_a_00019

Baesens, B., Setiono, R., Mues, C., & Vanthienen, J. (2003). Using neural network rule extraction and decision tables for Credit-Risk evaluation. *Management Science, 49*(3), 312–329. DOI: 10.1287/mnsc.49.3.312.12739

Bahrammirzaee, A. (2010). A comparative survey of artificial intelligence applications in finance: Artificial neural networks, expert system and hybrid intelligent systems. *Neural Computing & Applications, 19*(8), 1165–1195. DOI: 10.1007/s00521-010-0362-z

Bitzenis, A., & Koutsoupias, N. (2023A). Foreign Direct Investment And Sustainability: A Visualized Bibliometric Review. *South-Eastern Europe Journal of Economics, 1*, 41–52. https://doi.org/DOI: 10.17605/osf.io/pcaxg

Bitzenis, A., & Koutsoupias, N. (2023B, December). Visualizing Economics and Business in the field of Education: A Quantitative Analysis of Scholarly Literature. *Global Business & Economics Anthology. Volumes I, II.* Advance online publication. DOI: 10.47341/gbea.23126

Bitzenis, A., & Koutsoupias, N. (2024). Big Data in Economics Research. In Tsounis, N., & Vlachvei, A. (Eds.), *Applied Economic Research and Trends* (pp. 1063–1072). Springer Nature Switzerland., DOI: 10.1007/978-3-031-49105-4_6

Bitzenis, A., Koutsoupias, N., & Boutsiouki, S. (2023). Business Research and Data Mining: a Bibliometric Analysis. *2023 3rd International Conference on Electrical, Computer, Communications and Mechatronics Engineering (ICECCME)*, 1–6. https://doi.org/DOI: 10.1109/iceccme57830.2023.10252699

Bitzenis, A., Koutsoupias, N., & Nosios, M. (2025A). Artificial intelligence and machine learning in production efficiency enhancement and sustainable development: A comprehensive bibliometric review. *Frontiers in Sustainability*, *5*. Advance online publication. DOI: 10.3389/frsus.2024.1508647

Bitzenis, A., Koutsoupias, N., & Nosios, M. (2025B). Public Perceptions of Tax Evasion and Informal Economy in Greece. *Proceedings of XXIII. International Balkan and Near Eastern Social Sciences Congress Series on Economics, Business and Management*, 80–90. https://doi.org/DOI: 10.17605/OSF.IO/V3YCS

Bitzenis, A., Koutsoupias, N., & Nosios, M. (2025C). Theoretical Advancements in Logistics: Digitalization, Big Data, and Machine Learning in Decision Making. *Proceedings of XXIII. International Balkan and Near Eastern Social Sciences Congress Series on Economics, Business and Management*, 91–101. https://doi.org/DOI: 10.17605/OSF.IO/G7H43

Bitzenis, A., Koutsoupias, N., & Nosios, M. (2025D). A Meta-Systematic Review of Research Trends in Artificial Intelligence and Machine Learning for Business and Economic Applications [dataset]. https://doi.org/DOI: 10.17605/OSF.IO/R9UYX

Bommasani, R., Hudson, D. A., Adeli, E., Altman, R., Arora, S., Von Arx, S., Bernstein, M. S., Bohg, J., Bosselut, A., Brunskill, E., Brynjolfsson, E., Buch, S., Card, D., Castellon, R., Chatterji, N., Chen, A., Creel, K., Davis, J. Q., Demszky, D., . . . Liang, P. (2021). On the Opportunities and Risks of Foundation Models. *arXiv (Cornell University)*. https://doi.org//arxiv.2108.07258DOI: 10.48550

Bose, I., & Mahapatra, R. K. (2001). Business data mining — A machine learning perspective. *Information & Management*, *39*(3), 211–225. DOI: 10.1016/s0378-7206(01)00091-x

Brynjolfsson, E., & Mitchell, T. (2017). What can machine learning do? Workforce implications. *Science, 358*(6370), 1530–1534. DOI: 10.1126/science.aap8062

Burnham, J. F. (2006). Scopus database: A review. *Biomedical Digital Libraries, 3*(1), 1. DOI: 10.1186/1742-5581-3-1

Cao, L. (2022). AI in Finance: Challenges, Techniques, and Opportunities. *ACM Computing Surveys, 55*(3), 1–38. DOI: 10.1145/3502289

Chowdhury, S., Budhwar, P., Dey, P. K., Joel-Edgar, S., & Abadie, A. (2022). AI-employee collaboration and business performance: Integrating knowledge-based view, socio-technical systems and organisational socialisation framework. *Journal of Business Research, 144*, 31–49. DOI: 10.1016/j.jbusres.2022.01.069

Cubric, M. (2020). Drivers, barriers and social considerations for AI adoption in business and management: A tertiary study. *Technology in Society, 62*, 101257. DOI: 10.1016/j.techsoc.2020.101257

Di Vaio, A., Palladino, R., Hassan, R., & Escobar, O. (2020). Artificial intelligence and business models in the sustainable development goals perspective: A systematic literature review. *Journal of Business Research, 121*, 283–314. DOI: 10.1016/j.jbusres.2020.08.019

Donthu, N., Kumar, S., Mukherjee, D., Pandey, N., & Lim, W. M. (2021). How to conduct a bibliometric analysis: An overview and guidelines. *Journal of Business Research, 133*, 285–296. DOI: 10.1016/j.jbusres.2021.04.070

Einav, L., & Levin, J. (2014). Economics in the age of big data. *Science, 346*(6210). Advance online publication. DOI: 10.1126/science.1243089

Ellegaard, O., & Wallin, J. A. (2015). The bibliometric analysis of scholarly production: How great is the impact? *Scientometrics, 105*(3), 1809–1831. DOI: 10.1007/s11192-015-1645-z

Enholm, I. M., Papagiannidis, E., Mikalef, P., & Krogstie, J. (2022). Artificial Intelligence and Business Value: A Literature Review. *Information Systems Frontiers, 24*(5), 1709–1734. DOI: 10.1007/s10796-021-10186-w

Gao, H., Kou, G., Liang, H., Zhang, H., Chao, X., Li, C., & Dong, Y. (2024). Machine learning in business and finance: A literature review and research opportunities. *Financial Innovation, 10*(1). Advance online publication. DOI: 10.1186/s40854-024-00629-z

Ghoddusi, H., Creamer, G. G., & Rafizadeh, N. (2019). Machine learning in energy economics and finance: A review. *Energy Economics, 81*, 709–727. DOI: 10.1016/j.eneco.2019.05.006

Gu, S., Kelly, B., & Xiu, D. (2020). Empirical asset pricing via machine learning. *Review of Financial Studies, 33*(5), 2223–2273. DOI: 10.1093/rfs/hhaa009

Huang, M., & Rust, R. T. (2020). A strategic framework for artificial intelligence in marketing. *Journal of the Academy of Marketing Science, 49*(1), 30–50. DOI: 10.1007/s11747-020-00749-9

Koutsoupias, N., & Nosios, M. (2025A). Hierarchical Clustering in Social Sciences and Humanities: A Review. In S. D. Anastasiadou, T. G. Chadjipadelis, Nikolaos Koutsoupias, Angelos Markos, & George Menexes (Eds.), *Modern International Developments in Data Analysis and Multivariate Statistical Analysis.* IGI Global Scientific Publishing. https://doi.org/DOI: 10.4018/979-8-3693-9400-7

Koutsoupias, N., & Nosios, M. (2025B). Sentiment and Geopolitical Analysis in Sino-American Relations. In S. D. Anastasiadou, T. G. Chadjipadelis, Nikolaos Koutsoupias, Angelos Markos, & George Menexes (Eds.), *Modern International Developments in Data Analysis and Multivariate Statistical Analysis.* IGI Global Scientific Publishing. https://doi.org/DOI: 10.4018/979-8-3693-9400-7

Kumar, S., Kumar, V., Bhatt, I. K., & Kumar, S. (2023). Mapping Research Trends on Smart Tourism: A Bibliometric analysis. In *Tourism, hospitality & event management* (pp. 87–109). https://doi.org/DOI: 10.1007/978-3-031-31682-1_5

Lee, J., Suh, T., Roy, D., & Baucus, M. (2019). Emerging technology and business model innovation: The case of artificial intelligence. *Journal of Open Innovation, 5*(3), 44. DOI: 10.3390/joitmc5030044

Loureiro, S. M. C., Guerreiro, J., & Tussyadiah, I. (2021). Artificial intelligence in business: State of the art and future research agenda. *Journal of Business Research, 129*, 911–926. DOI: 10.1016/j.jbusres.2020.11.001

Mariani, M. M., Machado, I., Magrelli, V., & Dwivedi, Y. K. (2022). Artificial intelligence in innovation research: A systematic review, conceptual framework, and future research directions. *Technovation, 122*, 102623. DOI: 10.1016/j.technovation.2022.102623

Mhlanga, D. (2020). Industry 4.0 in Finance: The impact of Artificial intelligence (AI) on digital financial inclusion. *International Journal of Financial Studies, 8*(3), 45. DOI: 10.3390/ijfs8030045

Mousa, B. A., & Al-Khateeb, B. (2023). Predicting medicine demand using deep learning techniques: A review. *Journal of Intelligent Systems*, *32*(1). Advance online publication. DOI: 10.1515/jisys-2022-0297

Mullainathan, S., & Spiess, J. (2017). Machine Learning: An Applied Econometric approach. *The Journal of Economic Perspectives*, *31*(2), 87–106. DOI: 10.1257/jep.31.2.87

Nazareth, N., & Reddy, Y. V. R. (2023). Financial applications of machine learning: A literature review. *Expert Systems with Applications*, *219*, 119640. DOI: 10.1016/j.eswa.2023.119640

Ozbayoglu, A. M., Gudelek, M. U., & Sezer, O. B. (2020). Deep learning for financial applications : A survey. *Applied Soft Computing*, *93*, 106384. DOI: 10.1016/j.asoc.2020.106384

Page, M. J., McKenzie, J. E., Bossuyt, P. M., Boutron, I., Hoffmann, T. C., Mulrow, C. D., Shamseer, L., Tetzlaff, J. M., Akl, E. A., Brennan, S. E., Chou, R., Glanville, J., Grimshaw, J. M., Hróbjartsson, A., Lalu, M. M., Li, T., Loder, E. W., Mayo-Wilson, E., McDonald, S., & Moher, D. (2021). The PRISMA 2020 statement: An updated guideline for reporting systematic reviews. *BMJ (Clinical Research Ed.)*, (71). Advance online publication. DOI: 10.1136/bmj.n71

Passas, I. (2024). Bibliometric Analysis: The main steps. *Encyclopedia*, *4*(2), 1014–1025. DOI: 10.3390/encyclopedia4020065

Schotten, M., Aisati, M. E., Meester, W. J. N., Steiginga, S., & Ross, C. A. (2017). A brief history of Scopus: the world's largest abstract and citation database of scientific literature. In *Auerbach Publications eBooks* (pp. 31–58). https://doi.org/DOI: 10.1201/9781315155890-3

Sjödin, D., Parida, V., Palmié, M., & Wincent, J. (2021). How AI capabilities enable business model innovation: Scaling AI through co-evolutionary processes and feedback loops. *Journal of Business Research*, *134*, 574–587. DOI: 10.1016/j.jbusres.2021.05.009

Thomos, K., Bitzenis, A., & Koutsoupias, N. (2023, December). Credit Rating in Business and Economics Research: Europe (2000-2022). *Global Business & Economics Anthology. Volumes I, II*. Advance online publication. DOI: 10.47341/gbea.23128

Toorajipour, R., Sohrabpour, V., Nazarpour, A., Oghazi, P., & Fischl, M. (2020). Artificial intelligence in supply chain management: A systematic literature review. *Journal of Business Research*, *122*, 502–517. DOI: 10.1016/j.jbusres.2020.09.009

Wamba-Taguimdje, S., Wamba, S. F., Kamdjoug, J. R. K., & Wanko, C. E. T. (2020). Influence of artificial intelligence (AI) on firm performance: The business value of AI-based transformation projects. *Business Process Management Journal, 26*(7), 1893–1924. DOI: 10.1108/bpmj-10-2019-0411

Zhu, Y., Zhou, L., Xie, C., Wang, G., & Nguyen, T. V. (2019). Forecasting SMEs' credit risk in supply chain finance with an enhanced hybrid ensemble machine learning approach. *International Journal of Production Economics, 211*, 22–33. DOI: 10.1016/j.ijpe.2019.01.032

Zourna, C., Papavassiliou-Alexia, I., Koutsoupias, N., & Papakota, A. (2021). *A mixed methods research approach to investigate undergraduate students' perceptions of changes enforced due to COVID-19*. Advance., DOI: 10.31124/advance.13606409.v1

Zupic, I., & Čater, T. (2014). Bibliometric methods in management and organization. *Organizational Research Methods, 18*(3), 429–472. DOI: 10.1177/1094428114562629

Chapter 5
Clustering Strategies on Data Cubes With Independent "Slices"

Zacharenia Kyrana
http://orcid.org/0000-0001-9269-0675
School of Agriculture, Aristotle University of Thessaloniki, Greece

Christos Dordas
http://orcid.org/0000-0002-7027-474X
School of Agriculture, Aristotle University of Thessaloniki, Greece

Nikolaos Papafilippou
http://orcid.org/0009-0003-3148-7229
School of Agriculture, Aristotle University of Thessaloniki, Greece

Angelos Markos
http://orcid.org/0000-0002-4204-3573
School of Education, Democritus University of Thrace, Greece

Emmanouil D. Pratsinakis
http://orcid.org/0000-0002-3725-3525
School of Agriculture, Aristotle University of Thessaloniki, Greece

Georgios C. Menexes
http://orcid.org/0000-0002-1034-7345
School of Agriculture, Aristotle University of Thessaloniki, Greece

ABSTRACT

Data cubes are p-dimensional data structures ($p \geq 3$). This study proposes alternative clustering strategies for four-dimensional data cubes ($p = 4$) with independent slices. In biological sciences, the key point of Statistical-Data Analysis is the study of variability focusing on its structure and components, while interactions between slices and hyper-slices are often of scientific interest. The dimensionality reduction strategy decomposes the cube's total variability into variability between and within slices and hyper-slices. The first clustering strategy projects the extracted principal components as points in Euclidean space, the second projects them onto a differentiable manifold, and the third is based on Procrustes distances among matrices. The real dataset "Basil" is used, consisting of three irrigation levels (hyper-slices), five

DOI: 10.4018/979-8-3373-6926-6.ch005

basil varieties (slices), seven quantitative traits, and 60 basil plants. These strategies highlight the need for a holistic approach to the cube, so that its underlying sources of variability can be studied in depth and from different perspectives.

INTRODUCTION

In most scientific fields, data are represented as complex, multidimensional phenomena in the form of data cubes. Data cubes are p-dimensional data structures, where $p \geq 3$ (Kyrana et al., 2026). For example, in a three-dimensional data cube, $p=3$. In a four-dimensional data cube, $p=4$, and so on. p can take any positive integer value greater than or equal to three, depending on the structure of the data. The first dimension of a three-dimensional data cube ($p=3$) consists of objects (e.g., different plants, persons, or animals and, in general, different experimental or sampling units). The second dimension consists of dependent or response variables (e.g., quantitative characteristics of objects). The third dimension consists of the variable of "slices", that is an independent, usually categorical, variable (e.g., different plants' varieties, different experimental treatments, and in the field of agricultural experimentation different blocks of experimental plots or different locations or years of experimentation). If an additional fourth dimension (variable of "hyper-slices") is added, that is another independent variable (e.g., different irrigation levels, additional experimental treatments, or other qualitative characteristics of the units), the data cube will become four-dimensional ($p=4$), and so on.

This study focuses exclusively on four-dimensional data cubes, where $p=4$. It is worth mentioning that the "slices" and "hyper-slices" variables are structural components of a data cube, which are usually considered independent variables. Investigating their effect on the overall structure of the data cube is crucial, as it can result in either simpler or more complex data cube management and statistical analysis practices.

According to Kroonenberg (2008, p. 17), the main research question that can be answered when processing and analyzing a data cube is "Which groups of objects behave differently, in which variables, and under which conditions?". Therefore, data cubes are used to explore and analyze multidimensional data from various perspectives, answer complex questions, and extract more information (Suh & Chung, 2016).

Data Cubes' Structure

In international scientific literature, multidimensional data appear under different names, according to their structural characteristics (Kroonenberg, 2008; Tenenhaus

& Tenenhaus, 2014). For example, data with repeated measurements of the same objects under different conditions are commonly called multi-way data (Acar & Yener, 2009; Kolda & Bader, 2009; Kroonenberg, 2008). On the other hand, data with different objects and the same variables per "group" are commonly called multi-group data (Codesido et al., 2021; Tenenhaus & Tenenhaus, 2014), while data with the same objects and different variables per "block" are commonly called multi-block data (Tenenhaus & Tenenhaus, 2014).

In the case of data cubes with independent "slices" and "hyper-slices", when the number of objects is equal within each "slice" and "hyper-slice", the cube is considered balanced. On the other hand, when the number of objects is unequal within each "slice" and "hyper-slice", the cube is considered unbalanced (Kyrana et al., 2026).

In most biological sciences, as well as in the present study, the objects are different and equal in number per "slice" and "hyper-slice" (i.e., balanced data cubes), and the variables are quantitative and the same per "slice" and "hyper-slice", while the "slices" and "hyper-slices" are categorical and independent (Kroonenberg, 2008; Pavoine et al., 2007).

Methodological Approaches for Managing and Analyzing Balanced Four-Dimensional Data Cubes With Independent "Slices" and "Hyper-Slices"

There are two basic methodological approaches for the analysis of data cubes with independent "slices" and "hyper-slices". The first is based on analyzing the data cube as a two-dimensional mixed-type dataset (with categorical and scale variables), in which the "slices" and "hyper-slices" are considered additional (usually categorical) variables (Kyrana et al., 2025). The second is based on analyzing a data cube as a "stacked" data matrix, in which the "slices" and "hyper-slices" do not lose their conceptual and structural role (Kyrana et al., 2026).

This study will focus on the second methodological approach. According to this, the mathematical background of a balanced four-dimensional data cube with independent "slices" and "hyper-slices" is presented below.

Let

$$\underline{\mathbf{X}} = \left[\mathbf{X}_{11}, \mathbf{X}_{21}, \ldots, \mathbf{X}_{K1}, \mathbf{X}_{12}, \mathbf{X}_{22}, \ldots, \mathbf{X}_{K2}, \ldots, \mathbf{X}_{1G}, \mathbf{X}_{2G}, \mathbf{X}_{KG}\right]$$

be a four-dimensional $I \times J \times K \times G$ balanced data cube (p=4), with x_{ijkg} elements, where i= 1,2,…,I, j= 1,2,…,J, k= 1,2,…,K and g= 1,2,…,F. The first dimension I denotes the rows (experimental/sampling units or objects) of the data cube, which are different and equal in number per "slice" and "hyper-slice". The second dimension

J denotes the columns (traits or variables) of the data cube. The third dimension *K* denotes the independent "slices" of the data cube. The fourth dimension *G* denotes the independent "hyper-slices" of the data cube. In other words, the data cube $\underline{\mathbf{X}}$ can be seen as a collection of either three-dimensional data cubes $\underline{\mathbf{X}}_k$, with dimensions $IK \times J \times G$, or two-dimensional matrices $\mathbf{X}_{kg}$, with dimensions $IKG \times J$, where each matrix represents a "slice" *k* within "hyper-slice" *g* of a data cube.

The most classic way to manage such a data cube is to transform it into a two-dimensional data matrix, through vertical concatenation (Codesido et al., 2021). Specifically, data cube $\underline{\mathbf{X}}$ is transformed into a "stacked" data matrix **X** with dimensions $IKG \times J$ and x_{ijkg} elements, where $i = 1,2,\ldots,I$, $j = 1,2,\ldots,J$, $k = 1,2,\ldots,K$ and $g = 1,2,\ldots,G$ (see Figure 1).

*Figure 1. Transformation of a four-dimensional data cube $\underline{\mathbf{X}}$, with independent "slices" and "hyper-slices", and with different and equal number of objects per "slice" and "hyper-slice", into a "stacked" data matrix **X** (through vertical concatenation)*

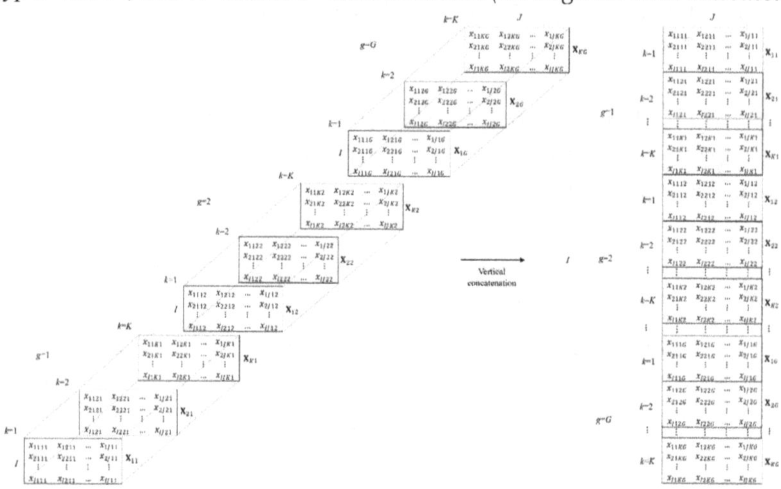

Dimensionality Reduction

Dimensionality reduction methods aim to provide a compressed representation of the original dataset, smaller in "volume" but maintaining critical and informative content (Dash et al., 1997; Sharma, 1996).

In international scientific literature, there are several dimensionality reduction methods for both multivariate and multidimensional data. The most widely used methods are Principal Components Analysis (PCA) (Anderson, 1984; Hair et al., 2010; Jolliffe, 2002; Jolliffe & Cadima, 2016; Kaiser, 1958; Song et al., 2018),

Factor Analysis (FA) (Anderson, 1984; Hair et al., 2010; Jolliffe, 2002), Multiple Correspondence Analysis (MCA) (Greenacre & Blasius, 2006; Menexes, 2006; Messaoud et al., 2007), Categorical Principal Components Analysis with optimal scaling (CATPCA) (Gifi, 1990; Linting et al., 2007; Markos et al., 2020; Tabachnick & Fidell, 2007), Factor Analysis for Mixed Data (FAMD) (Kassambara, 2017; Markos et al., 2020; Mothobi et al., 2021; Pagès, 2014), Simultaneous Components Analysis (SCA) (Smilde et al., 2022; Tenenhaus & Tenenhaus, 2014; Timmerman & Kiers, 2003), Multi-group PCA (Eslami et al., 2013; Rotari et al., 2024; Tenenhaus & Tenenhaus, 2014) and Common PCA (Eslami et al., 2013; Rotari et al., 2024; Tenenhaus & Tenenhaus, 2014).

However, these methods are not applicable in the context of data cubes, either because they are applied directly on two-dimensional datasets, where "slices" and "hyper-slices" lose their structural and conceptual role (Greenacre & Blasius, 2006; Hair et al., 2010; Markos et al., 2020), or because they are applied to multi-group and/or multi-block data (Eslami et al., 2013; Rotari et al., 2024; Smilde et al., 2022; Tenenhaus & Tenenhaus, 2014; Timmerman & Kiers, 2003). Furthermore, based on Kyrana et al. (2025) and Kyrana et al. (2026), the application of the above "traditional" dimensionality reduction methods depends on the scientific field, the objectives of the study, the transformation of the data cube, the observed data and the type of data cube. Therefore, it is more appropriate to discuss analysis strategies rather than a "global" dimensionality reduction method suitable for every case, in order to increase the range of applications for each method and extract more usable results.

According to Kyrana et al. (2026), there are several dimensionality reduction strategies, which can be applied to three-dimensional data cubes (p=3) with independent "slices". Some strategies are based on the idea of decomposing the total variability of the data cube into between-"slices" and within-"slices" variability. Other strategies either ignore the effect of "slices" (Codesido et al., 2021; Eslami et al., 2013) or consider it on the overall data cube structure (Eslami et al., 2013). Some other strategies initially ignore the effect of "slices" and add it at a second level based on the French School of Data Analysis (Benzécri & Collaborateurs, 1973). All these dimensionality reduction strategies can also be applied to four-dimensional data cubes (p=3), and so on.

The present study focuses exclusively on the variability decomposition strategy for balanced four-dimensional data cubes with independent "slices" and "hyper-slices", so that clustering strategies can be applied. However, it is worth noting that in the case of unbalanced four-dimensional data cubes with independent "slices" and "hyper-slices", the variability decomposition strategy is different, more complex and constitutes a controversial scientific issue (Searle, 1987).

The proposed dimensionality reduction strategy is based on PCA, as it is one of the most well-known linear dimensionality reduction methods (Greenacre et al.,

2022; Jolliffe & Cadima, 2016) of Data Analysis (Papafilippou et al., 2025). Also, many methods are generalizations (Bro, 1997) and/or extensions of PCA (Bishop, 2006; Mair, 2018), while according to Kyrana et al. (2025), PCA outperforms other well-known methods (FA, MCA, CATPCA, and FAMD), in terms of the combination of satisfactory reduction of mathematical dimensions, faster results execution times in Python (regardless of the analysis strategy), and its applicability across three different statistical software programs (Python, R, and IBM SPSS Statistics), thus allowing the application of most analysis strategies. Additionally, in the field of Agriculture, PCA is an important tool for Exploratory Data Analysis (i.e., the detection of patterns, clusters, extreme values, etc.) through visualizations, in order to identify the key characteristics of a dataset (Jolliffe, 2002; Shaukat et al., 2016; Okasha et al., 2022). Also, both PCA and the proposed dimensionality reduction strategy constitute a preprocessing stage for Machine Learning algorithms (Papafilippou et al., 2025). Particularly, they constitute feature extraction techniques that contribute to the understanding of data and the interpretation of the results obtained, so that useful conclusions and valid predictions can be extracted, and that correct decisions can be made by researchers (Papafilippou et al., 2025).

This study, following the philosophy of the French School of Data Analysis, attempts to combine the proposed dimensionality reduction strategy with alternative clustering strategies (Beaudouin, 2016; Benzécri & Collaborateurs, 1973).

Clustering

Clustering methods aim to group objects (sampling or experimental units) according to their common characteristics (Hair et al., 2010). Their primary objective is to develop a typology that partitions a set of objects into clusters such that objects in the same cluster are more similar to each other than to objects in other clusters, based on certain predefined characteristics (variables) (Hair et al., 2010; Kaufman & Rousseeuw, 1990; Lattin et al., 2003; Sharma, 1996). The core objectives of clustering include, either individually or in combination, the exploration of "useful" conceptual patterns for grouping objects, the formulation of hypotheses arising from Exploratory Data Analysis, the verification and testing of hypotheses related to the data (in the sense of revealing structures and types proposed or determined by other procedures), as well as dimensionality reduction (Hair et al., 2010).

Clustering methods always lead to a "solution" (when the data analysis is computationally feasible), which may differ depending on the distance measure and/or the linkage method employed. For this reason, it is necessary to determine whether the clusters formed are real, conceptually interpretable, and not merely "imposed" by the specific clustering method used (Everitt et al., 2011; Hair et al., 2010; Sharma, 1996).

Clustering – Distance measures

In international scientific literature, various distance measures are employed. The most widely used metrics for quantitative data are the Euclidean distance (Blanco-Mallo et al., 2023; Pratsinakis et al., 2020) and the Manhattan distance (Blanco-Mallo et al., 2023). Other common dissimilarity measures include the Squared Euclidean distance (Blanco-Mallo et al., 2023; Pratsinakis et al., 2020), which is used in this study, and Pearson's correlation coefficient distance (Solo, 2019), the latter of which is a non-metric measure. For additional quantitative distance measures, see Everitt (2011).

In this study, the Squared Euclidean distance is used, which is defined as (Blanco-Mallo et al., 2023; Pratsinakis et al., 2020):

$$d^2(i,j) = \sum_{k=1}^{n} \left(x_{ik} - x_{jk}\right)^2,$$

where i and j are two objects of a dataset $\mathbf{X}$, k=1,…,n are the variables of the dataset, x_{ik} is the value of variable k for object i, and x_{jk} is the value of variable k for object j.

Another type of measures consists of geodesic distances, which calculate the shortest possible distance between two points on a Riemannian manifold, by following the intrinsic geometry (curvature) of the space (do Carmo, 1992; Pizer & Marron, 2017). For example, in this study the arc-cosine distance (Srivastava & Klassen, 2016) is used, which measures the angle (in radians) between two vectors on the unit sphere (i.e., the length of the shortest arc connecting them), and is defined as (Zheng & Molina, 1998):

$$d(i,j) = arccos\left(\frac{\langle x_i, x_j \rangle}{\|x_i\| \|x_j\|}\right),$$

where $\langle x_i, x_j \rangle$ denotes the inner product of vectors x_i and x_j, and $\| \cdot \|$ denotes the Euclidean norm. If the vectors are unit vectors ($\| x_i \| = \| x_j \| = 1$), then it is true that (Zheng & Molina, 1998):

$$d(i,j) = arccos\left(\langle x_i, x_j \rangle\right).$$

The arc-cosine distance between two vectors on the unit sphere is a special case of the Riemannian distance (i.e., a distance defined on a Riemannian manifold) (Bauer et al., 2019; Chikuse, 2003). It is also worth noting that there are several types of manifold, including the Grassmannian (Edelman et al., 1998; Srivastava & Klassen, 2004).

Distances designed exclusively for categorical data also exist, such as the Jaccard distance, which measures dissimilarity between two datasets or binary vectors (Pratsinakis et al., 2020; Van de Velden et al., 2024).

Furthermore, there are also well-known metric similarity distances measuring the distance between two or more matrices (composed of the same variables), such as the Procrustes distance or its generalization (Generalized Procrustes distance) (Gower, 1971 and 1975). The mathematical formulation of Procrustes Orthogonal Projection and/or Rotation and its generalization are presented below.

Clustering – Procrustes Orthogonal Projection and/or Rotation

The Procrustes Orthogonal Projection and/or Rotation method is used to compare two matrices (Gower, 1971). Let two matrices $\mathbf{X}(n \times p)$ and $\mathbf{Y}(n \times p)$, where $\mathbf{X}$ is considered the reference matrix, be optimally projected (after rotation) onto a common reference (or else target) space. After centering the matrices, their columns have zero mean. The objective of the method is to determine an orthogonal rotation matrix $\mathbf{R}$ $(p \times p)$, satisfying $\mathbf{R}^{\mathrm{T}}\mathbf{R} = \mathbf{I}$, such that matrix $\mathbf{XR}$ optimally approximates matrix $\mathbf{Y}$ and minimizes the distance (Menexes et al., 2012; Gower & Dijksterhuis, 2004):

$$\| X - YR \|_F^2,$$

where $\| \cdot \|_F$ denotes the Frobenius norm (sum of squared elements of the matrix). In practice, minimization is achieved via the Singular Value Decomposition (SVD), and the resulting distance expresses the degree of similarity between the two matrices. Specifically, $\mathbf{Y}^{\mathrm{T}}\mathbf{X} = \mathbf{UDV}^{\mathrm{T}}$, and the optimal rotation matrix is given by $\mathbf{R} = \mathbf{UV}^{\mathrm{T}}$. The Procrustes distance is defined as:

$$d(\mathbf{X},\mathbf{Y}) = \| \mathbf{X} - \mathbf{YR} \|_F.$$

A standardized version of distance $d(\mathbf{X},\mathbf{Y})$ is given by (Sibson, 1978):

$$d'(\mathbf{X},\mathbf{Y}) = \frac{d(\mathbf{X},\mathbf{Y})}{\mathrm{trace}(\mathbf{XX}^{\mathrm{T}})},$$

where $\mathrm{trace}(\mathbf{XX}^{\mathrm{T}})$ denotes the sum of the diagonal elements of matrix $\mathbf{X}$.

Clustering – Generalized Procrustes Orthogonal Projection and/or Rotation

The Generalized Procrustes Analysis (GPA) method is a generalization of Procrustes analysis and is used to compare multiple matrices by optimally projecting them (after rotation) onto a common reference space (Gower, 1975). Let c matrices $\mathbf{X}_1, \mathbf{X}_2, \ldots, \mathbf{X}_c$ of dimensions $n \times p$. After centering the matrices $\mathbf{X}_i$ (i=1,...,c), their columns have zero mean and represent deviations of the corresponding points from their centroid. The objective of the method is to determine orthogonal rotation matrices $\mathbf{R}_i(p \times p)$, satisfying $\mathbf{R}_i^{\mathrm{T}}\mathbf{R}_i = \mathbf{I}$, such that the matrices $\mathbf{X}_i\mathbf{R}_i$ are aligned as closely as possible in a common reference space $\mathbf{M}(n \times p)$ and minimize the sum of squared distances of all aligned matrices from $\mathbf{M}$ (Gower, 1975):

$$\sum_{i=1}^{c} \left\| \mathbf{X}_i\mathbf{R}_i - \mathbf{M} \right\|_F^2.$$

As in the previous case, minimization is achieved via SVD, and the final distance expresses the degree of similarity among the matrices after alignment. Specifically, it is true that $\mathbf{X}_i^{\mathrm{T}}\mathbf{M} = \mathbf{U}_i\mathbf{D}_i\mathbf{V}_i^{\mathrm{T}}$ and the optimal rotation matrices are given by $\mathbf{R}_i = \mathbf{U}_i\mathbf{V}_i^{\mathrm{T}}$. Subsequently, the "new" $\mathbf{M}$ (mean of the aligned matrices) is computed as:

$$\mathbf{M} = \tfrac{1}{c}\sum_{i=1}^{c} \mathbf{X}_i\mathbf{R}_i,$$

and the procedure is repeated until the convergence of matrix $\mathbf{M}$. The final Generalized Procrustes distance is defined as:

$$d = \sqrt{\sum_{i=1}^{c} \left\| \mathbf{X}_i\mathbf{R}_i - \mathbf{M} \right\|_F^2}.$$

Alternatively, the mean Generalized Procrustes distance is defined as:

$$\bar{d} = \sqrt{\tfrac{1}{c}\sum_{i=1}^{c} \left\| \mathbf{X}_i\mathbf{R}_i - \mathbf{M} \right\|_F^2}.$$

A standardized version of distance d is given by:

$$d' = \frac{d}{trace(\mathbf{M}\mathbf{M}^{\mathrm{T}})},$$

where $trace(\mathbf{M}\mathbf{M}^{\mathrm{T}})$ denotes the sum of the diagonal elements of matrix $\mathbf{M}$.

Clustering – Linkage methods

Linkage methods aim at clustering (grouping) objects (experimental or sampling units) and are classified into Hierarchical and Non-Hierarchical methods (Hair et al., 2010; Jobson, 1992; Lattin et al., 2003; Sharma, 1996).

In Hierarchical clustering (HCL) methods, the number of clusters is not known *a priori* (Hair et al., 2010; Sharma, 1996), and objects are initially considered as independent clusters, each containing a single object, which are merged at each step of the algorithm according to their proximity (Hair et al., 2010; Jobson, 1992; Lattin et al., 2003). The linkage algorithms used may be either divisive, operating "backwards" (initially all objects belong to a single cluster, which is partitioned at each step until the algorithm results in as many clusters as objects), or agglomerative, operating "forwards" (initially each object constitutes a separate cluster, and at each step the most similar clusters are merged until a final cluster is formed) (Hair et al., 2010; Jobson, 1992; Lattin et al., 2003).

The present study focuses exclusively on hierarchical agglomerative linkage methods applied to an appropriate distance matrix. In particular, the most important hierarchical agglomerative linkage methods are the following:

- Nearest Neighbor (Single Linkage), which computes the distance between two clusters as the minimum distance between an observation belonging to one cluster and an observation belonging to another cluster (Hair et al., 2010; Sharma, 1996; Sneath, 1957) and tends to produce clusters with high variability (Everitt et al., 2011).
- Furthest Neighbor (Complete Linkage), which computes the distance between two clusters as the maximum distance between an observation in one cluster and an observation in another cluster (Hair et al., 2010; Lattin et al., 2003; Sharma, 1996; Sørensen, 1948) and tends to produce clusters with low variability (Everitt et al., 2011).
- Average Between Groups, which computes the distance between two clusters as the average of the distances between observations of one cluster and observations of the other (Hair et al., 2010; Lattin et al., 2003; Sharma, 1996; Sokal & Michener, 1958) and tends to produce clusters with low variability (Everitt et al., 2011).
- Average Within Groups, which computes the distance between two clusters as the average of all distances among observations of the cluster formed by merging the two clusters (Karlis, 2005) and produces dendrograms with small differences compared to the Nearest Neighbor method.

- Centroid Method, which computes the distance between the centroids of two clusters (Hair et al., 2010; Lattin et al., 2003; Sokal & Michener, 1958), resulting in ultimately homogeneous clusters.
- Median Method, which computes the distance between the median values of the observations of two clusters, under the assumption that cluster centroids have equal weight during cluster merging, regardless of the number of observations in each cluster (Gower, 1967).
- Ward's Minimum Variance Method, which is based on the application of Analysis of Variance to cluster observations. In other words, it minimizes within-cluster variability and maximizes between-cluster variability (Lattin et al., 2003; Ward, 1963). Specifically, it aims to minimize the increase in the total within-cluster sum of squares at each step of the algorithm, and the clusters produced by this method tend to have approximately equal sizes in terms of number of observations (Everitt et al., 2011; Lattin et al., 2003; Menexes & Angelopoulos, 2008).

In Non-Hierarchical (or Partitioning) clustering methods, observations are grouped into a predefined number of clusters (Hair et al., 2010; Izenman, 2008; Sharma, 1996). The most widely known method is *K*-Means and its variants (Hair et al., 2010; Jobson, 1992; Sharma, 1996).

Another category of clustering methods includes Model-Based Methods, which assume that each cluster follows a specific statistical model whose parameters are estimated, and each object is subsequently assigned to the cluster with the highest estimated probability of membership (Fraley & Raftery, 2002).

Furthermore, in the context of multidimensional data, well-known methods include Three-Way Clustering for multi-way data (Kolda & Bader, 2009; Kroonenberg, 2008; Shashua et al., 2006) and Clusterwise Simultaneous Component Analysis (Clusterwise SCA) for multi-group data (De Roover et al., 2013; Smilde et al., 2022; Tenenhaus & Tenenhaus, 2014). However, these methods are not applicable in the context of four-dimensional data cubes with independent "slices" and "hyper-slices".

For further details about clustering, see Charrad et al. (2014), Everitt et al. (2011), Pratsinakis et al. (2020), and Saxena et al. (2017).

Contribution of the Study

Regarding the second methodological approach, and specifically the proposed dimensionality reduction strategy, there are several comparative studies among different strategies and methods applied to multi-group and multi-block data (Codesido et al., 2021; Eslami et al., 2013; Tenenhaus & Tenenhaus, 2014), which focus mainly on highlighting (a) the application of multi-block methods to multi-group data (Codesido et al., 2021; Eslami et al., 2013), (b) the outperformance of PCA (in terms of effective dimensionality reduction) to both multi-block and multi-group data (Tenenhaus & Tenenhaus, 2014), (c) the fact that most methods are extensions or generalizations of PCA (Tenenhaus & Tenenhaus, 2014), (d) the relationships among variables (Jansen et al., 2005), (e) patterns within each group (people emotion categories) or block (wine quality characteristics), taking into account the variability of each group or block (Tenenhaus & Tenenhaus, 2014), and (f) the common patterns among groups (iris plants per species, number of olive oils per region of Italy, animals per farms) (Eslami et al., 2013).

There are also studies (Ali et al., 2021; De Haan et al., 2006; Jansen et al., 2005; Smilde et al., 2005; Thiel et al., 2017; Zwanenburg et al., 2011) that generally follow similar methodologies (application of ANOVA/MANOVA extensions and combination with PCA to variability data matrices), mainly in the field of Veterinary Medicine, in order to (a) improve the visualization and interpretation of results (De Haan et al., 2006; Jansen et al., 2005; Smilde et al., 2005; Zwanenburg et al., 2011), (b) highlight the relationships among main effects, interactions, and variables (De Haan et al., 2006; Jansen et al., 2005; Smilde et al., 2005), (c) demonstrate the applicability of several methods to both balanced and unbalanced experimental designs (Ali et al., 2021; Thiel et al., 2017), and (d) study all sources of variability (Ali et al., 2021).

However, to the best of the author's knowledge, there are no studies focusing on multidimensional data in the form of four-dimensional data cubes with independent "slices" and "hyper-slices" (especially from the field of Agriculture). As a result, the conceptual and structural role of the cube's "slices" and "hyper-slices", as well as their interaction, are not considered. It is worth noting that investigating the effect of "slices" and "hyper-slices" on the overall data cube structure is crucial, as it can lead to simpler or more complex practices for managing and analyzing a data cube.

Moreover, according to Rencher (2002), Williams (1972), and Zetterberg (2013), there are no studies that present explicitly, analytically, and clearly the mathematical expressions of the variability data matrices. From this perspective, the present study provides a detailed presentation of the mathematical expressions of the variability data matrices. The row and column elements of these matrices are ready for direct application of either PCA or any other alternative (linear or non-linear) dimensionality reduction method.

Regarding the proposed clustering strategies, there are several studies that focus on clustering methods for multidimensional data. For example, the Three-Way Clustering method is applied to multi-way data (Kolda & Bader, 2009; Kroonenberg, 2008; Shashua et al., 2006) and the Clusterwise Simultaneous Component Analysis (Clusterwise SCA) method is applied to both multi-group and multi-block data (De Roover et al., 2013; Smilde et al., 2022; Tenenhaus & Tenenhaus, 2014). However, these methods are not applicable in the context of four-dimensional data cubes with independent "slices" and "hyper-slices".

Furthermore, to the best of the author's knowledge, there are no comparative studies between different clustering strategies (in terms of different distance matrices, linkage methods and geometric representations of the data) aiming to conduct an in-depth analysis and reveal latent underlying directions of data variability from different perspectives. Finally, there are no studies that apply clustering between matrices that are structured a four-dimensional balanced data cube, through the Procrustes distance matrix.

It is worth noting that, in the context of the second methodological approach, PCA or any other (linear or non-linear) dimensionality reduction method can be applied directly to the selected variability data matrix (the corresponding mathematical expressions are presented below). Alternatively, SVD can be applied to the corresponding correlation or variance-covariance matrix. Also, all clustering strategies can be applied either to PCA (factor) scores or directly to the selected variability data matrix, in order to cluster the objects (experimental or sampling units) of the "stacked" data matrix.

Aims and Outline of the Study

The aims of this study are to propose alternative clustering strategies for balanced four-dimensional data cubes with independent "slices" and "hyper-slices", and to highlight the importance of applying different analysis strategies in the interpretation of results.

The outline of the study is as follows. The Materials and Methods section introduces the real dataset used for the analyses, as well as the proposed dimensionality reduction and clustering strategies. The Results section presents the outcomes of both the dimensionality reduction (PCA loading plot) and clustering (HCL dendrograms) strategies. The Discussion section provides an in-depth analysis and comparison of the results. The Conclusions section summarizes the study's findings, highlights its originality and contribution to the international scientific community, and discusses its limitations and recommendations for future research.

MATERIALS AND METHODS

The proposed dimensionality reduction strategy is based on the study of variability (inertia), which is the key point of Statistical-Data Analysis in biological sciences and especially in agricultural sciences (Kitchen & Clay, 2016).

The proposed dimensionality reduction strategy is also based on the PCA method without rotation (Greenacre et al., 2022; Jolliffe & Cadima, 2016). Alternatively, FA or SVD on the appropriate data matrix (i.e., the correlation matrix) can be used (Smilde et al., 2022). In other cases, such as where the data lie in non-Euclidean spaces, there are some other methods for dimensionality reduction such as Kernel PCA (Anowar et al., 2021). For practical purposes, including visualization and interpretation, only the first two PCs are selected.

Furthermore, the proposed clustering strategies can be used complementarily to all previously proposed methodological approaches and dimensionality reduction strategies. In this study, the application of the proposed clustering strategies 1 and 2 is illustrated indicatively on the variability data matrix $\mathbf{X}_{KG}$ of the interaction between "slices" and "hyper-slices", whereas the application of the proposed clustering strategy 3 is illustrated indicatively on the initial "stacked" data matrix **M**. The choice of interaction effect is not arbitrary, as it constitutes a central focus of investigation in the majority of agricultural experiments (Vargas et al., 2015).

It is worth noting that all clustering methods can be applied either to PCA (factor) scores or directly to the selected variability data matrix, in order to cluster the objects (experimental or sampling units) of the dataset. The statistical software packages used for the analyses were IBM SPSS Statistics v29.0 (SPSS) and R v4.3.2 (R).

Dataset

For the implementation of the proposed dimensionality reduction and clustering strategies, the real agricultural dataset "Basil" is used (Kalamartzis et al., 2020). This dataset covers basil plants cultivated and studied at the Aristotle University of Thessaloniki Farm between 2016 and 2017 (Stage III of basil plant development).

The sample consists of 60 basil plants, seven quantitative characteristics, three irrigation levels, and five basil varieties. More specifically, the "Basil" dataset is considered as a balanced four-dimensional data cube $\underline{\mathbf{X}}(4 \times 7 \times 5 \times 3)$ with independent "slices" and "hyper-slices". Data cube $\underline{\mathbf{X}}$ is transformed into a "stacked" data matrix $\mathbf{X}(60 \times 7)$ through vertical concatenation. The first dimension consists of different and equal number of objects (basil plants) per "slice" (I=4). The second dimension consists of the same seven continuous variables (traits) per "slice" (J=7). Specifically, these were the measurements of Height (cm), Weight (gr), Leaf Area Index (LAI) (m^2/m^2), Leaf Temperature (labeled as Leaf Temp) (°C), Photosynthesis (μmol $CO_2\,m^{-2}\,s^{-1}$), Water Use Efficiency (WUE) (gr/L), and Water Potential (MPa). The third dimension is a categorical variable denoting five "slices" (K=5) corresponding to five basil varieties [Mrs Burns (labeled as Burns), Cinnamon, Sweet, Red Rubin (labeled as Red), Thai]. The fourth dimension is a categorical variable denoting three "hyper-slices" (G=3) corresponding to three irrigation levels (40%, 70%, 100%). Also, the number of basil plants in the gth "hyper-slice" across all "slices" are IG=12, while the number of basil plants in the kth "slice" across all "hyper-slices" are IK=20. It is worth noting that, the "small" dataset ("Basil") is used for practical reasons, in order to facilitate the visualization of the results.

Variability Decomposition Strategy on Balanced Four-Dimensional Data Cubes With Independent "Slices" And "Hyper-Slices"

Based on Zetterberg et al. (2013) and Bertinetto et al. (2020), for balanced four-dimensional data cubes, it is true that:

Total variability = Between-"hyper-slices" variability + Between-"slices" variability + Interaction between "hyper-slices" and "slices" variability + Within "hyper-slices" and "slices" variability (1)

Let **X** be a balanced "stacked" data matrix with different objects per "slice" and "hyper-slice", with dimensions $IKG \times J$ and x_{ijkg} elements, where i= 1,2,…,I, j= 1,2,…,J, k= 1,2,…,K and g= 1,2,…,G. The equation (1) is expressed mathematically as follows:

$$\mathbf{X}_\mathrm{T} = \mathbf{X}_\mathrm{G} + \mathbf{X}_\mathrm{K} + \mathbf{X}_\mathrm{KG} + \mathbf{X}_\mathrm{W} \quad \mathbf{X}_\mathrm{t} = \mathbf{X}_\mathrm{g} + \mathbf{X}_\mathrm{k} + \mathbf{X}_\mathrm{kg} + \mathbf{X}_\mathrm{w}$$

Also,

$$\mathbf{x}_{ikg} = \begin{bmatrix} x_{i1kg} \\ x_{i2kg} \\ \vdots \\ x_{iJkg} \end{bmatrix}_{J\times 1}$$

is the J-dimensional vector of variables for the object i in the kth "slice" within g^{th} "hyper-slice",

$$\bar{\mathbf{x}}_{.k.} = \frac{1}{IG}\sum_{g=1}^{G}\sum_{i=1}^{I}\mathbf{x}_{ikg} = \begin{bmatrix} \bar{x}_{.1k.} \\ \bar{x}_{.2k.} \\ \vdots \\ \bar{x}_{.Jk.} \end{bmatrix}_{J\times 1}$$

is the J-dimensional vector of means for the kth "slice",

$$\bar{\mathbf{x}}_{..g} = \frac{1}{IK}\sum_{k=1}^{K}\sum_{i=1}^{I}\mathbf{x}_{ikg} = \begin{bmatrix} \bar{x}_{.1.g} \\ \bar{x}_{.2.g} \\ \vdots \\ \bar{x}_{.J.g} \end{bmatrix}_{J\times 1}$$

is the J-dimensional vector of means for the gth "hyper-slice",

$$\bar{\mathbf{x}}_{.kg} = \frac{1}{I}\sum_{i=1}^{I}\mathbf{x}_{ikg} = \begin{bmatrix} \bar{x}_{.1kg} \\ \bar{x}_{.2kg} \\ \vdots \\ \bar{x}_{.Jkg} \end{bmatrix}_{J\times 1}$$

is the J-dimensional vector of means for the kth "slice" within the gth "hyper-slice", and

$$\bar{\mathbf{x}}_{...} = \frac{1}{IKG}\sum_{g=1}^{G}\sum_{k=1}^{K}\sum_{i=1}^{I}\mathbf{x}_{ikg} = \begin{bmatrix} \bar{x}_{.1..} \\ \bar{x}_{.2..} \\ \vdots \\ \bar{x}_{.J..} \end{bmatrix}_{J\times 1}$$

is the J-dimensional vector of means for the "stacked" data matrix **X**.

Then, it is true that the $J \times J$ Sum of Squares and Cross-Products (SSCP) matrix of the total variability is defined as

$$\mathbf{X}_{\mathbf{t}} = \sum_{g=1}^{G}\sum_{k=1}^{K}\sum_{i=1}^{I}\left(\mathbf{x}_{ikg} - \bar{\mathbf{x}}_{...}\right)\left(\mathbf{x}_{ikg} - \bar{\mathbf{x}}_{...}\right)^{\mathrm{T}}.$$

The $J \times J$ SSCP matrix of the variability between-"hyper-slices" is defined as

$$\mathbf{X}_{\mathbf{g}} = IK\sum_{g=1}^{G}\left(\bar{\mathbf{x}}_{..g} - \bar{\mathbf{x}}_{...}\right)\left(\bar{\mathbf{x}}_{..g} - \bar{\mathbf{x}}_{...}\right)^{T}.$$

The $J \times J$ SSCP matrix of the variability between-"slices" is defined as

$$\mathbf{X_k} = IG\sum_{k=1}^{K}(\bar{\mathbf{x}}_{.k.} - \bar{\mathbf{x}}_{...})(\bar{\mathbf{x}}_{.k.} - \bar{\mathbf{x}}_{...})^T.$$

The $J \times J$ SSCP matrix of the variability of interaction between "hyper-slices" and "slices" is defined as

$$\mathbf{X_{kg}} = I\sum_{g=1}^{G}\sum_{k=1}^{K}(\bar{\mathbf{x}}_{.kg} - \bar{\mathbf{x}}_{..g} - \bar{\mathbf{x}}_{.k.} + \bar{\mathbf{x}}_{...})(\bar{\mathbf{x}}_{.kg} - \bar{\mathbf{x}}_{..g} - \bar{\mathbf{x}}_{.k.} + \bar{\mathbf{x}}_{...})^T.$$

The $J \times J$ SSCP matrix of the variability within "hyper-slices" and "slices" is defined as

$$\mathbf{X_w} = \sum_{g=1}^{G}\sum_{k=1}^{K}\sum_{i=1}^{I}\left(\mathbf{x}_{ikg} - \bar{\mathbf{x}}_{.kg}\right)\left(\mathbf{x}_{ikg} - \bar{\mathbf{x}}_{.kg}\right)^T.$$

Furthermore, it is true that the $IKG \times J$ data matrix of the total variability is defined as $\mathbf{X_T} = \mathbf{X} - 1_{IKG}\bar{\mathbf{x}}_{...}{}^{\mathrm{T}}$, where for example 1_n is the n-vector of ones. The $IKG \times J$ data matrix of the between-"hyper-slices" variability is defined as

$$\mathbf{X_G} = \begin{bmatrix} 1_{IK}\bar{\mathbf{x}}_{..1}{}^{\mathrm{T}} \\ 1_{IK}\bar{\mathbf{x}}_{..2}{}^{\mathrm{T}} \\ \vdots \\ 1_{IK}\bar{\mathbf{x}}_{..G}{}^{\mathrm{T}} \end{bmatrix} - 1_{IKG}\bar{\mathbf{x}}_{...}{}^{\mathrm{T}}.$$

The $IKG \times J$ data matrix of the between-"slices" variability is defined as

$$\mathbf{X_K} = repmat\left(\begin{bmatrix} 1_I\bar{\mathbf{x}}_{.1.}{}^{\mathrm{T}} \\ 1_I\bar{\mathbf{x}}_{.2.}{}^{\mathrm{T}} \\ \vdots \\ 1_I\bar{\mathbf{x}}_{.K.}{}^{\mathrm{T}} \end{bmatrix}, G\right) - 1_{IKG}\bar{\mathbf{x}}_{...}{}^{\mathrm{T}},$$

where the function $repmat(\mathbf{X_K}, G)$ repeats the matrix $\mathbf{X_K}$ vertically G times. The $IKG \times J$ variability data matrix of the interaction between "hyper-slices" and "slices" is defined as

$$\mathbf{X}_{\mathbf{KG}} = \begin{bmatrix} 1_I\bar{\mathbf{x}}_{.11}{}^{\mathrm{T}} \\ 1_I\bar{\mathbf{x}}_{.21}{}^{\mathrm{T}} \\ \vdots \\ 1_I\bar{\mathbf{x}}_{.KG}{}^{\mathrm{T}} \end{bmatrix} - \begin{bmatrix} 1_{IK}\bar{\mathbf{x}}_{..1}{}^{\mathrm{T}} \\ 1_{IK}\bar{\mathbf{x}}_{..2}{}^{\mathrm{T}} \\ \vdots \\ 1_{IK}\bar{\mathbf{x}}_{..G}{}^{\mathrm{T}} \end{bmatrix} - repmat\left(\begin{bmatrix} 1_I\bar{\mathbf{x}}_{.1.}{}^{\mathrm{T}} \\ 1_I\bar{\mathbf{x}}_{.2.}{}^{\mathrm{T}} \\ \vdots \\ 1_I\bar{\mathbf{x}}_{.K.}{}^{\mathrm{T}} \end{bmatrix}, G\right) + 1_{IKG}\bar{\mathbf{x}}_{...}{}^{\mathrm{T}}.$$

The $IKG \times J$data matrix of the within "hyper-slices" and "slices" variability is defined as

$$\mathbf{X}_{\mathbf{W}} = \mathbf{X} - \begin{bmatrix} 1_I\bar{\mathbf{x}}_{.11}{}^{\mathrm{T}} \\ 1_I\bar{\mathbf{x}}_{.21}{}^{\mathrm{T}} \\ \vdots \\ 1_I\bar{\mathbf{x}}_{.KG}{}^{\mathrm{T}} \end{bmatrix}.$$

The steps of the proposed dimensionality reduction strategy are the following:

Step 1: Construct the data matrix $\mathbf{X}_{\mathbf{T}}$ with the total variability of the data cube.
Step 2: Construct the data matrix $\mathbf{X}_{\mathbf{G}}$ with the variability between-"hyper-slices".
Step 3: Construct the data matrix $\mathbf{X}_{\mathbf{K}}$ with the variability between-"slices".
Step 4: Construct the data matrix $\mathbf{X}_{\mathbf{KG}}$ with the variability of the interaction between "hyper-slices" and "slices".
Step 5: Construct the data matrix $\mathbf{X}_{\mathbf{W}}$ with the variability within "hyper-slices" and "slices" of the cube.
Step 6: Apply PCA to the correlation matrices $\mathbf{R}_{\mathbf{T}}$, $\mathbf{R}_{\mathbf{G}}$, $\mathbf{R}_{\mathbf{K}}$, $\mathbf{R}_{\mathbf{KG}}$, and $\mathbf{R}_{\mathbf{W}}$ of the variability matrices $\mathbf{X}_{\mathbf{T}}$, $\mathbf{X}_{\mathbf{G}}$, $\mathbf{X}_{\mathbf{K}}$, $\mathbf{X}_{\mathbf{KG}}$, and $\mathbf{X}_{\mathbf{W}}$.

It is worth noting that linear and non-linear dimensionality reduction methods can be applied and compared directly to the proposed variability data matrices (i.e., between and within "slices" and "hyper-slices", etc.). These methods either assume linear (e.g., PCA, FA, etc.) or non-linear (e.g., Kernel PCA, t-distributed Stochastic Neighbor Embedding – t-SNE) relationships between variables (Anowar et al., 2021).

Clustering Strategies on Balanced Four-Dimensional Data Cubes With Independent "Slices" And "Hyper-Slices"

The proposed clustering strategies aim to explore and compare different clustering approaches for experimental/sampling units, depending on the nature of the data and their underlying geometric structure. Specifically, they are based on the Squared Euclidean distance between principal components (PCs) projected onto a plane, the arc-cosine geodesic distance between PCs projected onto a circle, as well as the Procrustes distance between matrices. Therefore, clusters are able to capture underlying sources of variability from different perspectives by offering a holistic approach to data analysis. The steps of the proposed strategies are presented below.

Clustering Strategy 1

Step 1.1: Compute the factor (PCA) scores of the significant PCs of the variability matrices $\mathbf{X}_T$, $\mathbf{X}_G$, $\mathbf{X}_K$, $\mathbf{X}_{KG}$ and $\mathbf{X}_W$ (continuation of the dimensionality reduction strategy).
Step 1.2: Construct the matrices $\mathbf{T}_T$, $\mathbf{T}_G$, $\mathbf{T}_K$, $\mathbf{T}_{KG}$, and $\mathbf{T}_W$ with the Squared Euclidean distances of the significant PCs for each variability matrix.
Step 1.3: Apply HCL using Ward's method to each distance matrix **T**.
Step 1.4: Analyze the cluster profiles.

Clustering Strategy 2

Step 2.1: Compute the factor (PCA) scores of the significant PCs of the variability matrices $\mathbf{X}_T$, $\mathbf{X}_G$, $\mathbf{X}_K$, $\mathbf{X}_{KG}$ and $\mathbf{X}_W$ (continuation of the dimensionality reduction strategy).
Step 2.2: Transform the PCA scores of the significant PCs, in order to project them onto a circle, sphere, or "hyper-sphere". For example, in the case of the first two PCs (PC1 and PC2), the transformation is given by:

$$PC_1^* = \frac{PC_1}{\sqrt{PC_1^2 + PC_2^2}}, PC_2^* = \frac{PC_2}{\sqrt{PC_1^2 + PC_2^2}},$$

for which $PC_1^{*2} + PC_2^{*2} = 1$, since the PCA scores lie on the unit circle (see Figure 2). When three PCs are extracted, this transformation projects them onto a sphere, whereas with four PCs it projects them onto a "hyper-sphere", and so on (Bishop, 2006).
Step 2.3: Construct the matrices $\mathbf{C}_T$, $\mathbf{C}_G$, $\mathbf{C}_K$, $\mathbf{C}_{KG}$ and $\mathbf{C}_W$ containing the arc-cosine geodesic distances of the significant PCs for each variability matrix.
Step 2.4: Apply HCL using the Average Between Groups method to each distance matrix **C**.
Step 2.5: Analyze the cluster profiles.

Figure 2. Scatter plot (a) of the original PCA scores of the first two PCs of the interaction variability matrix $\mathbf{X}_{KG}$ *between "hyper-slices" and "slices" and (b) of the transformed PCA scores of the first two PCs of the interaction variability matrix* $\mathbf{X}_{KG}$ *between "hyper-slices" and "slices" from the "Basil" dataset. The axes represent the first two PCs (PC1 and PC2) (visualization produced in SPSS)*

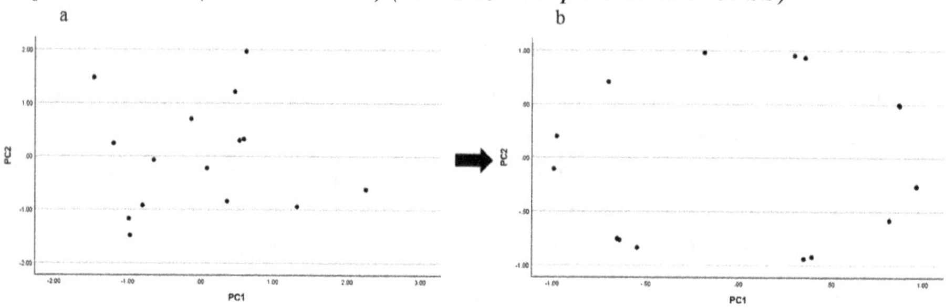

Clustering Strategy 3

> **Step 3.1:** Construct the submatrices $\mathbf{X}_{kg}$ of the original data for each combination of "slice" and "hyper-slice".
> **Step 3.2:** Construct the matrix **P** containing the Procrustes distances between all pairs of submatrices $\mathbf{X}_{kg}$.
> **Step 3.3:** Apply HCL using Ward's method to distance matrix **P**.
> **Step 3.4:** Analyze the cluster profiles.

RESULTS

Results from the Dimensionality Reduction Strategy

The PCA loading diagram of $\mathbf{X}_{KG}$ (variability data matrix of interaction between "slices" and "hyper-slices") is presented below (Figures 3).

Figure 3. PCA loading plot of the interaction variability data matrix $\mathbf{X}_{KG}$ *between "slices" (basil varieties) and "hyper-slices" (irrigation levels). The axes represent the first two PCs (PC1-Dim 1, PC2-Dim 2) with the corresponding percentages of the variance explained by each principal component and the vectors (arrows) represent the loadings of each variable on the principal components (analysis and visualization from R)*

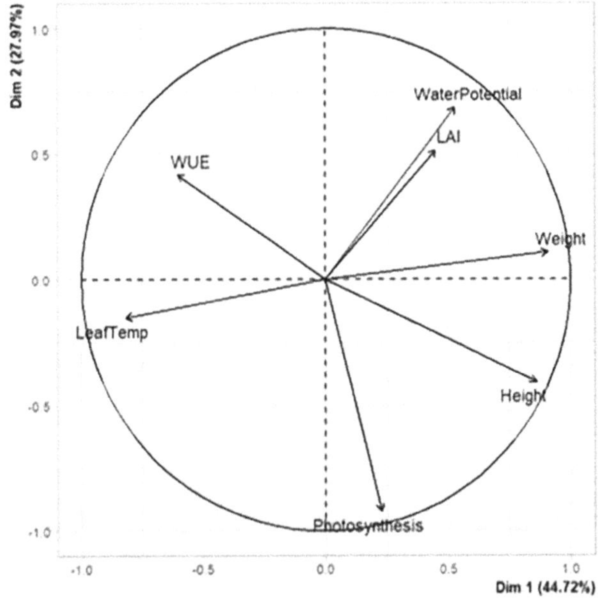

The percentage of total variance explained by the first two PCs of $\mathbf{X}_{KG}$ is 72.69%. As for the main correlations between the variables, there appears to be a strong positive correlation between Weight and Height, as well as between WaterPotential and LAI. In contrast, LeafTemp is negatively correlated with Weight. Regarding the contribution of the variables to the first two PCs, it is observed that the variables Weight and Height contribute positively to PC1, while the variables LeafTemp and WUE contribute negatively to PC1. In contrast, the variables LAI and WaterPotential contribute positively to PC2, while the variable Photosynthesis contributes negatively to PC2.

Results From the Clustering Strategies

The HCL dendrogram for the clustering strategy 1 is presented below (see Figures 4).

Figure 4. Dendrogram based on the original PCA scores of the first two PCs for basil plants derived from the interaction variability data matrix between "slices" (basil varieties) and "hyper-slices" (irrigation levels). The input distance matrix is the matrix of Squared Euclidean distances, and Ward is the linkage method. The red line indicates the dendrogram cut-off height, the horizontal axis represents the basil plants of the variability data matrix, and the vertical axis represents the dendrogram height (analysis and visualization from SPSS)

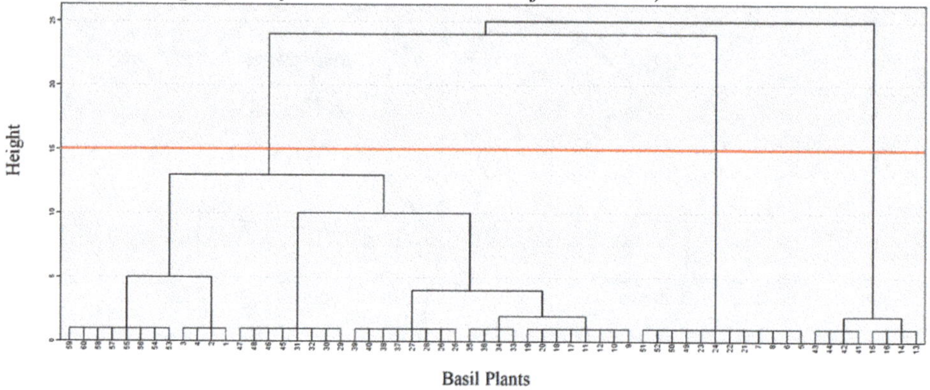

According to Kaufman and Rousseeuw (2009), the optimal number of clusters is determined by cutting the dendrogram (Figure 4) at the point of a sharp increase in clustering distance (height 15). Cluster profile analysis yields three clusters with the following characteristics:

- The first cluster consists of 40 objects. The PC1 centroid is –0.08 and the PC2 centroid is 0.51.
- The second cluster consists of 12 objects. The PC1 centroid is –0.92 and the PC2 centroid is –1.19.
- The third cluster consists of 8 objects. The PC1 centroid is 1.79 and the PC2 centroid is –0.78.

Figure 5 presents the bar chart of the standardized centroids of the PCs, while Figure 6 presents the bar chart of the corresponding effect sizes (partial η^2).

Figure 5. Bar chart with the standardized centroids (z-scores) of each cluster for the first two PCs (PC1 and PC2) from the first clustering strategy (visualization from Excel)

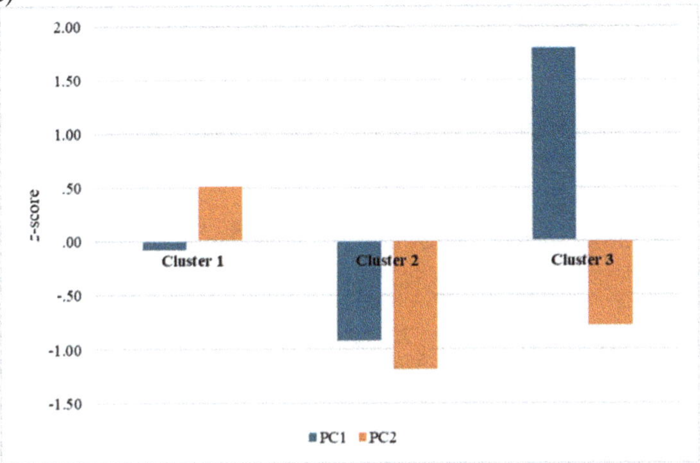

Figure 6. Bar chart with the effect sizes (partial η^2) of the first two PCs (PC1 and PC2) from the first clustering strategy (visualization from Excel)

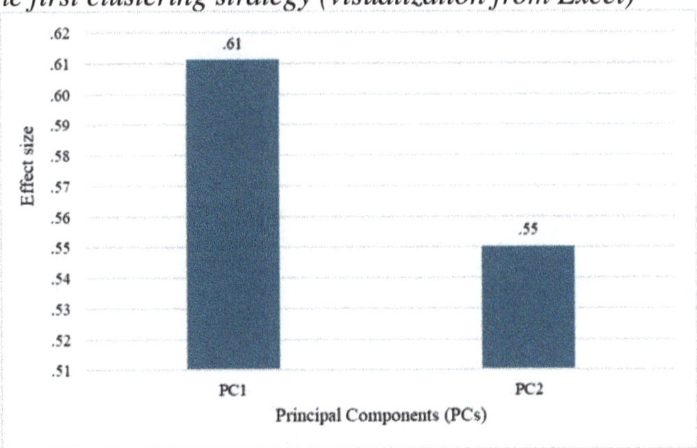

Based on the above, the first cluster includes the majority of the basil plants, which exhibit moderate water stress, as well as moderate morphological and physiological status, since the centroid of PC1 lies slightly below zero (low biological growth), while the centroid of PC2 lies slightly above zero (high values of physiological traits).

The second cluster consists of basil plants with low water stress and poor morphological and physiological status, with the centroids of both PC1 and PC2 lying below zero (low biological growth and low values of physiological traits).

The third cluster exhibits greater variability, with the centroid of PC1 lying above zero (high biological growth) and the centroid of PC2 lying below zero (low values of physiological traits).

According to the effect size (partial η^2), PC1 represents the biological growth of basil plants, with a larger effect size ($\eta^2 = 0.61$) than PC2, which represents the physiological traits of basil plants ($\eta^2 = 0.55$).

The HCL dendrogram for the clustering strategy 2 is presented below (Figures 7).

Figure 7. Dendrogram based on the transformed PCA scores of the first two PCs for basil plants derived from the interaction variability data matrix between "slices" (basil varieties) and "hyper-slices" (irrigation levels). The input distance matrix is the matrix of geodesic arc-cosine distances, and Average Between Groups is the linkage method. The red line indicates the dendrogram cut-off height, the horizontal axis represents the basil plants of the variability data matrix, and the vertical axis represents the dendrogram height (analysis and visualization from SPSS)

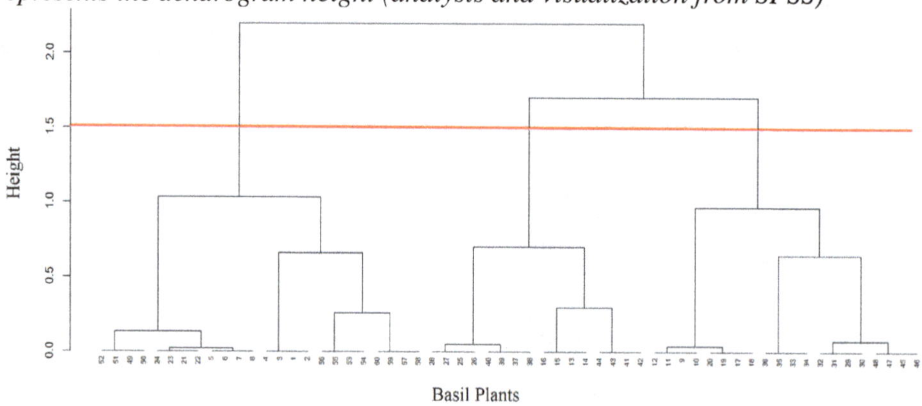

According to Kaufman and Rousseeuw (2009), the optimal number of clusters is determined by cutting the dendrogram (Figure 7) at the point of a sharp increase in clustering distance (height 1.5). Cluster profile analysis yields three clusters with the following characteristics:

- The first cluster consists of 24 objects. The PC1 centroid is −1.11 and the PC2 centroid is −0.33.
- The second cluster consists of 20 objects. The PC1 centroid is 0.61 and the PC2 centroid is 1.09.

- The third cluster consists of 16 objects. The PC1 centroid is 0.91 and the PC2 centroid is −0.88.

Figure 8 presents the bar chart of the standardized centroids of the PCs, while Figure 9 presents the bar chart of the corresponding effect sizes (partial η^2).

Figure 8. Bar chart with the standardized centroids (z-scores) of each cluster for the first two PCs (PC1 and PC2) from the first clustering strategy (visualization from Excel)

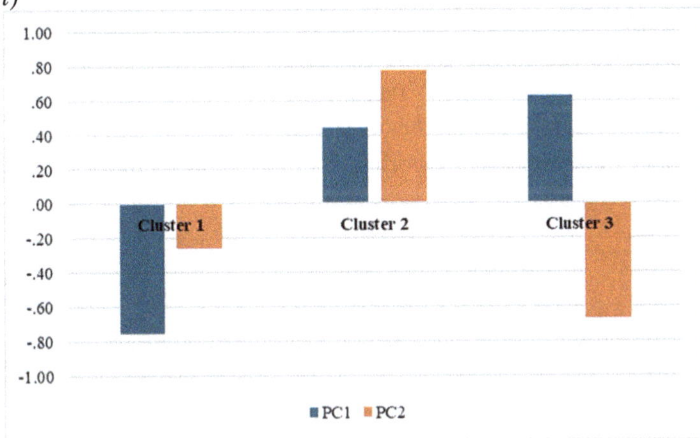

Figure 9. Bar chart with the effect sizes (partial η^2) of the first two PCs (PC1 and PC2) from the first clustering strategy (visualization from Excel)

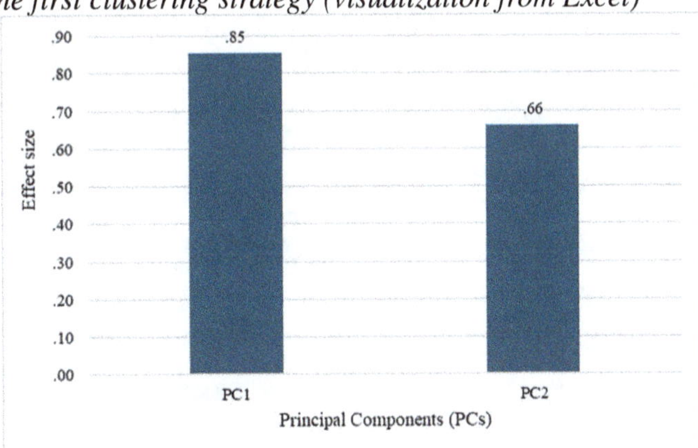

Based on the above, the first and second clusters include the majority of the basil plants. The first cluster consists of basil plants with low water stress and poor morphological and physiological status, with the centroids of both PC1 and PC2 lying below zero (low biological growth and low values of physiological traits).

The second cluster consists of basil plants with high water stress and high morphological and physiological status, with the centroids of both PC1 and PC2 lying above zero (high biological growth and high values of physiological traits).

The third cluster exhibits greater variability, with the centroid of PC1 lying above zero (high biological growth) and the centroid of PC2 lying below zero (low values of physiological traits).

According to the effect size (partial η^2), PC1 represents the biological growth of basil plants, with a larger effect size ($\eta^2 = 0.85$) than PC2, which represents the physiological traits of basil plants ($\eta^2 = 0.66$).

The HCL dendrogram for the clustering strategy 3 is presented below (Figures 10).

Figure 10. Dendrogram based on the Procrustes distances between all pairs of the 15 combined matrices $\mathbf{X}_{kg}$ *derived from the initial "stacked" data matrix* $\mathbf{X}$*. The red line indicates the dendrogram cut-off height, the vertical axis represents the dendrogram height, and the horizontal axis represents the objects (15 combined matrices: Matrix_1 [1st "slice" within the 1st "hyper-slice"], Matrix_2 [2nd "slice" within the 1st "hyper-slice"], Matrix_3 [3rd "slice" within the 1st "hyper-slice"], Matrix_4 [4th "slice" within the 1st "hyper-slice"], Matrix_5 [5th "slice" within the 1st "hyper-slice"], Matrix_6 [1st "slice" within the 2nd "hyper-slice"], Matrix_7 [2nd "slice" within the 2nd "hyper-slice"], Matrix_8 [3rd "slice" within the 2nd "hyper-slice"], Matrix_9 [4th "slice" within the 2nd "hyper-slice"], Matrix_10 [5th "slice" within the 2nd "hyper-slice"], Matrix_11 [1st "slice" within the 3rd "hyper-slice"], Matrix_12 [2nd "slice" within the 3rd "hyper-slice"], Matrix_13 [3rd "slice" within the 3rd "hyper-slice"], Matrix_14 [4th "slice" within the 3rd "hyper-slice"], and Matrix_15 [5th "slice" within the 3rd "hyper-slice"]) (analysis and visualization performed in R)*

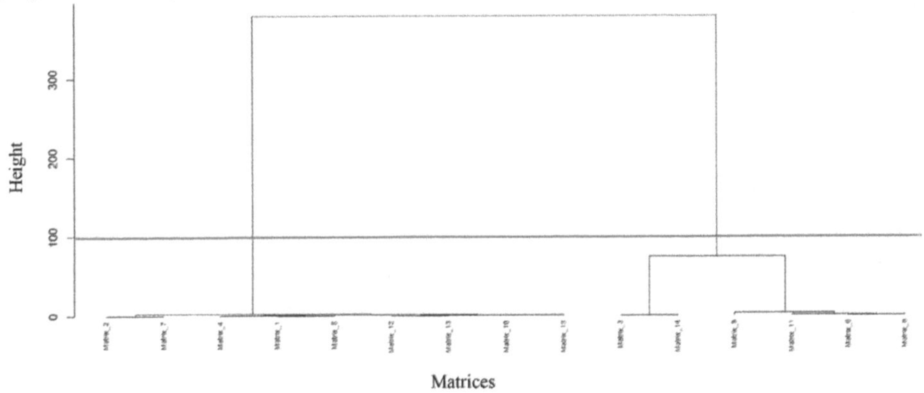

According to Kaufman and Rousseeuw (2009), the optimal number of clusters is determined by cutting the dendrogram (Figure 10) at the point of a sharp increase in clustering distance (height 100). Cluster profile analysis yields two clusters with the following characteristics:

- The first cluster consists of nine matrices representing combinations of "slices" and "hyper-slices". These matrices are the following:
    - Matrix_1 (1st "slice" within the 1st "hyper-slice")
    - Matrix_2 (2nd "slice" within the 1st "hyper-slice")
    - Matrix_4 (4th "slice" within the 1st "hyper-slice")
    - Matrix_5 (5th "slice" within the 1st "hyper-slice")
    - Matrix_7 (2nd "slice" within the 2nd "hyper-slice")

    - Matrix_10 (5th “slice” within the 2nd “hyper-slice”)
    - Matrix_12 (2nd “slice” within the 3rd “hyper-slice”)
    - Matrix_13 (3rd “slice” within the 3rd “hyper-slice”)
    - Matrix_15 (5th “slice” within the 3rd “hyper-slice”)
- The second cluster consists of six matrices representing combinations of “slices” and “hyper-slices”. These matrices are the following:
    - Matrix_3 (3rd “slice” within the 1st “hyper-slice”)
    - Matrix_6 (1st “slice” within the 2nd “hyper-slice”)
    - Matrix_8 (3rd “slice” within the 2nd “hyper-slice”)
    - Matrix_9 (4th “slice” within the 2nd “hyper-slice”)
    - Matrix_11 (1st “slice” within the 3rd “hyper-slice”)
    - Matrix_14 (4th “slice” within the 3rd “hyper-slice”)

Based on the above, the first cluster consists mainly of the first and third “hyper-slices” (40% and 100% irrigation levels), while the second cluster consists mainly of the second “hyper-slice” (70% irrigation level). In addition, the first cluster consists mainly of the second and fifth “slices” (Cinnamon and Thai), while the second cluster consists mainly of the first, third, and fourth “slices” (Burns, Sweet, and Red).

DISCUSSION

Dimensionality reduction strategy shows that the variability of interaction between basil varieties and irrigation levels is significant, as each variety responds differently to different irrigation levels. More specifically, PC1 represents the biological growth of basil plants with characteristics (height and biomass) that show positive PCA loadings, while leaf temperature and water use efficiency show negative PCA loadings. On the other hand, PC2 represents physiological characteristics of basil plants, such as photosynthesis (negative PCA loading) and water potential (positive PCA loading).

To the best of the author’s knowledge, there are no studies focusing on multidimensional data in the form of four-dimensional data cubes with independent “slices” and “hyper-slices”. Additionally, this study provides a detailed presentation of the mathematical expressions of the variability data matrices, to which PCA or any other alternative dimensionality reduction method can be applied directly. The proposed dimensionality reduction strategy can also be applied complementary to the “traditional” MANOVA method providing more information about the structure and components of variability.

In addition to the second methodological approach of managing and analyzing data cubes, and by extension of the proposed dimensionality reduction strategy (which is based on variability decomposition and PCA), alternative clustering strategies are also proposed. These clustering strategies vary in terms of the choice of distance matrix and linkage method.

Specifically, it is possible to either display the extracted factor scores as points on a plane or display them as points on a differentiable manifold (circle, sphere, "hyper-sphere"). The first strategy is based on Ward's agglomerative clustering method and the matrix with the Squared Euclidean distances between the objects of the first two extracted PCs (from the application of PCA to the interaction variability matrix between "hyper-slices" and "slices"), which are projected onto a plane. The second strategy is based on the Average Between Groups method and the matrix with the arc-cosine geodesic distances between the objects of the transformed first two extracted PCs (from the application of PCA to the interaction variability matrix between "hyper-slices" and "slices"), which are projected onto the unit circle. The third strategy is based on Ward's method and the matrix with the Procrustes distances between the submatrices (in pairs) per combination of "slices" and "hyper-slice", from the initial "stacked" data matrix.

Clustering strategies show that in the first clustering strategy, the first cluster represents basil plants with moderate water stress and moderate morphological and physiological status. The second cluster represents basil plants with low water stress and poor morphological and physiological status, while the third cluster exhibits greater variability.

In the second clustering strategy, the first cluster represents basil plants with low water stress and poor morphological and physiological status. The second cluster consists of basil plants with high water stress and high morphological and physiological status, while the third cluster exhibits greater variability.

In the third clustering strategy, the results indicate clear differentiation among basil varieties in combination with different irrigation levels. More specifically, the Cinnamon and Thai basil varieties under 40% and 100% irrigation levels differ markedly from the Burns, Sweet, and Red varieties under the 70% irrigation level, with respect to their hydrological status, as well as their morphological and physiological traits.

To the best of the author's knowledge, there are no studies focusing on clustering methods for multidimensional data in the form of four-dimensional data cubes with independent "slices" and "hyper-slices". Furthermore, there are no comparative studies between different clustering strategies (in terms of different distance matrices, linkage methods and geometric representations of the data) aiming to conduct an in-depth analysis and reveal latent underlying directions of data variability from different perspectives. Finally, there are no studies that apply clustering between matrices structuring a balanced four-dimensional data cube through a Procrustes distance matrix.

It is worth noting that, in the context of the second methodological approach, PCA or any other linear or non-linear dimensionality reduction method can be applied directly to the selected variability data matrix. Alternatively, SVD can be applied to the corresponding correlation or variance-covariance matrix. Also, all clustering strategies can be applied either to PCA (factor) scores or directly to the selected variability data matrix, in order to cluster the objects of the "stacked" data matrix.

CONCLUSION

The proposed clustering strategies highlight the importance of a holistic approach to the data cube, so that its underlying sources of variability can be examined in depth from different perspectives. It is worth noting that the second clustering strategy (using arc-cosine distances) identifies underlying directions of variability that the first strategy (using Squared Euclidean distances) does not, due to the circular structure of the data and the different distance measurement.

For future research, we propose the development of new and innovative analysis strategies on data cubes with independent "slices" and "hyper-slices", for dimensions $p \geq 4$. These strategies can be applied on both real and simulated data cubes with independent "slices" and "hyper-slices".

This study applied and compared three clustering strategies, as well as a dimensionality reduction strategy, on a specific real dataset. Both the dataset and the analysis strategies used were limited to the scope of this study. Therefore, caution should be exercised when generalizing the findings to other contexts or datasets.

ACKNOWLEDGMENT

We would like to thank Prof Christos Dordas, Dr Iakovos Kalamartzis, and the Laboratory of Agronomy, School of Agriculture, Aristotle University of Thessaloniki, for granting us access to the experiment's primary data.

COMPETING INTERESTS

The authors of this publication declare there are no competing interests.

FUNDING

This research received no specific grant from any funding agency in the public, commercial, or not-for-profit sectors. Funding for this research was covered by the author(s) of the article.

REFERENCES

Acar, E., & Yener, B. (2009). Unsupervised Multiway Data Analysis: A Literature Survey. *IEEE Transactions on Knowledge and Data Engineering*, *21*(1), 6–20. DOI: 10.1109/TKDE.2008.112

Ali, N., Jansen, J., Van Den Doel, A., Tinnevelt, G. H., & Bocklitz, T. (2021). WE-ASCA: The Weighted-Effect ASCA for Analyzing Unbalanced Multifactorial Designs—A Raman Spectra-Based Example. *Molecules (Basel, Switzerland)*, *26*(1), 66. DOI: 10.3390/molecules26010066 PMID: 33375623

Anderson, T. W. (1984). *An Introduction to Multivariate Statistical Analysis* (2nd ed.). John Willey and Sons Inc.

Anowar, F., Sadaoui, S., & Selim, B. (2021). Conceptual and empirical comparison of dimensionality reduction algorithms (PCA, KPCA, LDA, MDS, SVD, LLE, ISOMAP, LE, ICA, t-SNE). *Computer Science Review*, *40*, 100378. DOI: 10.1016/j.cosrev.2021.100378

Bauer, M., Charon, N., & Younes, L. (2019). Metric registration of curves and surfaces using optimal control. In Kimmel, R., & Tai, X. C. (Eds.), *Handbook of numerical analysis* (pp. 613–646)., DOI: 10.1016/bs.hna.2019.03.001

Beaudouin, V. (2016). Statistical analysis of textual data: Benzécri and the French School of data analysis. *Glottometrics*, *33*, 56–72.

Benzécri, J. P. & Collaborateurs. (1973). *L'Analyse des Données. Vol. 1: Taxinomie. Vol. 2: Analyse des Correspondances*. Dunod.

Bertinetto, C., Engel, J., & Jansen, J. (2020). ANOVA simultaneous component analysis: A tutorial review. *Analytica Chimica Acta: X*, *6*, 100061. DOI: 10.1016/j.acax.2020.100061 PMID: 33392497

Bishop, C. M. (2006). *Pattern Recognition and Machine Learning*. Springer.

Blanco-Mallo, E., Morán-Fernández, L., Remeseiro, B., & Bolón-Canedo, V. (2023). Do all roads lead to Rome? Studying distance measures in the context of machine learning. *Pattern Recognition*, *141*, 109646. DOI: 10.1016/j.patcog.2023.109646

Bro, R. (1997). PARAFAC. Tutorial and applications. *Chemometrics and Intelligent Laboratory Systems*, *38*(2), 149–171. DOI: 10.1016/s0169-7439(97)00032-4

Charrad, M., Ghazzali, N., Boiteau, V., & Niknafs, A. (2014). NBClust: ANRPackage for determining the relevant number of clusters in a data set. *Journal of Statistical Software*, *61*(6). Advance online publication. DOI: 10.18637/jss.v061.i06

Chikuse, Y. (2003). The special manifolds and related multivariate topics. In *Lecture notes in statistics* (pp. 1–26). Springer., DOI: 10.1007/978-0-387-21540-2_1

Codesido, S., Hanafi, M., Gagnebin, Y., González-Ruiz, V., Rudaz, S., & Boccard, J. (2021). Network principal component analysis: A versatile tool for the investigation of multigroup and multiblock datasets. *Bioinformatics (Oxford, England)*, *37*(9), 1297–1303. DOI: 10.1093/bioinformatics/btaa954 PMID: 33165510

Dash, M., Liu, H., & Yao, J. (1997). Dimensionality reduction of unsupervised data. In Anon (Ed.), *Proceedings of the International Conference on Tools with Artificial Intelligence* (pp. 532-539). IEEE. https://doi.org/DOI: 10.1109/TAI.1997.632300

De Haan, J. R., Wehrens, R., Bauerschmidt, S., Piek, E., Van Schaik, R. C., & Buydens, L. M. C. (2006). Interpretation of ANOVA models for microarray data using PCA. *Bioinformatics (Oxford, England)*, *23*(2), 184–190. DOI: 10.1093/bioinformatics/btl572 PMID: 17105717

De Roover, K., Ceulemans, E., Timmerman, M. E., Nezlek, J. B., & Onghena, P. (2013). Modeling differences in the dimensionality of multiblock data by means of clusterwise simultaneous component analysis. *Psychometrika*, *78*(4), 648–668. DOI: 10.1007/s11336-013-9318-4 PMID: 24092482

do Carmo, M. P. (1992). *Riemannian Geometry*. Birkhäuser.

Edelman, A., Arias, T. A., & Smith, S. T. (1998). The Geometry of Algorithms with Orthogonality Constraints. *SIAM Journal on Matrix Analysis and Applications, 20*(2), 303–353. DOI: 10.1137/s0895479895290954

Eslami, A., Qannari, E. M., Kohler, A., and Bougeard, S. (2013). General overview of methods of analysis of multi-group datasets. *Revue des Nouvelles Technologies de l'Information. 25.*

Everitt, B. S., Landau, S., Leese, M., & Stahl, D. (2011). *Cluster analysis.* John Wiley & Sons.

Fraley, C., & Raftery, A. E. (2002). Model-Based clustering, discriminant analysis, and density estimation. *Journal of the American Statistical Association, 97*(458), 611–631. DOI: 10.1198/016214502760047131

Gifi, A. (1990). *Nonlinear Multivariate Analysis.* John Willey and Sons Inc.

Gower, J. C. (1967). A comparison of some methods of cluster analysis. *Biometrics, 23*(4), 623–637. DOI: 10.2307/2528417 PMID: 6080200

Gower, J. C. (1971). A general coefficient of similarity and some of its properties. *Biometrics, 27*(4), 857. DOI: 10.2307/2528823

Gower, J. C. (1975). Generalized Procrustes analysis. *Psychometrika, 40*(1), 33–51. DOI: 10.1007/bf02291478

Gower, J. C., & Dijksterhuis, G. B. (2004). *Procrustes problems.* https://doi.org/ DOI: 10.1093/acprof:oso/9780198510581.001.0001

Greenacre, M., Groenen, P. J. F., Hastie, T., Iodice D'Enza, A., Markos, A., & Tuzhilina, E. (2022). Principal component analysis. *Nature Reviews. Methods Primers, 2*, 100. DOI: 10.1038/s43586-022-00184-w

Greenacre, M. J., & Blasius, J. (2006). Multiple Correspondence Analysis and Related Methods. In *Chapman and Hall/CRC eBooks.* https://doi.org/DOI: 10.1201/9781420011319

Hair, J. F., Black, W. C., Babin, B. J., & Anderson, R. E. (2010). *Multivariate Data Analysis: A Global Perspective* (7th ed.). Pearson Education Inc.

Izenman, A. J. (2008). *Modern Multivariate Statistical Techniques: Regression, Classification, and Manifold Learning.* Springer., DOI: 10.1007/978-0-387-78189-1

Jansen, J. J., Hoefsloot, H. C. J., Van Der Greef, J., Timmerman, M. E., Westerhuis, J. A., & Smilde, A. K. (2005). ASCA: Analysis of multivariate data obtained from an experimental design. *Journal of Chemometrics, 19*(9), 469–481. DOI: 10.1002/cem.952

Jobson, J. D. (1992). *Applied multivariate data analysis: Volume II: Categorical and Multivariate methods*. Springer-Verlag.

Jolliffe, I. T. (2002). *Principal component analysis* (2nd ed.). Springer.

Jolliffe, I. T., & Cadima, J. (2016). Principal component analysis: A review and recent developments. *Phil Trans R Soc A, 374*(2065), 20150202. DOI: 10.1098/rsta.2015.0202 PMID: 26953178

Kaiser, H. F. (1958). The varimax criterion for analytic rotation in factor analysis. *Psychometrika, 23*, 187–200. DOI: 10.1007/BF02289233

Kalamartzis, I., Dordas, C., Georgiou, P., & Menexes, G. (2020). The Use of Appropriate Cultivar of Basil (Ocimum basilicum) Can Increase Water Use Efficiency under Water Stress. *Agronomy (Basel), 10*(1), 70. DOI: 10.3390/agronomy10010070

Karlis, D. (2005). *Multivariate Statistical Analysis*. Ath. Stamoulis Publications. (In Greek)

Kassambara, A. (2017). *Practical Guide to Cluster Analysis in R: Unsupervised Machine Learning* (Vol. 1). STHDA.

Kaufman, L., & Rousseeuw, L. (1990). *Finding Groups in Data. An Introduction to Cluster Analysis*. John Wiley & Sons.

Kaufman, L., & Rousseeuw, P. J. (2009). *Finding Groups in Data: An Introduction to Cluster Analysis*. John Wiley & Sons.

Kitchen, N. R., & Clay, S. A. (2016). Understanding and Identifying Variability. *Agronomy, Horticulture and Plant Science Faculty Publications. 69*. https://openprairie.sdstate.edu/plant_faculty_pubs/69

Kolda, T. G., & Bader, B. W. (2009). Tensor Decompositions and Applications. *SIAM Review, 51*, 455–500. DOI: 10.1137/07070111X

Kroonenberg, P. M. (2008). *Applied Multiway Data Analysis*. Wiley Series in Probability and Statistics.

Kyrana, Z., Pratsinakis, E. D., Papafilippou, N., Markos, A., Dordas, C., & Menexes, G. C. (2025). Evaluating dimensionality reduction strategies on mixed-type datasets: A comparative analysis using Python, R and SPSS. *International Journal of Sustainable Agricultural Management and Informatics, 11*(4), 445–469. DOI: 10.1504/IJSAMI.2024.10065202

Kyrana, Z., Pratsinakis, E. D., Papafilippou, N., Michaelidou, A. M., Kiranas, E., & Menexes, G. C. (2026). Dimensionality Reduction in Data Cubes With Independent Slices. In Anastasiadou, S., Chadjipadelis, T., Koutsoupias, N., Markos, A., & Menexes, G. (Eds.), *Modern International Developments in Data Analysis and Multivariate Statistical Analysis* (pp. 37–72). IGI Global Scientific Publishing., DOI: 10.4018/979-8-3693-9400-7.ch002

Lattin, J. M., Carroll, J. D., & Green, P. E. (2003). *Analyzing multivariate data.* Duxbury Press.

Linting, M., Meulman, J. J., Groenen, P. J., & Van der Koojj, A. J. (2007). Nonlinear principal components analysis: Introduction and application. *Psychological Methods, 12*(3), 336–358. DOI: 10.1037/1082-989X.12.3.336 PMID: 17784798

Mair, P. (2018). *Modern Psychometrics with R.* Springer International., DOI: 10.1007/978-3-319-93177-7

Markos, A., Moschidis, O., & Chadjipantelis, T. (2020). Sequential dimension reduction and clustering of mixed-type data. *Int. J. Data Analysis Techniques and Strategies, 12*(3), 228–246. DOI: 10.1504/IJDATS.2020.108043

Menexes, G. (2006). *Experimental Designs in Data Analysis.* Doctoral dissertation, University of Macedonia, Thessaloniki, Greece (in Greek).

Menexes, G., & Angelopoulos, S. (2008). Proposals for the financing and development of Greek farms based on a clustering method for categorical data. *EuroMed Journal of Business, 3*(3), 263–285. DOI: 10.1108/14502190810906437

Menexes, G., Markos, A., & Farmakis, N. (2012). *Convergence Index of Data Groups toward a Target Group: An Application to Energy Input–Output Data in Agroecosystems.* Data Analysis Bulletin. (In Greek)

Messaoud, R. B., Boussaïd, O., & Loudcher-Rabaseda, S. (2007). A Multiple Correspondence Analysis to Organize Data Cubes. *Frontiers in Artificial Intelligence and Applications, 155*(1), 133–146. https://halshs.archives-ouvertes.fr/halshs-00476483

Mothobi, N., Van Ryneveld, L., & Graham, M. A. (2021). A Cross-Country Comparison of Mathematics Teachers' Beliefs About Technology in Education. [IJICTE]. *International Journal of Information and Communication Technology Education, 17*(4), 1–13. DOI: 10.4018/IJICTE.20211001.oa13

Okasha, A. M., Deraz, N., Elmetwalli, A. H., Elsayed, S., Falah, M. W., Farooque, A. A., & Yaseen, Z. M. (2022). Effects of irrigation method and water flow rate on irrigation performance, soil salinity, yield, and water productivity of cauliflower. *Agriculture, 12*(8), 1164. DOI: 10.3390/agriculture12081164

Pagès, J. (2014). *Multiple Factor Analysis by Example Using R*. CRC Press.

Papafilippou, N., Kyrana, Z., Pratsinakis, E., Kiranas, E., Michailidou, A., Markos, A., & Menexes, G. (2025). Integrating Data Analysis Methods with Machine Learning Algorithms for Mixed Data Types: Does This Combination Improve Predictive Models' Accuracy? *Journal of Data Science and Intelligent Systems*. https://doi.org/ DOI: 10.47852/bonviewjdsis52023906

Pavoine, S., Blondel, J., Baguette, M., & Chessel, D. (2007). A new technique for ordering asymmetrical three-dimensional data sets in ecology. *Ecology, 88*(2), 512–523. DOI: 10.1890/05-1806 PMID: 17479768

Pizer, S. M., & Marron, J. (2017). Object statistics on curved manifolds. In Zheng, G., Li, S., & Székely, G. (Eds.), *Statistical Shape and Deformation Analysis* (pp. 137–164). Academic Press., DOI: 10.1016/b978-0-12-810493-4.00007-9

Pratsinakis, E. D., Ntoanidou, S., Polidoros, A., Dordas, C., Madesis, P., Eleftherohorinos, I., & Menexes, G. (2020). Comparison of hierarchical clustering methods for binary data from molecular markers. *International Journal of Data Analysis Techniques and Strategies, 12*(3), 190. DOI: 10.1504/ijdats.2020.108036

Rencher, A. C. (2002). *Methods of Multivariate Analysis* (2nd ed.). John Wiley & Sons.

Rotari, M., Diaz, V. F., De Ketelaere, B., & Kulahci, M. (2024). An extension of PARAFAC to analyze multi-group three-way data. *Chemometrics and Intelligent Laboratory Systems, 246*, 105089. DOI: 10.1016/j.chemolab.2024.105089

Saxena, A., Prasad, M., Gupta, A., Bharill, N., Patel, O. P., Tiwari, A., Er, M. J., Ding, W., & Lin, C. (2017). A review of clustering techniques and developments. *Neurocomputing, 267*, 664–681. DOI: 10.1016/j.neucom.2017.06.053

Searle, S. R. (1987). *Linear models for unbalanced data*. Wiley.

Sharma, S. (1996). *Applied Multivariate Techniques*. John Willey and Sons Inc.

Shashua, A., Zass, R., & Hazan, T. (2006). Multi-way clustering using Super-Symmetric non-negative tensor factorization. In Leonardis, A., Bischof, H., & Pinz, A. (Eds.), (pp. 595–608). Lecture notes in computer science. Springer., DOI: 10.1007/11744085_46

Shaukat, S. S., Rao, T. A., & Khan, M. A. (2016). Impact of sample size on principal component analysis ordination of an environmental data set: effects on eigenstructure. *Ochrana PríRody Slovenska/EkolóGia, 35*(2), 173–190. https://doi.org/DOI: 10.1515/eko-2016-0014

Sibson, R. (1978). Studies in the Robustness of Multidimensional Scaling: Procrustes Statistics. *Journal of the Royal Statistical Society. Series B, Statistical Methodology, 40*(2), 234–238. DOI: 10.1111/j.2517-6161.1978.tb01669.x

Smilde, B. J., Botman, E., de Ruiter, R. D., Smit, J. M., Teunissen, B. P., Lubbers, W. D., Schwarte, L. A., Schober, P., & Eekhoff, E. M. W. (2022). Monitoring and Management of Fibrodysplasia Ossificans Progressiva: Current Perspectives. *Orthopedic Research and Reviews, 14*, 113–120. DOI: 10.2147/ORR.S337491 PMID: 35480068

Sneath, P. H. A. (1957). The Application of Computers to Taxonomy. *Journal of General Microbiology, 17*, 201–226. DOI: 10.1099/00221287-17-1-201 PMID: 13475686

Sokal, R. R., & Michener, C. D. (1958). A Statistical Methods for Evaluating Relationships. *The University of Kansas Science Bulletin, 38*, 1409–1448.

Solo, V. (2019). Pearson Distance is not a Distance. *arXiv (Cornell University).* https://doi.org//arxiv.1908.06029DOI: 10.48550

Song, Y., Li, Y., & Qu, J. (2018). A new approach for supervised dimensionality reduction. *International Journal of Data Warehousing and Mining, 14*(4), 20–37. DOI: 10.4018/ijdwm.2018100102

Sørensen, T. (1948). A Method of Establishing Groups of Equal Amplitude in Plant Sociology Based on Similarity of Species Content and Its Application to Analyses of the Vegetation on Danish Commons. *Biologiske Skrifter/Kongelige Danske Videnskabernes Selskab, 5*, 1–34.

Srivastava, A., & Klassen, E. P. (2004). Bayesian and geometric subspace tracking. *Advances in Applied Probability, 36*(1), 43–56. DOI: 10.1239/aap/1077134463

Srivastava, A., & Klassen, E. P. (2016). Motivation for Function and Shape Analysis. In *Functional and Shape Data Analysis*. Springer., DOI: 10.1007/978-1-4939-4020-2_1

Suh, I., & Chung, Y. D. (2016). A Workload Assignment Strategy for Efficient ROLAP Data Cube Computation in Distributed Systems. *International Journal of Data Warehousing and Mining, 12*(3), 51–71. DOI: 10.4018/ijdwm.2016070104

Tabachnick, B. G., & Fidell, L. S. (2007). *Using Multivariate Statistics* (5th ed.). Allyn and Bacon/Pearson Education.

Tenenhaus, A., & Tenenhaus, M. (2014). Regularized generalized canonical correlation analysis for multiblock or multigroup data analysis. *European Journal of Operational Research, 238*(2), 391–403. DOI: 10.1016/j.ejor.2014.01.008

Thiel, M., Féraud, B., & Govaerts, B. (2017). ASCA+ and APCA+: Extensions of ASCA and APCA in the analysis of unbalanced multifactorial designs. *Journal of Chemometrics, 31*(6). Advance online publication. DOI: 10.1002/cem.2895

Timmerman, M. E., & Kiers, H. A. L. (2003). Four simultaneous component models for the analysis of multivariate time series from more than one subject to model intraindividual and interindividual differences. *Psychometrika, 68*(1), 105–121. DOI: 10.1007/BF02296656

Van de Velden, M., Iodice D'Enza, A., Markos, A., & Cavicchia, C. (2024). A general framework for implementing distances for categorical variables. *Pattern Recognition, 153*, 115547.

Vargas, M., Glaz, B., Alvarado, G., Pietragalla, J., Morgounov, A., Zelenskiy, Y., & Crossa, J. (2015). Analysis and interpretation of interactions in agricultural research. *Agronomy Journal, 107*(2), 748–762. DOI: 10.2134/agronj13.0405

Ward, J. H. (1963). Hierarchical grouping to optimize an objective function. *Journal of the American Statistical Association, 58*(301), 236–244. DOI: 10.1080/01621459.1963.10500845

Williams, J. D. (1972). Two-way fixed effects analysis of variance with disproportionate cell frequencies. *Multivariate Behavioral Research, 7*(1), 67–83. DOI: 10.1207/s15327906mbr0701_4 PMID: 26804962

Zetterberg, H., Smith, D. H., & Blennow, K. (2013). Biomarkers of mild traumatic brain injury in cerebrospinal fluid and blood. *Nature Reviews. Neurology, 9*(4), 201–210. DOI: 10.1038/nrneurol.2013.9 PMID: 23399646

Zheng, S., & Molina, C. G. (1998). An empirical comparison of arc-cosine distance, generalised Fisher ratio and normalised entropy criteria for model selection. *Neural Networks for Signal Processing VIII. Proceedings of the 1998 IEEE Signal Processing Society Workshop (Cat. No.98TH8378)*, 214–223. https://doi.org/DOI: 10.1109/NNSP.1998.710651

Zwanenburg, G., Hoefsloot, H. C., Westerhuis, J. A., Jansen, J. J., & Smilde, A. K. (2011). ANOVA–principal component analysis and ANOVA–simultaneous component analysis: A comparison. *Journal of Chemometrics*, *25*(10), 561–567. DOI: 10.1002/cem.1400

KEY TERMS AND DEFINITIONS

Concatenation: The transformation of data cubes with independent "slices" and "hyper-slices" into "stacked" data matrices.

Data cube: A p-dimensional data structure, where $p \geq 3$.

Four-dimensional data cube: A p-dimensional data structure, where $p=4$

Hyper-Slice: A submatrix of a data cube.

Multidimensional: A dataset with multiple dimensions.

Multi-group: A dataset consisting of independent groups, where each group is described by the same set of variables, but contains different objects (sampling/ experimental units)

Slice: A sub-submatrix of a data cube.

Variability: Heterogeneity of the data.

Chapter 6
Comparison of Dimensionality Reduction Methods and Strategies in Mixed-Type Data From the Healthcare Field

Emmanouil D. Pratsinakis
http://orcid.org/0000-0002-3725-3525
School of Agriculture, Institute of Applied Biosciences Centre for Research and Technology, Aristotle University of Thessaloniki, Greece

Zacharenia Kyrana
http://orcid.org/0000-0001-9269-0675
School of Agriculture, Aristotle University of Thessaloniki, Greece

Nikolaos Papafilippou
http://orcid.org/0009-0003-3148-7229
School of Agriculture, Aristotle University of Thessaloniki, Greece

Christos Dordas
http://orcid.org/0000-0002-7027-474X
School of Agriculture, Aristotle University of Thessaloniki, Greece

George Menexes
http://orcid.org/0000-0002-1034-7345
School of Agriculture, Aristotle University of Thessaloniki, Greece

DOI: 10.4018/979-8-3373-6926-6.ch006

ABSTRACT

Mixed-type data consists of a mix of both scale and categorical data within the same dataset. Analyzing mixed-type data presents unique challenges because traditional statistical methods often require variables to be of the same type. Thus, special techniques and strategies are needed to handle and analyze mixed-type data effectively. One of these strategies refers to the encoding of variables. One approach, advocated by the Dutch School of Data Analysis (GIFI System), suggests transforming categorical data into scale data to address this issue. Conversely, the French School of Data Analysis proposes converting scale data into categorical. However, these transformations may result in a loss of original data information. The aim of this study is to compare various encoding strategies to be used simultaneously in the same dimensionality reduction analysis, at the same dataset, to highlight the importance of applying different strategies of encoding data until a satisfactory solution of dimensionality reduction is found or the validity of the results is reinforced.

INTRODUCTION

Mixed-type datasets (or mixed data) combine different variable types. These types of data most commonly include categorical (ordinal and nominal) and scale (continuous) (Costa et al., 2023; Ebrahimi Warkiani & Moattar, 2025; Kyrana et al., 2024; Markos et al., 2020; Moschidis et al., 2023; Papafilippou et al., 2025; Pratsinakis et al., 2025; Singh & Singh, 2024). Nominal variables are qualitative or discrete variables that are divided into distinct categories or groups. Scale variables are continuous and can take an infinite number of values within a range. Ordinal variables have internal order and are differentiated from scale data because they lack a consistent scale. The majority of datasets are used across various scientific disciplines, including Biology, Social Sciences, Economics, and Health Sciences. (Ahmad & Dey, 2007; Ahmad & Khan, 2019; Ebrahimi Warkiani & Moattar, 2025; Hennig & Liao, 2013; Morlini & Zani, 2010), are mixed data where scale, nominal, and ordinal data can be found simultaneously (Grané et al., 2021; Kuo & Wang, 2022).

Analyzing mixed-type datasets within the same multivariate, multidimensional analysis is challenging because of the heterogeneity of data types. To address this issue and ensure that the datasets are homogeneous, two approaches were proposed: the first one from the Dutch School's Gifi System that employs optimal scaling to quantify categorical variables (van Rijckevorsel & de Leeuw, 1988; Young, 1981), and the second one from the French School that employs the transforms of quantitative variables into categories (Pagès, 2004; Papadimitriou, 1994). Both proposals scope to address the challenge of simultaneously analyzing the three data types

(Markos et al., 2020; Pagès, 2004). However, converting these datasets may result in one that has less information compared to the original dataset. (Kyrana et al., 2024; Menexes, 2006; Papafilippou et al., 2025).

Dimensionality reduction techniques transform high-dimensional datasets into a lower-dimensional space while preserving most of the structure. Their primary objective is to reduce the number of variables in a dataset (Kyrana et al., 2025; Papafilippou et al., 2025; Sharma, 1996). However, these methods also come with inherent disadvantages, such as the "curse of dimensionality" (Kyrana et al., 2024, 2025; Nguyen & Holmes, 2019; Papafilippou et al., 2025), challenges in determining the number of significant dimensions, high computational requirements (Kyrana et al., 2024), and issues with handling missing values, outliers, and extreme values, as well as difficulties in visualizing the results (Hair et al., 2010; Menexes, 2006). Dimensionality reduction techniques are used as a preliminary step in data preprocessing at various statistical analyses, for example classification, regression, clustering, or feature extraction in Machine Learning and can be achieved through both linear and nonlinear methods (Castillo-Girones et al., 2025; Deng et al., 2025; Li et al., 2024; Madoune et al., 2025; Markos et al., 2020; Muyama et al., 2024; Orsenigo & Vercellis, 2012; Papafilippou et al., 2026; Pratsinakis et al., 2025; Wang et al., 2020; Yao et al., 2023; Zeng et al., 2023). Dimensionality reduction methods aim to provide a more compact representation of the original dataset, reduced in "volume" while preserving essential and informative content (Kyrana et al., 2024; Sharma, 1996).

The main objective of this study is to compare the results of six dimensionality reduction techniques by applying the same encoding strategies to the same dataset, using methods appropriate for dimensionality reduction and for the measurement scales of the input variables. The focus is primarily on the components and structure of the observed variability (inertia) in the measured variables (characteristics, features). From a different perspective, dimensionality reduction methods are essential for identifying meaningful patterns and decreasing computational complexity in subsequent statistical analyses, such as model-based approaches or machine learning techniques. This study emphasizes the significance of using various data encoding strategies for reducing the dimensions of mixed-type data until an effective and interpretable solution is achieved. Overall, it is preferable to focus on specific analytical strategies rather than relying on a single "global" dimensionality reduction method.

MATERIALS AND METHODS

The dimensionality reduction techniques used in this study are the Multiple Correspondence Analysis (MCA), the Categorical Principal Component Analysis

(CATPCA), the Principal Component Analysis (PCA), the Multiple Factor Analysis (MFA), the Factor Analysis for Mixed Data (FAMD), and the Non-Linear Canonical Correlation Analysis (NLCCA), used with different analytical strategies. The strategies used depend on the type of data, nominal, ordinal, and/or scale, and mainly on the researcher's willingness on how the variables should be handled (nominal, ordinal, scale) in a specific scientific frame (Gifi, 1990). Note that in some strategies, ordinal data are considered as "quasi scale" variables with equal distance intervals, Factor Analysis can be used also instead of PCA, and that in some strategies all variables are considered as one group, and in others, the variables were split into groups (multi-block) according to their type. In addition, continuous variables are categorized into five classes, each one in 4 cut points (20% of cases in each class), and so transformed into ordinal variables.

Analyses are conducted using eight different strategies:

- Strategy 1: After transforming scale variables to ordinal, treat all variables as nominal and perform MCA.
- Strategy 2: Perform CATPCA to the raw data (nominal, ordinal, scale).
- Strategy 3: After transforming scale variables to ordinal, treat variables as nominal and ordinal and perform MCA, considering all of them as nominal, (Strategy 3.1) or CATPCA (Strategy 3.2) on nominal and ordinal variables.
- Strategy 4: Perform MFA (Strategy 4.1) or FAMD (Strategy 4.2) to the nominal (consider the ordinal as nominal too) and scale variables.
- Strategy 5: After transforming scale variables to ordinal, treat variables as nominal and ordinal and perform NLCCA.
- Strategy 6: After transforming scale variables to ordinal perform MCA on nominal variables (group or block 1) and CATPCA or PCA on ordinal variables (group or block 2) and divide the columns of the corresponding 0-1 (each categorical variable with m modalities is transformed into a set of m binary variables coded 0 or 1) logical matrix of nominal variables by the square root of the maximum eigenvalue of MCA and the original coded values of ordinal variables by the square root of the maximum eigenvalue of CATPCA. This division balances the influence of variable blocks variability. Finally, apply PCA to the transformed data.
- Strategy 7: After transforming scale variables to ordinal perform MCA on nominal and CATPCA on ordinal variables and replace original values with optimal quantified values of the first MCA and CATPCA axis, respectively. Finally, apply PCA to the quantified data.
- Strategy 8: After transforming scale variables to ordinal perform divide the columns of the corresponding 0-1 logical matrix of nominal variables by the square root of the probability of each category (group or block 1) and perform

CATPCA on ordinal variables (group or block 2) and divide the original coded values of ordinal variables by the square root of the maximum eigenvalue of CATPCA. Finally, apply PCA to the transformed data.

THE DIMENSIONALITY REDUCTION TECHNIQUES USED

Principal Component Analysis (PCA)

PCA is designed for continuous (quantitative) variables and is used to derive principal components by considering the correlation between these variables (Tauro et al., 2022). PCA is less suitable for categorical data, as it assumes linear relationships and continuous measurement scales (Belaïd et al., 2021; Choi et al., 2023; Tauro et al., 2022).

Multiple Correspondence Analysis (MCA)

MCA is an extension of correspondence analysis for more than two categorical variables and is the equivalent of PCA for categorical data (Belaïd et al., 2021; Chauvin et al., 2013; Choi et al., 2023; Golob & Hensher, 2007; Greenacre, 2010; Roccetti et al., 2021; Sicsic et al., 2012; Tauro et al., 2022; Van Ness et al., 2012). MCA detects structures and patterns of association among variables by representing data as points in a low-dimensional Euclidean space (Belaïd et al., 2021; Chauvin et al., 2013; Golob & Hensher, 2007; Greenacre, 2010). MCA is not suitable for continuous variables and is best applied when all variables are categorical (Sicsic et al., 2012; Tauro et al., 2022).

Categorical Principal Component Analysis (CATPCA)

CATPCA is a variant of PCA for categorical data (Magkanas et al., 2023; Tauro et al., 2022). CATPCA reduces dimensionality by projecting data onto a low-dimensional plane without assuming linear relationships among variables (Roccetti et al., 2021). CATPCA and MCA are used for categorical data, but CATPCA can handle nonlinear relationships (Roccetti et al., 2021). CATPCA is suitable when the dataset is mostly categorical (Roccetti et al., 2021; Tauro et al., 2022).

Multiple Factor Analysis (MFA)

MFA combines PCA and correspondence analysis to analyze mixed data, taking into account dimensionality (Magkanas et al., 2023). MFA is suitable for datasets with both categorical and scale variables, allowing for the simultaneous study of both types (Magkanas et al., 2023; Tauro et al., 2022). MFA is similar to FAMD in its ability to handle mixed data (Magkanas et al., 2023).

Factor Analysis for Mixed Data (FAMD)

For datasets containing both scale and categorical variables, FAMD is used (Magkanas et al., 2023; Tauro et al., 2022). FAMD combines PCA for scale data and MCA for categorical data. MCA projecting data onto orthogonal dimensions to maximize the variability (Magkanas et al., 2023; Tauro et al., 2022). MCA used correlation coefficients for the scale variables and squared correlation ratios for the categorical variables to extract dimensions that best illustrate the data structure (Magkanas et al., 2023; Tauro et al., 2022). FAMD is recommended when both types of variables are present and need to be analyzed together (Magkanas et al., 2023; Tauro et al., 2022).

Non-Linear Canonical Correlation Analysis (NLCCA)

To analyze mixed data without assuming linearity NLCCA can be used. NLCCA exploring relationships between sets of variables and is suitable for mixed data (Theodosiou et al., 2008).

To conclude, PCA is suitable for scale data, MCA and CATPCA for categorical data, and FAMD, MFA, and NLCCA for mixed data, FAMD and MFA were the most suited for simultaneous analysis of both categorical and scale variables.

DATASET

A simulated dataset is used throughout the analyses. 192 patients and 15 variables: four (4) nominal binary variables (diabetes, hypertension, smoking, gender), one (1) nominal (drug groups with three different drug types), three (3) ordinal (alcohol consumption with three ordered categories, health condition with four ordered categories and severity index with four ordered categories), and six (6) continuous variables (three blood indexes and three biochemical indexes). Data analyses were performed with IBM SPSS Statistics v.26.0 and R v.4.3.0.

RESULTS

Strategy 1 and Strategy 3.1: Every Variable in the Dataset is Treated as Nominal

In those strategies, all variables are treated as nominal (after transforming scale variables to ordinal), and MCA is performed. The results show that the first two dimensions explained 15% of the total inertia without correction. Severity index, Blood index 2, and Blood index 3 have the main contribution to Dimension 1, and Biochemical index 1, Biochemical index 2, and Biochemical index 3 have the main contribution to Dimension 2 (see Table 1 and Figure 1).

Table 1. MCA discrimination indices for Dimensions 1 and 2.

Discrimination indices		
	Dimension	
	1	2
Drug Type	0.027	0.006
Health Condition	0.004	0.023
Severity Index	0.588	0.087
Sex	0.029	0.075
Smoking	0.042	0.174
Alcohol consumption	0.005	0.119
Diabetes	0.006	0.003
Hypertension	0.000	0.256
Age	0.095	0.050
Blood Index 1	0.187	0.091
Blood Index 2	0.541	0.308
Blood Index 3	0.553	0.023
Biochemical Index 1	0.023	0.511
Biochemical Index 2	0.387	0.618
Biochemical Index 3	0.440	0.511

Figure 1. MCA loadings plot, factorial plane 1×2. (DT: Drug Type, HC: Health Condition, SI: Severity Index, Db: Diabetes, Hp: Hypertension, BI1: Blood Index 1, BI2: Blood Index 2, BI3: Blood Index 3, BC1: Biochemical Index 1, BC2: Biochemical Index 2, BC3: Biochemical Index 3).

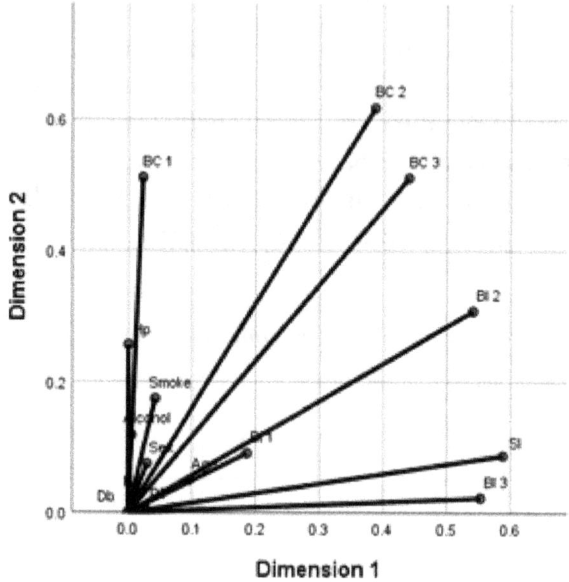

Strategy 2: Perform Analysis on the Raw Data

In this strategy, the raw data are analyzed by performing CATPCA. The results show that the first two dimensions accounted for 32.6% of the total inertia. Biochemical index 1, Biochemical index 2, and Biochemical index 3 have the main contribution to Dimension 1 and Severity index, Blood index 3, and Blood index 1 have the main contribution to Dimension 2 (see Table 2 and Figure 2).

Figure 2. CATPCA on raw data loadings plot, factorial plane 1×2. (DT: Drug Type, HC: Health Condition, SI: Severity Index, Db: Diabetes, Hp: Hypertension, BI1: Blood Index 1, BI2: Blood Index 2, BI3: Blood Index 3, BC1: Biochemical Index 1, BC2: Biochemical Index 2, BC3: Biochemical Index 3).

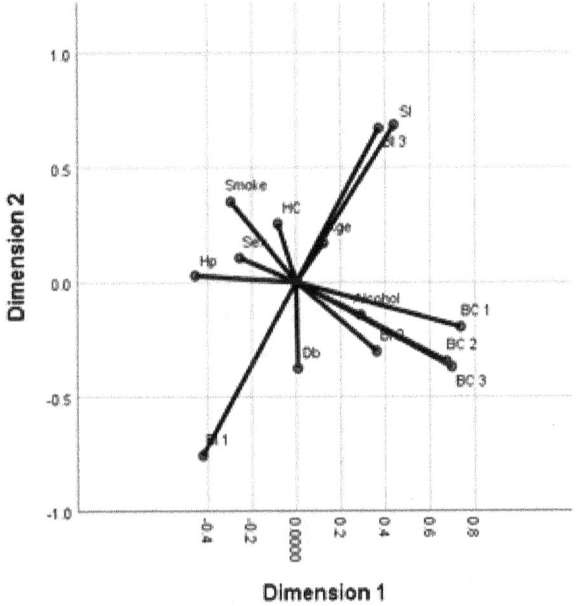

Table 2. CATPCA on raw data discrimination indices for Dimensions 1 and 2.

Discrimination indices		
	Dimension	
	1	**2**
Health Condition	-0.082	0.255
Severity Index	0.440	0.686
Age	0.121	0.170
Sex	-0.254	0.106
Smoke	-0.294	0.351
Alcohol	0.289	-0.145
Diabetes	0.006	-0.376
Hypertension	-0.454	0.029
Blood Index 1	-0.421	-0.758
Blood Index 2	0.361	-0.303

continued on following page

Table 2. Continued

Discrimination indices		
	Dimension	
	1	**2**
Blood Index 3	0.370	0.672
Biochemical Index 1	0.737	-0.197
Biochemical Index 2	0.674	-0.346
Biochemical Index 3	0.698	-0.371
Drug Type	-0.151	-0.434

Strategy 3.2: Transform Scale Variables to Ordinal and Perform Analyses on Nominal and Ordinal Data

In this strategy, all variables are treated as nominal and ordinal (after transforming scale variables to ordinal), and a CATPCA is performed on nominal and ordinal variables. The results showed that the first two dimensions explained 34.63% of the total inertia. Biochemical index 1, Biochemical index 2, and Biochemical index 3 have the main contribution to Dimension 1 and Severity index, Blood index 1, and Blood index 3 have the main contribution to Dimension 2 (see Table 3 and Figure 3).

Figure 3. CATPCA on nominal and ordinal data loadings plot, factorial plane 1×2. (DT: Drug Type, HC: Health Condition, SI: Severity Index, Db: Diabetes, Hp: Hypertension, BI1: Blood Index 1, BI2: Blood Index 2, BI3: Blood Index 3, BC1: Biochemical Index 1, BC2: Biochemical Index 2, BC3: Biochemical Index 3).

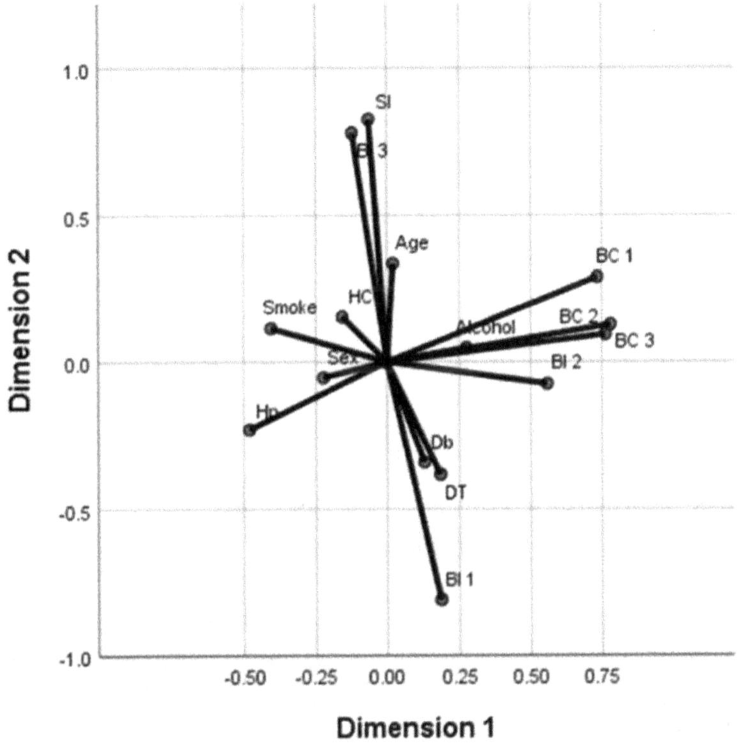

Table 3. CATPCA on nominal and ordinal data discrimination indices for Dimensions 1 and 2.

Discrimination indices		
	Dimension	
	1	**2**
Health Condition	-0.156	0.153
Severity Index	-0.063	0.826
Sex	-0.223	-0.053
Smoke	-0.406	0.114
Alcohol	0.276	0.048

continued on following page

Table 3. Continued

Discrimination indices		
	Dimension	
	1	**2**
Diabetes	0.129	-0.341
Hypertension	-0.480	-0.229
Drug Type	0.184	-0.384
Age	0.021	0.335
Blood Index 1	0.186	-0.810
Blood Index 2	0.557	-0.075
Blood Index 3	-0.121	0.780
Biochemical Index 1	0.734	0.288
Biochemical Index 2	0.763	0.093
Biochemical Index 3	0.781	0.127

Strategy 4: Nominal (Consider the Ordinal as Nominal Too) and Scale Data

In Strategy 4.1, the variables are treated as nominal (considering ordinal data nominal as well) and scale, and an MFA is performed. The results show that the first two dimensions explained 32.2% of the total inertia. Biochemical index 1, Biochemical index 2, Biochemical index 3, hypertension, smoking, alcohol, Severity index, and Blood index 1 have the main contribution to Dimension 1, and Severity index, Blood index 1, Blood index 3, Diabetes, Smoking, and Drug type have the main contribution to Dimension 2 (see Figure 4).

Figure 4. MFA loadings plot, factorial plane 1×2, and contribution plots for variables. (A1: Blood Index 1, A2: Blood Index 2, A3: Blood Index 3, B1: Biochemical Index 1, B2: Biochemical Index 2, B3: Biochemical Index 3)

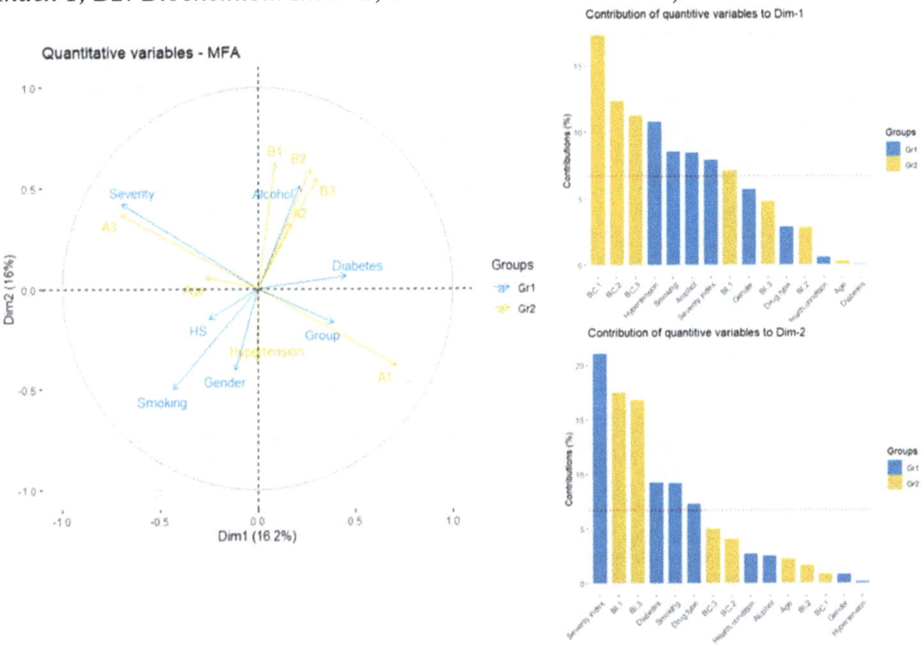

In Strategy 4.2, variables are treated as nominal (consider the ordinal as nominal too) and scale, and FAMD is performed. The results show that the first two dimensions explained 24.5% of the total inertia. Biochemical index 1, Biochemical index 2, Biochemical index 3, Blood index 1 have the main contribution to Dimension 1, and Severity index, Blood index 1, Blood index 3, Drug type have the main contribution to Dimension 2 (see Figure 5).

Figure 5. FAMD loadings plot, factorial plane 1×2, and contribution plots for variables.

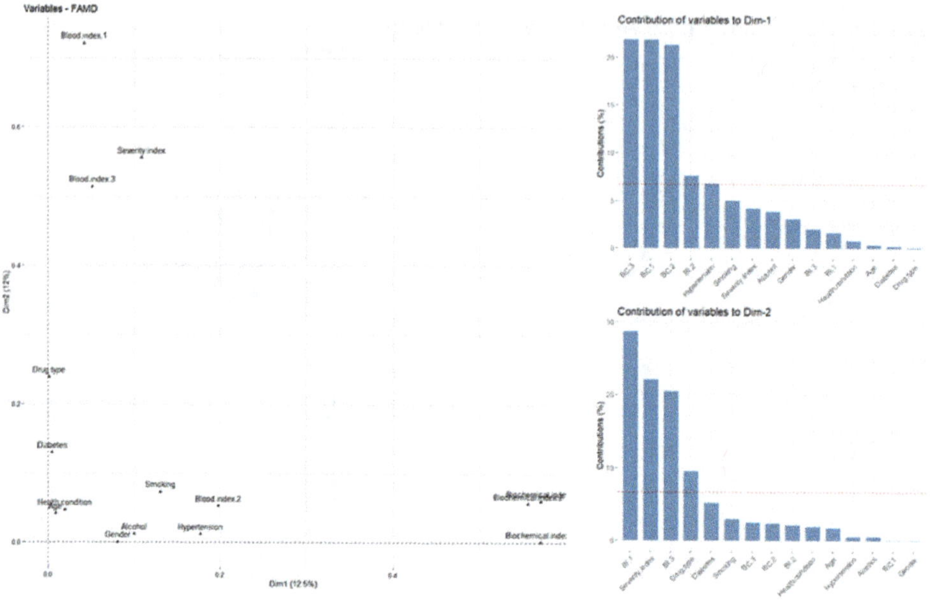

Strategy 5: Nominal and Ordinal (After Transforming Scale Variables to Ordinal) Data

In this Strategy, data are treated as nominal and ordinal (after transforming scale variables to ordinal), and Non-Linear Canonical Correlation Analysis NLCCA is performed. The model identified a connection or correlation between the variables indicated by the eigenvalues and the high fit too (see Table 4). Blood index 1, Diabetes, and Severity index have the main contribution to Dimension 1, and Alcohol, Biochemical index 2, and Smoking have the main contribution to Dimension 2 (see Table 5 and Figure 6).

Table 4. NLCCA model summary

Summary of Analysis				
		Dimension		
		1	2	Sum
Loss	Set 1	0.072	0.123	0.195
	Set 2	0.072	0.123	0.195
	Mean	0.072	0.123	0.195
Eigenvalue		0.928	0.877	
Fit				1.805

Figure 6. NLCCA loadings plot, factorial plane 1×2. (DT: Drug Type, HC: Health Condition, SI: Severity Index, Db: Diabetes, Hp: Hypertension, BI1: Blood Index 1, BI2: Blood Index 2, BI3: Blood Index 3, BC1: Biochemical Index 1, BC2: Biochemical Index 2, BC3: Biochemical Index 3).

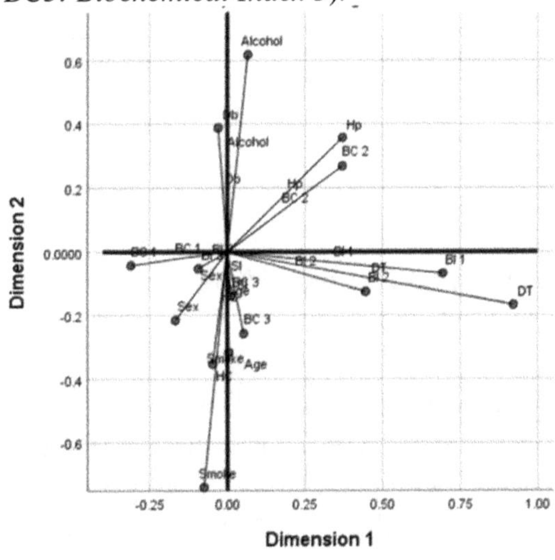

Table 5. NLCCA variable contributions (loadings) for Dimensions 1 and 2

Multiple fit			
		Dimension	
Set		1	2
1	Health Condition	0.009	0.173
	Severity Index	0.273	0.088
	Alcohol	0.011	0.290
	Age	0.002	0.057
	Blood Index 1	0.566	0.117
	Blood Index 2	0.132	0.004
	Blood Index 3	0.022	0.004
	Biochemical index 1	0.113	0.018
	Biochemical index 2	0.106	0.261
	Biochemical index 3	0.005	0.154
2	Drug Type	0.808	0.069
	Sex	0.037	0.005
	Smoke	0.012	0.539
	Diabetes	0.005	0.077
	Hypertension	0.024	0.238

Strategy 7: Nominal and Ordinal (After Transforming Scale Variables to Ordinal) Data

In this strategy, data are treated as nominal and ordinal (after transforming scale variables to ordinal), perform MCA on nominal and CATPCA on ordinal variables, and replace original values with optimal quantified values of the first MCA and CATPCA axis, respectively. Finally, apply PCA to quantified data. The results show that the first two dimensions explained 33.03% of the total inertia. Biochemical index 1, Biochemical index 2, Biochemical index 3, and Blood index 2 have the main contribution to Dimension 1, and Blood index 1, Drug type, and hypertension have the main contribution to Dimension 2 (see Table 6 and Figure 7)

Figure 7. PCA on the quantified data loadings plot, factorial plane 1×2. (Group_MCA: Drug Type, HC_CATPCA: Health Condition, Smoke_MCA: Smoking, Alcohol_CATPCA: Alcohol, Gender_MCA: Gender, Age_CATPCA: Age, Db_MCA: Diabetes, Hp_MCA: Hypertension, BI1_CATPCA: Blood Index 1, BI2_CATPCA: Blood Index 2, BI3_CATPCA: Blood Index 3, BC1_CATPCA: Biochemical Index 1, BC2_CATPCA: Biochemical Index 2, BC3_CATPCA: Biochemical Index 3).

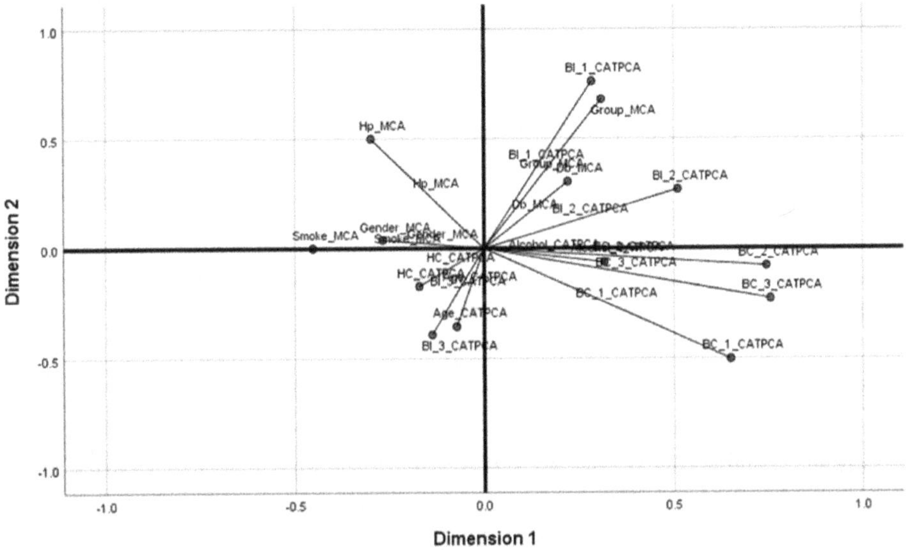

Table 6. PCA on the quantified data discrimination indices for Dimensions 1 and 2. Only discrimination indices greater than 0.5 are presented.

Discrimination indices		
	Dimension	
	1	2
Biochemical index 3	0.753	
Biochemical index 2	0.742	
Biochemical index 1	0.648	
Blood index 2	0.510	
Smoking		
Alcohol		
Gender		
Blood index 1		0.761

continued on following page

Table 6. Continued

Discrimination indices		
	Dimension	
	1	2
Drug Type		0.679
Hp_MCA		0.500
Blood index 3		
Age		
Diabetes		
Health Condition		

Strategy 8: Nominal and Ordinal (After Transforming Scale Variables to Ordinal) Data

In this strategy, data are treated as nominal and ordinal (after transforming scale variables to ordinal) divide the columns of the corresponding 0-1 of logical matrix of nominal variables by the square root of the probability of each category (group or block 1), perform CATPCA on ordinal variables (group or block 2) and divide the original coded values of ordinal variables by the square root of the maximum eigenvalue of CATPCA. Finally, apply PCA to the transformed data. The results show that the first two dimensions explained 30.96% of the total inertia. Smoking and Biochemical index 1 have the main contribution to Dimension 1 and Hypertension (yes or no), Blood index 1, Drug B, and Placebo drug have the main contribution to Dimension 2 (see Table 7 and Figure 8)

Table 7. PCA on the transformed data discrimination indices for Dimensions 1 and 2. Only discrimination indices greater than 0.5 are presented.

Discrimination indices		
	Dimension	
	1	2
Smoker	-0.759	
Non smoker	0.759	
Alcohol	0.516	
Biochemical index 3		
Biochemical index 1		

continued on following page

Table 7. Continued

Discrimination indices		
	Dimension	
	1	2
Female		
Male		
Biochemical index 2		
Health condition		
Drug A		
Blood index 1		-0.717
Drug_B		-0.586
No Hypertension		0.584
Hypertension		-0.584
Placebo		0.581
Diabetes		
No Diabetes		
Blood index 3		
Severity Index		
Age		
Blood index 2		

Figure 8. Principal Component Analysis (PCA) on the transformed data loadings plot, factorial plane 1×2. (Drug_A_prob, Drug_B_prob, and Plac_prob: Drug type, HC_CATPCA: Health Condition, Smoke_yes_prob and Smoke_no_prob: Smoking, Alcohol_CATPCA: Alcohol, Male_prob and Female_prob: Gender, Age_CATPCA: Age, Hp_yes_prob and Hp_no_prob: Hypertension, Db_yes_prob and Db_no_prob: Diabetes, BI1_CATPCA: Blood Index 1, BI2_CATPCA: Blood Index 2, BI3_CATPCA: Blood Index 3, BC1_CATPCA: Biochemical Index 1, BC2_CATPCA: Biochemical Index 2, BC3_CATPCA: Biochemical Index 3).

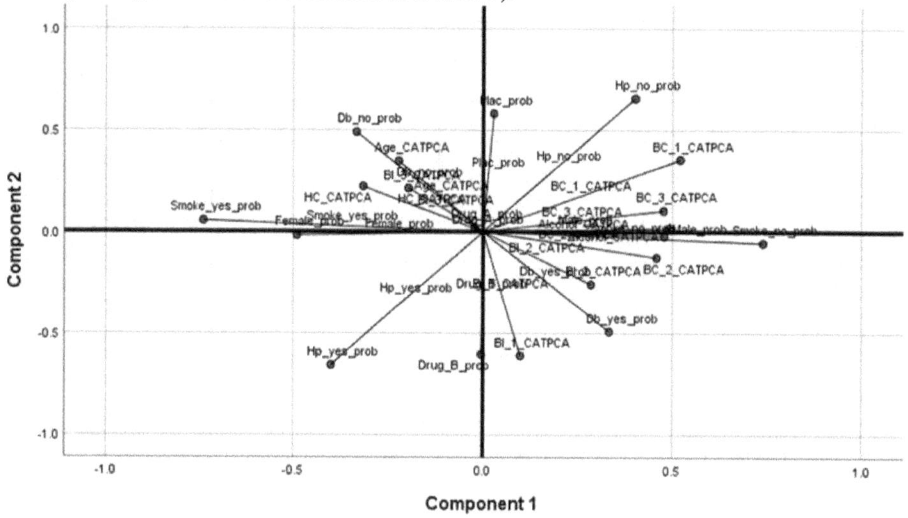

DISCUSSION

The analyses highlight various strategies for dimensionality reduction of mixed-type datasets, depending on the coding and measurement scales of the input variables. However, the results are different according to the analysis strategy, highlighting once again that, when dealing with mixed-type datasets, the "true" structure of variability reflects the analyses performed on the data. Although data remained constant across all tests, the eight strategies gave diverse results of the dataset's principal components, confirming that the choice of encoding and measurement scale is crucial in dimensionality reduction techniques.

In terms of results, Strategies 1, 2, 3.1, 3.2, and 4.2 show a common structure of variability but at different dimensions. Additionally, results from Strategy 5 show a common structure of variability with those from Strategy 6. Results from Strategies 7 and 8 had a different structure from those of any other strategy. Results from Strategy 4.1 had a completely different structure from those of the others and included more variables. The three blood indices and three biochemical indices were significant across nearly all Strategies, indicating that physiological markers had the most significant influence on the patient. Furthermore, clinical indicators such as the Severity Index, Drug Type, and Hypertension were important in defining patient profiles. Lifestyle factors, specifically alcohol consumption and smoking status also contributed significantly, particularly in strategies that prioritized non-linear associations. These structural similarities and differences are further reflected in the explanatory power of each method. Specifically, Strategies 1 and 3.1 (MCA) explained the lowest percentage of total inertia, the use of CATPCA in Strategies 2 and 3.2 explained the highest percentage of total inertia among all approaches. For mixed-type data, MFA (Strategy 4.1) and FAMD (Strategy 4.2) explained 32.2% and 24.5% of the inertia, respectively. Meanwhile, the PCA variations used in Strategies 6, 7, and 8 explained between 30% and 33% of total inertia. Finally, the high fit and eigenvalues in Strategy 5 confirm that the NLCCA model effectively captured the underlying correlations between the analyzed variables. Overall, strategies that use the same dimensionality reduction techniques return similar results.

The challenges highlighted by the study's results suggest that relying on a single dimensionality-reduction technique is insufficient for complex, mixed-type datasets. The study indicates that it is wiser to apply different analysis strategies depending on the objectives of the research and the researcher's willingness on how the variables should be handled (nominal, ordinal, scale) in a specific scientific frame because the proposed strategies provide more and sometimes different insights into the structure of variability.

In addition, Papafilippou et al. (2026) have employed dimensionality reduction methods on mixed data as a preparatory step before applying machine learning algorithms, also known as "data preprocessing". This methodological approach brings together exploratory data analysis and dimensionality reduction. The study utilizes techniques such as PCA and other multivariate methods to prepare the data before applying machine learning algorithms. The purpose of these methods is to reduce dimensionality, improve interpretability, and enhance the predictive accuracy of the machine learning models used in the subsequent analyses.

CONCLUSION

The general conclusion of the proposed categorical data analysis methodology is that the choice of an appropriate dimension-reduction strategy depends mainly on the nature of the data and the research objectives. The analysis showed that there is no "universally" best method, but instead that the use of different approaches provides more and, often, other information about the structure of variability in the data. Researchers must compare various encoding strategies—considering variables as nominal, ordinal, or scale—until a solution is found that is both statistically satisfactory and scientifically interpretable.

COMPETING INTERESTS

The authors of this publication declare there are no competing interests.

FUNDING

This research received no specific grant from any funding agency in the public, commercial, or not-for-profit sectors. Funding for this research was covered by the author(s) of the article.

REFERENCES

Ahmad, A., & Dey, L. (2007). A k-mean clustering algorithm for mixed numeric and categorical data. *Data and Knowledge Engineering, 63*(2), 503–527. *Scopus.* Advance online publication. DOI: 10.1016/j.datak.2007.03.016

Ahmad, A., & Khan, S. S. (2019). Survey of State-of-the-Art Mixed Data Clustering Algorithms. *IEEE Access, 7*, 31883–31902. *Scopus.* Advance online publication. DOI: 10.1109/ACCESS.2019.2903568

Belaïd, F., Ranjbar, Z., & Massié, C. (2021). Exploring the cost-effectiveness of energy efficiency implementation measures in the residential sector. *Energy Policy, 150*, 112122. DOI: 10.1016/j.enpol.2020.112122

Castillo-Girones, S., Munera, S., Martínez-Sober, M., Blasco, J., Cubero, S., & Gómez-Sanchis, J. (2025). Artificial Neural Networks in Agriculture, the core of artificial intelligence: What, When, and Why. *Computers and Electronics in Agriculture, 230*, 109938. DOI: 10.1016/j.compag.2025.109938

Chauvin, C., Lardjane, S., Morel, G., Clostermann, J.-P., & Langard, B. (2013). Human and organisational factors in maritime accidents: Analysis of collisions at sea using the HFACS. *Accident; Analysis and Prevention, 59*, 26–37. DOI: 10.1016/j.aap.2013.05.006 PMID: 23764875

Choi, Y., Choi, B. Y., Kim, S. I., Choi, J., Kim, J., Park, B. Y., Kim, S. M., Kim, S.-W., Choi, J. Y., Song, J. Y., Kim, Y. J., Kim, H. Y., Lee, J.-S., Kim, J. H., Jun, Y. H., Lee, M., & Seong, J. (2023). Effect of characteristics on the clinical course at the initiation of treatment for human immunodeficiency virus infection using dimensionality reduction. *Scientific Reports, 13*(1), 5547. DOI: 10.1038/s41598-023-31916-x PMID: 37016006

Costa, E., Papatsouma, I., & Markos, A. (2023). Benchmarking distance-based partitioning methods for mixed-type data. *Advances in Data Analysis and Classification, 17*(3), 701–724. DOI: 10.1007/s11634-022-00521-7

Deng, Z., Li, T., Zhang, P., Liu, K., Yuan, Z., & Deng, D. (2025). Feature selection for label distribution learning based on neighborhood fuzzy rough sets. *Applied Soft Computing, 169*, 112542. DOI: 10.1016/j.asoc.2024.112542

Ebrahimi Warkiani, M., & Moattar, M. H. (2025). A comprehensive survey on recent feature selection methods for mixed data: Challenges, solutions and future directions. *Neurocomputing, 623*, 129372. DOI: 10.1016/j.neucom.2025.129372

Gifi, A. (1990). *Nonlinear Multivariate Analysis*. Wiley.

Golob, T. F., & Hensher, D. A. (2007). The trip chaining activity of Sydney residents: A cross-section assessment by age group with a focus on seniors. *Journal of Transport Geography, 15*(4), 298–312. DOI: 10.1016/j.jtrangeo.2006.09.005

Grané, A., Salini, S., & Verdolini, E. (2021). Robust multivariate analysis for mixed-type data: Novel algorithm and its practical application in socio-economic research. *Socio-Economic Planning Sciences. Statistical Methods & Models for the Evaluation Systems of the Public Sector, 73*, 100907. DOI: 10.1016/j.seps.2020.100907

Greenacre, M. (2010). Correspondence Analysis. In Peterson, P., Baker, E., & McGaw, B. (Eds.), *International Encyclopedia of Education* (3rd ed., pp. 103–111). Elsevier., DOI: 10.1016/B978-0-08-044894-7.01317-8

Hair, J. F., Black, W. C., Babin, B. J., & Anderson, R. E. (2010). *Multivariate Data Analysis: A Global Perspective* (7th ed.). Pearson Education Inc.

Hennig, C., & Liao, T. F. (2013). How to find an appropriate clustering for mixed-type variables with application to socio-economic stratification. *Journal of the Royal Statistical Society. Series C: Applied Statistics, 62*(3), 309–369. *Scopus*. Advance online publication. DOI: 10.1111/j.1467-9876.2012.01066.x

Kuo, T., & Wang, K.-J. (2022). A hybrid *k*-prototypes clustering approach with improved sine-cosine algorithm for mixed-data classification. *Computers & Industrial Engineering, 169*, 108164. DOI: 10.1016/j.cie.2022.108164

Kyrana, Z., Pratsinakis, E. D., Papafilippou, N., Markos, A., Dordas, C., & Menexes, G. C. (2024). Evaluating dimensionality reduction strategies on mixed-type datasets: A comparative analysis using Python, R and SPSS. *International Journal of Sustainable Agricultural Management and Informatics, 1*(1), 10065202. DOI: 10.1504/IJSAMI.2024.10065202

Kyrana, Z., Pratsinakis, E. D., Papafilippou, N., Markos, A., Dordas, C., & Menexes, G. C. (2025). Evaluating dimensionality reduction strategies on mixed-type datasets: A comparative analysis using Python, R and SPSS. *International Journal of Sustainable Agricultural Management and Informatics, 11*(4), 445–469. *Scopus*. Advance online publication. DOI: 10.1504/IJSAMI.2025.149223

Li, R., Zhou, G., Li, X., Jia, L., & Shang, Z. (2024). Semi-supervised multi-label dimensionality reduction learning based on minimizing redundant correlation of specific and common features. *Knowledge-Based Systems, 294*, 111789. DOI: 10.1016/j.knosys.2024.111789

Madoune, S. A., Senouci, S., Jiang, D. D., Senouci, M. R., Daoud, M. A., Anwar Mohammed Alawad, R., & Madoune, Y. (2025). A novel approach for real-time DDoS detection in SDN using dimensionality reduction and ensemble learning. *Journal of Information Security and Applications, 94*, 104195. DOI: 10.1016/j.jisa.2025.104195

Magkanas, G., Bagán, H., Sistach, M. C., & García, J. F. (2023). *Artomics*: A holistic approach to the study of artworks integrating their compositional and formal characteristics. Application on the *Liber Feudorum Maior. Microchemical Journal, 185*, 108276. DOI: 10.1016/j.microc.2022.108276

Markos, A., Moschidis, O., & Chadjipantelis, T. (2020). Sequential dimension reduction and clustering of mixed-type data. *International Journal of Data Analysis Techniques and Strategies, 12*(3), 228–246. *Scopus*. Advance online publication. DOI: 10.1504/IJDATS.2020.108043

Menexes, G. (2006). *Experimental designs in data analysis* ([Doctoral dissertation, University of Macedonia]).

Morlini, I., & Zani, S. (2010). Comparing approaches for clustering mixed mode data: An application in marketing research. *Data Analysis and Classification*, 49–57. Scopus.

Moschidis, O., Markos, A., & Chadjipadelis, T. (2023). Hierarchical clustering of mixed-type data based on barycentric coding. *Behaviormetrika, 50*(1), 465–489. *Scopus*. Advance online publication. DOI: 10.1007/s41237-022-00165-z

Muyama, L., Neuraz, A., & Coulet, A. (2024). Machine learning approaches for the discovery of clinical pathways from patient data: A systematic review. *Journal of Biomedical Informatics, 160*, 104746. DOI: 10.1016/j.jbi.2024.104746 PMID: 39537000

Nguyen, L. H., & Holmes, S. (2019). Ten quick tips for effective dimensionality reduction. *PLoS Computational Biology, 15*(6). *Scopus.* Advance online publication. DOI: 10.1371/journal.pcbi.1006907 PMID: 31220072

Orsenigo, C., & Vercellis, C. (2012). Kernel ridge regression for out-of-sample mapping in supervised manifold learning. *Expert Systems with Applications, 39*(9), 7757–7762. DOI: 10.1016/j.eswa.2012.01.060

Pagès, J. (2004). Analyse factorielle de données mixtes. [Scopus.]. *Revue de Statistique Appliquee, 52*(4), 93–111.

Papadimitriou, G. (1994). *Data analysis methods: University lectures.* University of Macedonia Economics and Social Sciences.

Papafilippou, N., Kyrana, Z., Pratsinakis, E., Kiranas, E., Michailidou, A.-M., Markos, A., & Menexes, G. (2026). Integrating Data Analysis Methods with Machine Learning Algorithms for Mixed Data Types: Does This Combination Improve Predictive Models' Accuracy? *Journal of Data Science and Intelligent Systems, 4*(1), 39–50. DOI: 10.47852/bonviewJDSIS52023906

Papafilippou, N., Kyrana, Z., Pratsinakis, E. D., Dordas, C., & Menexes, G. C. (2025). Dimensionality Reduction Techniques for Multivariate Categorical Data. In *Modern International Developments in Data Analysis and Multivariate Statistical Analysis* (pp. 1–36). Scopus., DOI: 10.4018/979-8-3693-9400-7.ch001

Pratsinakis, E. D., Kyrana, Z., Papafilippou, N., Karapetsi, L., Dordas, C., & Markos, A. (2025). Clustering Mixed-Type Data: A Comparative Study Using Python and SPSS. In *Modern International Developments in Data Analysis and Multivariate Statistical Analysis* (pp. 73–89). Scopus. https://doi.org/DOI: 10.4018/979-8-3693-9400-7.ch003

Roccetti, M., Delnevo, G., Casini, L., & Mirri, S. (2021). An alternative approach to dimension reduction for pareto distributed data: A case study. *Journal of Big Data, 8*(1), 39. DOI: 10.1186/s40537-021-00428-8 PMID: 33649714

Sharma, S. (1996). *Applied Multivariate Techniques.* John Willey and Sons Inc.

Sicsic, J., Le Vaillant, M., & Franc, C. (2012). Intrinsic and extrinsic motivations in primary care: An explanatory study among French general practitioners. *Health Policy (Amsterdam), 108*(2), 140–148. DOI: 10.1016/j.healthpol.2012.08.020 PMID: 22995769

Singh, J., & Singh, D. (2024). A comprehensive review of clustering techniques in artificial intelligence for knowledge discovery: Taxonomy, challenges, applications and future prospects. *Advanced Engineering Informatics, 62*, 102799. DOI: 10.1016/j.aei.2024.102799

Tauro, E., Gorini, A., Caglio, C., Gabanelli, P., & Caiani, E. G. (2022). COVID-19 and mental disorders in healthcare Personnel: A novel framework to develop Personas from an online survey. *Journal of Biomedical Informatics, 126*, 103993. DOI: 10.1016/j.jbi.2022.103993 PMID: 35026414

Theodosiou, T., Angelis, L., & Vakali, A. (2008). Non-linear correlation of content and metadata information extracted from biomedical article datasets. *Journal of Biomedical Informatics, 41*(1), 202–216. DOI: 10.1016/j.jbi.2007.06.004 PMID: 17643352

Van Ness, P. H., Murphy, T. E., Araujo, K. L. B., & Pisani, M. A. (2012). Multivariate graphical methods provide an insightful way to formulate explanatory hypotheses from limited categorical data. *Journal of Clinical Epidemiology, 65*(2), 179–188. DOI: 10.1016/j.jclinepi.2011.06.007 PMID: 21889310

van Rijckevorsel, J. L. A., & de Leeuw, J. (1988). *Component and correspondence analysis. Dimension reduction by functional approximation*. Wiley.

Wang, A., Zhao, S., Liu, J., Yang, J., Liu, L., & Chen, G. (2020). Locality adaptive preserving projections for linear dimensionality reduction. *Expert Systems with Applications, 151*, 113352. DOI: 10.1016/j.eswa.2020.113352

Yao, Y., Meng, H., Gao, Y., Long, Z., & Li, T. (2023). Linear dimensionality reduction method based on topological properties. *Information Sciences, 624*, 493–511. DOI: 10.1016/j.ins.2022.12.098

Young, F. W. (1981). Quantitative analysis of qualitative data. *Psychometrika, 46*(4), 357–388. *Scopus*. Advance online publication. DOI: 10.1007/BF02293796

Zeng, R., Ye, Y., Ou, H., Hua, Y., Su, Y., Hu, J., Lu, H., Tang, J., Liu, J., Xiao, T., Wu, Z., Tang, W., Li, Z.-Y., Lin, S., Zhuang, S., Xu, G., Lin, Y., Li, Y., Huang, F., & Zhang, H.-T. (2023). Early osteoarthritis diagnosis based on near-infrared spectroscopy combined with aquaphotomics. *Spectrochimica Acta. Part A: Molecular and Biomolecular Spectroscopy, 302*, 123120. DOI: 10.1016/j.saa.2023.123120 PMID: 37453381

Chapter 7
Exploring Brand Equity Transition Using the Construct of Social Media Advertisement Abstract

Rajinder Minhas
http://orcid.org/0000-0002-2428-3688
Lovely Professional University, India

ABSTRACT

Businesses can cultivate and pursue all such activities that improve perceived brand equity vis a vis increased awareness of the customers of the company. Social media advertisement can be one of the important constructs in contemporary business times. Indicators like image and brand recognition as well as customer retention can be used a benchmark to understand and innovate for an excellence. It is, therefore, very necessary to assess how social media marketing affects brand equity. To cater this, a context of social media marketing is taken to do the assessment of the effectiveness of social media advertisement on brand equity transitions. Structured questionnaire using convenient sampling approach, on sample size of one hundred and forty-two (142) respondents, living in the Punjab State of India Country is the research framework. The emerging data is analyzed using statistical tool of Regression Analysis.

INTRODUCTION

In the digital age, social media marketing is tool which helps both the business and the customer due to the fact that in the digital era the social media tool is

DOI: 10.4018/979-8-3373-6926-6.ch007

widely used for customer retention and brand equity. Quality content, interaction and personalization helps the company to engage the customer. It is observed that at the age of eighteen people are active on social media like: Facebook, Instagram, LinkedIn. Hence, it becomes easy for a company to target such customers and get leveraged using said platforms. According to the survey approx. 60-70% of people are active users on Instagram which gives the company a mover advantage to target their customer in high quantity (Artha et al., 2022). Through social media marketing, brands can tell stories that effectively interact with their target audience, initiate conversations and evoke strong emotions. Every piece of content, from impactful tweets to visually appealing Instagram pictures, acts as a touchpoint for interacting with customer and enhancing brand identity and recognition. Moreover, the real time nature of social media allows organizations to remain fluid and flexible and modify their communications to align with evolving customer taste and preference and prevailing trends. Beyond superficial metrics such as like and shares, social media has a significant impact on brand equity and is essential for building long-term customer relationships and retention. By delivering content that adds value, exceptional customer service, fostering engaging interactions, brands can develop a devoted customer base that remains steadfast amidst competition. In conclusion, social media marketing has transformed the industry by allowing companies to engage with clients directly and build strong relationships. By implementing tailored social media campaigns that prioritize brand recognition and perception, company may achieve ongoing success, in a world digital. In this way, company can also increase their customer retention by using personalization by involvement of the customer.

REVIEW OF LITERATURE

In the digital age, social media is becoming more than basically a tool for communication. It is proved that in a dynamic ecosystem that allows brands to really connect with their audience in an authentic way, affects the organisation and its values (Artha et al., 2022; Rofiq et al., 2020; Rootman & Cupp, n.d.). Undoubtedly, brands can create stories that truly resonate with their target audience through social media, sparking conversations and strong emotions evoking. Every piece of content, from visually gorgeous Instagram photos to provocative tweets, acts as a touchpoint for customer connection, increasing recall and brand identification (Adejuwon, 2022). In addition to providing awareness, social media gives brands a platform to develop a distinctive brand identity that embodies their values, character, and unique selling proposition (USP) (Bowen & Ozuem, 2015). Companies can differentiate themselves from competition and connect more deeply with their target audience by using visual branding and consistent messaging. Moreover, brands can promote brand advocacy and loyalty by interacting with customers through messages, comments, and user-generated content (Dr, n.d.; Kumar, 2023). Social media plays a critical role in building long-term customer relationships and retention, and its influence on brand equity goes beyond vanity metrics like likes and shares (Jamil et al., 2022).

In summary, social media marketing has completely changed the industry by enabling businesses to interact with customers on a personal level and create enduring bonds (Aldaihani et al., 2020; Nuseir, 2016).Through the implementation of focused social media campaigns that emphasize brand awareness and perception, companies may set themselves up for long-term success in an increasingly digital environment (Duffett, 2017; Kankam Boadu, 2019).In conclusion, methods focused on boosting either of the two variables social media advertisement and consumer involvement appear to be substantial predictors of the dependent variable, indicating that doing so could have a favorable effect on the intended result (Santoso & Dewi, 2018; Suharto et al., 2022).Comprehensive studies that explore the long-term effects of customized social media initiatives on client retention are desperately needed (Elareshi et al., 2023; Maecker et al., 2016; Putra et al., 2022; Yang et al., 2022).Although a great deal of research has been done on the broad impacts of social media marketing and engagement on consumer behavior and retention, little is known about the ways in which distinct social media content kinds, engagement strategies, and platform-specific techniques affect customer loyalty in diverse business settings (Farook & Abeysekara, n.d.).Businesses looking to improve their digital marketing strategies in order to increase client retention and loyalty will benefit from this (Hasan & Sohail, 2021).

Research Gap: - The existing literature on social media marketing and customer retention reveals an important research gap. There are not many in-depth real time studies that concentrate on the long-term impacts of particular social media strategies on client loyalty and retention across a range of industry. Although a great deal of research has been done on the broad impacts of social media marketing and engagement on consumer behavior and retention, little is known about the ways in which distinct social media content kinds, engagement strategies, and platform-specific techniques affect customer loyalty in diverse business settings (Farook & Abeysekara, n.d.). Future research on the complex relationships between particular social media behaviors and the long-term results of customer retention is made possible by the current research void.

RESEARCH METHODOLOGY

Research Type: Primary Research using Structured Questionnaire on a sample of One hundred and forty-two respondents using convenient sampling approach.

Components of the conceptual framework: The conceptual framework incorporates into account elements that affect brand recognition, brand image, repurchase intention, and ultimate consumer loyalty. These elements further include trendiness, interactivity, word-of-mouth, customization, entertainment, commitment, satisfaction, trust, and relationship quality.

Research Design: The study utilized a cross-sectional design with data collected through an online survey to analyze the effects of various social media marketing activities on brand equity components like brand awareness and image.

Data Collection Method: Data was collected through an online survey from valid responses to analyze the effects of different social media marketing activities on brand equity components like brand awareness and image.

Procedure for Data Collection: The data collection process involved administering an online survey to participants to gather responses related to their perceptions of various social media marketing activities.

Sample Size: One hundred and forty-two respondents (142) from the State of Punjab in India Country.

Sampling Approach: Convenient Sampling

Objectives of this research: -

1. To understand relationship between customer engagement with presence of social media advertisement.
2. To relate customer buying decision with presence of social media advertisement.
3. To conclude satisfaction of customer in term of buying experience vis-a- vis social media advertisement.

Figure 1. Research Model

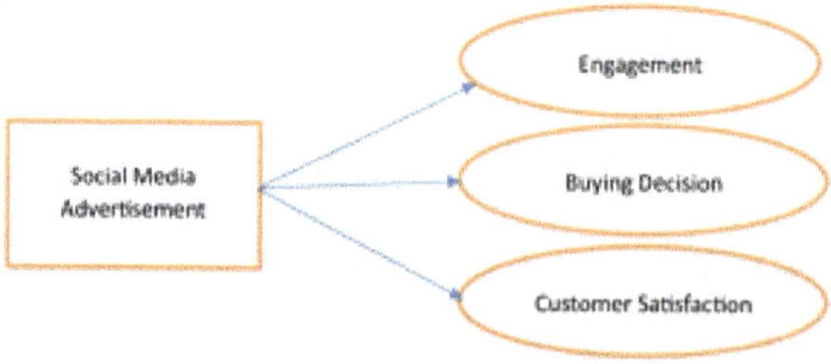

(Source: Author)

HYPOTHESES DEVELOPMENT

1. H01: There is not significant relationship between customer engagement and social media advertisement.
2. H11: There is a significant relationship between customer engagement and social media advertisement.
3. H20: There is not a significant relationship between Customer Buying Decision with presence of Social Media Advertisement.
4. H21: There is a significant relationship between Customer Buying Decision with presence of Social Media Advertisement.
5. H31: There is not a significant relationship between Customer buying experience with social media advertisement.

6.H30: There is a significant relationship between Customer buying experience with social media advertisement.

DATA ANALYSIS

Data Analysis Method: Correlation, Regression & ANOVA is used to analyze the Data.

Table 1. Data sources from questionnaire (Source: Authors)

	(Data in %age)					
Research Questions	Very Unlikely	Unlikely	Neutral	Likely	Very Likely	Total
Do you make purchases from a brand as a result of seeing a promotion or advertisement on social media?	4.82	8.45	35.21	39.44	11.97	100
Do you feel more connected to brands due to their presence on social media platforms?	2.82	7.04	26.06	47.18	17.61	100
Compared to brands that do not have a strong social media presence, do you feel more loyal to a brand because of active engagement on social media platforms?	0.00	7.75	31.69	45.07	15.49	100
While considering purchasing from a brand, do you think social media reviews and testimonials are important in the decision-making process?	3.03	2.11	28.17	44.37	22.54	100
Do you feel that a brand's social media presence adds value to your overall experience as a customer?	3.03	0.00	30.99	43.66	22.54	100

Objective No.1

To understand relationship between customer engagement with presence of social media advertisement

Independent Variable(X): Social Media Advertisement

Dependent Variable(Y): Customer Engagement

Table 2.

SUMMARY OUTPUT

Regression Statistics	
Multiple R	0.924421111
R Square	0.854554391
Adjusted R Square	0.806072521
Standard Error	7.102654635
Observations	5

ANOVA

	df	SS	MS	F	Significance F
Regression	1	889.2046914	889.204691	17.62627	0.024657489
Residual	3	151.3431086	50.4477029		
Total	4	1040.5478			

	Coefficients	Standard Error	t Stat	P-value	Lower 95%	Upper 95%	Lower 95.0%	Upper 95.0%
Intercept	3.152007587	5.117970528	0.6158706	0.581554	-13.13565881	19.43967	-13.13565881	19.43967399
X Variable 1	0.842399621	0.200649456	4.19836483	0.024657	0.203843499	1.480956	0.203843499	1.480955742

Multiple R coefficient and adjusted R square of 0.92 states strong correlation between the two variables viz social media advertising and customer engagement. R square value and adjusted R Square of 0.85 and 0.80 clearly support the goodness fit of the model, the explanatory variable is significantly explained by a relationship between the input variable. F value of 17.63 means differences in group means are significant and significance F value of 0.025 clearly indicates that the model best fits to the data. The p value 0.02 is higher than the standard of 0.05 clearly supports the adoption of Null Hypothesis, H01: There is not significant relationship between customer engagement and social media advertisement and rejection of Alternate Hypothesis, H21: There is significant relationship between customer engagement and social media advertisement.

Objective No.2

To relate customer buying decision with presence of social media advertisement.

Independent Variable (X): Social Media Advertisement

Dependent Variable (Y): Customer Buying Decision

Table 3.

SUMMARY OUTPUT

Regression Statistics	
Multiple R	0.982859009
R Square	0.966011852
Adjusted R Square	0.954682443
Standard Error	3.885874033
Observations	5

ANOVA

	df	SS	MS	F	Significance F
Regression	1	1290.17024	1290.17024	85.26601073	0.002687002
Residual	3	45.39335999	15.13112		
Total	4	1335.5636			

	Coefficients	Standard Error	t Stat	P-value	Lower 95%	Upper 95%	Lower 95.0%	Upper 95.0%
Intercept	-0.294146706	2.80293238	-0.104942491	0.923044404	-9.214328503	8.626035091	-9.214328503	8.626035091
X Variable 1	1.014707335	0.109888647	9.233959645	0.002687002	0.664992615	1.364422055	0.664992615	1.364422055

Multiple R statistics of 0.98 state very high correlation between the two variables *viz.* social media advertising and Customer buying decision. R square value and adjusted R square value of 0.96 and 0.95 respectively, clearly supports the goodness fit of the model, the explanatory variable (dependent variable) is very significantly explained by a relationship with the input variable (independent variable). F value of 85.26 means differences in group means are very much significant and significance F value of 0.00268 superbly best fits model to the data. The p value of 0.0026 is appreciably lower than the standard 0.05 and clearly supports the rejection of Null Hypothesis, H20: There is not a significant relationship between Customer Buying Decision with presence of Social Media Advertisement and acceptance of Alternative Hypothesis, H21: There is a significant relationship between Customer Buying Decision with presence of Social Media Advertisement.

Objective No. 3

To conclude satisfaction of customer in term of buying experience vis-a- vis social media advertisement.

Independent Variable(X): Social Media Advertisement

Dependent Variable(Y): Buying Experience

Table 4.

SUMMARY OUTPUT

Regression Statistics	
Multiple R	0.959999047
R Square	0.92159817
Adjusted R Square	0.895464227
Standard Error	5.992198594
Observations	5

ANOVA

	df	SS	MS	F	Significance F
Regression	1	1266.219668	1266.22	35.26441	0.009545886
Residual	3	107.719332	35.90644		
Total	4	1373.939			

	Coefficients	Standard Error	t Stat	P-value	Lower 95%	Upper 95%	Lower 95.0%	Upper 95.0%
Intercept	-0.104895177	4.317807549	-0.02429	0.982144	-13.84608586	13.6362955	-13.8460859	13.6362955
X Variable 1	1.005244759	0.169279157	5.938385	0.009546	0.46652293	1.543966587	0.46652293	1.543966587

There exists a strong relationship between the variable of Social Media Advertisement and the Customer Buying Experience. R square value of 0.92 clearly supports the goodness fit of the model, the explanatory variable is very significantly explained by a relationship with the dependent variable. F value of 36.26 means differences in group means are very significant and significance F value of 0.0095 supportively best fits model to the data. P value 0.0095 is much lower than the standard of 0.05 and clearly evidently supports the rejection of Null Hypothesis H30: There is not a significant relationship between Customer buying experience with social media advertisement and adoption of Alternative Hypothesis H31: There is a significant relationship between Customer buying experience with social media advertisement.

FINDINGS OF THE STUDY

It is found from the study that:

1. Social media advertisement cannot be appreciated as engagement tools. Businesses need to advent to make social media engaging the audiences for imminence
2. Social media advertisement affects the positively the customer buying decisions.
3. Social media advertisements are positively related to the buying experiences of the customers.

LIMITATIONS OF THE STUDY

The research is primarily done using structured questionnaire as tool of research on respondents living in Punjab State of India country, selected using convenient sampling. There is limitation of the questions and also bias of the customers in answering the questions cannot be ruled out.

SCOPE FOR FUTURE RESEARCH

There is need to do more research taking the constructs of social media advertisement and customer satisfaction to find the novel symmetry in the brand equity transformation, when the respondents are taken from different part of the World.

REFERENCES

Adejuwon, J. A. (2022). Social Media Marketing And Customer Retention Of Selected Small And Medium Enterprises (SMEs) In South-West Nigeria. *International Journal of Management and Economics Invention, 8*(6). Advance online publication. DOI: 10.47191/ijmei/v8i6.01

Aldaihani, F. M. F., Ali, N. A. B., Hashim, H. B., & Kamal, N. (2020). Impact of Social Customer Relationship Management on Customer Retention of Islamic Banks in Kuwait: The Mediating Role of Customer Empowerment. 9(1).

Artha, B., Zahara, I., Bahri, & Permata Sari, N. (2022). Customer Retention: A Literature Review. Social Science Studies, 2(1), 030–045. https://doi.org/DOI: 10.47153/sss21.2952022

Bowen, G., & Ozuem, W. (Eds.). (2015). *Computer-Mediated Marketing Strategies: Social Media and Online Brand Communities. IGI Global.* Department of Management and Accounting, Lead City University., DOI: 10.4018/978-1-4666-6595-8

Dr, M. W. (n.d.). social media marketing communications effect on attitudes among millennials in South Africa. 8(3).

Duffett, R. G. (2017). Influence of social media marketing communications on young consumers' attitudes. *Young Consumers, 18*(1), 19–39. DOI: 10.1108/YC-07-2016-00622

Elareshi, M., Habes, M., Safori, A., Attar, R. W., Noor Al Adwan, M., & Al-Rahmi, W. M. (2023). Understanding the Effects of Social Media Marketing on Customers' Bank Loyalty: A SEM Approach. *Electronics (Basel), 12*(8), 1822. DOI: 10.3390/electronics12081822

Farook, F. S., & Abeysekara, N. (n.d.). Influence of Social Media Marketing on Customer Engagement.

Hasan, M., & Sohail, M. S. (2021). The Influence of Social Media Marketing on Consumers' Purchase Decision: Investigating the Effects of Local and Nonlocal Brands. *Journal of International Consumer Marketing, 33*(3), 350–367. DOI: 10.1080/08961530.2020.1795043

Jamil, K., Dunnan, L., Gul, R. F., Shehzad, M. U., Gillani, S. H. M., & Awan, F. H. (2022). Role of Social Media Marketing Activities in Influencing Customer Intentions: A Perspective of a New Emerging Era. *Frontiers in Psychology, 12*, 808525. DOI: 10.3389/fpsyg.2021.808525 PMID: 35111111

Kankam Boadu, A. A. (2019). Customer Relationship Management and Customer Retention. SSRN Electronic Journal. https://doi.org/DOI: 10.2139/ssrn.3472492

Maecker, O., Barrot, C., & Becker, J. U. (2016). The effect of social media interactions on customer relationship management. *Business Research*, *9*(1), 133–155. DOI: 10.1007/s40685-016-0027-6

Nuseir, M. T. (2016). Exploring the use of Online Marketing Strategies and Digital Media to Improve the Brand Loyalty and Customer Retention. *International Journal of Business and Management*, *11*(4), 228. DOI: 10.5539/ijbm.v11n4p228

Putra, A., Suhud, U., & Handaru, A. W. (2022). The Role of Brand Reputation on Customer Retention of Social Media Users. https://doi.org/DOI: 10.5281/ZENODO.6132552

Rofiq, M., Firdi, A., & Respati, H. (2020). The Effect of Brand Image and Social Media on Customer Retention through Customer Satisfaction at Kaliwatu Adventure. *International Journal of Innovative Science and Research Technology*, *5*(8), 589–594. DOI: 10.38124/IJISRT20AUG293

Rootman, C., & Cupp, N. (n.d.). The impact of social media on customer satisfaction and retention in the banking industry: views of clients and managers.

Santoso, R. K., & Dewi, N. F. (2018). The Influence of Social Media Against Customer Retention (Case Study on J.Co). *KnE Social Sciences*, *3*(11), 1436. DOI: 10.18502/kss.v3i11.2860

Suharto, S., Junaedi, I. W. R., Muhdar, H. M., Firmansyah, A., & Sarana, S. (2022). Consumer loyalty of Indonesia e-commerce SMEs: The role of social media marketing and customer satisfaction. *International Journal of Data and Network Science*, *6*(2), 383–390. DOI: 10.5267/j.ijdns.2021.12.016

Yang, Q., Hayat, N., Al Mamun, A., Makhbul, Z. K. M., & Zainol, N. R. (2022). Sustainable customer retention through social media marketing activities using hybrid SEM-neural network approach. plos one, 17(3), e0264899. https://doi.org/.DOI: 10.1371/journal.pone.0264899

Chapter 8
Exploring Student Attitudes Towards Artificial Intelligence

Christoforos Karachristos
University of Western Macedonia, Greece

Lamprini Seremeti
http://orcid.org/0000-0002-0663-5408
University of Western Macedonia, Greece

Sofia Anastasiadou
http://orcid.org/0000-0001-6404-5003
University of Western University, Greece

ABSTRACT

Artificial intelligence (AI) has unprecedented applications across education. AI algorithms learn from data, make in-formed decisions, interact with their environment, and integrate seamlessly into educational settings. AI can support personalized learning, facilitate language acquisition, address individual student needs, offer real-time feedback, and enhance teacher-student interactions. This research investigates students' attitudes by exploring their emotional responses, perceptions of cognitive impact, and resulting behavioral intentions regarding AI. The SATAI scale (Students' Attitudes Towards Artificial Intelligence) was employed to measure these attitudes. The scale comprises 26 statements rated on a five-point Likert scale, divided into three dimensions: affective, cognitive, and behavioral factors. A total of 216 stu-dents participated in the study. Data analysis was conducted using factor analysis. Results indicated that emotional and cognitive factors significantly shape students' behavioral intentions toward AI integration in educational contexts.

DOI: 10.4018/979-8-3373-6926-6.ch008

1. INTRODUCTION

The use of artificial intelligence (AI) in education offers significant advantages for students (Crompton & Burke, 2023). One of the primary benefits is personalized learning, as AI algorithms can adapt educational content to each student's individual needs and skill level. This facilitates more effective learning and addresses individual knowledge gaps. Additionally, AI provides real-time feedback, helping students immediately identify their mistakes and improve. Furthermore, AI incorporates applications such as language learning and simulation creation, making the educational experience more interactive and engaging.

However, there are also disadvantages to using AI in education (Bates et al., 2020). One of the primary concerns is the potential dependence of students on AI tools, which could limit the development of their critical thinking and autonomy. Furthermore, concerns are raised regarding privacy protection and the security of students' personal data, as AI relies on large amounts of data. Additionally, increased reliance on AI may exacerbate social inequalities, as students with limited access to technological infrastructure might not equally benefit from these tools.

Conducting research on students' attitudes toward artificial intelligence (AI) is necessary to understand their perceptions, concerns, and expectations regarding the use of these technologies in education (Al-Zahrani & Alasmari, 2024). Given the rapid integration of AI into educational processes, such as automated assessment, personalized learning, and digital assistants, it is crucial to investigate how students perceive the role and capabilities of AI. Such research may reveal potential challenges, including trust in technology, privacy concerns, or fears about the replacement of traditional teaching methods. The findings will contribute to improving AI integration, taking into consideration students' actual needs and preferences.

Weichert & Eldardiry (2024) research findings reveal that computer science students generally hold favorable views regarding the benefits of artificial intelligence (AI) and regularly utilize AI tools. Despite this enthusiasm, students express significant concerns about the ethical implications associated with both existing and future AI technologies. Additionally, their survey highlights that nearly half of the respondents show an interest in AI policy as a possible career direction, yet only one-third feel that their current academic programs effectively equip them with the necessary knowledge and skills to actively engage in meaningful conversations around AI policies and regulations (Weichert & Eldardiry, 2024). Their results underscore a clear need for educational institutions to strengthen curricula by integrating comprehensive discussions of ethical considerations and regulatory frameworks related to AI. This enhancement could better prepare students for future roles that require them to navigate complex policy issues, fostering not only technical proficiency but also a well-rounded understanding of the societal impact and governance of AI technologies (Weichert & Eldardiry, 2024).

Farhi et al., 2023 claimed that Artificial Intelligence (AI) is being integrated into education to guide, support, and assist students in tailoring their learning experiences. According to Farhi et al. (2023) nowadays, students have greater access to AI-driven writing tools that offer immediate feedback and corrections in grammar, punctuation, and clarity of expression. They added that these advanced tools help students refine sentence structure, tone, and vocabulary choices, significantly enhancing the overall quality of their written work. Additionally, AI tools often include chatbots that suggest self-study techniques, allowing students to easily access information, find answers to their questions, and benefit from AI-powered problem-solving assistance (Farhi et al., 2023).

Accordig to Katsantonis and Katsantonis (2024), the most significant factor influencing cognitive, behavioral, and emotional attitudes toward artificial intelligence (AI) among students was identified as their expected future frequency of AI usage. Following closely, the general sense of safety and trust students have toward technology also substantially impacts their attitudes. Overall, students demonstrated predominantly positive emotional and cognitive perspectives regarding AI. They argued that these findings highlight that the social backgrounds of students considerably shape their attitudes towards AI, emphasizing the importance of context and individual differences. Students who anticipate frequent future engagement with AI technologies tend to exhibit stronger positive attitudes, suggesting a direct relationship between perceived relevance and acceptance (Katsantonis and Katsantonis, 2024).

In this context of inquiry, the present research focuses on students' attitudes toward the use of artificial intelligence in the learning process, examining their emotions, perceptions about their knowledge, and behavior. The research employed the SATAI scale (Student Attitudes toward AI), which comprises three factors: affective, cognitive, and behavioral. The analysis was conducted using factor analysis on data from a sample of 216 students, with results indicating that emotional and cognitive factors influence the behavioral factor.

2. THE RESEARCH INSTRUMENT: STUDENT ATTITUDES TOWARD AI (SATAI) SCALE

The research instrument, the Student Attitudes toward AI (SATAI) scale (Suh & Ahn, 2022), is divided into three distinct groups/conceptual constructs consisting of 26 items.

The first group corresponds to the conceptual construct known as the "Behavioral Component" (BC), which includes 12 items (BCi) (e.g., BC1: I want to work in the cognitive area of Artificial Intelligence (AI)). The second group corresponds to the "Affective Component" (AC), comprising 10 items (ACi) (e.g., AC5: I will need Artificial Intelligence (AI) in my future life). The third group corresponds to the "Cognitive Component" (CC), consisting of 4 items (CCi) (e.g., CC4: "Every student should learn about Artificial Intelligence (AI) at university").

These three conceptual constructs constitute a latent variable named "Student Attitudes toward AI (SATAI) ()." The items of the scale are presented in Table 1.

The reliability of the scale, in terms of internal consistency, was evaluated using Cronbach's alpha coefficient (Anastasiadou, 2019; Anastasiadou & Taraza, 2019). Cronbach's alpha for the overall scale was 0.801 indicating a very satisfactory reliability (Anastasiadou & Karakos, 2011; Anastasiadou, 2013; Papadaki & Anastsasiadou, S.D. 2019), while for the Behavioral, Affective, and Cognitive components, it was 0.726, 0.616, and 0.827, respectively (Papademetriou et al., 2023; Papademetriou et al., 2022; Anastasiadou & Tiliakou, 2016; Papadaki, et al., 2023).

Table 1. Student Attitudes toward Artificial Intelligence

	Student Attitudes toward Artificial Intelligence
Conceptual Construct	**Items**
Behavioral Component	
	BC1. I want to work in the cognitive field of Artificial Intelligence (AI).
	BC2. I will choose a job in the cognitive field of Artificial Intelligence (AI).
	BC3. I would like to participate in a club related to Artificial Intelligence (AI), if such a club exists.
	BC4. I like using topics related to Artificial Intelligence (AI).
	BC5. Learning about Artificial Intelligence (AI) is enjoyable.
	BC6. I want to continue learning about Artificial Intelligence (AI).
	BC7. I am interested in TV programs or online videos related to Artificial Intelligence (AI).
	BC8. I want to create something that makes human life more convenient through Artificial Intelligence (AI).
	BC9. I am interested in the development of Artificial Intelligence (AI).
	BC10. It is interesting to use Artificial Intelligence (AI).
	BC11. More class time should be dedicated to Artificial Intelligence (AI).
	BC12. I can handle Artificial Intelligence (AI) well.
Affective Component	
	AC1. Artificial Intelligence (AI) is essential for societal development.

continued on following page

Table 1. Continued

	Student Attitudes toward Artificial Intelligence
	AC2. Artificial Intelligence (AI) makes people's lives more convenient.
	AC3. Artificial Intelligence (AI) is relevant to my life.
	AC4. I will use Artificial Intelligence (AI) to solve everyday life problems.
	AC5. I will need Artificial Intelligence (AI) in my future life.
	AC6. Artificial Intelligence (AI) helps me solve real-life problems.
	AC7. Artificial Intelligence (AI) is necessary for everyone.
	AC8. Artificial Intelligence (AI) produces more good than harm.
	AC9. Artificial Intelligence (AI) is worth studying.
	AC10. Most jobs in the future will require knowledge related to Artificial Intelligence (AI).
Cognitive Component	
	CC1. It is necessary for students to learn about Artificial Intelligence (AI) at school.
	CC2. Courses in Artificial Intelligence (AI) are important.
	CC3. Courses related to Artificial Intelligence (AI) should be taught at the students' university.
	CC4. Every student should learn about Artificial Intelligence (AI) at their university.

3. RESEARCH SAMPLE

The research sample consists of 216 participants, of whom 78 (36.1%) were female and 138 (63.9%) were male.

Regarding the age of respondents, 112 (51.9%) were between 18-20 years old, 52 (24.1%) were between 20-22 years old, 25 (11.6%) were between 22-24 years old, and finally, 27 (12.5%) were over 24 years old.

Concerning place of residence, out of 216 respondents, 168 (77.8%) reported living in urban areas, 43 (19.9%) in semi-urban areas, and 5 (2.3%) in rural areas.

Regarding faculty enrollment, 136 (63%) were from the School of Engineering, 57 (26.4%) from the School of Sciences, 13 (6%) from the School of Health Sciences, 6 (2.8%) from the School of Economics and Social Sciences, and finally, 4 (1.9%) from the School of Humanities.

Concerning the year of studies, 84 (38.9%) were in their first year, 48 (22.2%) in their second year, 24 (11.1%) in their third year, 11 (10.2%) in their fourth year, 14 (6.5%) in their fifth year, 14 (6.5%) in their sixth year, 4 (1.9%) were final-year undergraduate students, and 6 (2.8%) were enrolled in postgraduate or doctoral programs (Table 2).

Table 2. Demographic Characteristics

Demographic Data	Category	Frequency N	Relative Frequency (%)
Gender	Male	138	63,9
	Female	78	36,1
Age	18-20	112	51,9
	20-22	52	24,1
	22-24	25	11,6
	>24	27	12,5
Place of Residence	Urban area	86	77,5
	Semi-urban area	22	19,8
	Rural area	3	2,7
Faculty of Enrollment	School of Engineering	136	63
	School of Sciences	57	26,4
	School of Health Sciences	13	6
	School of Economics and Social Sciences	6	2,8
	School of Humanities	4	1,9
Year of Study	1st year	84	38,9
	2nd year	48	22,2
	3rd year	24	11,1
	4th year	22	10,2
	5th year	14	6,5
	6th year	14	6,5
	Final-year undergraduate	4	1,9
	Postgraduate or doctoral program	6	2,8

4. METHODOLOGY

During the research process, absolute and relative frequencies were recorded for 34 item-variables using classical statistical methods. Subsequently, each of the 34 item-variables was categorized into three classes, resulting in a total of 105 classes represented in a logical table (0-1). Additionally, the demographic variable "gender" was categorized into two classes (male-female), and the variable "years of service" into four classes.

The categorization of variables resulted in a two-way frequency table (absolute and relative frequencies) of dimensions 105x105, known as a Burt table. Each column of the Burt table is treated as a vector in a 105-dimensional space. The Burt table allowed the analysis of each class primarily, then each variable individually, and subsequently, the cross-classification of the variables' categories.

The primary aim of determining these relationships is achieved through the use of n×n two-way frequency tables known as Burt tables. These tables contain all the categories into which the variables have been divided, arranged in both rows and columns. Consequently, each element in the Burt table depends exclusively on two variables, thereby revealing the relationship between them. Data processing employed methods of Data Analysis, as this study required no a priori hypotheses. This condition is fully satisfied by Data Analysis methods, also referred to as Multivariate Statistical Analysis without models. These methods were selected because traditional statistical assumptions regarding the behavior of the phenomenon described by the analyzed table are not utilized; instead, a more specific determination of their structure is pursued. By identifying the characteristics of variables that influence respondents' behavior and attitudes, it becomes possible to approach the actual dimensions of students' attitudes toward AI.

The approach of a posteriori categorization of electronic store customers' attitudes, as revealed through questionnaires, is achieved through factorial axes—complex variables—and factorial planes, which provide a more comprehensive visual representation. These enable the qualitative relationships among all variables to be highlighted and defined (Ntotsi & Anastasiadou, 2019).

Among the previously mentioned Data Analysis methods, Factorial Correspondence Analysis (Analyse Factorielle des Correspondances) was selected for data analysis. Factorial Correspondence Analysis allows contemporary statistical processing of categorized qualitative and quantitative variables (Benzécri, 1973; Karapistolis, 2015; Papadimitriou, 2007; Anastasiadou, 2016). This method facilitates grouping dominant clusters of observations, providing an almost universal description of the phenomenon represented by the analyzed table, utilizing a reduced number of new composite variables—factors (Papadimitriou, 1994). These factors, mutually independent, are created by combining groups of initial variables, significantly simplifying the search for relationships among variables and providing a comprehensive and more nuanced depiction of the examined phenomenon. Factors can take the form of axes, pairing to form factorial planes, enabling graphical representation of variables.

Subsequently, contribution and correlation indices are presented, serving as criteria for selecting variables in the construction and interpretation of axes and the corresponding factorial planes.

1. The contribution of a row and column point to the construction of a factorial axis: If λk represents the total inertia along axis k, and λk(i) represents the inertia of point i in the cloud along the respective axis k, then the contribution is denoted by ctr(i,k) and is given by equation (4): $ctr(i,k) = \lambda k(i) / \lambda k$ (4) where $\lambda k = \Sigma\ \lambda k(i)$ for each axis k. (5)

Similarly, the contribution of points j in the cloud is defined.

The contribution, as defined, represents the percentage of inertia of a point relative to the inertia explained by the factorial axis.

Because the contribution index reveals the points primarily contributing to the axis's construction, we seek points with high ctr(i,k) values, which potentially serve as a basis for interpreting the axis, a critical aspect in understanding the phenomenon (Dro

2. The squared cosine (or relative contribution) indicates the quality of representation of a point by the factorial axis and essentially represents a form of correlation between point i and factorial axis k. It is denoted by $\cos^2(i,k)$ and given by equation (6): $\cos^2(i,k) = \lambda k(i) / d^2(i,G)$ (6) where $d^2(i,G)$ is the squared distance of point i from the center of gravity (Drosos, 2004).

A high $\cos^2(i,k)$ value implies a small angle between the point and the axis, indicating a strong correlation between point i and axis k, thus representing a high-quality projection of point i onto axis k. According to this, $\cos^2(i,k)$ expresses the proportion of inertia of point i explained by axis k.

Points with very high $\cos^2(i,k)$ usually also show high ctr(i,k) values. If points have high $\cos^2(i,k)$ values but low ctr(i,k), it means they have good projection quality on the axis but do not contribute significantly to its construction (Papadimitriou, 2007).

Conversely, if points have low $\cos^2(i,k)$ but high ctr(i,k), it means they contribute significantly to the axis's construction but are better projected onto another axis, to which they may contribute more substantially (Drosos, 2004; Papadimitriou, 2007; Anastasiadou, 2016).

5. RESULTS

The indices used in interpreting the results of this particular factorial correspondence analysis (FCA) were the well-known "inertia" and "contribution" indices (Benzécri, 1980; Papadimitriou, 1994). These indices enable the immediate identification of the most significant and influential variables or items contributing to the creation of factorial axes. We interpreted the results of this factorial analysis using inertia, explained by each factorial axis, and ultimately the contribution.

The analysis of the data table with FCA initially produces Table 1, which presents the characteristic values of the Burt table and the inertia percentages for each factorial axis. Table 1 allows the identification of the main factorial axes most suitable for interpreting the results. The inertia percentage for each factorial axis indicates the relative importance each axis represents.

According to the values accompanied by the histogram (Table 2), the important percentage of the first factorial axis is 28.43%, the second axis 66.05%, the third axis 9.28%, the fourth axis 5.98%, etc. The cumulative information provided by the 12 factorial axes amounts to 89.05%, as illustrated in the table below (Table 3).

Table 3. Inertia - Eigenvalues

Total Inertia 0,13631				
Axis	Inertia	% of Explained Inertia	cumulative %	Eigenvalues Histogram
01	0,0387465	28,43	28,43	|***
02	0,0218723	26,05	54,47	|***********************
03	0,0126458	9,28	63,75	|*****************
04	0,0081520	5,98	69,73	|************
05	0,0051416	3,77	73,50	|*********
06	0,0044757	3,28	76,79	|*******
07	0,0038076	2,79	79,58	|*****
08	0,0030408	2,23	81,81	|****
09	0,0027762	2,04	83,85	|***
10	0,0026903	1,97	85,85	|**
11	0,0023708	1,74	87,56	|*
12	0,0020390	1,50	89,06	|*

Based on the cumulative frequency, the first three factorial axes explain 64.74% of the total data variance (Table 1). This percentage is considered sufficient for data interpretation (Karapistolis, 2015). Subsequently, from the factorial correspondence analysis results table and according to the previously mentioned selected criteria (inertia, correlation, and contribution), we identify the variables contributing to the formation of the first two factorial axes using MAD software (Karapistolis, 2000). The mentioned variables are selected based on two criteria: correlation ($Cor \geq 200$, criterion 2) and contribution (Ctr $\geq 1000/97 \approx 10.30928 \approx 11$, criterion 3) (Karapistolis, 2015; Fotiadis & Anastasiadou, 2018).

The First Factorial Plane $e_1 \times e_2$: The variables most significant for the first factorial plane $e_1 \times e_2$, based on the criteria of inertia, contribution, and correlation, are analyzed in detail below.

The first factorial plane $e_1 \times e_2$ (Diagram 4) explains 54.47% of the total inertia—information, which is a satisfactory percentage. The first factorial axis contrasts the extreme cases, while the second axis contrasts the intermediate cases between extremes.

In the first factorial plane and specifically in the first quadrant(e_1+, e_2+), we identify a group of respondents who either believe it is not necessary for students to learn about Artificial Intelligence (AI) at school (CC11) or hold no specific opinion on the matter. This group is characterized by a neutral stance. More specifically, this group does not have an opinion on whether AI courses are important (CC22), whether they want to continue learning about AI (BC62), whether they are interested in AI-related television programs or online videos (BC72) and the development of AI (BC92), whether they will need AI in their future life (AC52), whether most future jobs will require AI-related knowledge (AC102), and finally, whether AI is necessary for everyone (AC72).

n the second quadrant(e_1-, e_2+), we primarily encounter female students who, although uncertain whether Artificial Intelligence (AI) produces more good than harm (AC82), believe it is not enjoyable to learn about AI (BC53). However, they express a desire to participate in an AI-related club if one exists (BC33), as they acknowledge that AI makes people's lives more convenient (AC23) and is worth studying (AC93).

In the third quadrant (e_1-, e_2-), respondents strongly believe it is necessary for students to learn about AI at university (CC13) because AI produces more good than harm (AC83). Nonetheless, they indicate that AI is not essential for everyone (AC711), as it does not help them solve real-life problems (AC61).

In the fourth quadrant (e_1+, e_2-), respondents appear undecided about whether they will choose a career in the cognitive field of Artificial Intelligence (AI) (BC22). They do not believe AI makes people's lives more convenient (AC21) and do not think more class time should be dedicated to AI (BC111), primarily because they cannot determine if it is necessary for students to learn about AI in school (CC12), tending to believe it is not necessary (CC11). Consequently, they assert that AI is not worth studying (AC91) as they do not believe it produces more good than harm (AC81). Additionally, they believe most future jobs will not require AI-related knowledge (AC101). Moreover, they indicate uncertainty about their ability to handle

AI effectively (BC12), would not wish to participate in an AI-related club even if one existed (BC31), and ultimately find learning about cutting-edge technologies like AI not enjoyable at all (BC51).

Figure 1. First Factorial Plane $e_1 \times e_2$

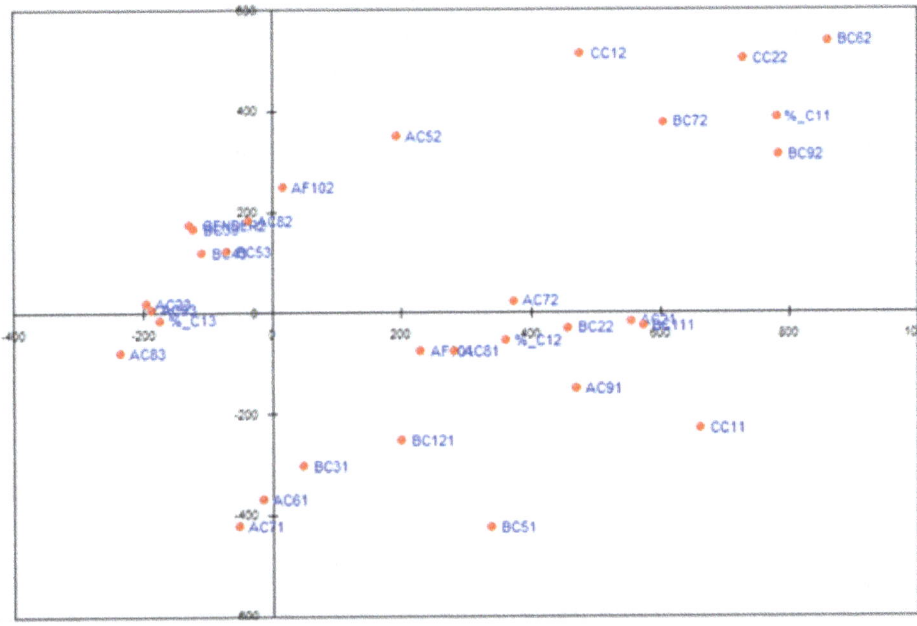

The Second Factorial Plane $e_1 \times e_3$: The Second Factorial Plane $e_1 \times e_3$ (Figure 2) explains 37.71% of the total inertia—information, which is a satisfactory percentage.

In the first quadrant, we observe respondents who hold negative attitudes regarding the conceptual constructs "Affective Component," "Cognitive Component," and "Behavioral Component." More specifically, within the first quadrant of this factorial plane, respondents are characterized by their lack of desire to continue learning about Artificial Intelligence (AI) (BC61), lack of interest in AI-related television programs or online videos (BC71), and the belief that AI does not deserve to be studied or taught (AC91) because it does not produce more good than harm (AC81). Moreover, they consider that most future jobs will not require AI-related knowledge (AC101) and believe AI does not make people's lives more convenient (AC21). Finally, these respondents either view learning about AI at school as unnecessary (CC11) or have no opinion on this matter (CC12).

In the second quadrant $(e_1 -, e_3 +)$, we find respondents aged over 24, residing in semi-urban areas, enrolled in schools of sciences, who find it interesting to use Artificial Intelligence (AI) (BC103).

In the third quadrant $(e_1 - ,e_3+)$, we encounter a distinct group that believes it is necessary for students to learn about Artificial Intelligence (AI) at school (CC13), as they consider that AI makes people's lives more convenient (AC23).

In the fourth quadrant $(e_1 + ,e_3-)$, we find respondents primarily holding a neutral stance regarding the "Behavioral Component." Specifically, respondents in this quadrant come from urban areas, are aged 18-20, and are enrolled in the School of Engineering. They do not have a clear opinion on whether it is interesting to use Artificial Intelligence (AI) (BC102), whether they are interested in AI-related television programs or online videos (BC72), or whether they generally have an interest in the development of AI (BC92). Additionally, they have not decided whether they want to continue learning about AI (BC6) or whether AI courses are important (CC2).

Figure 2. Second Factorial Plane $e_1 \times e_3$

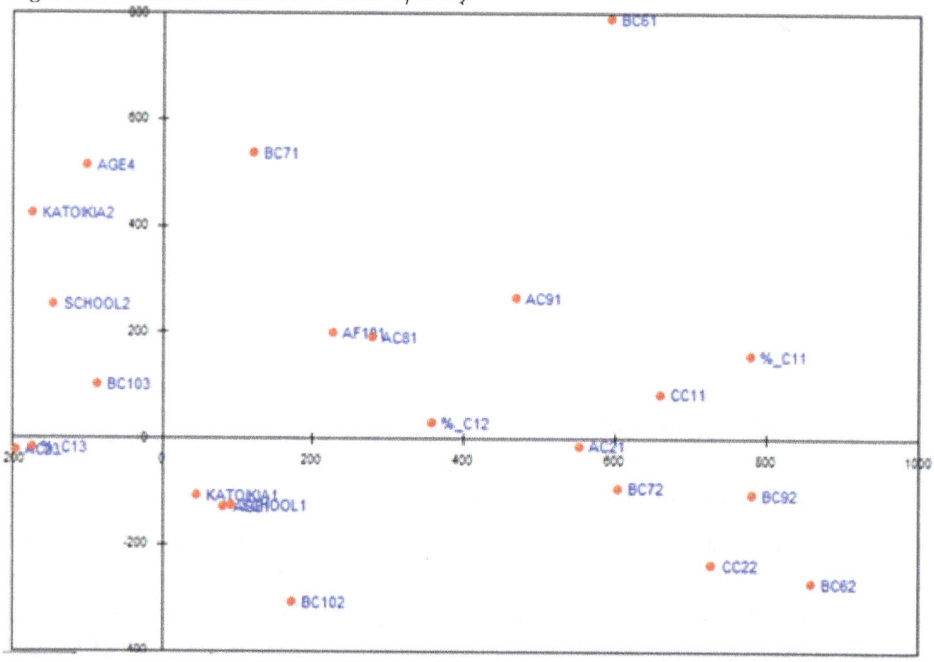

6. CONCLUSION

This research contributes to understanding students' attitudes toward artificial intelligence (AI), emphasizing the importance of emotional and cognitive factors in shaping their opinions and behaviors. More especially, this research significantly contributes to the understanding of students' attitudes toward artificial intelligence (AI), highlighting how emotional responses and cognitive perceptions shape their opinions and subsequent behaviors. The findings underscore that emotional factors, such as anxiety, curiosity, and enthusiasm, alongside cognitive elements, including knowledge and understanding of AI, play a pivotal role in determining students' acceptance and interaction with AI technologies. These findings suggest that education and awareness regarding AI can positively influence students' behavior and acceptance, with practical implications for designing educational programs.

The study indicates that targeted educational initiatives aimed at increasing AI literacy can effectively reduce misconceptions and apprehensions, promoting a more positive attitude among students. By incorporating comprehensive AI education into curricula, educators can foster an environment that encourages informed curiosity, critical thinking, and constructive engagement with emerging technologies.

Furthermore, this research emphasizes the necessity of addressing emotional responses, suggesting that educational programs should not solely focus on factual content but also engage students emotionally. Interactive learning experiences, practical demonstrations, and real-world applications of AI can help students relate better to AI technologies, reducing emotional barriers and enhancing acceptance.

Practically, the results offer valuable insights for educational institutions, curriculum designers, and policymakers. Effective AI-related educational programs should integrate emotional intelligence components, tailored to address students' fears, expectations, and aspirations regarding AI. Such comprehensive programs can prepare students to navigate and thrive in a rapidly evolving technological landscape, ultimately fostering a more AI-literate and adaptable future workfor

Specifically, according to the present research, there are varying attitudes towards Artificial Intelligence (AI). There is a group of students with an indifferent or neutral stance, another group with a positive stance, a group with a strongly positive stance, and a group with a negative stance.

The affective and cognitive factors are those determining the behavioral factor. Positive emotions lead to active behavior regarding AI use, doubts or negative emotions lead to passive behavior, and positive recognition of AI reinforces learning behavior.

The relationship between cognitive and behavioral factors is significant. Particularly, understanding the value of AI leads to positive behavior. Perceptions about AI education result in participation and commitment to its use. Those with limited knowledge exhibit passive behavior, while conversely, individuals with knowledge and confidence demonstrate increased engagement.

Addressing these behaviors related to students' attitudes toward artificial intelligence (AI) necessitates additional research, particularly through the use of artificial intelligence (Souravlas & Anastasiadou, 2022; Souravlas et al., 2020), cloud computing (Souravlas et al., 2021a; 2021b; 2021c), cutting-edge technologies, and innovative educational approaches. Such research is critical due to the significance and necessity of comprehensively grasping emotional and cognitive factors toward AI (Souravlas et al., 2022a; 2022b; 2023).

REFERENCES

Al-Zahrani, A. M., & Alasmari, T. M. (2024). Exploring the impact of artificial intelligence on higher education: The dynamics of ethical, social, and educational implications. *Humanities & Social Sciences Communications, 11*(912). Advance online publication. DOI: 10.1057/s41599-024-03432-4

Anastasiadou, S. (2013). Developing and Evaluating a Structural Equation Model Measuring Leadership Changes in a Lifelong Learning World. *The International Journal of Educational Organization and Leadership, 19*(2), 1–17. DOI: 10.18848/2329-1656/CGP/v19i02/48520

Anastasiadou, S. (2016). Evaluation of the Implementation of TQM principles in Tertiary Education using the EFQM Excellence Model -Research in Educational Departments of Greek Universities. Published Master's thesis, Greek Open University, Patra, Greece.

Anastasiadou, S. (2019). Comparison of contemporary advanced statistical methods regarding construct validity evaluation of TEIque-SF instrument: Statistical Implicative Analysis vs. Principal Components Analysis. *9ème Colloque International sur Analyse Statistique Implicative (ASI 10)*. Belfort – France. pp. 148-163.

Anastasiadou, S., & Karakos, A. (2011). The beliefs of electrical and computer engineering students´ regarding computer programming. *International Journal of Technology, Knowledge and Society, 7*(1), 37–52. DOI: 10.18848/1832-3669/CGP/v07i01/56170

Anastasiadou, S., & Taraza, E. (2019). Total quality management: implementation of the six sigma methodology for improving quality in higher education, ICERI2019, the 12th annual International Conference of Education, Research and Innovation, Seville (Spain), ICERI2019, pp. 9533-9537.

Anastasiadou, S., & Tiliakou, C. (2016). Evaluation of the discriminating ability of the Greek state foreign language exam (KPG) for English by means of the factorial analysis of correspondences. *International Journal of Learning and Teaching, 8*(2), 129–140. DOI: 10.18844/ijlt.v8i2.518

Bates, T., Cobo, C., Marino, O., & Wheeler, S. (2020). Can artificial intelligence transform higher education? *International Journal of Educational Technology in Higher Education, 17*(42). Advance online publication. DOI: 10.1186/s41239-020-00218-x

Benzécri, J. P. (1973). *Analyse des Données.*

Crompton, H., & Burke, D. (2023). Artificial intelligence in higher education: The state of the field. *International Journal of Educational Technology in Higher Education, 20*(22). Advance online publication. DOI: 10.1186/s41239-023-00392-8

Farhi, F., Jeljeli, R., & Aburezeq, I. Fawzi Fayez Dweikat, Samer Ali Al-shami, Slamene, R. (2023). Analyzing the students' views, concerns, and perceived ethics about chatGPT usage, Computers and Education: Artificial Intelligence, Volume 5, 2023, 100180, ISSN 2666-920X,https://doi.org/DOI: 10.1016/j.caeai.2023.100180

Fotiadis, Th., & Anastasiadou, S. (2018). Contemporary advanced statistical methods for the science of marketing: Principal Components Analysis vs Analysee Factorielle des Correspondances. Proceeding of the ICME 2018- 1st International Conference on Marketing and Entrepreneuship. Cyprus. https://hephaestus.nup.ac.cy/handle/11728/11392

Karapistolis, D. (2015). *Multivariate Statistical Analysis* (Altintzis, A., Ed.).

Katsantonis, A., & Katsantonis, I. G. (2024). University Students' Attitudes toward Artificial Intelligence: An Exploratory Study of the Cognitive, Emotional, and Behavioural Dimensions of AI Attitudes. *Education in Science, 14*, 988. DOI: 10.3390/educsci14090988

Ntotsi, P., & Anastasiadou, S. D. (2019). Contemporary advanced statistical methods for the science of educational research: Principal components analysis versus L' analysee factorielle des correspondances. *New Trends and Issues Proceedings on Humanities and Social Sciences*. [Online]. 6(1), pp 246–255. Available from from: www.prosoc.eu

Papadaki, Z., Anastasiadou, S., Masouras, A., & Papalexandris, S. (2023). Factors Influencing the Use of Digital Marketing by Telemedicine Services. 10th International Conference on Strategic Innovative Marketing and Tourism 2023. Zakynthos, Ionian Islands, Greece. pp. 855-862. In A. Kavoura et al. (eds.), Strategic Innovative Marketing and Tourism, Springer Proceedings in Business and Economics, https://doi.org/DOI: 10.1007/978-3-031-51038-0_92

Papadaki, Z. E., & Anastsasiadou, S. D. (2019). Evaluating Perception, Expectation of Consumers, and Service Quality Gap in Greek Banking in a Period of Financial Crisis and Capital Controls. In Sykianakis, N., Polychronidou, P., & Karasavvoglou, A. (Eds.), *Economic and Financial Challenges for Eastern Europe. Springer Proceedings in Business and Economics* (pp. 67–80). Springer., DOI: 10.1007/978-3-030-12169-3_5

Papademetriou, C., Anastasiadou, S., Kondeos, G., & Papalexandris, S. (2022). COVID-19 Pandemic: The Impact of the Social Media Technology on Higher Education. *Education in Science, 12*(4), 261. DOI: 10.3390/educsci12040261

Papademetriou, C., Anastasiadou, S., & Papalexandris, S. (2023). The impact of sustainable HRM practices on service quality, customer satisfaction, and organizational performance in hotel industry. Sustainability, mdpi. *Sustainability, 15*(10), 8251. DOI: 10.3390/su15108251

Papadimitriou, I. (2007). Data Analysis. Tipothito Eds. Athens, Greece.

Souravlas, S., & Anastasiadou, S. (2020). Pipelined Dynamic Scheduling of Big Data Streams. *Applied Sciences (Basel, Switzerland), 10*(14), 4796. DOI: 10.3390/app10144796

Souravlas, S., & Anastasiadou, S. (2022). On Implementing Social Community Clouds Based on Markov Models. *IEEE Transactions on Computational Social Systems, 2022*. Advance online publication. DOI: 10.1109/TCSS.2022.3213273

Souravlas, S., Anastasiadou, S., Economides, Th., & Katsavounis, S. (2023). Probabilistic Community Detection in Social Networks. IEEE Access, Journal: IEEE Access, Publication Date: 2023, Volume: 11, On Page(s): 25629-25641, Print ISSN: 2169-3536, Online ISSN: 2169-3536, Digital Object Identifier: DOI: 10.1109/ACCESS.2023.3257021

Souravlas, S., Anastasiadou, S., & Katsavounis, S. (2021b). A Survey on the Recent Advances of Deep Community Detection. *Applied Sciences (Basel, Switzerland), 11*(16), 7179. DOI: 10.3390/app11167179

Souravlas, S., Anastasiadou, S., & Katsavounis, S. (2021c). More on Pipelined Dynamic Scheduling of Big Data Streams. *Applied Sciences (Basel, Switzerland), 11*(1), 61. DOI: 10.3390/app11010061

Souravlas, S. Anastasiadou, S. & Kostoglou, I. (2022b). A Novel Method For General Hierarchical System Modeling Via Colored Petri Nets Based on Transition Extractions From Real Data Sets. Appl. Sci. 2023, 13, 339. https://doi.org/DOI: 10.3390/app13010339

Souravlas, S., Anastasiadou, S., Tantalaki, N., & Katsavounis, S. (2021a). A Dynamic Load Balanced Task Distribution Strategy for Heterogeneous Cloud Platforms Based on Markov Process Modeling. *IEEE Access : Practical Innovations, Open Solutions, 10*, 2169–3536. https://ieeexplore.ieee.org/abstract/document/9729723

Souravlas, S., Anastasiadou, S. D., Tantalaki, N., & Katsavounis, S. (2022a). A Fair, Dynamic Load Balanced Task Distribution Strategy for Heterogeneous Cloud Platforms Based on Markov Process Modeling," in IEEE Access, vol. 10, pp. 26149-26162, 2022, doi: DOI: 10.1109/ACCESS.2022.3157435

Souravlas, S., Katsavounis, S., & Anastasiadou, S. (2020). On Modeling and Simulation of Resource Allocation Policies in Cloud Computing Using Colored Petri Nets. *Applied Sciences (Basel, Switzerland)*, *10*(16), 5644. DOI: 10.3390/app10165644

Suh, W., & Ahn, S. (2022). Development and Validation of a Scale Measuring Student Attitudes toward Artificial Intelligence. *SAGE Open*, *2022*(12), 215824402211004.

Weichert, J., & Eldardiry, H. (2024). Computer Science Student Attitudes Towards AI Ethics and Policy: A Preliminary Investigation. *2024 IEEE International Symposium on Technology and Society (ISTAS)*, Puebla, Mexico, 2024, pp. 1-5, doi: DOI: 10.1109/ISTAS61960.2024.10732801

Chapter 9
Exploring Students' Mental Strategies in Algebraic Function Tasks Through Multivariate–Multidimensional Data Analysis

Nikolaos Papafilippou
http://orcid.org/0009-0003-3148-7229
School of Agriculture, Aristotle University of Thessaloniki, Greece

Christos Dordas
http://orcid.org/0000-0002-7027-474X
School of Agriculture, Aristotle University of Thessaloniki, Greece

Zacharenia Kyrana
http://orcid.org/0000-0001-9269-0675
School of Agriculture, Aristotle University of Thessaloniki, Greece

Thomas Koutsos
http://orcid.org/0000-0003-4035-7971
School of Agriculture, Aristotle University of Thessaloniki, Greece

Emmanouil D. Pratsinakis
http://orcid.org/0000-0002-3725-3525
School of Agriculture, Aristotle University of Thessaloniki, Greece

Angelos Markos
http://orcid.org/0000-0002-4204-3573
School of Education, Democritus University of Thrace, Greece

ABSTRACT

This chapter examines Grade 12 students' mental strategies when solving functional tasks in a graphical environment. Forty-two students in Greece participated in clinical interviews requiring mental computation without external tools. They solved tasks with pairs of functions—linear–constant, quadratic–constant, or two

DOI: 10.4018/979-8-3373-6926-6.ch009

linear—by finding their sum or difference. Students' verbal and gestural responses were coded into categories capturing strategy type, task context, and accuracy. Using Correspondence Analysis, Biplot Analysis, Hierarchical Cluster Analysis, and Kriging Interpolation, the study revealed associations among strategies and tasks, clusters of adaptive reasoning, and spatial "cognitive landscapes" showing gradients of success. Findings indicate that reasoning in mental mathematics is emergent and shaped by interactions among cognitive, representational, and contextual factors. Grounded in cognitive activation theory and enactivism, the study shows that mathematical knowledge is enacted through coordinated action with the environment.

INTRODUCTION

The study of students' reasoning processes with functions has long been considered a central theme in mathematics education. Functions constitute a fundamental concept, yet they are notoriously challenging for learners due to the multiplicity of their representations—algebraic, graphical, tabular, and verbal—and the cognitive demand of translating between these (Dubinsky & Harel, 1992; Duval, 2006; Eisenberg, 1992). While substantial research has focused on students' difficulties and misconceptions with functions, less attention has been given to how students mentally manage operations on functions in non-symbolic or graphical contexts.

Mental mathematics, traditionally associated with arithmetic operations, has been shown to foster number sense, flexibility, and adaptive reasoning (Threlfall, 2002, 2009). However, its extension to other mathematical objects, such as functions, remains relatively unexplored (Proulx, 2015). Investigating how students mentally add or subtract functions in a graphical environment provides a unique opportunity to examine the strategies they develop when algebraic expressions are absent or de-emphasized. Such inquiry can reveal the extent to which students rely on holistic graphical reasoning, algebraic-parametric manipulation, or hybrid approaches that combine representational modes.

In addition, the notion of strategic flexibility—the ability to select and shift between strategies depending on the task context and cognitive resources—has emerged as a key dimension of mathematical proficiency (Star & Rittle-Johnson, 2008). Understanding flexibility in the context of functional reasoning is essential, as students must often coordinate multiple representations and strategies in order to interpret or construct function graphs. The study of mental strategies in this domain thus contributes both to the theory of mathematical cognition and to the practical challenge of supporting representational fluency in the classroom.

The present chapter builds on empirical research with 42 Greek Grade 12 students who engaged in clinical interviews involving mental operations on pairs of functions. Their discourse—verbal explanations, gestures, and reasoning processes—was analyzed using advanced multivariate and multidimensional statistical techniques. By applying Simple Correspondence Analysis (CA), Bi-plot Analysis, Hierarchical Cluster Analysis (HCA), and Kriging Interpolation, the study aims to uncover the hidden structures in students' strategies, visualize the associations between tasks and reasoning modes, and generate "cognitive landscapes" that reveal gradients of performance across the factorial space.

The contribution of this work is threefold: (a) theoretically, it extends the scope of mental mathematics research beyond numbers to include functions, highlighting strategic behavior and flexibility; (b) methodologically, it demonstrates the integration of statistical and geostatistical techniques in the analysis of discourse data; and (c) pedagogically, it offers insights into how teachers may recognize and leverage students' reasoning patterns to design instruction that supports deeper understanding of functions.

THE IMPORTANCE OF FUNCTIONS IN MATHEMATICS LEARNING

The notion of function is widely recognized as one of the cornerstones of secondary mathematics curricula. Eisenberg (1992) argues that the development of function sense should be regarded as the equivalent of number sense in primary education. Similarly, Dubinsky and Harel (1992) emphasize that understanding functions is a prerequisite for grasping many other mathematical ideas and for bridging classical and modern mathematics. This makes functions not only a fundamental mathematical object but also a critical cognitive structure for students' progression in algebra, calculus, and modeling. Functions are also deeply connected to everyday experiences, since they describe covariation between quantities such as distance and time, pressure and age, or profit and production (Gagatsis & Shiakalli, 2004). This dual nature—abstract yet applicable—makes the teaching and learning of functions both essential and challenging.

Students' Difficulties and Misconceptions

Despite its importance, research consistently shows that functions are among the least understood concepts for high school and even undergraduate students (Sierpinska, 1992; Vinner & Dreyfus, 1989). Difficulties arise in at least three domains:

- The basic concept and definition: Many students confuse "function" with "formula" or believe that only one-to-one correspondences qualify as functions (Vinner, 1983).
- Multiple representations: Students often struggle to connect algebraic, graphical, tabular, and verbal representations. They may rely heavily on algebraic forms even when a graphical or numerical approach would be more efficient (Knuth, 2000; Eisenberg & Dreyfus, 1994).
- Covariation and dependency: Students often fail to interpret how changes in one variable affect another, treating functions as static instead of dynamic relationships (Carlson, 1998).

Sfard (1992) highlights that students tend to view functions procedurally (as processes of computation) rather than structurally (as objects), which restricts their conceptual flexibility. Duval (2006) further shows that learning difficulties stem from the challenge of translating between semiotic registers; meaningful understanding requires recognizing the same mathematical object across symbolic, graphical, and verbal forms.

The Role of Representations and Visualization

Representation is now considered a central principle in mathematics learning (NCTM, 2000). Research indicates that external representations, including graphs, diagrams and algebraic formulas serve not merely as illustrations but as cognitive tools that shape reasoning (Pape & Tchoshanov, 2001). Presmeg (1998) emphasizes the importance of visualization in mathematical thought, while Arcavi (2003) notes that graphical reasoning allows students to see structures and patterns that may remain hidden in symbolic manipulation. Scholars such as Janvier (1987), Kaput (1992), and Moschkovich et al. (2012) have emphasized representational fluency as a critical component of functional understanding. Students' reasoning often reveals whether they perceive representations as distinct entities or as interconnected views of the same mathematical object. Studying how learners mentally operate on functions in graphical settings provides a window into their representational competence and the cognitive resources they mobilize when algebraic symbolism is not foregrounded.

Mental Computation, Strategies, and Flexibility

Scholarly research recognizes mental computation as an essential dimension of mathematical expertise. Early definitions emphasized accurate calculation without external aids (Wandt & Brown, 1957; Trafton, 1978), while later perspectives highlighted the distinction between exact calculation and estimation (Reys, 1984;

Sowder, 1988). More recent work frames mental computation as the execution of arithmetic or algebraic processes through strategies, often involving informal, personal methods rather than algorithmic procedures (Maclellan, 2001; Thompson, 2010; Threlfall, 2002).

A central construct within this literature is the notion of strategies. Mental strategies are not simply memorized procedures but adaptive processes that learners construct to support problem solving. Researchers distinguish flexibility—the readiness to move across alternative strategies—from adaptivity—the competence to select the most effective strategy in a particular situation. (Heinze et al., 2009; Selter, 2009; Verschaffel et al., 2009). Strategic flexibility and adaptivity have been associated with deeper conceptual understanding and the development of adaptive expertise.

While research has traditionally focused on numbers and arithmetic, there is growing interest in extending mental computation to other mathematical domains, including algebra, geometry, and functions (Proulx, 2015). In these settings, mental computation emphasizes reasoning with symbolic structures and graphical representations rather than reliance on written algorithms. For instance, in the case of functions, mental tasks may involve adding or subtracting function graphs without resorting to formal algebraic manipulation, requiring students to mobilize conceptual and representational knowledge.

Recent theoretical perspectives argue that strategies should not be seen as fixed tools selected from a repertoire but rather as emergent phenomena arising from the interaction between learner and task (Threlfall, 2009; Proulx, 2013). From an inactive standpoint (Maturana & Varela, 1992), strategies are contextually generated, shaped by both the structure of the problem and the learner's prior experiences. Such a perspective shifts the emphasis away from listing predetermined strategies and toward understanding students' activity in the process of task engagement.

Within this framework, the study of mental computation with functions contributes to a broader conception of mental mathematics—not limited to number sense, but encompassing "graph sense," "symbol sense," and "process sense" (Caney & Watson, 2003). Investigating how learners develop and adapt strategies in graphical environments provides a powerful lens for examining flexibility, representation, and meaning-making in mathematics.

Research on Mental Management of Functions

Within this context, the emerging field of research on mental management of functions (Proulx, 2014, 2015) provides a unique lens. Proulx conducted multiple case studies with Grade 11 students, asking them to mentally perform operations such as the addition or subtraction of functions within a graphical environment, without pencil, paper, or computational aids. His findings revealed three distinct strategic approaches:

- Algebraic-parametric strategy: relying on symbolic manipulation of expressions, even when only graphs were provided.
- Graphical-geometrical strategy: treating functions as shapes or curves, emphasizing shifts, parallels, and geometric transformations.
- Graphical-arithmetic strategy: focusing on specific points on the graph, estimating values numerically, and constructing the resulting function point by point.

These strategies highlight that students do not simply "apply rules" but actively generate approaches based on the interplay of prior knowledge, task constraints, and representational affordances. Moreover, the study showed that students tended to default to algebraic reasoning, reflecting the curriculum's heavy emphasis on algebra, but also demonstrated creative geometric and numerical reasoning in novel contexts.

This research provides the immediate backdrop for the present study, which extends the exploration of mental strategies for functions to Grade 12 students in Greece, examining both the distribution of strategies and their relationship with achievement levels.

MULTIVARIATE-MULTIDIMENSIONAL METHODS IN DISCOURSE DATA ANALYSIS

Simple Correspondence Analysis

Correspondence Analysis (CA) is an exploratory multivariate technique designed for the geometric investigation of associations within categorical data structures. Rather than testing predefined hypotheses, CA seeks to uncover latent relational patterns embedded in contingency tables by transforming frequency information into a low-dimensional spatial configuration (Benzécri, 1992; Greenacre, 2017; Beh & Lombardo, 2021).

In the case of two categorical variables X and Y, with k and l categories respectively, the analysis begins with the construction of the correspondence matrix $P=(p_{ij})$, obtained by standardizing the contingency table frequencies f_{ij} (Table 1) by the grand total n, such that:

$$p_{ij} = \frac{f_{ij}}{n}$$

Row and column profiles are defined through the marginal proportions $r_i = n_{i.}/n$ and $c_j = n_{.j}/n$, which act as weights (masses) in the geometric representation.

Table 1. Contingency table of categorical variables X and Y

	Categories of variable Y				
Categories of variable X	Y_1	Y_2	...	Y_l	Row sum (total)
X	f_{11}	f_{12}	...	f_{1l}	$n_{1.}$
$\mathbf{X_2}$	f_{21}	f_{22}	...	f_{2l}	$n_{2.}$
⋮	⋮	⋮	...	⋮	⋮
$\mathbf{X_k}$	f_{kl}	f_{k2}	...	f_{kl}	$n_{k.}$
Columns sum (total)	$n_{.1}$	$n_{.2}$	...	$n_{.l}$	n

The relational structure between profiles is assessed using the chi-square metric introduced by Benzécri. Distances between row profiles (or column profiles) are computed by weighting squared deviations with respect to the inverse of the corresponding masses. This metric ensures that deviations in rarely occurring categories receive appropriate emphasis. The overall dispersion of the cloud of profiles in the multidimensional space is quantified through total inertia, which reflects the departure from independence. It is well established that total inertia equals the chi-square statistic divided by the sample size:

$$I = \frac{Q}{n}$$

Thus, inertia may be interpreted as a normalized measure of association strength within the contingency structure.

CA proceeds through the singular value decomposition (SVD) of the matrix of standardized residuals:

$$S = (s_{ij}) = \frac{p_{ij} - r_i c_j}{\sqrt{r_i c_j}}$$

where p_{ij} is the (i,j) element of the correspondence table, and r_i, c_j are the masses of the *i-th* row and *j-th* column, respectively.

The decomposition extracts orthogonal factorial axes that successively maximize explained inertia. The dimensionality of the solution is bounded by $p = \min\{k-1, l-1\}$. Each axis s is associated with singular value d_s and corresponding eigenvalue $\lambda_s = d_s^2$. The relative contribution of each axis is computed as:

$\frac{\lambda_s}{I} \times 100.$

Through this procedure, both row and column categories are simultaneously projected onto a common factorial space, typically two- or three-dimensional, preserving as much of the original association structure as possible.

To evaluate the interpretative relevance of projected points, three complementary indices are commonly examined:

- CTR (Contribution): quantifies how strongly a category influences the construction of a factorial axis.
- $\cos^2$ (Squared Correlation): indicates the degree to which a point is well represented on a specific axis.
- QLT (Quality of Representation): summarizes the adequacy of representation across retained dimensions.

Categories exhibiting high contribution and satisfactory representation values are typically retained for substantive interpretation of factorial dimensions.

Different normalization approaches alter the graphical emphasis of CA without modifying eigenvalues or the underlying association structure. Symmetrical normalization balances row and column dispersion, whereas row-principal and column-principal normalizations privilege one set of categories over the other. The principal normalization traditionally associated with the French school redistributes inertia separately to rows and columns, yielding the classical factorial representation. These alternative scaling modify interpretative perspective but do not affect the statistical core of the solution.

Although CA provides a comprehensive geometric depiction of association patterns, standard factorial maps emphasize mutual positioning rather than directional relational strength. To further enhance interpretability—particularly when asymmetry between rows and columns is substantively meaningful—Bi-plot approaches may be employed as complementary analytical tools.

Bi-Plot Analysis

The geometric interpretation of these indices is based on projections onto bi-plot axes (Gabriel, 1971, 2002, 2004; Kroonenberg, 1995; Blasius & Greenacre, 1998; Gower, 2004; Cuadras et al., 2006; Greenacre, 2009). Within the factorial space, any selected category—row or column—may be used to define a directional reference passing through the origin. This direction functions as an interpretative axis along which the categories of the complementary set can be examined. By projecting these categories perpendicularly onto the reference direction, their relative positioning becomes comparable on a single continuum.

The ordering that emerges along this direction reflects the intensity of association: projections located nearer to the defining category indicate stronger relational proximity, whereas more distant projections correspond to weaker connections. Consequently, each such directional construction allows an ordered comparison between rows and columns, moving beyond the purely symmetric visual inspection of the factorial map.

To evaluate how faithfully a category aligns with the chosen direction, the squared cosine ($\cos^2$) between its position vector and the reference direction is considered. This index expresses the proportion of the point's variance that is explained by the axis. Values approaching unity indicate that the category lies nearly along the direction itself, implying stable interpretability. Lower values suggest that the point's configuration is influenced by other latent dimensions and should therefore be interpreted cautiously.

Through this combined use of directional projection and angular diagnostics, the bi-plot framework refines the interpretation of associations by quantifying not only their existence but also their relative strength and representational adequacy.

Hierarchical Cluster Analysis (HCA)

Hierarchical Cluster Analysis (HCA) (Everitt et al., 2011) is a foundational multivariate technique within unsupervised learning (Bishop, 2016) that seeks to identify hierarchical relationships among observations based on their similarity or dissimilarity. Whereas partitioning techniques like k-means assume a fixed number of clusters defined a priori, HCA derives a multilevel clustering structure directly from the data. The resulting hierarchy is represented graphically in the form of a dendrogram. This representation provides insight into both fine-grained and broad relationships among cases, allowing the researcher to examine multiple levels of clustering simultaneously. The theoretical basis of HCA lies in multivariate statistical theory, pattern recognition, and unsupervised machine learning. It assumes that within a dataset, there exist latent structural relationships that can be discovered through iterative similarity comparisons (Murtagh & Contreras, 2011, 2017). The process involves calculating a similarity or distance matrix—using metrics such as Euclidean, Manhattan, Benzécri's chi-squared or correlation distance—and successively merging or dividing clusters according to specific linkage criteria. Clustering solutions may be constructed using several linkage strategies, including single and complete linkage, average linkage, and Ward's approach, which merges clusters so as to achieve the smallest possible growth in within-group dispersion. (Everitt et al., 2011).

Mathematically, if X= $\{x_1, x_2, ..., x_n\}$ denotes a dataset of n observations, HCA begins with each observation as a separate cluster and iteratively combines the two closest clusters A and B based on their linkage distance d (A, B). The process continues until all elements are grouped into a single cluster, forming a hierarchy of nested relationships. The resulting structure can be interpreted at various levels of similarity depending on the researcher's analytical purpose.

In the field of education, HCA provides a theoretically coherent framework for exploring learner diversity, institutional classification, and educational system typologies. Educational phenomena are often inherently hierarchical—students belong to classes, classes to schools, and schools to districts—making HCA conceptually compatible with the structure of educational data (Romero & Ventura, 2020). By identifying nested groupings, HCA enables researchers to reveal patterns of academic performance, engagement behaviors, or contextual influences that operate at different levels of aggregation (Macfadyen & Dawson, 2009).

From a theoretical standpoint, HCA aligns with constructivist and systems perspectives on education. Constructivist theory posits that learning is a cumulative process shaped by relationships among cognitive elements (Lerner, 2015b). Similarly, systems theory views education as a multilevel network of interdependent units. HCA operationalizes these perspectives by statistically modeling how educational entities are linked in hierarchical structures based on shared attributes or behaviors.

Moreover, HCA supports the principles of differentiated instruction and learning analytics, which emphasize that learners exhibit diverse profiles that can be empirically identified through data analysis (Tomlinson, 2014; Siemens, 2013). By clustering students or institutions into meaningful hierarchical groups, educational stakeholders can tailor interventions and policies to the unique characteristics of each subgroup.

Kriging Interpolation

Kriging is a geostatistical interpolation method that estimates unknown spatial values by exploiting the spatial correlation among observed data points. Developed by D. G. Krige and theoretically formalized by Georges Matheron in the 1960s, it constitutes one of the most robust frameworks in spatial statistics, combining concepts from probability theory, stochastic processes, and spatial autocorrelation (Matheron, 1963; Goovaerts, 1997). Its main premise is that spatial phenomena exhibit systematic spatial dependence—nearby locations tend to have more similar values than distant ones (Isaaks & Srivastava, 1989).

At its core, Kriging is based on the theory of regionalized variables, which assumes that any spatially distributed attribute $Z(x)$ can be represented as a combination of a deterministic trend component $\mu(\mathrm{x})$ and a random, spatially correlated component $\varepsilon(x)$:

$$Z(x)=\mu(x)+\varepsilon(x)$$

where $\mu(x)$ captures large-scale spatial trends (for example, gradual regional differences in educational performance), while $\varepsilon(x)$ represents local random variations that are spatially correlated. This formulation allows Kriging to produce not only a prediction of the variable at unsampled locations but also an estimation of the prediction variance. This feature sets Kriging apart from deterministic techniques, including IDW and spline interpolation, by explicitly modeling spatial dependence. (Cressie, 1993).

At the heart of Kriging lies the concept of the variogram, a function that models how similarity (covariance) between two points decreases as their spatial distance increases. The variogram quantifies spatial dependence as:

$$\gamma(h)=\frac{1}{2}E[Z(x)-Z(x+h)]^2$$

where $\gamma(h)$ is the semivariance for lag distance h, $Z(x)$ denotes the value of the spatial variable at location x, and $E\,[\cdot]$ represents the expected value operator. The parameters of the variogram—nugget, sill, and range—define the degree of spatial continuity and serve as the basis for weighting nearby observations during interpolation. Kriging uses these spatial weights to ensure that the predicted value at each location is the best linear unbiased estimator (BLUE) under the assumed covariance structure (Goovaerts, 1997).

MATERIALS AND METHODS

Participants

The study involved 42 Grade 12 students from general secondary school in Greece. All participants had completed the standard national curriculum in algebra and functions, including linear, quadratic, and constant functions, and were familiar with their graphical representations. The sample was constructed through a purposive selection procedure, aiming to include comparable numbers of students from different achievement levels—based on their mathematics grades and teacher recommendations. Participation was voluntary, and all data collection procedures adhered to ethical guidelines for research in education, ensuring anonymity and informed consent.

Data Collection Procedure

Data were collected through individual clinical interviews, each lasting approximately 25–30 minutes. In these sessions, students engaged in mental tasks that required performing addition and subtraction of functions displayed in graphical form. The interviews emphasized mental reasoning, meaning that no written calculations or external computational aids were permitted. Students were encouraged to verbalize their thought processes or indicate their reasoning through gestures or pointing to features of the graphs.

All interviews were audio-recorded and transcribed verbatim. The researcher maintained detailed field notes capturing the students' gestures, pauses, and shifts in strategy. These verbal and nonverbal data formed the basis for subsequent discourse analysis and coding.

Coding Procedure

The analysis and processing of the qualitative data followed principles of grounded theory methodology (Creswell, 2012, pp. 423–447). At the first level of analysis, all interview transcripts were read in detail in order to identify excerpts—verbal statements or reasoning episodes—that corresponded to one of the predefined strategy categories. At the second level, these excerpts were coded according to the specific type of strategy they represented. At the third level, the individual codes were grouped based on similarities in structure, reasoning patterns, and representational processes, allowing the emergence of higher-order categories. More specifically, six strategy codes were used: AP (algebraic/parametric), GG (graphical/geometric), GA (graphical/arithmetic), AP–GG (combined algebraic/parametric and graphical/geometric), AP–GA (combined algebraic/parametric and graphical/arithmetic), and GG–GA (combined graphical/geometric and graphical/arithmetic). Students' responses were additionally coded as C (correct), W (wrong), or NA (no answer), while each participant was labeled as Si (i student). This coding structure provided a consistent framework for transforming qualitative reasoning processes into categorical data suitable for multivariate analysis (see Appendix A).

Research Instrument

The research instrument was designed by adapting tasks from Proulx (2015), modified for the Greek educational context. It consisted of six groups of tasks, each designed to elicit specific types of reasoning and to investigate how representational features (presence or absence of algebraic expressions) influenced strategic behavior:

Group 1 (Task 1.1–Task 1.2): In the first group, both graphical and algebraic representations of a linear and a constant function (Task 1.1) and of a quadratic and a constant function (Task 1.2) were presented on the same Cartesian plane. Students were asked to determine mentally the sum or difference of the two functions.

Figure 1. Tasks of the first group (Proulx, 2015, pg. 6)

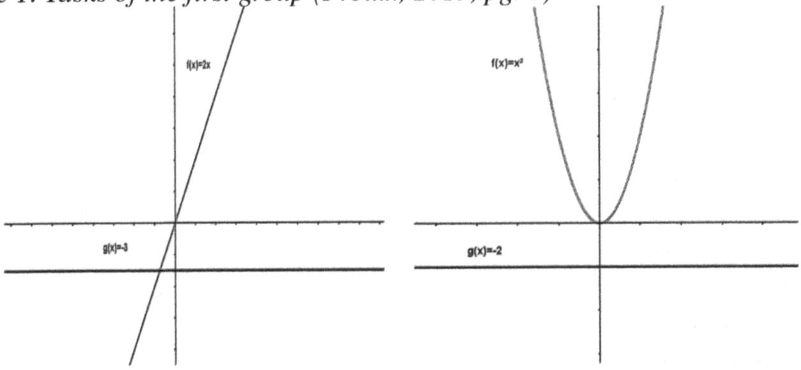

This group was designed to investigate whether the presence of algebraic expressions would prompt students to adopt an algebraic–parametric strategy—first adding the algebraic forms (for example $f(x)+g(x)$) and then mentally visualizing the resulting graph—or whether they would engage in a graphical–geometric strategy, reasoning holistically that adding a constant translates a graph vertically upward or downward depending on its sign. An additional aim was to assess whether students would approach linear and quadratic cases differently, revealing sensitivity to the visual and functional structure of each task.

Group 2 (Task 2.1-Task 2.2): In the second group, students were shown the graphs only—a linear–constant pair (Task 2.1) and a quadratic–constant pair (Task 2.2)—without any symbolic expressions provided. They were asked to find graphically and mentally the sum of the two functions.

Figure 2. Tasks of the second group (Proulx, 2015, pg. 9)

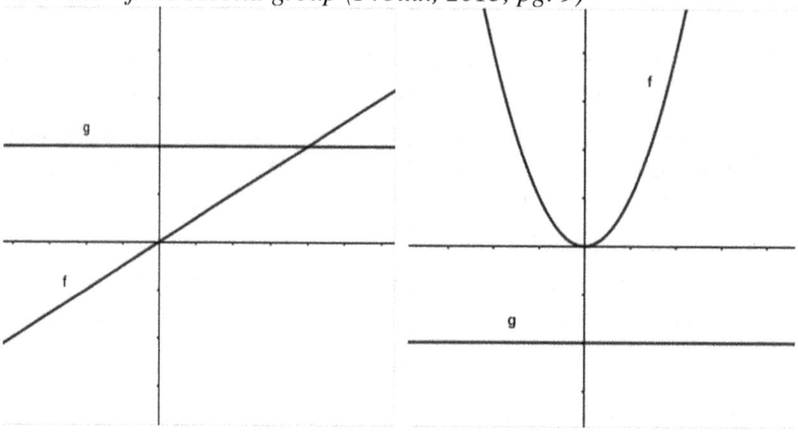

The absence of algebraic formulas aimed to test whether students would rely on visual transformations and a holistic reading of the graph ("adding a constant shifts the function vertically")—that is, a graphical–geometric strategy—or whether they would reconstruct implicit algebraic forms (for example, $f(x)=ax$ or $f(x)=ax^2$, and $g(x)=c$) and mentally combine them, reflecting an algebraic–parametric approach. By comparing linear and quadratic tasks, this group explored whether strategic reasoning varies with the complexity of functional form.

Group 3 (Task 3): In the third task, both the original function $f(x)$ and the resulting function $f(x)+g(x)$ were displayed on the same Cartesian plane. Students were asked to infer the unknown function g(x) mentally.

Here, both $f(x)$ and $f(x)+g(x)$ represented square-root functions plus a constant. The task examined whether students would reason visually, identifying that the result corresponds to a vertical translation of the initial curve (indicating a constant positive or negative offset)—a graphical–geometric strategy—or whether they would combine algebraic and arithmetic reasoning, computing approximate vertical differences between points (for example, $g=(f+g)-f$, thus exhibiting a graphical–arithmetic or mixed strategy.

Figure 3. Task of the third group (Proulx, 2015, pg. 6)

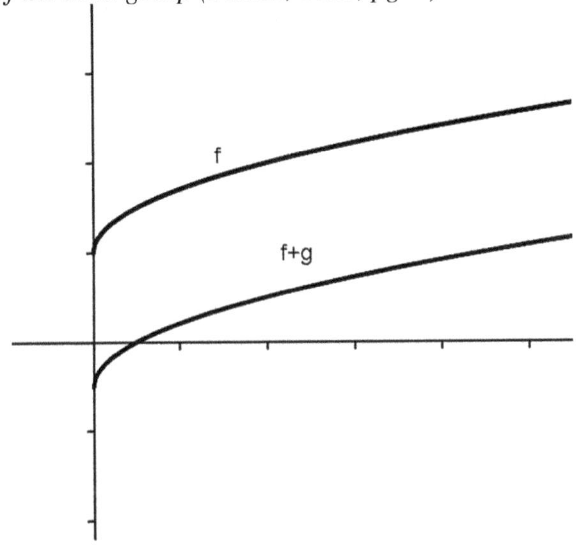

Group 4 (Task 4): The fourth task involved two intersecting linear functions whose meeting point was located on the x-axis at $x \neq 0$. Students were asked to determine $f-g$ or $g-f$ mentally.

Figure 4. Task of the fourth group (Proulx, 2015, pg. 9)

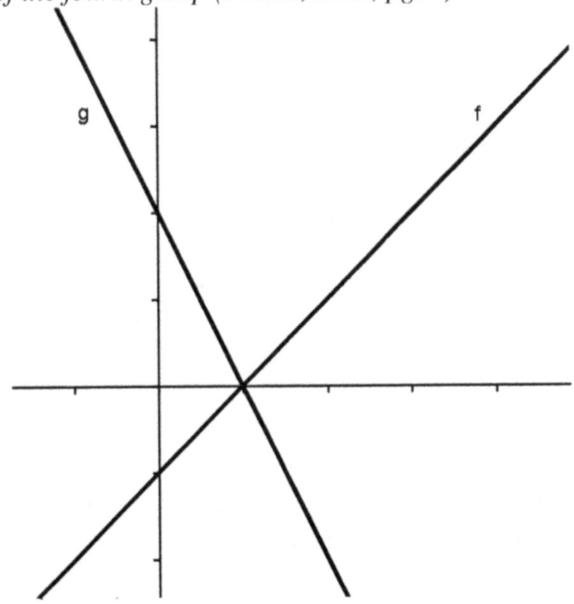

The goal was to identify whether students would reason algebraically, assigning symbolic expressions (for example, $f(x)=ax+b$, $g(x)=cx+d$ and mentally computing the difference $(f-g)(x)=(a-c)x+(b-d)$ or use a graphical–arithmetic strategy, focusing on specific points such as intercepts or intersection coordinates to estimate relative distances.

Students' ability to combine these approaches was also examined, as evidence of strategic flexibility under cognitive constraints.

Group 5 (Task 5.1-Task 5.2): In this group, only algebraic expressions were provided—initially the functions $f(x)=|x|$ and $g(x)=x$ (Task 5.1), followed by $f(x)=x^2$ and $g(x)=x$ (Task 5.2) (Proulx, 2015, pg. 7). Students were asked to mentally visualize the graph of the sum $f+g$. These tasks required translating a purely symbolic representation into a mental graphical image, thus evaluating students' ability to construct a conceptual link between algebraic manipulation and graphical structure. Students who added the symbolic expressions directly (for example, $(f+g)(x)=0$ for $x<0$ and $(f+g)(x)=x$ for $x>0$) demonstrated an algebraic–parametric strategy, while those who reasoned through sample point evaluations or estimated local values to shape the graph demonstrated a graphical–arithmetic strategy. A secondary objective was to observe whether students differentiated their strategies between the linear and quadratic forms.

Group 6 (Task 6): The final task displayed two symmetrical linear functions on the same Cartesian plane, and students were asked to find $f+g$ mentally.

Figure 5. Task of the sixth group (Proulx, 2015, pg. 13)

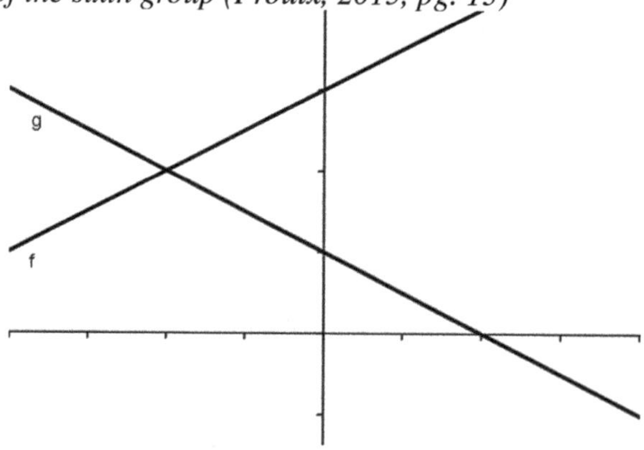

This task investigated whether students would recognize graphical symmetry and infer that the sum would yield a constant function with a value equal to twice the ordinate of the intersection point—a graphical–geometric reasoning pattern—or whether they would attend to the algebraic parameters (for example, opposite slopes, equal intercepts) to deduce that the sum equals the sum of intercepts, representing an algebraic–parametric strategy. A third possibility involved graphical–arithmetic reasoning, where students estimated values at specific points (intercepts, intersections) to mentally reconstruct the resulting function. This final task thus served to reveal integrative reasoning, combining symmetry, structure, and arithmetic estimation.

Taken together, these six groups of tasks formed a systematically varied set of stimuli that manipulated representational format (algebraic vs. graphical), functional type (linear, quadratic, absolute value, constant), and operation (addition or subtraction).

This design allowed the identification of shifts between reasoning modes, the emergence of hybrid strategies, and the role of representational cues in activating distinct forms of mental mathematical reasoning.

RESULTS

All analyses involving Correspondence Analysis (CA), Biplot Axis Interpretation, and Hierarchical Cluster Analysis (HCA) were performed using the CHIC Analysis software (Markos et al., 2010), which provides an integrated environment for the geometric exploration of categorical data and supports all normalization schemes, biplot projections, and clustering procedures applied in the present study.

Simple Correspondence Analysis (CA)

Results obtained from Simple Correspondence Analysis under symmetrical normalization indicated that a coherent factorial structure explaining 77.6% of the total inertia across the first two dimensions. Dimension 1, which accounted for 45.06% of the explained variance, represented the dominant structural contrast within the data and clearly differentiated algebraic–parametric reasoning from graphical–geometric approaches. On the positive side of this axis, the Algebraic–Parametric (AP) strategy displayed the strongest coordinate (F1 = 0.866), accompanied by high representational quality (*QLT* = 0.787) and the largest contribution to axis construction (*CTR* = 0.430). This confirms that the AP strategy was the principal driver of variation along Dimension 1, defining the algebraic pole of the configuration. In contrast, the Graphical–Geometric (GG) and the hybrid Algebraic–Graphical (AP–GG) strategies occupied the negative side of the axis with coordinates –0.359 and –0.485 respectively. Both categories showed high overall quality (*QLT* = 0.986 and 0.924), strong correlations with the dimension, and meaningful contributions (*CTR* = 0.137 and 0.144), indicating that they shaped the geometric end of the first axis. Other strategy types, including Graphical–Arithmetic (GA), Algebraic–Arithmetic (AP–GA), and Graphical–Arithmetic hybrids (GG–GA), were positioned closer to the origin, reflecting weaker or intermediate association patterns and reduced influence on the primary algebraic–geometric contrast.

Figure 6. Factorial plane 1 × 2 from Correspondence Analysis with SN (plotted with CHIC Analysis, where AP: Algebraic Parametric, GG: Graphical Geometric, GA: Graphical Arithmetic, AP-GG: Algebraic Parametric-Graphical Geometric, AP-GA: Algebraic Parametric- Graphical Arithmetic, GG-GA: Graphical Geometric-Graphical Arithmetic, T1-T6 the Task's number.)

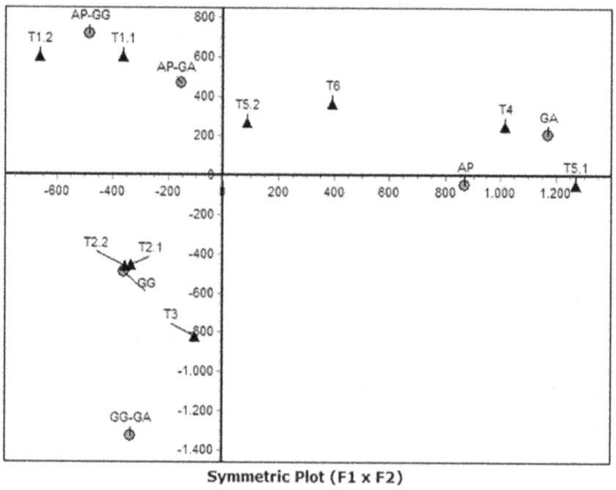

Dimension 2, accounting for 32.56% of inertia, revealed a second layer of differentiation linked to students' combined or transitional reasoning processes. Here, the strongest contributors were AP–GG (F2 = 0.718, *CTR* = 0.435) and GG–GA (F2 = –1.327, *CTR* = 0.108), indicating that the axis captured a contrast between pure geometric reasoning and geometric–arithmetic hybrid approaches. The GG strategy also contributed substantially to this dimension (*CTR* = 0.359, *COR* = 0.645), occupying the lower region of the factorial plane. The AP strategy, which dominated Dimension 1, showed almost no contribution to Dimension 2 (*CTR* = 0.002), highlighting that its influence is confined to the algebraic–geometric opposition and plays no role in shaping the secondary structure of the data.

The distribution of tasks across the factorial map further clarified the cognitive landscape emerging from the students' responses. On Dimension 1, tasks T5.1 and T4 formed the strongest positive contributors, with T5.1 showing the highest correlation (*COR* = 0.747) and contribution (*CTR* = 0.399), confirming its strong association with algebraic processing. Task T4 displayed a similar pattern (F1 = 1.013, *CTR* = 0.263), positioning itself clearly within the algebraic quadrant. Task T6 also appeared on the positive side, though with a smaller contribution, suggesting a partial alignment with algebraic reasoning. On the negative side of Dimension 1, tasks T1.1 and T1.2 exhibited strong negative coordinates (–0.363 and –0.664) and moderate contributions, reflecting their strong graphical nature. Similarly, tasks T2.1 and T2.2 aligned closely, indicating a consistent pattern in which the absence of algebraic expressions elicited more holistic, visually driven strategies. Task T3, although positioned negatively, contributed minimally to the construction of Dimension 1.

Along Dimension 2, task T3 emerged as the most distinctive element in the configuration, showing the highest correlation ($COR = 0.923$) and largest contribution ($CTR = 0.331$). This confirms that T3 played a unique role in shaping the second axis, consistent with its cognitive demand: inferring a vertical shift of a non-linear function. Tasks T1.1 and T1.2 also contributed to Dimension 2, highlighting the complexity introduced by providing both graphs and symbolic expressions. Tasks T5.2 and T6 occupied intermediate positions, while T5.1 and T4 were nearly orthogonal to Dimension 2, reflecting their predominantly algebraic character.

Overall, the CA configuration revealed a robust and theoretically meaningful structure. The first dimension captured the fundamental contrast between algebraic–parametric and graphical–geometric reasoning, while the second dimension illuminated differences among geometric sub-strategies, particularly between holistic visual processing and pointwise or arithmetic-based graphical reasoning. Tasks aligned systematically with the strategies they elicited, forming coherent clusters across the factorial space. This dual structure offers strong empirical support for the idea that students' mental strategies are not random but emerge systematically from the representational and cognitive affordances of the tasks.

Bi-Plot Analysis

The bi-plot representation provided an integrated view of the relationships between strategy categories and tasks by projecting both sets of points onto the same factorial plane. The configuration aligned closely with the structure identified in the CA but enriched the interpretation by revealing which specific tasks were most strongly associated with each strategic approach. Interpretation follows the standard criterion that shorter distances indicate stronger geometric proximity, while higher $\cos^2$ values indicate better representation of a task or a given strategy direction (Table 2, Figure 7).

Table 2. Distances and cos2 (cos square-CosSq) for rows (Strategies)

Order T1.1	**AP-GG**	**AP-GA**	**GG**	**GA**	**AP**	**GG-GA**
Distance	0.220	0.299	1.341	1.444	1.567	2.377
CosSq	0.998	0.954	0.206	0.098	0.292	0.550
Order T1.2	AP-GG	AP-GA	GG	GA	AP	GG-GA
Distance	0.340	0.594	1.567	1.668	1.789	2.588
CosSq	0.945	0.768	0,034	0.323	0.571	0.272
Order T2.1	GG	GA	AP	AP-GA	GG-GA	AP-GG
Distance	0.687	0.699	0.733	1.220	1.270	1.674
CosSq	1.000	0.501	0.260	0.397	0.870	0.164
Order T2.2	GG	GA	AP	AP-GA	GG-GA	AP-GG
Distance	0.718	0.731	0.764	1.230	1.290	1.685
CosSq	0.999	0.522	0.278	0.377	0.855	0.149
Order T3	AP	GA	GG-GA	GG	AP-GA	AP-GG
Distance	0.756	0.818	0.825	0.880	1.742	2.230
CosSq	0.003	0.090	0.987	0.790	0.844	0.613
Order T4	GG	GA	AP	AP-GA	GG-GA	AP-GG
Distance	1.311	1.318	1.338	1.648	1.697	2.006
CosSq	0.563	0.995	0.901	0.001	0.217	0.087
Order T5.1	AP	GA	GG	GG-GA	AP-GA	AP-GG
Distance	1.419	1.447	1.477	1.501	2.068	2.476
CosSq	1.000	0.946	0.270	0.033	0.109	0.320
Order T5.2	AP-GA	GG	GA	AP	AP-GG	GG-GA
Distance	0.483	0.707	0.802	0.919	0.954	1.708
CosSq	0.694	0.915	0.217	0.053	0.434	0.995
Order T6	AP-GA	GG	GA	AP	AP-GG	GG-GA
Distance	0.833	0.897	0.966	1.056	1.203	1.751
CosSq	0.225	0.963	0.685	0.437	0.052	0.720

Figure 7. Biplot axes for rows (Strategies) on Factorial plane 1 × 2 from CA (plotted with CHIC Analysis, where AP: Algebraic Parametric, GG: Graphical Geometric, GA: Graphical Arithmetic, AP-GG: Algebraic Parametric-Graphical Geometric, AP-GA: Algebraic Parametric- Graphical Arithmetic, GG-GA: Graphical Geometric- Graphical Arithmetic and T1.1-T6 the Tasks' number. The dots (.) represent the intersection points of the perpendicular projections of the line points onto the Biplot axes.)

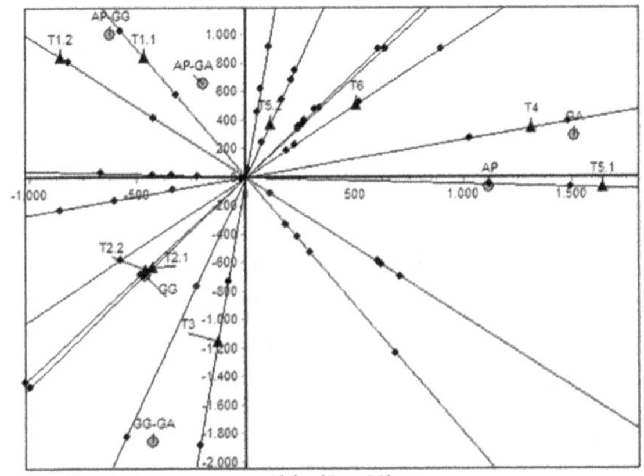

Biplot (F1 x F2)

The bi-plot axis analysis provided a detailed understanding of the association between the six mental strategies (AP, GA, GG, AP–GA, AP–GG, GG–GA) and the nine tasks of the study. Examination of the distances and squared cosines showed that Tasks T1.1 and T1.2 were predominantly associated with the mixed AP–GG and AP–GA strategies. T1.1, in particular, was represented almost perfectly by AP–GG ($\cos^2 = 0.998$) and very strongly by AP–GA ($\cos^2 = 0.954$), indicating that students relied on hybrid reasoning combining algebraic manipulation with graphical interpretation. A similar pattern was observed for T1.2, where AP–GG ($\cos^2 = 0.945$) and AP–GA ($\cos^2 = 0.768$) again dominated, suggesting that even when algebraic expressions were not directly used for computation, students spontaneously blended symbolic and visual structures when dealing with shifts of functions.

Task T3 demonstrated a strong association with the GG–GA mixed strategy, with a very high squared cosine (0.987), accompanied by substantial alignment with GG ($\cos^2 = 0.79$) and AP–GA ($\cos^2 = 0.844$). These results indicate that students combined graphical observation of vertical shifts with a partial algebraic–numeric estimation, rather than adopting a purely algebraic approach ($\cos^2 = 0.003$ for AP). This profile is consistent with the nature of the task, which involved a less familiar function (square root), encouraging students to interpret its shape visually before considering arithmetic differences between corresponding points.

Task T4 revealed a distinct pattern centered around the GA strategy, which displayed the highest representation ($\cos^2 = 0.995$), followed by strong alignment with the algebraic strategy AP ($\cos^2 = 0.901$) and moderate alignment with GG ($\cos^2 = 0.563$). Students thus appeared to integrate geometric reasoning (slopes, intersections, relative position) with algebraic parameter comparison to determine the difference between the two linear functions. The minimal involvement of the mixed strategies (AP–GG, AP–GA, GG–GA) suggests that T4 cued a more structured geometric–algebraic approach rather than blended or holistic reasoning.

Task T5.1 constituted the clearest example of a pure algebraic task. It showed perfect representation by the AP strategy ($\cos^2 = 1.000$), making it the strongest algebraic alignment in the dataset. Its second-highest association was with GA ($\cos^2 = 0.946$), which is expected given that students ultimately needed to imagine the resulting graph after performing algebraic additions of expressions. All other strategies contributed very little, confirming that this task required symbolic decomposition, case analysis (as with $|x|$), and recomposition into a mental graph. Task T5.2, although also involving algebraic expressions, elicited a more blended strategic profile. Its strongest alignment was with the GG–GA strategy ($\cos^2 = 0.995$), closely followed by the graphical strategy GG ($\cos^2 = 0.915$). These findings indicate that students alternated between symbolic manipulation, geometric visualization, and pointwise checking of values, especially due to the piecewise behaviour of the absolute value and the gradual curvature of the square function. The task therefore induced a multi-modal reasoning process.

Finally, Task T6 showed its highest representation in the GG strategy ($\cos^2 = 0.963$), with substantial contributions from the mixed GG–GA strategy ($\cos^2 = 0.720$) and the GA strategy ($\cos^2 = 0.685$). Students primarily perceived the symmetry of the two linear functions and used it holistically to infer that their sum would be constant, while secondarily noting algebraic features such as opposite slopes and identical intercept relationships. The presence of moderate AP representation ($\cos^2 = 0.437$) suggests that some students incorporated symbolic reasoning, but the overall picture is that T6 was solved mainly through geometric insight and symmetry detection.

Overall, the biplot analysis identified three robust clusters of tasks: (a) purely graphical tasks (T2.1, T2.2, T6), which elicited primarily holistic visual strategies; (b) purely algebraic tasks (T5.1), which depended almost exclusively on symbolic manipulation; and (c) mixed-strategy tasks (T1.1, T1.2, T3, T4, T5.2), each activating different blends of algebraic, geometric, and numeric reasoning depending on the representational demands imposed by the task. This structure provides strong evidence for the dynamic, enactive character of students' mental strategies, which adapt to the features of each functional environment rather than reflecting stable, fixed preferences.

The projection of the strategy categories revealed a clearly structured configuration anchored by three dominant poles of reasoning (Table 3, Figure 8).

Table 3. Distances and cos2 (cos square-CosSq) for columns (Tasks)

Order AP	**T4**	**T5.1**	**T6**	**T5.2**	**T3**	**T2.1**	**T2.2**	**T1.1**	**T1.2**
Distance	0.165	0.521	0.645	1.029	1.180	1.510	1.538	1.639	2.026
CosSq	0.149	0.954	0.855	0.109	0.946	0.999	0.098	0.292	1.000
Order GG	T2.2	T2.1	T1.1	T3	T1.2	T5.2	T6	T4	T5.1
Distance	0.719	0.720	0.726	0.804	0.869	0.882	1.148	1.850	2.183
CosSq	0.323	0.790	0.571	0.217	0.053	0.694	0.987	0.613	0.768
Order GA	5.1	T4	T6	T5.2	T3	T2.1	T2.2	T1.1	T1.2
Distance	0.412	0.433	1.083	1.449	1.595	1.917	1.944	2.043	2.425
CosSq	0.397	0.087	0.217	0.225	0.685	0.563	0.501	0.260	0.437
Order AP-GG	T1.1	T1.2	T2.2	T2.1	T3	T5.2	T6	T4	T5.1
Distance	0.979	0.989	1.001	1.009	1.150	1.238	1.509	2.194	2.519
CosSq	0.278	0.206	0.522	0.270	0.998	0.550	0.033	0.320	0.377
Order AP-GA	T2.1	T3	T2.2	T1.1	T5.2	T1.2	T6	T4	T5.1
Distance	0.656	0.661	0.664	0.698	0.716	0.926	0.954	1.648	1.982
CosSq	0.915	0.945	0.090	0.003	0.272	0.034	0.995	0.434	0.844
Order GG-GA	T2.1	T2.2	T1.1	T3	T5.2	T1.2	T6	T4	T5.1
Distance	1.883	1.884	1.892	1.898	1.924	1.972	2.039	2.468	2.712
CosSq	0.963	0.995	0.901	0.164	0.870	1.000	0.720	0.052	0.001

Figure 8. Biplot axes for columns (Tasks) on Factorial plane 1 × 2 from CA (plotted with CHIC Analysis, where AP: Algebraic Parametric, GG: Graphical Geometric, GA: Graphical Arithmetic, AP-GG: Algebraic Parametric-Graphical Geometric, AP-GA: Algebraic Parametric- Graphical Arithmetic, GG-GA: Graphical Geometric- Graphical Arithmetic and T1.1-T6 the Tasks' number. The dots (.) represent the intersection points of the perpendicular projections of the line points onto the Biplot axes.)

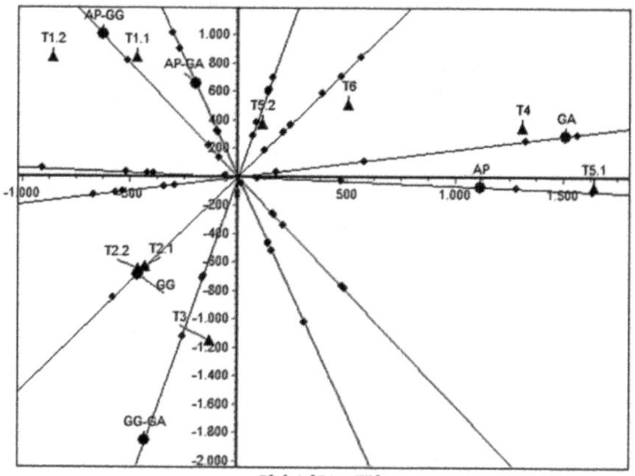

The algebraic–parametric strategy (AP) exhibited a clear and distinctive profile, showing strong activation in tasks where explicit algebraic structure or piecewise symbolic reasoning could be applied efficiently. Its strongest association was with T1.2, which displayed the highest squared cosine ($cos^2 = 1.000$) and the largest distance (2.026), indicating that this task defined the direction of the AP axis and was almost perfectly explained by the algebraic–parametric mode. A similarly strong relationship emerged with T2.1 ($cos^2 = 0.999$; distance = 1.510), confirming that students frequently reconstructed explicit formulas even when only graphical information was provided. The AP strategy also showed strong representation in T5.1 ($cos^2 = 0.954$; distance = 0.521) and T3 ($cos^2 = 0.946$; distance = 1.180), illustrating that students often preferred symbolic decomposition—such as piecewise definitions for absolute value or approximate algebraic manipulation of root functions—over relying solely on graphical cues. Moderate involvement appeared in T2.2 and T1.1 ($cos^2 = 0.098$ and 0.292), reflecting that a subset of students blended algebraic reconstruction with partial visual checks. In contrast, very weak representation was observed for T4 and T6 ($cos^2 = 0.149$ and 0.109), where tasks favored geometric symmetry or slope-based inference that reduced the need for symbolic manipulation. Overall, the AP profile suggests that students heavily relied on algebraic formulations whenever they perceived the task as symbolically tractable or when formal expressions could be mentally reconstructed even from purely graphical stimuli.

The graphical–geometric strategy (GG) showed a highly coherent profile, clustering tightly around the tasks that required students to perform mental operations solely through perceptual inspection of graphs. Its strongest associations were with T2.2 and T2.1, which both involved determining vertical translations of functions presented only in graphical form. The minimal distances (0.719 and 0.720) and high squared cosine values (0.323 and 0.790) indicate that GG was the dominant reasoning approach for these tasks. A similarly strong alignment appeared with T1.1 ($\cos^2 = 0.571$; distance = 0.726), indicating that even when algebraic expressions were present, a substantial portion of students favored holistic shape recognition. Moderate associations were observed with T3 and T5.2 ($\cos^2 = 0.217$ and 0.694), suggesting that students frequently relied on geometric intuition or pointwise visual comparisons when the underlying functional form (e.g., square-root or quadratic) made symbolic manipulation less straightforward. In contrast, GG exhibited weak involvement in algebraically structured tasks, particularly T4 and T5.1, which showed very large distances (1.850 and 2.183) and high $\cos^2$ for other strategies. This confirms that GG is primarily activated when visual structure is the dominant cue and algebraic engagement is either unnecessary or cognitively taxing.

The geometric–algebraic strategy (GA) demonstrated a balanced profile that blends geometric interpretation with parametric reasoning. Its strongest alignment was with T5.1 (distance = 0.412; $\cos^2 = 0.397$) and T4 (distance = 0.433; $\cos^2 = 0.087$), indicating that tasks requiring students to infer slopes, intercepts, or structural composition of functions strongly activated GA processing. The close association with T6 (distance = 1.083; $\cos^2 = 0.217$) suggests that symmetry-based tasks also trigger parametric reasoning, particularly when students leverage slope relationships or intercept symmetry to perform mental addition. Moderate connections to T5.2, T3, T2.1, and T2.2 ($\cos^2$ between 0.225 and 0.685) reveal that GA is used flexibly when a task can be interpreted through local geometric features combined with inferred algebraic properties. However, the largest distances and weakest quality of representation were observed for T1.1 and T1.2, indicating that when algebraic information is directly provided, students tend to shift toward purely symbolic (AP) or hybrid (AP–GG) strategies rather than GA. Overall, GA appears as an intermediate reasoning mode bridging symbolic and geometric forms, especially in tasks involving linear structures, symmetry, or manageable algebraic decomposition.

The AP–GG strategy, reflecting a blended use of symbolic cues and holistic visual reasoning, showed its strongest associations with T1.1 and T1.2, where distances were small (0.979 and 0.989) and squared cosines substantial (0.278 and 0.206). These tasks provided both algebraic expressions and graphical representations, encouraging students to combine symbolic structure with perceptual cues. AP–GG also showed moderate alignment with T2.2 and T2.1 ($\cos^2 = 0.522$ and 0.270), indicating that when algebraic information was absent but graphical structure was simple, a subset of students still attempted symbolic reconstruction mentally before confirming visually. The extremely high squared cosine for T3 ($\cos^2 = 0.998$), despite a larger distance (1.150), reveals that the hybrid strategy contributes significantly to shaping the dimension on which T3 is projected, reflecting attempts by some students to integrate symbolic approximations with geometric reasoning for the square-root transformation. In contrast, AP–GG showed weak involvement in T6, T4, and especially T5.1, where distances exceeded 2.0 and squared cosines dropped sharply. These results indicate that AP–GG emerges mostly in tasks that present dual representation formats or require complementary use of both symbolic and visual heuristics.

The AP–GA strategy showed a distinct preference for tasks that involved either implicit algebraic structure or moderately complex geometric transformations. Its strongest associations appeared with T2.1 and T3 ($\cos^2 = 0.915$ and 0.945; distances = 0.656 and 0.661), revealing that students frequently combined reconstructed symbolic expressions with geometric features when processing pure graph tasks or unfamiliar nonlinear functions. The association with T2.2 and T1.1 ($\cos^2 = 0.090$ and 0.003) was weaker but still indicative of occasional reliance on symbolic–parametric cues. Moderate alignment with T5.2 ($\cos^2 = 0.272$; distance = 0.716) and T1.2 ($\cos^2 = 0.034$; distance = 0.926) suggests that AP–GA plays a secondary role when symbolic decomposition is possible but not dominant. Weak associations with T6, T4, and T5.1 (large distances between 1.648 and 1.982) indicate that AP–GA is least likely to appear when tasks strongly prefer either purely symbolic (AP) or purely geometric (GG) processing. Overall, AP–GA emerges as a flexible but transitional reasoning mode used primarily when students attempt to impose symbolic structure onto graph-only tasks or mentally reconcile symbolic and geometric cues in nonlinear transformations.

The GG–GA strategy, characterized by local pointwise comparisons and visual estimation, showed its strongest alignment with tasks T2.1 and T2.2, which exhibited the smallest distances (1.883 and 1.884) and extremely high squared cosines (0.963 and 0.995). These results confirm that tasks requiring vertical-shift inference from graphs prompted students to rely heavily on local vertical distance judgments. Similarly, T1.1 and T3 ($\cos^2 = 0.901$ and 0.164) showed substantial representation, indicating reliance on numeric–visual estimation when students mentally compared corresponding points on multiple curves. The strategy aligned strongly with T5.2 as well ($\cos^2 = 0.870$), revealing that students often evaluated specific x-values mentally to approximate the sum of nonlinear expressions. In contrast, T6, T4, and particularly T5.1 showed very weak associations, with squared cosines dropping to near-zero and distances exceeding 2.4. This indicates that when symbolic structure is transparent or geometric symmetry eliminates the need for pointwise estimation, GG–GA becomes irrelevant. Overall, the hybrid GG–GA strategy is the primary mode of reasoning for tasks involving local comparison, vertical-distance estimation, or nonlinear function behavior, especially when symbolic manipulation is difficult or unavailable.

Cluster Analysis

The hierarchical cluster analysis (HCA), which carried out with Ward's linkage and Benzécri's chi-squared distances, revealed a clear and interpretable structure among the six strategies (AP, GA, GG, AP–GA, AP–GG, GG–GA). The dendrogram (Figure 9) indicates that GG and its combined form GG–GA constitute the first and tightest cluster, reflecting their close conceptual affinity as predominantly graphical–geometric strategies. Their minimal linkage distance suggests that students who used GG tended also to employ GG–GA in closely related contexts. A second cluster emerged between AP–GG and AP–GA, which grouped together at a moderate distance. These two hybrid strategies represent intermediate forms that combine algebraic–parametric reasoning with graphical-geometric components. Their clustering suggests that students who shift between algebraic and visual reasoning did so in a structurally similar manner across tasks.

At a higher level, the dendrogram shows that these four strategies (GG, GG–GA, AP–GG, AP–GA) merge into a broader cluster, which stands in contrast to the more distinctly algebraic strategy AP and its conceptual counterpart GA. AP and GA formed a separate pair at a relatively larger linkage distance, indicating that students who relied on strictly algebraic–parametric approaches did so systematically and independently of the mixed or graphical strategies. The final merge between the AP/GA group and the graphical-hybrid cluster occurred only at the highest distance, highlighting a strong methodological divide between pure algebraic and pure/combined graphical strategic approaches.

Overall, the HCA results support the presence of two dominant families of reasoning strategies: a graphical–geometric cluster (GG, GG–GA) with adjacent hybrid forms (AP–GG, AP–GA), and an algebraic–parametric cluster (AP, GA). This organization reinforces the findings from the CA and Biplot analysis, showing that students' strategy use follows a structured continuum from fully algebraic reasoning to fully graphical reasoning, with mixed strategies occupying the intermediate conceptual space.

Figure 9. Hierarchical Cluster Analysis of Strategies (Ward Method, Benzécri's chi-squared Distances). Dendrogram illustrating the clustering relationships among the six mental strategies (AP, GA, GG, AP–GA, AP–GG, GG–GA plotted with CHIC Analysis, where AP: Algebraic Parametric, GG: Graphical Geometric, GA: Graphical Arithmetic, AP-GG: Algebraic Parametric-Graphical Geometric, AP-GA: Algebraic Parametric- Graphical Arithmetic, GG-GA: Graphical Geometric-Graphical Arithmetic)

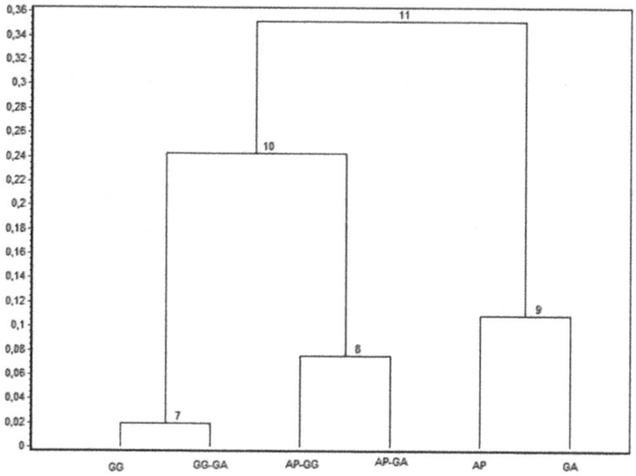

The HCA for the nine tasks (T1.1, T1.2, T2.1, T2.2, T3, T4, T5.1, T5.2, T6) produced an equally coherent structure, revealing how different graphical and algebraic demands prompted specific patterns of mental strategies (Figure 10). At the lowest distances, the twin variants T2.1 and T2.2 clustered together, reflecting their near-identical cognitive demands as tasks requiring mental addition of a function and a constant in purely graphical settings. Their tight coupling confirms that students responded to these two tasks in almost the same way, regardless of small representational differences. Shortly after, T3 joined this cluster, indicating that students approached the "reverse sum" task (deriving g from f and f+g) using reasoning closely aligned with their approaches to T2.1/T2.2. This grouping highlights a shared reliance on local, pointwise graphical reasoning across these tasks.

A second cluster was formed between T1.1 and T1.2, which involved mental addition with explicit algebraic expressions available. Their proximity indicates that students relied on a consistent mixture of algebraic and graphical reasoning in both versions. This T1 cluster merged with the T2–T3 cluster at a moderate height, forming a broader group of tasks characterized by transformations involving vertical shifts and functional composition.

On a different branch, T5.2 and T6 grouped together at low distance. Both tasks require students to interpret more relational or structural graphical features (symmetry, composite transformations, or non-linear curves), and their clustering suggests that these tasks activated similar high-level reasoning patterns.

At a larger distance, T4 joined this cluster, reflecting its somewhat different but still graphically–structured nature (difference of two lines). Finally, T5.1 merged only at the highest hierarchical level, indicating that it elicited the most distinct cognitive profile among all tasks. This isolation is consistent with its unique demand: transforming purely algebraic expressions ($|x| + x$, $x^2 + x$) into a mental graphical representation without any supporting diagram.

Overall, the HCA task dendrogram reveals three functional families of tasks: a vertical-shift and pointwise reasoning cluster (T2.1, T2.2, T3, T1.1, T1.2), a graphical–structural cluster (T5.2, T6, T4), and a distinct algebra-to-graph translation task (T5.1), standing uniquely apart. This organization aligns closely with the theoretical expectations of Proulx's taxonomy and with the CA and Biplot findings, which consistently characterize T5.1 as a uniquely challenging algebraic–conceptual transformation task.

Figure 10. Hierarchical Cluster Analysis of Tasks (Ward Method, Benzécri's chi-squared Distances). Dendrogram showing the hierarchical grouping of the nine tasks (T1.1–T6, plotted with CHIC Analysis, where Ti the Tasks' number).

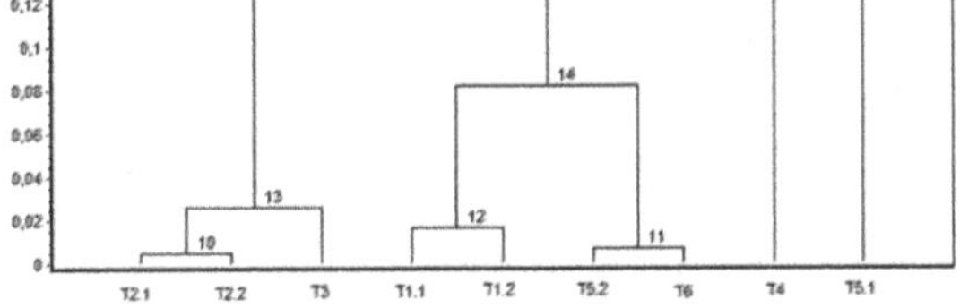

Kriging Interpolation

The Kriging interpolation projected students' success rates (Table 4) onto the factorial plane derived from the Correspondence Analysis, generating a continuous "cognitive performance landscape" over the strategy–task space. The resulting contour map (Figure 11) illustrates how performance gradients vary across regions dominated by different strategies and tasks, revealing coherent patterns in students' mental management of functions.

Table 4. Total successes and percentage of them per task

TASK	T1.1	T1.2	T2.1	T2.2	T3	T4	T5.1	T5.2	T6
Successes	40	41	41	40	25	21	14	10	14
Percentage	95.2%	97.6%	97.6%	95.2%	59.5%	50%	33.3%	23.8%	33.3%

Figure 11. The Kriging interpolation surface visualizes the distribution of student success rates across the factorial plane (1× 2) obtained from Correspondence Analysis. Darker regions represent areas of higher predicted accuracy, whereas lighter regions indicate lower performance levels. This spatial visualization highlights performance clusters and reveals how task positioning in the factorial space relates to student achievement.

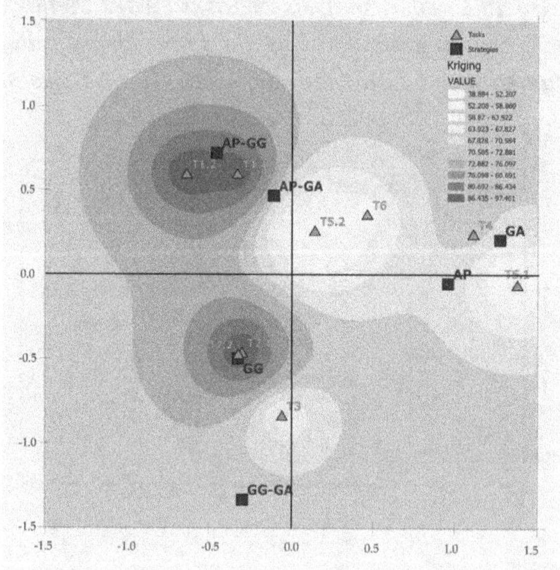

A clear high-performance region (>90% success) emerges in the upper-left quadrant, where the graphical–geometric (GG) and mixed strategies (AP–GG, AP–GA) are located. This zone coincides with Tasks T1.1, T1.2, T2.1, and T2.2, all of which exhibit exceptionally high success rates (95.2%–97.6%). These tasks involve vertical shifts of functions—either with or without explicit algebraic expressions—an operation that students appear to manage efficiently through holistic graphical reasoning. The concentration of high contour values around these tasks confirms a strong alignment between geometrical/graphical strategies and student success, reinforcing earlier findings from CA and the biplot.

In contrast, the lower-left region of the map, where Task T3 is situated, shows a pronounced drop in performance (59.5%). This task required identifying the function g from f and f+g, presented as square-root curves. The contour distribution in this area reflects increased cognitive demand, likely because the task requires combining geometric reasoning with approximate numerical judgments. This intermediate success level forms a "saddle zone" between the high-performing vertical-shift cluster and the low-performing algebra-to-graph tasks.

The lowest performance cluster (<35%) appears in the right-hand side of the map, particularly in the lower-right quadrant where Tasks T5.1, T5.2, and T6 are projected. These tasks required mentally constructing the graph of f+g from purely algebraic expressions (T5.1), combining algebraic and graphical structures (T5.2), or processing symmetry-based linear-function addition (T6). Success rates drop sharply to 33.3%, 23.8%, and 33.3% respectively. The contour map forms deep "valleys" around these task coordinates, indicating persistent difficulty. These low-performance zones overlap with the location of the algebraic–parametric strategy (AP) and the GA strategy, suggesting that tasks demanding symbolic reconstruction or algebra-to-graph translation are significantly more challenging for students.

Interestingly, Task T4, which required graphically determining f–g or g–f from intersecting lines, appears in an intermediate region of the contour map (50% success). Its position between the GG-domain and AP-domain reflects its hybrid cognitive structure: while it is grounded in graphical reasoning, it also requires pointwise comparisons or implicit algebraic thinking. The Kriging surface around this task shows moderate gradient levels, consistent with mixed-strategy engagement.

DISCUSSION

The primary aim of this study was to examine how students mentally manage functional relationships by engaging in tasks requiring mental computation with graphical and algebraic representations. The multivariate analyses conducted—Correspondence Analysis, Biplot axis interpretation, Hierarchical Cluster Analysis, and Kriging interpolation—revealed that students' strategies do not emerge arbitrarily. Rather, they appear as structured patterns of enacted reasoning shaped by the representational configuration of each task and the students' previous experiences with functions. The findings align with enactivist perspectives (Maturana &

Varela, 1992; Proulx, 2015), which argue that cognition arises through the dynamic interaction between the learner and the task environment, producing strategies that are inseparable from the activity itself. What this study contributes is an empirical validation of these theoretical claims through multivariate geometric methods rarely used in mathematics education research, providing a systematic, data-driven mapping of how strategies emerge in context.

Across the factorial space of the CA, a clear contrast emerged between algebraic/parametric strategies (AP, GA) and graphical/geometric or graphical/arithmetic strategies (GG, GG–GA). This indicates that students activate qualitatively different modes of reasoning depending on whether the task provides explicit symbolic information or primarily graphical cues. The fact that the first two CA dimensions captured over 77% of total inertia shows that students' mental strategies form a low-dimensional, coherent structure rather than a dispersed collection of idiosyncratic responses. In line with earlier research (Dreyfus & Eisenberg, 1991; Duval, 2006), the representational format of the tasks significantly constrained the strategies that students considered viable. However, the present study extends this literature by demonstrating that these constraints can be visualized and quantified geometrically, revealing not only broad tendencies but also the strength and stability of the associations across multiple tasks.

The Bi-plot analysis provided a more fine-grained view of these relationships, revealing asymmetries between tasks and strategies. Tasks with strong visual cues and invariant characteristics—particularly Tasks 1.1, 1.2 and 2.1, 2.2—were closely associated with the graphical–geometric (GG) and graphical–arithmetic (GA) strategies. These tasks required students to perceive vertical translations or simple additive combinations of known function shapes. Students tended to engage in rapid, holistic reading of the graph, consistent with the idea that geometric configurations offer immediate perceptual affordances (Arcavi, 2003). Conversely, tasks involving algebraically defined functions (Task 5.1 in particular) attracted algebraic/parametric approaches, suggesting that symbolic expressions invite students to manipulate formulas mentally even when the ultimate goal requires a graphical interpretation. This supports earlier claims that symbolic forms often dominate students' reasoning (Booth et al., 2016), but the present study contributes uniquely by ranking the relative strength of these associations, showing which tasks pull students most strongly toward specific forms of reasoning. This ranking capability, absent from standard CA, highlights the differential cognitive pull exerted by individual tasks—an insight that can inform the intentional design of instructional sequences.

The Bi-plot further revealed that hybrid strategies (AP–GG, AP–GA) occupied intermediate positions, bridging symbolic and graphical reasoning. This demonstrates that some students form blended modes of activity—estimating values graphically while coordinating them with algebraic structures. Such hybrid strategies echo research on representational flexibility, suggesting that proficient students integrate multiple forms of representation instead of adhering to a single dominant approach (Ainsworth, 2006). However, the relatively low cosine-squared values for several hybrid associations indicate that this flexible coordination was not frequent across the sample. Mental computation under time constraints may limit students' ability to shift between representational registers (Presmeg, 2006).

The hierarchical clustering analysis enriched this picture by revealing that both strategies and tasks formed meaningful clusters. Tasks grouped into two main families: those emphasizing perceptual invariants (for example, vertical shifts or slopes) and those requiring structural manipulation of symbolic expressions. Strategies mirrored this division, showing that learners tend to commit consistently to a cluster of reasoning modes rather than switching fluidly across tasks. This suggests a stable cognitive organization of mental strategies, shaped both by students' prior knowledge and by the immediate structure of the tasks, consistent with enactivist claims that reasoning emerges from recurrent patterns of action-in-context (Varela, 1996; Proulx, 2013). A unique contribution of this study is that clustering shows the "patterns" of strategies use across tasks, revealing stable cognitive profiles rather than isolated behaviors—something previous studies did not empirically map.

The Kriging interpolation results provided an additional, unique perspective by revealing gradients of performance across the task space. The darkest regions—indicating the highest success rates—corresponded to tasks involving simple graphical structures (Tasks 1.1–2.2), where mental visualization required minimal transformation. Conversely, regions corresponding to Tasks 3–6 exhibited lower performance, reflecting the increasing cognitive demands of interpreting non-linear functions, combining symbolic and graphical information, or mentally reconstructing composite functions. The spatial distribution of success indicates that students' difficulties are not task-specific anomalies but rather reflect a continuous cognitive landscape, where increases in functional complexity or representational ambiguity systematically depress performance. Kriging thus adds a novel contribution by showing how performance varies smoothly across the "task space," revealing structural cognitive gradients that have not been documented in previous function-learning research.

Taken together, these findings demonstrate that students' mental management of functions is shaped jointly by representational form, task structure, and embodied interaction with graphical cues. Strategy emergence reflects not only prior knowledge but also the moment-to-moment activation of perceptual features that guide students' reasoning. The results reinforce the view that functional thinking in mental-computation contexts is a dynamic, situated activity rather than a purely internal symbolic process.

CONCLUSION

The present study advanced the analysis of students' mental management of functions by integrating a suite of multivariate and geostatistical techniques—Correspondence Analysis, Biplot mapping, Hierarchical Clustering, and Kriging interpolation. This methodological synthesis offered a multidimensional perspective on how students coordinate algebraic, graphical, and hybrid strategies when solving functional tasks under mental-computation conditions. Rather than focusing on isolated response patterns, the study revealed the structural organization of students' reasoning: which strategies tend to emerge together, which tasks elicit similar forms of thinking, and how performance gradients unfold across a shared cognitive space.

A key contribution of the study lies in showing that mental-processing behavior in functions is not random but forms coherent, interpretable landscapes. Algebraic–parametric strategies consolidated around symbolically structured tasks, whereas graphical–geometric and graphical–arithmetic strategies aligned with tasks involving visual transformations. The interpolation of success rates further demonstrated that performance is closely tied to the cognitive structure of the tasks themselves rather than merely to individual variability.

Beyond illuminating these internal structures, the study highlights the value of adopting multidimensional analytic frameworks in mathematics education research. Traditional qualitative or quantitative approaches alone could not have captured the latent geometry of students' reasoning uncovered here. By contrast, the multivariate–geostatistical approach employed provides a robust blueprint for future studies seeking to explore complex interaction patterns in student thinking. Ultimately, the findings underscore the need to design learning environments and instructional sequences that account for the interplay of representational forms, mental strategies, and cognitive demands rather than treating them as separate instructional components.

Implications for Teaching

The findings of this study offer several important implications for the teaching and learning of functions, particularly when students are required to reason mentally in graphical environments. First, the consistent dominance and high success rates of graphical–geometrical strategies indicate that instruction should deliberately build on students' intuitive visual reasoning. Teachers can leverage this strength by designing tasks that encourage students to identify global features (for example, shifts, reflections, intersections) before engaging in symbolic manipulation. Such an approach can help students develop a more flexible understanding of functions as dynamic objects rather than static algebraic formulas.

Second, the difficulties observed in algebraic–parametric reasoning highlight the need for more explicit and structured support in connecting algebraic and graphical representations. Students must not only learn how algebraic changes affect graphs but also learn to mentally coordinate these changes without external cues. Instruction should therefore include opportunities for students to engage in "representation translation" activities, where they move intentionally between symbolic, numeric, and graphical forms. Dynamic mathematics environments (for example, GeoGebra), before transitioning to mental imagery, may serve as scaffolds that strengthen the internalization of algebraic structures.

Third, the emergence of hybrid strategies (AP–GA, AP–GG) suggests that many students attempt to blend representational forms, but these attempts are not always successful. Teachers can support these emerging strategies by helping students articulate and justify their reasoning, making explicit the connections between visual patterns and algebraic rules. Strategy sharing, think-aloud protocols, and guided discovery of multiple solution paths can foster greater strategic flexibility.

Finally, the results underscore the importance of time constraints and mental-processing conditions. When students work without pencil and paper, their reasoning becomes more reliant on intuitive or perceptual strategies. Teachers might consider integrating mental-visual tasks into regular instruction—not to replace written work, but to promote the development of deeper conceptual understanding and more adaptive problem-solving behaviors.

Limitations and Future Research

Although the study offers valuable insights into students' mental management of functions, several limitations should be acknowledged. First, the sample size, while sufficient for exploratory multivariate analysis, constrains the generalizability of findings to broader student populations. Future research should include larger and more diverse samples across grade levels, school contexts, and mathematical backgrounds to capture the full variability of students' strategic behaviors.

Second, the study relied on short interviews conducted under time pressure, a condition intentionally designed to elicit spontaneous mental strategies. However, this design may also have restricted students' ability to reflect deeply or articulate reasoning that emerges over longer periods. Future studies could combine real-time mental tasks with delayed reflective interviews or written explanations to better understand strategy evolution.

Third, the research focused exclusively on function addition and subtraction. While these operations provided a rich context for observing mental-graphical reasoning, they represent only one part of the broader function landscape. Future studies should extend the analysis to more complex function operations (for example, composition, transformation sequences, piecewise functions, inverse relations) to determine whether similar strategic patterns persist.

Finally, although the use of multivariate techniques (CA, Biplot analysis, HCA) and geostatistical visualization (Kriging interpolation) provided a powerful analytical framework, these methods are exploratory and descriptive. Future research might incorporate confirmatory statistical models, such as latent class analysis or structural equation modeling, to validate the structure of students' strategic profiles.

COMPETING INTERESTS

The authors of this publication declare there are no competing interests.

FUNDING

This research received no specific grant from any funding agency in the public, commercial, or not-for-profit sectors. Funding for this research was covered by the author(s) of the article.

REFERENCES

Ainsworth, S. (2006). DeFT: A conceptual framework for considering learning with multiple representations. *Learning and Instruction, 16*(3), 183–198. DOI: 10.1016/j.learninstruc.2006.03.001

Arcavi, A. (2003). The role of visual representations in the learning of mathematics. *Educational Studies in Mathematics, 52*(3), 215–241. DOI: 10.1023/a:1024312321077

Beh, E. J., & Lombardo, R. (2021). An Introduction to correspondence analysis. In *Wiley series in probability and statistics*. https://doi.org/DOI: 10.1002/9781119044482

Benzécri, J.-P. (1992). *Correspondence A nalysis Handbook*. Marcel Dekker, Inc.

Bishop, C. M. (2016). *Pattern recognition and machine learning*. Springer.

Blasius, J., & Greenacre, M. L. (1998). Visualization of categorical data. In *Elsevier eBooks*. https://doi.org/DOI: 10.1016/b978-0-12-299045-8.x5000-1

Booth, J. L., McGinn, K. M., Barbieri, C., & Young, L. K. (2016). Misconceptions and learning algebra. In *And the rest is just algebra* (pp. 63–78). Springer International Publishing., DOI: 10.1007/978-3-319-45053-7_4

Caney, A., & Watson, J. M. (2003). Mental computation strategies for part-whole numbers. In *AARE 2003 Conference papers, International Education Research*. https://ecite.utas.edu.au/28319

Creswell, J. W. (2012). *Educational research: Planning*. Conducting, and Evaluating Quantitative and Qualitative Research.

Cuadras, C. M., Cuadras, D., & Greenacre, M. J. (2006). A comparison of different methods for representing categorical data. *Communications in Statistics. Simulation and Computation, 35*(2), 447–459. DOI: 10.1080/03610910600591875

Dubinsky, E., & Harel, G. (1992). The Concept of function: aspects of epistemology and pedagogy. In *Mathematical Association of America eBooks*. http://ci.nii.ac.jp/ncid/BA23271623

Duval, R. (2006). A cognitive analysis of problems of comprehension in a learning of mathematics. *Educational Studies in Mathematics, 61*(1–2), 103–131. DOI: 10.1007/s10649-006-0400-z

Eisenberg, T. (1992). On the development of a sense for functions. In Harel, G., & Dubinsky, E. (Eds.), *The concept of function: Aspects of epistemology and pedagogy. MAA Notes, 25* (pp. 153–174). Mathematical Association of America.

Everitt, B. S., Landau, S., Leese, M., & Stahl, D. (2011). Cluster analysis. In *Wiley series in probability and statistics*. https://doi.org/DOI: 10.1002/9780470977811

Gabriel, K. R. (1971). The biplot graphic display of matrices with application to principal component analysis. *Biometrika, 58*(3), 453–467. DOI: 10.1093/biomet/58.3.453

Gabriel, K. R. (2002). Goodness of fit of biplots and correspondence analysis. *Biometrika, 89*(2), 423–436. DOI: 10.1093/biomet/89.2.423

Gagatsis, A., & Shiakalli, M. (2004). Ability to Translate from One Representation of the Concept of Function to Another and Mathematical Problem Solving. *Educational Psychology, 24*(5), 645–657. DOI: 10.1080/0144341042000262953

Gower, J. C. (2004). The geometry of biplot scaling. *Biometrika, 91*(3), 705–714. DOI: 10.1093/biomet/91.3.705

Greenacre, M. (2009). *Biplots in practice*. https://econpapers.repec.org/RePEc:fbb:booklb:2011113

Greenacre, M. (2017a). Correspondence analysis in practice. In *Chapman and Hall/CRC eBooks*. https://doi.org/DOI: 10.1201/9781315369983

Greenacre, M. (2017b). *Correspondence analysis in practice*. CRC Press.

Heinze, A., Star, J. R., & Verschaffel, L. (2009). Flexible and adaptive use of strategies and representations in mathematics education. *ZDM, 41*(5), 535–540. DOI: 10.1007/s11858-009-0214-4

Janvier, C. (1987). *Problems of Representations in the Learning and Teaching of Mathematics*. Lawrence Erlbaum Associates.

Kaput, J. (1992). Notations and representations as mediators of constructive processes. In Glasersfeld, E. (Ed.), *Radical Constructivism in Mathematics Education* (pp. 53–74). Kluwer Academic Publishers., DOI: 10.1007/0-306-47201-5_3

Knuth, E. J. (2000). Student understanding of the Cartesian connection: An exploratory study. *Journal for Research in Mathematics Education, 31*(4), 500–514.

Lerner, R. M. (2015b). *Handbook of Child Psychology and Developmental Science.*, DOI: 10.1002/9781118963418

Macfadyen, L. P., & Dawson, S. (2009). Mining LMS data to develop an "early warning system" for educators: A proof of concept. *Computers & Education, 54*(2), 588–599. DOI: 10.1016/j.compedu.2009.09.008

Maclellan, E. (2001). Mental Calculation: Its place in the development of numeracy. *Westminster Studies in Education, 24*(2), 145–154. DOI: 10.1080/0140672010240205

Markos, A., Menexes, G., & Papadimitriou, I. (2010). The CHIC Analysis Software V1.0. In *Studies in classification, data analysis, and knowledge organization* (pp. 409–416). https://doi.org/DOI: 10.1007/978-3-642-10745-0_44

Maturana, H. R., & Varela, F. J. (1992). The Tree of Knowledge: the biological roots of human understanding. In *Medical Entomology and Zoology*. https://ci.nii.ac.jp/ncid/BA04994769

Moschkovich, J., Schoenfeld, A. H., & Arcavi, A. (2012). Aspects of understanding: On multiple perspectives and representations of linear relations and connections among them. In *Integrating research on the graphical representation of functions* (pp. 69–100). Routledge.

Murtagh, F., & Contreras, P. (2011). Algorithms for hierarchical clustering: An overview. *Wiley Interdisciplinary Reviews. Data Mining and Knowledge Discovery, 2*(1), 86–97. DOI: 10.1002/widm.53

Murtagh, F., & Contreras, P. (2017). Algorithms for hierarchical clustering: An overview, II. *Wiley Interdisciplinary Reviews. Data Mining and Knowledge Discovery, 7*(6). Advance online publication. DOI: 10.1002/widm.1219

Pape, S. J., & Tchoshanov, M. A. (2001). The Role of Representation(s) in Developing Mathematical Understanding. *Theory into Practice, 40*(2), 118–127. DOI: 10.1207/s15430421tip4002_6

Presmeg, N. C. (1998). Metaphoric and metonymic signification in mathematics. *The Journal of Mathematical Behavior*, *17*(1), 25–32. DOI: 10.1016/s0732-3123(99)80059-5

Proulx, J. (2013). Mental mathematics, emergence of strategies, and the enactivist theory of cognition. *Educational Studies in Mathematics*, *84*(3), 309–328. DOI: 10.1007/s10649-013-9480-8

Proulx, J. (2014). Mental mathematics and operations on functions. *Proceedings of the . . . PME Conference*. https://files.eric.ed.gov/fulltext/ED599991.pdf

Proulx, J. (2015). Mental mathematics with mathematical objects other than numbers: The case of operation on functions. *The Journal of Mathematical Behavior*, *39*, 156–176. DOI: 10.1016/j.jmathb.2015.07.001

Reys, R. E. (1984). Mental computation and estimation: Past, present, and future. *The Elementary School Journal*, *84*(5), 547–557. DOI: 10.1086/461383

Romero, C., & Ventura, S. (2020). Educational data mining and learning analytics: An updated survey. *Wiley Interdisciplinary Reviews. Data Mining and Knowledge Discovery*, *10*(3). Advance online publication. DOI: 10.1002/widm.1355

Selter, C. (2009). Creativity, flexibility, adaptivity, and strategy use in mathematics. *ZDM*, *41*(5), 619–625. DOI: 10.1007/s11858-009-0203-7

Sfard, A. (1992). Operational origins of mathematical objects and the quandary of reification-the case of function. *The concept of function: Aspects of epistemology and pedagogy, 25*, 59-84.

Siemens, G. (2013). Learning analytics: The emergence of a discipline. *The American Behavioral Scientist*, *57*(10), 1380–1400.

Sierpinska, A. (1992). Theoretical perspectives for development of the function concept. *The concept of function: Aspects of epistemology and pedagogy. MAA Notes*, *25*, 23–58.

Sowder, J. T. (1988). Mental computation and number comparison: Their roles in the development of number sense and computational estimation. *Number concepts and operations in the middle grades, 2*, 182-197.

Thompson, I. (2010). 12 Getting your head around mental calculation. *Issues In Teaching Numeracy In Primary Schools*, 161.

Threlfall, J. (2002). Flexible mental calculation. *Educational Studies in Mathematics*, *50*(1), 29–47. DOI: 10.1023/a:1020572803437

Threlfall, J. (2009). Strategies and flexibility in mental calculation. *ZDM, 41*(5), 541–555. DOI: 10.1007/s11858-009-0195-3

Tomlinson, C. A. (2014). *The differentiated classroom: Responding to the needs of all learners*. Ascd.

Trafton, P. R. (1978). Estimation and Mental Arithmetic: Important Components of Computation. *NCTM Yearbook, 196*(213), 78. https://eric.ed.gov/?id=EJ182166

Verschaffel, L., Luwel, K., Torbeyns, J., & Van Dooren, W. (2009). Conceptualizing, investigating, and enhancing adaptive expertise in elementary mathematics education. *European Journal of Psychology of Education, 24*(3), 335–359. DOI: 10.1007/bf03174765

Vinner, S. (1983). Concept definition, concept image and the notion of function. *International Journal of Mathematical Education in Science and Technology, 14*(3), 293–305. DOI: 10.1080/0020739830140305

Vinner, S., & Dreyfus, T. (1989). Images and definitions for the concept of function. *Journal for Research in Mathematics Education, 20*(4), 356–366. DOI: 10.5951/jresematheduc.20.4.0356

Wandt, E., & Brown, G. W. (1957). Non-Occupational Uses of Mathematics Mental and Written—Approximate and Exact. *The Arithmetic Teacher, 4*(4), 151–154. DOI: 10.5951/at.4.4.0151

KEY TERMS AND DEFINITIONS

Biplot Analysis: A graphical statistical method that simultaneously represents rows and columns of a data matrix in the same low-dimensional space, allowing joint interpretation of relationships among categories.

Correspondence Analysis: A multivariate method that reveals structural relationships among categorical variables by projecting them into a shared low-dimensional space.

Enactivism: A view of cognition as emerging through interaction with the environment, where strategies arise dynamically rather than being stored in advance.

Hierarchical Cluster Analysis: A multivariate method for grouping items into sets based on similarity, providing insight into patterns or structures within a dataset.

Kriging Interpolation: A spatial estimation technique that predicts values across a continuous surface, generating smooth gradients and visualizing underlying patterns or performance distributions.

Mathematical Cognition: The mental processes involved in understanding, representing, and manipulating mathematical concepts, including reasoning, problem solving, visualization, memory, and the coordination of symbolic and graphical information.

Mental Management of Functions: The mental processing and manipulation of functions without external aids, including visualization of graphs, estimation of values, and mental combination of functional expressions.

Strategies behavior: Purposeful methods or approaches that individuals employ to accomplish a task, solve a problem, or achieve a goal, based on available information and contextual demands.

APPENDIX A: ILLUSTRATIVE STUDENT RESPONSES AND STRATEGY CODING

To enhance transparency regarding the coding process and to illustrate how students' reasoning was classified into the six strategy categories, this appendix presents representative excerpts from student interviews. Each example is accompanied by the corresponding strategy label assigned during the grounded-theory–based coding.

- **Student 2 (Task 2.1, GG Strategy):**
  "Because g is a positive constant, f will shift parallel upward."
  (Graphical–Geometric reasoning based on perceiving vertical translation.)
- **Student 4 (Task 2.1, GG–GA Strategy):**
  "Since g = c, the function f is shifted vertically, and in fact its intersection with the y-axis becomes (c, 0) instead of (0, 0)."
  (Combination of geometric visualization and numerical estimation.)
- **Student 14 (Task 2.1, AP–GA Strategy):**
  "f is of the form $f(x) = \alpha x$ with $\alpha > 0$ and $g(x) = c$ with $c > 0$, so $(f+g)(x) = \alpha x + c$. This results from a vertical shift of by c units upward, meaning it now passes through (0, c)."
  (Blend of algebraic manipulation with arithmetic interpretation of constants.)
- **Student 25 (Task 2.1, AP–GG Strategy):**
  "f is of the form $f(x) = \alpha x$ with $\alpha > 0$ and $g(x) = c$ with $c > 0$, hence $(f+g)(x) = \alpha x + c$. Its graph is therefore obtained by shifting f(x) vertically upward by c units."
  (Combination of algebraic/parametric reasoning with geometric interpretation.)
- **Student 17 (Task 2.1, AP Strategy):**
  "f is of the form $f(x) = \alpha x$ with $\alpha > 0$ and $g(x) = \beta$ with $\beta > 0$, so $(f+g)(x) = \alpha x + \beta$, meaning it is a straight line parallel to f at distance β."
  (Purely algebraic–parametric manipulation of symbolic expressions.)
- **Student 4 (Task 4, GA Strategy):**
  "At the point where the two lines intersect, their difference is zero. Then I find the vertical distance d between their intercepts on the y-axis. So $f - g$ will be a line passing through (d, 0) and their intersection point."
  (Graphical–Arithmetic reasoning using pointwise vertical differences.)

These examples illustrate how students' statements were mapped onto the conceptual framework of strategy types, and they provide qualitative grounding for the quantitative multivariate analyses presented in the main text.

Chapter 10
Generative AI and Learning Analytics in Education:
Methods, Risks, and Compliance With the EU AI Act

Lazaros Mitsou
http://orcid.org/0000-0002-6297-4738
Democritus University of Thrace, Greece

Theodora Vainterli
http://orcid.org/0009-0009-0363-7908
Democritus University of Thrace, Greece

ABSTRACT

This article examines the convergence of Generative Artificial Intelligence and Learning Analytics in education through a structured literature review. It highlights how large language models expand analytical capabilities by enabling the interpretation of unstructured learner data and supporting automated feedback, personalized learning, and multimodal analysis. At the same time, the study identifies critical risks, including hallucinations, bias, opacity, over-reliance, and threats to academic integrity and privacy. Particular emphasis is placed on the EU AI Act, which classifies many educational AI applications as high-risk and introduces strict requirements for transparency, documentation, and human oversight. The article argues for responsible-by-design adoption, integrating governance frameworks, explainability mechanisms, and AI literacy for educators. It concludes by outlining future research needs related to long-term learning impact, fairness, and institutional AI governance.

DOI: 10.4018/979-8-3373-6926-6.ch010

INTRODUCTION

The rapid evolution of artificial intelligence has significantly transformed education, with Generative AI emerging as a major catalyst for change. At the same time, Learning Analytics (LA) has matured as a data-driven approach for understanding and optimizing learning processes. Their convergence marks a new paradigm, as LA's traditional reliance on structured data is now complemented by large language models (LLMs) capable of analyzing unstructured text such as essays, discussions, and reflections. This integration expands learner modelling, supports personalized feedback, and enables dynamic, adaptive educational systems.

While offering substantial pedagogical opportunities, Generative-AI-supported analytics also raise concerns. LLMs may hallucinate, reproduce biases, or reduce transparency, affecting student understanding, assessment validity, and equity. Issues of privacy, data governance, and human oversight are increasingly critical, especially as institutions deploy AI to evaluate performance, make admissions-related decisions, or personalize learning pathways. These challenges intensify under the EU AI Act, which classifies many educational AI applications as "high-risk," requiring strict standards for documentation, transparency, risk management, and human oversight.

This study synthesizes recent empirical research, systematic reviews, and international policy frameworks to explore how Generative AI is integrated into LA, the opportunities it creates, the risks it poses, and the regulatory obligations that shape its use. It offers a literature-based analysis—without primary data collection—given the rapid evolution of AI technologies and the complexity of emerging governance requirements. The chapter contributes a structured overview of the field, identifies pedagogical benefits and ethical challenges, and highlights the need for responsible, compliant, and human-centered adoption of AI in education. Ultimately, the work situates Generative AI and LA within broader debates on trust, governance, and the future of educational technology, setting the foundation for the chapters that follow.

THEORETICAL AND CONCEPTUAL BACKGROUND

The evolution of Learning Analytics (LA) and Generative Artificial Intelligence (Generative AI) has profoundly influenced contemporary educational research, pedagogical practice, and institutional strategy. Understanding the theoretical foundations of both fields, as well as the ways they intersect, is essential for analyzing how Generative-AI-driven approaches reshape data-informed learning environments. This chapter provides a comprehensive conceptual overview, beginning with the origins and analytical traditions of Learning Analytics, progressing to the theoretical underpinnings of transformer-based generative models, and culminating in a synthesis of how these domains converge within modern educational ecosystems.

Learning Analytics emerged during the early 2010s as educational systems increasingly adopted digital platforms, producing vast quantities of learner-generated data. Siemens (2013) described LA as "the measurement, collection, analysis, and reporting of data about learners and their contexts" to optimize learning processes. This framing positioned LA as a multidisciplinary field integrating educational theory, computer science, statistics, cognitive psychology, and instructional design. Early research in the field drew heavily from Educational Data Mining (EDM), which focused on identifying patterns in learner behavior using supervised learning, clustering, regression, and classification techniques (Baker & Inventado, 2014; Chatti et al., 2014). These methods were well-suited to the structured data available at the time—such as clickstreams, quiz attempts, assignment submissions, and timestamped interaction logs. As Romero and Ventura (2024) emphasize in their updated survey of the field, these traditional methods reliably supported predictive modeling, early-warning systems, and performance analytics, forming a robust methodological backbone that many institutions continue to use today.

A useful representation of the traditional LA workflow, synthesizing insights from Chatti et al. (2014) and Baker and Inventado (2014), can be expressed in the following analytic cycle (Table 1).

Table 1. The Learning Analytics Cycle (Synthesized from Chatti et al., 2014; Baker & Inventado, 2014; Siemens, 2013)

Phase	Description	Traditional Methods
1. Data Collection	Capture of behavioral, interaction, or performance data from digital learning ecosystems.	LMS logs, clickstream data, assessment records.
2. Data Processing & Feature Engineering	Transformation, cleaning, and structuring of data for modeling.	Statistical preprocessing, normalization, time-on-task metrics.
3. Modeling & Analysis	Use of computational techniques to identify patterns or build predictive models.	Regression, clustering (k-means), classification (SVM, random forests), sequence mining.
4. Interpretation & Visualization	Translation of analytic outputs into interpretable insights for educators and learners.	Dashboards, heatmaps, learning curves.
5. Intervention & Decision-Making	Application of insights to improve learning, personalize pathways, or design support actions.	Early warning alerts, adaptive feedback, tutor interventions.
6. Evaluation & Refinement	Assessment of intervention impact and iterative improvement of models.	A/B testing, learning outcome analysis.

These foundational models reflect a rationalistic and data-driven view of learning processes, emphasizing prediction, pattern detection, and optimization. While highly effective in many contexts, traditional LA approaches face notable limitations: they rely heavily on structured, quantitative data; they struggle to capture complex cognitive or affective states; and they are limited in their ability to interpret rich linguistic or multimodal evidence of learning (Berland et al., 2014; Chatti et al., 2014). As learning increasingly unfolds in digital, collaborative, and multimodal environments, these limitations have become more pronounced.

The emergence of Generative AI, particularly large language models (LLMs), transformed the landscape by enabling the analysis of unstructured and natural language data at scale. Generative AI is grounded in deep learning architectures that model complex patterns in language, images, and other modalities. The key breakthrough occurred with the introduction of the transformer architecture (Vaswani et al., 2017), which uses self-attention mechanisms to encode contextual relationships across sequences. This architecture paved the way for models such as BERT (Devlin et al., 2018), GPT-3 (Brown et al., 2020), and GPT-4 (OpenAI, 2023), which demonstrated unprecedented capabilities in natural language understanding and generation.

Theoretically, LLMs function as high-dimensional probabilistic models trained on massive text corpora. They learn latent semantic representations and can generate coherent outputs that align with linguistic, syntactic, and contextual cues. This ability allows them to summarize text, generate explanations, translate content, evaluate argumentation, and interact in conversational modes. Systematic reviews indicate that LLMs are rapidly being integrated into educational contexts across diverse disciplines. Dong et al. (2024) highlight their expanding use in tutoring, code evaluation, content generation, knowledge explanation, and simulation-based instruction, while Guizani et al. (2025) emphasize their value for personalization, learner support, and scaffolding in higher education. Emirtekin et al. (2025) demonstrate how LLM-powered automated assessment tools are increasingly used to evaluate essays, coding assignments, and discipline-specific reasoning, thereby extending the range of tasks that AI systems can support in formal learning environments.

The convergence of Learning Analytics and Generative AI marks a conceptual shift from traditional data-driven approaches to more holistic, semantic, and interpretive forms of analysis. Whereas classic LA techniques analyze patterns in structured data, LLMs can process unstructured text such as essays, reflections, forum posts, group discussions, and student feedback. This enables a deeper examination of learner cognition, motivation, misconceptions, emotional states, and metacognitive strategies. As Saleh et al. (2025) note, LLMs exhibit a capacity to infer latent conceptual relationships, evaluate coherence and argumentative quality, and identify motivational cues. These capabilities transform the analytic space by allowing more nuanced insights into learning processes that were previously inaccessible through quantitative log data alone.

This expanded analytical capacity aligns with emerging models of multimodal learning analytics, which integrate text, images, clickstream patterns, audio, and other modalities to create a holistic representation of learning. Generative AI acts as both an analytic engine and a content generator, bridging the gap between analysis and pedagogical intervention. For example, the same model that analyzes the structure and content of a learner's written response can also generate personalized feedback, suggest resources, or scaffold the next step in a learning trajectory. This dual capacity introduces what can be described as a unified analysis-and-intervention loop, representing a shift from a traditional linear LA workflow toward a more dynamic and interactive AI-supported process.

The integration of Generative AI within LA is also shaped by theoretical models emphasizing human oversight and transparency. Human-in-the-loop (HITL) frameworks underscore the importance of maintaining educator judgment as central to AI-supported decision-making. In such models, AI systems provide insights or generate recommendations, but humans retain control, interpret outputs, validate their relevance, and make final decisions. UNESCO's (2023) guidance on generative AI in education highlights HITL principles as essential for ensuring accountability, pedagogical appropriateness, and contextual sensitivity, particularly in high-stakes environments such as assessment.

Another critical theoretical dimension involves explainable AI (XAI). While traditional LA models such as regression or decision trees offer interpretable outputs, LLMs are often opaque, operating through complex internal representations that defy simple explanation. Peters et al. (2025) demonstrate how LLMs may oversimplify or distort scientific content, underscoring the need for robust interpretability mechanisms. Transparency requirements, model documentation, data provenance, and error analysis become essential to ensure that generative models used in educational analytics are trustworthy. These issues gain additional significance in light of regulatory frameworks such as the EU AI Act (European Union, 2024), which mandates transparency, risk management, and human oversight for AI systems used in sensitive domains including education.

Underlying all these developments is an expanding discourse on responsible AI, algorithmic fairness, and data governance. Educational institutions must consider not only the capabilities of Generative AI but also the ethical and regulatory implications of its use. UNESCO's global frameworks (2021, 2023, 2024) highlight principles of learner agency, equity, privacy, and accountability, emphasizing the need to ensure that AI systems do not reproduce or amplify existing biases. The integration of Generative AI into LA must therefore be accompanied by governance structures that protect data integrity, ensure fairness, and promote ethical use, especially in contexts involving assessment, student profiling, or personalized interventions.

In conclusion, the theoretical and conceptual background that frames the convergence of Learning Analytics and Generative AI is built upon a decade of developments across data science, education, AI research, and policy. Learning Analytics has matured into a robust field grounded in structured data analysis and predictive modeling. Generative AI introduces new analytic modalities capable of interpreting unstructured and multimodal data while simultaneously generating pedagogical content. Their convergence creates unprecedented opportunities for understanding learning processes, personalizing instruction, and supporting educators. However, it also raises significant challenges relating to interpretability, governance, equity, and regulatory compliance. These conceptual foundations establish the groundwork for subsequent chapters, which examine methodological considerations, practical applications, risks, and the implications of regulatory frameworks such as the EU AI Act.

METHODOLOGY AND LITERATURE REVIEW PROCESS

The present study adopts a structured literature review methodology that combines elements of both narrative synthesis and systematic review in order to capture the rapidly evolving landscape surrounding Generative Artificial Intelligence and Learning Analytics in education. Due to the pace of technological advancement, a purely systematic review would risk excluding important recent sources, while a purely narrative approach would lack the methodological transparency and rigor required for a scholarly book chapter. Therefore, a hybrid methodology was employed, drawing from established guidelines for systematic educational reviews while retaining the flexibility needed to integrate policy documents, high-impact reports, and regulatory frameworks such as the EU AI Act (European Union, 2024; UNESCO, 2023).

The review process began by defining the temporal and conceptual boundaries of the literature. Because transformer-based Generative AI models emerged after 2017 and gained widespread educational relevance after 2020, the period of interest for this review was set from 2018 to 2025. This temporal window ensured the inclusion of foundational work on Learning Analytics (such as Siemens, 2013; Baker & Inventado, 2014), while focusing primarily on recent studies addressing LLM-based educational applications (Dong et al., 2024; Guizani et al., 2025; Emirtekin et al., 2025). Literature was retrieved from major academic databases including Scopus, Web of Science, IEEE Xplore, ACM Digital Library, ERIC, and Google Scholar. Additional sources, such as UNESCO's AI in Education reports, OECD policy documents, and the official text of the EU AI Act, were incorporated to provide regulatory and governance context not typically captured in journal databases.

The search strategy was based on a combination of controlled vocabulary and free-text keywords. Common terms included "learning analytics," "educational data mining," "generative artificial intelligence," "large language models," "ChatGPT in education," "AI-driven assessment," "explainable AI," "human-in-the-loop education," and "AI Act education compliance." Boolean combinations enabled targeted queries capturing intersections such as "Generative AI AND learning analytics," "LLMs AND educational data," or "AI regulation AND education." The diversity of search terms was necessary given the interdisciplinary nature of the topic, spanning computer science, educational technology, data science, and legal studies.

To maintain transparency and methodological rigor, the study employed predefined inclusion and exclusion criteria. Eligible sources needed to meet three requirements: they had to be published after 2018, except for foundational LA works prior to that date; they had to directly address Learning Analytics, Generative AI, educational data analysis, or relevant regulatory frameworks; and they had to be peer-reviewed publications or authoritative policy documents. Excluded were opinion articles lacking empirical or conceptual rigor, technical AI papers unrelated to education, sources with unverifiable publication details, and preprints without sufficient academic use or citation. This approach ensured the reliability of the corpus while allowing the incorporation of recent publications crucial for understanding an evolving technology.

During the screening process, 247 initial records were identified. After removing duplicates and evaluating abstracts, 81 publications were retained for full-text assessment. Following the application of inclusion criteria, 42 journal articles, 9 conference papers, 7 policy documents, and 1 regulatory text were selected. This distribution reflects the global research trend, wherein much of the early work on LLMs in education has appeared in conference proceedings and preprint repositories before transitioning into journal publication (Dong et al., 2024; Saleh et al., 2025). To document the screening stages, a simplified literature flow representation was created to enhance methodological transparency.

The analysis of the selected corpus followed a thematic coding process. After multiple rounds of reading, the literature was grouped into four overarching thematic categories that reflect the central concerns of the field: applications of Generative AI in learning analytics; pedagogical benefits and opportunities; risks and ethical implications; and regulatory and compliance issues, particularly those emerging from the EU AI Act. These categories emerged inductively from the literature but align well with existing reviews such as Guizani et al. (2025), Emirtekin et al. (2025), and UNESCO's global frameworks (UNESCO, 2023).

A summary of the thematic classification is presented below (Table 2).

Table 2. Thematic Categories Identified in the Literature Corpus

Category	Description	Representative Sources
Applications	Use of LLMs in assessment, feedback, tutoring, learner modeling, and multimodal analytics.	Dong et al. (2024); Emirtekin et al. (2025)
Benefits	Personalization, scalability, cognitive support, accessibility, data richness, early diagnostics.	Saleh et al. (2025); Guizani et al. (2025)
Risks	Bias, hallucinations, opacity, privacy issues, over-reliance, academic integrity, misrepresentation.	Peters et al. (2025); UNESCO (2023)
Compliance	Regulatory requirements for high-risk systems, transparency obligations, human oversight.	European Union (2024); Future of Life Institute (2024)

Although the categories are analytically distinct, they overlap in practice. For example, studies reporting benefits often simultaneously acknowledge risks, particularly when discussing the scalability of automated feedback. Research documenting applications frequently touches upon compliance concerns where LLM-powered assessment tools might be classified as high-risk under Annex III of the EU AI Act. This overlap reinforces the necessity of analyzing the literature holistically rather than in isolation.

The synthesis process involved integrating findings within and across categories. For instance, studies on automated assessment consistently highlight both the potential efficiency gains (Emirtekin et al., 2025) and the dangers of misrepresentation or hallucination, which Peters et al. (2025) identify as inherent risks in generative models. These findings were aligned with policy insights emphasizing the need for human oversight and transparent documentation (UNESCO, 2023; European Union, 2024). Similarly, literature on learner modeling using LLMs was compared to traditional LA methods to identify points of methodological convergence and divergence. This comparative approach strengthened the conceptual foundation for analyzing how Generative AI extends or challenges established practices in Learning Analytics.

Overall, the methodological strategy employed in this study ensures a rigorous, transparent, and comprehensive examination of the rapidly expanding field of Generative-AI-enhanced Learning Analytics. The hybrid narrative-systematic approach captures both empirical evidence and conceptual developments, providing a robust foundation for the subsequent chapters on applications, risks, ethics, and compliance.

APPLICATIONS AND OPPORTUNITIES OF GENERATIVE AI IN LEARNING ANALYTICS

The integration of Generative Artificial Intelligence into Learning Analytics represents one of the most transformative shifts in contemporary educational technology. While Learning Analytics traditionally relied on structured data such as clickstream logs, quiz scores, and time-on-task indicators, the emergence of large language models (LLMs) has expanded the analytic landscape to include unstructured linguistic, discursive, and multimodal evidence of learning. This evolution has enabled new forms of interpretation, personalization, and pedagogical support, with significant implications for both educators and learners.

At the heart of this transformation lies the ability of LLMs to process, interpret, and generate human-like language at scale. Dong et al. (2024) show that LLMs such as GPT-4 can evaluate student writing, summarize discussions, detect misconceptions, and produce explanatory material with accuracy levels that approximate expert educators in specific domains. This capability supports the enrichment of learner modeling by incorporating qualitative dimensions—such as argument structure, conceptual fluency, emotional tone, and metacognitive reflection—that were previously inaccessible through conventional Learning Analytics. As a result, institutions appear increasingly capable of developing more holistic profiles of learners, supporting deeper diagnostics and more meaningful intervention strategies.

One of the most impactful applications of Generative AI within Learning Analytics is the automation of feedback. Feedback is widely recognized as one of the most powerful drivers of learning, yet it is time-consuming and inconsistently delivered in many educational settings. LLMs can generate detailed formative feedback on essays, problem-solving explanations, code, and reflective journals, offering learners immediate and personalized guidance. Emirtekin et al. (2025) document that AI-powered automated assessment systems already provide feedback on writing quality, argument clarity, accuracy of reasoning, and structural coherence across disciplines ranging from language learning to computer science. The immediacy of this feedback supports self-regulated learning by enabling students to revise their work iteratively without waiting for instructor response. When embedded within Learning Analytics dashboards, AI-generated feedback can contribute directly to learner-facing indicators, such as progress over time or conceptual mastery.

Generative AI also contributes to the personalization of learning pathways. Traditional LA systems use prediction models to estimate risk levels or recommend resources based on structured data. In contrast, LLMs can dynamically tailor content, explanations, difficulty levels, and practice activities based on nuanced linguistic evidence of learner needs. Saleh et al. (2025) report that LLMs can generate adaptive explanations or problem variations aligned with a learner's demonstrated competency profile. This allows Learning Analytics not only to diagnose challenges but also to operationalize interventions by generating targeted pedagogical material. Personalization thus becomes more fluid and conversational, allowing learners to engage with AI-driven support that mimics the responsiveness of human tutoring.

Another emerging opportunity involves the creation of synthetic data for educational modeling. Traditional LA research often suffers from limited data availability due to privacy concerns, small sample sizes, or contextual variability. LLMs can generate synthetic datasets that simulate realistic student responses or performance trajectories, enabling institutions to prototype dashboards, test predictive models, or train machine learning algorithms on non-sensitive data. While this application is still developing, the potential to reduce privacy risk and democratize access to training data is significant, particularly for smaller institutions or researchers who lack access to large-scale datasets. Preliminary findings in the broader AI literature show that LLM-generated synthetic data can approximate the statistical and linguistic properties of real data, although careful validation is required to avoid amplifying biases (UNESCO, 2023).

In higher education, the integration of LLMs into Learning Analytics is accelerating rapidly. Universities use AI-supported systems to analyze student writing across disciplines, provide feedback in writing-intensive courses, assist with programming assignments, and monitor discussion forum engagement. Guizani et al. (2025) show that higher education institutions are leveraging LLMs to support academic advising, supplement peer feedback, and scaffold complex assignments. Because university learners engage in diverse forms of linguistic production—from essays to research proposals and peer critiques—Generative AI provides a rich analytic layer that complements traditional numerical indicators.

Lifelong learning environments exhibit similar trends. Professional learners in reskilling programs or corporate training often interact with digital platforms where AI-driven analysis can identify knowledge gaps, recommend micro-learning modules, and generate personalized learning sequences. The flexibility of LLMs makes them well-suited to adult learning contexts, where personalization must account for varied backgrounds, goals, and schedules. Dong et al. (2024) highlight applications in medical education, programming bootcamps, and simulations that provide learners with scenario-based explanations or domain-specific reasoning, offering evidence that LLMs can serve as cognitive partners in professional development.

To illustrate the breadth of applications, the following table (Table 3) synthesizes representative uses of Generative AI across different educational levels, based on recurring findings in Dong et al. (2024), Emirtekin et al. (2025), and Guizani et al. (2025).

Table 3. Representative Applications of Generative AI in Learning Analytics

Educational Context	Analytic Functions	Generative Functions	Benefits Identified
Higher Education	Evaluation of student discourse, writing analytics, detection of misconceptions	Automated feedback, generation of examples, code review	Improved feedback quality, support for academic writing, scalable assessment
Professional & Lifelong Learning	Competency mapping, skill-gap analysis, trace analysis	Scenario generation, personalized micro-content	Targeted reskilling pathways, higher learner autonomy
K–12 and Introductory Courses	Early risk detection, monitoring engagement	Explanation of concepts, adaptive hints	Enhanced understanding, improved motivation

The opportunities introduced by Generative AI extend beyond instructional benefits to include substantial advantages for educators. Time savings in grading and feedback provision allow instructors to reallocate effort toward mentoring, curriculum design, and higher-order pedagogical tasks. LA systems enriched with AI-generated insights can help instructors identify patterns that would otherwise remain hidden, such as recurring conceptual difficulties across cohorts or sentiment patterns in discussion forums. These analytic enhancements can also inform the redesign of courses, identification of materials requiring revision, and evaluation of pedagogical interventions, thereby strengthening evidence-based decision-making.

From an institutional perspective, Generative-AI-enhanced analytics contribute to higher levels of scalability and responsiveness. Administrators increasingly rely on real-time dashboards to monitor student progression, evaluate program effectiveness, and anticipate support needs. LLMs enable more sophisticated analyses of open-ended survey responses, retention-related writings, or advising discussions, improving institutional awareness of learner well-being, motivation, and challenges. In contexts where learners produce large volumes of qualitative data, institutions can achieve an analytic maturity level previously unattainable with manual methods alone.

Nevertheless, assessing the maturity of Generative-AI-enabled Learning Analytics requires careful consideration. While some applications, such as automated feedback on grammar or syntactic structure, are relatively mature and widely validated, others—particularly those involving high-stakes assessment, deep cognitive inference, or prediction of learner capabilities—remain at an early stage. Peters et al. (2025) demonstrate that LLMs may oversimplify or misinterpret scientific content, posing risks for accuracy. UNESCO (2023) repeatedly emphasizes that while AI-driven personalization and feedback hold enormous promise, they require strong human oversight and transparent design principles. In this sense, the maturity of current systems depends not only on technical performance but also on the presence of governance structures, evaluation protocols, and responsible deployment practices.

In summary, the integration of Generative AI into Learning Analytics offers vast opportunities across multiple educational contexts. LLMs expand analytic capabilities into new semantic territories, enabling deeper insights into learner reasoning, discourse, and motivation. They support scalable personalized learning, automate feedback, generate synthetic data, and enhance institutional decision-making. At the same time, the maturity and reliability of these applications depend on thoughtful governance, careful validation, and alignment with ethical and regulatory frameworks. These opportunities set the stage for the next chapter, which examines the corresponding risks and challenges associated with deploying Generative-AI-driven Learning Analytics in education.

PEDAGOGICAL, METHODOLOGICAL AND ETHICAL RISKS

The integration of Generative Artificial Intelligence into Learning Analytics has generated considerable enthusiasm due to its potential to enhance learner modeling, automate feedback, and support personalized instruction. Yet the same capabilities that make generative models attractive also introduce substantial pedagogical, methodological, and ethical risks. These risks reflect not only technical limitations of large language models (LLMs) but also the broader implications of embedding AI into instructional processes, assessment practices, and educational decision-making. Understanding these risks is essential to ensuring that the deployment of AI-driven Learning Analytics remains pedagogically sound, ethically responsible, and aligned with regulatory frameworks.

One of the most widely documented technical risks of Generative AI involves hallucinations, the phenomenon in which LLMs generate plausible but incorrect information. Peters et al. (2025) demonstrate that LLMs routinely simplify or distort scientific studies, sometimes fabricating details or omitting critical nuances. In educational contexts, such distortions can mislead learners, undermine conceptual understanding, and compromise the integrity of formative assessment. When hallucinated outputs appear in feedback systems, they may reinforce misconceptions instead of correcting them. Even small inaccuracies can have amplified consequences when learners rely on AI-generated guidance during the early stages of concept acquisition. This makes hallucinations a methodological as well as pedagogical concern, particularly when LLM outputs are integrated directly into Learning Analytics dashboards or automated feedback loops.

Bias represents another foundational technical challenge. LLMs inherit the statistical patterns, stereotypes, and imbalances present in their training data. As UNESCO (2023) notes, generative models may reproduce discriminatory patterns related to gender, race, socioeconomic status, or linguistic background. When such models are used for learner modeling or predictions in Learning Analytics, they may skew interpretations of student ability or performance. Bias in automated assessment, for instance, can lead to inequitable evaluations, particularly for learners whose linguistic expressions deviate from dominant language norms. Studies such as Guizani et al. (2025) warn that unfair system responses may reinforce academic inequalities and perpetuate structural biases already present in educational systems. Bias is therefore both a technical and a social risk, as it influences not only the accuracy of AI-generated outputs but also the fairness of educational decisions informed by those outputs.

A related methodological challenge arises from the lack of explainability. Unlike traditional Learning Analytics models—for example, regression, decision trees, or transparent classification approaches—LLMs operate through opaque internal representations that offer limited insight into the reasoning behind their outputs. This opacity creates barriers for educators attempting to interpret AI-supported analytics or validate AI-generated feedback. UNESCO (2023) emphasizes that when educational stakeholders cannot understand why a system produces a given result, they are less likely to trust or appropriately use the system. The lack of explainability also complicates compliance with the EU AI Act (European Union, 2024), which requires transparency, documentation, and human oversight for AI systems, especially those used in high-stakes educational contexts such as assessment and decision-making about learners.

Beyond technical concerns, Generative AI poses several pedagogical risks. One such risk involves the potential erosion of learner autonomy. If students rely excessively on AI-generated solutions, explanations, or drafts, they may bypass essential cognitive processes that foster deep learning. Over-reliance on AI tools can transform learning into a passive consumption process rather than an active construction of knowledge. Evidence from higher education indicates that frequent use of generative systems may encourage surface-level engagement, particularly when learners substitute AI output for their own reasoning. Dong et al. (2024) suggest that while LLMs can support learning, they can also inhibit independent problem-solving when learners view them as authoritative sources rather than as tools requiring critical evaluation.

Pedagogical challenges also emerge in relation to academic integrity. Because LLMs can generate human-like text, code, and arguments, distinguishing between authentic student work and AI-generated content becomes increasingly difficult. This ambiguity poses significant challenges for assessment validity. If educators cannot reliably determine whether student work reflects genuine learning, they cannot accurately evaluate performance or provide meaningful feedback. Peters et al. (2025) also highlight concerns that generative models may mask the depth—or lack thereof—of student understanding, enabling students to present polished but conceptually shallow work. This not only threatens academic integrity but also compromises the broader educational mission of fostering critical thinking and originality.

The integration of Generative AI into Learning Analytics also carries ethical risks related to fairness, accountability, privacy, and data ownership. Learning Analytics traditionally involves the analysis of student data, and the addition of LLM-based systems intensifies these concerns. UNESCO (2023) emphasizes that AI systems must respect data privacy and limit the collection of sensitive information. However, many generative systems require exposure to textual data that may contain personal or identifiable information. If used without careful governance, such systems may violate privacy rights or inadvertently expose learner data to third-party vendors. This becomes particularly problematic in contexts where institutional data infrastructures rely on cloud-based AI services that operate beyond the institution's direct control.

Accountability emerges as a further ethical concern. When AI systems produce errors, discriminatory outcomes, or misleading feedback, it may be unclear who bears responsibility: the educator deploying the system, the institution adopting it, or the developers designing it. The EU AI Act (European Union, 2024) seeks to address such ambiguities by assigning specific obligations to providers and deployers of high-risk AI systems. Yet operationalizing accountability within educational institutions remains complex, especially when systems integrate both analytics and generative components that interact dynamically. Without clear lines of responsibility, institutions risk deploying tools whose negative impacts may go unaddressed or unmonitored.

Issues of data ownership and consent further complicate the ethical landscape. Students may not be fully aware that their contributions—including essays, discussion posts, or assignments—are being used to train or refine AI systems. Even when personal identifiers are removed, the use of student-generated data for system improvement raises questions about rights, consent, and control. UNESCO (2023) argues that learners must retain agency over their data, including the right to know how it will be used and the ability to opt out of non-essential data processing. This requirement aligns with legal obligations under the EU AI Act and broader data governance frameworks.

The cumulative impact of these risks on educational equity is significant. If LLMs provide higher-quality feedback to students with strong linguistic skills, or misinterpret the work of students from marginalized groups, they may exacerbate existing achievement gaps. Similarly, students with greater digital literacy or access to technology may benefit disproportionately from AI-enhanced Learning Analytics, while others may struggle to navigate the complexities of AI-driven tools. These dynamics underscore the importance of treating Generative AI not merely as a technological innovation but as an intervention with potential social consequences.

The interplay of risks can be summarized through a conceptual matrix drawing from Peters et al. (2025), UNESCO (2023), and the EU AI Act, illustrating how technical, pedagogical, and ethical concerns intersect and amplify each other.

Table 4. Conceptual Matrix of Risks in Generative-AI-Enhanced Learning Analytics

Risk Domain	Core Issue	Educational Impact	Representative Source
Technical	Hallucinations, bias, opacity	Misleading analytics, unfair feedback, unreliable assessment	Peters et al. (2025)
Pedagogical	Over-reliance, surface learning, reduced agency	Compromised learning quality, weakened autonomy	Dong et al. (2024)
Ethical	Privacy, fairness, accountability	Inequity, loss of trust, regulatory violations	UNESCO (2023); European Union (2024)

Trust emerges as one of the most fragile dimensions within this matrix. When learners, instructors, or institutions lose confidence in AI-supported analytics, the legitimacy of educational decisions becomes uncertain. Trust is undermined not only by technical inaccuracies but also by opaque system behavior, insufficient human oversight, and inadequate communication about system capabilities and limitations. Saleh et al. (2025) emphasize that robust evaluation frameworks, transparent design, and continuous monitoring are essential to sustaining trust in LLM-supported educational tools. Without such safeguards, institutions risk adopting systems that appear effective on the surface yet introduce unintended harms.

In conclusion, while Generative AI offers significant opportunities for enhancing Learning Analytics, its deployment introduces substantial technical, pedagogical, and ethical risks. Hallucinations, bias, and opacity challenge methodological soundness. The potential erosion of learner autonomy and academic integrity raises pedagogical concerns. Issues of fairness, privacy, accountability, and data ownership introduce deep ethical complexities. Understanding these risks is a prerequisite for responsible adoption and forms the essential foundation for the next chapter, which addresses institutional governance and compliance frameworks.

REGULATORY AND POLICY FRAMEWORK: THE EU AI ACT

The regulation known as the EU AI Act marks a watershed moment in the governance of artificial intelligence across the European Union. The regulation establishes a risk-based framework, categorizing AI systems according to the level of risk they pose to safety, fundamental rights, and societal functions (European Union, 2024; European Commission, 2024). Under this framework, AI systems deemed to present an "unacceptable risk" are prohibited, those classified as "high-risk" are subject to stringent obligations, while "limited risk" and "minimal risk" systems face increasingly lighter regulatory burdens. The notion of "high-risk" is particularly pertinent to educational environments, where AI systems can affect access to education, assessment outcomes, and learners' trajectories.

As illustrated in Figure 1, the European Commission conceptualizes AI regulation through a hierarchical, risk-based pyramid structure distinguishing unacceptable, high, limited, and minimal risk levels (European Commission, 2021). This model frames the logic of the EU AI Act and clarifies why educational applications often fall under "high-risk" categories.

Figure 1. Risk-based regulatory pyramid of the European Commission (European Commission, 2021).

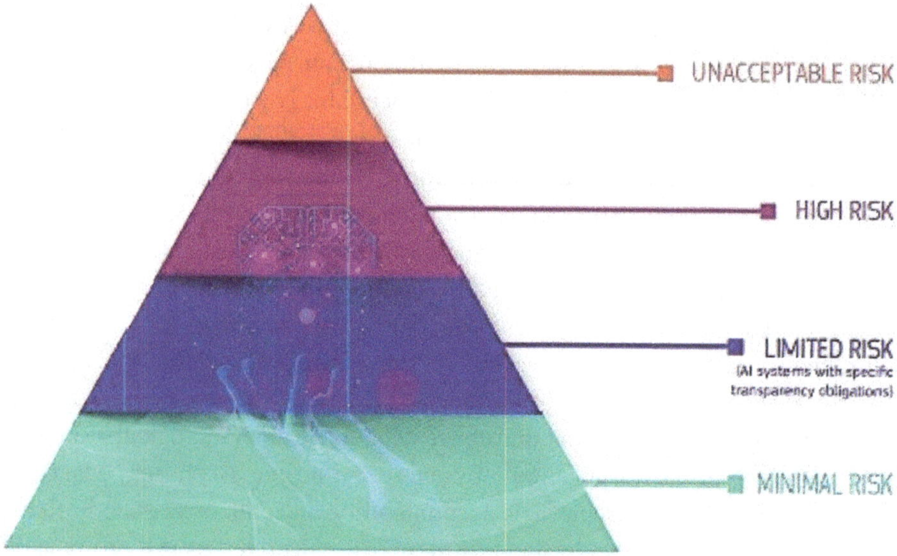

Article 6 of the EU AI Act outlines the rules for classification of high-risk AI systems, specifying that systems listed in Annex III are automatically considered high-risk (unless the system in question demonstrably poses no significant risk) (EU AI Act, Art. 6). Annex III explicitly includes AI systems used for "determining access to education or vocational training institutions or programmes," "evaluating learning outcomes of persons," "assessing the appropriate level of education for an individual," or "monitoring and detecting prohibited behaviour of students during examinations or tests" (Recital 56; EU AI Act, 2024). Given this inclusion, many AI applications in the education sector—such as automated grading tools, admission decision support systems, and exam-proctoring analytics—fall squarely into the high-risk category (FeedbackFruits, 2025). This classification has major implications for educational institutions, EdTech providers and policymakers.

The EU AI Act does not merely categorize systems: it imposes a robust set of obligations on providers and deployers of high-risk AI systems. These include requirements for human oversight, risk assessment, documentation and transparency, quality of datasets, robustness, cybersecurity measures, logging of incidents, and post-deployment monitoring (EU AI Act, 2024; IAPP, 2023). For example, providers must undertake a conformity assessment prior to placing a high-risk AI system on the market, ensuring it meets the prescribed standards (Future of Life Institute, 2024). Deployer obligations include the use of the system in accordance with instructions, training of personnel, monitoring of system performance in context, and reporting of serious incidents (RTR, 2024). Moreover, the EU regulation retains an extraterritorial effect: non-EU providers whose systems are marketed in the EU will also be captured under these obligations (Digital Strategy – European Commission, 2024).

In the educational context, the implications of these obligations are significant. Consider an EdTech company that develops an AI system to automatically assign learners to courses based on performance data, or a university that deploys an AI-driven analysis of student essays and forum posts to predict dropout risk and deliver tailored feedback. Under the EU AI Act, such systems must first evaluate whether they fall in the high-risk category. If so, they must undertake risk classification, ensure conformity, maintain detailed technical documentation, perform impact assessments (including human rights and fundamental rights impact), and secure transparent user information. Importantly, human oversight must remain integral: educators must be able to override or interpret AI decisions, and learners must be informed when they interact with an AI system in a decision-influencing capacity (EU AI Act, Art. 13; Digital Strategy – European Commission, 2024).

The link between the EU AI Act and existing data-protection regulation, namely the GDPR, is also critical. Educational institutions already handling sensitive personal data of learners must now address not only the safeguarding of personal data under GDPR but also the transparency, accountability and human-rights obligations introduced by the AI Act. The AI Act explicitly states that compliance with data-protection requirements or sectoral regulation does not exempt providers or deployers from its obligations (Recital 71). For example, an automated grading system that processes essay submissions and behavioral data may comply with GDPR in terms of lawful basis and data minimization; yet under the AI Act, it must also satisfy additional obligations such as robustness of outputs, human-in-loop governance, log retention, and impact reporting.

For educational institutions, the practical implications of the EU AI Act are manifold. Firstly, there is a need for organizational governance structures: institutions must map their use of AI systems, classify them, conduct impact assessments, and ensure oversight frameworks. EdTech providers must embed legal-compliance features into the design of their systems, including documentation, versioning, incident logging, and transparency disclosures. Policymakers must foster ecosystem support, verification infrastructure and training initiatives to ensure that the education sector can comply without stifling innovation. The timeline for implementation is strict: while the Act entered into force on 1 August 2024, many obligations for high-risk systems become applicable two years after entry (IAPP, 2023; Digital Strategy – European Commission, 2024). Thus, there is a window of preparation—but institutions must act now.

To illustrate major compliance obligations for high-risk AI systems in education, one may consider the following schematic overview (Table 5):

Table 5. Selected Obligations for High-Risk AI Systems under the EU AI Act

Obligation	Description	Educational Example
Risk Management System	Set up a quality-management and risk-mitigation framework across the lifecycle	An institution implements dashboards tracking AI-guided assignment recommendations and student outcomes to detect bias or drift
Conformity Assessment	External/internal audit and certification prior to deployment	EdTech vendor conducts third-party audit of its automated admission-tool before licensing to European universities
Transparency & Information to Users	Provide clear documentation, indicate AI usage to end-users	Students are informed when their essays are evaluated by an AI-system and are given human contact for appeal
Human Oversight	Ensure human review of AI decisions and intervention capability	A tutor reviews automated feedback and overrides unexpected score anomalies before final grade issuance
Post-Market Monitoring & Incident Reporting	Log incidents, update models responsibly, notify authorities of serious errors	Institution reports erroneous grouping by AI-system to national regulator, retrains model and informs affected learners

This overview provides a conceptual scaffold that helps educational stakeholders plan compliance and governance efforts in a structured manner. While the table format is presented here for clarity, the obligations are deeply interconnected and must be embedded into institution-wide AI governance frameworks.

The classification of educational applications as high risk carries broader ramifications for innovation and market dynamics. Some EdTech firms may face enhanced certification costs, audit burdens, and longer time-to-market for AI-driven products. On the other hand, the regulation also signals a maturation of the sector: clear rules reduce uncertainty, enhance trust among users and institutions, and may become a competitive differentiator for compliant providers. Policymakers face the balancing challenge of enforcing safeguards while avoiding wholesale suppression of AI innovation in education. The European Commission supports this via the AI Pact and the Service Desk for AI compliance, aimed at assisting smaller players and educational institutions (Digital Strategy – European Commission, 2024).

In conclusion, the regulatory and policy framework established by the EU AI Act transforms how AI systems are developed, deployed and governed within the education sector. By introducing a risk-based classification, assigning high-risk status to key educational AI use-cases, and imposing foundational obligations such as human oversight, transparency, documentation, and conformity assessment, the Act sets the stage for trustworthy AI in education. For educational institutions, EdTech companies and policymakers, the Act presents both a challenge and an opportunity: the challenge of compliance and governance adaptation, and the opportunity to embed ethical, transparent, and robust AI systems that earn the trust of educators and learners alike.

TOWARD RESPONSIBLE-BY-DESIGN ADOPTION

The rapid expansion of Generative Artificial Intelligence within educational ecosystems has accelerated discussions about how institutions can adopt such technologies responsibly and sustainably. As Learning Analytics becomes increasingly intertwined with language-model-based systems, the requirements for transparency, accountability, fairness, and ethical alignment grow correspondingly in importance. The notion of *responsible-by-design* shifts the focus from reactive governance toward proactive integration of ethical, technical, and pedagogical safeguards from the earliest stages of system development and deployment. This chapter examines the principles, practices, and institutional strategies that can guide such an approach, drawing on established frameworks from UNESCO, the EU AI Act, and contemporary AI governance research.

Responsible adoption begins with the recognition that the opacity and probabilistic nature of LLMs demand robust mechanisms for explainability. Traditional Learning Analytics models have often relied on relatively interpretable statistical techniques, enabling educators to understand and scrutinize outputs. By contrast, LLMs function through high-dimensional internal representations that obscure causal pathways, raising concerns about interpretability and trust. UNESCO (2023) emphasizes that explainability is fundamental to maintaining user trust, enabling human oversight, and ensuring that learners understand when and how AI influences their educational experiences. Explainability does not require exposing internal model weights; instead, it relies on meaningful explanations tailored to users' needs, such as model rationales, counterexamples, feature attributions, and structured documentation (e.g., model cards). These approaches help educators critically assess AI outputs rather than treating them as authoritative.

The importance of data governance grows proportionally with the complexity and sensitivity of the data that LLM-driven analytics systems process. As learning environments increasingly generate unstructured textual data—reflections, essays, discussions—educational institutions must adopt strengthened frameworks for data minimization, secure storage, provenance tracking, and responsible data sharing. UNESCO (2021) stresses that learners must retain agency over their data, and institutions must maintain transparent policies regarding how data is used, stored, and repurposed. A responsible-by-design approach extends beyond basic compliance with GDPR to include robust internal governance mechanisms such as designated data stewards, ethical review boards for analytics projects, and systematic monitoring of potential data misuse. These structures ensure not only legal compliance but also alignment with the values of educational integrity and learner protection.

Accountability frameworks constitute another central pillar of responsible adoption. The EU AI Act (European Union, 2024) places explicit responsibility on both providers and deployers of high-risk systems. Yet even beyond statutory obligations, institutions must cultivate internal accountability structures that define roles and responsibilities clearly. Educators must know when they are accountable for interpreting AI outputs; administrators must ensure that governance processes function effectively; and developers or vendors must provide clear documentation, risk assessments, and transparent system behaviors. Saleh et al. (2025) argue that accountability strengthens the reliability of AI-enhanced Learning Analytics, ensuring that errors are traceable and remediable.

To operationalize responsible AI, a variety of tools and practices have emerged. Model cards represent structured documentation that outlines key information about an AI model, including intended use cases, limitations, ethical considerations, training data characteristics, and known biases. Such documentation supports transparency and enables educators to understand the constraints of LLMs used in analytic applications. Bias audits complement model cards by assessing the model's performance across demographic groups or linguistic profiles. As studies such as Guizani et al. (2025) show, LLMs may perform unevenly across learners with varied language backgrounds, requiring systematic evaluation to ensure fairness. Bias audits, whether internal or third-party, identify disparities and inform model retraining or adjustments to deployment strategies.

Impact assessments also serve as critical governance tools, especially within the EU regulatory framework. The EU AI Act mandates assessments focused on risk, safety, and fundamental rights, but educational institutions may expand these assessments to include pedagogical and learning impacts. For example, institutions might evaluate how an AI-driven feedback tool influences learners' motivation, autonomy, or sense of competence. Integrating such findings into iterative design cycles ensures that AI systems augment rather than undermine learning processes. This approach aligns with the broader goal of responsible-by-design integration by ensuring that ethical and pedagogical values shape and constrain technological development from the outset.

Given the centrality of human oversight in both pedagogical practice and regulatory compliance, the professional development of educators becomes a cornerstone of responsible adoption. Educators must be equipped not only to use AI tools effectively but also to critically interrogate their outputs and understand their limitations. Emirtekin et al. (2025) demonstrate that automated assessment systems can support instructors substantially, but only when educators are able to review, validate, and contextualize AI-generated feedback. Professional development programs must therefore encompass foundational AI literacy, critical evaluation of model outputs, recognition of bias, and understanding of risk mitigation practices. Such training ensures that educators remain in control of instructional decisions and that AI systems serve as augmentative tools rather than replacements for human judgment.

At the institutional level, responsible-by-design adoption requires coherent policies and organizational structures. Institutions must establish AI governance committees, develop guidelines for procurement, ensure that AI systems undergo ethical and technical vetting, and create reporting channels for incidents or system failures. Policies should articulate acceptable uses of AI, delineate boundaries for automated assessment, and outline processes for appealing AI-influenced decisions. Furthermore, institutions should promote learner transparency by informing students when AI systems are used, how their data is processed, and how they can contest or request human review of AI-generated outcomes. UNESCO (2023) emphasizes that such transparency practices are essential for maintaining trust and protecting learner rights.

Figure 1 below synthesizes UNESCO's responsible AI framework, which highlights the interplay between ethical principles, governance structures, and stakeholder involvement. Although presented in simplified form, this conceptual diagram supports an integrated understanding of responsible-by-design adoption within education.

As illustrated in Figure 2, UNESCO's Competency Framework for Teachers outlines the key AI-related knowledge, skills and values required in contemporary education.

Figure 2. UNESCO AI Competency Framework for Teachers (UNESCO, 2024)

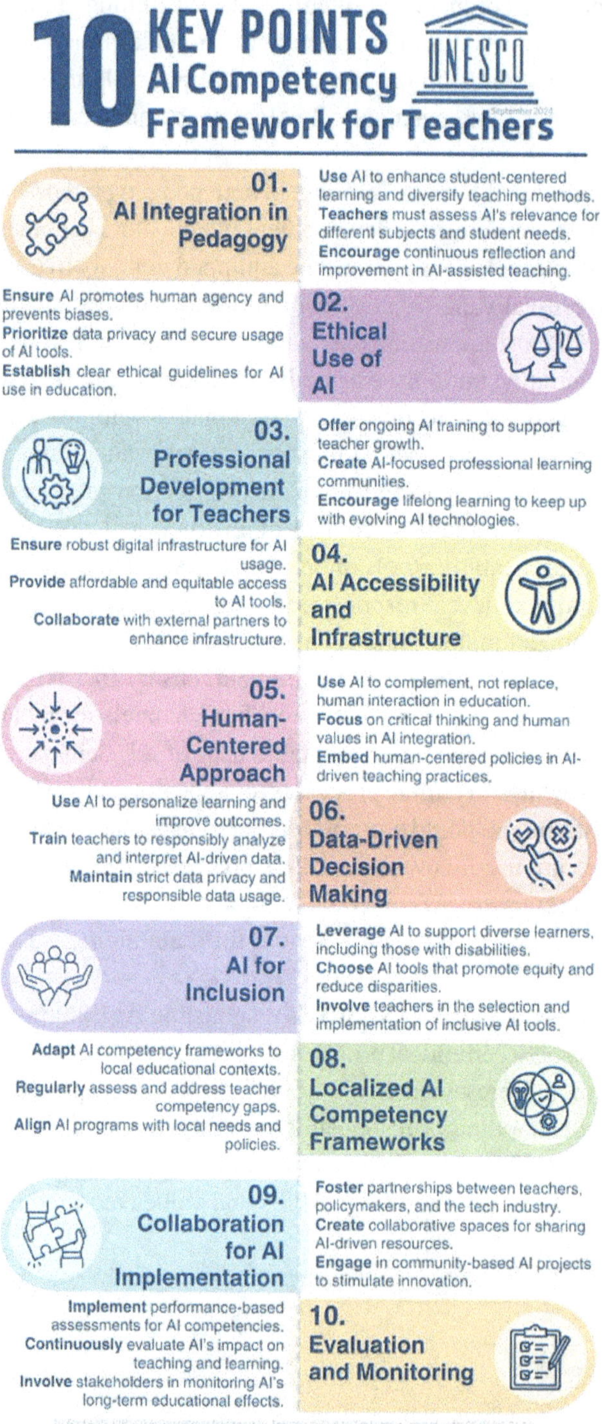

The adoption of Generative AI in Learning Analytics also requires alignment between institutional policies and national or regional regulatory frameworks. The EU AI Act establishes legally enforceable obligations, but institutions must internalize these within their strategic planning processes. For example, an AI-based early-warning system for dropout detection may be classified as high-risk under Annex III of the Act; therefore, the institution must implement documentation practices, incident reporting mechanisms, and human-in-the-loop governance. By integrating EU regulatory mandates with internal ethical guidelines, institutions can create a cohesive and robust governance ecosystem.

Ultimately, responsible-by-design adoption reflects an evolving understanding of AI's role in education. Rather than viewing Generative AI as a neutral tool, institutions must recognize that its influence is shaped by design choices, data structures, documentation practices, and the competencies of educators who use it. A mature approach to Learning Analytics enhanced by LLMs requires continuous monitoring, iterative improvement, and engagement with learners, educators, developers, and policymakers. In doing so, educational institutions can harness AI's transformative potential while safeguarding the values of fairness, trust, and human-centered learning.

DISCUSSION

The synthesis of findings across the preceding chapters underscores the profound shifts that Generative Artificial Intelligence introduces into the field of Learning Analytics. The central objective of this study was to explore how LLM-enhanced analytic practices transform pedagogical processes, reshape feedback mechanisms, and impose new governance and regulatory responsibilities on educational institutions. The literature consistently shows that the convergence of LA and generative models extends analytic capabilities beyond structured datasets toward multimodal, semantically rich sources of learner information (Dong et al., 2024; Emirtekin et al., 2025). This expansion supports more nuanced understanding of student reasoning, misconceptions, and learning trajectories, yet it simultaneously introduces methodological uncertainties, ethical challenges, and the risk of over-dependence.

Comparing earlier generations of LA systems with contemporary LLM-based approaches clarifies the magnitude of this transformation. Traditional Learning Analytics relied primarily on statistical models, classification algorithms, and pattern detection techniques grounded in structured interactional data such as clickstreams, quiz attempts, and time-on-task indicators (Baker & Inventado, 2014; Romero & Ventura, 2024). Such methods offered predictive value but were limited in their capacity to interpret qualitative or textual dimensions of learning. The advent of transformer-based architectures enables analyses previously unattainable, including discourse evaluation, sentiment extraction, conceptual mapping, feedback generation, and multimodal reasoning (Guizani et al., 2025). This shift suggests a movement from analytics as measurement toward analytics as co-participation in learning processes, blurring traditional distinctions between assessment and instruction.

From a pedagogical standpoint, the literature reflects a dual narrative. On one hand, LLM-driven feedback can accelerate formative assessment cycles, enhance learner autonomy, and provide personalized support that responds dynamically to student needs (Saleh et al., 2025). Learners benefit from immediate explanations, targeted examples, and fine-grained feedback, particularly in writing-intensive or problem-solving contexts. On the other hand, the risk of epistemic over-reliance becomes increasingly salient: when generative systems produce highly polished yet potentially shallow explanations, students may develop a false sense of understanding or minimize the cognitive effort invested in learning. As Peters et al. (2025) show, the potential for oversimplification, hallucinations, or distorted interpretation of scientific content requires vigilant human oversight. Thus, while Generative AI enhances learning opportunities, it also reinforces the need for pedagogical models that promote critical engagement with AI outputs rather than passive acceptance.

To support a structured understanding of the interplay between opportunities, risks, and institutional obligations, a consolidated summary of the literature's recurring themes is provided in Table 6. This table synthesizes representative findings across the main analytical dimensions of this study and clarifies how the combined evidence advances the broader discussion.

Table 6. Synthesis of Key Themes Identified in the Literature

Dimension	Core Themes Identified in Literature	Representative Sources
Analytical Capabilities	Expansion from structured to multimodal data; richer semantic interpretation; automated feedback and reasoning support	Dong et al. (2024); Emirtekin et al. (2025)
Pedagogical Impact	Enhanced personalization; risk of over-reliance; potential for surface learning; shifting role of feedback	Saleh et al. (2025); Peters et al. (2025)
Ethical & Social Considerations	Bias, opacity, privacy concerns, unequal learner impacts; influence on academic integrity	UNESCO (2023); Guizani et al. (2025)
Regulatory & Institutional Demands	High-risk categorization under EU AI Act; need for transparency, oversight, documentation; increased governance complexity	European Union (2024)
Future Challenges	Limited longitudinal evidence; inconsistent performance across languages; need for educator training; evolving regulatory norms	UNESCO (2021); Romero & Ventura (2024)

The table illustrates how the discussion does not rest on isolated observations but emerges from interconnected, multi-level considerations. Pedagogical, methodological, and ethical dimensions intersect in ways that shape institutional responsibilities and influence student experiences. For instance, stronger analytic capabilities open the door to more effective personalization, yet the presence of bias or opacity in LLMs may compromise fairness and equity when used in assessment or learner modeling. Similarly, regulatory obligations introduced by the EU AI Act reinforce the need for structured documentation, bias audits, and human oversight, all of which reframe institutional routines and professional development requirements for educators.

The broader social implications of these developments are significant. Educational AI systems participate in shaping learners' identities, opportunities, and evaluative outcomes. UNESCO (2023) emphasizes the risk of entrenching existing inequalities if AI systems perform unevenly across linguistic or demographic groups. Conversely, when properly governed, LLM-enhanced analytics may promote more inclusive support structures by identifying at-risk learners earlier, offering personalized scaffolding, and reducing workload barriers for educators.

Despite the promising directions highlighted throughout this study, several limitations constrain the generalizability of current findings. Much of the research on LLMs in education is recent and exploratory, with limited longitudinal evidence or cross-context validation. There remains a notable imbalance in empirical studies across educational sectors; while higher education is well represented, K–12 and multilingual contexts appear underexplored (Guizani et al., 2025). Additionally, given the rapid evolution of commercial LLMs, system performance may vary significantly across model versions, posing challenges for replicability and sustained evaluation. Regulatory impacts, particularly those stemming from the EU AI Act, are still unfolding, limiting the availability of empirical studies examining institutional compliance practices.

In sum, the discussion reveals a field in transition: Generative AI enhances the analytic and pedagogical capacities of Learning Analytics while simultaneously intensifying ethical and regulatory demands. These dynamics reinforce the need for responsible-by-design frameworks that integrate transparency, data governance, and human oversight as foundational principles. As the field advances, sustained interdisciplinary collaboration among educators, data scientists, policymakers, and learners will be essential to ensure that AI-enhanced Learning Analytics fulfills its potential while safeguarding educational values and equity.

CONCLUSION: FUTURE DIRECTIONS

This study has examined the evolving convergence between Learning Analytics and Generative Artificial Intelligence, highlighting both the significant pedagogical opportunities and the complex ethical, methodological, and regulatory challenges that accompany this transformation. Across the chapters, a recurring theme emerged: the integration of large language models into educational data analysis marks a substantial departure from earlier analytic paradigms, enabling richer interpretation of learner behavior while simultaneously increasing institutional responsibility for oversight, transparency, and governance. The findings suggest that the potential benefits of LLM-enhanced analytics—such as improved feedback, personalized learning pathways, multimodal data processing, and early identification of learning barriers—are inseparable from concerns about bias, fairness, accountability, and regulatory compliance. Thus, the contribution of this study lies in synthesizing these dimensions and situating them within the broader European policy landscape, particularly the implications of the EU AI Act for educational practice.

The review demonstrated that Generative AI expands analytic capabilities by incorporating semantic understanding, narrative reasoning, and dynamic content generation, which move beyond the limitations of earlier forms of Learning Analytics. Works such as those of Dong et al. (2024) and Emirtekin et al. (2025) underscore the extent to which LLMs can enhance interpretation of textual data, automate assessment processes, and provide cognitively responsive feedback. These developments represent a methodological shift from descriptive or predictive analytics toward interactive and interventionist applications, where AI not only analyzes but actively shapes learning trajectories. At the same time, the literature stresses that such power must be balanced with mechanisms of human oversight and pedagogical deliberation to mitigate risks associated with hallucinations, misalignment, and over-reliance on machine-generated reasoning (Peters et al., 2025).

The study also emphasizes that the transformative potential of Generative AI in education must be understood through the lens of ethics and governance. UNESCO (2023) highlights the centrality of human-centered AI design, advocating for transparency, privacy protections, and fairness as foundational components of responsible educational adoption. These concerns resonate strongly with the requirements introduced by the EU AI Act, which classifies many educational AI tools as high-risk systems and therefore subject to stringent obligations for documentation, continuous monitoring, risk assessment, and human-in-the-loop decision-making (European Union, 2024). This alignment between pedagogical ethics and regulatory expectations reinforces the notion that Learning Analytics enhanced by LLMs is not merely a technical innovation but a governance challenge that demands institutional readiness, structured policies, and educator training.

Despite the progress documented in recent literature, several gaps remain that point toward critical avenues for future research. One major area concerns the lack of longitudinal evidence on how LLM-driven systems influence actual learning outcomes. While initial studies report promising improvements in feedback quality and learner engagement, there is limited empirical validation of long-term learning gains or the sustained reliability of AI-generated explanations across different subjects, cultures, or linguistic groups (Guizani et al., 2025). This suggests a need for multi-year, mixed-methods research designs that investigate both cognitive and affective impacts of AI-mediated learning.

Another major line of future research involves systematic measurement of bias and fairness in educational applications of Generative AI. Existing studies demonstrate that LLMs may exhibit uneven performance across students with different linguistic or cultural backgrounds, raising concerns about equity and academic integrity. Future research should develop more robust methodologies for detecting, quantifying, and mitigating bias, including controlled evaluation frameworks, third-party audits, and comparative analyses across multiple model versions or providers (Saleh et al., 2025). Such work would provide evidence-based guidance for institutions adopting AI systems and contribute to the refinement of international standards for educational fairness.

Further investigation is needed regarding the development and validation of ethical and governance frameworks tailored specifically to educational contexts. While UNESCO and the EU AI Act provide high-level guidance, additional empirical research could explore how institutions interpret, implement, and operationalize these guidelines in practice. Areas for future exploration include the design of institutional AI governance committees, the integration of risk assessment into curriculum planning, and the development of pedagogically aligned human oversight protocols that maintain learner agency and avoid algorithmic overreach. Research into educators' AI literacy and professional development needs also remains limited, despite strong evidence that teacher readiness significantly shapes the effectiveness and ethical use of AI-enhanced Learning Analytics (UNESCO, 2021).

From a policy perspective, the findings of this study suggest a strong need for continued collaboration between European policymakers, educational institutions, and AI developers to ensure harmonized implementation of the EU AI Act across member states. This includes clarifying compliance expectations for educational systems classified as high-risk, supporting institutions with capacity-building resources, and facilitating cross-national exchanges of best practices. As the regulatory environment continues to evolve, policy development must address emerging challenges such as AI explainability in assessment, accountability for hybrid human–AI decisions, and the rights of learners to contest AI-influenced evaluations. Effective policy harmonization at the European level may support more equitable deployment of AI technologies and reduce disparities in institutional readiness across the EU.

In conclusion, the integration of Generative AI into Learning Analytics presents both unprecedented opportunities and formidable challenges. This study has synthesized the available evidence to provide a holistic view of how LLM-enhanced analytics reshape learning processes, pedagogical models, and regulatory obligations. The future of the field will depend on sustained interdisciplinary collaboration, rigorous empirical research, and the development of robust institutional and policy frameworks that ensure AI enhances rather than undermines human-centered education. As the European regulatory landscape matures and Generative AI technologies advance, the ongoing dialogue between educators, policymakers, developers, and researchers will remain essential for shaping an equitable and trustworthy future for AI in education.

REFERENCES

Artificial Intelligence Act. (n.d.). *Annex III: High-risk AI systems referred to in Article 6(2).* https://artificialintelligenceact.eu/annex/3/

Baker, R. S., & Inventado, P. S. (2014). Educational data mining and learning analytics. In Larusson, J. A., & White, B. (Eds.), *Learning analytics* (pp. 61–75). Springer.

Berland, M., Baker, R. S., & Blikstein, P. (2014). Educational data mining and learning analytics: Applications to constructionist research. *Technology. Knowledge and Learning, 19*, 205–220.

Chatti, M. A., Dyckhoff, A. L., Schroeder, U., & Thüs, H. (2014). Learning analytics: Challenges and future research directions. *eLearning and Education (eleed).*

Devlin, J., Chang, M.-W., Lee, K., & Toutanova, K. (2018). BERT: Pre-training of deep bidirectional transformers for language understanding. https://arxiv.org/abs/1810.04805

Digital Strategy – European Commission. (2024). *AI Act: Shaping Europe's digital future.* https://digital-strategy.ec.europa.eu/en/policies/regulatory-framework-ai

Dong, B., Bai, J., Xu, T., & Zhou, Y. (2024). Large language models in education: A systematic review. In *Proceedings of the 2024 International Conference on Computer Science and Technologies in Education (CSTE).* IEEE.

Emirtekin, E., Yilmaz, H., Kose, U., & Deperlioglu, O. (2025). Large language model-powered automated assessment: A systematic review. *Applied Sciences (Basel, Switzerland), 15*(10), 5683.

European Commission. (2021). *AI risk-based regulatory pyramid infographic.*

European Union. (2024). *Regulation (EU) 2024/1689 of the European Parliament and of the Council on artificial intelligence (AI Act).* Official Journal of the European Union.

FeedbackFruits. (2025, February 12). What is the EU AI Act? A comprehensive overview. https://feedbackfruits.com/blog/from-regulation-to-innovation-what-the-eu-ai-act-means-for-edtech

Future of Life Institute. (2024). *High-level summary of the EU AI Act.* https://artificialintelligenceact.eu

Guizani, S., Mazhar, T., Shahzad, T., Ahmad, W., Bibi, A., & Hamam, H. (2025). A systematic literature review to implement large language models in higher education: Issues and solutions. *Discover Education*, *4*(35).

IAPP. (2023, December). *EU AI Act cheat sheet.* International Association of Privacy Professionals. https://iapp.org/resources/article/eu-ai-act-cheat-sheet/

OpenAI. (2023). *GPT-4 technical report.*

Peters, U.. (2025). AI chatbots oversimplify scientific studies and gloss over critical details—The newest models are especially guilty. *Royal Society Open Science.*

Référé – RTR Austrian Regulatory Authority. (2024). *Deployer obligations – EU AI Act.* https://www.rtr.at/rtr/service/ki-servicestelle/ai-act/Deployer_obligations.en.html

Romero, C., & Ventura, S. (2024). Educational data mining and learning analytics: An updated survey. *arXiv:2402.07956.*

Saleh, Y., Abu Talib, M., Nasir, Q., & Dakalbab, F. (2025). Evaluating large language models: A systematic review of efficiency, applications, and future directions. *Frontiers of Computer Science*, *7*, 1523699.

Siemens, G. (2013). Learning analytics: The emergence of a discipline. *The American Behavioral Scientist*, *57*(10), 1380–1400.

UNESCO. (2021). *AI and education: Guidance for policymakers.* UNESCO Publishing.

UNESCO. (2023). *Guidance for generative AI in education and research.* UNESCO Publishing.

UNESCO. (2024). *AI competency framework for teachers.* UNESCO Publishing.

Vaswani, A., Shazeer, N., Parmar, N., Uszkoreit, J., Jones, L., Gomez, A. N., Kaiser, Ł., & Polosukhin, I. (2017). Attention is all you need. In *Advances in Neural Information Processing Systems.*

Chapter 11
Managing the European Energy Dilemma Through the Energy Quadrilemma Index

Kerasia Kalkitsa
http://orcid.org/0000-0003-0446-901X
Democritus University of Thrace, Greece

Giannoula Florou
http://orcid.org/0000-0002-2621-2832
Democritus University of Thrace, Greece

Anastasios Karasavboglou
Democritus University of Thrace, Greece

Vasileios Zoumboulidis
http://orcid.org/0009-0005-3304-1620
Democritus University of Thrace, Greece

ABSTRACT

This chapter, according to the authors, examines the European energy dilemma through an expanded analytical framework that builds on established approaches to energy system assessment. The chapter introduces the Energy Quadrilemma, which extends the conventional three-dimensional perspective by explicitly incorporating Technology as a fourth pillar alongside energy security, environmental sustainability, and energy equity. Technology is defined as a latent, human-centered, and governance-related construct reflecting education and skills development, digital inclusion, knowledge-intensive employment, and government effectiveness. Using

DOI: 10.4018/979-8-3373-6926-6.ch011

statistical data from 27 European Union member states for the period 2010–2022, Exploratory Factor Analysis is applied to empirically validate the Technology dimension. Based on this framework, the Energy Quadrilemma Index is constructed as a composite indicator integrating energy outcomes with enabling technological and institutional capacities, supporting comparative analysis of energy governance performance in Europe.

1. INTRODUCTION

Over the past decade, the European Union (EU) has been confronted with a growing set of interrelated challenges that have fundamentally reshaped the landscape of energy policy and governance. Climate change mitigation, energy security, and social equity have emerged as core priorities of the European Green Deal and the Union's long-term vision for a climate-neutral economy (Kanellakis et al., 2013). However, the pursuit of these objectives has proven increasingly complex, as progress in one dimension often generates trade-offs in others. This structural tension has crystallized into what is commonly described as the European energy dilemma: the difficulty of simultaneously ensuring secure energy supply, environmental sustainability, and affordable access to energy for households and firms (Solorio & Jörgens, 2020).

This dilemma has been further exacerbated by recent geopolitical developments, most notably the Russia-Ukraine conflict, which exposed the EU's persistent dependence on imported fossil fuels and heightened its vulnerability to external supply shocks and energy price volatility (Estrada & Koutronas, 2022; Ostrowski, 2022). The disruption of natural gas flows, combined with escalating global energy demand and inflationary pressures, has underscored the fragility of Europe's energy system and the limitations of existing policy frameworks. As a result, energy security has re-emerged as a strategic priority, sometimes in apparent contradiction with decarbonization goals and climate commitments (Siddi, 2023; Joi a et al., 2023). These developments have intensified the need for analytical frameworks capable of capturing the multidimensional and dynamic nature of contemporary energy policy challenges.

Within this context, the World Energy Trilemma has become one of the most widely used conceptual and empirical tools for assessing national energy performance. Developed by the World Energy Council, the Trilemma framework evaluates countries across three core dimensions: energy security, environmental sustainability, and energy equity. The associated World Energy Trilemma Index (WETI) has been extensively employed by policymakers, researchers, and international organizations as a benchmarking instrument to compare energy systems and inform strategic decision-making (World Energy Council & Oliver Wyman, 2019). By emphasizing balance among competing objectives, the Trilemma has contributed significantly to the discourse on sustainable energy transitions, consistent with the broader sustainability paradigm articulated in Brundtland Report (Brundtland, 1987).

Nevertheless, as energy systems evolve in response to technological progress, digitalization, and the knowledge-based economy, the adequacy of the Trilemma framework has increasingly been called into question. Contemporary energy transitions are no longer driven solely by fuel substitution or infrastructure expansion but are deeply embedded in broader socio-economic transformations (Ostrowski, 2022). Advances in digital technologies, data analytics, smart grids, and human capital development play a pivotal role in enhancing energy efficiency, integrating renewable energy sources, and strengthening system resilience. Despite this, technology remains largely implicit within the traditional Trilemma framework, rather than being explicitly conceptualized and empirically measured as a distinct and foundational dimension of energy policy (Siddi, 2023; Joi a et al., 2023).

This omission represents a critical gap in both theoretical and empirical assessment of energy systems. Technology functions not merely as a supporting instrument but as a structural enabler that shapes the interactions among energy security, sustainability, and equity. The capacity of countries to innovate, adopt digital solutions, develop green skills, and govern technological change effectively determines their ability to navigate the trade-offs inherent in the energy transition. In the absence of a systematic integration of technology into energy performance metrics, existing indices risk underestimating the true drivers of sustainable and resilient energy systems.

Against this backdrop, the present chapter argues that the European energy dilemma cannot be adequately addressed within a purely trilemmatic framework. Instead, it proposes an expanded analytical perspective, the Energy Quadrilemma, which incorporates Technology as a fourth, autonomous pillar alongside energy security, environmental sustainability, and energy equity. By reconceptualizing technology as a latent, human-centered construct, the chapter advances a more comprehensive and policy-relevant model for evaluating energy governance in the European Union.

The Energy Quadrilemma framework builds on the premise that technological capacity is inherently multidimensional. It encompasses not only innovation and infrastructure but also human capital formation, digital inclusion, labor market structures, and institutional quality. Adult participation in lifelong learning, employment in knowledge-intensive and high-technology sectors, access to digital technologies, and government effectiveness collectively shape the technological ecosystem within which energy transitions unfold. These elements influence how societies produce, distribute, and consume energy, as well as how they respond to environmental and geopolitical shocks.

Methodologically, this chapter contributes to the literature by employing advanced data analysis techniques to operationalize the Technology dimension as a latent construct. Using statistical data from the 27 EU member states over the period 2010-2022, the study applies Exploratory Factor Analysis (EFA) to examine whether a set of theoretically grounded indicators can be statistically consolidated into a single, coherent Technology factor. This approach aligns with contemporary methodological standards in sustainability research, where composite indicators and latent variable modeling are increasingly used to capture complex, multidimensional phenomena.

By integrating factor analysis into the construction of a composite energy governance index, the chapter demonstrates how quantitative methods can bridge the gap between theory and empirical observation. The resulting Energy Quadrilemma Index (EQI) extends the analytical capacity of existing energy metrics by explicitly accounting for the technological foundations of sustainable energy systems. In doing so, it offers a robust and replicable framework that can support evidence-based policymaking and comparative analysis across countries.

The contribution of this chapter is threefold. First, it advances the theoretical literature on energy policy by redefining the conventional Energy Trilemma as a broader Energy Quadrilemma, thereby acknowledging the central role of technology in contemporary energy transitions. Second, it provides a methodological contribution by illustrating the application of EFA in the development and validation of composite indicators for policy analysis. Third, it offers practical insights for policymakers by highlighting how investments in education, digital inclusion, innovation, and institutional effectiveness can enhance the coherence and resilience of energy strategies within the European Union.

The remainder of the chapter is structured as follows. The next section revisits the conceptual foundations of the Energy Trilemma and discusses its limitations in the context of modern energy systems. Subsequently, the chapter introduces the Energy Quadrilemma framework and elaborates on the role of technology as a human-centered and governance-related dimension. The literature review situates the proposed framework within existing research on energy policy, technological innovation, and institutional quality. The methodological section details the data sources, variable selection, and factor analysis techniques employed in the study. Empirical results from the EFA are then presented and discussed. The chapter concludes with policy implications, future research directions, and concluding remarks on the relevance of the Energy Quadrilemma for advancing sustainable and resilient energy governance in Europe.

2. THE ENERGY TRILEMMA REVISITED

The concept of the Energy Trilemma has emerged as one of the most influential analytical frameworks in contemporary energy policy analysis (Siddi, 2023; Joi a et al., 2023). Introduced and popularized by the World Energy Council, the framework was designed to capture the inherent trade-offs policymakers face when attempting to design energy systems that are simultaneously secure, environmentally sustainable, and socially equitable (World Energy Council & Oliver Wyman, 2019). At its core, the Trilemma recognizes that energy policy constitutes a multidimensional challenge, requiring the balancing of competing and often conflicting objectives.

The three pillars of the Energy Trilemma: energy security, environmental sustainability, and energy equity reflect the fundamental concerns of modern energy governance. Energy security refers to the ability of a country or region to ensure reliable and uninterrupted access to energy resources in both the short and long term, encompassing supply diversification, infrastructure adequacy, and system resilience (Winzer, 2012; Ang et al., 2015). Environmental sustainability captures the need to minimize the environmental footprint of energy production and consumption, particularly in relation to greenhouse gas emissions and climate change mitigation, while supporting the transition toward low-carbon and renewable energy sources (Cohen et al., 2011; Blum & Legey, 2012). Energy equity addresses the social dimension of energy policy, emphasizing affordability, accessibility, and fairness in energy provision, and is closely linked to broader debates on energy justice and social inclusion (Heffron et al., 2015; Barlow et al., 2022).

The appeal of the Energy Trilemma lies in its intuitive structure and strong policy relevance. By framing energy performance as a matter of balance rather than the optimization of a single objective, the framework has encouraged a more holistic understanding of energy transitions. Its empirical extension, the World Energy Trilemma Index, has further enhanced its practical value by providing a standardized benchmarking tool for assessing national energy systems across countries and over time (World Energy Council & Oliver Wyman, 2019). As a result, the Trilemma has become a widely adopted reference point in both academic research and policy discourse.

Despite its widespread use, the Energy Trilemma framework exhibits important limitations in the context of accelerating technological change and the systemic transformation of energy systems. The original formulation of the Trilemma emerged at a time when energy transitions were primarily conceptualized in terms of fuel substitution, supply diversification, and regulatory reform. Contemporary energy systems, however, are increasingly shaped by digitalization, innovation dynamics, and the growing role of knowledge-intensive activities, developments that are not explicitly captured within the traditional Trilemma framework.

In practice, technological capabilities influence all three pillars of the Energy Trilemma. Advanced technologies enhance energy security by enabling smart grids, storage solutions, and improved system flexibility; they support environmental sustainability by facilitating the integration of renewable energy sources and improving energy efficiency; and they affect energy equity by shaping access to modern energy services and the distribution of transition costs and benefits across society. Yet, within the Trilemma framework, technology remains largely implicit, treated as a secondary or supporting factor rather than as a core analytical dimension.

A further limitation of the traditional Trilemma lies in its limited engagement with the human and institutional foundations of energy transitions. Energy systems are embedded in broader socio-economic and governance structures, where human capital, education, digital skills, and institutional effectiveness condition the capacity to adopt, adapt, and govern technological change. Without adequate investment in these enabling factors, even well-designed energy policies may fail to deliver inclusive and sustainable outcomes. Such dimensions, however, remain largely outside the scope of the conventional Trilemma model and its associated index.

The European Union provides a particularly illustrative case of these limitations. Despite ambitious climate and energy targets, EU member states exhibit significant heterogeneity in technological readiness, institutional capacity, and policy implementation. Recent geopolitical shocks, most notably the Russia–Ukraine conflict, have further exposed structural vulnerabilities in Europe's energy system, demonstrating that balancing the three traditional Trilemma dimensions is necessary but not sufficient for navigating complex energy crises and long-term transitions.

In response to these challenges, an expanding body of literature has called for the reconceptualization or extension of the Energy Trilemma framework. Rather than viewing technology merely as an auxiliary instrument, these perspectives emphasize its role as a transformative and enabling force that reshapes energy systems, policy trade-offs, and governance structures. Revisiting the Energy Trilemma through this lens underscores the need for a more comprehensive analytical framework that explicitly incorporates technological capacity as a central pillar of energy policy.

Building on these insights, this chapter proposes an extension of the traditional Energy Trilemma into an Energy Quadrilemma framework. By introducing Technology as a fourth, human-centered and governance-related dimension, the proposed model responds directly to the conceptual and empirical gaps identified in the Trilemma literature. The following section elaborates on this transition in greater detail, outlining the conceptual foundations of the Energy Quadrilemma and clarifying the role of technology as an integrative and enabling force in sustainable energy governance.

3. FROM THE ENERGY TRILEMMA TO THE ENERGY QUADRILEMMA: TECHNOLOGY AS THE FOURTH PILLAR

The limitations of the traditional Energy Trilemma framework become increasingly evident in the context of contemporary energy transitions. While the Trilemma provides a useful lens for understanding the trade-offs among energy security, environmental sustainability, and energy equity, it does not fully capture the enabling conditions that allow countries to manage these trade-offs effectively. Among these conditions, Technology has emerged as a decisive but underrepresented factor in conventional energy policy analysis.

Recent research highlights that technological progress plays a central role in shaping energy system performance across all dimensions of sustainability. Innovation in renewable energy technologies, digital infrastructure, and energy efficiency solutions enhances energy security by reducing dependence on imported fuels and improving system resilience (Chakraborty & Mazzanti, 2020). At the same time, technological advancements support environmental sustainability by facilitating the integration of renewable energy sources and lowering emissions, while also influencing energy equity through access to modern energy services and the affordability of clean technologies (Cevik, 2024). However, the benefits of technological progress are neither automatic nor evenly distributed, underscoring the need for a broader, governance-oriented perspective.

In this chapter, Technology is not conceptualized narrowly as physical infrastructure or innovation output. Instead, it is treated as a multidimensional, human-centered construct encompassing education and skills development, digital inclusion, knowledge-intensive employment, and institutional effectiveness. Adult participation in lifelong learning enhances societies' capacity to adapt to technological change and supports the diffusion of green technologies, while digital inclusion reduces information asymmetries and enables more efficient energy consumption through data-driven systems (European Commission, 2021; Sun & You, 2023). Employment in knowledge-intensive and high-technology sectors reflects the depth of innovation systems and contributes to long-term productivity, energy efficiency, and structural transformation (Mohelska et al., 2020).

Institutional quality further conditions the impact of technology on energy outcomes. Government effectiveness plays a critical role in designing, implementing, and enforcing policies that support technological innovation and sustainable energy transitions (Sareen, 2021; Song & Majeed, 2023). Empirical evidence suggests that strong institutions enhance the capacity of technological progress to translate into improved environmental and energy performance, whereas weak governance can undermine these potential benefits (Khan et al., 2023; Zang & Xiong, 2020). As such, technology and governance are deeply intertwined within national energy systems.

Taken together, these dimensions indicate that Technology functions as an integrative and enabling force linking energy security, environmental sustainability, and energy equity. This insight motivates the transition from the Energy Trilemma to the Energy Quadrilemma framework. By explicitly incorporating Technology as a fourth, autonomous pillar, the Energy Quadrilemma recognizes that the ability to balance competing energy objectives depends fundamentally on human capital, digital capacity, labor market structures, and institutional effectiveness.

The relevance of this expanded framework is particularly pronounced in the European Union. Despite operating under a common policy architecture, EU member states exhibit substantial heterogeneity in technological readiness, digital inclusion, and governance capacity. These differences help explain divergent energy outcomes and varying resilience to environmental and geopolitical shocks, even when formal energy policy objectives are shared. The Energy Quadrilemma framework provides a more comprehensive analytical perspective for capturing this heterogeneity and assessing energy governance performance across countries.

Building on this conceptual foundation, the following section translates the Energy Quadrilemma framework into an empirical model. The Technology pillar is operationalized as a latent construct using a set of theoretically grounded indicators, and advanced data analysis techniques are applied to validate its structure and integrate it into the Energy Quadrilemma Index.

4. LITERATURE REVIEW

4.1 Energy Policy and Sustainability

Energy policy has become a central pillar of sustainable development strategies, particularly in regions facing simultaneous environmental, economic, and geopolitical pressures. In the European Union, energy policy is closely intertwined with climate change mitigation, economic competitiveness, and social cohesion, reflecting the multidimensional nature of sustainability challenges. A substantial body of research highlights that EU energy policy has evolved within a complex institutional and regulatory environment, shaped by long-term climate objectives and security concerns (Kanellakis et al., 2013; Solorio & Jörgens, 2020). The transition toward a low-carbon and climate-neutral energy system therefore requires not only technological change but also coherent policy frameworks capable of balancing competing objectives and managing systemic risks (Strambo et al., 2015).

A growing strand of the literature identifies the existence of a persistent energy security dilemma in the European context, arising from the tension between environmental sustainability and the security of energy supply. While ambitious decarbonization targets necessitate a rapid reduction in fossil fuel consumption, many EU member states remain structurally dependent on imported energy resources, exposing them to geopolitical shocks and price volatility (Elbassoussy, 2019; Mišík, 2022). This dependency has been further amplified by recent geopolitical developments, reinforcing the vulnerability of European energy systems and complicating the implementation of climate-oriented energy policies (Keypour & Ahmadzada, 2022).

The Energy Trilemma framework has been widely adopted as a conceptual tool for capturing these tensions within energy policy analysis. By emphasizing the balance among energy security, environmental sustainability, and energy equity, the framework offers a structured approach for assessing national and regional energy systems (World Energy Council & Oliver Wyman, 2019). However, several scholars argue that the Trilemma provides only a partial representation of contemporary energy challenges, particularly in advanced economies undergoing rapid technological and institutional transformation (Strambo et al., 2015; Solorio & Jörgens, 2020).

Recent research increasingly suggests that sustainability-oriented energy policy should prioritize long-term systemic resilience rather than short-term efficiency gains. From this perspective, climate change mitigation and energy security are not competing objectives but interdependent components of a unified sustainability agenda (Mišík & Nosko, 2023). This reframing highlight that the energy dilemma may function both as a constraint and as a catalyst for structural change, depending on the adaptive capacity of energy systems and the effectiveness of policy coordination (Elbassoussy, 2019).

The European Union's response to recent energy crises illustrates this evolving understanding of sustainability in energy policy. Policy measures aimed at accelerating renewable energy deployment, improving energy efficiency, and diversifying supply sources have increasingly been complemented by interventions addressing affordability and social protection. These developments reflect a growing recognition that sustainable energy policy extends beyond environmental outcomes to encompass social and distributional dimensions, consistent with the equity pillar of the Energy Trilemma (Mišík, 2022).

At the same time, empirical evidence indicates that progress toward sustainable energy systems remains uneven across EU member states. Variations in energy mixes, institutional capacity, and economic structures lead to heterogeneous policy outcomes, even within a shared regulatory framework (Kanellakis et al., 2013; Keypour & Ahmadzada, 2022). This heterogeneity raises important questions regarding the adequacy of existing analytical tools for capturing national energy performance and guiding policy interventions. In particular, it suggests that sustainability outcomes are shaped not only by policy targets but also by underlying capabilities that enable or constrain policy implementation.

Within this context, scholars increasingly call for analytical frameworks that move beyond static representations of energy systems and incorporate the political and institutional dimensions of policy design and evaluation. Research on the politics of measurement and energy efficiency policy highlights that indicators and performance metrics are not neutral instruments but shape policy priorities and outcomes (Dunlop, 2019; Dunlop & Völker, 2023). This insight further underscores the need for expanded conceptual models that account for the dynamic and governance-related drivers of sustainability.

Overall, this strand of the literature provides a strong foundation for the present chapter's argument that sustainability-oriented energy policy cannot be fully understood without explicitly accounting for the technological and governance dimensions that underpin energy transitions. By situating energy policy within a broader sustainability framework, the Energy Quadrilemma approach seeks to address these limitations and offer a more comprehensive basis for assessing energy performance in the European Union.

4.2 Technology and Innovation Systems

Technology and innovation systems play a central role in shaping contemporary energy transitions, particularly in advanced economies seeking to reconcile sustainability objectives with economic competitiveness and energy security. Recent literature increasingly emphasizes that the transition toward low-carbon energy systems is not merely a technological shift but a systemic transformation involving institutions, skills, markets, and social practices. Within this broader perspective, technology functions both as a driver of structural change and as an enabling condition for effective and sustainable energy policy.

Innovation in energy-related technologies has been consistently identified as a key determinant of reductions in energy intensity and greenhouse gas emissions. Empirical evidence suggests that green innovation and technological upgrading contribute significantly to improved environmental performance, particularly when supported by coherent policy frameworks and sustained investment in research and development (Chakraborty & Mazzanti, 2020). Technological progress facilitates the integration of renewable energy sources, enhances energy efficiency, and supports the decarbonization of energy-intensive sectors, thereby reinforcing the sustainability dimension of energy policy.

Beyond innovation outputs, however, the effectiveness of technology-driven energy transitions depends critically on the capacity of societies to absorb, diffuse, and utilize new technologies. This capacity is closely linked to human capital development and lifelong learning. Adult participation in education and training is increasingly recognized as a core component of innovation systems, as it equips the workforce with the skills required to adapt to digitalization, automation, and green technologies (European Commission, 2021). Human capital development not only supports technological innovation but also enhances public awareness and social acceptance of energy transition policies.

Digitalization constitutes another fundamental pillar of contemporary innovation systems. Digital inclusion defined as equitable access to and effective use of digital technologies enables advanced monitoring, data-driven decision-making, and optimization of energy consumption. The literature highlights that digital technologies can reduce information asymmetries, improve resource allocation, and enhance energy efficiency across households, firms, and energy networks (Usman et al., 2021). In the context of energy systems, digital tools such as smart meters, digital platforms, and data analytics contribute to more flexible, responsive, and resilient energy infrastructures.

At the same time, digital transformation raises important concerns related to equity and inclusiveness. Unequal access to digital infrastructure and digital skills may reinforce existing socio-economic disparities, limiting the ability of certain population groups or regions to benefit from technological advancements. Recent studies emphasize that digital inclusion plays a critical role in ensuring that energy transitions are socially sustainable and broadly shared (Sareen, 2021; Song & Majeed, 2023). Consequently, innovation systems that fail to integrate social and educational dimensions risk exacerbating inequalities and undermining the legitimacy of energy policy interventions.

The structure of employment further reflects the technological orientation and innovation capacity of an economy. Employment in high and medium-high technology manufacturing and knowledge-intensive services is widely used as an indicator of knowledge-based economic activity and technological capability. Empirical research suggests that such employment structures are associated with higher productivity, stronger innovation spillovers, and improved energy efficiency outcomes (Mohelska et al., 2020). Knowledge-intensive sectors contribute to the development and diffusion of energy-saving technologies and support the long-term competitiveness of sustainable energy systems.

Taken together, these strands of the literature underscore that technology should be conceptualized as a multidimensional system rather than a single input or output. Innovation systems encompass not only technological artifacts but also human capital, digital infrastructure, and labor market dynamics. This systemic perspective supports the argument that technology constitutes a distinct and autonomous pillar of energy governance, shaping countries capacity to manage the trade-offs inherent in energy policy.

In the European Union, disparities in innovation systems and technological readiness among member states have significant implications for energy policy outcomes. Differences in education systems, digital inclusion, and employment structures contribute to uneven progress toward sustainability goals, even under shared regulatory frameworks. These variations highlight the need for analytical models that explicitly incorporate technological and innovation-related dimensions when assessing energy performance.

This body of literature provides strong theoretical justification for integrating Technology as a core component of the Energy Quadrilemma framework. By recognizing innovation systems as foundational to sustainable energy transitions, the chapter conceptualizes technology as a latent, human-centered construct that influences energy security, environmental sustainability, and energy equity. The following section builds on this perspective by examining the role of government effectiveness and institutional quality in governing technological change and energy transitions.

4.3 Government Effectiveness and Energy Governance

Government effectiveness and institutional quality are increasingly recognized as central determinants of energy policy outcomes and sustainable development. Effective governance frameworks shape the capacity of states to design, implement, and enforce policies that support energy transitions, technological innovation, and environmental protection. Within the field of energy governance, institutions mediate the interaction between policy objectives, technological capabilities, and socio-economic conditions, thereby influencing the overall performance of energy systems (Bennett & Satterfield, 2018; Lange et al., 2019).

The concept of government effectiveness, as operationalized in widely used governance indicators, captures key dimensions of public sector performance, including policy formulation, regulatory quality, public service delivery, and institutional credibility.

A growing body of empirical research demonstrates that countries exhibiting higher levels of government effectiveness tend to achieve superior environmental outcomes and more efficient allocation of public resources (Rodríguez-Pose & Di Cataldo, 2015; Khan et al., 2023). In the context of energy policy, effective governance is particularly critical due to the long-term, capital-intensive, and highly regulated nature of energy systems.

Energy transitions require coordinated policy action across multiple sectors and governance levels. Governments play a pivotal role in setting regulatory frameworks, providing incentives for technological innovation, and managing the distributional effects of energy policies. Institutional weaknesses such as regulatory instability, limited administrative capacity, or insufficient policy coherence can significantly undermine the effectiveness of energy reforms and delay the diffusion of clean technologies (Lange et al., 2019). Conversely, strong and credible institutions enhance investor confidence and facilitate the adoption of innovative energy solutions.

The literature further emphasizes that government effectiveness moderates the relationship between technological innovation and environmental performance. Technological progress alone does not guarantee sustainability outcomes; rather, its impact depends on the institutional context in which it is embedded. Empirical studies examining governance-environment nexuses reveal that higher-quality institutions strengthen the capacity of technological innovation to translate into lower emissions and improved energy efficiency (Liu et al., 2020; Khan et al., 2023). This insight highlights the importance of integrating governance considerations into analytical frameworks assessing energy policy performance.

In the European Union, the role of government effectiveness in energy governance is particularly salient. Although EU member states operate under a common regulatory and policy framework, substantial variation persists in institutional capacity, administrative efficiency, and policy implementation. These disparities contribute to heterogeneous energy outcomes and help explain why similar policy targets often yield divergent results across countries (Rodríguez-Pose & Di Cataldo, 2015). The EU experience illustrates that supranational coordination must be complemented by strong national institutions to achieve sustainable and equitable energy transitions.

Moreover, government effectiveness plays a crucial role in shaping the social acceptability and equity of energy policies. Transparent decision-making processes, inclusive governance arrangements, and effective communication mechanisms enhance public trust and societal support for energy reforms. This dimension becomes particularly important in periods of rising energy prices and distributional stress, where weak governance may exacerbate social tensions and undermine policy legitimacy (Hassan et al., 2020; Jamil et al., 2021).

From a conceptual perspective, the integration of government effectiveness into energy policy analysis aligns with broader governance-based approaches to sustainability. Energy systems are increasingly understood as socio-technical systems, in which technological innovation, human capital, and institutional quality interact dynamically. Within such systems, governance quality determines the extent to which technological and human resources can be mobilized to achieve long-term policy objectives (Bennett & Satterfield, 2018).

This strand of the literature provides strong theoretical support for including government effectiveness as a core component of the Technology pillar within the Energy Quadrilemma framework. By recognizing the institutional foundations of energy transitions, the Quadrilemma approach captures the enabling role of governance in balancing energy security, environmental sustainability, and energy equity. Building on this literature review, the following section presents the data sources and methodological framework used to operationalize the Energy Quadrilemma Index and empirically assess the latent role of technology and governance in European energy systems.

5. DATA AND METHODOLOGICAL FRAMEWORK

This section presents the data sources, variable selection, and methodological approach used to operationalize the Energy Quadrilemma framework and construct the Energy Quadrilemma Index (EQI). Building on the conceptual foundations developed in the previous sections, the empirical analysis focuses on capturing the enabling role of Technology as a distinct pillar of energy governance in the European Union.

5.1 Data Sources and Sample

The empirical analysis draws on secondary data obtained from internationally recognized and widely used databases to ensure reliability, comparability, and policy relevance. The use of secondary data is particularly appropriate for cross-country energy policy research, where harmonized indicators allow systematic comparison across countries and over time (Hakim, 1982; Dale et al., 2008).

The sample comprises the 27 member states of the European Union over the period 2010–2022. To ensure methodological consistency and satisfy the independence assumption required for factor analysis, all indicators were aggregated to the country level by computing average values over the study period for each member state (N = 27). This approach allows for cross-sectional analysis while capturing long-term structural characteristics of national energy systems.

Energy-related indicators: energy security, environmental sustainability, and energy equity were derived from the World Energy Trilemma Index and its underlying dimensions, as published by the World Energy Council (World Energy Council & Oliver Wyman, 2019; World Energy Council, 2024). Socio-economic and technology-related indicators were obtained from Eurostat and capture adult participation in learning, digital inclusion, and employment in high- and medium-high technology manufacturing and knowledge-intensive services (Eurostat, 2022). Governance quality was measured using the Government Effectiveness indicator from the Worldwide Governance Indicators of the World Bank (World Bank, 2023).

5.2 Variable Selection and Conceptual Mapping

Variable selection was guided by the conceptual structure of the Energy Quadrilemma framework. The analysis distinguishes between three outcome-oriented energy pillars: energy security, environmental sustainability, energy equity and one enabling pillar, Technology. Technology is conceptualized as a human-centered and governance-related latent construct reflecting four dimensions: education and skills development (adult participation in learning), digital inclusion (internet usage), knowledge intensity of the labor market (employment in high- and medium-high technology manufacturing and knowledge-intensive services), and institutional quality (government effectiveness).

Importantly, energy outcome indicators are not included in the Technology construct, thereby avoiding conceptual overlap and double counting within the Energy Quadrilemma framework. All indicators were measured on an annual basis and subsequently averaged across the period 2010–2022 to obtain country-level values suitable for cross-sectional analysis as shown in Table 1.

Table 1. Indicators Used for the Construction of the Energy Quadrilemma Index (EQI)

Indicator	Measurement Unit	Source	Period
World Energy Trilemma Index	Composite percentage score reflecting the average performance across Energy Security, Energy Equity, and Environmental Sustainability	World Energy Council	2010–2022
Adult Participation in Learning	Percentage of men and women aged 25–64 participating in education and training	Eurostat	2010–2022
Digital Inclusion	Percentage of individuals using the internet	Eurostat	2010–2022
Employment in High- and Medium-High Technology Manufacturing and Knowledge-Intensive Services	Percentage of total employment	Eurostat	2010–2022
Government Effectiveness	Percentile rank (upper bound of the 90% confidence interval)	World Bank – Worldwide Governance Indicators	2010–2022

All indicators are measured on an annual basis and harmonized to ensure cross-country comparability across EU member states.

5.3 Exploratory Factor Analysis (EFA)

Exploratory Factor Analysis (EFA) was employed to examine whether the selected non-energy indicators could be statistically consolidated into a single latent factor representing Technology. EFA is particularly well suited for identifying underlying structures in multivariate datasets and for validating theoretically informed latent constructs. Prior to factor extraction, the suitability of the data for factor analysis was assessed using the Kaiser-Meyer-Olkin (KMO) measure of sampling adequacy and Bartlett's Test of Sphericity.

Factor extraction was conducted using Principal Axis Factoring, which is appropriate for data that may deviate from strict normality assumptions. Given the theoretical expectation of a unidimensional construct, a single-factor solution was retained. The internal consistency of the resulting Technology construct was evaluated using Cronbach's alpha to assess scale reliability, a widely used measure of scale reliability in social and economic research (Morera & Stokes, 2016; Ekolu & Quainoo, 2019).

5.4 Construction of the Energy Quadrilemma Index

Following the validation of the Technology pillar, the Energy Quadrilemma Index (EQI) was constructed by combining four core dimensions: energy security, environmental sustainability, energy equity, and technology. To ensure comparability across dimensions, all four pillars were standardized using z-scores. Equal weights were assigned to each pillar, reflecting their equivalent conceptual importance within the Energy Quadrilemma framework and avoiding arbitrary weighting schemes.

The EQI for each country was computed as the arithmetic mean of the four standardized pillars, providing a composite measure of overall energy governance performance. This approach allows the EQI to capture both energy system outcomes and the underlying technological and institutional capacities that enable sustainable and resilient energy transitions.

6. EMPIRICAL RESULTS

This section presents the empirical findings of the study, focusing on the validation of the Technology pillar and the construction and application of the Energy Quadrilemma Index (EQI). The analysis proceeds in four stages: (i) validation of the Technology construct through Exploratory Factor Analysis, (ii) assessment of internal consistency, (iii) construction of the EQI, and (iv) comparison between the EQI and the World Energy Trilemma Index (WETI).

6.1 Exploratory Factor Analysis Results

Exploratory Factor Analysis was conducted to examine whether the selected indicators could be statistically grouped into a single latent factor representing Technology. Prior to factor extraction, the suitability of the data for factor analysis was assessed using the Kaiser–Meyer–Olkin (KMO) measure of sampling adequacy and Bartlett's Test of Sphericity as shown in Table 2.

Table 2. KMO and Bartlett's Test for the Technology Indicators (N = 27)

Measure	Statistic
Kaiser–Meyer–Olkin (KMO) Measure of Sampling Adequacy	0.845
Bartlett's Test of Sphericity (Approx. χ^2)	98.873
Degrees of Freedom (df)	6
Significance (p-value)	< 0.001

The Kaiser-Meyer-Olkin measure indicates meritorious sampling adequacy. Bartlett's test of sphericity is statistically significant ($p < .05$), confirming that the correlation matrix is suitable for factor analysis.

Table 3. Total Variance Explained by the Technology Factor

Factor	Eigenvalue (Total)	% of Variance	Cumulative %
1	3.261	81.516	81.516

Extraction Method: Principal Axis Factoring

Factor extraction using Principal Axis Factoring revealed a single dominant factor with an eigenvalue greater than one. The extracted factor explains 81.52% of the total variance, providing strong empirical support for the unidimensional structure of the Technology construct as shown in Table 3.

Table 4. Factor Loadings for the Technology Latent Construct

Indicator	Factor Loading
Adult Participation in Learning	0.814
Employment in High- and Medium-High Technology Manufacturing and Knowledge-Intensive Services	0.887
Digital Inclusion	0.979
Government Effectiveness	0.923

Extraction Method: Principal Axis Factoring. One Factor was Extracted

All selected indicators load strongly and positively on the extracted Technology factor, with factor loadings ranging from 0.814 to 0.979. These results indicate a high degree of convergence among the indicators and confirm that education and skills development, digital inclusion, knowledge-intensive employment, and government effectiveness jointly form a coherent and integrated Technology construct. The strength of the loadings further supports the conceptualization of Technology as a human-centered and governance-related pillar within the Energy Quadrilemma framework as shown in Table 4.

6.2 Reliability Analysis

To assess the internal consistency of the extracted latent factor, reliability analysis was conducted using Cronbach's alpha as shown in Table 5.

Table 5. Reliability Statistics (Cronbach's Alpha)

Measure	Value
Cronbach's Alpha	0.937
Cronbach's Alpha (Standardized Items)	0.945
Number of Items	4

The internal consistency of the Technology construct was assessed using Cronbach's alpha. The results indicate excellent reliability, with Cronbach's alpha equal to 0.937 and standardized alpha equal to 0.945. These values are well above commonly accepted thresholds, confirming that the four indicators consistently measure a single, coherent latent Technology dimension within the Energy Quadrilemma framework as shown in Table 5.

6.3 Construction of the Energy Quadrilemma Index (EQI)

Following the validation of the Technology pillar, the Energy Quadrilemma Index (EQI) was constructed to provide a composite measure of overall energy governance performance across EU member states. The EQI integrates four core dimensions: energy security, environmental sustainability, energy equity, and technology.

To ensure comparability across dimensions measured on different scales, all four pillars were standardized using z-scores. Equal weights were assigned to each pillar, reflecting their equivalent conceptual importance within the Energy Quadrilemma framework and avoiding arbitrary weighting schemes. The EQI for each country was computed as the arithmetic mean of the four standardized pillars, as shown in Equation (1):

$$EQI\_i = \frac{Z(Security\_i) + Z(Sustainability\_i) + Z(Equity\_i) + Z(Technology\_i)}{4}$$

Table 6. Descriptive Statistics of the Energy Quadrilemma Pillars (N = 27)

Pillar	Minimum	Maximum	Mean	Standard Deviation
Energy Security	32.50	75.90	61.90	10.76
Environmental Sustainability	64.90	87.50	76.21	5.01
Energy Equity	70.80	99.80	91.16	6.07
Technology (Factor Score)	−2.01	1.52	0.00	0.99

Values refer to country-level averages for the period 2010–2022. Technology is measured using standardized factor scores derived from Exploratory Factor Analysis as shown in Table 6.

The descriptive statistics indicate substantial variation across the four Energy Quadrilemma pillars, reflecting heterogeneity in both energy outcomes and enabling capacities among EU member states. The Technology pillar, measured through factor scores, exhibits a mean close to zero and a standard deviation close to one, as expected from standardized latent variables as shown in Table 6.

Table 7. Descriptive Statistics of the Energy Quadrilemma Index (EQI)

Statistic	Value
Minimum	−4.50
Maximum	4.12
Mean	0.00
Standard Deviation	2.24
Number of Countries	27

The resulting EQI displays a balanced distribution, with values ranging from −4.50 to 4.12 and a mean equal to zero. This variation confirms that the index captures meaningful cross-country differences in overall energy governance performance. Importantly, the dispersion of EQI values suggests that no single pillar dominates the composite indicator, underscoring the analytical value of integrating energy outcomes with technological and institutional capacities as shown in Table 7.

By construction, the EQI enables transparent and replicable cross-country comparison while preserving the conceptual distinction between energy system outcomes and the enabling role of technology. As such, the Energy Quadrilemma

Index provides a robust empirical foundation for assessing multidimensional energy governance performance in the European Union.

6.4 Country Rankings and Comparison with the World Energy Trilemma Index

This subsection presents the country rankings derived from the Energy Quadrilemma Index (EQI) and compares them with the World Energy Trilemma Index (WETI) in order to assess the added analytical value of incorporating Technology as a fourth pillar.

Table 8. Energy Quadrilemma Index (EQI) and Country Rankings

Country	EQI	EQI Rank
Sweden	4.12	1
Denmark	3.41	2
France	3.17	3
Austria	2.92	4
Finland	2.74	5
Germany	1.58	6
Spain	1.45	7
Slovenia	1.21	8
Belgium	1.02	9
Luxembourg	0.42	10
Ireland	0.41	11
Czech Republic	0.21	12
Portugal	−0.01	13
Hungary	−0.04	14
Slovakia	−0.12	15
Latvia	−0.31	16
Italy	−0.32	17
Croatia	−0.32	18
Netherlands	−0.53	19
Romania	−1.14	20
Estonia	−1.54	21
Greece	−1.54	22
Lithuania	−1.70	23

continued on following page

Table 8. Continued

Country	EQI	EQI Rank
Malta	−2.70	24
Poland	−3.81	25
Cyprus	−4.10	26
Bulgaria	−4.50	27

Higher EQI values indicate stronger overall energy governance performance.

The EQI-based rankings reveal a clear and theoretically consistent pattern across EU member states. Northern European countries including Sweden, Denmark, Finland, and Austria occupy the top positions, reflecting strong performance across all four pillars, particularly in technology, governance effectiveness, and human capital development. Large continental economies such as France and Germany also rank highly, indicating balanced energy outcomes supported by robust technological and institutional capacities as shown in Table 8.

In contrast, several Central and Eastern European countries appear at the lower end of the ranking. Their weaker performance is primarily associated with lower scores in the Technology pillar, highlighting gaps in digital inclusion, skills development, and institutional effectiveness, even where energy outcomes are moderate. Southern European countries tend to cluster around the middle of the distribution, illustrating heterogeneous performance across the Energy Quadrilemma dimensions as shown in Table 8.

Table 9. Correlation Between EQI and the World Energy Trilemma Index (WETI)

Variables	Pearson Correlation (r)	p-value	N
EQI – WETI	0.957	< 0.001	27

The comparison between the Energy Quadrilemma Index and the World Energy Trilemma Index reveals a strong but imperfect positive correlation ($r = 0.957$, $p < 0.001$) as shown in Table 9. This finding indicates that the EQI captures the core dimensions of energy system performance reflected in the Trilemma Index, while simultaneously extending its analytical scope.

Importantly, the correlation is not perfect, suggesting that the inclusion of the Technology pillar introduces additional explanatory power. Differences in country rankings underscore the role of human capital, digital inclusion, and government effectiveness as enabling conditions that shape energy governance outcomes beyond conventional energy performance indicators. As such, the EQI provides a more comprehensive assessment of national energy systems by integrating both energy outcomes and the technological and institutional capacities required for sustainable and resilient energy transitions.

7. DISCUSSION

The purpose of this chapter was to address a key conceptual and empirical gap in contemporary energy policy analysis by extending the traditional Energy Trilemma framework to incorporate Technology as a fourth, autonomous pillar. The empirical results provide strong support for this extension and demonstrate that technological and institutional capacities play a decisive role in shaping energy governance outcomes across European Union member states.

The empirical validation of Technology as a coherent latent construct reinforces its role as a foundational pillar of contemporary energy governance. The construction of the Energy Quadrilemma Index further highlights the analytical value of explicitly integrating Technology into energy performance assessment. While the strong correlation between the EQI and the World Energy Trilemma Index indicates that the proposed index captures core aspects of energy system outcomes, the observed differences in country rankings demonstrate that the inclusion of Technology adds meaningful explanatory power. Countries with comparable energy security, sustainability, or equity outcomes diverge significantly in their overall performance once differences in human capital, digital capacity, and institutional effectiveness are taken into account. This suggests that conventional energy metrics may underestimate the role of structural enabling conditions in shaping long-term energy resilience.

The country-level results reveal clear and theoretically consistent patterns across the European Union. Northern European countries dominate the upper end of the EQI distribution, reflecting not only strong energy outcomes but also high levels of technological readiness, effective governance, and investment in skills and digital infrastructure. In contrast, several Central and Eastern European member states rank lower, primarily due to weaker performance in the Technology pillar, despite in some cases moderate energy outcomes. Southern European countries tend to occupy intermediate positions, highlighting heterogeneous combinations of energy performance and enabling capacities. These patterns underscore that differences in energy governance across the EU are not solely the result of energy policy choices, but also reflect deeper socio-economic and institutional structures.

From a conceptual perspective, the findings support the argument that the European energy dilemma cannot be fully understood within a purely trilemmatic framework. Balancing energy security, environmental sustainability, and energy equity is necessary but insufficient in the absence of adequate technological and institutional capacity. Technology operates as an integrative force that mediates trade-offs among the three traditional dimensions, enhancing the ability of countries to pursue decarbonization without compromising security or social inclusion. The Energy Quadrilemma framework captures this dynamic by repositioning Technology as a foundational pillar rather than a residual or implicit factor.

Methodologically, the chapter demonstrates the usefulness of combining factor analysis with composite indicator construction in energy policy research. By validating a theoretically grounded latent construct and integrating it into a transparent and replicable index, the study bridges the gap between abstract conceptual frameworks and empirical measurement. At the same time, the reliance on country-level averages reflects a deliberate choice to prioritize structural and long-term characteristics of national energy systems, rather than short-term fluctuations. This approach is well suited to comparative governance analysis, although it also points to avenues for future research using richer datasets and dynamic modeling techniques.

Overall, the discussion highlights that effective energy governance in the European Union depends not only on energy system design but also on investments in people, institutions, and digital capacity. The Energy Quadrilemma framework provides a more comprehensive lens through which to assess these interdependencies and offers a foundation for more integrated and forward-looking energy policy analysis.

8. POLICY IMPLICATIONS

The findings of this chapter carry important implications for energy policy and governance in the European Union. By extending the Energy Trilemma to an Energy Quadrilemma, the analysis demonstrates that successful energy transitions depend not only on balancing energy security, environmental sustainability, and energy equity, but also on the technological and institutional capacities that enable this balance in practice.

First, the results underscore the central role of human capital in shaping energy governance outcomes. Countries that perform well in adult education, skills development, and knowledge-intensive employment consistently achieve higher overall Energy Quadrilemma Index scores. This suggests that investments in lifelong learning, reskilling, and workforce adaptability should be considered integral components of energy policy, rather than complementary social measures. Energy transitions are, to a significant extent, skills transitions, and policy frameworks that neglect this dimension risk undermining long-term system resilience.

Second, digital inclusion emerges as a critical enabler of sustainable and equitable energy systems. The strong contribution of digital inclusion to the Technology pillar highlights the importance of digital infrastructure, access to information technologies, and data-driven energy management. Policies that promote smart grids, digital monitoring, and consumer participation through digital platforms can enhance energy efficiency, improve system flexibility, and reduce information asymmetries, thereby supporting all three traditional dimensions of the Energy Trilemma.

Third, the findings emphasize the importance of institutional quality and effective governance. Government effectiveness plays a key role in translating technological potential into tangible energy outcomes. This has direct implications for policy coordination, regulatory capacity, and administrative efficiency at both national and EU levels. Strengthening institutional frameworks, improving policy coherence, and reducing implementation gaps are essential for ensuring that investments in clean energy and technology yield their intended benefits.

Fourth, the observed cross-country heterogeneity within the European Union suggests that a "one-size-fits-all" approach to energy policy may be insufficient. While EU-wide targets and regulatory frameworks remain crucial, the Energy Quadrilemma results indicate that member states face distinct challenges depending on their technological readiness and institutional capacity. Tailored policy instruments that account for these structural differences particularly in Central and Eastern European countries—can enhance convergence and support a more inclusive energy transition.

9. CONCLUSIONS

This chapter addressed a key limitation of existing energy performance frameworks by explicitly incorporating Technology into the assessment of national energy systems. Building on the Energy Trilemma, the proposed Energy Quadrilemma framework conceptualizes Technology as a human-centered and governance-related pillar that conditions how countries manage trade-offs among energy security, environmental sustainability, and energy equity. By repositioning Technology as an enabling and structurally embedded dimension, the framework advances a more comprehensive understanding of contemporary energy governance.

Empirically, the chapter validated the Technology dimension as a coherent latent construct and demonstrated its relevance through the construction of the Energy Quadrilemma Index. The findings indicate that while conventional energy performance indicators capture important outcome-based aspects of energy systems, they often overlook the institutional and technological capacities that underpin long-term resilience and policy effectiveness. By integrating technological and governance-related dimensions, the Energy Quadrilemma Index offers a more forward-looking and multidimensional assessment of energy system performance within the European Union.

The results further highlight that countries with strong human capital, high levels of digital inclusion, and effective governance structures are better positioned to navigate complex energy challenges and respond to environmental and geopolitical shocks. Conversely, weaknesses in these enabling conditions may constrain energy transitions even in contexts where policy ambition and energy outcomes appear favorable. This underscores the importance of adopting a holistic approach to energy policy that extends beyond infrastructure development and market design to include people, institutions, and digital capacity as central components of energy governance.

Several limitations should be acknowledged. The analysis relies on country-level averages and focuses on the European Union, which may limit the generalizability of the findings. Future research could extend the Energy Quadrilemma framework to broader comparative contexts, longer time horizons, or alternative indicator configurations in order to further enhance its robustness and policy relevance.

REFERENCES

Ang, B. W., Choong, W. L., & Ng, T. S. (2015). Energy security: Definitions, dimensions and indexes. *Renewable & Sustainable Energy Reviews*, *42*, 1077–1093. DOI: 10.1016/j.rser.2014.10.064

Barlow, J., Tapio, R., & Tarekegne, B. (2022). Advancing the state of energy equity metrics. *The Electricity Journal*, *35*(10), 107208. DOI: 10.1016/j.tej.2022.107208

Bennett, N. J., & Satterfield, T. (2018). Environmental governance: A practical framework to guide design, evaluation, and analysis. *Conservation Letters*, *11*(6), e12600. DOI: 10.1111/conl.12600

Blum, H., & Legey, L. F. (2012). The challenging economics of energy security: Ensuring energy benefits in support to sustainable development. *Energy Economics*, *34*(6), 1982–1989. DOI: 10.1016/j.eneco.2012.08.013

Brundtland, G. H. (1987). *Our common future*. Oxford University Press.

Cevik, S. (2024). Climate change and energy security: The dilemma or opportunity of the century? *Environmental Economics and Policy Studies*, *26*(3), 653–672. DOI: 10.1007/s10018-023-00391-z

Chakraborty, S. K., & Mazzanti, M. (2020). Energy intensity and green energy innovation: Checking heterogeneous country effects in the OECD. *Structural Change and Economic Dynamics*, *52*, 328–343. DOI: 10.1016/j.strueco.2019.12.002

Cohen, G., Joutz, F., & Loungani, P. (2011). Measuring energy security: Trends in the diversification of oil and natural gas supplies. *Energy Policy*, *39*(9), 4860–4869. DOI: 10.1016/j.enpol.2011.06.034

Dale, A., Wathan, J., & Higgins, V. (2008). *Secondary analysis of quantitative data sources. The SAGE Handbook of Social Research Methods*. SAGE Publications Ltd.

Dunlop, T. (2019). Mind the gap: A social sciences review of energy efficiency. *Energy Research & Social Science*, *56*, 101216. DOI: 10.1016/j.erss.2019.05.026

Dunlop, T., & Völker, T. (2023). The politics of measurement and the case of energy efficiency policy in the European Union. *Energy Research & Social Science*, *96*, 102918. DOI: 10.1016/j.erss.2022.102918

Ekolu, S. O., & Quainoo, H. (2019). Reliability of assessments in engineering education using Cronbach's alpha, KR and split-half methods. *Global journal of engineering education, 21*(1), 24-29.

Elbassoussy, A. (2019). European energy security dilemma: Major challenges and confrontation strategies. *Review of Economics and Political Science*, *4*(4), 321–343. DOI: 10.1108/REPS-02-2019-0019

Estrada, M. A. R., & Koutronas, E. (2022). The impact of the Russian aggression against Ukraine on the Russia-EU trade. *Journal of Policy Modeling*, *44*(3), 599–616. DOI: 10.1016/j.jpolmod.2022.06.004

European Commission. (2021). *The European Pillar of Social Rights Action Plan*. Publications Office of the European Union. https://op.europa.eu/webpub/empl/european-pillar-of-social rights/downloads/KE0921008ENN.pdf

Eurostat, Statistics Explained, (2022), Archive: EU energy mix and import dependency, 104551.pdf

Hakim, C. (1982). *Secondary analysis in social research: A guide to data sources and methods with examples*. Unwin Hyman (Firm).

Hassan, S. T., Khan, S. U. D., Xia, E., & Fatima, H. (2020). Role of institutions in correcting environmental pollution: An empirical investigation. *Sustainable Cities and Society*, *53*, 101901. DOI: 10.1016/j.scs.2019.101901

Heffron, R. J., McCauley, D., & Sovacool, B. K. (2015). Resolving society's energy trilemma through the Energy Justice Metric. *Energy Policy*, *87*, 168–176. DOI: 10.1016/j.enpol.2015.08.033

Joi a, D., Panait, M., Dobrotă, C. E., Dini ă, A., Neac a, A., & Naghi, L. E. (2023). The European dilemma-Energy security or green transition. *Energies*, *16*(9), 3849. DOI: 10.3390/en16093849

Kanellakis, M., Martinopoulos, G., & Zachariadis, T. (2013). European energy policy—A review. *Energy Policy*, *62*, 1020–1030. DOI: 10.1016/j.enpol.2013.08.008

Keypour, J., & Ahmadzada, U. (2022). Consolidating EU energy security by relying on energy de-politicisation. *European Security*, *31*(1), 135–157. DOI: 10.1080/09662839.2021.1970538

Khan, A., Sampene, A. K., & Ali, S. (2023). Towards environmental degradation mitigation: The role of regulatory quality, technological innovation and government effectiveness in the CEMAC countries. *Heliyon*, *9*(6).

Lange, P., Bornemann, B., & Burger, P. (2019). Sustainability impacts of governance modes: Insights from Swiss energy policy. *Journal of Environmental Policy and Planning*, *21*(2), 174–187. DOI: 10.1080/1523908X.2019.1566062

Liu, X., Latif, K., Latif, Z., & Li, N. (2020). Relationship between economic growth and CO2 emissions: Does governance matter? *Environmental Science and Pollution Research International*, *27*(14), 17221–17228. DOI: 10.1007/s11356-020-08142-3

Mišík, M. (2022). The EU needs to improve its external energy security. *Energy Policy*, *165*, 112930. DOI: 10.1016/j.enpol.2022.112930

Mišík, M., & Nosko, A. (2023). Each one for themselves: Exploring the energy security paradox of the European Union. *Energy Research & Social Science*, *99*, 103074. DOI: 10.1016/j.erss.2023.103074

Mohelska, H., Sokolova, M., Cierniak-Emerych, A., & Dziuba, S. T. (2020). Employment in high-technology industries in the european union and job satisfaction-case study Czech Republic and Poland. *Economic research-. Ekonomska Istrazivanja*, *33*(1), 639–651. DOI: 10.1080/1331677X.2019.1697723

Morera, O. F., & Stokes, S. M. (2016). Coefficient α as a measure of test score reliability: Review of 3 popular misconceptions. *American Journal of Public Health*, *106*(3), 458–461.

Ostrowski, W. (2022). The twenty years' crisis of European energy security: Central and Eastern Europe and the US. *Geopolitics*, *27*(3), 875–897. DOI: 10.1080/14650045.2020.1835863

Rodríguez-Pose, A., & Di Cataldo, M. (2015). Quality of government and innovative performance in the regions of Europe. *Journal of Economic Geography*, *15*(4), 673–706. DOI: 10.1093/jeg/lbu023

Sareen, S. (2021). Digitalisation and social inclusion in multi-scalar smart energy transitions. *Energy Research & Social Science*, *81*, 102251. DOI: 10.1016/j.erss.2021.102251

Siddi, M. (2023). Europe's energy dilemma: War and the green transition. *Current History (New York, N.Y.)*, *122*(842), 83–88. DOI: 10.1525/curh.2023.122.842.83

Solorio, I., & Jörgens, H. (2020). Contested energy transition? Europeanization and authority turns in EU renewable energy policy. *Journal of European Integration*, *42*(1), 77–93. DOI: 10.1080/07036337.2019.1708342

Song, C., & Majeed, M. T. (2023). Digital inclusion to enhance energy sustainability: Public participation and environmental governance in the new media era to achieve energy sustainable goals. *Environmental Science and Pollution Research International*, *30*(59), 123633–123642. DOI: 10.1007/s11356-023-30837-6

Strambo, C., Nilsson, M., & Månsson, A. (2015). Coherent or inconsistent? Assessing energy security and climate policy interaction within the European Union. *Energy Research & Social Science*, *8*, 1–12. DOI: 10.1016/j.erss.2015.04.004

Sun, Y., & You, X. (2023). Do digital inclusive finance, innovation, and entrepreneurship activities stimulate vitality of the urban economy? Empirical evidence from the Yangtze River Delta, China. *Technology in Society*, *72*, 102200. DOI: 10.1016/j.techsoc.2023.102200

Usman, A., Ozturk, I., Hassan, A., Zafar, S. M., & Ullah, S. (2021). The effect of ICT on energy consumption and economic growth in South Asian economies: An empirical analysis. *Telematics and Informatics*, *58*, 101537. DOI: 10.1016/j.tele.2020.101537

World Bank. (2023). *Worldwide Governance Indicators*. https://info.worldbank.org/governance/wgi/

World Energy Council. (2024). *World Energy Trilemma 2024: Evolving with resilience and justice*. World Energy Council.

World Energy Council & Oliver Wyman. (2019). *World Energy Trilemma Index 2019*. https://www.worldenergy.org/publications/entry/world-energy-trilemma-index-2019

Zang, L., & Xiong, F. (2020). How (when) does technological innovation improve government effectiveness? An empirical investigation with cross-national evidence. *Science & Public Policy*, *47*(1), 103–113. DOI: 10.1093/scipol/scz050

ADDITIONAL READING

Abdullah, F. B., Iqbal, R., Ahmad, S., El-Affendi, M. A., & Kumar, P. (2022). Optimization of multidimensional energy security: An index based assessment. *Energies*, *15*(11), 3929. DOI: 10.3390/en15113929

Brodny, J., & Tutak, M. (2023). Assessing the energy security of European Union countries from two perspectives–A new integrated approach based on MCDM methods. *Applied Energy*, *347*, 121443. DOI: 10.1016/j.apenergy.2023.121443

Fragkos, P., Fragkiadakis, K., Sovacool, B., Paroussos, L., Vrontisi, Z., & Charalampidis, I. (2021). Equity implications of climate policy: Assessing the social and distributional impacts of emission reduction targets in the European Union. *Energy*, *237*, 121591. DOI: 10.1016/j.energy.2021.121591

Guivarch, C., & Monjon, S. (2017). Identifying the main uncertainty drivers of energy security in a low-carbon world: The case of Europe. *Energy Economics, 64*, 530–541. DOI: 10.1016/j.eneco.2016.04.007

Lu, Y., Khan, Z. A., Alvarez-Alvarado, M. S., Zhang, Y., Huang, Z., & Imran, M. (2020). A critical review of sustainable energy policies for the promotion of renewable energy sources. *Sustainability, 12*(12), 5078. DOI: 10.3390/su12125078

Pérez-Lombard, L., Ortiz, J., & Velázquez, D. (2013). Revisiting energy efficiency fundamentals. *Energy Efficiency, 6*(2), 239–254. DOI: 10.1007/s12053-012-9180-8

Trotta, G. (2020). Assessing energy efficiency improvements and related energy security and climate benefits in Finland: An ex post multi-sectoral decomposition analysis. *Energy Economics, 86*, 104640. DOI: 10.1016/j.eneco.2019.104640

KEY TERMS AND DEFINITIONS

Composite Indicator: A quantitative index created by aggregating multiple indicators into a single measure to capture complex and multidimensional phenomena, such as sustainability, governance quality, or energy system performance.

Energy Governance: The set of institutional arrangements, policies, regulatory frameworks, and decision-making processes through which energy systems are managed, coordinated, and transformed at national and supranational levels.

Energy Quadrilemma Index (EQI): A composite indicator that aggregates energy security, environmental sustainability, energy equity, and technology into a single standardized measure, enabling cross-country comparison of overall energy governance performance.

Energy Quadrilemma: An expanded analytical framework that extends the traditional Energy Trilemma by incorporating Technology as a fourth pillar alongside energy security, environmental sustainability, and energy equity. The framework captures the enabling role of human capital, digitalization, and governance capacity in shaping sustainable energy transitions.

Energy Trilemma: A conceptual framework used to assess energy system performance based on the balance among energy security, environmental sustainability, and energy equity, highlighting the inherent trade-offs faced in energy policy design.

Exploratory Factor Analysis (EFA): A multivariate statistical technique used to identify latent structures underlying a set of observed variables, commonly applied in the development of composite indicators and the exploration of multidimensional constructs.

Technology (Energy Governance Context): A multidimensional, human-centered enabling capacity encompassing education and skills development, digital inclusion, knowledge-intensive employment, and institutional quality, which conditions the ability of energy systems to evolve in a sustainable, resilient, and equitable manner.

Chapter 12

Preference of Medium of Study in Schools for Higher Secondary (10+2) Level:

An Insights Study From India

Tripti Basuri
Uttar Dum Dum Vidyapith, India

Kamal Hossain Gazi
http://orcid.org/0000-0001-7179-984X
Maulana Abul Kalam Azad University of Technology, West Bengal, India

Prodip Bhaduri
Maulana Abul Kalam Azad University of Technology, West Bengal, India

Srabani Guria Das
NSHM Knowledge Campus, Durgapur, India

Soheil Salahshour
Faculty of Engineering and Natural Sciences, Istanbul Okan University, Istanbul, Turkey

Sankar Prasad Mondal
http://orcid.org/0000-0003-4690-2598
Maulana Abul Kalam Azad University of Technology, West Bengal, India

ABSTRACT

In a country like India, where language diversity is present, it becomes essential to choose the medium of instruction for higher study. In this chapter, we aim to determine which medium of instruction will receive the most preference for studying in schools at the Higher Secondary (10+2) level. Here, Triangular Neutrosophic Numbers (TNNs) are used to incorporate uncertainty into the dataset. Here, two

DOI: 10.4018/979-8-3373-6926-6.ch012

MCDM methods, namely CRITIC and COPRAS, are applied. The CRITIC method is applied to evaluate the criteria weight and the ranking of alternatives is performed by using the COPRAS method.

1. INTRODUCTION

Education forms the foundation of a developing country. Therefore, it is essential to establish a well-structured educational system (Aktar, 2021; Kumar et al., 2021). There are various languages used for communication in different parts of our country. Thus, the students of those particular regions are comfortable speaking and understanding their regional language. There are educational policies that enable students to continue their preliminary studies in their native language. But when they want to take admission in the higher secondary (10+2) level, then they may choose their medium of instruction for the betterment of their future study and career. Several factors may influence (Mezhoudi et al., 2023; Sabharwal, 2021) the choice of medium of instruction for the higher secondary (10+2) level, including accessibility, future employability, parental preference, and economic affordability. In India (Kumar & Choudhury, 2021), Hindi is the official language, English is an associate official language and there are also 22 regional languages which can be used in education, official purposes, etc.

1.1 Motivation of This Study

Choosing the medium of instruction for Higher Secondary, i.e., (10+2) level, is a complex and critical task which represents the diversity of languages across India. The decision of choosing an appropriate medium directly impacts students' academic performance, accessibility for higher qualifications and various career opportunities. The decision of choosing a suitable medium is dependent upon multiple factors, including the location and financial situation of the family. There are some cognitive benefits of studying in one's mother tongue, but at the same time, studying in English medium provides an edge in career trajectories. Therefore, there is a pressing need for an effective decision-making model to select the most suitable medium of instruction by considering various conflicting criteria. Using a triangular neutrosophic fuzzy environment (Fahmi et al., 2021) paired with a hybrid CRITIC MARCOS-based MCDM (Bilişik et al., 2024; Demir et al., 2024; Divya et al., 2020) strategy, this study aims to evaluate a consistent balanced methodology for selecting the most suitable language as a medium of instruction for students in High Secondary studies.

1.2 Novelties of this Research

The novelties of this chapter are discussed in this section. The selection of the medium of instruction is an important as well as a critical task. The novelties of this chapter are as follows:

1. Many obstacles are taken into deliberation and examined for the selection of the medium of instruction.
2. Numerous aspects like economic affordability (Patel, 2022), accessibility (Sabharwal, 2021), quality of education (Baranwal, 2024), employability (Mezhoudi et al., 2023), socio-cultural factors (Mishra, 2013), etc., are taken into consideration.
3. Two strategies of MCDM are used to construct the proposed model, namely the CRiteria Importance Through Intercriteria Correlation (CRITIC) (Bilişik et al., 2024) and the Measurement of Alternatives and Ranking according to Compromise Solution (MARCOS) (Demir et al., 2024) techniques.
4. Linguistic inputs are taken from three DMs.
5. A triangular neutrosophic fuzzy (Fahmi et al., 2021) environment is involved to deal with the uncertainties.

1.3 Structure of this Chapter

The structure of this paper is described in this section. Section 1 analyses the introduction, motivation and novelties of this work. A brief literature survey on the school education system, triangular neutrosophic fuzzy and MCDM strategies are discussed in Section 2. Section 3 describes the preliminaries of fuzzy sets and triangular neutrosophic fuzzy numbers. Two MCDM methodologies named CRITIC and MARCOS are discussed in Section 4. Section 5 outlines the various criteria for selecting the medium of study. Section 6 deals with the proposed alternatives for the medium of instruction. Section 7 describes the formulation of the model and data collection from three DMs. Numerical illustration is completed in Section 8. Finally, the conclusion is drawn and the scope of future research is analysed in Section 9.

2. LITERATURE REVIEW OF THIS CHAPTER

This section presents the literature review for this study. Initially, the literature on school education is discussed, followed by an introduction to triangular neutrosophic fuzzy sets. Finally, the methodologies of MCDM (Divya et al., 2020) are briefly discussed.

2.1 Literature on the Role of Medium of Instruction in School Education

The choice of medium of instruction for students studying at the higher secondary level in India is shaped by various conflicting cultural, socio-economic and policy factors. The interest of students and parents in English medium schools is rapidly increasing, as evident in a study by Azam, Chin, and Prakash (Azam et al., 2013). Meanwhile, research by Nakamura et al. (Nakamura et al., 2023) highlights the pedagogical difficulties that arise when adopting English as the primary medium for students from non-English backgrounds. Classroom studies by Lightfoot (Lightfoot et al., 2022) further reveal that rigid monolingual norms may not accurately reflect the real-world experiences of students in code-mixing and translanguaging. The study by Endow (Endow, 2018) examines the dilemma of harmonising accessibility and equity in education within a global and primarily nation-wise competitive environment. Affordable private English-medium schools usually promise upward mobility but often compromise on the quality of education.

2.2 Literature on Triangular Neutrosophic Fuzzy Set

In the current era of mathematical and statistical analysis, uncertainty is a key concept. Fuzzy set theory primarily deals with measuring the uncertainty of complex problems in the real world. It was first introduced in 1965 by a mathematician named Lotfi A. Zadeh (Zadeh, 1965). Fuzzy sets and fuzzy numbers have various extensions, including triangular fuzzy sets (Kahraman et al., 2016), trapezoidal fuzzy sets (Xiao et al., 2012), intuitionistic fuzzy sets (Afful-Dadzie et al., 2017), neutrosophic fuzzy sets (Broumi et al., 2018) and interval-valued neutrosophic number (Adhikari et al., 2025). Florentin Smarandache (Smarandache, 2003) introduced the concept of the neutrosophic fuzzy set in 2003. A triangular neutrosophic fuzzy number (Fahmi et al., 2021) is used to evaluate an accurate representation of uncertainty and ambiguity in a fuzzy environment to obtain feasible and effective decision-making results. In numerous complex problems, such as solving differential equations, difference equations, integral equations (Divya & Ganesan, 2025), fuzzy numbers and neutrosophic numbers are used. Some scenarios of using triangular neutrosophic numbers include triangular neutrosophic topology (Al-subhi et al., 2021), applications in linear programming (Tripath et al., 2024) and the critical path problem (Pratyusha & Kumar, 2024), among others.

2.3 Literature on MCDM Methodologies

In the field of operations research, one of the most crucial tools is Multi-Criteria Decision Making (MCDM) (Divya et al., 2020), which addresses complex decision-making problems involving conflicting criteria. There are multiple approaches, procedures, and methodologies for calculating the weight of the criteria and thus ranking and comparing the most suitable alternatives to make the best possible decision. We have numerous methods for evaluating the weight of the criteria, such as SWARA (Pajić et al., 2024) and Entropy (Ribeiro et al., 2021), and several techniques for arranging the alternatives according to their priorities, including MOORA (Singh et al., 2024) and VIKOR (Abdul et al., 2024). These MCDM methodologies (Momena et al., 2025) help decision-makers select the most suitable alternative in complex situations involving conflicting criteria. There are various instances of using MCDM for restaurant ranking (Gazi et al., 2023), site selection for a new school (Basuri et al., 2025), PhD supervisor selection (Mandal et al., 2024), canteen selection in an educational institution (Biswas et al., 2024) and so on.

In this chapter, we have employed the Criteria Importance Through Intercriteria Correlation (CRITIC) (Bilişik et al., 2024) method for evaluating the weights of the criteria and the Measurement Alternatives and Ranking (MARCOS) (Demir et al., 2024) method for comparing and ranking the alternatives. Diakoulaki, D. et al. (Diakoulaki et al., 1995) first introduced the CRITIC method for determining the weights of the criteria in 1995. Further, Stević, Ž. et al. (Stević et al., 2020) invented the MARCOS method for ranking alternatives based on multiple conflicting criteria and alternatives. Some recent studies on CRITIC and MARCOS methodologies are as follows: choosing a material for sintered pulley (Ranjan et al., 2023), analysis of sustainable food supplier selection (Wang et al., 2024), measures for zero carbon measures for sustainable transportation in smart cities (Krishankumar et al., 2023), analyzing performance of steel industry (Dwivedi et al., 2021), model selection for internal transport technology (Huskanović et al., 2023), modeling low-carbon logistics service provider (Su et al., 2025) and financial performance analysis of airlines (Su et al., 2025).

3. PRELIMINARIES OF MATHEMATICAL TOOLS

The preliminaries of the mathematical tools are discussed in detail in this section. Initially, we discuss fuzzy sets (Zadeh, 1965) and their properties. Next, a brief discussion of the neutrosophic fuzzy set (Broumi et al., 2018), the neutrosophic fuzzy number and the triangular neutrosophic number (Fahmi et al., 2021) has been provided.

3.1 Fuzzy Sets and Fuzzy Numbers

Lotfi A. Zadeh (Zadeh, 1965) introduced fuzzy sets in 1965 to address the uncertainty and vagueness in systems. In a fuzzy set, every element has two components, the element itself and its membership value, which describes the belongingness of the element in the set. A fuzzy set can be defined as follows:

Definition 1. [Fuzzy Set] (Gazi et al., 2023)

Let us assume, η is an arbitrary element of $\widetilde{A}$ where hv is a universal set. So, the fuzzy set $\widetilde{A}$ on hv can be defined as,

$$\widetilde{A} = \{(\eta, \mu_{\widetilde{A}}(\eta)) : \eta \in hv\} \tag{1}$$

where the membership value of the element η in $\widetilde{A}$ is $\mu_{\widetilde{A}}(\eta) \in [0,1]$.

Example 1. Let the respective set of players in boxing club is $Q = \{r_1, r_2, r_3, r_4, r_5\}$. By using the word "strong" as a fuzzy term, consider $\widetilde{U}$ to be the fuzzy set of "strong" players in the boxing club. So, the required set is $\widetilde{M} = \{(r_1, 0.73), (r_2, 0.62), (r_3, 1), (r_4, 0.81), (r_5, 0.92)\}$, where the player r_1 is strong of 73% and so on.

Definition 2. [Fuzzy Number] (Mandal et al., 2024)

The following properties must be fulfilled for a fuzzy set $\widetilde{K}$ on the set of real numbers ($\mathbb{R}$), such as

1. $\widetilde{K}$ needs to be a normal fuzzy set, i.e., there exists an element, $c \in \mathbb{R}$ such that $\mu_{\widetilde{K}}(c) = 1$.
2. ${}^{\alpha}\widetilde{K}$ must be a closed interval for every $\alpha \in (0,1]$, where, ${}^{\alpha}\widetilde{K} = \{c : \mu_{\widetilde{K}}(c) \geq \alpha\}$ is closed.
3. ${}^{\alpha}\widetilde{K}$ needs to be a convex fuzzy set, i.e., $\mu_{\widetilde{K}}(\lambda c_1 + (1-\lambda)c_2) \geq \max\{\mu_{\widetilde{K}}(c_1), \mu_{\widetilde{K}}(c_2)\}; \forall\, c_1, c_2 \in \widetilde{K}$ and $\lambda \in [0,1]$.
4. $\widetilde{K}$ must be bounded support within a specific range.
5. The membership function of $\widetilde{K}$ should be piecewise continuous.

Then we call it a fuzzy number.

Example 2. Suppose that Rajendri scored 'Good' marks in the final semester exam. The word 'Good' is incapable of portraying her particular marks, and the term 'Good' differs from one individual to another. So, we can use the idea of the fuzzy number by using it as an object. So, from 0 ('Not good' in fuzzy concept) to 1 ('Fully good' in fuzzy concept) is the membership function of the narrated object.

3.2 Neutrosophic Fuzzy Set

A neutrosophic fuzzy set is an extension of a fuzzy set that was invented by Florentin Smarandache (Smarandache, 2003) in 2003. In the neutrosophic fuzzy set (Biswas et al., 2024), every element has three membership values instead of one and represents the position of the element more specifically. The membership functions are in belongness, indeterminacy and non-belongness, respectively. The neutrosophic fuzzy set can be defined as follows:

Definition 3. [Neutrosophic Fuzzy Set] (Basuri et al., 2025)

Let X be the universal set and a single-valued neutrosophic fuzzy set $\tilde{\mathscr{A}}$ can be defined as,

$$\tilde{\mathscr{A}} = \left\{\left(a, \mathscr{T}_{\tilde{\mathscr{A}}}(a), \mathscr{I}_{\tilde{\mathscr{A}}}(a), \mathscr{F}_{\tilde{\mathscr{A}}}(a)\right) : a \in X\right\} \tag{2}$$

where $\mathscr{T}_{\tilde{\mathscr{A}}}(a), \mathscr{I}_{\tilde{\mathscr{A}}}(a)$ and $\mathscr{F}_{\tilde{\mathscr{A}}}(a)$ are the degree of membership, the degree of indeterminacy and the degree of non-membership functions, respectively. Here, $\mathscr{T}_{\tilde{\mathscr{A}}}(a), \mathscr{I}_{\tilde{\mathscr{A}}}(a), \mathscr{F}_{\tilde{\mathscr{A}}}(a) : X \to [0,1]$ for all $a \in X$ with the primary condition that $0 \le \mathscr{T}_{\tilde{\mathscr{A}}}(a) + \mathscr{I}_{\tilde{\mathscr{A}}}(a) + \mathscr{F}_{\tilde{\mathscr{A}}}(a) \le 3$.

Definition 4. [Neutrosophic Number (NN)] (Biswas et al., 2024)

A Neutrosophic fuzzy number $\tilde{\mathscr{A}}$ is originally a single-valued neutrosophic fuzzy set on the set of real numbers ($\mathbb{R}$), which satisfies the conditions given below

1. $\tilde{\mathscr{A}}$ is normal if $\exists a_0 \in \mathbb{R}$, for which $\mathscr{T}_{\tilde{\mathscr{A}}}(a_0) = 1$, and $\mathscr{I}_{\tilde{\mathscr{A}}}(a_0) = \mathscr{F}_{\tilde{\mathscr{A}}}(a_0) = 0$.
2. $\tilde{\mathscr{A}}$ is a convex set for the membership function $\mathscr{T}_{\tilde{\mathscr{A}}}(a)$, indeterministic function $\mathscr{I}_{\tilde{\mathscr{A}}}(a)$ and non-membership function $\mathscr{F}_{\tilde{\mathscr{A}}}(a)$, such that
    a. $\mathscr{T}_{\tilde{\mathscr{A}}}(\gamma a_1 + (1-\gamma) a_2) \ge \min\{\mathscr{T}_{\tilde{\mathscr{A}}}(a_1), \mathscr{T}_{\tilde{\mathscr{A}}}(a_2)\}$; $\forall a_1, a_2 \in \mathbb{R}$ and $\gamma \in [0,1]$,
    b. $\mathscr{I}_{\tilde{\mathscr{A}}}(\gamma a_1 + (1-\gamma) a_2) \le \min\{\mathscr{I}_{\tilde{\mathscr{A}}}(a_1), \mathscr{I}_{\tilde{\mathscr{A}}}(a_2)\}$; $\forall a_1, a_2 \in \mathbb{R}$ and $\gamma \in [0,1]$,
    c. $\mathscr{F}_{\tilde{\mathscr{A}}}(\gamma a_1 + (1-\gamma) a_2) \le \min\{\mathscr{F}_{\tilde{\mathscr{A}}}(a_1), \mathscr{F}_{\tilde{\mathscr{A}}}(a_2)\}$; $\forall a_1, a_2 \in \mathbb{R}$ and $\gamma \in [0,1]$.

3.3 Triangular Neutrosophic Number (TNN)

Triangular Neutrosophic Number (TNN) (Biswas et al., 2024) is a special type of neutrosophic number where the membership functions are in triangular form. TNNs are applied in various fields to capture the uncertainty and vagueness of models and datasets. TNN may be defined as follows:

Definition 5. [Triangular Neutrosophic Number (TNN)] (Biswas et al., 2024)

Here, we will utilise Triangular Neutrosophic Numbers (TNNs) (Das et al., 2020) to incorporate the uncertainty and vagueness inherent in the systems. A single-valued Triangular Neutrosophic Number (TNN) $\widetilde{\mathscr{P}} = \langle (p_1, p_2, p_3) \; ; \alpha_{\widetilde{\mathscr{P}}}, \beta_{\widetilde{\mathscr{P}}}, \delta_{\widetilde{\mathscr{P}}} \rangle$ is a Neutrosophic set on $\mathbb{R}$, whose membership function $\mathscr{T}_{\widetilde{\mathscr{P}}}(x)$, indeterministic function $\mathscr{I}_{\widetilde{\mathscr{P}}}(x)$ and non-membership function $\mathscr{F}_{\widetilde{\mathscr{P}}}(x)$ are described as follows

$$\mathscr{T}_{\widetilde{\mathscr{P}}}(x) = \begin{cases} \alpha_{\widetilde{\mathscr{P}}} \dfrac{x - p_1}{p_2 - p_1} & ; where\ p_1 \le x < p_2 \\ \alpha_{\widetilde{\mathscr{P}}} & ; where\ x = p_2 \\ \alpha_{\widetilde{\mathscr{P}}} \dfrac{p_3 - x}{p_3 - p_2} & ; where\ p_2 < x \le p_3 \\ 0 & ; otherwise \end{cases} \tag{3}$$

$$\mathscr{I}_{\widetilde{\mathscr{P}}}(x) = \begin{cases} \dfrac{(p_2 - x) + (x - p_1)\beta_{\widetilde{\mathscr{P}}}}{p_2 - p_1} & ; where\ p_1 \le x < p_2 \\ \beta_{\widetilde{\mathscr{P}}} & ; where\ x = p_2 \\ \dfrac{(x - p_2) + (p_3 - x)\beta_{\widetilde{\mathscr{P}}}}{p_3 - p_2} & ; where\ p_2 < x \le p_3 \\ 0 & ; otherwise \end{cases} \tag{4}$$

and

$$\mathscr{F}_{\widetilde{\mathscr{P}}}(x) = \begin{cases} \dfrac{(p_2 - x) + (x - p_1)\delta_{\widetilde{\mathscr{P}}}}{p_2 - p_1} & ; where\ p_1 \le x < p_2 \\ \delta_{\widetilde{\mathscr{P}}} & ; where\ x = p_2 \\ \dfrac{(x - p_2) + (p_3 - x)\delta_{\widetilde{\mathscr{P}}}}{p_3 - p_2} & ; where\ p_2 < x \le p_3 \\ 0 & ; otherwise \end{cases} \tag{5}$$

where $\alpha_{\widetilde{\mathscr{P}}}, \beta_{\widetilde{\mathscr{P}}}, \delta_{\widetilde{\mathscr{P}}} \in [0,1]$, $p_1, p_2, p_3 \in \mathbb{R}$ and $p_1 \le p_2 \le p_3$.

3.4 Arithmetic Operations on TNNs

Let us consider two single-valued Triangular Neutrosophic Numbers (TNNs) $\widetilde{\mathscr{P}} = \langle (p_1, p_2, p_3) \; ; \alpha_{\widetilde{\mathscr{P}}}, \beta_{\widetilde{\mathscr{P}}}, \delta_{\widetilde{\mathscr{P}}} \rangle$ and $\widetilde{\mathscr{Q}} = \langle (q_1, q_2, q_3) \; ; \alpha_{\widetilde{\mathscr{Q}}}, \beta_{\widetilde{\mathscr{Q}}}, \delta_{\widetilde{\mathscr{Q}}} \rangle$ defined on the universal set of discourse $\mathbb{R}$ and $\lambda(> 0)$ be a scalar. Then the arithmetic operations (Biswas et al., 2024) of TNNs $\widetilde{\mathscr{P}}$ and $\widetilde{\mathscr{Q}}$ are described as follows:

A. Addition of two TNNs

$$\widetilde{\mathscr{P}} + \widetilde{\mathscr{Q}} = \langle (p_1, p_2, p_3) \; ; \alpha_{\widetilde{\mathscr{P}}}, \beta_{\widetilde{\mathscr{P}}}, \delta_{\widetilde{\mathscr{P}}} \rangle + \langle (q_1, q_2, q_3) \; ; \alpha_{\widetilde{\mathscr{Q}}}, \beta_{\widetilde{\mathscr{Q}}}, \delta_{\widetilde{\mathscr{Q}}} \rangle$$

$$= \langle (p_1 + q_1, p_2 + q_2, p_3 + q_3) \; ; min\{ \alpha_{\widetilde{\mathscr{P}}}, \alpha_{\widetilde{\mathscr{Q}}} \}, max\{ \beta_{\widetilde{\mathscr{P}}}, \beta_{\widetilde{\mathscr{Q}}} \}, max\{ \delta_{\widetilde{\mathscr{P}}}, \delta_{\widetilde{\mathscr{Q}}} \} \rangle$$

B. Subtraction of two TNNs

$$\widetilde{\mathscr{P}} - \widetilde{\mathscr{Q}} = \langle (p_1, p_2, p_3) \; ; \alpha_{\widetilde{\mathscr{P}}}, \beta_{\widetilde{\mathscr{P}}}, \delta_{\widetilde{\mathscr{P}}} \rangle - \langle (q_1, q_2, q_3) \; ; \alpha_{\widetilde{\mathscr{Q}}}, \beta_{\widetilde{\mathscr{Q}}}, \delta_{\widetilde{\mathscr{Q}}} \rangle$$

$$= \langle (p_1 - q_3, p_2 - q_2, p_3 - q_1) \; ; min\{ \alpha_{\widetilde{\mathscr{P}}}, \alpha_{\widetilde{\mathscr{Q}}} \}, max\{ \beta_{\widetilde{\mathscr{P}}}, \beta_{\widetilde{\mathscr{Q}}} \}, max\{ \delta_{\widetilde{\mathscr{P}}}, \delta_{\widetilde{\mathscr{Q}}} \} \rangle$$

C. Scalar Multiplication of TNN

$$\lambda\widetilde{\mathscr{P}} = \lambda \times \widetilde{\mathscr{P}} = \lambda \times \langle (p_1, p_2, p_3) \; ; \alpha_{\widetilde{\mathscr{P}}}, \beta_{\widetilde{\mathscr{P}}}, \delta_{\widetilde{\mathscr{P}}} \rangle$$

$$= \langle (\lambda p_1, \lambda p_2, \lambda p_3) \; ; \alpha_{\widetilde{\mathscr{P}}}, \beta_{\widetilde{\mathscr{P}}}, \delta_{\widetilde{\mathscr{P}}} \rangle$$

where $\lambda(> 0)$ be a positive scalar number.

D. Multiplication of two TNNs

$$\widetilde{\mathscr{P}} \times \widetilde{\mathscr{Q}} = \langle (p_1, p_2, p_3) \; ; \alpha_{\widetilde{\mathscr{P}}}, \beta_{\widetilde{\mathscr{P}}}, \delta_{\widetilde{\mathscr{P}}} \rangle \times \langle (q_1, q_2, q_3) \; ; \alpha_{\widetilde{\mathscr{Q}}}, \beta_{\widetilde{\mathscr{Q}}}, \delta_{\widetilde{\mathscr{Q}}} \rangle$$

$$= \langle (p_1 q_1, p_2 q_2, p_3 q_3); min\{ \alpha_{\widetilde{\mathscr{P}}}, \alpha_{\widetilde{\mathscr{Q}}} \}, max\{ \beta_{\widetilde{\mathscr{P}}}, \beta_{\widetilde{\mathscr{Q}}} \}, max\{ \delta_{\widetilde{\mathscr{P}}}, \delta_{\widetilde{\mathscr{Q}}} \} \rangle$$

for $p_1 > 0$ and $q_1 > 0$.

E. Division of two TNNs

$$\frac{\widetilde{\mathscr{P}}}{\widetilde{\mathscr{Q}}} = \langle \left(\frac{p_1}{q_3}, \frac{p_2}{q_2}, \frac{p_3}{q_1}\right); \min\{\alpha_{\widetilde{\mathscr{P}}}, \alpha_{\widetilde{\mathscr{Q}}}\}, \max\{\beta_{\widetilde{\mathscr{P}}}, \beta_{\widetilde{\mathscr{Q}}}\}, \max\{\delta_{\widetilde{\mathscr{P}}}, \delta_{\widetilde{\mathscr{Q}}}\}\rangle$$

for $p_3 > 0$ and $q_3 > 0$.

3.5 Ranking of Triangular Neutrosophic Numbers (TNNs)

Score and accuracy functions (Basuri et al., 2025) are used to compare two Triangular Neutrosophic Numbers (TNNs). Since there is no order pair in Triangular Neutrosophic Numbers (TNNs), to order the TNNs, de-neutrosophication, score or accuracy functions (Adhikari et al., 2025; Biswas et al., 2024; Momena et al., 2025) are needed. There are several methodologies used for these numerical computations, but in this study, we used score and accuracy functions described below.

Definition 6. [Score and Accuracy functions on TNN] (Basuri et al., 2025)

Let $\widetilde{\mathscr{P}} = \langle (p_1, p_2, p_3)\ ; \alpha_{\widetilde{\mathscr{P}}}, \beta_{\widetilde{\mathscr{P}}}, \delta_{\widetilde{\mathscr{P}}}\rangle$ be a TTN. Then the Score function $\mathcal{S}_f(\widetilde{\mathscr{P}})$ and the Accuracy function $\mathbb{A}_f(\widetilde{\mathscr{P}})$ are defined on TTN $\widetilde{\mathscr{P}}$, as follows

$$\mathcal{S}_f(\widetilde{\mathscr{P}}) = \frac{1}{5}(2p_1 + p_2 + 2p_3)(\alpha_{\widetilde{\mathscr{P}}} - \beta_{\widetilde{\mathscr{P}}} - 2\delta_{\widetilde{\mathscr{P}}}) \tag{6}$$

$$\mathbb{A}_f(\widetilde{\mathscr{P}}) = \frac{1}{5}(p_1 + p_2 + p_3)(2 + \alpha_{\widetilde{\mathscr{P}}} - 3\beta_{\widetilde{\mathscr{P}}} + \delta_{\widetilde{\mathscr{P}}}) \tag{7}$$

Theorem: Let $\widetilde{\mathscr{P}} = \langle (p_1, p_2, p_3)\ ; \alpha_{\widetilde{\mathscr{P}}}, \beta_{\widetilde{\mathscr{P}}}, \delta_{\widetilde{\mathscr{P}}}\rangle\, and\, \widetilde{\mathscr{Q}} = \langle (q_1, q_2, q_3)\ ; \alpha_{\widetilde{\mathscr{Q}}}, \beta_{\widetilde{\mathscr{Q}}}, \delta_{\widetilde{\mathscr{Q}}}\rangle$ to be two single-valued Triangular Neutrosophic Numbers (TNNs). Then the relation between two TNNs $\widetilde{\mathscr{P}}$ and $\widetilde{Q}$, are define as

1. If $\mathcal{S}_f(\widetilde{\mathscr{P}}) \succ \mathcal{S}_f(\widetilde{\mathscr{Q}}) \Longrightarrow \widetilde{\mathscr{P}} \succ \widetilde{\mathscr{Q}}$;
2. If $\mathcal{S}_f(\widetilde{\mathscr{P}}) \prec \mathcal{S}_f(\widetilde{\mathscr{Q}}) \Longrightarrow \widetilde{\mathscr{P}} \prec \widetilde{\mathscr{Q}}$;
3. If $\mathcal{S}_f(\widetilde{\mathscr{P}}) = \mathcal{S}_f(\widetilde{\mathscr{Q}})$, then
   a. If $\mathbb{A}_f(\widetilde{\mathscr{P}}) \prec \mathbb{A}_f(\widetilde{\mathscr{Q}}) \Longrightarrow \widetilde{\mathscr{P}} \prec \widetilde{\mathscr{Q}}$;
   b. If $\mathbb{A}_f(\widetilde{\mathscr{P}}) \succ \mathbb{A}_f(\widetilde{\mathscr{Q}}) \Longrightarrow \widetilde{\mathscr{P}} \succ \widetilde{\mathscr{Q}}$;
   c. If $\mathbb{A}_f(\widetilde{\mathscr{P}}) = \mathbb{A}_f(\widetilde{\mathscr{Q}}) \Longrightarrow \widetilde{\mathscr{P}} = \widetilde{\mathscr{Q}}$.

4. PROPOSED MCDM METHODOLOGIES

MCDM is a powerful mathematical technique used to address complex decision-making problems (Momena et al., 2025) that involve multiple criteria and alternatives. In this work, two MCDM methods, namely CRITIC (Biswas et al., 2024) and COPRAS (Ecer & Pamucar, 2021), are used. We will discuss these methodologies briefly as follows:

4.1 CRITIC Methodology

The Criteria Importance Through Intercriteria Correlation (CRITIC) method (Biswas et al., 2024) is a well-known MCDM technique used to evaluate the weight associated with each criterion. The CRITIC method was introduced by Diakoulaki, D. et al. (Diakoulaki et al., 1995) in 1995. It is one of the most popular MCDM-based methods for weight calculation.

Let there be $\mathscr{U}$ number of criteria and $\mathscr{V}$ number of alternatives. Let $\mathscr{R}$ number of decision makers to be considered who will provide their opinions to rank the alternatives. The steps of the CRITIC method are evaluated as follows:

A. **Formulation of Decision Matrices:** In this step, decision matrices are formulated by using the opinions of decision experts. Decision experts provided their opinion in linguistic terms and those are further converted to Triangular Neutrosophic Numbers (TNNs). There are a total $\mathscr{R}$ decision experts, so $\mathscr{R}$ numbers of decision matrices are constructed. The decision matrix formulated by ξ^{th} decision expert is denoted by $\widetilde{\mathfrak{D}}_\xi$ where $\xi = 1,2,\ldots,\mathscr{R}$ and defined as,

$$\widetilde{\mathfrak{D}}_\xi = \begin{bmatrix} \left(\widetilde{\mathscr{P}}_{11}\right)_\xi & \left(\widetilde{\mathscr{P}}_{12}\right)_\xi & \cdots & \left(\widetilde{\mathscr{P}}_{1n}\right)_\xi & \cdots & \left(\widetilde{\mathscr{P}}_{1\mathscr{U}}\right)_\xi \\ \left(\widetilde{\mathscr{P}}_{21}\right)_\xi & \left(\widetilde{\mathscr{P}}_{22}\right)_\xi & \cdots & \left(\widetilde{\mathscr{P}}_{2n}\right)_\xi & \cdots & \left(\widetilde{\mathscr{P}}_{2\mathscr{U}}\right)_\xi \\ \vdots & \vdots & \ddots & \cdots & \ddots & \vdots \\ \left(\widetilde{\mathscr{P}}_{m1}\right)_\xi & \left(\widetilde{\mathscr{P}}_{m2}\right)_\xi & \cdots & \left(\widetilde{\mathscr{P}}_{mn}\right)_\xi & \cdots & \left(\widetilde{\mathscr{P}}_{m\mathscr{U}}\right)_\xi \\ \vdots & \vdots & \ddots & \vdots & \vdots & \vdots \\ \left(\widetilde{\mathscr{P}}_{\mathscr{V}1}\right)_\xi & \left(\widetilde{\mathscr{P}}_{\mathscr{V}2}\right)_\xi & \cdots & \left(\widetilde{\mathscr{P}}_{\mathscr{V}n}\right)_\xi & \cdots & \left(\widetilde{\mathscr{P}}_{\mathscr{V}\mathscr{U}}\right)_\xi \end{bmatrix}_{\mathscr{V}\times\mathscr{U}} \tag{8}$$

i.e., $\widetilde{\mathfrak{D}}_\xi = \left[\left(\widetilde{\mathscr{P}}_{mn}\right)_\xi\right]_{\mathscr{V}\times\mathscr{U}} = \left[\left(\left(\widetilde{\widetilde{\mathscr{P}}}\right)_{mn}\right)_\xi\right]_{\mathscr{V}\times\mathscr{U}}$, where $m = 1,2,\ldots,\mathscr{V}$, $n = 1,2,\ldots,\mathscr{U}$ and $\xi = 1,2,\ldots,\mathscr{R}$. Each element $\left(\widetilde{\mathscr{P}}_{mn}\right)_\xi$ is of the form,

$$\left(\left(\widetilde{\widetilde{\mathscr{P}}}\right)_{mn}\right)_\xi =$$

$$\left\langle\left(\left((\mathcal{P}_1)_{mn}\right)_\xi, \left((\mathcal{P}_2)_{mn}\right)_\xi, \left((\mathcal{P}_3)_{mn}\right)_\xi; ((\alpha_{\tilde{\mathcal{P}}})_{mn})_\xi, ((\beta_{\tilde{\mathcal{P}}})_{mn})_\xi, ((\gamma_{\tilde{\mathcal{P}}})_{mn})_\xi\right\rangle \tag{9}$$

B. **Construction of Aggregated Decision Matrix:** In this step, all decision matrices are converted into a single decision matrix by using the following equations,

$$\begin{cases} (\mathcal{P}_1)_{mn} = \min_{\xi=1,2,\ldots,\mathcal{R}}((\mathcal{P}_1)_{mn})_\xi \\ (\mathcal{P}_2)_{mn} = \sqrt[\mathcal{R}]{\prod_{\xi=1}^{\mathcal{R}}((\mathcal{P}_2)_{mn})_\xi} \\ (\mathcal{P}_3)_{mn} = \max_{\xi=1,2,\ldots,\mathcal{R}}((\mathcal{P}_3)_{mn})_\xi \\ (\alpha_{\tilde{\mathcal{P}}})_{mn} = \min_{\xi=1,2,\ldots,\mathcal{R}}((\alpha_{\tilde{\mathcal{P}}})_{mn})_\xi \\ (\beta_{\tilde{\mathcal{P}}})_{mn} = \min_{\xi=1,2,\ldots,\mathcal{R}}((\beta_{\tilde{\mathcal{P}}})_{mn})_\xi \\ (\gamma_{\tilde{\mathcal{P}}})_{mn} = \min_{\xi=1,2,\ldots,\mathcal{R}}((\gamma_{\tilde{\mathcal{P}}})_{mn})_\xi \end{cases} \tag{10}$$

where $m = 1,2,\ldots,\mathcal{V}$ and $n = 1,2,\ldots,\mathcal{U}$. So, the aggregated decision matrix is of the form $\tilde{\mathfrak{D}}_a = [\tilde{\mathcal{P}}_{mn}]_{\mathcal{V}\times\mathcal{U}}$, where

$$\tilde{\mathcal{P}}_{mn} = \langle((\mathcal{P}_1)_{mn}, (\mathcal{P}_2)_{mn}, (\mathcal{P}_3)_{mn}), (\alpha_{\tilde{\mathcal{P}}})_{mn}, (\beta_{\tilde{\mathcal{P}}})_{mn}, (\gamma_{\tilde{\mathcal{P}}})_{mn}\rangle \tag{11}$$

C. **Score value of the decision matrix:** In this step, each element of the aggregated decision matrix, which is given in the form of a Triangular Neutrosophic Number (TNN), is converted to an equivalent score value by using Equation (6). The score valued decision matrix is of the form $\mathfrak{D} = [(\mathcal{b}_{mn})]_{\mathcal{V}\times\mathcal{U}}$, where $\mathcal{b}_{mn}$ is the assigned crisp value corresponding to the Triangular Neutrosophic Numbers (TNNs) $(\tilde{\mathcal{P}}_{mn})$.

D. **Normalisation of the Score Valued Decision Matrix:** In this step, the normalisation of the score valued decision matrix is performed by using the formula,

$$\mathcal{b}'_{mn} = \frac{\mathcal{b}_{mn} - \mathcal{b}_{mn}^{wort}}{\mathcal{b}_{mn}^{best} - \mathcal{b}_{mn}^{worst}} \tag{12}$$

where $\begin{cases} \mathcal{b}_{mn}^{best} = \max_{m=1,2,\ldots,\mathcal{V}} \mathcal{b}_{mn} \\ \mathcal{b}_{mn}^{worst} = \min_{m=1,2,\ldots,\mathcal{V}} \mathcal{b}_{mn} \end{cases}$ and the normalized decision matrix takes the form of

$$\mathfrak{D}_{\mathcal{N}} = [(\mathcal{b}'_{mn})]_{\mathcal{V}\times\mathcal{U}} = [(\mathcal{b}')_{mn}]_{\mathcal{V}\times\mathcal{U}} \tag{13}$$

E. **Evaluating the Standard deviation of each criterion:** In this step, the Standard deviation σ_n related to each criterion is evaluated with the help of the following equation,

$$\sigma_n = \sqrt{\frac{\sum_{n=1}^{\gamma}(\mathscr{b}_n - \overline{\mathscr{b}}_n)}{\mathscr{U} - 1}} \tag{14}$$

where $\overline{\mathscr{b}}_n$ is the population mean and $\mathscr{U}$ is the number of criteria.

F. **Finding the linear Correlation coefficient $(\widetilde{\theta}_{nn})$ between the criteria c_n and criteria c_n**: In this step, we will consider the matrix of $\mathscr{V} \times \mathscr{U}$ order with the elements $\mathscr{b}_{\widetilde{mn}}$. The Correlation coefficient between the criteria c_n and $c_{n'}$ is represented by $\widetilde{\theta}_{nn'}$.

G. **Determining the conflict created by the criteria:** In this step, the conflict ($\mathscr{M}_n$) created by the criterion is evaluated by using the formula,

$$\mathscr{M}_n = \sum_{n=1}^{\mathscr{U}}(1 - \widetilde{\theta}_{nn}) \tag{15}$$

where $n = 1,2,\ldots,\mathscr{U}$.

H. **Determining the quality of information:** In this step, the quality of information $(\mathscr{Q}_n)$ in relation to each criterion is determined by using the following formula,

$$\mathscr{Q}_n = \sigma_n \times \mathscr{M}_n \tag{16}$$

where $n = 1,2,\ldots,\mathscr{U}$.

I. **Finding Criterion weight:** $\mathscr{W}_n$ represents the criterion weight corresponding to n^{th} criteria and it is obtained by applying the equation

$$\mathscr{W}_n = \frac{\mathscr{Q}_n}{\sum_{n=1}^{\mathscr{U}}\mathscr{Q}_n} \tag{17}$$

for $n = 1,2,\ldots,\mathscr{U}$.

From the $\mathscr{W}_n$ values evaluated in Equation (17), describe the criteria weight for the CRITIC method for $n = 1,2,\ldots,\mathscr{U}$, which is further used for numerical computations.

4.2 MARCOS Methodology

Measurement of Alternatives and Ranking according to Compromise Solution (MARCOS) is a popular MCDM method developed by Stević, Ž. Et al. (Stević et al., 2020) in 2020. This method (Ecer & Pamucar, 2021) is used to find the rank of alternatives where multiple criteria are present in a decision-making problem. In this method, both the ideal solutions and the anti-ideal solutions are considered to identify the best alternative.

Let there be $\mathscr{U}$ number of criteria and $\mathscr{V}$ number of alternatives. Let $\mathscr{R}$ number of decision makers be considered who will provide their opinions to rank the alternatives. The mathematical procedure of the MARCOS methodology is described as follows:

1. **Construction of Decision matrices:** In this step $\mathscr{R}$ number of decision matrices are formulated in the same way as mentioned in Step A of the CRITIC method.
2. **Formulation of Aggregated Decision Matrix:** In this step, a total $\mathscr{R}$ number of decision matrices is converted to a single Aggregated decision matrix in a similar manner as we discussed in Step B of the CRITIC method.
3. **Extension of the Decision Matrix:** In this step, the extension of the decision matrix is done by including an Ideal solution (AI) and an Anti-Ideal solution (AAI). Thus, the Extended Decision matrix is,

$$\widetilde{\mathfrak{D}}_{\mathscr{E}} = \begin{pmatrix} \widetilde{\mathscr{P}}^{AAI}_{n} \\ \widetilde{\mathscr{P}}_{mn} \\ \widetilde{\mathscr{P}}^{AI}_{n} \end{pmatrix}_{(\mathscr{V}+2)\times\mathscr{U}} = \begin{bmatrix} \widetilde{\mathscr{P}}^{AAI}_{1} & \widetilde{\mathscr{P}}^{AAI}_{2} & \cdots & \widetilde{\mathscr{P}}^{AAI}_{\mathscr{U}} \\ \widetilde{\mathscr{P}}_{11} & \widetilde{\mathscr{P}}_{12} & \cdots & \widetilde{\mathscr{P}}_{1\mathscr{U}} \\ \vdots & \vdots & \ddots & \vdots \\ \widetilde{\mathscr{P}}_{m1} & \widetilde{\mathscr{P}}_{m2} & & \widetilde{\mathscr{P}}_{m\mathscr{U}} \\ \vdots & \vdots & \ddots & \vdots \\ \widetilde{\mathscr{P}}_{\mathscr{V}1} & \widetilde{\mathscr{P}}_{\mathscr{V}2} & \cdots & \widetilde{\mathscr{P}}_{\mathscr{V}\mathscr{U}} \\ \widetilde{\mathscr{P}}^{AI}_{1} & \widetilde{\mathscr{P}}^{AI}_{2} & & \widetilde{\mathscr{P}}^{AI}_{\mathscr{U}} \end{bmatrix} \tag{18}$$

The best alternative is noted as the Ideal solution (AI) and the worst alternative is noted as the Anti-Ideal solution (AAI). AAI and AI are evaluated by using the following formulas,

$$\begin{cases} AAI = \begin{cases} \min_{m} \widetilde{\mathscr{P}}_{mn}\,;\ if\, n \in B \\ \max_{m} \widetilde{\mathscr{P}}_{mn}\,;\ if\, n \in C \end{cases} \\ AI = \begin{cases} \max_{m} \widetilde{\mathscr{P}}_{mn}\,;\ if\, n \in B \\ \min_{m} \widetilde{\mathscr{P}}_{mn}\,;\ if\, n \in C \end{cases} \end{cases} \tag{19}$$

where $\mathscr{B}$ represents a benefit group of criteria and $\mathscr{C}$ is known as a group of Cost criteria with $m = 1,2,\ldots,\mathscr{V}$ and $n = 1,2,\ldots,\mathscr{U}$.

4. **Score value of decision matrix**: In this step, the score value of the decision matrix was evaluated by using Equation (6) and the score valued matrix $(\mathfrak{D}_{\mathfrak{N}})$ takes the form of $\mathfrak{D}_{\mathfrak{N}} = [\mathcal{G}_{mn}]_{(\mathcal{V}+2)\times\mathcal{U}}$.
5. **Normalization of the Score Valued Decision Matrix:** The extended score valued decision matrix is normalized by using the following formulas,

$$\widetilde{\mathcal{N}}_{mn} = \begin{cases} \dfrac{\mathcal{G}_{mn}^{AII}}{\mathcal{G}_{mn}}\,;\, if\, n \in C \\ \dfrac{\mathcal{G}_{mn}}{\mathcal{G}_{mn}^{AI}}\,;\, if\, n \in B \end{cases} \tag{20}$$

and the normalized matrix takes the form as, $\widetilde{\mathfrak{D}}_{\mathfrak{N}} = [\widetilde{\mathcal{N}}_{mn}]_{(\mathcal{V}+2)\times\mathcal{U}}$ where $m = 1,2,\ldots,\mathcal{V}$ and $n = 1,2,\ldots,\mathcal{U}$.

6. **Construction of Weighted Normalized Matrix:** In this step, the weighted normalized matrix $(\mathfrak{D}_{\mathfrak{WN}})$, using Equation (17), as follows

$$\mathfrak{D}_{\mathfrak{WN}} = [\hat{k}_{mn}]_{(\mathcal{V}+2)\times\mathcal{U}} = [\widetilde{\mathcal{N}}_{mn} \times \mathcal{W}_{n}]_{(\mathcal{V}+2)\times\mathcal{U}} \tag{21}$$

where $\mathcal{W}_n$ is the weight associated with the criteria n $(n = 1,2,\ldots,\mathcal{U})$.

7. **Calculating the Utility Degree:** The utility degree of alternatives $\mathcal{K}_m^{+}$ and $\mathcal{K}_m^{-}$ are calculated by using the following equation,

$$\begin{cases} \mathcal{K}_m^{-} = \dfrac{\mathcal{S}_m}{\mathcal{S}_{AAI}} \\ \mathcal{K}_m^{+} = \dfrac{\mathcal{S}_m}{\mathcal{S}_{AI}} \end{cases} \tag{22}$$

where $\mathcal{S}_m$ $(m = 1,2,\ldots,\mathcal{V})$ is the sum of the elements of the mth row of the Weighted normalized matrix $\mathfrak{D}_{\mathfrak{WN}}$, i.e., $\mathcal{S}_m = \sum_{m=1}^{\mathcal{V}} \hat{k}_{mn}$.

8. **Determining the Utility Function:** The utility function corresponding to each alternative is evaluated in this step. It is evaluated by using the following formula,

$$(\mathcal{K}_m) = \frac{(\mathcal{K}_m^{+} + \mathcal{K}_m^{-})}{1 + \dfrac{1 - f(\mathcal{K}_m^{+})}{f(\mathcal{K}_m^{+})} + \dfrac{1 - f(\mathcal{K}_m^{-})}{f(\mathcal{K}_m^{-})}} \tag{23}$$

where, $\ell(\mathcal{K}_m^-)$ is the utility function associated with the Anti-Ideal solution and it is calculated with the help of the equation, $\ell(\mathcal{K}_m^-) = \frac{\mathcal{K}_m^+}{(\mathcal{K}_m^+ + \mathcal{K}_m^-)}$ and $\ell(\mathcal{K}_m^+)$ is the utility function related to the Ideal solution and it is evaluated by using the equation, $\ell(\mathcal{K}_m^+) = \frac{\mathcal{K}_m^-}{(\mathcal{K}_m^+ + \mathcal{K}_m^-)}$ with $m = 1,2,\ldots,\mathcal{V}$.

9. **Ranking of Alternatives:** Depending on the value of the utility function $(\ell(\mathcal{K}_m))$, the ranking of alternatives is performed where alternatives are $m = 1,2,\ldots,\mathcal{V}$. An alternative that obtains the highest value of the utility function receives the first rank; similarly, an alternative that obtains the second-highest value of the utility function receives the second rank and so on.

5. CRITERIA SELECTION FOR MEDIUM OF STUDY

Choosing a medium of study in higher secondary education depends on several crucial factors, including accessibility, academic performance, future employability and economic affordability. Private English medium schools are mostly situated in urban areas, whereas state board regional language schools are mostly found in rural areas. Hindi-medium schools can be found in both areas, but in smaller numbers, unless the regional language is Hindi. Private English medium schools often provide more facilities with more proficient teachers who can effortlessly teach complex subjects like science and mathematics in English. Although students from rural areas face financial difficulties in affording it, those from urban areas often study in expensive English-medium schools as a status symbol. All the criteria are discussed in detail below:

5.1 Accessibility $(\mathcal{C}_1)$:

Accessibility (Sabharwal, 2021) plays a crucial role in determining the medium of study for students during their high school years. In rural and semi-urban areas, government schools primarily offer the medium of instruction in the regional language, which is often the only option available to a vast student population. On the contrary, English-medium schools are generally located in the urban areas. Moreover, it is challenging to have a sufficient supply of proficient teachers who can effectively teach complex subjects like Biology, Physics, and chemistry in fluent English. This shortage of quality educators often influences students' decisions to choose English as their primary medium for higher secondary studies.

5.2 Academic Performance $(\mathscr{C}_2)$:

There is a genuine connection between academic performance (Baranwal, 2024; Mezhoudi et al., 2023) and the medium of instruction. Students generally perform well when they study in their native language. Studying in the mother tongue enhances the conceptual clarity and critical thinking of the students, making them more likely to understand the depth of the subject. But on the contrary, to perform well in national-level exams like JEE or NEET, one must study in the English medium, as there is no option available to give the exam in any other language except English. Moreover, all the available study materials are also only in English. As a result, many students choose English as the medium of study to gain an advantage in competitive examinations, despite facing some initial difficulties.

5.3 Future Employability $(\mathscr{C}_3)$:

To thrive in India's competitive job market, it is essential to have fluency in English. Proficiency in English has a significant impact on an individual's employability (Mezhoudi et al., 2023). The capability of speaking in English is often considered a key skill in multinational companies, corporations and startups. Better communication skills offer a greater potential for career advancement. To achieve professionalism and secure anticipated jobs, students often opt for English over their native language.

5.4 Preference of Parent $(\mathscr{C}_4)$:

The preference of parents (Kumar & Choudhury, 2021) often plays a crucial role in choosing the medium of study for their children. Involvement of parent in making decisions often reflects their own ambitions, social status and experience in schooling. Most parents view English-medium schools as the gateway to success and social recognition. The parents who are not fluent in English believe that studying in English would provide opportunities to their children that they never had. As a result, the parents' decision undermines the student's comfort in their higher secondary studies.

5.5 Quality of Education $(\mathscr{C}_5)$:

Quality of education (Baranwal, 2024) in a school often determines the choice of medium of instruction. In India, English-medium private schools often provide a higher-quality of education, complemented by superior infrastructure, smaller class sizes, modern teaching methodologies and various extracurricular activities. On the contrary, government funded Hindi medium or regional language medium schools are lacking in providing the facilities as the private English medium schools. These differences encourage families to invest more in a better learning environment and achieve superior academic results.

5.6 Economic Affordability $(\mathscr{C}_6)$:

Economic affordability (Patel, 2022) is an essential factor for most of families in India. There is a huge difference in the fee structure between English medium private schools and government sponsored Hindi medium and regional medium schools. Private English-medium schools often charge a high amount, including tuition fees, transportation fees, library fees, laboratory fees, games fees, and development fees, among others. This huge financial burden often limits many parents from choosing English medium schools for their children. As a result, many students choose government sponsored regional and Hindi medium schools as the only affordable option due to the economic barrier of their families.

5.7 Socio-Cultural factors $(\mathscr{C}_7)$:

Socio-cultural factors (Mishra, 2013) often play a significant role in determining the medium of instruction for higher secondary studies. There exists a significant urban-rural division when making a decision in this matter. Students from urban areas mostly choose to study in the English medium as a status symbol, whereas students from rural areas prefer the Hindi medium, especially the state language medium, for studying, as it fosters a stronger bond with the regional language. Psychologically, fluency in speaking English often conveys modernism and confidence, implying a higher social and financial standing. On the contrary, regional languages are more closely associated with preserving culture and traditions.

6. PROPOSED ALTERNATIVES

We can categorize the schools in India mainly into three sections based on the medium of study offered by them. Every state has its own regional language and schools offer the medium of instruction in the state language. Hindi is understood by most Indians, especially in the north. So, there exist a plenty number of Hindi medium schools all over India. However, in modern times, the growth in the number of English-medium schools is significant. Primarily, ICSE and CBSE boards offer English-medium schools, which are mostly private. All the alternative languages are discussed below:

6.1 English $(\mathscr{A}_1)$:

English medium schools are emerging significantly in the modern era. The ICSE and CBSE boards primarily offer English-medium schools all over India. English medium schools are mostly private and generally offer high-quality services to their students. The classrooms, washrooms and school buildings are generally cleaned on a regular basis, making hygiene a key attraction for students and parents. They conduct pedagogical training for teachers on a regular basis and provide numerous extracurricular activities for the students, but the expense is substantial. Families from urban areas often prefer English medium schools as a status symbol. Fluency in English provides students with an advantage in corporate and multinational company jobs.

6.2 Hindi $(\mathscr{A}_2)$:

Hindi is the official language of India, along with English. Hindi is understood throughout India, particularly in northern India. Hindi-medium schools are primarily sponsored by the state government, with some also receiving support from the central government. Parents who have transferred jobs often prefer Hindi as the medium of instruction for their child because it is unlikely to find the same atmosphere in any other state.

6.3 Regional Language $(\mathscr{A}_3)$:

India is a country of diversity. Every state has their own regional language. As a result, many state schools offer various languages as a medium of instruction, depending on their location. For example, West Bengal primarily offers Bengali-medium schools, Gujarat offers Gujarati-medium schools, Maharashtra offers Marathi-medium schools, Punjab offers Punjabi-medium schools, etc. Though there are some private schools offering state language as the medium, but most of the state board schools are sponsored by the state government of that particular region. Students mostly from rural areas choose state board schools, preserving their cultural values.

7. MODEL FORMULATION AND DATA COLLECTION

In this section, we will discuss about the model formulation and data collection process. Here, we want to design a model composed of two popular MCDM techniques, namely CRITIC and the MARCOS method. In this chapter, we have included Triangular Neutrosophic Numbers to incorporate the uncertainty in the dataset. Here, a total of 7 criteria and 3 alternatives are considered to develop the framework and 3 decision experts have given their decision in linguistic terms with the help of Table 1. The specifics of these three DMs are given as follows:

DM1: A policymaker from the Ministry of Education.
DM2: A professor in the education department at a university.
DM3: An administrative head of the department of education in a district.

Table 1. Conversion table between linguistic terms and Triangular Neutrosophic Number

Linguistic term	**Triangular Neutrosophic Number**	**Score Value**	**Accuracy Value**
Absolutely Important (AI)	< (9,9.5,10); 0.90,0.06,0.08 >	9.5	10.3
Strongly Important (SI)	< (8.5,9,9.5); 0.85,0.09,0.12 >	9.0	9.2
Very Important (VI)	< (8,8.5,9); 0.82,0.10,0.14 >	8.5	8.5
Equally Important (EI)	< (7.5,8,8.5); 0.78,0.14,0.18 >	8.0	7.4
Moderately Important (MI)	< (7,7.5,8); 0.73,0.19,0.22 >	7.4	6.2
Poor Important (PI)	< (6.5,7,7.5); 0.69,0.25,0.28 >	7.0	5.1
Less Important (LI)	< (6,6.5,7); 0.66,0.28,0.31 >	6.5	4.4

Based on the opinions of decision experts, three 3×7 decision matrices are formulated using linguistic terms. These three decision matrices are shown in Table 2. Further, each entry of these decision matrices is converted to an equivalent Triangular Neutrosophic Number with the help of Table 1. These decision matrices are taken into account for further evaluation.

Table 2. Decision matrices in linguistic terms given by three decision makers

	Criteria vs Alternative	Accessibility $(\mathscr{C}_1)$	Academic Performance $(\mathscr{C}_2)$	Future Employability $(\mathscr{C}_3)$	Preference of Parent $(\mathscr{C}_4)$	Quality of Education $(\mathscr{C}_5)$	Economic Affordability $(\mathscr{C}_6)$	Socio-Cultural factors $(\mathscr{C}_7)$
DM1	English $(\mathscr{A}_1)$	SI	AI	VI	VI	SI	VI	SI
	Hindi $(\mathscr{A}_2)$	MI	VI	MI	EI	VI	SI	VI
	Regional Language $(\mathscr{A}_3)$	VI	MI	VI	MI	EI	MI	MI
DM2	English $(\mathscr{A}_1)$	MI	SI	AI	SI	MI	VI	MI
	Hindi $(\mathscr{A}_2)$	AI	VI	SI	MI	SI	MI	EI
	Regional Language $(\mathscr{A}_3)$	SI	SI	MI	VI	MI	EI	VI
DM3	English $(\mathscr{A}_1)$	AI	VI	SI	MI	AI	MI	EI
	Hindi $(\mathscr{A}_2)$	SI	MI	MI	SI	MI	VI	MI
	Regional Language $(\mathscr{A}_3)$	MI	SI	VI	EI	EI	MI	VI

8. NUMERICAL ILLUSTRATION

In this section, we will describe about the numerical calculation. At first, we have performed the CRITIC method as discussed in Subsection 4.1. Here we aggregate these 3 decision matrices into a single Aggregated decision matrix and then calculate the score value of each entry of the aggregated decision matrix using Equation (6). After that, proceeding step by step as mentioned in the CRITIC method, we finally evaluated the weight associated with each criterion. Each criterion, along with its associated weight, is shown in Table 3.

Table 3. Weight of the criteria evaluated by the CRITIC method

Criteria	Weight
Accessibility $(\mathscr{C}_1)$	0.130
Academic Performance $(\mathscr{C}_2)$	0.152
Future Employability $(\mathscr{C}_3)$	0.149
Preference of Parent $(\mathscr{C}_4)$	0.104
Quality of Education $(\mathscr{C}_5)$	0.076
Economic Affordability $(\mathscr{C}_6)$	0.219
Socio-Cultural factors $(\mathscr{C}_7)$	0.171

Remark: From Table 3, we have come to know that the criterion Economic Affordability $(\mathscr{C}_6)$ acquired the weight 0.219, which is the highest weight among all criteria, the criterion Socio-Cultural factors $(\mathscr{C}_7)$ takes the 2nd highest weight, i.e., 0.171 and so on. Figure 1 shows the Pie diagram helps to visualize the criteria along with their weight.

Figure 1. Pi diagram of the criteria weights

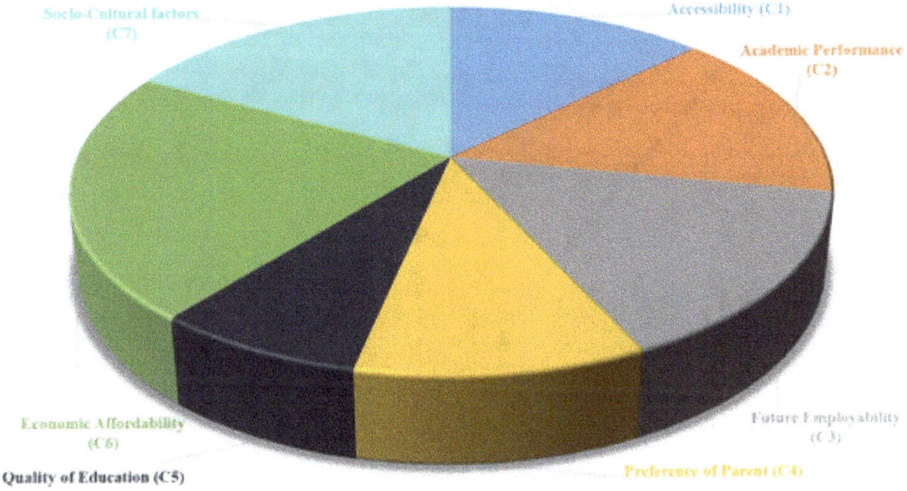

After finding the criteria weight, we have applied the MARCOS method. In this method, after constructing the Aggregated decision matrix, we have formulated an Extended decision matrix including an Ideal solution (AI) and an Anti-Ideal solution (AAI). Then we have converted to a crisp valued Extended decision matrix using the score function given in Equation (6). Further, we have proceeded as mentioned in the MARCOS method and finally, we have evaluated the Utility degrees $\mathscr{K}^{+}_{m}$, $\mathscr{K}^{-}_{m}$ and Utility function $f(\mathscr{K}_{m})$ of alternatives which are shown in Table 4.

Table 4. Alternatives ranking by the MARCOS method with associated data

Alternatives	k^+	k^-	$k^+ + k^-$	$f(k^+)$	$f(k^-)$	$\frac{(1-f(k^+))}{f(k^+)}$	$\frac{(1-f(k^+))}{f(k^+)}$	$f(k)$	Rank
English $(\mathscr{A}_1)$	0.994	1.366	2.360	0.579	0.421	0.727	1.375	0.761	1
Hindi $(\mathscr{A}_2)$	0.753	1.036	1.789	0.579	0.421	0.727	1.375	0.577	2
Regional Language $(\mathscr{A}_3)$	0.729	1.002	1.731	0.579	0.421	0.727	1.375	0.558	3

From Table 4., depending on the value of Utility function, we have obtained that the alternative English $(\mathscr{A}_1)$ pursued the 1st ranking, Hindi $(\mathscr{A}_2)$ achieved the 2nd ranking and the alternative Regional Language $(\mathscr{A}_3)$ got the 3rd ranking. Figure 2 represents the bar graph, which shows the value of the utility function of each alternative, and it helps us to visualise how these value helps to rank the alternatives.

Figure 2. Bar diagram of the different medium of study with their $\boldsymbol{f(k)}$ *score*

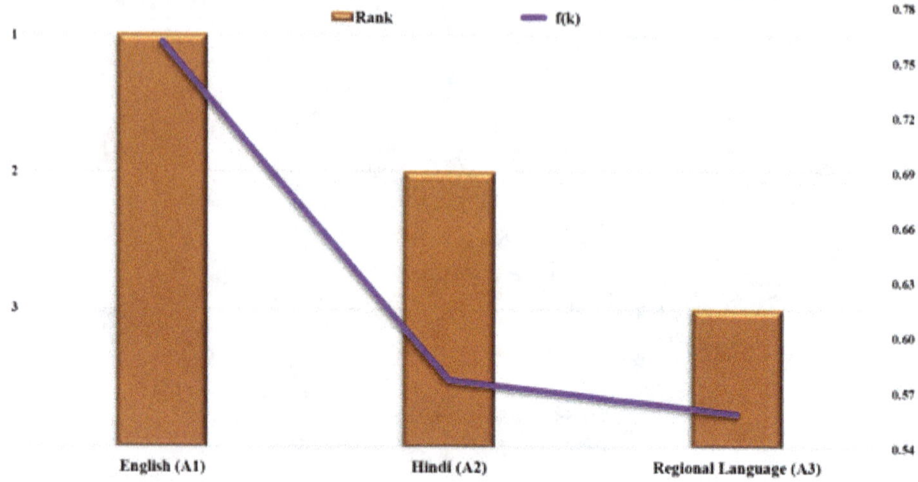

9. CONCLUSION

In a country like India, there is significant linguistic diversity. In the process of providing learning opportunities at the higher secondary level, the medium of instruction plays a vital role. In this chapter, we have formulated a CRITIC-MARCOS-based framework in a Triangular Neutrosophic Number environment to identify the best alternative language as a medium of instruction at the higher secondary level. Here, we have considered 7 factors as criteria and 3 language options as alternatives. After collecting the data set from 3 decision-making experts, we have obtained that the criterion Economic Affordability $(\mathscr{C}_6)$ has the highest weightage and the criterion Quality of Education $(\mathscr{C}_5)$ has the lowest weightage in this decision-making problem. In our final result after considering all factors, we have evaluated that the alternative English $(\mathscr{A}_1)$ is the best option as a medium of instruction in higher secondary level.

This model will be very impactful in improving our educational policies and advancing educational facilities. There are also some future research scopes. In this paper, we have included two MCDM-based optimization approaches, whereas one can include some other effective MCDM techniques. Here, we have applied triangular neutrosophic numbers to account for uncertainty in the data; one can also use other newly developed fuzzy numbers. Here, we have considered regional languages as one alternative, but one can consider specific languages belonging to this category as distinct alternatives. Thus, the number of alternatives will be increased.

REFERENCES

Abdul, D., Wenqi, J., Tanveer, A., & Sameeroddin, M. (2024). Comprehensive analysis of renewable energy technologies adoption in remote areas using the integrated delphi-fuzzy AHP-VIKOR approach. *Arabian Journal for Science and Engineering*, *49*(5), 7585–7610.

Adhikari, D., Gazi, K. H., Basuri, T., Giri, B. C., Mandal, S., Ramalingam, S., & Mondal, S. P. (2025). Contribution of Education in Women Empowerment: An Innovative Neutrosophic Approach on MCDM Method. Journal of Uncertain Systems, 1-32.

Afful-Dadzie, E., Oplatkova, Z. K., & Beltran Prieto, L. A. (2017). Comparative state-of-the-art survey of classical fuzzy set and intuitionistic fuzzy sets in multi-criteria decision making. *International Journal of Fuzzy Systems*, *19*(3), 726–738.

Aktar, S. (2021). New education policy 2020 of India: A theoretical analysis. *International Journal of Business and Management Research*, *9*(3), 302–306.

Al-subhi, S. H., Papageorgiou, E. I., Pérez, P. P., Mahdi, G. S. S., & Acuna, L. A. (2021). Triangular neutrosophic cognitive map for multistage sequential decision-making problems. *International Journal of Fuzzy Systems*, *23*(3), 657–679.

Azam, M., Chin, A., & Prakash, N. (2013). The returns to English-language skills in India. *Economic Development and Cultural Change*, *61*(2), 335–367.

Baranwal, R. (2024). Quality-deterioration, English Studies, Problems and Challenges in Higher Education System of India. *The SPL Journal of Literary Hermeneutics: A Biannual International Journal of Independent Critical Thinking*, *4*(2), 78-95.

Basuri, T., Gazi, K. H., Bhaduri, P., Das, S. G., & Mondal, S. P. (2025). Decision-analytics-based sustainable location problem-neutrosophic CRITIC-COPRAS assessment model. *Management Science Advances*, *2*(1), 19–58.

Bilişik, Ö. N., Duman, N. H., & Taş, E. (2024). A novel interval-valued intuitionistic fuzzy CRITIC-TOPSIS methodology: An application for transportation mode selection problem for a glass production company. *Expert Systems with Applications*, *235*, 121134.

Biswas, A., Gazi, K. H., Bhaduri, P., & Mondal, S. P. (2024). Neutrosophic fuzzy decision-making framework for site selection. *Journal of Decision Analytics and Intelligent Computing*, *4*(1), 187–215.

Broumi, S., Bakali, A., & Bahnasse, A. (2018). Neutrosophic sets: An overview. Infinite Study, 410(1).

Demir, G., Chatterjee, P., Kadry, S., Abdelhadi, A., & Pamučar, D. (2024). Measurement of alternatives and ranking according to compromise solution (MARCOS) method: a comprehensive bibliometric analysis. *Decision making: applications in management and engineering, 7*(2), 313-336.

Diakoulaki, D., Mavrotas, G., & Papayannakis, L. (1995). Determining objective weights in multiple criteria problems: The critic method. *Computers & Operations Research, 22*(7), 763–770.

Divya, B., & Ganesan, K. (2025). Solution of Second Order Fuzzy Differential Equations using Sumudu Transform under Neutrosophic Environment. [IJNS]. *International Journal of Neutrosophic Science, 26*(1).

Divya, C., Raju, L. S., & Singaravel, B. (2020). Application of MCDM methods for process parameter optimization in turning process—a review. *Recent Trends in Mechanical Engineering: Select Proceedings of ICIME 2020*, 199-207.

Dwivedi, R., Prasad, K., Jha, P. K., & Singh, S. (2021). An integrated CRITIC-MARCOS technique for analysing the performance of steel industry. In *Data-Driven Optimization of Manufacturing Processes* (pp. 115–127). IGI Global Scientific Publishing.

Ecer, F., & Pamucar, D. (2021). MARCOS technique under intuitionistic fuzzy environment for determining the COVID-19 pandemic performance of insurance companies in terms of healthcare services. *Applied Soft Computing, 104*, 107199.

Endow, T. (2018). Inferior outcomes: Learning in low-cost English-medium private schools—A survey in Delhi and National Capital Region. *Indian Journal of Human Development, 12*(1), 1–19.

Fahmi, A., Amin, F., & Ullah, H. (2021). Multiple attribute group decision making based on weighted aggregation operators of triangular neutrosophic cubic fuzzy numbers. *Granular Computing, 6*(2), 421–433.

Gazi, K. H., Mondal, S. P., Chatterjee, B., Ghorui, N., Ghosh, A., & De, D. (2023). A new synergistic strategy for ranking restaurant locations: A decision-making approach based on the hexagonal fuzzy numbers. *Operations Research, 57*(2), 571–608.

Huskanović, E., Stević, Ž., & Simić, S. (2023). Objective-subjective CRITIC-MARCOS model for selection forklift in internal transport technology processes. *Mechatronics and Intelligent Transportation Systems, 2*(1), 20–31.

Kahraman, C., Öztayşi, B., & Çevik Onar, S. (2016). A comprehensive literature review of 50 years of fuzzy set theory. International Journal of Computational Intelligence Systems, 9(sup1), 3-24.

Krishankumar, R., Mishra, A. R., Rani, P., Ecer, F., & Ravichandran, K. S. (2023). Assessment of zero-carbon measures for sustainable transportation in smart cities: A CRITIC-MARCOS framework based on Q-rung fuzzy preferences. *IEEE Internet of Things Journal, 10*(21), 18651–18662.

Kumar, D., & Choudhury, P. K. (2021). Determinants of private school choice in India: All about the family backgrounds? *Journal of School Choice, 15*(4), 576–602.

Kumar, K., Prakash, A., & Singh, K. (2021). How National Education Policy 2020 can be a lodestar to transform future generation in India. *Journal of Public Affairs, 21*(3), e2500.

Lightfoot, A., Balasubramanian, A., Tsimpli, I., Mukhopadhyay, L., & Treffers-Daller, J. (2022). Measuring the multilingual reality: Lessons from classrooms in Delhi and Hyderabad. *International Journal of Bilingual Education and Bilingualism, 25*(6), 2208–2228.

Mandal, S., Gazi, K. H., Salahshour, S., Mondal, S. P., Bhattacharya, P., & Saha, A. K. (2024). Application of interval valued intuitionistic fuzzy uncertain mcdm methodology for ph. d supervisor selection problem. Results in control and optimization, 15, 100411.

Mezhoudi, N., Alghamdi, R., Aljunaid, R., Krichna, G., & Düştegör, D. (2023). Employability prediction: A survey of current approaches, research challenges and applications. *Journal of Ambient Intelligence and Humanized Computing, 14*(3), 1489–1505.

Mishra, U. K. (2013). Learning English for development and economy in India: A socio-cultural perspective. *English Language Teacher Education in a Diverse Environment*, 186.

Momena, A. F., Biswas, A., Gazi, K. H., & Mondal, S. P. (2025, January). Adaptation Challenges of Electric Vehicles in Third World Countries. In 2025 *9th International Conference on Management Engineering, Software Engineering and Service Sciences (ICMSS)* (pp. 63-67). IEEE.

Nakamura, P., Molotsky, A., Zarzur, R. C., Ranjit, V., Haddad, Y., & De Hoop, T. (2023). Language of instruction in schools in low-and middle-income countries: A systematic review. *Campbell Systematic Reviews, 19*(4), e1351.

Pajić, V., Andrejić, M., Jolović, M., & Kilibarda, M. (2024). Strategic warehouse location selection in business logistics: A novel approach using imf SWARA–MARCOS—A case study of a Serbian logistics service provider. *Mathematics, 12*(5), 776.

Patel, V. (2022). Affordability and Equity Concerns in Private Higher Education Institutions. In *India Higher Education Report 2021* (pp. 205–225). Routledge India.

Pratyusha, M. N., & Kumar, R. (2024). Advancements in critical path method using neutrosophic theory: a review. *Uncertainty discourse and applications, 1*(1), 73-78.

Ranjan, R., Rajak, S., & Chatterjee, P. (2023). Material selection for sintered pulley in automobile: An integrated CRITIC-MARCOS model. *Reports in Mechanical Engineering, 4*(1), 225–240.

Ribeiro, M., Henriques, T., Castro, L., Souto, A., Antunes, L., Costa-Santos, C., & Teixeira, A. (2021). The entropy universe. *Entropy (Basel, Switzerland), 23*(2), 222.

Sabharwal, N. S. (2021). Nature of access to higher education in India: emerging pattern of social and spatial inequalities in educational opportunities. In *Reflections on 21st Century Human Habitats in India: Felicitation Volume in Honour of Professor MH Qureshi* (pp. 345–369). Springer Singapore.

Sarıgül, S. S., Ünlü, M., & Yaşar, E. (2023). Financial performance analysis of airlines operating in Europe: CRITIC based MAUT and MARCOS methods. *International Journal of Business and Economic Studies, 5*(2), 76–97.

Singh, R., Pathak, V. K., Kumar, R., Dikshit, M., Aherwar, A., Singh, V., & Singh, T. (2024). A historical review and analysis on MOORA and its fuzzy extensions for different applications. *Heliyon, 10*(3).

Smarandache, F. Neutrosophic Logic -A Generalization of the Intuitionistic Fuzzy Logic. In Proceedings of the *3rd Conference of the European Society for Fuzzy Logic and Technology*, Zittau, Germany, 10–12 September 2003.

Stević, Ž., Pamučar, D., Puška, A., & Chatterjee, P. (2020). Sustainable supplier selection in healthcare industries using a new MCDM method: Measurement of alternatives and ranking according to COmpromise solution (MARCOS). *Computers & Industrial Engineering, 140*, 106231.

Su, J., Xu, B., Liu, H., Chen, Y., & Tingting, L. (2025). An improved CRITIC–MARCOS method based on a group consensus model for selecting low-carbon logistics service providers. *Kybernetes*.

Tripath, S. K., Dey, A., & Broumi, S. (2024). Exploring neutrosophic linear programming in advanced fuzzy contexts. *Neutrosophic sets and systems, 66*, 170-184.

Wang, Y., Wang, W., Wang, Z., Deveci, M., Roy, S. K., & Kadry, S. (2024). Selection of sustainable food suppliers using the Pythagorean fuzzy CRITIC-MARCOS method. *Information Sciences*, *664*, 120326.

Xiao, Z., Xia, S., Gong, K., & Li, D. (2012). The trapezoidal fuzzy soft set and its application in MCDM. *Applied Mathematical Modelling*, *36*(12), 5844–5855.

Zadeh, L. A. (1965). Fuzzy sets. *Information and Control*, *8*(3), 338–353.

Chapter 13
Study of the Opinions of Pedagogical Department Students on the Existence of School Bullying in Primary and Secondary Education With the Help of AFC

Amalia Karamitrou
http://orcid.org/0009-0005-1248-5089
Hellenic Open University, Greece

ABSTRACT

This study investigates, identifies, and examines in depth the views, perceptions, and attitudes of first-year students about bullying in education, and specifically about bullying as they experienced it during their years of secondary education. More specifically, it studies the attitudes of 182 students who stated that they experienced bullying to a small or large degree, either in middle school or high school. The instrument used is the Child Adolescent Bullying Scale (CABS), constructed by Strout et al. (2018), which consists of 20 items. The reliability of CABS was particularly high. Factorial Correspondence Analysis was applied for the data analysis. The results, among other findings, revealed distinct groups of students for whom the effects of school bullying during their school years were so unpleasant that they even developed a tendency to withdraw from school life or change their school environment.

DOI: 10.4018/979-8-3373-6926-6.ch013

THEORETICAL FRAMEWORK

The phenomenon of school bullying has taken on enormous proportions (Björkqvist, 1994; Beale, 2001; Cabrera et al., 2022; Zhang et al., 2020). Cabrera & Guerrero (2019) argue that bullying has serious negative effects on many primary school children and secondary school adolescents. Possibly, multicultural society has caused many negative reactions in the global social sphere. Strout et al. (2017) reports that these effects are so unpleasant for students that they can even cause health problems requiring pediatric medical care in order to be treated. Zhang et al. (2020) add that bullying victimization among school students has raised serious public health concerns, as it is directly related to multiple problems associated with mental health.

According to international literature, school bullying is categorized into four types: verbal bullying, physical bullying, emotional or relational bullying, and sexual bullying (Valdivia-Salas et al., 2021; U.S. Department of Education, *Preventing Bullying: A Manual for Schools and Communities*, Washington, DC, USA, 1998). Donnelly et al. (2019) add another category of bullying, which is cyberbullying, or bullying in cyberspace (malicious or offensive messages, comments, or photos on the Internet). The authors add that all five aforementioned types of school bullying are characterized by unique features and defined dimensions that are used with the aim of harassing the victim (Donnelly et al., 2019).

Verbal bullying is a form of verbal aggression that includes insults, threats, mockery, laughter, and teasing remarks, which usually refer to the victim's body shape and overall appearance (Strout et al., 2018; Tania et al., 2018).

RESEARCH AIM

The aim of the present study is to investigate and conduct an in-depth analysis of the opinions, perceptions, and attitudes of first-year university students regarding bullying in education, and more specifically, the bullying they experienced during their secondary education years. The study is carried out with the help of Correspondence Factor Analysis (Benzecri, 1973; Anastasiadou, 2016; Papadimitriou, 1994) and the MAD software (Karapistolis, 2015).

RESEARCH TOOL

The tool used in this study is the Child Adolescent Bullying Scale (CABS) by Strout et al. (2018), which consists of 20 statements rated on a 5-point Likert scale, where 1 corresponds to strongly disagree, 2 to disagree, 3 to neither agree nor disagree, 4 to agree, and 5 to strongly agree. The statements explore the extent to which respondents experienced, during their school years, situations such as classmates intentionally trying to make them feel bad, one or more children behaving badly toward them, being mocked to feel bad, attempts to turn others against them, being put in trouble, experiencing bullying at school, having their belongings taken or destroyed on purpose, being hurt intentionally by another student, being threatened in a harmful way, feeling reluctant to attend school due to intimidation, wishing to attend another school because of bullying, pretending to be sick to stay home from school, being deliberately ignored by other children, having malicious or offensive messages, comments, or photos posted about them online.

Additionally, the statements examine if classmates teased or annoyed them in ways they found disturbing, whether such teasing bothered them, whether they worried about bullying so much that they could not concentrate at school, if classmates spoke behind their backs, shared secrets, or spread rumors, if they were excluded or ignored for being different, and whether they have upsetting memories of bullying.

Regarding respondents' demographic information, the variables included were gender (male, female), age, school location (rural, semi-urban, urban), school track (theoretical, scientific, technological), field of study (Social Sciences, Economics and Law, Health Sciences, Physical Sciences), and year of study (first, second, third, fourth, graduate).

Sample

The demographic characteristics of the 182 respondents in the study are presented in the following Table 1.

Table 1. Demographic Characteristics

Demographic characteristics	Category	Frequency (N=182)	Relative Frequency (%)
Gender	Male	88	48,4
	Female	94	51,6
Age	19	19	10,4
	20	58	31,9
	21	42	23,1
	22	33	18,1
	≥22	30	16.4
School Location	Rural	91	50

continued on following page

Table 1. Continued

Demographic characteristics	Category	Frequency (N=182)	Relative Frequency (%)
	Semi-urban	55	30,2
	Urban	36	19,8
School Track	Theoretical	27	14,8
	Scientific	138	70,3
	Technological	27	14,8
Field of Study	Social Sciences	56	.30,8
	Economics	12	6,6
	Law	35	19,2
	Health Sciences	45	24,7
	Sciences	34	18,7
Year of Study	First	137	40.9
	Second	154	46
	Third	35	10,4
	Fourth	5	1,5
	Graduate	4	1,2

METHODOLOGY

Within the framework of the research process, absolute and relative frequencies were recorded using classical statistical methods for the 20 statements/variables of the Child Adolescent Bullying Scale (CABS) by Strout et al. (2018). These were categorized into three classes, each representing 25%, 50%, and 25%, respectively, as well as for the six demographic variables related to the participants' characteristics. Specifically, the demographic variable gender was categorized into two classes (male–female), age into five, school location into three, school track into three, field of study into five, and year of study into five.

Subsequently, the 25 statements/variables/items, categorized into their respective classes, resulted in a total of 78 elements in our study, which were represented in a logical 0–1 table. This categorization produced a k × k contingency table of absolute and relative frequencies, known as a Burt table. Each column of the Burt table is considered a vector in a k-dimensional space. The Burt table allowed the study of each class both primarily and secondarily for each variable individually, and then the cross-analysis of variable classes.

With the main goal of identifying these relationships, the k × k contingency tables (Burt tables) were used, containing in their rows and columns all the classes into which the CABS scale statements (Strout et al., 2018) and the supplementary demographic variables were divided. Consequently, each element of the Burt table depends exclusively on two variables, thus revealing the relationship between them.

This research required no a priori assumptions, and therefore, data processing was conducted using Data Analysis methods. This condition was fully met by the methods of Multidimensional Statistical Analysis without models (Benzecri, 1973; Anastasiadou, 2016; Karapistolis, 2015; Menexes, 2007; Papadimitriou, 1994). The choice of these methods is based on the fact that traditional statistical assumptions are not applied to analyze the phenomenon described by the data table. Instead, the methods aim for a more detailed identification of the underlying structure. By determining the characteristics of the variables that influence participants' behaviors and attitudes, it becomes possible to approach the actual dimensions that bullying takes in our country.

From the Data Analysis methods mentioned earlier, Correspondence Factor Analysis (Analyse Factorielle des Correspondances) was selected for the data analysis (Anastasiadou, 2019). Correspondence Factor Analysis allows the simultaneous statistical processing of categorized qualitative and quantitative variables (Benzecri, 1980; Anastasiadou, 2016; Karapistolis, 2015; Papadimitriou, 1994; Florou, 1997).

Using this method, dominant groups of observations are clustered, achieving an almost complete description of the phenomenon represented by the analyzed table through a smaller number of new composite variables—factors (Papadimitriou, 1994). These factors, which are mutually independent in pairs, are created by combining groups of original variables, greatly simplifying the process of identifying relationships between variables and providing a more comprehensive and detailed picture of the phenomenon under study. Factors can be represented as axes and, in pairs, form factorial planes, allowing the graphical visualization of variables.

Next, the contribution and correlation indices are presented, which serve as criteria for selecting variables in constructing and interpreting the axes, and consequently, the factorial planes. The contribution of a row or column point to the construction of each axis is considered. Let λ be the total inertia along axis k, and let λ be the partial inertia along part of axis k and $f_i F_k^2(i)$ is the inertia of point i corresponding to the cloud N_I along a given axis k, then the contribution of that point $Ctr_k(i)$ is calculated using the formula, $Ctr_k(i) = \frac{f_i F_k^2(i)}{\lambda_k}$ with $\sum_{i=1}^{n} Ctr_k(i) = 1$ for each axis k. This contribution represents the percentage of the point's inertia relative to the inertia explained by the factorial axis.

Points with a high contribution $Ctr_k(i)$ significantly influence the interpretation of the axis (Anastasiadou, 2000; Drosos, 2004; Moschidis, 2003; Papadimitriou, 2007).

The squared cosine $\cos_k{}^2(i)$, corresponding to the relative contribution, reflects the quality of representation of a point on the factorial axis and essentially shows a form of correlation between point i and the factorial axis k corresponding to the relative contribution, reflects the quality of representation of a point i on the factorial axis and essentially shows a form of correlation between point i and the factorial axis k it is denoted by $Cor_k(i)$ and defined as $Cor_k(i) = \frac{F_k^2(i)}{d^2(G,i)} = \cos^2\omega$, with $d^2(G,i)$ the distance between i from the centroid (Drosos, 2004).

A high value of $Cor_k(i)$indicates a small angle ω between the point ι and the axis, meaning a strong correlation of point *i* with the axis and thus a good quality of projection of *i*on that axis. This index $Cor_k(i)$expresses the percentage of the inertia of point *i* that is explained by axis *k* (Anastasiadou, 2000; Drosos, 2004; Menexes, 2007; Markos, 2007; Papadimitriou, 2007).

Points that have very high *Cor* values also have high *Ctr* values. When they show high *Cor* values and low *Ctr* values, this means that they have good projection quality on the axis but do not contribute to its construction (Papadimitriou, 2007). When they have low *Cor* values and high *Ctr* values, this means that they contribute to the construction of the axis but are projected better on another axis to which they may contribute more significantly (Anastasiadou, 2016; Karapistolis, 2000; Papadimitriou, 2007).

RESULTS

The reliability of the Child Adolescent Bullying Scale (CABS) developed by Strout et al. (2018) was particularly high. Specifically, the reliability of the scale was assessed using the Cronbach's alpha coefficient, which was found to be 0.907, a value considered very high (Anastasiadou et al., 2010; Anastasiadou, 2011, 2018, 2019; Anastasiadou & Dimitriadou, 2011; Taraza & Anastasiadou, 2019; Papadaki & Anastasiadou, 2017).The indices used in the interpretation of the results of this correspondence factor analysis were: *Inertia*, and *Contribution* (Benzécri, 1980; Papadimitriou, 1994; Florou, 1997). These indices allow for the distinction between the most significant and decisive variables or items that contribute to the formation of the factorial axes. Furthermore, the results of this factor analysis were examined by taking into account both the inertia of each factorial axis and the corresponding contribution. The data analysis was carried out using the MAD method (Karapistolis, 2000; Karapistolis, 2015).

The analysis of the data table using Correspondence Factor Analysis (CFA), with the help of the MAD computation, produces the characteristic values of the Burt table as well as the inertia percentages of each factorial axis, allowing us to distinguish the main factorial axes, which are the most important for interpreting the results. The inertia percentage of each factorial axis indicates the degree of significance that each one represents.

The significance percentage of the first factorial axis is 45.11%, of the second 21.16%, of the third 14.31%, and of the fourth 5.23%, etc. The total amount of information provided by the 12 factorial axes amounts to 98.52%. The cumulative frequency of the first three factorial axes reaches 80.58% of the total data variance. This percentage is quite satisfactory for interpreting the data (Karapistolēs, 2000, 2015). The interpretation of the factorial axes resulting from the Correspondence Factor Analysis was based on the criteria of inertia, correlation, and contribution. In the present study, the first, second, and third factorial axes will be interpreted based on these criteria (Papadaki & Anastasiadou, 2017).

Interpretation of the First Factorial Axis e_1: Specifically, based on the respondents' answers as derived from the factorial analysis, the first axis–factor e_1, with an eigenvalue of 0.069, which explains 45.11% of the total variance, is constructed from those classes of variables that strongly emphasize the recognition of the negative impacts of bullying and its various forms.At first, we encounter the views of respondents who admitted that they experienced bullying at school (*Cor = 744, Ctr = 72*), and that there were times when they did not want to attend school because they were being intimidated (*Cor = 752, Ctr = 76*). Some respondents wished they could transfer to another school due to bullying (*Cor = 7914, Ctr = 85*), and as a result, pretended to be sick in order to stay home and avoid school (*Cor = 742, Ctr = 109*).

The main reason for such behavior was that they had been threatened by another student in a harmful or malicious way (*Cor = 693, Ctr = 87*), had been deliberately hurt by another student (*Cor = 703, Ctr = 62*), and that someone had taken or intentionally damaged their belongings (*Cor = 725, Ctr = 62*). Moreover, some students had posted or written malicious or offensive messages, comments, or photos about them on the Internet (*Cor = 694, Ctr = 87*), and talked behind their backs, shared their secrets, or spread rumors (*Cor = 688, Ctr = 94*).

Additionally, the gender of the respondents located on the left side of the first factorial axis (e1) corresponds to girls. On the right side of the factorial axis e_1, we find variables associated with students who are not particularly worried about bullying at school, to the extent that it would distract them from learning (*Cor = 831, Ctr = 89*), and who generally have not experienced bullying (*Cor = 821, Ctr = 75*). Therefore, they do not retain unpleasant memories of bullying (*Cor = 764, Ctr = 68*), even though their classmates might have teased or joked with them in a way that did not bother them (*Cor = 689, Ctr = 67*) and thus did not feel disturbed by their peers' teasing (*Cor = 649, Ctr = 63*). Furthermore, the gender of the respondents positioned on the right side of the first factorial axis e_1 corresponds to boys.

In conclusion, the first factorial axis reflects a strong contrast between the intense presence of bullying at school, its common forms and consequences and its absence.

Interpretation of the Second Factorial Axis e_2: Specifically, based on the respondents' answers as derived from the factorial analysis, the second axis–factor

e_2, with an eigenvalue of 0.045, explains 14.31% of the total data variance. More precisely, on the left side of the second factorial axis e_2, we find those classes of variables that express a neutral attitude regarding the extent to which respondents felt that other children at school mocked them to make them feel bad (*Cor = 766, Ctr = 128*), believed that other children at school tried to turn others against them (*Cor = 745, Ctr = 102*), or felt that other children tried to get them into trouble (*Cor = 690, Ctr = 91*).

Interpretation of the Third Factorial Axis e3: The third axis–factor e3, with an eigenvalue of 0.018, explains 5.23% of the total data variance. Specifically, on the left side of the third factorial axis e_3, we find those classes of variables that strongly express the belief that a dominant reason for the existence of bullying (*Cor* = 659, *Ctr* = 72) is diversity. More precisely, the respondents located on the left side of this axis support the view that their classmates exclude them from school activities or ignore them because they are different (*Cor* = 618, *Ctr* = 96), and that they were deliberately ignored (*Cor* = 607, *Ctr* = 102). On the right side of this axis are the respondents who state that children did not exclude or ignore them because of their differences (*Cor* = 789, *Ctr* = 182), did not intentionally try to make them feel bad (*Cor* = 730, *Ctr* = 126), and that none of the children behaved badly toward them (*Cor* = 683, *Ctr* = 99), nor did anyone ever deliberately try to make them feel uncomfortable. Consequently, it can be concluded that the third factorial axis e_3 differentiates respondents in terms of bullying behavior based on diversity.

CONCLUSIONS AND SUGGESTIONS FOR FUTURE RESEARCH

This study examined the opinions, perceptions, and attitudes of first-year university students regarding bullying, as experienced during their secondary education years. The attitudes of 182 students were analyzed, who reported experiencing bullying at school from a minor to a significant degree, or not at all, during their middle and high school years. The Child Adolescent Bullying Scale (CABS) by Strout et al. (2018) was used as the measurement tool, showing high reliability. Data were processed using Correspondence Factor Analysis with the support of the MAD software.

The results revealed distinct groups of respondents: some reported that the effects of school bullying were so severe that they led to tendencies to leave school or change school environments, while another group reported never being victims of bullying. It was also found that diversity plays a role in differentiating verbal, physical, and other forms of attacks. Finally, among demographic variables, only gender influenced victimization in bullying situations. The sample consisted of 88 male and 94 female students.

Future research could further explore this significant issue of school bullying by including other countries with diverse cultural identities and larger samples. Big Data applications and related algorithms, such as those for Dynamic Scheduling of Big Data Streams, could facilitate the easier and faster collection of large-scale data from multiple higher education institutions (Souravlas et al., 2021a; 2021b; Souravlas & Anastasiadou, 2024; Tantalaki et al., 2020).

Artificial intelligence can play a decisive role by leveraging ontologies (Seremeti & Kameas, 2009; Kameas & Seremeti, 2011). AI uses ontologies to achieve effective and consistent knowledge exchange across different systems and applications (Panagiotopoulos et al., 2011; Pruvost et al., 2009; Seremeti & Anastasiadou, 2025; Seremeti & Kougias, 2013). Through ontologies, information acquires a unified, structured form, allowing systems to "understand" and collaborate despite technological or functional differences. In this way, ontologies serve as the foundation for developing intelligent, adaptive, and interoperable applications that better respond to user needs and environmental contexts (Seremeti & Kameas, 2008; 2009; 2010).

By leveraging Big Data collection through applications and algorithms related to Dynamic Scheduling of Big Data Streams (Souravlas et al., 2021c; 2021d; 2022; Kontis et al., 2025), the multidimensional issue of bullying can be studied in depth, along with its negative consequences on academic achievement, school dropout, and students' mental health worldwide.

REFERENCES

Anastasiadou, S. (2000). *Determination of students' attitudes toward statistics using methods of multivariate statistical analysis* Doctoral Dissertation, Department of Applied Informatics, University of Macedonia, Thessaloniki, Greece.

Anastasiadou, S. (2011). Reliability and validity testing of a new scale for monitoring attitudes toward learning statistics with technology. *Acta Didactica Napocencia*, *4*(1), 1–10. http://adn.teaching.ro/

Anastasiadou, S. (2016). Evaluation of the Implementation of TQM Principles in Higher Education Using the EFQM Excellence Model – A Study in Pedagogical Departments of Greek Universities. Master's Thesis, Hellenic Open University (EAP).

Anastasiadou, S. (2018). Leadership according to EFQM model in tertiary education: The case of Greek universities. In *Proceedings of the 10th International Conference: The Economies of the Balkan and the Eastern European Countries in the Changing World (EBEEC 2018)*, Warsaw, Poland (pp. 20–24).

Anastasiadou, S. (2019). Comparison of contemporary advanced statistical methods regarding construct validity evaluation of TEIque-SF instrument: Statistical implicative analysis vs. principal components analysis. In *Actes du 9ème Colloque International sur l'Analyse Statistique Implicative (ASI 10)* (pp. 148–163). Belfort, France.

Anastasiadou, S., Anastasiadis, L., Angeletos, T., & Vandikas, J. (2010). A Multidimensional Statistical Analysis of Students' Attitudes toward Physics. *The International Journal of Diversity in Organisations, Communities and Nations*, *16*(5), 341–356.

Anastasiadou, S., & Dimitriadou, C. (2011). What does critical thinking mean? A statistical data analysis of pre-service teachers' defining statements. International Journal of Humanities and Social Science, 1(7, Special Issue), 73–83.

Beale, A. V. (2001). Bully busters: Using drama to empower students to take a stand against bullying behavior. *Professional School Counseling*, *2001*(4), 300–305.

Björkqvist, K. (1994). Sex differences in physical, verbal, and indirect aggression: A review of recent research. *Sex Roles*, *1994*(30), 177–188.

Cabrera, A. F., & Guerrero, A. J. M. (2019). Sánchez. S.P., and García, Antonio-Manuel R. (2022). Bullying among Teens: Are Ethnicity and Race Risk Factors for Victimization? A Bibliometric Research. *Education in Science*, *9*, 220. DOI: 10.3390/educsci9030220

Donnelly, H. K., Han, Y., Song, J., & Song, T. M. (2019). Application of Social Big Data to Identify Trends of School Bullying Forms in South Korea. *International Journal of Environmental Research and Public Health, 2019*(16), 2596. DOI: 10.3390/ijerph16142596 PMID: 31330879

Drosos, G. (2004). Statistical Analysis of Linguistic Information Data. Doctoral Dissertation, University of Macedonia, Thessaloniki, Greece.

Florou, G. (1997). Determination of the Ideal Distance Metric and the Best Clustering Method in Various Hierarchical Agglomerative Classification Methods. Doctoral Dissertation, Department of Applied Informatics, University of Macedonia, Thessaloniki, Greece.

Kameas, A., & Seremeti, L. (2011). Ontology-based knowledge management in NGAIEs. In Minker, W., & Heinroth, T. (Eds.), *Next Generation Intelligent Environments* (pp. 85–126). Springer., DOI: 10.1007/978-1-4614-1299-1_3

Karapistolis, D. (2000). *MAD Data Analysis Method Software*. Athanasiou Altintzis Publishing.

Karapistolis, D. (2015). *Multidimensional Statistical Analysis*. Athanasiou Altintzis Publishing.

Kontis, S., Anastasiadou, S., Anastasiadis, L., & Seremeti, L. (2025). Legal entropy in AI governance. In Anastasiadou, S., Seremeti, L., Masouras, A., & Anastasiadis, L. (Eds.), *Modern perspectives on artificial intelligence and law* (pp. 193–206). IGI Global Scientific Publishing., DOI: 10.4018/979-8-3693-9576-9.ch010

Markos, A. (2007). *Assistance in the Interpretation of Correspondence Factor Analysis Results & Algorithms for Constructing and Analyzing Special Input Tables*. Doctoral Dissertation, Department of Applied Informatics, University of Macedonia, Thessaloniki, Greece.

Menexes, G. (2007). *Experimental Designs in Data Analysis*. Doctoral Dissertation, Department of Applied Informatics, University of Macedonia, Thessaloniki, Greece.

Moschidis, O. (2003). *Contribution to the Study of Evaluation Scales Using Multidimensional Data Analysis Methods*. Doctoral Dissertation, Department of Applied Informatics, University of Macedonia, Thessaloniki, Greece.

Panagiotopoulos, I., Seremeti, L., & Kameas, A. (2011). An Alignable User Profile Ontology for Ambient Intelligence Environments. In *Proceedings of the Seventh International Conference on Intelligent Environments*, Nottingham, UK, pp. 270-276. https://doi.org/DOI: 10.1109/IE.2011.15

Papadaki, Z., & Anastasiadou, S. (2017). Study of Bank Customers' Attitudes toward Service Quality during the Early Period of Capital Controls Using Correspondence Factor Analysis. Data Analysis Notebooks. Retrieved from http://www.gsda.gr/journal/archives/586

Pruvost, G., Kameas, A., Heinroth, T., Seremeti, L., & Minker, W. (2009). Combining Agents and Ontologies to Support Task-Centred Interoperability in Ambient Intelligent Environments. In *Proceedings of the Ninth International Conference on Intelligent Systems Design and Applications*, Pisa, Italy, pp. 55-60. https://doi.org/DOI: 10.1109/ISDA.2009.195

Seremeti, L., & Anastasiadou, S. (2025). The transformative impact of artificial intelligence (AI) on strategic decision-making. In Kavoura, A., Kefallonitis, E., & Theodoridis, P. (Eds.), *Strategic innovative marketing and tourism* (pp. 427–435). Springer., DOI: 10.1007/978-3-031-81962-9_47

Seremeti, L., & Kameas, A. (2008). Ontology-based high level task composition in ubiquitous computing applications. In *Proceedings of the IET 4th International Conference on Intelligent Environments*, Seattle, WA, USA, pp. 1-5. https://doi.org/DOI: 10.1049/cp:20081142

Seremeti, L., & Kameas, A. (2009). A Task-Based Ontology Engineering Approach for Novice Ontology Developers. In *Proceedings of the Fourth Balkan Conference in Informatics*, Thessaloniki, Greece, pp. 85-89. https://doi.org/DOI: 10.1109/BCI.2009.46

Seremeti, L., & Kougias, I. (2013). Networks of Aligned Ontologies Through a Category Theoretic Approach. Journal of Emerging Trends in Computing and Information Sciences. Vol. 4, No. 10, pp.785-794. Seremeti, L., Kameas, A. (2010). Tools for Ontology Engineering and Management. In: Poli, R., Healy, M., Kameas, A. (eds) Theory and Applications of Ontology: Computer Applications. Springer, Dordrecht, pp. 131-154. https://doi.org/DOI: 10.1007/978-90-481-8847-5_6

Souravlas, Katsavounis, and Anastasiadou. (2021d). On Modeling and Simulation of Resource Allocation Policies in Cloud Computing Using Colored Petri Nets. *Applied Sciences*. 10.16 (2021): 5644

Souravlas, S., Anastasiadou, S. & Katsavounis. (2021c). A Survey on the Recent Advances of Deep Community Detection." *Applied Sciences.* 11.16 (2021): 7179.

Souravlas, S. & Anastasiadou, S. (2021a). Pipelined Dynamic Scheduling of Big Data Streams. *Applied Sciences.* 10.14 (2021): 4796.

Souravlas, S., Anastasiadou, S. & Katsavounis, S (2021b). More on Pipelined Dynamic Scheduling of Big Data Streams. *Appl. Sci.* 11.1, 61; https://doi.org/.DOI: 10.3390/app11010061

Souravlas, S., & Anastasiadou, S. D. (2024). On implementing social community clouds based on Markov models. *IEEE Transactions on Computational Social Systems, 11*(1), 89–100. DOI: 10.1109/TCSS.2022.3213273

Strout, T. D., Vessey, J. A., Difazio, R. L., & Ludlow, L. H. (2018). The Child Adolescent Bullying Scale (CABS): Psychometric evaluation of a new measure. *Research in Nursing & Health, 41*, 1–13. PMID: 29504650

Strout, T. D., Vessey, J. A., DiFazio, R. L., & Ludlow, L. H. (2018). The Child Adolescent Bullying Scale (CABS): Psychometric evaluation of a new measure. *Research in Nursing & Health, 2018*, 1–13. DOI: 10.1002/nur.21871 PMID: 29504650

Tantalaki, S., Souravlas, S., Roumeliotis, M., & Katsavounis, S. (2020). Pipeline-Based Linear Scheduling of Big Data Streams in the Cloud. *IEEE Access : Practical Innovations, Open Solutions, 8*, 117182–117202. DOI: 10.1109/ACCESS.2020.3004612

Taraza, E., & Anastasiadou, S. (2019). EFQM Excellence Model in Vocational Lyceum: Reliability and Validity of EFQM Instrument. Proceedings of 13th annual International Technology, Education and Development Conference (INTED2019), Valencia, Spain, pp. 2273-2285.

USA Department of Education. (1998). *Preventing Bullying: A Manual for Schools and Communities*. USA Department of Education.

Valdivia-Salas, S., Jiménez, T. I., Lombas, A. S., & López-Crespo, G. (2021). School Violence towards Peers and Teen Dating Violence: The Mediating Role of Personal Distress. *International Journal of Environmental Research and Public Health, 2021*(18), 310. DOI: 10.3390/ijerph18010310 PMID: 33406621

Zhang, S., Gong, M., & Li, W. (2020). W., Wang, W., Wu, R., Lan Guo, L. and Lu C. (2020). Patterns of Bullying Victimization and Associations with Mental Health Problems in Chinese Adolescents: A Latent Class Analysis. *International Journal of Environmental Research and Public Health, 17*, 779. DOI: 10.3390/ijerph17030779 PMID: 32012686

Chapter 14

The Correlation of the Spoken Language in Combination With Religion With the Main Settlements of the Northern Regions of Greece

Petros Trantas
University of the Aegean, Greece

Elias Athanasiadis
University of the Aegean, Greece

Sofia Anastasiadou
http://orcid.org/0000-0001-6404-5003
University of Western Macedonia, Greece

ABSTRACT

The present study investigates this intersection in relation to location in the main settlements of Epirus, Macedonia, Thrace, and Thessaly, utilizing data analysis methods. The terminology associated with language, religion, and location is consistent with employed in the aforementioned census. This census encompasses data pertaining to the Greek area from 1922 to the onset of World War II. Regarding Thessaloniki town, apart from the Greek-speaking Orthodox Christian population,

DOI: 10.4018/979-8-3373-6926-6.ch014

there are also significant communities of Jewish Spanish-speaking, Russian-speaking Orthodox Christian, Armenian-speaking, and Roma communities, as well as a notable Greek-speaking Catholic population. In Ioannina, the population is comprised of Greek-speaking Orthodox Christians, Muslim Jews, and Orthodox Christians who speak either Albanian or Kutsovalach. In the city of Ekaterini, the religious groups present include Greek-speaking Protestants. In the cities of western Macedonia, Orthodox Christians utilize a multitude of linguistic varieties, including Greek, Macedonian-Slavic, Turkish, and Kutsovalach.

INTRODUCTION

Following the conclusion of the Balkan Wars and the delineation of the contemporary northern borders, a population exchange was initiated between Greece and Bulgaria. Subsequently, Greece engaged in armed conflict with Turkey, resulting in a decisive defeat for the former and becoming known as the Asia Minor Catastrophe. The official conclusion of the war was signified by the Treaty of Lausanne in 1923. In accordance with the terms of the treaty, which were signed by both states, a population exchange was to be conducted between the former combatants based solely on religious affiliation (Pelagidis, 2003; Dalègre & Tzimakas, 2015; Winter, 2023). In addition to the considerable number of individuals impacted by this criterion, there was the matter of Turkish-speaking Orthodox Christians in Turkey and Greek-speaking Muslims in Greece, whose ancestors had inhabited the region on either side of the Aegean for centuries. Notably, the treaty made exceptions for the Muslims of Thrace and the predominantly Greek-speaking Orthodox Christians of Constantinople. Subsequent data indicates that a few years later, Muslims, predominantly Albanian-speaking, were documented in Epirus. Furthermore, minor proportions of Muslims were documented in other regions due to intermarriages or professional and other considerations (Hellenic Statistical Authority, 1929a; Hellenic Statistical Authority, 2022; Mazower, 2002, 2006). It seems reasonable to posit that a similar situation may have occurred in Turkey.

In 1928, a general population census was conducted in Greece. It is noteworthy that the Dodecanese Islands were incorporated into Greece's national territory a mere twenty years later and, consequently, were not included in the census (Hellenic Statistical Authority, 1929b). Accordingly, the census pertains to the then-existing state of affairs. The 1928 census is a singular event in the history of Greece. The census records not only the distribution of inhabitants by spoken language and religion but also categorizes them based on simultaneous characteristics in a manner that is unique in Greece's history. The importance of this census at the time is clear, given the context of population relocations.

The present study is concerned with the processing of data from the four northernmost regions of Greece. The regions in question are Macedonia, Epirus, Thrace (referred to as Western Thrace), and Thessaly. The analysis is focused on the residents of municipalities and large communities. The following table provides an initial overview of the situation in the regions not analyzed in detail, as this is done on a more granular level.

Table 1. Distribution of census population in four regions by religion combined with language spoken.

	Thessaly	Macedonia	Epirus	W. Thrace
OrthodoxGreek-speaking	486.314	1.161.191	283.413	132.958
OrthodoxTurkish-speaking	2.830	70.032	1.796	9.124
Muslim Turkish-speaking	108	1.399	141	84.584
OrthodoxMacedonian-Slavic-speaking	59	80.608	2	1.059
JewsSpanish-speaking	691	59.073	5	2.882
OrthodoxArmenian-speaking	652	10.743	53	796
CatholicGreek-speaking	323	1.569	71	121
OrthodoxKutsovalach-speaking	906	13.456	5.227	68
Muslim Albanian-speaking	51	1.041	17.008	205
Muslim Bulgarian-speaking	3	12	-	16.740
JewsGreek-speaking	1.671	1.013	2.631	76
ProtestantsGreek-speaking	92	1.649	71	32
OrthodoxRoma-speaking	17	3.200	4	590
OrthodoxRussian-speaking	61	1.872	14	83
CatholicItalian-speaking	28	636	15	56
Muslim Greek-speaking	33	131	2.000	60

RESEARCH DATA AND METHODOLOGY

The municipalities and key communities included in the analysis are as follows:

- Larissa, Volos, Karditsa, and Trikala for Thessaly;
- Veria, Thessaloniki, Naousa, Katerini, Kavala, Kozani, Giannitsa, Edessa, Serres, Florina, Polygyros for Macedonia;
- Arta, Ioannina, Preveza for Epirus; and
- Alexandroupolis, Didymoteicho, Soufli, Komotini, and Xanthi for Thrace.

The population can be further subdivided into the following categories: Orthodox Greek-speaking, Orthodox Turkish-speaking, Muslim Turkish-speaking, Orthodox Macedonian-Slavic-speaking, Spanish-speaking Jews, Orthodox Armenian-speaking, Catholic Greek-speaking, Orthodox Vlach-speaking, Muslim Albanian-speaking, Muslim Bulgarian-speaking, Jewish Greek-speaking, Protestant Greek-speaking, Orthodox Romani-speaking, Orthodox Russian-speaking, Catholic Italian-speaking, and Muslim Greek-speaking. These categories serve as the variables of the analysis, forming the columns of the table that is analyzed using data analysis methods (Benzécri, 1992; Greenacre & Blasius, 1994; Papadimitriou, 2007).

The double-entry table, comprising rows representing settlements (municipalities and large communities) and columns representing combinations of religion and spoken language (as presented in Table 1), was subjected to analysis using correspondence factor analysis and hierarchical classification.

PRESENTATION OF CORRESPONDENCE FACTOR ANALYSIS RESULTS

The eigenvalues and percentages of the histogram of the analysis are shown in Figure 1.

Figure 1. Eigenvalues and percentages of quality characteristics

HISTOGRAMME DES 15 PREMIERES VALEURS PROPRES

NUMERO	VALEUR PROPRE	POURCENTAGE	POURCENTAGE CUMULE	
1	0.3179	42.98	42.98	***
2	0.1619	21.89	64.87	***
3	0.1138	15.38	80.26	******************************
4	0.0537	7.25	87.51	**************
5	0.0370	5.00	92.51	**********
6	0.0272	3.67	96.18	*******
7	0.0188	2.54	98.72	*****
8	0.0046	0.62	99.35	**
9	0.0020	0.27	99.62	*
10	0.0012	0.17	99.78	*
11	0.0010	0.14	99.92	*
12	0.0004	0.05	99.98	*
13	0.0001	0.01	99.99	*
14	0.0000	0.01	100.00	*
15	0.0000	0.00	100.00	*

The initial three factor axes are as follows:

- The 1[st]axis ($\lambda 1 = 0.3179$, $\tau 1 = 42.98\%$) facilitates the expansion of settlements belonging to the EDESSA, FLORINA, GIANNITSA, THESSALONIKI,

IOANNINA, and KATERINI regions, which are inhabited by Orthodox Kutsoalach and Israelite Greek populations. The Orthodox Macedonian-Slavic and Protestant Greek populations are situated in contrast to the settlements of Komotini, Xanthi, Didymoteicho, and Alexandroupoli, which are inhabited by Turkish Muslims, Bulgarian Muslims, and Armenian Orthodox Christians.

- The 2[nd]axis ($\lambda 2= 0{,}1619$, $\tau 2= 21{,}89\%$)represents an expansion of the settlements of THESSALONIKI, DIDYMOTICHO, and KOMOTINI, which include populations of Israelis of Spanish, Catholics of Italian, Orthodox of Russian, and Catholics of Greek descent. The settlements of EDESSA, GIANNITSA, FLORINA, BEROIA, KATERINI, and KASTRORIA, with populations of Orthodox Macedonian-Slavic, Orthodox Kuchovlach, Orthodox Turkish, and Protestant Greek, are also included.
- The 3[rd]axis ($\lambda 3= 0.1138$, $\tau 3= 15.38\%$) serves to expand the scope of the study by including the settlements EDESSSA, FLORINA, GIANNITSA, THESSALONIKI, KOMOTINI, and DIDYMOTEICHO, which have populations of Orthodox Macedonian-Slavic, Israelite-Spanish, The Catholic-Italian, Orthodox Russian, and on the other hand the settlements of IOANNINA, ARTA, PREVEZA, KATERINI, TRIKALA, and VOLOS with populations of Israelis Greek, Muslims Greek, Protestants Greek, and Muslims Albanian.

The intersection of the characteristics of the first three axes are shown in Figures 1, 2 and 3.

Figure 2. Diagram 1x2

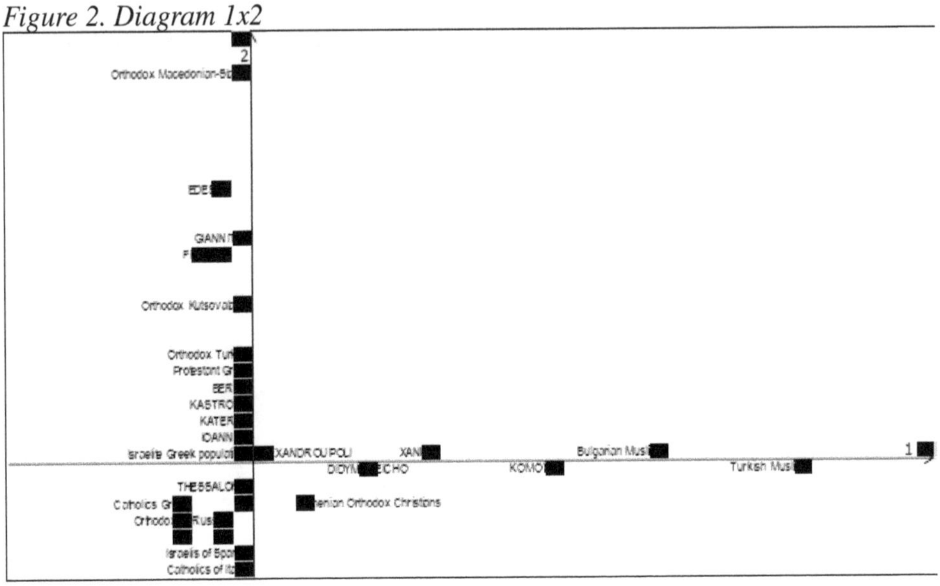

As illustrated in Figure 2., the settlements of Thrace are notable for the prevalence of Turkish-speaking and Bulgarian-speaking Muslims. Armenian-speaking Orthodox Christians are present in the vicinity of Didymoteicho, while Spanish-speaking Jews, Russian-speaking Orthodox Christians, and Catholics are located in Thessaloniki. Jews are documented in Ioannina, while non-Greek-speaking Orthodox Christians are present in settlements in Western Macedonia.

Figure 3. Diagram 1x3

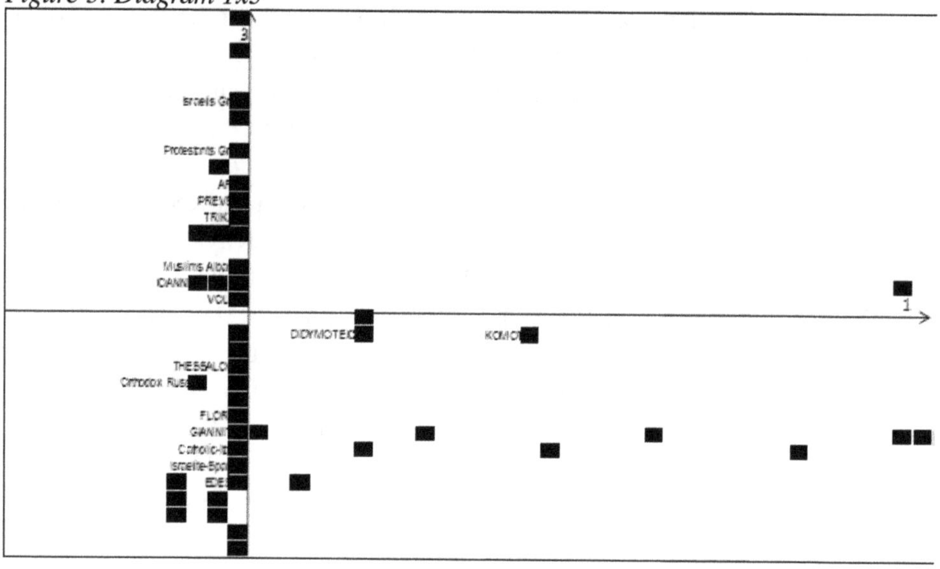

Figure 3., through the 3rd axis, expands the Greek-speaking non-Orthodox with the non-Greek-speaking populations.

Figure 4. Diagram 2x3

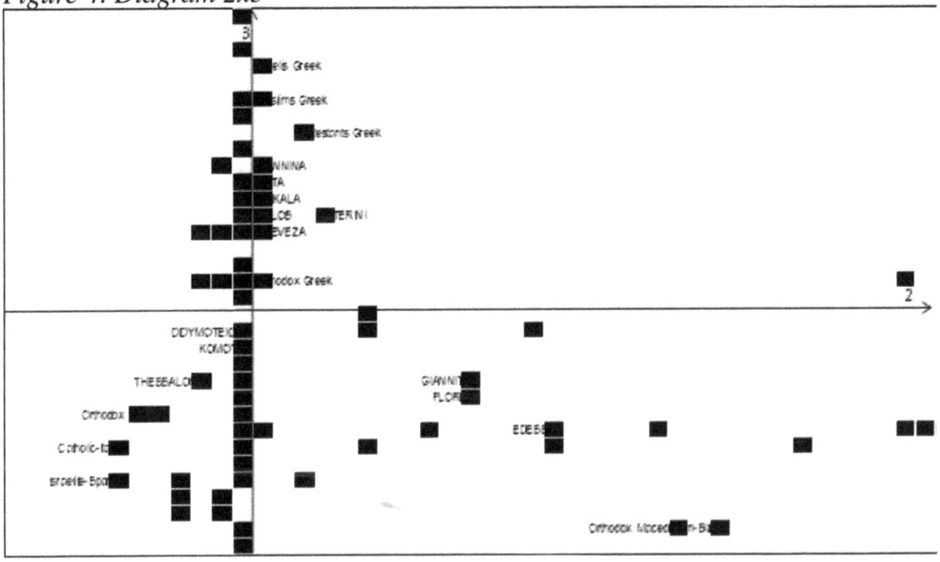

In Figure 4 we observe that the Orthodox Macedonian-Slavic language speakers are projected on the side of the settlements of GIANNITSA, FLORINA and EDESSAS.

Presentation of Hierarchical Classification

As illustrated in Figure 4, the SPAD program presents the option of selecting dendrograms with either four or seven classes.

Figure 5. Hierarchical classification dendrogram

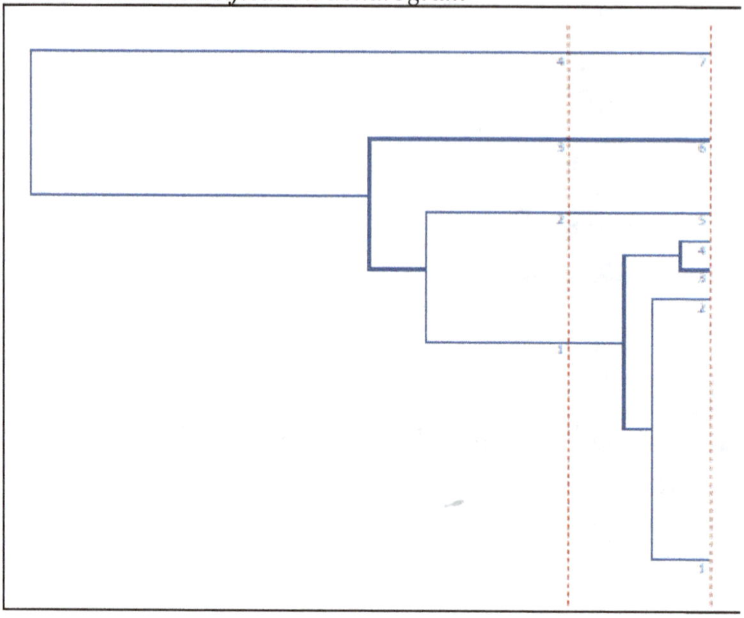

The hierarchical classification dendrogram with four classes (Figure 6) shows that the first class includes the populations of Orthodox Greek-speakers, Israelites Greek-speakers, Orthodox Kutsovalach-speakers, Protestant Greek-speakers, Muslim Greek-speakers and Orthodox Turkish-speakers in the areas/settlements of VOLOS, KAVALA, LARISSA, KOZANI, TRIKALA, SOUFLI, KARDITSA, POLYGYROS, DRAMA, NAOUSA, VEROIA, SERRES, KASTRIA, ARTA, IOANNINA, PREVEZA and ALEXANDROUPOLI. The second class includes the populations of Israeli Spanish-speakers, Orthodox Armenian-speakers, Catholic Greek-speakers, Orthodox Russian-speakers, and Orthodox Roma-speakers from THESSALONIKI. The third class includes the populations Orthodox Macedonian-Slavic-speakers, Orthodox Turkish-speakers, Orthodox Kutsovalach-speakers from FLORINA, GIANITSA and EDESSA. Finally, the fourth class includes the populations of Muslims Turkish-speakers, Orthodox Armenian-speakers and Muslims Bulgarian-speakers from XANTHI, KOMOTINI and DIDYMOTEICHO.

Figure 6. Hierarchical classification dendrogram with 4 classes

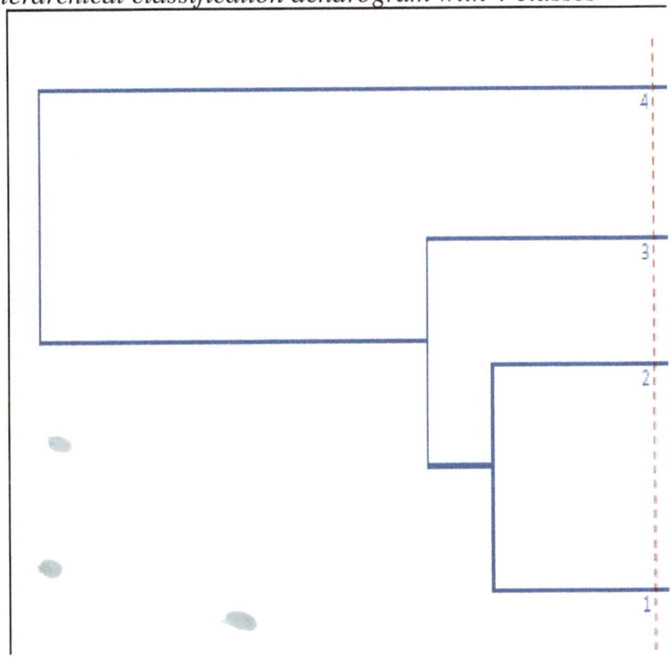

Similarly, the hierarchical classification dendrogram with seven classes (Figure 6) demonstrates that the initial class encompasses populations of Orthodox Greek-speakers, Israelites Greek-speakers, and Orthodox Roma-speakers residing in the regions/settlements of KAVALA, LARISA, VOLOS, KOZANI, SOUFLI, KARDITSA, POLYGROS, TRIKALA, DRAMA, KASTRIA, NAOUSA, SERRES, ARTA, PREVEZA, and ALEXANDROPOLI. The second class encompasses the following populations: Israelites Greek-speakers, Muslims Albanian-speakers, Muslims, Orthodox Greek-speakers, and Orthodox Kutsovalach-speakers from IOANNINA. The third class encompasses the populations of Orthodox Kutsovalach-speakers and Orthodox Turkish-speakers, as well as the Muslim Albanian-speakers from VEROIA. The fourth class includes the Protestant Greek-speakers, Orthodox Turkish-speakers, Orthodox Kutsovalach-speakers, and Orthodox Greek-speakers populations from AIKATERINI. The fifth class includes the populations of Israelites Spanish-speakers, Orthodox Armenian-speakers, Catholics Greek-speakers, Catholics Italian-speakers, Orthodox Russian-speakers, and Orthodox Roma-speakers from THESSALONIKI. The sixth class encompasses the populations of Orthodox Macedonian-Slavic-speakers, Orthodox Turkish-speakers, and Orthodox Kutsovalach-speakers from FLORINA, GIANNITSA, and EDESSA. The seventh class includes the populations of Muslim Turkish-speakers, Orthodox Armenian-speakers, and Muslim Bulgarian-speakers from XANTHI, KOMOTINI, and DIDYMOTEICHO.

Figure 7. Hierarchical classification dendrogram with 7 classes

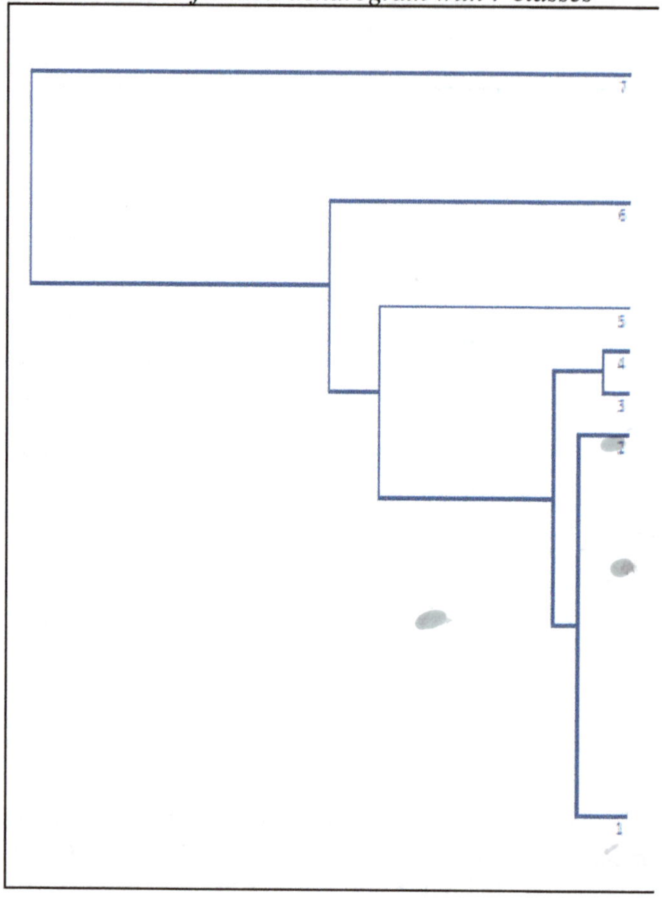

Finally, we can observe the projection of the centres of the four or seven classes onto the projective planes of the combinations of the first three axes as depicted in Figures 8, 9, and 10.

Figure 8. Projective diagram of classes in the plane 1x2

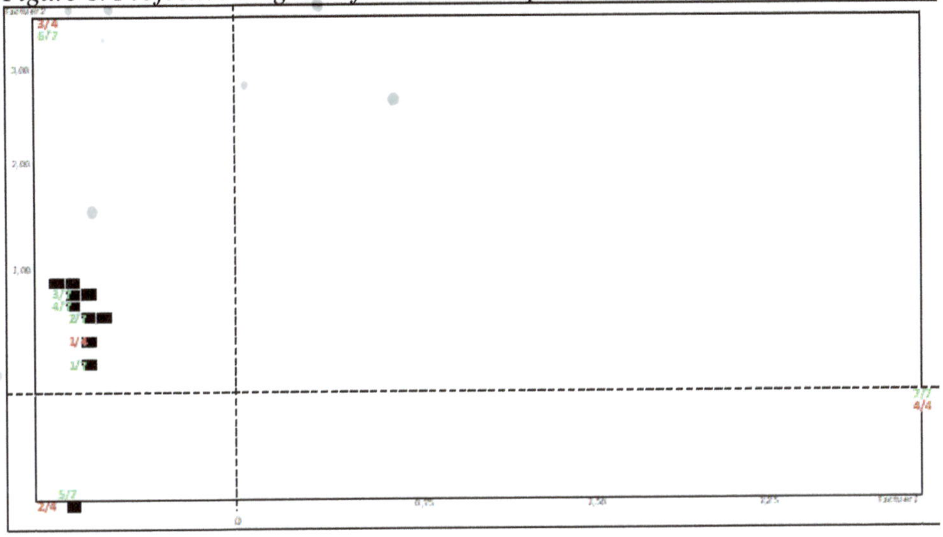

Figure 9. Projective diagram of classes in the plane 1x3

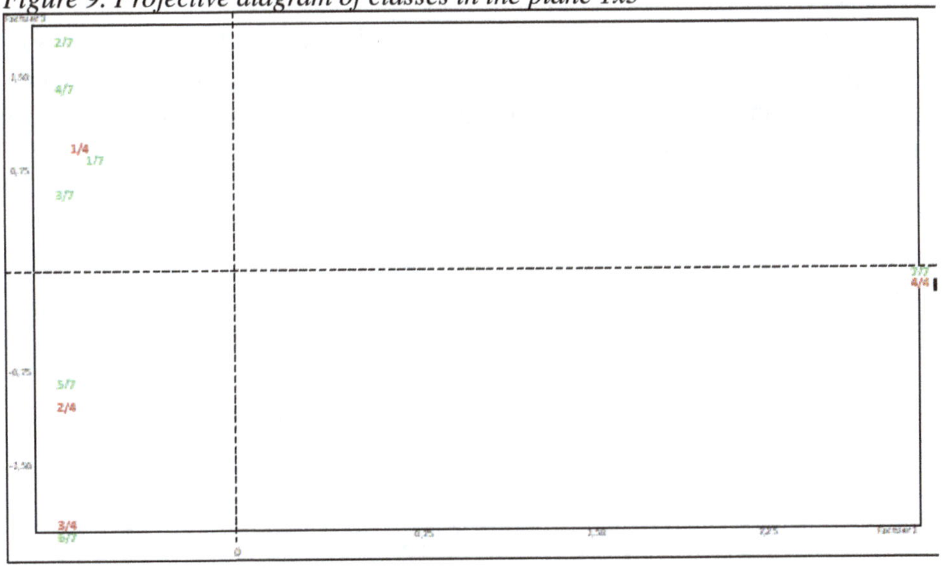

Figure 10. Projective diagram of classes in the plane 2x3

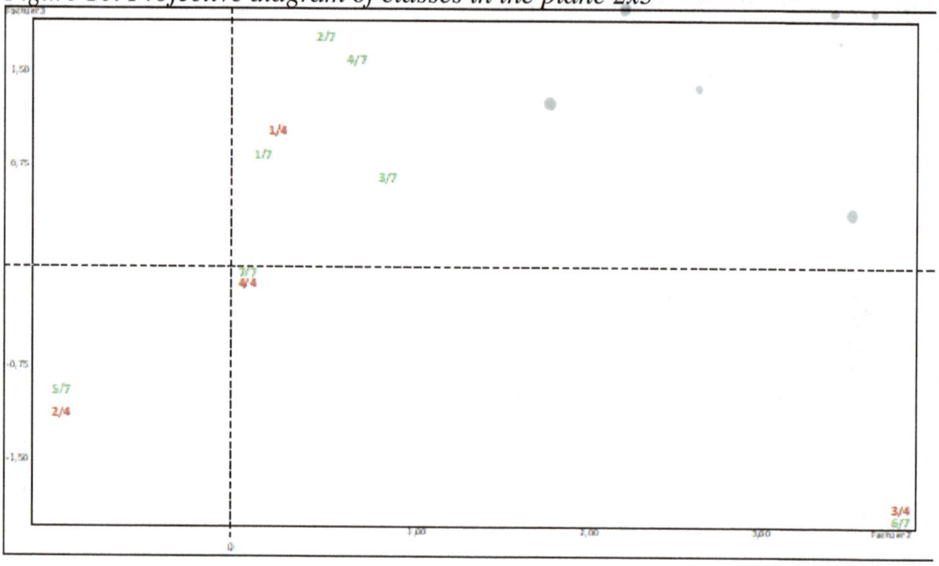

In conclusion, the 1928 Census provides evidence of the existing multiculturalism in Northern Greece and Thessaly. For the first time, the 1928 Census records combinations of spoken language and religion that are differentiated from each other in municipalities and large communities in the geographical areas under examination. The statistical analysis identifies the dominant local specificities of these language and religion combinations.

REFERENCES

Benzécri, J.-P. (1992). *Correspondence Analysis Handbook*. Marcel Dekker., DOI: 10.1201/9780585363035

Dalègre, J., & Tzimakas, M. (2015). *Les populations de la Macédoine grecque au XXe siècle*. L'Harmattan.

Greenacre, M., & Blasius, J. (1994). *Correspondence Analysis in the Social Sciences*. Academic Press.

Hellenic Statistical Authority. (1929a). Census of the population of Greece on 19 December 1920. http://dlib.statistics.gr/Book/GRESYE_02_0101_00011.pdf

Hellenic Statistical Authority. (1929b). Population de la Grece d aprel le recensement du 15-16 Mai 1928. http://dlib.statistics.gr/portal/page/portal/ESYE/showdetails?p_id=16690436&p_derive=book&p_topic=10007862

Hellenic Statistical Authority. (2022). *Census of refugees carried out in April 1923*. http://dlib.statistics.gr/Book/GRESYE_02_0101_00107.pdf

Mazower, M. (2002). *The Balkans*. Patakis.

Mazower, M. (2006).*Thessaloniki, the city of ghosts, Christians, Muslims, and Jews 1430-1950* Alexandreia. ISBN: 960221354X.

Papadimitriou, G. (2007). *The data analysis*. Tipothito.

Pelagidis, S. (2003). *Refugee Greece (1913-1930). The pain and the glory*. Adelfoi Kyriakidi.

Winter, J. (2023). *The day the Great War ends*. Ed.Pedio.

Compilation of References

Aayog, N. I. T. I. (2024, July). SDG India Index 2023–24. Government of India. Retrieved in February, 2025 from https://www.niti.gov.in/sites/default/files/2024-7/SDG_India_Index_ 2023-24.pdf

Abul, O., Bonchi, F., & Nanni, M. (2008). Never Walk Alone: Uncertainty for Anonymity in Moving Objects Databases. *2008 IEEE 24th International Conference on Data Engineering*, 376–385. https://doi.org/DOI: 10.1109/icde.2008.4497446

Acar, E., & Yener, B. (2009). Unsupervised Multiway Data Analysis: A Literature Survey. *IEEE Transactions on Knowledge and Data Engineering*, *21*(1), 6–20. DOI: 10.1109/TKDE.2008.112

Adejuwon, J. A. (2022). Social Media Marketing And Customer Retention Of Selected Small And Medium Enterprises (SMEs) In South-West Nigeria. *International Journal of Management and Economics Invention*, *8*(6). Advance online publication. DOI: 10.47191/ijmei/v8i6.01

Agrawal, A., Gans, J., & Goldfarb, A. (2018). *Prediction machines: The Simple Economics of Artificial Intelligence*. Harvard Business Press.

Ahmad, A., & Dey, L. (2007). A k-mean clustering algorithm for mixed numeric and categorical data. *Data and Knowledge Engineering*, *63*(2), 503–527. *Scopus*. Advance online publication. DOI: 10.1016/j.datak.2007.03.016

Ahmad, A., & Khan, S. S. (2019). Survey of State-of-the-Art Mixed Data Clustering Algorithms. *IEEE Access*, *7*, 31883–31902. *Scopus*. Advance online publication. DOI: 10.1109/ACCESS.2019.2903568

Ainsworth, S. (2006). DeFT: A conceptual framework for considering learning with multiple representations. *Learning and Instruction*, *16*(3), 183–198. DOI: 10.1016/j.learninstruc.2006.03.001

Akter, S., Michael, K., Uddin, M. R., McCarthy, G., & Rahman, M. (2022). Transforming business using digital innovations: The application of AI, blockchain, cloud and data analytics. *Annals of Operations Research, 308*(1–2), 7–39. DOI: 10.1007/s10479-020-03620-w

Aldahdouh, M. M., & AlDahdooh, R. M. (2019). Social media network analysis with NodeXL. *International Journal of Innovative Research in Computer and Communication Engineering*, *7*(9).

Aldaihani, F. M. F., Ali, N. A. B., Hashim, H. B., & Kamal, N. (2020). Impact of Social Customer Relationship Management on Customer Retention of Islamic Banks in Kuwait: The Mediating Role of Customer Empowerment. 9(1).

Ali, N., Jansen, J., Van Den Doel, A., Tinnevelt, G. H., & Bocklitz, T. (2021). WE-ASCA: The Weighted-Effect ASCA for Analyzing Unbalanced Multifactorial Designs—A Raman Spectra-Based Example. *Molecules (Basel, Switzerland)*, *26*(1), 66. DOI: 10.3390/molecules26010066 PMID: 33375623

Al-Zahrani, A. M., & Alasmari, T. M. (2024). Exploring the impact of artificial intelligence on higher education: The dynamics of ethical, social, and educational implications. *Humanities & Social Sciences Communications*, *11*(912). Advance online publication. DOI: 10.1057/s41599-024-03432-4

Alzboon, M. S., Aljarrah, E., Alqaraleh, M., & Alomari, S. A. (2021). NodeXL tool for social network analysis. *Turkish Journal of Computer and Mathematics Education*, *12*(14), 202–216.

Anastasiadou, S. (2000). *Determination of students' attitudes toward statistics using methods of multivariate statistical analysis* Doctoral Dissertation, Department of Applied Informatics, University of Macedonia, Thessaloniki, Greece.

Anastasiadou, S. (2016). Evaluation of the Implementation of TQM Principles in Higher Education Using the EFQM Excellence Model – A Study in Pedagogical Departments of Greek Universities. Master's Thesis, Hellenic Open University (EAP).

Anastasiadou, S. (2016). Evaluation of the Implementation of TQM principles in Tertiary Education using the EFQM Excellence Model -Research in Educational Departments of Greek Universities. Published Master's thesis, Greek Open University, Patra, Greece.

Anastasiadou, S., & Dimitriadou, C. (2011). What does critical thinking mean? A statistical data analysis of pre-service teachers' defining statements. International Journal of Humanities and Social Science, 1(7, Special Issue), 73–83.

Anastasiadou, S., & Taraza, E. (2019). Total quality management: implementation of the six sigma methodology for improving quality in higher education, ICERI2019, the 12th annual International Conference of Education, Research and Innovation, Seville (Spain), ICERI2019, pp. 9533-9537.

Anastasiadou, S. (2011). Reliability and validity testing of a new scale for monitoring attitudes toward learning statistics with technology. *Acta Didactica Napocencia, 4*(1), 1–10. http://adn.teaching.ro/

Anastasiadou, S. (2013). Developing and Evaluating a Structural Equation Model Measuring Leadership Changes in a Lifelong Learning World. *The International Journal of Educational Organization and Leadership, 19*(2), 1–17. DOI: 10.18848/2329-1656/CGP/v19i02/48520

Anastasiadou, S. (2018). Leadership according to EFQM model in tertiary education: The case of Greek universities. In *Proceedings of the 10th International Conference: The Economies of the Balkan and the Eastern European Countries in the Changing World (EBEEC 2018)*, Warsaw, Poland (pp. 20–24).

Anastasiadou, S. (2019). Comparison of contemporary advanced statistical methods regarding construct validity evaluation of TEIque-SF instrument: Statistical Implicative Analysis vs. Principal Components Analysis. *9ème Colloque International sur Analyse Statistique Implicative (ASI 10)*. Belfort – France. pp. 148-163.

Anastasiadou, S. (2019). Comparison of contemporary advanced statistical methods regarding construct validity evaluation of TEIque-SF instrument: Statistical implicative analysis vs. principal components analysis. In *Actes du 9ème Colloque International sur l'Analyse Statistique Implicative (ASI 10)* (pp. 148–163). Belfort, France.

Anastasiadou, S., Anastasiadis, L., Angeletos, T., & Vandikas, J. (2010). A Multidimensional Statistical Analysis of Students' Attitudes toward Physics. *The International Journal of Diversity in Organisations, Communities and Nations, 16*(5), 341–356.

Anastasiadou, S., & Karakos, A. (2011). The beliefs of electrical and computer engineering students´ regarding computer programming. *International Journal of Technology, Knowledge and Society, 7*(1), 37–52. DOI: 10.18848/1832-3669/CGP/v07i01/56170

Anastasiadou, S., & Tiliakou, C. (2016). Evaluation of the discriminating ability of the Greek state foreign language exam (KPG) for English by means of the factorial analysis of correspondences. *International Journal of Learning and Teaching, 8*(2), 129–140. DOI: 10.18844/ijlt.v8i2.518

Anderson, T. W. (1984). *An Introduction to Multivariate Statistical Analysis* (2nd ed.). John Willey and Sons Inc.

Ang, B. W., Choong, W. L., & Ng, T. S. (2015). Energy security: Definitions, dimensions and indexes. *Renewable & Sustainable Energy Reviews*, *42*, 1077–1093. DOI: 10.1016/j.rser.2014.10.064

Anowar, F., Sadaoui, S., & Selim, B. (2021). Conceptual and empirical comparison of dimensionality reduction algorithms (PCA, KPCA, LDA, MDS, SVD, LLE, ISOMAP, LE, ICA, t-SNE). *Computer Science Review*, *40*, 100378. DOI: 10.1016/j.cosrev.2021.100378

API documentation - EXPORTCOMMENTS.COM. (n.d.). ExportComments. Retrieved May 17, 2024, from https://exportcomments.com/api

Arcavi, A. (2003). The role of visual representations in the learning of mathematics. *Educational Studies in Mathematics*, *52*(3), 215–241. DOI: 10.1023/a:1024312321077

Aria, M., & Cuccurullo, C. (2017). bibliometrix : An R-tool for comprehensive science mapping analysis. *Journal of Informetrics*, *11*(4), 959–975. DOI: 10.1016/j.joi.2017.08.007

Arrieta, A. B., Díaz-Rodríguez, N., Del Ser, J., Bennetot, A., Tabik, S., Barbado, A., Garcia, S., Gil-Lopez, S., Molina, D., Benjamins, R., Chatila, R., & Herrera, F. (2019). Explainable Artificial Intelligence (XAI): Concepts, taxonomies, opportunities and challenges toward responsible AI. *Information Fusion*, *58*, 82–115. DOI: 10.1016/j.inffus.2019.12.012

Artha, B., Zahara, I., Bahri, & Permata Sari, N. (2022). Customer Retention: A Literature Review. Social Science Studies, 2(1), 030–045. https://doi.org/DOI: 10.47153/sss21.2952022

Artificial Intelligence Act. (n.d.). *Annex III: High-risk AI systems referred to in Article 6(2)*. https://artificialintelligenceact.eu/annex/3/

Asaad, C., & Baïna, K. (2018). NoSQL Databases – seek for a design methodology. In *Lecture notes in computer science* (pp. 25–40). https://doi.org/DOI: 10.1007/978-3-030-00856-7_2

Athey, S., & Imbens, G. W. (2019). Machine learning methods that economists should know about. *Annual Review of Economics*, *11*(1), 685–725. DOI: 10.1146/annurev-economics-080217-053433

Baas, J., Schotten, M., Plume, A., Côté, G., & Karimi, R. (2020). Scopus as a curated, high-quality bibliometric data source for academic research in quantitative science studies. *Quantitative Science Studies*, *1*(1), 377–386. DOI: 10.1162/qss_a_00019

Baesens, B., Setiono, R., Mues, C., & Vanthienen, J. (2003). Using neural network rule extraction and decision tables for Credit-Risk evaluation. *Management Science*, *49*(3), 312–329. DOI: 10.1287/mnsc.49.3.312.12739

Bahrammirzaee, A. (2010). A comparative survey of artificial intelligence applications in finance: Artificial neural networks, expert system and hybrid intelligent systems. *Neural Computing & Applications*, *19*(8), 1165–1195. DOI: 10.1007/s00521-010-0362-z

Baker, R. S., & Inventado, P. S. (2014). Educational data mining and learning analytics. In Larusson, J. A., & White, B. (Eds.), *Learning analytics* (pp. 61–75). Springer.

Barlow, J., Tapio, R., & Tarekegne, B. (2022). Advancing the state of energy equity metrics. *The Electricity Journal*, *35*(10), 107208. DOI: 10.1016/j.tej.2022.107208

Bates, T., Cobo, C., Marino, O., & Wheeler, S. (2020). Can artificial intelligence transform higher education? *International Journal of Educational Technology in Higher Education*, *17*(42). Advance online publication. DOI: 10.1186/s41239-020-00218-x

Bauer, M., Charon, N., & Younes, L. (2019). Metric registration of curves and surfaces using optimal control. In Kimmel, R., & Tai, X. C. (Eds.), *Handbook of numerical analysis* (pp. 613–646)., DOI: 10.1016/bs.hna.2019.03.001

Beale, A. V. (2001). Bully busters: Using drama to empower students to take a stand against bullying behavior. *Professional School Counseling*, *2001*(4), 300–305.

Beaudouin, V. (2016). Statistical analysis of textual data: Benzécri and the French School of data analysis. *Glottometrics*, *33*, 56–72.

Bebbington, J., & Unerman, J. (2020). Advancing research into accounting and the UN Sustainable Development Goals. *Accounting, Auditing & Accountability Journal*, *33*(7), 1657–1670. DOI: 10.1108/aaaj-05-2020-4556

Beh, E. J., & Lombardo, R. (2021). An Introduction to correspondence analysis. In *Wiley series in probability and statistics*. https://doi.org/DOI: 10.1002/9781119044482

Belaïd, F., Ranjbar, Z., & Massié, C. (2021). Exploring the cost-effectiveness of energy efficiency implementation measures in the residential sector. *Energy Policy*, *150*, 112122. DOI: 10.1016/j.enpol.2020.112122

Bennett, N. J., & Satterfield, T. (2018). Environmental governance: A practical framework to guide design, evaluation, and analysis. *Conservation Letters, 11*(6), e12600. DOI: 10.1111/conl.12600

Benzécri, J. P. & Collaborateurs. (1973). *L'Analyse des Données. Vol. 1: Taxinomie. Vol. 2: Analyse des Correspondances.* Dunod.

Benzécri, J. P. (1973). *Analyse des Données.*

Benzécri, J.-P. (1992). *Correspondence A nalysis Handbook.* Marcel Dekker, Inc.

Benzécri, J.-P. (1992). *Correspondence Analysis Handbook.* Marcel Dekker., DOI: 10.1201/9780585363035

Beretta, V., Demartini, M. C., & Trucco, S. (2024). SDG disclosure and financial performance: Evidence from Europe. *Sustainable Development.* Advance online publication. DOI: 10.1108/MBE-05-2024-0054

Berland, M., Baker, R. S., & Blikstein, P. (2014). Educational data mining and learning analytics: Applications to constructionist research. *Technology. Knowledge and Learning, 19*, 205–220.

Bertinetto, C., Engel, J., & Jansen, J. (2020). ANOVA simultaneous component analysis: A tutorial review. *Analytica Chimica Acta: X, 6*, 100061. DOI: 10.1016/j.acax.2020.100061 PMID: 33392497

Bhagawan, P., & Mukhopadhyay, J. P. (2024). Does mandatory expenditure on CSR affect firm value? Empirical evidence from Indian firms. *Journal of Accounting Literature.* Advance online publication. DOI: 10.1108/jal-10-2023-0184

Bishop, C. M. (2006). *Pattern Recognition and Machine Learning.* Springer.

Bishop, C. M. (2016). *Pattern recognition and machine learning.* Springer.

Bitzenis, A., & Koutsoupias, N. (2024A). Big data in economics research. In *Springer proceedings in business and economics* (pp. 1063–1072). https://doi.org/DOI: 10.1007/978-3-031-49105-4_61

Bitzenis, A., & Koutsoupias, N. (2024B). A Scientometric Review regarding FDI in SouthEast Europe (2005–2024). *Global Business & Economics Anthology, I&II*(2024), 117–128. https://doi.org/DOI: 10.47341/gbea.241210

Bitzenis, A., Koutsoupias, N., & Boutsiouki, S. (2023). Business Research and Data Mining: a Bibliometric Analysis. *2023 3rd International Conference on Electrical, Computer, Communications and Mechatronics Engineering (ICECCME)*, 1–6. https://doi.org/DOI: 10.1109/iceccme57830.2023.10252699

Bitzenis, A., Koutsoupias, N., & Nosios, M. (2025D). A Meta-Systematic Review of Research Trends in Artificial Intelligence and Machine Learning for Business and Economic Applications [dataset]. https://doi.org/DOI: 10.17605/OSF.IO/R9UYX

Bitzenis, A., & Koutsoupias, N. (2023A). Foreign Direct Investment And Sustainability: A Visualized Bibliometric Review. *South-Eastern Europe Journal of Economics, 1*, 41–52. https://doi.org/DOI: 10.17605/osf.io/pcaxg

Bitzenis, A., & Koutsoupias, N. (2023A). FOREIGN DIRECT INVESTMENT AND SUSTAINABILITY: A VISUALIZED BIBLIOMETRIC REVIEW. *South-Eastern Europe Journal of Economics, 1*, 41–52. https://doi.org/DOI: 10.17605/OSF.IO/PCAXG

Bitzenis, A., & Koutsoupias, N. (2023B, December). Visualizing Economics and Business in the field of Education: A Quantitative Analysis of Scholarly Literature. *Global Business & Economics Anthology. Volumes I, II.* Advance online publication. DOI: 10.47341/gbea.23126

Bitzenis, A., & Koutsoupias, N. (2024). Big Data in Economics Research. In Tsounis, N., & Vlachvei, A. (Eds.), *Applied Economic Research and Trends* (pp. 1063–1072). Springer Nature Switzerland., DOI: 10.1007/978-3-031-49105-4_6

Bitzenis, A., Koutsoupias, N., & Nosios, M. (2025A). Artificial intelligence and machine learning in production efficiency enhancement and sustainable development: A comprehensive bibliometric review. *Frontiers in Sustainability, 5*. Advance online publication. DOI: 10.3389/frsus.2024.1508647

Bitzenis, A., Koutsoupias, N., & Nosios, M. (2025B). Public Perceptions of Tax Evasion and Informal Economy in Greece. *Proceedings of XXIII. International Balkan and Near Eastern Social Sciences Congress Series on Economics, Business and Management*, 80–90. https://doi.org/DOI: 10.17605/OSF.IO/V3YCS

Bitzenis, A., Koutsoupias, N., & Nosios, M. (2025C). Theoretical Advancements in Logistics: Digitalization, Big Data, and Machine Learning in Decision Making. *Proceedings of XXIII. International Balkan and Near Eastern Social Sciences Congress Series on Economics, Business and Management*, 91–101. https://doi.org/DOI: 10.17605/OSF.IO/G7H43

Björkqvist, K. (1994). Sex differences in physical, verbal, and indirect aggression: A review of recent research. *Sex Roles, 1994*(30), 177–188.

Blanco-Mallo, E., Morán-Fernández, L., Remeseiro, B., & Bolón-Canedo, V. (2023). Do all roads lead to Rome? Studying distance measures in the context of machine learning. *Pattern Recognition, 141*, 109646. DOI: 10.1016/j.patcog.2023.109646

Blasius, J., & Greenacre, M. L. (1998). Visualization of categorical data. In *Elsevier eBooks*. https://doi.org/DOI: 10.1016/b978-0-12-299045-8.x5000-1

Blum, H., & Legey, L. F. (2012). The challenging economics of energy security: Ensuring energy benefits in support to sustainable development. *Energy Economics*, *34*(6), 1982–1989. DOI: 10.1016/j.eneco.2012.08.013

Bommasani, R., Hudson, D. A., Adeli, E., Altman, R., Arora, S., Von Arx, S., Bernstein, M. S., Bohg, J., Bosselut, A., Brunskill, E., Brynjolfsson, E., Buch, S., Card, D., Castellon, R., Chatterji, N., Chen, A., Creel, K., Davis, J. Q., Demszky, D., . . . Liang, P. (2021). On the Opportunities and Risks of Foundation Models. *arXiv (Cornell University)*. https://doi.org//arxiv.2108.07258DOI: 10.48550

Booth, J. L., McGinn, K. M., Barbieri, C., & Young, L. K. (2016). Misconceptions and learning algebra. In *And the rest is just algebra* (pp. 63–78). Springer International Publishing., DOI: 10.1007/978-3-319-45053-7_4

Bose, I., & Mahapatra, R. K. (2001). Business data mining — A machine learning perspective. *Information & Management*, *39*(3), 211–225. DOI: 10.1016/s0378-7206(01)00091-x

Bowen, G., & Ozuem, W. (Eds.). (2015). *Computer-Mediated Marketing Strategies: Social Media and Online Brand Communities. IGI Global*. Department of Management and Accounting, Lead City University., DOI: 10.4018/978-1-4666-6595-8

Bro, R. (1997). PARAFAC. Tutorial and applications. *Chemometrics and Intelligent Laboratory Systems*, *38*(2), 149–171. DOI: 10.1016/s0169-7439(97)00032-4

Brundtland, G. H. (1987). *Our common future*. Oxford University Press.

Brynjolfsson, E., & Mitchell, T. (2017). What can machine learning do? Workforce implications. *Science*, *358*(6370), 1530–1534. DOI: 10.1126/science.aap8062

Burnham, J. F. (2006). Scopus database: A review. *Biomedical Digital Libraries*, *3*(1), 1. DOI: 10.1186/1742-5581-3-1

Cabrera, A. F., & Guerrero, A. J. M. (2019). Sánchez. S.P., and García, Antonio-Manuel R. (2022). Bullying among Teens: Are Ethnicity and Race Risk Factors for Victimization? A Bibliometric Research. *Education in Science*, *9*, 220. DOI: 10.3390/educsci9030220

Calabrese, A., Costa, R., Gastaldi, M., Ghiron, N. L., & Montalvan, R. A. V. (2021). Implications for Sustainable Development Goals: A framework to assess company disclosure in sustainability reporting. *Journal of Cleaner Production*, *319*, 128624. DOI: 10.1016/j.jclepro.2021.128624

Caney, A., & Watson, J. M. (2003). Mental computation strategies for part-whole numbers. In *AARE 2003 Conference papers, International Education Research.* https://ecite.utas.edu.au/28319

Cao, L. (2022). AI in Finance: Challenges, Techniques, and Opportunities. *ACM Computing Surveys*, *55*(3), 1–38. DOI: 10.1145/3502289

Caporale, G. M., Gil-Alana, L. A., Plastun, A., & Makarenko, I. (2022). Persistence in ESG and conventional stock market indices. *Journal of Economics and Finance*, *46*(4), 678–703. DOI: 10.1007/s12197-022-09580-0

Castillo-Girones, S., Munera, S., Martínez-Sober, M., Blasco, J., Cubero, S., & Gómez-Sanchis, J. (2025). Artificial Neural Networks in Agriculture, the core of artificial intelligence: What, When, and Why. *Computers and Electronics in Agriculture*, *230*, 109938. DOI: 10.1016/j.compag.2025.109938

Cattell, R. (2011). Scalable SQL and NoSQL data stores. *SIGMOD Record*, *39*(4), 12–27. DOI: 10.1145/1978915.1978919

Cevik, S. (2024). Climate change and energy security: The dilemma or opportunity of the century? *Environmental Economics and Policy Studies*, *26*(3), 653–672. DOI: 10.1007/s10018-023-00391-z

Chakraborty, S. K., & Mazzanti, M. (2020). Energy intensity and green energy innovation: Checking heterogeneous country effects in the OECD. *Structural Change and Economic Dynamics*, *52*, 328–343. DOI: 10.1016/j.strueco.2019.12.002

Charrad, M., Ghazzali, N., Boiteau, V., & Niknafs, A. (2014). NBClust: ANRPackage for determining the relevant number of clusters in a data set. *Journal of Statistical Software*, *61*(6). Advance online publication. DOI: 10.18637/jss.v061.i06

Chatti, M. A., Dyckhoff, A. L., Schroeder, U., & Thüs, H. (2014). Learning analytics: Challenges and future research directions. *eLearning and Education (eleed).*

Chauvin, C., Lardjane, S., Morel, G., Clostermann, J.-P., & Langard, B. (2013). Human and organisational factors in maritime accidents: Analysis of collisions at sea using the HFACS. *Accident; Analysis and Prevention*, *59*, 26–37. DOI: 10.1016/j.aap.2013.05.006 PMID: 23764875

Chen, Z., Xu, M., Ren, F., & Xiong, X. (2025). SDG performance and stock returns: Fresh insights from China. *Journal of International Money and Finance*, *152*, 103264. DOI: 10.1016/j.jimonfin.2024.103264

Chikuse, Y. (2003). The special manifolds and related multivariate topics. In *Lecture notes in statistics* (pp. 1–26). Springer., DOI: 10.1007/978-0-387-21540-2_1

Choi, Y., Choi, B. Y., Kim, S. I., Choi, J., Kim, J., Park, B. Y., Kim, S. M., Kim, S.-W., Choi, J. Y., Song, J. Y., Kim, Y. J., Kim, H. Y., Lee, J.-S., Kim, J. H., Jun, Y. H., Lee, M., & Seong, J. (2023). Effect of characteristics on the clinical course at the initiation of treatment for human immunodeficiency virus infection using dimensionality reduction. *Scientific Reports, 13*(1), 5547. DOI: 10.1038/s41598-023-31916-x PMID: 37016006

Chowdhury, S., Budhwar, P., Dey, P. K., Joel-Edgar, S., & Abadie, A. (2022). AI-employee collaboration and business performance: Integrating knowledge-based view, socio-technical systems and organisational socialisation framework. *Journal of Business Research, 144*, 31–49. DOI: 10.1016/j.jbusres.2022.01.069

Codesido, S., Hanafi, M., Gagnebin, Y., González-Ruiz, V., Rudaz, S., & Boccard, J. (2021). Network principal component analysis: A versatile tool for the investigation of multigroup and multiblock datasets. *Bioinformatics (Oxford, England), 37*(9), 1297–1303. DOI: 10.1093/bioinformatics/btaa954 PMID: 33165510

Cohen, G., Joutz, F., & Loungani, P. (2011). Measuring energy security: Trends in the diversification of oil and natural gas supplies. *Energy Policy, 39*(9), 4860–4869. DOI: 10.1016/j.enpol.2011.06.034

Costa, E., Papatsouma, I., & Markos, A. (2023). Benchmarking distance-based partitioning methods for mixed-type data. *Advances in Data Analysis and Classification, 17*(3), 701–724. DOI: 10.1007/s11634-022-00521-7

Creswell, J. W. (2012). *Educational research: Planning*. Conducting, and Evaluating Quantitative and Qualitative Research.

Crompton, H., & Burke, D. (2023). Artificial intelligence in higher education: The state of the field. *International Journal of Educational Technology in Higher Education, 20*(22). Advance online publication. DOI: 10.1186/s41239-023-00392-8

Cuadras, C. M., Cuadras, D., & Greenacre, M. J. (2006). A comparison of different methods for representing categorical data. *Communications in Statistics. Simulation and Computation, 35*(2), 447–459. DOI: 10.1080/03610910600591875

Cubric, M. (2020). Drivers, barriers and social considerations for AI adoption in business and management: A tertiary study. *Technology in Society, 62*, 101257. DOI: 10.1016/j.techsoc.2020.101257

Dale, A., Wathan, J., & Higgins, V. (2008). *Secondary analysis of quantitative data sources. The SAGE Handbook of Social Research Methods*. SAGE Publications Ltd.

Dalègre, J., & Tzimakas, M. (2015). *Les populations de la Macédoine grecque au XXe siècle*. L'Harmattan.

Dash, M., Liu, H., & Yao, J. (1997). Dimensionality reduction of unsupervised data. In Anon (Ed.), *Proceedings of the International Conference on Tools with Artificial Intelligence* (pp. 532-539). IEEE. https://doi.org/DOI: 10.1109/TAI.1997.632300

De Haan, J. R., Wehrens, R., Bauerschmidt, S., Piek, E., Van Schaik, R. C., & Buydens, L. M. C. (2006). Interpretation of ANOVA models for microarray data using PCA. *Bioinformatics (Oxford, England)*, *23*(2), 184–190. DOI: 10.1093/bioinformatics/btl572 PMID: 17105717

De Roover, K., Ceulemans, E., Timmerman, M. E., Nezlek, J. B., & Onghena, P. (2013). Modeling differences in the dimensionality of multiblock data by means of clusterwise simultaneous component analysis. *Psychometrika*, *78*(4), 648–668. DOI: 10.1007/s11336-013-9318-4 PMID: 24092482

Denecke, K. (2008). Using SentiWordNet for multilingual sentiment analysis. *2008 IEEE 24th International Conference on Data Engineering Workshop*, 507–512. https://doi.org/DOI: 10.1109/icdew.2008.4498370

Deng, Z., Li, T., Zhang, P., Liu, K., Yuan, Z., & Deng, D. (2025). Feature selection for label distribution learning based on neighborhood fuzzy rough sets. *Applied Soft Computing*, *169*, 112542. DOI: 10.1016/j.asoc.2024.112542

Deraman, N. A., Samah, K. A. F. A., Jono, M. N. H. H., & Isa, S. M. A. M., & Saad, [Initial(s)]. (2021). A social media mining using topic modeling and sentiment analysis on tourism in Malaysia during COVID-19. *IOP Conference Series. Earth and Environmental Science*, *704*, 012020. Advance online publication. DOI: 10.1088/1755-1315/704/1/012020

Devlin, J., Chang, M.-W., Lee, K., & Toutanova, K. (2018). BERT: Pre-training of deep bidirectional transformers for language understanding. https://arxiv.org/abs/1810.04805

Di Vaio, A., Palladino, R., Hassan, R., & Escobar, O. (2020). Artificial intelligence and business models in the sustainable development goals perspective: A systematic literature review. *Journal of Business Research*, *121*, 283–314. DOI: 10.1016/j.jbusres.2020.08.019

Digital Strategy – European Commission. (2024). *AI Act: Shaping Europe's digital future.* https://digital-strategy.ec.europa.eu/en/policies/regulatory-framework-ai

do Carmo, M. P. (1992). *Riemannian Geometry.* Birkhäuser.

Dong, B., Bai, J., Xu, T., & Zhou, Y. (2024). Large language models in education: A systematic review. In *Proceedings of the 2024 International Conference on Computer Science and Technologies in Education (CSTE).* IEEE.

Donnelly, H. K., Han, Y., Song, J., & Song, T. M. (2019). Application of Social Big Data to Identify Trends of School Bullying Forms in South Korea. *International Journal of Environmental Research and Public Health, 2019*(16), 2596. DOI: 10.3390/ijerph16142596 PMID: 31330879

Donthu, N., Kumar, S., Mukherjee, D., Pandey, N., & Lim, W. M. (2021). How to conduct a bibliometric analysis: An overview and guidelines. *Journal of Business Research, 133*, 285–296. DOI: 10.1016/j.jbusres.2021.04.070

Dr, M. W. (n.d.). social media marketing communications effect on attitudes among millennials in South Africa. 8(3).

Drosos, G. (2004). Statistical Analysis of Linguistic Information Data. Doctoral Dissertation, University of Macedonia, Thessaloniki, Greece.

Dubinsky, E., & Harel, G. (1992). The Concept of function: aspects of epistemology and pedagogy. In *Mathematical Association of America eBooks*. http://ci.nii.ac.jp/ncid/BA23271623

Duffett, R. G. (2017). Influence of social media marketing communications on young consumers' attitudes. *Young Consumers, 18*(1), 19–39. DOI: 10.1108/YC-07-2016-00622

Dunlop, T. (2019). Mind the gap: A social sciences review of energy efficiency. *Energy Research & Social Science, 56*, 101216. DOI: 10.1016/j.erss.2019.05.026

Dunlop, T., & Völker, T. (2023). The politics of measurement and the case of energy efficiency policy in the European Union. *Energy Research & Social Science, 96*, 102918. DOI: 10.1016/j.erss.2022.102918

Dutta, E., Diwan, S., & Chakrabarty, S. P. (2024, January 26). ESG driven pairs algorithm for sustainable trading: Analysis from the Indian market [Preprint]. arXiv. https://arxiv.org/abs/2401.14761

Duval, R. (2006). A cognitive analysis of problems of comprehension in a learning of mathematics. *Educational Studies in Mathematics, 61*(1–2), 103–131. DOI: 10.1007/s10649-006-0400-z

Ebrahimi Warkiani, M., & Moattar, M. H. (2025). A comprehensive survey on recent feature selection methods for mixed data: Challenges, solutions and future directions. *Neurocomputing, 623*, 129372. DOI: 10.1016/j.neucom.2025.129372

Edelman, A., Arias, T. A., & Smith, S. T. (1998). The Geometry of Algorithms with Orthogonality Constraints. *SIAM Journal on Matrix Analysis and Applications, 20*(2), 303–353. DOI: 10.1137/s0895479895290954

Einav, L., & Levin, J. (2014). Economics in the age of big data. *Science, 346*(6210). Advance online publication. DOI: 10.1126/science.1243089

Eisenberg, T. (1992). On the development of a sense for functions. In Harel, G., & Dubinsky, E. (Eds.), *The concept of function: Aspects of epistemology and pedagogy. MAA Notes, 25* (pp. 153–174). Mathematical Association of America.

Ekolu, S. O., & Quainoo, H. (2019). Reliability of assessments in engineering education using Cronbach's alpha, KR and split-half methods. *Global journal of engineering education, 21*(1), 24-29.

Elareshi, M., Habes, M., Safori, A., Attar, R. W., Noor Al Adwan, M., & Al-Rahmi, W. M. (2023). Understanding the Effects of Social Media Marketing on Customers' Bank Loyalty: A SEM Approach. *Electronics (Basel), 12*(8), 1822. DOI: 10.3390/electronics12081822

Elbassoussy, A. (2019). European energy security dilemma: Major challenges and confrontation strategies. *Review of Economics and Political Science, 4*(4), 321–343. DOI: 10.1108/REPS-02-2019-0019

Ellegaard, O., & Wallin, J. A. (2015). The bibliometric analysis of scholarly production: How great is the impact? *Scientometrics, 105*(3), 1809–1831. DOI: 10.1007/s11192-015-1645-z

Emirtekin, E., Yilmaz, H., Kose, U., & Deperlioglu, O. (2025). Large language model-powered automated assessment: A systematic review. *Applied Sciences (Basel, Switzerland), 15*(10), 5683.

Enholm, I. M., Papagiannidis, E., Mikalef, P., & Krogstie, J. (2022). Artificial Intelligence and Business Value: A Literature Review. *Information Systems Frontiers, 24*(5), 1709–1734. DOI: 10.1007/s10796-021-10186-w

Erin, O. A., & Bamigboye, O. A. (2021). Evaluation and analysis of SDG reporting: Evidence from Africa. *Journal of Accounting & Organizational Change, 18*(3), 369–396. DOI: 10.1108/jaoc-02-2020-0025

Erin, O. A., Bamigboye, O. A., & Oyewo, B. M. (2022). Sustainable development goals (SDG) reporting: An analysis of disclosure. *Journal of Accounting in Emerging Economies, 12*(5), 761–789. DOI: 10.1108/JAEE-02-2020-0037

Erin, O., Ackers, B., & Bamigboye, O. (2024). The State of SDGs and Sustainability Practices of Public Sector Entities: Evidence from an under-investigated Context. *Journal of Cleaner Production, 465*, 142772. DOI: 10.1016/j.jclepro.2024.142772

Eskandari, F., Lake, A. A., & Butler, M. (2022). COVID-19 pandemic and food poverty conversations: Social network analysis of Twitter data. *Nutrition Bulletin, 47*(1), 93–105. DOI: 10.1111/nbu.12547 PMID: 36045084

Eslami, A., Qannari, E. M., Kohler, A., and Bougeard, S. (2013). General overview of methods of analysis of multi-group datasets. *Revue des Nouvelles Technologies de l'Information. 25.*

Estrada, M. A. R., & Koutronas, E. (2022). The impact of the Russian aggression against Ukraine on the Russia-EU trade. *Journal of Policy Modeling, 44*(3), 599–616. DOI: 10.1016/j.jpolmod.2022.06.004

European Commission. (2021). *AI risk-based regulatory pyramid infographic.*

European Commission. (2021). *The European Pillar of Social Rights Action Plan.* Publications Office of the European Union. https://op.europa.eu/webpub/empl/european-pillar-of-social rights/downloads/KE0921008ENN.pdf

European Union. (2024). *Regulation (EU) 2024/1689 of the European Parliament and of the Council on artificial intelligence (AI Act).* Official Journal of the European Union.

Eurostat, Statistics Explained, (2022), Archive: EU energy mix and import dependency, 104551.pdf

Everitt, B. S., Landau, S., Leese, M., & Stahl, D. (2011). Cluster analysis. In *Wiley series in probability and statistics.* https://doi.org/DOI: 10.1002/9780470977811

Everitt, B. S., Landau, S., Leese, M., & Stahl, D. (2011). *Cluster analysis.* John Wiley & Sons.

Fahad, P., & Rahman, P. M. (2020). Impact of corporate governance on CSR disclosure. *International Journal of Disclosure and Governance, 17*(2–3), 155–167. DOI: 10.1057/s41310-020-00082-1

Farhi, F., Jeljeli, R., & Aburezeq, I. Fawzi Fayez Dweikat, Samer Ali Al-shami, Slamene, R. (2023). Analyzing the students' views, concerns, and perceived ethics about chatGPT usage, Computers and Education: Artificial Intelligence, Volume 5, 2023, 100180, ISSN 2666-920X,https://doi.org/DOI: 10.1016/j.caeai.2023.100180

Farook, F. S., & Abeysekara, N. (n.d.). Influence of Social Media Marketing on Customer Engagement.

FeedbackFruits. (2025, February 12). What is the EU AI Act? A comprehensive overview. https://feedbackfruits.com/blog/from-regulation-to-innovation-what-the-eu-ai-act-means-for-edtech

Fenton, A., & Procter, C. (2019). Studying social media communities: Blending methods with netnography. In *Sage research methods cases.* SAGE Publications., DOI: 10.4135/9781526468901

Ferrero-Ferrero, I., Muñoz-Torres, M. J., Rivera-Lirio, J. M., Escrig-Olmedo, E., & Fernández-Izquierdo, M. Á. (2023). Sustainable development goals in the hospitality industry: A dream or reality? *Journal of Accounting & Organizational Change, 20*(5), 773–796. DOI: 10.1108/jaoc-09-2022-0146

Flores-Ruiz, D., Elizondo-Salto, A., & Barroso-González, M. D. L. O. (2021). Using social media in tourist sentiment analysis: A case study of Andalusia during the COVID-19 pandemic. *Sustainability, 13*(7), 3836. Advance online publication. DOI: 10.3390/su13073836

Florou, G. (1997). Determination of the Ideal Distance Metric and the Best Clustering Method in Various Hierarchical Agglomerative Classification Methods. Doctoral Dissertation, Department of Applied Informatics, University of Macedonia, Thessaloniki, Greece.

Fotiadis, Th., & Anastasiadou, S. (2018). Contemporary advanced statistical methods for the science of marketing: Principal Components Analysis vs Analysee Factorielle des Correspondances. Proceeding of the ICME 2018- 1st International Conference on Marketing and Entrepreneuship. Cyprus. https://hephaestus.nup.ac.cy/handle/11728/11392

Fragkoulis, M., Carbone, P., Kalavri, V., & Katsifodimos, A. (2023). A survey on the evolution of stream processing systems. *The VLDB Journal, 33*(2), 507–541. DOI: 10.1007/s00778-023-00819-8

Fraley, C., & Raftery, A. E. (2002). Model-Based clustering, discriminant analysis, and density estimation. *Journal of the American Statistical Association, 97*(458), 611–631. DOI: 10.1198/016214502760047131

Future of Life Institute. (2024). *High-level summary of the EU AI Act.* https://artificialintelligenceact.eu

Gabriel, K. R. (1971). The biplot graphic display of matrices with application to principal component analysis. *Biometrika, 58*(3), 453–467. DOI: 10.1093/biomet/58.3.453

Gabriel, K. R. (2002). Goodness of fit of biplots and correspondence analysis. *Biometrika, 89*(2), 423–436. DOI: 10.1093/biomet/89.2.423

Gagatsis, A., & Shiakalli, M. (2004). Ability to Translate from One Representation of the Concept of Function to Another and Mathematical Problem Solving. *Educational Psychology, 24*(5), 645–657. DOI: 10.1080/0144341042000262953

Gao, H., Kou, G., Liang, H., Zhang, H., Chao, X., Li, C., & Dong, Y. (2024). Machine learning in business and finance: A literature review and research opportunities. *Financial Innovation, 10*(1). Advance online publication. DOI: 10.1186/s40854-024-00629-z

Ghauri, P. N. (2022). The role of multinational enterprises in achieving sustainable development goals. *AIB Insights, 22*(1). Advance online publication. DOI: 10.46697/001c.31077

Ghoddusi, H., Creamer, G. G., & Rafizadeh, N. (2019). Machine learning in energy economics and finance: A review. *Energy Economics, 81*, 709–727. DOI: 10.1016/j.eneco.2019.05.006

Gifi, A. (1990). *Nonlinear Multivariate Analysis*. John Willey and Sons Inc.

Golbeck, J. (2015). Analyzing networks. In *Introduction to social media investigation* (pp. 221–235). Elsevier., DOI: 10.1016/B978-0-12-801656-5.00021-4

Golob, T. F., & Hensher, D. A. (2007). The trip chaining activity of Sydney residents: A cross-section assessment by age group with a focus on seniors. *Journal of Transport Geography, 15*(4), 298–312. DOI: 10.1016/j.jtrangeo.2006.09.005

Gower, J. C. (1967). A comparison of some methods of cluster analysis. *Biometrics, 23*(4), 623–637. DOI: 10.2307/2528417 PMID: 6080200

Gower, J. C. (1971). A general coefficient of similarity and some of its properties. *Biometrics, 27*(4), 857. DOI: 10.2307/2528823

Gower, J. C. (1975). Generalized Procrustes analysis. *Psychometrika, 40*(1), 33–51. DOI: 10.1007/bf02291478

Gower, J. C. (2004). The geometry of biplot scaling. *Biometrika, 91*(3), 705–714. DOI: 10.1093/biomet/91.3.705

Gower, J. C., & Dijksterhuis, G. B. (2004). *Procrustes problems*. https://doi.org/DOI: 10.1093/acprof:oso/9780198510581.001.0001

Grané, A., Salini, S., & Verdolini, E. (2021). Robust multivariate analysis for mixed-type data: Novel algorithm and its practical application in socio-economic research. *Socio-Economic Planning Sciences. Statistical Methods & Models for the Evaluation Systems of the Public Sector, 73*, 100907. DOI: 10.1016/j.seps.2020.100907

Greenacre, M. (2009). *Biplots in practice*. https://econpapers.repec.org/RePEc:fbb:booklb:2011113

Greenacre, M. (2017a). Correspondence analysis in practice. In *Chapman and Hall/CRC eBooks*. https://doi.org/DOI: 10.1201/9781315369983

Greenacre, M. J., & Blasius, J. (2006). Multiple Correspondence Analysis and Related Methods. In *Chapman and Hall/CRC eBooks*. https://doi.org/DOI: 10.1201/9781420011319

Greenacre, M. (2010). Correspondence Analysis. In Peterson, P., Baker, E., & Mc-Gaw, B. (Eds.), *International Encyclopedia of Education* (3rd ed., pp. 103–111). Elsevier., DOI: 10.1016/B978-0-08-044894-7.01317-8

Greenacre, M. (2017b). *Correspondence analysis in practice*. CRC Press.

Greenacre, M., & Blasius, J. (1994). *Correspondence Analysis in the Social Sciences*. Academic Press.

Greenacre, M., Groenen, P. J. F., Hastie, T., Iodice D'Enza, A., Markos, A., & Tuzhilina, E. (2022). Principal component analysis. *Nature Reviews. Methods Primers*, *2*, 100. DOI: 10.1038/s43586-022-00184-w

Guizani, S., Mazhar, T., Shahzad, T., Ahmad, W., Bibi, A., & Hamam, H. (2025). A systematic literature review to implement large language models in higher education: Issues and solutions. *Discover Education*, *4*(35).

Gulati, S. (2022). Tapping public sentiments on Twitter for tourism insights: A study of famous Indian heritage sites. *International Hospitality Review*, *36*(2), 244–257. DOI: 10.1108/IHR-03-2021-0021

Gu, S., Kelly, B., & Xiu, D. (2020). Empirical asset pricing via machine learning. *Review of Financial Studies*, *33*(5), 2223–2273. DOI: 10.1093/rfs/hhaa009

Hair, J. F., Black, W. C., Babin, B. J., & Anderson, R. E. (2010). *Multivariate Data Analysis: A Global Perspective* (7th ed.). Pearson Education Inc.

Hakim, C. (1982). *Secondary analysis in social research: A guide to data sources and methods with examples*. Unwin Hyman (Firm).

Hall, M., & Holmes, G. (2003). Benchmarking attribute selection techniques for discrete class data mining. *IEEE Transactions on Knowledge and Data Engineering*, *15*(6), 1437–1447. DOI: 10.1109/tkde.2003.1245283

Hansen, D. L., Shneiderman, B., & Smith, M. A. (2011). *Analyzing social media networks with NodeXL: Insights from a connected world*. Elsevier.

Hasan, M., & Sohail, M. S. (2021). The Influence of Social Media Marketing on Consumers' Purchase Decision: Investigating the Effects of Local and Nonlocal Brands. *Journal of International Consumer Marketing*, *33*(3), 350–367. DOI: 10.1080/08961530.2020.1795043

Hassan, S. T., Khan, S. U. D., Xia, E., & Fatima, H. (2020). Role of institutions in correcting environmental pollution: An empirical investigation. *Sustainable Cities and Society*, *53*, 101901. DOI: 10.1016/j.scs.2019.101901

Hays, S., Page, S. J., & Buhalis, D. (2013). Social media as a destination marketing tool: Its use by national tourism organisations. *Current Issues in Tourism*, *16*(3), 211–239. DOI: 10.1080/13683500.2012.662215

Heffron, R. J., McCauley, D., & Sovacool, B. K. (2015). Resolving society's energy trilemma through the Energy Justice Metric. *Energy Policy*, *87*, 168–176. DOI: 10.1016/j.enpol.2015.08.033

Heinze, A., Star, J. R., & Verschaffel, L. (2009). Flexible and adaptive use of strategies and representations in mathematics education. *ZDM*, *41*(5), 535–540. DOI: 10.1007/s11858-009-0214-4

Hellenic Statistical Authority. (1929a). Census of the population of Greece on 19 December 1920. http://dlib.statistics.gr/Book/GRESYE_02_0101_00011.pdf

Hellenic Statistical Authority. (1929b). Population de la Grece d aprel le recensement du 15-16 Mai 1928. http://dlib.statistics.gr/portal/page/portal/ESYE/showdetails?p_id=16690436&p_derive=book&p_topic=10007862

Hellenic Statistical Authority. (2022). *Census of refugees carried out in April 1923*. http://dlib.statistics.gr/Book/GRESYE_02_0101_00107.pdf

He, N. H., & Garcia, E. (2009). Learning from Imbalanced Data. *IEEE Transactions on Knowledge and Data Engineering*, *21*(9), 1263–1284. DOI: 10.1109/tkde.2008.239

Hennig, C., & Liao, T. F. (2013). How to find an appropriate clustering for mixed-type variables with application to socio-economic stratification. *Journal of the Royal Statistical Society. Series C: Applied Statistics, 62*(3), 309–369. *Scopus*. Advance online publication. DOI: 10.1111/j.1467-9876.2012.01066.x

Huang, M., & Rust, R. T. (2020). A strategic framework for artificial intelligence in marketing. *Journal of the Academy of Marketing Science*, *49*(1), 30–50. DOI: 10.1007/s11747-020-00749-9

IAPP. (2023, December). *EU AI Act cheat sheet*. International Association of Privacy Professionals. https://iapp.org/resources/article/eu-ai-act-cheat-sheet/

Indices, N. S. E. (2025, March 28). Nifty 50. National Stock Exchange of India. Retreieved from https://www.niftyindices.com/indices/equity/NIFTY-50

Inoubli, W., Aridhi, S., Mezni, H., Maddouri, M., & Nguifo, E. M. (2018). An experimental survey on big data frameworks. *Future Generation Computer Systems, 86*, 546–564. DOI: 10.1016/j.future.2018.04.032

Izenman, A. J. (2008). *Modern Multivariate Statistical Techniques: Regression, Classification, and Manifold Learning*. Springer., DOI: 10.1007/978-0-387-78189-1

Jagadish, H. V., Gehrke, J., Labrinidis, A., Papakonstantinou, Y., Patel, J. M., Ramakrishnan, R., & Shahabi, C. (2014). Big data and its technical challenges. *Communications of the ACM, 57*(7), 86–94. DOI: 10.1145/2611567

Jamil, K., Dunnan, L., Gul, R. F., Shehzad, M. U., Gillani, S. H. M., & Awan, F. H. (2022). Role of Social Media Marketing Activities in Influencing Customer Intentions: A Perspective of a New Emerging Era. *Frontiers in Psychology, 12*, 808525. DOI: 10.3389/fpsyg.2021.808525 PMID: 35111111

Jansen, J. J., Hoefsloot, H. C. J., Van Der Greef, J., Timmerman, M. E., Westerhuis, J. A., & Smilde, A. K. (2005). ASCA: Analysis of multivariate data obtained from an experimental design. *Journal of Chemometrics, 19*(9), 469–481. DOI: 10.1002/cem.952

Janvier, C. (1987). *Problems of Representations in the Learning and Teaching of Mathematics*. Lawrence Erlbaum Associates.

Jobson, J. D. (1992). *Applied multivariate data analysis: Volume II: Categorical and Multivariate methods*. Springer-Verlag.

Joi a, D., Panait, M., Dobrotă, C. E., Dini ă, A., Neac a, A., & Naghi, L. E. (2023). The European dilemma-Energy security or green transition. *Energies, 16*(9), 3849. DOI: 10.3390/en16093849

Jolliffe, I. T. (2002). *Principal component analysis* (2nd ed.). Springer.

Jolliffe, I. T., & Cadima, J. (2016). Principal component analysis: A review and recent developments. *Phil Trans R Soc A, 374*(2065), 20150202. DOI: 10.1098/rsta.2015.0202 PMID: 26953178

Kaiser, H. F. (1958). The varimax criterion for analytic rotation in factor analysis. *Psychometrika, 23*, 187–200. DOI: 10.1007/BF02289233

Kalamartzis, I., Dordas, C., Georgiou, P., & Menexes, G. (2020). The Use of Appropriate Cultivar of Basil (Ocimum basilicum) Can Increase Water Use Efficiency under Water Stress. *Agronomy (Basel), 10*(1), 70. DOI: 10.3390/agronomy10010070

Kameas, A., & Seremeti, L. (2011). Ontology-based knowledge management in NGAIEs. In Minker, W., & Heinroth, T. (Eds.), *Next Generation Intelligent Environments* (pp. 85–126). Springer., DOI: 10.1007/978-1-4614-1299-1_3

Kanellakis, M., Martinopoulos, G., & Zachariadis, T. (2013). European energy policy—A review. *Energy Policy*, *62*, 1020–1030. DOI: 10.1016/j.enpol.2013.08.008

Kankam Boadu, A. A. (2019). Customer Relationship Management and Customer Retention. SSRN Electronic Journal. https://doi.org/DOI: 10.2139/ssrn.3472492

Kaput, J. (1992). Notations and representations as mediators of constructive processes. In Glasersfeld, E. (Ed.), *Radical Constructivism in Mathematics Education* (pp. 53–74). Kluwer Academic Publishers., DOI: 10.1007/0-306-47201-5_3

Karapistolis, D. (2000). *MAD Data Analysis Method Software*. Athanasiou Altintzis Publishing.

Karapistolis, D. (2015). *Multidimensional Statistical Analysis*. Athanasiou Altintzis Publishing.

Karapistolis, D. (2015). *Multivariate Statistical Analysis* (Altintzis, A., Ed.).

Karlis, D. (2005). *Multivariate Statistical Analysis*. Ath. Stamoulis Publications. (In Greek)

Kassambara, A. (2017). *Practical Guide to Cluster Analysis in R: Unsupervised Machine Learning* (Vol. 1). STHDA.

Katsantonis, A., & Katsantonis, I. G. (2024). University Students' Attitudes toward Artificial Intelligence: An Exploratory Study of the Cognitive, Emotional, and Behavioural Dimensions of AI Attitudes. *Education in Science*, *14*, 988. DOI: 10.3390/educsci14090988

Kaufman, L., & Rousseeuw, L. (1990). *Finding Groups in Data. An Introduction to Cluster Analysis*. John Wiley & Sons.

Kaufman, L., & Rousseeuw, P. J. (2009). *Finding Groups in Data: An Introduction to Cluster Analysis*. John Wiley & Sons.

Keypour, J., & Ahmadzada, U. (2022). Consolidating EU energy security by relying on energy de-politicisation. *European Security*, *31*(1), 135–157. DOI: 10.1080/09662839.2021.1970538

Khan, A., Sampene, A. K., & Ali, S. (2023). Towards environmental degradation mitigation: The role of regulatory quality, technological innovation and government effectiveness in the CEMAC countries. *Heliyon*, *9*(6).

Khanchel, I., Lassoued, N., & Baccar, I. (2023). Sustainability and firm performance: The role of environmental, social and governance disclosure and green innovation. *Management Decision*, *61*(9), 2720–2739. DOI: 10.1108/md-09-2021-1252

Kim, Y., Nordgren, R., & Emery, S. (2020). The story of goldilocks and three twitter's APIs: A pilot study on twitter data sources and disclosure. *International Journal of Environmental Research and Public Health*, *17*(3), 864. Advance online publication. DOI: 10.3390/ijerph17030864 PMID: 32019070

Kiran, M., Murphy, P., Monga, I., Dugan, J., & Baveja, S. S. (2015). Lambda architecture for cost-effective batch and speed big data processing. *2021 IEEE International Conference on Big Data (Big Data)*. https://doi.org/DOI: 10.1109/bigdata.2015.7364082

Kitchen, N. R., & Clay, S. A. (2016). Understanding and Identifying Variability. *Agronomy, Horticulture and Plant Science Faculty Publications. 69*. https://openprairie.sdstate.edu/plant_faculty_pubs/69

Knuth, E. J. (2000). Student understanding of the Cartesian connection: An exploratory study. *Journal for Research in Mathematics Education*, *31*(4), 500–514.

Kolda, T. G., & Bader, B. W. (2009). Tensor Decompositions and Applications. *SIAM Review*, *51*, 455–500. DOI: 10.1137/07070111X

Kontis, S., Anastasiadou, S., Anastasiadis, L., & Seremeti, L. (2025). Legal entropy in AI governance. In Anastasiadou, S., Seremeti, L., Masouras, A., & Anastasiadis, L. (Eds.), *Modern perspectives on artificial intelligence and law* (pp. 193–206). IGI Global Scientific Publishing., DOI: 10.4018/979-8-3693-9576-9.ch010

Koutsoupias, N., & Nosios, M. (2025). Data Engineering Research: A Systematic Review and Thematic Analysis of Methods and Frameworks [dataset]. https://doi.org/DOI: 10.17605/OSF.IO/87XEH

Koutsoupias, N., & Nosios, M. (2025A). Hierarchical Clustering in Social Sciences and Humanities: A Review. In S. D. Anastasiadou, T. G. Chadjipadelis, Nikolaos Koutsoupias, Angelos Markos, & George Menexes (Eds.), *Modern International Developments in Data Analysis and Multivariate Statistical Analysis*. IGI Global Scientific Publishing. https://doi.org/DOI: 10.4018/979-8-3693-9400-7

Kroonenberg, P. M. (2008). *Applied Multiway Data Analysis*. Wiley Series in Probability and Statistics.

Kumar, S., Kumar, V., Bhatt, I. K., & Kumar, S. (2023). Mapping Research Trends on Smart Tourism: A Bibliometric analysis. In *Tourism, hospitality & event management* (pp. 87–109). https://doi.org/DOI: 10.1007/978-3-031-31682-1_5

Kuo, T., & Wang, K.-J. (2022). A hybrid *k*-prototypes clustering approach with improved sine-cosine algorithm for mixed-data classification. *Computers & Industrial Engineering*, *169*, 108164. DOI: 10.1016/j.cie.2022.108164

Kyrana, Z., Pratsinakis, E. D., Papafilippou, N., Markos, A., Dordas, C., & Menexes, G. C. (2025). Evaluating dimensionality reduction strategies on mixed-type datasets: A comparative analysis using Python, R and SPSS. *International Journal of Sustainable Agricultural Management and Informatics*, *11*(4), 445–469. DOI: 10.1504/IJSAMI.2024.10065202

Kyrana, Z., Pratsinakis, E. D., Papafilippou, N., Markos, A., Dordas, C., & Menexes, G. C. (2025). Evaluating dimensionality reduction strategies on mixed-type datasets: A comparative analysis using Python, R and SPSS. *International Journal of Sustainable Agricultural Management and Informatics, 11*(4), 445–469. *Scopus.* Advance online publication. DOI: 10.1504/IJSAMI.2025.149223

Kyrana, Z., Pratsinakis, E. D., Papafilippou, N., Michaelidou, A. M., Kiranas, E., & Menexes, G. C. (2026). Dimensionality Reduction in Data Cubes With Independent Slices. In Anastasiadou, S., Chadjipadelis, T., Koutsoupias, N., Markos, A., & Menexes, G. (Eds.), *Modern International Developments in Data Analysis and Multivariate Statistical Analysis* (pp. 37–72). IGI Global Scientific Publishing., DOI: 10.4018/979-8-3693-9400-7.ch002

Lange, P., Bornemann, B., & Burger, P. (2019). Sustainability impacts of governance modes: Insights from Swiss energy policy. *Journal of Environmental Policy and Planning*, *21*(2), 174–187. DOI: 10.1080/1523908X.2019.1566062

Lassala, C., Orero-Blat, M., & Ribeiro-Navarrete, S. (2021). The financial performance of listed companies in pursuit of the Sustainable Development Goals (SDG). *Economic Research-Ekonomska Istraživanja*, *34*(1), 427–449. DOI: 10.1080/1331677X.2021.1877167

Lattin, J. M., Carroll, J. D., & Green, P. E. (2003). *Analyzing multivariate data.* Duxbury Press.

Lee, J., Han, J., & Li, X. (2008). Trajectory Outlier Detection: A Partition-and-Detect Framework. *2008 IEEE 24th International Conference on Data Engineering*, 140–149. https://doi.org/DOI: 10.1109/icde.2008.4497422

Lee, J., Suh, T., Roy, D., & Baucus, M. (2019). Emerging technology and business model innovation: The case of artificial intelligence. *Journal of Open Innovation*, *5*(3), 44. DOI: 10.3390/joitmc5030044

Lerner, R. M. (2015b). *Handbook of Child Psychology and Developmental Science.*, DOI: 10.1002/9781118963418

Li, N. J., Tang, N. J., Li, N. Y., & Luo, N. Q. (2008). RIMOM: A dynamic multistrategy Ontology alignment framework. *IEEE Transactions on Knowledge and Data Engineering*, *21*(8), 1218–1232. DOI: 10.1109/tkde.2008.202

Linting, M., Meulman, J. J., Groenen, P. J., & Van der Koojj, A. J. (2007). Nonlinear principal components analysis: Introduction and application. *Psychological Methods*, *12*(3), 336–358. DOI: 10.1037/1082-989X.12.3.336 PMID: 17784798

Li, R., Zhou, G., Li, X., Jia, L., & Shang, Z. (2024). Semi-supervised multi-label dimensionality reduction learning based on minimizing redundant correlation of specific and common features. *Knowledge-Based Systems*, *294*, 111789. DOI: 10.1016/j.knosys.2024.111789

Liu, X., Latif, K., Latif, Z., & Li, N. (2020). Relationship between economic growth and CO2 emissions: Does governance matter? *Environmental Science and Pollution Research International*, *27*(14), 17221–17228. DOI: 10.1007/s11356-020-08142-3

Loureiro, S. M. C., Guerreiro, J., & Tussyadiah, I. (2021). Artificial intelligence in business: State of the art and future research agenda. *Journal of Business Research*, *129*, 911–926. DOI: 10.1016/j.jbusres.2020.11.001

Macfadyen, L. P., & Dawson, S. (2009). Mining LMS data to develop an "early warning system" for educators: A proof of concept. *Computers & Education*, *54*(2), 588–599. DOI: 10.1016/j.compedu.2009.09.008

Maclellan, E. (2001). Mental Calculation: Its place in the development of numeracy. *Westminster Studies in Education*, *24*(2), 145–154. DOI: 10.1080/0140672010240205

Madoune, S. A., Senouci, S., Jiang, D. D., Senouci, M. R., Daoud, M. A., Anwar Mohammed Alawad, R., & Madoune, Y. (2025). A novel approach for real-time DDoS detection in SDN using dimensionality reduction and ensemble learning. *Journal of Information Security and Applications*, *94*, 104195. DOI: 10.1016/j.jisa.2025.104195

Maecker, O., Barrot, C., & Becker, J. U. (2016). The effect of social media interactions on customer relationship management. *Business Research*, *9*(1), 133–155. DOI: 10.1007/s40685-016-0027-6

Magkanas, G., Bagán, H., Sistach, M. C., & García, J. F. (2023). *Artomics*: A holistic approach to the study of artworks integrating their compositional and formal characteristics. Application on the *Liber Feudorum Maior. Microchemical Journal*, *185*, 108276. DOI: 10.1016/j.microc.2022.108276

Mair, P. (2018). *Modern Psychometrics with R.* Springer International., DOI: 10.1007/978-3-319-93177-7

Mariani, M. M., Machado, I., Magrelli, V., & Dwivedi, Y. K. (2022). Artificial intelligence in innovation research: A systematic review, conceptual framework, and future research directions. *Technovation, 122*, 102623. DOI: 10.1016/j.technovation.2022.102623

Markos, A. (2007). *Assistance in the Interpretation of Correspondence Factor Analysis Results & Algorithms for Constructing and Analyzing Special Input Tables.* Doctoral Dissertation, Department of Applied Informatics, University of Macedonia, Thessaloniki, Greece.

Markos, A., Menexes, G., & Papadimitriou, I. (2010). The CHIC Analysis Software V1.0. In *Studies in classification, data analysis, and knowledge organization* (pp. 409–416). https://doi.org/DOI: 10.1007/978-3-642-10745-0_44

Markos, A., Moschidis, O., & Chadjipantelis, T. (2020). Sequential dimension reduction and clustering of mixed-type data. *Int. J. Data Analysis Techniques and Strategies, 12*(3), 228–246. DOI: 10.1504/IJDATS.2020.108043

Maturana, H. R., & Varela, F. J. (1992). The Tree of Knowledge: the biological roots of human understanding. In *Medical Entomology and Zoology*. https://ci.nii.ac.jp/ncid/BA04994769

Mazower, M. (2006).*Thessaloniki, the city of ghosts, Christians, Muslims, and Jews 1430-1950* Alexandreia. ISBN: 960221354X.

Mazower, M. (2002). *The Balkans*. Patakis.

Menexes, G. (2006). *Experimental designs in data analysis* ([Doctoral dissertation, University of Macedonia]).

Menexes, G. (2006). *Experimental Designs in Data Analysis*. Doctoral dissertation, University of Macedonia, Thessaloniki, Greece (in Greek).

Menexes, G. (2007). *Experimental Designs in Data Analysis.* Doctoral Dissertation, Department of Applied Informatics, University of Macedonia, Thessaloniki, Greece.

Menexes, G., & Angelopoulos, S. (2008). Proposals for the financing and development of Greek farms based on a clustering method for categorical data. *EuroMed Journal of Business, 3*(3), 263–285. DOI: 10.1108/14502190810906437

Menexes, G., Markos, A., & Farmakis, N. (2012). *Convergence Index of Data Groups toward a Target Group: An Application to Energy Input–Output Data in Agroecosystems*. Data Analysis Bulletin. (In Greek)

Messaoud, R. B., Boussaïd, O., & Loudcher-Rabaseda, S. (2007). A Multiple Correspondence Analysis to Organize Data Cubes. *Frontiers in Artificial Intelligence and Applications, 155*(1), 133–146. https://halshs.archives-ouvertes.fr/halshs-00476483

Mhlanga, D. (2020). Industry 4.0 in Finance: The impact of Artificial intelligence (AI) on digital financial inclusion. *International Journal of Financial Studies, 8*(3), 45. DOI: 10.3390/ijfs8030045

Mishra, M., Desul, S., & Santos, C. A. G.. (2024). A bibliometric analysis of sustainable development goals (SDGs): A review of progress, challenges, and opportunities. *Environment, Development and Sustainability, 26*, 11101–11143. DOI: 10.1007/s10668-023-03225-w PMID: 37362966

Mišík, M. (2022). The EU needs to improve its external energy security. *Energy Policy, 165*, 112930. DOI: 10.1016/j.enpol.2022.112930

Mišík, M., & Nosko, A. (2023). Each one for themselves: Exploring the energy security paradox of the European Union. *Energy Research & Social Science, 99*, 103074. DOI: 10.1016/j.erss.2023.103074

Mohelska, H., Sokolova, M., Cierniak-Emerych, A., & Dziuba, S. T. (2020). Employment in high-technology industries in the european union and job satisfaction-case study Czech Republic and Poland. *Economic research-. Ekonomska Istrazivanja, 33*(1), 639–651. DOI: 10.1080/1331677X.2019.1697723

Morera, O. F., & Stokes, S. M. (2016). Coefficient α as a measure of test score reliability: Review of 3 popular misconceptions. *American Journal of Public Health, 106*(3), 458–461.

Morlini, I., & Zani, S. (2010). Comparing approaches for clustering mixed mode data: An application in marketing research. *Data Analysis and Classification*, 49–57. Scopus.

Moschidis, O. (2003). *Contribution to the Study of Evaluation Scales Using Multidimensional Data Analysis Methods.* Doctoral Dissertation, Department of Applied Informatics, University of Macedonia, Thessaloniki, Greece.

Moschidis, O., Markos, A., & Chadjipadelis, T. (2023). Hierarchical clustering of mixed-type data based on barycentric coding. *Behaviormetrika, 50*(1), 465–489. *Scopus.* Advance online publication. DOI: 10.1007/s41237-022-00165-z

Moschkovich, J., Schoenfeld, A. H., & Arcavi, A. (2012). Aspects of understanding: On multiple perspectives and representations of linear relations and connections among them. In *Integrating research on the graphical representation of functions* (pp. 69–100). Routledge.

Mothobi, N., Van Ryneveld, L., & Graham, M. A. (2021). A Cross-Country Comparison of Mathematics Teachers' Beliefs About Technology in Education. [IJICTE]. *International Journal of Information and Communication Technology Education, 17*(4), 1–13. DOI: 10.4018/IJICTE.20211001.oa13

Mousa, B. A., & Al-Khateeb, B. (2023). Predicting medicine demand using deep learning techniques: A review. *Journal of Intelligent Systems, 32*(1). Advance online publication. DOI: 10.1515/jisys-2022-0297

Mullainathan, S., & Spiess, J. (2017). Machine Learning: An Applied Econometric approach. *The Journal of Economic Perspectives, 31*(2), 87–106. DOI: 10.1257/jep.31.2.87

Munappy, A. R., Bosch, J., & Olsson, H. H. (2020). Data Pipeline Management in Practice: Challenges and opportunities. In *Lecture notes in computer science* (pp. 168–184). https://doi.org/DOI: 10.1007/978-3-030-64148-1_11

Murtagh, F., & Contreras, P. (2011). Algorithms for hierarchical clustering: An overview. *Wiley Interdisciplinary Reviews. Data Mining and Knowledge Discovery, 2*(1), 86–97. DOI: 10.1002/widm.53

Murtagh, F., & Contreras, P. (2017). Algorithms for hierarchical clustering: An overview, II. *Wiley Interdisciplinary Reviews. Data Mining and Knowledge Discovery, 7*(6). Advance online publication. DOI: 10.1002/widm.1219

Muyama, L., Neuraz, A., & Coulet, A. (2024). Machine learning approaches for the discovery of clinical pathways from patient data: A systematic review. *Journal of Biomedical Informatics, 160*, 104746. DOI: 10.1016/j.jbi.2024.104746 PMID: 39537000

Nazareth, N., & Reddy, Y. V. R. (2023). Financial applications of machine learning: A literature review. *Expert Systems with Applications, 219*, 119640. DOI: 10.1016/j.eswa.2023.119640

Nguyen, L. H., & Holmes, S. (2019). Ten quick tips for effective dimensionality reduction. *PLoS Computational Biology, 15*(6). *Scopus*. Advance online publication. DOI: 10.1371/journal.pcbi.1006907 PMID: 31220072

Ntotsi, P., & Anastasiadou, S. D. (2019). Contemporary advanced statistical methods for the science of educational research: Principal components analysis versus L' analysee factorielle des correspondances. *New Trends and Issues Proceedings on Humanities and Social Sciences*. [Online]. 6(1), pp 246–255. Available from from: www.prosoc.eu

Nuseir, M. T. (2016). Exploring the use of Online Marketing Strategies and Digital Media to Improve the Brand Loyalty and Customer Retention. *International Journal of Business and Management*, *11*(4), 228. DOI: 10.5539/ijbm.v11n4p228

Okasha, A. M., Deraz, N., Elmetwalli, A. H., Elsayed, S., Falah, M. W., Farooque, A. A., & Yaseen, Z. M. (2022). Effects of irrigation method and water flow rate on irrigation performance, soil salinity, yield, and water productivity of cauliflower. *Agriculture*, *12*(8), 1164. DOI: 10.3390/agriculture12081164

OpenAI. (2023). *GPT-4 technical report.*

Orsenigo, C., & Vercellis, C. (2012). Kernel ridge regression for out-of-sample mapping in supervised manifold learning. *Expert Systems with Applications*, *39*(9), 7757–7762. DOI: 10.1016/j.eswa.2012.01.060

Ostrowski, W. (2022). The twenty years' crisis of European energy security: Central and Eastern Europe and the US. *Geopolitics*, *27*(3), 875–897. DOI: 10.1080/14650045.2020.1835863

Ozbayoglu, A. M., Gudelek, M. U., & Sezer, O. B. (2020). Deep learning for financial applications : A survey. *Applied Soft Computing*, *93*, 106384. DOI: 10.1016/j.asoc.2020.106384

Page, M. J., McKenzie, J. E., Bossuyt, P. M., Boutron, I., Hoffmann, T. C., Mulrow, C. D., Shamseer, L., Tetzlaff, J. M., Akl, E. A., Brennan, S. E., Chou, R., Glanville, J., Grimshaw, J. M., Hróbjartsson, A., Lalu, M. M., Li, T., Loder, E. W., Mayo-Wilson, E., McDonald, S., & Moher, D. (2021). The PRISMA 2020 statement: An updated guideline for reporting systematic reviews. *BMJ (Clinical Research Ed.)*, (71). Advance online publication. DOI: 10.1136/bmj.n71

Pagès, J. (2004). Analyse factorielle de données mixtes. [Scopus.]. *Revue de Statistique Appliquee*, *52*(4), 93–111.

Pagès, J. (2014). *Multiple Factor Analysis by Example Using R.* CRC Press.

Panagiotopoulos, I., Seremeti, L., & Kameas, A. (2011). An Alignable User Profile Ontology for Ambient Intelligence Environments. In *Proceedings of the Seventh International Conference on Intelligent Environments*, Nottingham, UK, pp. 270-276. https://doi.org/DOI: 10.1109/IE.2011.15

Papadaki, Z., & Anastasiadou, S. (2017). Study of Bank Customers' Attitudes toward Service Quality during the Early Period of Capital Controls Using Correspondence Factor Analysis. Data Analysis Notebooks. Retrieved from http://www.gsda.gr/journal/archives/586

Papadaki, Z., Anastasiadou, S., Masouras, A., & Papalexandris, S. (2023). Factors Influencing the Use of Digital Marketing by Telemedicine Services. 10th International Conference on Strategic Innovative Marketing and Tourism 2023. Zakynthos, Ionian Islands, Greece. pp. 855-862. In A. Kavoura et al. (eds.), Strategic Innovative Marketing and Tourism, Springer Proceedings in Business and Economics, https://doi.org/DOI: 10.1007/978-3-031-51038-0_92

Papadaki, Z. E., & Anastsasiadou, S. D. (2019). Evaluating Perception, Expectation of Consumers, and Service Quality Gap in Greek Banking in a Period of Financial Crisis and Capital Controls. In Sykianakis, N., Polychronidou, P., & Karasavvoglou, A. (Eds.), *Economic and Financial Challenges for Eastern Europe. Springer Proceedings in Business and Economics* (pp. 67–80). Springer., DOI: 10.1007/978-3-030-12169-3_5

Papademetriou, C., Anastasiadou, S., Kondeos, G., & Papalexandris, S. (2022). COVID-19 Pandemic: The Impact of the Social Media Technology on Higher Education. *Education in Science*, *12*(4), 261. DOI: 10.3390/educsci12040261

Papademetriou, C., Anastasiadou, S., & Papalexandris, S. (2023). The impact of sustainable HRM practices on service quality, customer satisfaction, and organizational performance in hotel industry. Sustainability, mdpi. *Sustainability*, *15*(10), 8251. DOI: 10.3390/su15108251

Papadimitriou, I. (2007). Data Analysis. Tipothito Eds. Athens, Greece.

Papadimitriou, G. (1994). *Data analysis methods: University lectures*. University of Macedonia Economics and Social Sciences.

Papadimitriou, G. (2007). *The data analysis*. Tipothito.

Papafilippou, N., Kyrana, Z., Pratsinakis, E., Kiranas, E., Michailidou, A., Markos, A., & Menexes, G. (2025). Integrating Data Analysis Methods with Machine Learning Algorithms for Mixed Data Types: Does This Combination Improve Predictive Models' Accuracy? *Journal of Data Science and Intelligent Systems*. https://doi.org/DOI: 10.47852/bonviewjdsis52023906

Papafilippou, N., Kyrana, Z., Pratsinakis, E., Kiranas, E., Michailidou, A.-M., Markos, A., & Menexes, G. (2026). Integrating Data Analysis Methods with Machine Learning Algorithms for Mixed Data Types: Does This Combination Improve Predictive Models' Accuracy? *Journal of Data Science and Intelligent Systems*, *4*(1), 39–50. DOI: 10.47852/bonviewJDSIS52023906

Pape, S. J., & Tchoshanov, M. A. (2001). The Role of Representation(s) in Developing Mathematical Understanding. *Theory into Practice*, *40*(2), 118–127. DOI: 10.1207/s15430421tip4002_6

Passas, I. (2024). Bibliometric Analysis: The main steps. *Encyclopedia*, *4*(2), 1014–1025. DOI: 10.3390/encyclopedia4020065

Patel, U. R., Ghaffarianhoseini, A., Ghaffarianhoseini, A., & Burgess, A. (2024). Digital Twin Technology for sustainable urban development: A review of its potential impact on SDG 11 in New Zealand. *Cities (London, England)*, *155*, 105484. DOI: 10.1016/j.cities.2024.105484

Pavoine, S., Blondel, J., Baguette, M., & Chessel, D. (2007). A new technique for ordering asymmetrical three-dimensional data sets in ecology. *Ecology*, *88*(2), 512–523. DOI: 10.1890/05-1806 PMID: 17479768

Pelagidis, S. (2003). *Refugee Greece (1913-1930). The pain and the glory*. Adelfoi Kyriakidi.

Peters, U.. (2025). AI chatbots oversimplify scientific studies and gloss over critical details—The newest models are especially guilty. *Royal Society Open Science*.

Pitchayadejanant, K., & Nakpathom, P. (2018). Data mining approach for arranging and clustering the agro-tourism activities in orchard. *Kasetsart Journal of Social Sciences*, *39*(3), 407–413. DOI: 10.1016/j.kjss.2017.07.004

Pizer, S. M., & Marron, J. (2017). Object statistics on curved manifolds. In Zheng, G., Li, S., & Székely, G. (Eds.), *Statistical Shape and Deformation Analysis* (pp. 137–164). Academic Press., DOI: 10.1016/b978-0-12-810493-4.00007-9

Pratsinakis, E. D., Kyrana, Z., Papafilippou, N., Karapetsi, L., Dordas, C., & Markos, A. (2025). Clustering Mixed-Type Data: A Comparative Study Using Python and SPSS. In *Modern International Developments in Data Analysis and Multivariate Statistical Analysis* (pp. 73–89). Scopus. https://doi.org/DOI: 10.4018/979-8-3693-9400-7.ch003

Pratsinakis, E. D., Ntoanidou, S., Polidoros, A., Dordas, C., Madesis, P., Eleftherohorinos, I., & Menexes, G. (2020). Comparison of hierarchical clustering methods for binary data from molecular markers. *International Journal of Data Analysis Techniques and Strategies*, *12*(3), 190. DOI: 10.1504/ijdats.2020.108036

Presmeg, N. C. (1998). Metaphoric and metonymic signification in mathematics. *The Journal of Mathematical Behavior*, *17*(1), 25–32. DOI: 10.1016/s0732-3123(99)80059-5

Proulx, J. (2014). Mental mathematics and operations on functions. *Proceedings of the . . . PME Conference*. https://files.eric.ed.gov/fulltext/ED599991.pdf

Proulx, J. (2013). Mental mathematics, emergence of strategies, and the enactivist theory of cognition. *Educational Studies in Mathematics*, *84*(3), 309–328. DOI: 10.1007/s10649-013-9480-8

Proulx, J. (2015). Mental mathematics with mathematical objects other than numbers: The case of operation on functions. *The Journal of Mathematical Behavior*, *39*, 156–176. DOI: 10.1016/j.jmathb.2015.07.001

Pruvost, G., Kameas, A., Heinroth, T., Seremeti, L., & Minker, W. (2009). Combining Agents and Ontologies to Support Task-Centred Interoperability in Ambient Intelligent Environments. In *Proceedings of the Ninth International Conference on Intelligent Systems Design and Applications*, Pisa, Italy, pp. 55-60. https://doi.org/DOI: 10.1109/ISDA.2009.195

Putra, A., Suhud, U., & Handaru, A. W. (2022). The Role of Brand Reputation on Customer Retention of Social Media Users. https://doi.org/DOI: 10.5281/ZENODO.6132552

Référé – RTR Austrian Regulatory Authority. (2024). *Deployer obligations – EU AI Act.* https://www.rtr.at/rtr/service/ki-servicestelle/ai-act/Deployer_obligations.en.html

Rencher, A. C. (2002). *Methods of Multivariate Analysis* (2nd ed.). John Wiley & Sons.

Reys, R. E. (1984). Mental computation and estimation: Past, present, and future. *The Elementary School Journal*, *84*(5), 547–557. DOI: 10.1086/461383

Roccetti, M., Delnevo, G., Casini, L., & Mirri, S. (2021). An alternative approach to dimension reduction for pareto distributed data: A case study. *Journal of Big Data*, *8*(1), 39. DOI: 10.1186/s40537-021-00428-8 PMID: 33649714

Rodríguez-Pose, A., & Di Cataldo, M. (2015). Quality of government and innovative performance in the regions of Europe. *Journal of Economic Geography*, *15*(4), 673–706. DOI: 10.1093/jeg/lbu023

Rofiq, M., Firdi, A., & Respati, H. (2020). The Effect of Brand Image and Social Media on Customer Retention through Customer Satisfaction at Kaliwatu Adventure. *International Journal of Innovative Science and Research Technology*, *5*(8), 589–594. DOI: 10.38124/IJISRT20AUG293

Romero, C., & Ventura, S. (2020). Educational data mining and learning analytics: An updated survey. *Wiley Interdisciplinary Reviews. Data Mining and Knowledge Discovery*, *10*(3). Advance online publication. DOI: 10.1002/widm.1355

Romero, C., & Ventura, S. (2024). Educational data mining and learning analytics: An updated survey. *arXiv:2402.07956.*

Rootman, C., & Cupp, N. (n.d.). The impact of social media on customer satisfaction and retention in the banking industry: views of clients and managers.

Rotari, M., Diaz, V. F., De Ketelaere, B., & Kulahci, M. (2024). An extension of PARAFAC to analyze multi-group three-way data. *Chemometrics and Intelligent Laboratory Systems*, *246*, 105089. DOI: 10.1016/j.chemolab.2024.105089

Saha, S., Hasan, A. R., Islam, K. R., & Priom, M. I. (2024). Sustainable Development Goals (SDGs) practices and firms' financial performance: Moderating role of country governance. *Green Finance*, *6*(1), 162–198. DOI: 10.3934/gf.2024007

Saleh, Y., Abu Talib, M., Nasir, Q., & Dakalbab, F. (2025). Evaluating large language models: A systematic review of efficiency, applications, and future directions. *Frontiers of Computer Science*, *7*, 1523699.

Santoso, R. K., & Dewi, N. F. (2018). The Influence of Social Media Against Customer Retention (Case Study on J.Co). *KnE Social Sciences*, *3*(11), 1436. DOI: 10.18502/kss.v3i11.2860

Sareen, S. (2021). Digitalisation and social inclusion in multi-scalar smart energy transitions. *Energy Research & Social Science*, *81*, 102251. DOI: 10.1016/j.erss.2021.102251

Sawadogo, P. N., Scholly, E., Favre, C., Ferey, E., Loudcher, S., & Darmont, J. (2019). New trends in databases and information systems. In *Communications in computer and information science*. https://doi.org/DOI: 10.1007/978-3-030-30278-8

Saxena, A., Prasad, M., Gupta, A., Bharill, N., Patel, O. P., Tiwari, A., Er, M. J., Ding, W., & Lin, C. (2017). A review of clustering techniques and developments. *Neurocomputing*, *267*, 664–681. DOI: 10.1016/j.neucom.2017.06.053

Schotten, M., Aisati, M. E., Meester, W. J. N., Steiginga, S., & Ross, C. A. (2017). A brief history of Scopus: the world's largest abstract and citation database of scientific literature. In *Auerbach Publications eBooks* (pp. 31–58). https://doi.org/DOI: 10.1201/9781315155890-3

Schramade, W. (2017). Investing in the UN Sustainable Development Goals: Opportunities for Companies and Investors. *Journal of Applied Corporate Finance, 29*(2), 87–99. DOI: 10.1111/jacf.12236

Searle, S. R. (1987). *Linear models for unbalanced data*. Wiley.

Selter, C. (2009). Creativity, flexibility, adaptivity, and strategy use in mathematics. *ZDM, 41*(5), 619–625. DOI: 10.1007/s11858-009-0203-7

Seremeti, L., & Kougias, I. (2013). Networks of Aligned Ontologies Through a Category Theoretic Approach. Journal of Emerging Trends in Computing and Information Sciences. Vol. 4, No. 10, pp.785-794. Seremeti, L., Kameas, A. (2010). Tools for Ontology Engineering and Management. In: Poli, R., Healy, M., Kameas, A. (eds) Theory and Applications of Ontology: Computer Applications. Springer, Dordrecht, pp. 131-154. https://doi.org/DOI: 10.1007/978-90-481-8847-5_6

Seremeti, L., & Anastasiadou, S. (2025). The transformative impact of artificial intelligence (AI) on strategic decision-making. In Kavoura, A., Kefallonitis, E., & Theodoridis, P. (Eds.), *Strategic innovative marketing and tourism* (pp. 427–435). Springer., DOI: 10.1007/978-3-031-81962-9_47

Seremeti, L., & Kameas, A. (2008). Ontology-based high level task composition in ubiquitous computing applications. In *Proceedings of the IET 4th International Conference on Intelligent Environments*, Seattle, WA, USA, pp. 1-5. https://doi.org/DOI: 10.1049/cp:20081142

Seremeti, L., & Kameas, A. (2009). A Task-Based Ontology Engineering Approach for Novice Ontology Developers. In *Proceedings of the Fourth Balkan Conference in Informatics*, Thessaloniki, Greece, pp. 85-89. https://doi.org/DOI: 10.1109/BCI.2009.46

Sfard, A. (1992). Operational origins of mathematical objects and the quandary of reification-the case of function. *The concept of function: Aspects of epistemology and pedagogy, 25*, 59-84.

Sharma, R., Chawla, S., Dagar, V., Kagzi, M., & Rao, A. (2025). SDG adoption and firm risk: The impact of ESG performance, investor confidence, and agency cost. *International Review of Economics & Finance, 101*, 104205. DOI: 10.1016/j.iref.2025.104205

Sharma, S. (1996). *Applied Multivariate Techniques*. John Willey and Sons Inc.

Shashua, A., Zass, R., & Hazan, T. (2006). Multi-way clustering using Super-Symmetric non-negative tensor factorization. In Leonardis, A., Bischof, H., & Pinz, A. (Eds.), (pp. 595–608). Lecture notes in computer science. Springer., DOI: 10.1007/11744085_46

Shaukat, S. S., Rao, T. A., & Khan, M. A. (2016). Impact of sample size on principal component analysis ordination of an environmental data set: effects on eigenstructure. *Ochrana PríRody Slovenska/EkolóGia, 35*(2), 173–190. https://doi.org/DOI: 10.1515/eko-2016-0014

Sibson, R. (1978). Studies in the Robustness of Multidimensional Scaling: Procrustes Statistics. *Journal of the Royal Statistical Society. Series B, Statistical Methodology, 40*(2), 234–238. DOI: 10.1111/j.2517-6161.1978.tb01669.x

Sicsic, J., Le Vaillant, M., & Franc, C. (2012). Intrinsic and extrinsic motivations in primary care: An explanatory study among French general practitioners. *Health Policy (Amsterdam), 108*(2), 140–148. DOI: 10.1016/j.healthpol.2012.08.020 PMID: 22995769

Siddi, M. (2023). Europe's energy dilemma: War and the green transition. *Current History (New York, N.Y.), 122*(842), 83–88. DOI: 10.1525/curh.2023.122.842.83

Siemens, G. (2013). Learning analytics: The emergence of a discipline. *The American Behavioral Scientist, 57*(10), 1380–1400.

Sierpinska, A. (1992). Theoretical perspectives for development of the function concept. *The concept of function: Aspects of epistemology and pedagogy. MAA Notes, 25*, 23–58.

Silva, S. (2021). Corporate contributions to the Sustainable Development Goals: An empirical analysis informed by legitimacy theory. *Journal of Cleaner Production, 292*, 125962. DOI: 10.1016/j.jclepro.2021.125962

Simitsis, A., Vassiliadis, P., & Sellis, T. (2005). State-space optimization of ETL workflows. *IEEE Transactions on Knowledge and Data Engineering, 17*(10), 1404–1419. DOI: 10.1109/tkde.2005.169

Singh, A. P., & Rahman, Z. (2021). Integrating corporate sustainability and sustainable development goals: Towards a multi-stakeholder framework. *Cogent Business & Management, 8*(1). Advance online publication. DOI: 10.1080/23311975.2021.1985686

Singh, J., & Singh, D. (2024). A comprehensive review of clustering techniques in artificial intelligence for knowledge discovery: Taxonomy, challenges, applications and future prospects. *Advanced Engineering Informatics, 62*, 102799. DOI: 10.1016/j.aei.2024.102799

Sjödin, D., Parida, V., Palmié, M., & Wincent, J. (2021). How AI capabilities enable business model innovation: Scaling AI through co-evolutionary processes and feedback loops. *Journal of Business Research, 134*, 574–587. DOI: 10.1016/j.jbusres.2021.05.009

Smilde, B. J., Botman, E., de Ruiter, R. D., Smit, J. M., Teunissen, B. P., Lubbers, W. D., Schwarte, L. A., Schober, P., & Eekhoff, E. M. W. (2022). Monitoring and Management of Fibrodysplasia Ossificans Progressiva: Current Perspectives. *Orthopedic Research and Reviews, 14*, 113–120. DOI: 10.2147/ORR.S337491 PMID: 35480068

Sneath, P. H. A. (1957). The Application of Computers to Taxonomy. *Journal of General Microbiology, 17*, 201–226. DOI: 10.1099/00221287-17-1-201 PMID: 13475686

Sokal, R. R., & Michener, C. D. (1958). A Statistical Methods for Evaluating Relationships. *The University of Kansas Science Bulletin, 38*, 1409–1448.

Solorio, I., & Jörgens, H. (2020). Contested energy transition? Europeanization and authority turns in EU renewable energy policy. *Journal of European Integration, 42*(1), 77–93. DOI: 10.1080/07036337.2019.1708342

Song, C., & Majeed, M. T. (2023). Digital inclusion to enhance energy sustainability: Public participation and environmental governance in the new media era to achieve energy sustainable goals. *Environmental Science and Pollution Research International, 30*(59), 123633–123642. DOI: 10.1007/s11356-023-30837-6

Song, L., Zhan, X., Zhang, H., Xu, M., Liu, J., & Zheng, C. (2022). How much is global business sectors contributing to sustainable development goals? *Sustainable Horizons, 1*, 100012. DOI: 10.1016/j.horiz.2022.100012

Song, Y., Li, Y., & Qu, J. (2018). A new approach for supervised dimensionality reduction. *International Journal of Data Warehousing and Mining, 14*(4), 20–37. DOI: 10.4018/ijdwm.2018100102

Sørensen, T. (1948). A Method of Establishing Groups of Equal Amplitude in Plant Sociology Based on Similarity of Species Content and Its Application to Analyses of the Vegetation on Danish Commons. *Biologiske Skrifter/Kongelige Danske Videnskabernes Selskab, 5*, 1–34.

Souravlas, Katsavounis, and Anastasiadou. (2021d). On Modeling and Simulation of Resource Allocation Policies in Cloud Computing Using Colored Petri Nets. *Applied Sciences*. 10.16 (2021): 5644

Souravlas, S. & Anastasiadou, S. (2021a). Pipelined Dynamic Scheduling of Big Data Streams. *Applied Sciences.* 10.14 (2021): 4796.

Souravlas, S. Anastasiadou, S. & Kostoglou, I. (2022b). A Novel Method For General Hierarchical System Modeling Via Colored Petri Nets Based on Transition Extractions From Real Data Sets. Appl. Sci. 2023, 13, 339. https://doi.org/DOI: 10.3390/app13010339

Souravlas, S., Anastasiadou, S. & Katsavounis. (2021c). A Survey on the Recent Advances of Deep Community Detection." *Applied Sciences.* 11.16 (2021): 7179.

Souravlas, S., Anastasiadou, S. D., Tantalaki, N., & Katsavounis, S. (2022a). A Fair, Dynamic Load Balanced Task Distribution Strategy for Heterogeneous Cloud Platforms Based on Markov Process Modeling," in IEEE Access, vol. 10, pp. 26149-26162, 2022, doi: DOI: 10.1109/ACCESS.2022.3157435

Souravlas, S., Anastasiadou, S., Economides, Th., & Katsavounis, S. (2023). Probabilistic Community Detection in Social Networks. IEEE Access, Journal: IEEE Access, Publication Date: 2023, Volume: 11, On Page(s): 25629-25641, Print ISSN: 2169-3536, Online ISSN: 2169-3536, Digital Object Identifier: DOI: 10.1109/ACCESS.2023.3257021

Souravlas, S., & Anastasiadou, S. (2020). Pipelined Dynamic Scheduling of Big Data Streams. *Applied Sciences (Basel, Switzerland)*, *10*(14), 4796. DOI: 10.3390/app10144796

Souravlas, S., & Anastasiadou, S. (2022). On Implementing Social Community Clouds Based on Markov Models. *IEEE Transactions on Computational Social Systems*, *2022*. Advance online publication. DOI: 10.1109/TCSS.2022.3213273

Souravlas, S., Anastasiadou, S., & Katsavounis, S. (2021b). A Survey on the Recent Advances of Deep Community Detection. *Applied Sciences (Basel, Switzerland)*, *11*(16), 7179. DOI: 10.3390/app11167179

Souravlas, S., Anastasiadou, S., & Katsavounis, S. (2021c). More on Pipelined Dynamic Scheduling of Big Data Streams. *Applied Sciences (Basel, Switzerland)*, *11*(1), 61. DOI: 10.3390/app11010061

Souravlas, S., Anastasiadou, S., Tantalaki, N., & Katsavounis, S. (2021a). A Dynamic Load Balanced Task Distribution Strategy for Heterogeneous Cloud Platforms Based on Markov Process Modeling. *IEEE Access : Practical Innovations, Open Solutions*, *10*, 2169–3536. https://ieeexplore.ieee.org/abstract/document/9729723

Souravlas, S., Katsavounis, S., & Anastasiadou, S. (2020). On Modeling and Simulation of Resource Allocation Policies in Cloud Computing Using Colored Petri Nets. *Applied Sciences (Basel, Switzerland), 10*(16), 5644. DOI: 10.3390/app10165644

Sowder, J. T. (1988). Mental computation and number comparison: Their roles in the development of number sense and computational estimation. *Number concepts and operations in the middle grades, 2*, 182-197.

Spulbar, C., Ejaz, A., Birau, R., & Trivedi, J. (2019). Sustainable investing based on momentum strategies in emerging stock markets: A case study for Bombay Stock Exchange (BSE) of India. *Scientific Annals of Economics and Business, 66*(3), 351–361. DOI: 10.47743/saeb-2019-0029

Srivastava, A., & Klassen, E. P. (2004). Bayesian and geometric subspace tracking. *Advances in Applied Probability, 36*(1), 43–56. DOI: 10.1239/aap/1077134463

Srivastava, A., & Klassen, E. P. (2016). Motivation for Function and Shape Analysis. In *Functional and Shape Data Analysis*. Springer., DOI: 10.1007/978-1-4939-4020-2_1

Strambo, C., Nilsson, M., & Månsson, A. (2015). Coherent or inconsistent? Assessing energy security and climate policy interaction within the European Union. *Energy Research & Social Science, 8*, 1–12. DOI: 10.1016/j.erss.2015.04.004

Strout, T. D., Vessey, J. A., Difazio, R. L., & Ludlow, L. H. (2018). The Child Adolescent Bullying Scale (CABS): Psychometric evaluation of a new measure. *Research in Nursing & Health, 41*, 1–13. PMID: 29504650

Suharto, S., Junaedi, I. W. R., Muhdar, H. M., Firmansyah, A., & Sarana, S. (2022). Consumer loyalty of Indonesia e-commerce SMEs: The role of social media marketing and customer satisfaction. *International Journal of Data and Network Science, 6*(2), 383–390. DOI: 10.5267/j.ijdns.2021.12.016

Suh, I., & Chung, Y. D. (2016). A Workload Assignment Strategy for Efficient ROLAP Data Cube Computation in Distributed Systems. *International Journal of Data Warehousing and Mining, 12*(3), 51–71. DOI: 10.4018/ijdwm.2016070104

Suh, W., & Ahn, S. (2022). Development and Validation of a Scale Measuring Student Attitudes toward Artificial Intelligence. *SAGE Open, 2022*(12), 215824402211004.

Sun, Y., & You, X. (2023). Do digital inclusive finance, innovation, and entrepreneurship activities stimulate vitality of the urban economy? Empirical evidence from the Yangtze River Delta, China. *Technology in Society, 72*, 102200. DOI: 10.1016/j.techsoc.2023.102200

Tabachnick, B. G., & Fidell, L. S. (2007). *Using Multivariate Statistics* (5th ed.). Allyn and Bacon/Pearson Education.

Tantalaki, S., Souravlas, S., Roumeliotis, M., & Katsavounis, S. (2020). Pipeline-Based Linear Scheduling of Big Data Streams in the Cloud. *IEEE Access : Practical Innovations, Open Solutions, 8,* 117182–117202. DOI: 10.1109/ACCESS.2020.3004612

Taraza, E., & Anastasiadou, S. (2019). EFQM Excellence Model in Vocational Lyceum: Reliability and Validity of EFQM Instrument. Proceedings of 13th annual International Technology, Education and Development Conference (INTED2019), Valencia, Spain, pp. 2273-2285.

Tauro, E., Gorini, A., Caglio, C., Gabanelli, P., & Caiani, E. G. (2022). COVID-19 and mental disorders in healthcare Personnel: A novel framework to develop Personas from an online survey. *Journal of Biomedical Informatics, 126,* 103993. DOI: 10.1016/j.jbi.2022.103993 PMID: 35026414

Tenenhaus, A., & Tenenhaus, M. (2014). Regularized generalized canonical correlation analysis for multiblock or multigroup data analysis. *European Journal of Operational Research, 238*(2), 391–403. DOI: 10.1016/j.ejor.2014.01.008

Theodosiou, T., Angelis, L., & Vakali, A. (2008). Non-linear correlation of content and metadata information extracted from biomedical article datasets. *Journal of Biomedical Informatics, 41*(1), 202–216. DOI: 10.1016/j.jbi.2007.06.004 PMID: 17643352

Thiel, M., Féraud, B., & Govaerts, B. (2017). ASCA+ and APCA+: Extensions of ASCA and APCA in the analysis of unbalanced multifactorial designs. *Journal of Chemometrics, 31*(6). Advance online publication. DOI: 10.1002/cem.2895

Thomos, K., Bitzenis, A., & Koutsoupias, N. (2023, December). Credit Rating in Business and Economics Research: Europe (2000-2022). *Global Business & Economics Anthology. Volumes I, II.* Advance online publication. DOI: 10.47341/gbea.23128

Thompson, I. (2010). 12 Getting your head around mental calculation. *Issues In Teaching Numeracy In Primary Schools,* 161.

Threlfall, J. (2002). Flexible mental calculation. *Educational Studies in Mathematics, 50*(1), 29–47. DOI: 10.1023/a:1020572803437

Threlfall, J. (2009). Strategies and flexibility in mental calculation. *ZDM, 41*(5), 541–555. DOI: 10.1007/s11858-009-0195-3

Timmerman, M. E., & Kiers, H. A. L. (2003). Four simultaneous component models for the analysis of multivariate time series from more than one subject to model intraindividual and interindividual differences. *Psychometrika, 68*(1), 105–121. DOI: 10.1007/BF02296656

Tomlinson, C. A. (2014). *The differentiated classroom: Responding to the needs of all learners*. Ascd.

Toorajipour, R., Sohrabpour, V., Nazarpour, A., Oghazi, P., & Fischl, M. (2020). Artificial intelligence in supply chain management: A systematic literature review. *Journal of Business Research, 122*, 502–517. DOI: 10.1016/j.jbusres.2020.09.009

Toshniwal, A., Taneja, S., Shukla, A., Ramasamy, K., Patel, J. M., Kulkarni, S., Jackson, J., Gade, K., Fu, M., Donham, J., Bhagat, N., Mittal, S., & Ryaboy, D. (2014). Storm@twitter. *SIGMOD '14: Proceedings of the 2014 ACM SIGMOD International Conference on Management of Data*, 147–156. https://doi.org/DOI: 10.1145/2588555.2595641

Trafton, P. R. (1978). Estimation and Mental Arithmetic: Important Components of Computation. *NCTM Yearbook, 196*(213), 78. https://eric.ed.gov/?id=EJ182166

UNESCO. (2021). *AI and education: Guidance for policymakers*. UNESCO Publishing.

UNESCO. (2023). *Guidance for generative AI in education and research*. UNESCO Publishing.

UNESCO. (2024). *AI competency framework for teachers*. UNESCO Publishing.

United Nations. (2015). Transforming our world: The 2030 Agenda for Sustainable Development. United Nations. Retrieved from https://sdgs.un.org/2030agenda

USA Department of Education. (1998). *Preventing Bullying: A Manual for Schools and Communities*. USA Department of Education.

Usman, A., Ozturk, I., Hassan, A., Zafar, S. M., & Ullah, S. (2021). The effect of ICT on energy consumption and economic growth in South Asian economies: An empirical analysis. *Telematics and Informatics, 58*, 101537. DOI: 10.1016/j.tele.2020.101537

Valdivia-Salas, S., Jiménez, T. I., Lombas, A. S., & López-Crespo, G. (2021). School Violence towards Peers and Teen Dating Violence: The Mediating Role of Personal Distress. *International Journal of Environmental Research and Public Health, 2021*(18), 310. DOI: 10.3390/ijerph18010310 PMID: 33406621

Van de Velden, M., Iodice D'Enza, A., Markos, A., & Cavicchia, C. (2024). A general framework for implementing distances for categorical variables. *Pattern Recognition*, *153*, 115547.

Van Ness, P. H., Murphy, T. E., Araujo, K. L. B., & Pisani, M. A. (2012). Multivariate graphical methods provide an insightful way to formulate explanatory hypotheses from limited categorical data. *Journal of Clinical Epidemiology*, *65*(2), 179–188. DOI: 10.1016/j.jclinepi.2011.06.007 PMID: 21889310

van Rijckevorsel, J. L. A., & de Leeuw, J. (1988). *Component and correspondence analysis. Dimension reduction by functional approximation*. Wiley.

Van Zanten, J. A., & Van Tulder, R. (2021). Analyzing companies' interactions with the Sustainable Development Goals through network analysis: Four corporate sustainability imperatives. *Business Strategy and the Environment*, *30*(5), 2396–2420. DOI: 10.1002/bse.2753

Vargas, M., Glaz, B., Alvarado, G., Pietragalla, J., Morgounov, A., Zelenskiy, Y., & Crossa, J. (2015). Analysis and interpretation of interactions in agricultural research. *Agronomy Journal*, *107*(2), 748–762. DOI: 10.2134/agronj13.0405

Vaswani, A., Shazeer, N., Parmar, N., Uszkoreit, J., Jones, L., Gomez, A. N., Kaiser, Ł., & Polosukhin, I. (2017). Attention is all you need. In *Advances in Neural Information Processing Systems.*

Vega, A. C., Sachs, L., Sachs, J. D., & Willis, B. (2025). The Cost: Lowering the Cost of Capital for Climate and SDG Finance in Emerging Markets and Developing Economies. SSRN Electronic Journal. https://doi.org/DOI: 10.2139/ssrn.5244304

Verschaffel, L., Luwel, K., Torbeyns, J., & Van Dooren, W. (2009). Conceptualizing, investigating, and enhancing adaptive expertise in elementary mathematics education. *European Journal of Psychology of Education*, *24*(3), 335–359. DOI: 10.1007/bf03174765

Vicente-Pascual, J. A., Del Carmen Paradinas Márquez, M., & González-Rodrigo, E. (2024). Key elements for achieving high impact and their relationship to the SDGs: Analysis of BCorp-certified companies in the primary sector. *Technological Forecasting and Social Change*, *201*, 123176. DOI: 10.1016/j.techfore.2023.123176

Vinner, S. (1983). Concept definition, concept image and the notion of function. *International Journal of Mathematical Education in Science and Technology*, *14*(3), 293–305. DOI: 10.1080/0020739830140305

Vinner, S., & Dreyfus, T. (1989). Images and definitions for the concept of function. *Journal for Research in Mathematics Education, 20*(4), 356–366. DOI: 10.5951/jresematheduc.20.4.0356

Wamba-Taguimdje, S., Wamba, S. F., Kamdjoug, J. R. K., & Wanko, C. E. T. (2020). Influence of artificial intelligence (AI) on firm performance: The business value of AI-based transformation projects. *Business Process Management Journal, 26*(7), 1893–1924. DOI: 10.1108/bpmj-10-2019-0411

Wandt, E., & Brown, G. W. (1957). Non-Occupational Uses of Mathematics Mental and Written—Approximate and Exact. *The Arithmetic Teacher, 4*(4), 151–154. DOI: 10.5951/at.4.4.0151

Wang, A., Zhao, S., Liu, J., Yang, J., Liu, L., & Chen, G. (2020). Locality adaptive preserving projections for linear dimensionality reduction. *Expert Systems with Applications, 151*, 113352. DOI: 10.1016/j.eswa.2020.113352

Ward, J. H. (1963). Hierarchical grouping to optimize an objective function. *Journal of the American Statistical Association, 58*(301), 236–244. DOI: 10.1080/01621459.1963.10500845

Weichert, J., & Eldardiry, H. (2024). Computer Science Student Attitudes Towards AI Ethics and Policy: A Preliminary Investigation. *2024 IEEE International Symposium on Technology and Society (ISTAS)*, Puebla, Mexico, 2024, pp. 1-5, doi: DOI: 10.1109/ISTAS61960.2024.10732801

Williams, J. D. (1972). Two-way fixed effects analysis of variance with disproportionate cell frequencies. *Multivariate Behavioral Research, 7*(1), 67–83. DOI: 10.1207/s15327906mbr0701_4 PMID: 26804962

Winter, J. (2023). *The day the Great War ends.* Ed.Pedio.

Woo Choi, J., & Young Kim, H. (2018). Tourism trend and network analysis utilizing big data on social media. International Journal of Engineering & Technology, 7(2.12), 312. https://doi.org/DOI: 10.14419/ijet.v7i2.12.11313

World Bank. (2023). *Worldwide Governance Indicators.* https://info.worldbank.org/governance/wgi/

World Energy Council & Oliver Wyman. (2019). *World Energy Trilemma Index 2019.* https://www.worldenergy.org/publications/entry/world-energy-trilemma-index-2019

World Energy Council. (2024). *World Energy Trilemma 2024: Evolving with resilience and justice.* World Energy Council.

Yang, Q., Hayat, N., Al Mamun, A., Makhbul, Z. K. M., & Zainol, N. R. (2022). Sustainable customer retention through social media marketing activities using hybrid SEM-neural network approach. plos one, 17(3), e0264899. https://doi.org/.DOI: 10.1371/journal.pone.0264899

Yao, Y., Meng, H., Gao, Y., Long, Z., & Li, T. (2023). Linear dimensionality reduction method based on topological properties. *Information Sciences*, *624*, 493–511. DOI: 10.1016/j.ins.2022.12.098

Yiu, M. L., Jensen, C. S., Huang, X., & Lu, H. (2008). SpaceTwist: Managing the Trade-Offs Among Location Privacy, Query Performance, and Query Accuracy in Mobile Services. *2008 IEEE 24th International Conference on Data Engineering*, 366–375. https://doi.org/DOI: 10.1109/icde.2008.4497445

Young, F. W. (1981). Quantitative analysis of qualitative data. *Psychometrika, 46*(4), 357–388. *Scopus.* Advance online publication. DOI: 10.1007/BF02293796

Yu, J., & Egger, R. (2021). Color and engagement in touristic Instagram pictures: A machine learning approach. *Annals of Tourism Research*, *89*, 103204. Advance online publication. DOI: 10.1016/j.annals.2021.103204

Zaharia, M., Xin, R. S., Wendell, P., Das, T., Armbrust, M., Dave, A., Meng, X., Rosen, J., Venkataraman, S., Franklin, M. J., Ghodsi, A., Gonzalez, J., Shenker, S., & Stoica, I. (2016). Apache Spark. *Communications of the ACM*, *59*(11), 56–65. DOI: 10.1145/2934664

Zang, L., & Xiong, F. (2020). How (when) does technological innovation improve government effectiveness? An empirical investigation with cross-national evidence. *Science & Public Policy*, *47*(1), 103–113. DOI: 10.1093/scipol/scz050

Zeng, R., Ye, Y., Ou, H., Hua, Y., Su, Y., Hu, J., Lu, H., Tang, J., Liu, J., Xiao, T., Wu, Z., Tang, W., Li, Z.-Y., Lin, S., Zhuang, S., Xu, G., Lin, Y., Li, Y., Huang, F., & Zhang, H.-T. (2023). Early osteoarthritis diagnosis based on near-infrared spectroscopy combined with aquaphotomics. *Spectrochimica Acta. Part A: Molecular and Biomolecular Spectroscopy*, *302*, 123120. DOI: 10.1016/j.saa.2023.123120 PMID: 37453381

Zetterberg, H., Smith, D. H., & Blennow, K. (2013). Biomarkers of mild traumatic brain injury in cerebrospinal fluid and blood. *Nature Reviews. Neurology*, *9*(4), 201–210. DOI: 10.1038/nrneurol.2013.9 PMID: 23399646

Zhang, L., Wen, J., Li, Y., Chen, J., Ye, Y., Fu, Y., & Livingood, W. (2021). A review of machine learning in building load prediction. *Applied Energy*, *285*, 116452. DOI: 10.1016/j.apenergy.2021.116452

Zhang, S., Gong, M., & Li, W. (2020). W., Wang, W., Wu, R., Lan Guo, L. and Lu C. (2020). Patterns of Bullying Victimization and Associations with Mental Health Problems in Chinese Adolescents: A Latent Class Analysis. *International Journal of Environmental Research and Public Health, 17*, 779. DOI: 10.3390/ijerph17030779 PMID: 32012686

Zhan, L., Cheng, M., & Zhu, J. (2024). Progress on image analytics: Implications for tourism and hospitality research. *Tourism Management, 100*, 104798. Advance online publication. DOI: 10.1016/j.tourman.2023.104798

Zheng, S., & Molina, C. G. (1998). An empirical comparison of arc-cosine distance, generalised Fisher ratio and normalised entropy criteria for model selection. *Neural Networks for Signal Processing VIII. Proceedings of the 1998 IEEE Signal Processing Society Workshop (Cat. No.98TH8378)*, 214–223. https://doi.org/DOI: 10.1109/NNSP.1998.710651

Zhou, B., & Pei, J. (2008). Preserving Privacy in Social Networks Against Neighborhood Attacks. *2008 IEEE 24th International Conference on Data Engineering*, 506–515. https://doi.org/DOI: 10.1109/icde.2008.4497459

Zhu, Y., Zhou, L., Xie, C., Wang, G., & Nguyen, T. V. (2019). Forecasting SMEs' credit risk in supply chain finance with an enhanced hybrid ensemble machine learning approach. *International Journal of Production Economics, 211*, 22–33. DOI: 10.1016/j.ijpe.2019.01.032

Zourna, C., Papavassiliou-Alexiou, I., Koutsoupias, N., & Papakota, A. (2021). *A mixed methods research approach to investigate undergraduate students' perceptions of changes enforced due to COVID-19*. Advance., DOI: 10.31124/advance.13606409.v1

Zupic, I., & Čater, T. (2014). Bibliometric methods in management and organization. *Organizational Research Methods, 18*(3), 429–472. DOI: 10.1177/1094428114562629

Zwanenburg, G., Hoefsloot, H. C., Westerhuis, J. A., Jansen, J. J., & Smilde, A. K. (2011). ANOVA–principal component analysis and ANOVA–simultaneous component analysis: A comparison. *Journal of Chemometrics, 25*(10), 561–567. DOI: 10.1002/cem.1400

About the Contributors

Sofia Anastasiadou is a Professor of Statistics and Research Methodology, Biostatistics and Biomedical Research Methodology at the School Health Sciences of the University of Western Macedonia (UOWM). She is the Dean of the Health Sciences of UOWM, Senate Member, and Member of post graduate studies committee. She is also a Member of the Senate and a MODIP Member of the same University. She is the president of the Greek Society of Data Analysis (GSDA). Her teaching focuses in the field of cognitive Research Methodology (Quantitative and Qualitative), Educational Research and Statistical Data Analysis, Big Data. She has written three books on Statistics and Research Methodology and has published over 300 articles in International and Greek Journals as well as in International and Greek Conferences. She has organized and co-organized Greek and International Scientific Conferences. She is also a Member of a number of Scientific Committees of International Conferences and is an Associate Editor in a number of International Journals.

Theodore Chadjipadelis is a Professor of Applied Statistics at the Department of Political Science in Aristotle University of Thessaloniki. He is the Head of Laboratory of Applied Political Research and also Director of the MSc programs Political Analysis and Governance-Regional Development. He is also the Head of the Research Centre "Observatory for Democracy in Balkans, Black Sea and Eastern Mediterranean". He taught Statistics, Mathematics, Electoral Analysis, Governance, Local and Regional Government, Decision Theory in the Aristotle University as well as in the University of Thessaly and the Hellenic Open University. He has published more than 100 papers in scientific journals and conference proceedings in Greece and abroad relating to Electoral Analysis, Public Opinion analysis, laboratory planning, Applied Statistics, Civil and Regional Planning. He is the Head of the Committee for Control of Public Surveys (established following agreement of the Committee with the Ministry of Media). From April 2010 till 2012 he was Board

Member of "Information Society SA" and since 2011 till 2015 he was President of the Managing Committee at the University of Western Macedonia. He was a member of the Special Scientific Committee of the Ministry of Interior Decentralization and E-government for the new architecture of Administration and Regional Administration as well as the Special Committee for the electoral law. He has been member of the National Committee for Administrative Reform of the Ministry of Interior, Public Administration and Decentralization (as a representative of Aristotle University). He has been also a member of the scientific Committee of the "Institute of Local Government" (K.E.Δ.K.E-T.E.Δ.K.N.A.). He has also been representative of the Hellenic Ministry of Education in EUROSTAT and national representative at FP6 Initiative 7 (Citizens and Governance in Knowledge Society).

Nikos Koutsoupias is a Professor of Applied Informatics & Data Analysis in the Department of International & European Studies of the School of Social Sciences, Humanities & Arts, University of Macedonia. He graduated from the Department of Computer Science, North Carolina State University (NCSU), Raleigh NC, USA and a PhD holder from the Department of Applied Informatics of the University of Macedonia. He worked as a Computing Lab Assistant at the Department of Computer Science and the Faculty of Social Sciences & Humanities, as a Teaching Assistant at the School of Electrical & Computer Engineering (NCSU) and as a Database Programmer of an International Insurance Group (ERGO). He taught IT & Data Analysis courses at the School of NCO Administration of the Hellenic Air Force and at the Departments of General Studies & Marketing of TEI of Thessaloniki. As Lecturer/pd407, Assistant and Associate Professor taught at the Aristotle University and later at the University of Western Macedonia.

Angelos Markos is a Professor of Data Analysis in the Social Sciences at the Democritus University of Thrace, School of Education (Greece), board member of the Greek Society of Data Analysis (GSDA) and additional member of the International Federation of Classification Societies (IFCS) Council. In 2017, he was Visiting Scholar at the Department of Statistics, Stanford University. He hold a PhD degree from the University of Macedonia, Greece (2007). His areas of interest include multivariate analysis (especially dimension reduction and clustering), psychological testing and measurement in the social sciences and statistics education. I am creator and maintainer of the R packages clustrd and idm.

George C. Menexes is a Professor of 'Biometry and Agricultural Experimentation' at the School of Agriculture of the Aristotle University of Thessaloniki. His research interests focused on the scientific research methodology, the development and application of statistical methods for the analysis of data resulted from experiments in the field of biological sciences and the methods of multivariate analysis of quantitative and categorical data. He has more than 240 publications (full articles) in scientific journals and conference proceedings and he has participated in 40 research programs. He has announced and/or presented more than 260 papers at National and International Conferences.

***

Elias Athanasiadis is a professor at Elementary Education Department, University of the Aegean, Rhodes, Greece

Yashmita Awasthi is a committed academician specializing in finance, entrepreneurship, and strategic business management. She holds a doctorate in management from Banaras Hindu University, Varanasi, and brings over 12 years of teaching experience across reputed institutions in Delhi NCR and Varanasi. Known for her research acumen, Dr. Awasthi has received several accolades and remains actively involved in academic conferences and workshops. She has made significant scholarly contributions through numerous research papers and articles published in esteemed journals. In addition to her research publications, she has authored academic books, co-edited research-oriented volumes, and contributed chapters on topics ranging from financial inclusion and sustainable business practices to strategic innovation and digital transformation in emerging markets.

Tripti Basuri is an Assistant Teacher in Uttar Dumdum Vidyapith (Girls) Primary Section, West Bengal, India. She completed her B.Sc in Mathematics Hons from St. Paul's Cathedral Mission College (under the University of Calcutta) in 2013, and M.Sc in Mathematics from Bethune College affiliated to the University of Calcutta in 2015. She also cleared the exams such as NET (rank-65) in 2020, SET in 2020 and GATE in 2021 in Mathematics Sciences. Now, she is working as a researcher and her areas of interest are fuzzy sets and it's applications, MCDM, Optimization theory, SDGs, and Educational policies.

Prodip Bhaduri is a postgraduate researcher in Applied Mathematics, affiliated with Maulana Abul Kalam Azad University of Technology, West Bengal, India. He detains an M.Sc. in Applied Mathematics and a B.Ed., with a bright background in applied mathematical modeling and mathematical analysis. He has heed in fields incorporate MCDM or multi-criteria decision-making techniques and to real-world applications in MCDM and it's problems surrounding decision making. He has co-authored various peer-reviewed research articles in international journal publications. His scholastic aim is aligned with advanced research and a long-term career in mathematics and higher academics.

Srabani Guria Das is an Assistant Professor in the Department of Basic Sciences, NSHM Institute of Engineering & Technology, West Bengal, India. She completed her Ph.D from the Indian Institute of Engineering Science and Technology, Shibpur. She already published several research articles in various reputed journals. Her research interests are Mathematical Biology, Stability, Optimal Control, Dynamics and Mathematical Modelling.

Christos Dordas is a Professor of Agronomy and since 2015 he is the Head of the Laboratory of Agronomy. He was the Deputy Head of the School of Agriculture (2013–2017) and Head of the School of Agriculture (2017–2022). His research work addresses several issues in the field crops and plant physiology. He participated in numerous competitive projects funded from EU and national agencies. He supervised 15 master's students, five PhD candidates and postdoctoral researchers in Greece and is the author of more than 200 scientific publications, including more than 82 papers in peer-reviewed journals (> 4,600 citations, h-index: 33).

Giannoula Florou is a professor at Department of Accounting and Finance Democritus University of Thrace, Campus of Kavala Agios Lucas, 65404 Kavala Greece

Kamal Hossain Gazi is a Research Scholar at Maulana Abul Kalam Azad University of Technology, West Bengal, India. He qualified for the CSIR NET in Mathematical Sciences in both June 2020 and June 2021.He received UGC JRF & SRF under the Maulana Azad National Fellowship (MANF) scheme in August 2022 and March 2025, respectively. He completed his B.Sc. (Honours) in Mathematics and M.Sc. in Mathematics (Pure) degrees from Aliah University, Kolkata, in 2016 and 2018, respectively. He has already published several research articles in various reputed journals. His research interests are Fuzzy sets, Optimization, Fuzzy Algebra, Linear Programming, Differential Equations, Operations Research, Data Analysis, MCDM and Mathematical Modelling.

Christoforos Karachristos is a PhD cditate at Midwifery Department, University of Western Macedonia, Greece

Thomas Koutsos is a member of the Laboratory Teaching Staff (ETS) at the Remote Sensing, Spectroscopy and Geographic Information Systems Laboratory, Department of Agriculture, School of Agriculture, Forestry and Natural Environment, Aristotle University of Thessaloniki. He holds a degree in

Geology, a master's degree in Applied and Environmental Geology, as well as a PhD in Geoinformatics and Geographic Information Systems. His research interests include geoinformatics in agriculture, spatial data analysis, GIS, environmental protection, data visualization and spatial statistics. He is a certified Microsoft Systems Engineer (MCSE + Internet) with expertise in SQL programming, Crystal Reports and database management. He has served as a reviewer for more than 35 high-impact scientific journals and has published over 50 scientific papers. He has also participated in at least 10 co-funded European research projects.

Zacharenia Kyrana holds a PhD in Biometry and Data Analysis from the School of Agriculture, Aristotle University of Thessaloniki. She holds an undergraduate degree in Statistics and Actuarial-Financial Mathematics and a postgraduate degree in Statistics and Data Analysis, from the School of Sciences, University of the Aegean. Her research interests include biometry, multivariate and multidimensional statistical-data analysis methods, and dimensionality reduction and clustering methods in data cubes and big data using various statistical software packages. She is the author of several scientific publications in peer-reviewed international journals, as well as in international and national conference proceedings

Sankar Prasad Mondal is an Assistant Professor in the Department of Applied Mathematics, Maulana Abul Kalam Azad University of Technology, West Bengal, India. Previously he was working as an Assistant Professor in the Department of Mathematics in Midnapore College (Autonomous) and the National Institute of Technology, Agartala. He completed his B.Sc. in Mathematics Hons. From Krishnagar Government College (under Kalyani University) in 2008, M.Sc. in Applied Mathematics from Bengal Engineering and Science University, Shibpur in 2010 and Ph.D from the Indian Institute of Engineering Science and Technology, Shibpur in 2014. He has 10 years of teaching and 14 years of research experience in the field of operations research, differential equations, fuzzy sets, mathematical biology, fuzzy differential equations, Soft Computing, Artificial Intelligence, and Optimization theory. He already published more than 150 research papers in reputed journals, book chapters and conferences. The Start-Up Research Grant FRPS (UGC) was received in August 2019.

Marios Nosios is a PhD candidate in the Department of International and European Studies at the University of Macedonia, Greece.

Nikolaos Papafilippou is a PhD candidate in Data Analysis at the School of Agriculture, Aristotle University of Thessaloniki. He holds a Bachelor's degree in Mathematics and Economics and a Postgraduate degree in Education Studies and Mathematics Didactic. His research interests are primarily centred on multivariate and multidimensional data analysis, with a particular emphasis on dimension reduction on big datasets with categorical data from the field of biological and education sciences. He is the author of several scientific publications in international and national conferences. He is a member of the Greek Statistical Institute and the Greek Society of Data Analysis.

Emmanouil D. Pratsinakis is a PhD candidate at the School of Agriculture, Aristotle University of Thessaloniki (AUTh). She graduated from the School of Agriculture of AUTh with Postgraduate studies in the School of Agriculture of AUTh. His current research interests focused on multivariate data analysis of mixed type data. In addition, his research utilises statistical and bioinformatics tools. He has published several publications in scientific journals and conference proceedings with full articles.

Soheil Salahshour received Ph.D. degree in Applied Mathematics in 2012. Since 2012, he has been a University Professor with the Department of Mathematics in different universities, and recently moved to the Istanbul Okan University. His research interests include fractional models and Calculus, Fuzzy expert systems, evolutionary algorithms, optical soliton solutions, data science and big data applications, in which he has published more than 220 works in international journals ISI, collaborated in more than 30 projects and research contracts. The current H-index is 40 on the list top-h scientists for Applied Mathematics. He is also the author of 5 research monographs and edited volumes covering various aspects of computational intelligence, data mining, and applied mathematics. He serves as a guest editor for 8 international journals, and is a member of the editorial committee of a number of international journals, and is a member of the "referees" committee of other ISI journals, such as the Fuzzy Sets and Systems, IEEE Transactions on Fuzzy Systems, Information Sciences, and among others. He has been awarded the best researcher at Bahceshir Unversity, Turkey, in 2021.Three times in a row, since 2020, he has been selected as top 2% scientist worldwide announced by Stanford University. He has presented and participated in more than 30 international conferences and has been invited as plenary speaker in more than 10 international conferences of applied mathematics and AI.

Shanu Singh is a dedicated academic professional with over 9.7 years of experience in commerce, finance, and accounting. She has completed B.Com (Honors), M.Com and Ph.D along with UGC-NET-JRF currently serving as an Assistant Professor at Christ University, Delhi NCR. She has previously held similar positions at institutions such as Amity University, Noida, Galgotias University, Greater Noida and AKS University, Madhya Pradesh. Previously, she has significantly contributed to academic administrations and holding key role as MOODLE Coordinator, Programme Leader, Placement Coordinator and IQAC Coordinator at departmental level. She is currently holding position of IQAC Coordinator and also involved in Media coordination, class mentorship, and strategic action planning. Her achievements include research publications in Scopus & UGC-Care listed journals and presentations at renowned conferences. Shanu has authored two academic books, co-edited research-oriented books, and contributed chapters on topics ranging from banking digitalization to women's health. Furthermore, she has completed several faculty development programs and certifications in research methodology and academic quality assurance, showcasing her commitment to continuous learning and academic excellence.

Surbhi Srivastava is an academician, researcher, and tax consultant. She has qualified UGC -NET exam and has done her doctorate from the University of Allahabad, India. Her area of interest is taxation, finance, auditing, business compliance & sustainability. She has published in international & national Scopus & Web of Science-indexed journals.

Petros Trantas is an assistant ptofessor, Department of Elementary Education / School of Humanities, University of the Aegean, Rhodes, Greece

Vassilios Zoumpoulidis received a four-year Business Management Diploma from Department of Business Management, University of Stuttgart, Germany and Dr. rer. nat. from the Department of Economic Geography, University Bayerische Julius Maximilian, Wuerzburg, Germany. Vassilios Zoumpoulidis is associate professor in the Department of Accounting and Finance of the Democritus University of Thrace, Campus of Kavala, Greece and Visiting Professor in Department of Economics, Democritus University of Thrace, Campus Komotini, Greece. He has published more than 40 papers in international journals and conferences. His research interests are in the areas Micro- and Macroeconomics, Foreign Direct Investments, Tourism Business Administration and Marketing in Tourism. His e-mail is: vzumpu at af.ihu.gr.

Index

A

B

C

D

E

F

T

V

W

X

www.ingramcontent.com/pod-product-compliance
Lightning Source LLC
LaVergne TN
LVHW062326300926
849161LV00007B/1590